D0853409

WITHDRAWN

AN AMERICAN OBSESSION

3 3503 00099 5898

AN AMERICAN OBSESSION

SCIENCE, MEDICINE, AND HOMOSEXUALITY IN MODERN SOCIETY

Jennifer Terry

State Library OF Ohio

SEO Library Center
40780 SR 821 * Caldwell, OH 43724

The University of Chicago Press · Chicago and London

Jennifer Terry is associate professor of comparative studies at The Ohio State University.

The University of Chicago Press, Chicago 60637
The University of Chicago Press, Ltd., London
© 1999 by The University of Chicago
All rights reserved. Published 1999
Printed in the United States of America
08 07 06 05 04 03 02 01 00 99   5 4 3 2 1

ISBN (cloth): 0-226-79366-4
ISBN (paper): 0-226-79367-2

Library of Congress Cataloging-in-Publication Data

Terry, Jennifer, Ph.D
    An American obsession : science, medicine, and homosexuality in modern society /
Jennifer Terry.
        p.   cm.
    Includes bibliographical references (p.   ) and index.
    ISBN 0-226-79366-4 (cl. : alk. paper). — ISBN 0-226-79367-2 (pbk.)
        1. Homosexuality—United States—History.   2. Homosexuality—History.   3.
Sexology—United States—History.   I. Title.
HQ76.3.U5T45   1999
307.76'6'0973—dc21   99-20809
                                                                                    CIP

⊗ The paper in this publication meets the minimum requirements of the American National
Standard for Information Sciences—Permanence of Paper for Printed Library Materials,
ANSI Z39.48-1992.

To Andrea

for her love,
compassion,
and humor

CONTENTS

PREFACE AND ACKNOWLEDGMENTS

This book is the product of years of research, writing, and, yes, obsessing. It has multiple points of origin. In a concrete sense, my inspiration for undertaking it dates from a cloudy winter afternoon in the early 1980s. Wandering around the East Village in Manhattan, I took relief from the biting winds by ducking into the Strand Bookstore, where I came upon a treasure: a scattered collection of used scientific texts on the subject of homosexuality, dating from the early years of the twentieth century. I bought up as many as I could carry back to San Francisco, where I was living at the time. Thus ensued what was to become a voracious habit of tracking down, collecting, and poring over amazingly rich material that captured my imagination for over a decade and a half.

These texts seduced me in a bizarre way: they were and were not about me—that is, about real, living people who engage in homosexuality. They were accurate and inaccurate at the same time. What I mean is that the texts spoke of things that were familiar to me: they offered details of homosexual desire not unlike what I had experienced, but they used these details to represent it in terms of repulsive stereotypes and to underscore the idea that homosexuality was an undesirable pathology. A queer person living in this society cannot help but have encountered and even, to a degree, incorporated such concepts, given the pressures of homophobia endemic to our time. But, curiously, rather than repel me, they drew me in as I sought to make sense of how the stereotypes were produced, what gave rise to them, how their production rhymed with larger cultural and historical anxieties. I learned from these texts a number of important things. First, they presented homosexuality as anomalous and, moreover, those who engaged in it as beings to be especially accounted for and thus contained in some way. This was not news to me. But probably for this very reason, the texts compelled me, for they offered specific evidence of how homosexual desire became such an intense focus for experts and for those who supported their efforts to account for people like me in a manner that was often insidiously oppressive. I guess, being a product of the Enlightenment, I believed that learning about such things could be a step toward countering them. Second, I learned that I was not alone as a queer person seeking information about how and why we represented something so strange, so potentially threatening, so different from people placed under the sign of normal. Many of the books, though coded in the languages of science and medicine, showed evidence of groups of people over many generations seeking, often under hostile circumstances and against great odds, to understand themselves and to make a case for their social acceptance. The books, many consisting of case histories compiled by doctors, required elaborate reading strategies to unearth self-affirming responses on the part of queer people to questions so frequently posed to them: How and why are you different? What do your unusual desires and attractions signify? What is wrong with you? I found, embedded in the putatively detached terms of science, evidence of a particular form of subjectivity, consisting of a sometimes urgent faith in medicine to offer psychic and social relief but also of struggles, of resistance, and of uneasy conciliation between homosexual subjects and experts whose discourses were aimed at making sense of people like me. I identified with the subjects. To do so entailed analyzing the heavily mediated terms of their representation, terms that often but not always underscored pervasive and damaging effects of stereotyping. Reading the texts deepened my sense of the poignancy of surviv ing as a queer person in a world we modern humans have built.

I was out of the academic loop at the time I came upon these books. They presented me with a means for tracing the history of the association of homosexual identity with disease, a matter that had profound significance for coming to terms with the cruel intensification of homophobia occasioned by the AIDS epidemic. At the time, I was involved in early AIDS activism in San Francisco, a ground zero for the epidemic, and was losing friends, co-workers, and neighbors to the disease in devastating numbers. In addition to grief and panic, I was struck daily by how the homophobia unleashed by AIDS was so immediate and so virulent. My not-so-brilliant hunch was that it must have been fueled by a longer history in which homosexuality and disease were not only conflated but made practically synonymous. I felt a pressing need to make sense of homophobia in the present by tracing its genealogy to the past. This as much as anything led me to dig up as many texts pertaining to this history as I could.

Several years later I applied to graduate school in the History of Consciousness program at the University of California, Santa Cruz, proposing a dissertation project aimed at excavating the taken-for-granted notion that homosexuality was itself a form of disease. This, I hoped, would not only help to combat the homophobia surrounding AIDS but would shed broader light on how and why scientific medicine for a long time has been an avenue for producing the terms in relation to which queer people, myself included, have been compelled to exist. From that point forward, my growing collection of primary sources became vehicles for analyzing not only the complexities of queer subjectivity but also the contexts and dominant ideas in relation to which homosexuality has become a cultural obsession in the United States. So while AIDS prompted a sense of urgency about the project, it finds a place only in the epilogue to this book. Perhaps this is a sign of my psychical defense against it—I do not want to give the epidemic any more than it has already taken. But, as I hope the book demonstrates, the longer history preceding the epidemic is not always as grim as we imagine. It does not simply underscore the idea that homosexuality and disease are one and the same. As much as I found a wide variety of subjective engagements in medical and scientific thinking among queers, I also discovered a complex history consisting of debates over whether, in fact, homosexuality as we know it might be a sign of modernity itself and thus be no more diseased than any of the other signifiers of cultural difference brought to the fore by modernity's rapid material transformations, its vexations over social heterogeneity, and its sense of urgency about recognizing, if not always valuing, the vast diversity of life.

Writing this book has been arduous and sometimes lonely. But such are the perils of an obsessive personality coupled with a diabolically ambitious topic. In truth, the book owes its fruition to the many mentors, colleagues, students, friends, and lovers with whom I have had invaluable conversations. My greatest sources of inspiration have been Andrea Slane, Jacqueline Urla, Patricia White, Joanne Meyerowitz, Donna Haraway, Teresa de Lauretis, and Carole Vance, who have given me so much in so many ways, believing that this book—from its beginnings—was worth writing, and then sharing their brilliance and empathy with me at vital steps along the way. I am very grateful to a number of friends and colleagues who have helped me with conceptual approaches and source materials in the history of sexuality. They are Mary Louise Adams, Donna Penn, Sharon Ullman, Vernon Rosario, Jonathan Ned Katz, Allan Berube, George Chauncey, Henry Minton, Martin Duberman, and Robert Moeller. I have been helped enormously by friends who have urged me, often by example through their own work, to think about events and discourses in culturally specific and historically dynamic terms that might bring us to more enlightened futures. They are Evelynn M. Hammonds, David Horn, Ara Wilson, Jessica Shubow, and Caren Kaplan.

A post-doctoral fellowship at the Pembroke Center for Teaching and Research on Women at Brown University vastly enhanced my thinking about the intersections of science, culture, and history. During that year, my work benefited greatly from critical readings by Leslie Camhi, Lisa Cartwright, Anne Fausto-Sterling, Carolyn Dean, Nancy Armstrong, and Elizabeth Weed. As a Resident Fellow at the SUNY Stony Brook Humanities Institute, I took further inspiration from the keen insights of Susan Squier, Ira Livingston, Iona Man-Cheong, Kathleen Wilson, Nicholas Mirzeoff, Nancy Tomes, and E. Ann Kaplan.

Several additional people have given me valuable advice, criticism, and inspiration at various points in this project. They are Gayle Rubin, Jeffrey Escoffier, Bert Hansen, Rhona Berenstein, Marilyn Schuster, and Margaret Cerullo. Colleagues at Ohio State University who have been especially supportive are David Horn, Judith Mayne, Julia Watson, Leigh Gilmore, Eugene Holland, Sabra Webber, Xiaomei Chen, Leila Rupp, Christian Zacher, Margaret Lynd, Christina Edbrooke, and Mary Margaret Fonow. Ohio State students whose thinking challenged me to ponder the overall implications of the project are Pippa Holloway, Jamie Lampidis, Susan Freeman, Heather Miller, James Fredal, Archana Pyati, Miles Rosenberg, Wendy Minkoff, Parissara Liewkeat, Michael Scarce, Jenrose Fitzgerald, T. Anne Dabb, and Mahalakshmi Jayaram.

Loved ones who have helped me through the project and offered me their generous friendship (and, in various cases, their couches to sleep on, their food to eat, their cigarettes to smoke, their shoulders to cry on, and their jokes to laugh at) are Andrea Slane, Patty White and Cynthia Schneider, Leyla Ezdinli, Rebecca Isaacs and Vanessa Schwartz, Evelynn Hammonds, Joanne Meyerowitz, Connie Samaras, Donna Penn, Bill Horrigan, Gillian Harkins, Catherine Gund and Melanie Hope, Cheryl Cole, Leigh Gilmore, Kay Diaz, Maureen McCarthy and Torie Smith, Judith Mayne and Terry Moore, Pippa Holloway, Melodie Calvert and Bonita Makuch, Dana Heller, Kimberly J. Dillon, Ara Wilson and Stephanie Grant, Caren Kaplan and Eric Smoodin, Rhona Berenstein, Ira Livingston, Iona Man-Cheong, Lisa Cartwright, Leslie Camhi, Michelle Lach, Cynthia Rothschild, and Negar Mottahedeh.

My mother, Patricia Terry, and brothers, Neal and Dane Terry, offered emotional support and playfully nudged me with important questions like, "When are you going to finish that book you've been talking about forever?! Does it really exist?" I would also like to acknowledge my father Richard Terry (1927–77) who passed away when I was nineteen. Though neither he nor I could have known then that I would go on to write this or, for that matter, any book, I have thought of him often through the course of composing it. In the face of many hardships, he, like my mother, maintained a love of learning, a deep sense of compassion, and a dedication to social justice. I am grateful for all the many ways that my family has helped me, from an early age, to value thinking, to care about the world, and to take important risks.

My archival research was facilitated through the assistance of Adele Lerner at the Payne-Whitney Clinic Archives at New York Hospital of the Cornell University Medical School, Linda Long at the Stanford University Archives, Barbara Paulson at the Columbia University School of Medicine Archives, Richard Wolfe at the Countway Library at Harvard Medical School, John LeGloahec and Anke Voss-Hubbard at the Rockefeller Archive Center, and Margaret Harter and Kath Pennavaria at the Kinsey Institute for Research in Sex, Gender, and Reproduction at Indiana University.

Previously formulated ideas manifesting themselves in new form here appeared originally in "Lesbians Under the Medical Gaze: Scientists Look for Remarkable Differences," *Journal of Sex Research* 27, no. 3 (1990): 317–40; "Theorizing Deviant Historiography," *differences* 3, no. 2 (1991): 55–74; revised and reprinted in Ann-Louise Shapiro, ed., *Feminists Revision History* (New Brunswick: Rutgers University Press, 1994), 276–303; "Anxious Slippages Between 'Us' and 'Them': A Brief History of the Scientific Search for Homosexual Bodies," in Jennifer Terry and Jacqueline Urla, eds., *Deviant Bodies: Critical Perspectives on Difference in Science and Popular Culture* (Bloomington: Indiana University Press, 1995), 129–69; "The Seduction of Science," in Judith Halberstam and Ira Livingston, eds., *Post-Human Bodies* (Bloomington: Indiana University Press, 1995), 135–61; revised and reprinted in Vernon A. Rosario III, *Science and Homosexualities* (New York: Routledge Press, 1996), 271–95; and "'Momism' and the Making of Treasonous Homosexuals," in Molly Ladd-Taylor and Lauri Umansky, eds., *'Bad' Mothers: The Politics of Blame in Twentieth-Century America* (New York: New York University Press, 1998), 169–90.

Heartfelt thanks to Douglas Mitchell and Richard Allen at University of Chicago Press for their care and feeding of a rough manuscript that has grown into a finished book. Thanks too to the anonymous readers of the draft manuscript whose comments helped to sharpen and deepen it. Finally I want to acknowledge the character and commitment of Jan Gay, whose elusive presence throughout this project has haunted and delighted me. Without her persistent devotion to understanding the joys and agonies of sex variance, this book would hardly have been possible.

Homosexuality, while socially stigmatized, has acquired a symboli-
cal centrality in American culture, figuring as a scandalous transgression against which notions of normalcy, in a vast array of domains, are defined. This book offers a history of how this came to be
so. Specifically, I examine the modern preoccupation with homosexuality by focusing on the efforts of scientists and physicians who have
been especially influential in stimulating and shaping discourse, opinion, and public policies on the subject. My broad argument is that the
topic of homosexuality, from its inception as an object of scientific
and medical inquiry, has allowed scientists, physicians, and those
whom they influence to set thresholds of permissible attitudes and
behavior concerning, most notably, the areas of gender and sexuality,
but in many other realms as well. In other words, by conceiving of
homosexuality as transgressive, experts (though seldom with this express purpose) have deployed it to conceptualize and delimit, by contradistinction, a range of acceptable habits, activities, gestures, relationships, identities, and desires in a manner that affects all of us in
countless monumental and minute ways. In the chapters that follow,
I attempt to show how scientific and medical discourses on homosexuality expose significant aspects of modern American culture, especially in terms of anxieties about gender and desire, as well as about
hygiene, bodily pleasures, population management, family life, race
relations, and democratic governing.

What are the causes and consequences of scientific and medical
inquiries into homosexuality? How have they contributed to making
homosexuality symbolically central, for better or worse? Who is
affected by their intense scrutiny? How are they affected? These questions provide a starting point for tracing how homosexuality, once
considered an obscure and unsettling violation, has become a topic of
obsessive national interest in American culture.

Initially, what motivated my undertaking was a pressing desire
to understand why homosexuality has been and continues to be
demonized in the United States. For nearly as long as I can remember, I have wondered why it is such a big deal, such a source of public

1

controversy and such a cause of private pain. What does it matter that people of the same sex are attracted to one another and express their desire in sexual relations? I pose the question again here in the pages of this book. My hope is that by attempting to answer it, I may help to dismantle what has become an endemic and taken-for-granted hostility toward homosexuality. Specifically, I am curious about how this demonization has been abetted by official and quotidian pronouncements that equate homosexuality with morbidity, mental derangement, and freakish bodily characteristics. To be sure, these notions, though not new, are no less common today than they have been in the past. From a decidedly presentist point of departure, I have attempted a genealogical analysis aimed at locating and mapping the emergence of why and how homosexuality has been imagined by experts to reside in anomalous bodies or to emanate from defective psyches and unfavorable social milieux. I attempt to show how these assumptions give rise to the idea that homosexuality qualifies those who engage in it habitually to be classified as discrete types of people who signify, to their proponents and opponents alike, transgression and dissent.

It is tempting to view this history in wholly tragic terms or, on the other hand, to presume that we have overcome the mistakes of the past to arrive at an enlightened and more tolerant present. I succumb to neither temptation in this book. Some readers will protest that, by focusing primarily on the roles of science and medicine in this history, I err on the side of pessimism and minimize the progress made by lesbians and gay men in making homosexuality more acceptable in American society over the past several decades. After all, is it not true that we find daily evidence of the public visibility of homosexuality in the United States today more than ever before? And have we not seen, over the last quarter of the twentieth century, a growing resistance among lesbians and gay men to medical and scientific proclamations about homosexuality?

In response to the first of these question, it is indeed true that several major American cities and a handful of private employers now have laws that forbid discrimination on the grounds of sexual orientation. Mainstream movies and television shows feature gay and lesbian characters. Celebrities are coming out of the closet every week, we have self-proclaimed homosexual politicians, and several major religious denominations have admitted gay and lesbian clergy and sanctioned homosexual marriage ceremonies. We now have openly gay and lesbian families raising children, openly gay postal carriers and school teachers, and lesbian flight attendants and presidential appointees who are "out" on the job. Clearly gay men and lesbians, through long and arduous struggles, have achieved unprecedented political clout and are now recognized as a significant constituency, which, though by no means homogenous or internally harmonious, is able to mobilize political resources and advance ethical claims for equality, respect, and tolerance. So I agree, it would be foolish, if not cynical, to deny that anti-homophobic social movements have changed the political landscape in the United States and, in many respects, made the lives of many gay men and lesbians more liveable. But there is nothing inevitable about this process; it is the result of committed struggles, often in the face of considerable homophobic backlashes which, in turn, are effected by the growing public visibility of homosexuality. And, as I hope to show, scientists and physicians have played a big role in bringing homosexuals into the view of the general public, sometimes for better, sometimes for worse.

The second question regarding recent skepticism among gay men and lesbians toward scientific and medical authority is equally complex. First, it should be said that homosexuals' skepticism toward science is not confined to recent history; it is evident during many of the episodes and specific contexts I trace in the chapters which follow, though it takes different forms and manifests itself with more intensity at particular moments. The same could be said of homosexuals' faith in scientific authority: it is present here and there, in the past as well as the present. But, again, its character and intensity shifts in particular contexts. Lesbian and gay rights movements, emerging in the recent past, called into question the role of scientific authority in constituting dominant ideas about homosexuality. But, as I show toward the end of the book, even in the light of homosexual liberation and rights movements, science and medicine continue to be appealing to at least some homosexual people as avenues for achieving greater knowledge about homosexuality which, it is presumed, will lead to the eradication of homophobic prejudice. In reality, ideas generated by scientists and doctors continue to fuel a variety of public opinions, some in favor and some opposed to homosexuality.

Neither the public's awareness of homosexuality nor the growing visibility of homosexuality necessarily lead to increasing tolerance on the part of the society as a whole. As I will argue, it is more historically sensible (and politically advisable) to view events of the past one hundred years or so as episodes in which debates about homosexuality brought the subject to the fore through a conflictual or dialectical process that at times promoted greater acceptance of homosexuality and at others led to its more pronounced condemnation. While the history I present cannot be characterized as wholly tragic, neither can it be described as the progressive unfolding of advancements that culminated in liberation from homophobia.

Because of the various ways that homosexuality has been figured as a transgression by those who either championed it or repudiated it, the subject came to be an agonistic rhetorical field of far-reaching cultural significance, equal in intensity to highly controversial matters concerning race, gender, and socioeconomic class. As such, homosexuality has allowed its advocates to launch liberatory critiques of oppressive features of the family, marriage, normative education, moralistic religious doctrines, and homophobic patriotism. At the same time, the public presence of homosexuality has allowed its detractors to instigate vociferous attacks on "the homosexual lifestyle" and "the gay agenda" as emblematic of the downfall of civilization and all that is good about it.

Hence, now, when homosexuality is perceived to be everywhere in the United States, we find the passage of the Defense of Marriage Act (DOMA), a federally promulgated law of the land that signals the nation's anxious commitment to protect the institution of marriage by limiting it to heterosexual couples. Its "defense" is a shoring-up strategy, necessitated, in the view of DOMA's proponents, by the unsavory encroachment of lesbians and gay men who seek the same moral, material, and legal privileges granted to "normal" people. We also find the proscriptive "Don't Ask, Don't Tell" military policy according to which officials are to refrain from conducting draconian inquisitions in exchange for homosexuals shutting up about their sexuality. The policy, which construes an individual's admission of homosexuality as itself a form of homosexual conduct, was touted by the Clinton administration as a moderate compromise that would end military witch hunts aimed at ferreting out homosexual military personnel and at the same time tame the troublesome tendency of homosexuals to be open about their identity and desires.

In this same historical moment, lesbian mothers around the country frequently lose legal custody of their children on the grounds that their sexual orientation subjects the children to an unhealthy home environment. In Florida, a father and convicted murderer was legally deemed more fit to raise his daughter, over her own protests, than was his lesbian ex-wife.[1] Cases of violent assaults and murders of lesbians and gay men have increased remarkably in the last fifteen years, a

symptom of the backlash against homosexuality fueled by AIDS phobia and by the general perception that homosexuals are dangerous and
gaining too much political power. Meanwhile, alarming numbers of
teenagers have attempted or committed suicide because of their fears
and anxieties about being homosexual. And the highly organized
Christian Right has launched an attack on "the gay agenda," charac-
terizing it as a secret moral campaign to use money and political influence to control the state, the media, and the schools as part of a
vast recruitment drive to draw innocent children and adults into the
"deadly lifestyle" of homosexual perversion. And "reparative therapies" to shock, nauseate, or otherwise dissuade patients from being
gay are championed by media-savvy psychiatrists who represent their
treatment regimes as a humane way to assist a purportedly increasing
number of unhappy homosexuals. In each of these matters, scientific
and medical authorities are summoned to offer expert opinions on
the subject of homosexuality. Their perspectives, though by no means
uniform, greatly influence the outcome of legal cases and the general
tide of public opinion. They are central players today, as they have
been over the past century, in public debates over the worth and significance of homosexuality in American society—debates, I argue,
that are evidence of the American obsession with homosexuality.

The process I trace in the book is not simply the step-by-step unfolding of a grand, thoroughly saturating obsession with homosexuality. Instead, what I document and analyze might be best described as
an episodic sedimenting process whereby medical and scientific theories about homosexuality came to form the ground upon which the
lines of public debate over the subject were drawn. These theories
and the surrounding cultural anxieties that fueled them emerged at
particular moments and were made possible by specific dynamics
within the overlapping histories of scientific invention, medical
knowledge and treatment, political discourses regarding proper citizenship, and moral discourses about what constituted normalcy.
Thus, homosexuality become a national obsession not in a gradual
but in an episodic fashion. These episodes took place in various cultural and professional locations which, at times but not always, were
conjoined. Furthermore, they did not follow a unidirectional teleological flow either toward ever-greater tolerance or toward increasing
repression. The obsession of which I write is just that: a symptomatic
cultural preoccupation taken up by politically diverse individuals and
institutions whose common feature is their appropriation of homo-

sexuality to register opinions on far-flung topics ranging from how to raise children properly to how to run the government of a world power, as well as vast phenomena in between.

Throughout the book I attempt to show evidence of American authorities' anxiety over how to maintain social and sexual order. I note especially how this anxiety was articulated through medico-scientific discourse as it suggested, sometimes explicitly but often implicitly, what was appropriate in the way of gender, race, and sexual relations in modern America. By the 1950s, it is evident how developments leading up to that point—in science and in the larger cultural arenas which it influenced—enabled the topic of homosexuality to become a national obsession. At that moment, the saliency of medical and scientific debates about homosexuality in society, as well as the prominence of lesbian and gay identities and subcultures, reached a critical intensity and visibility. But traces of an obsessive preoccupation with homosexuality are evident in earlier moments and took various forms: one can see how the recurring concern with homosexuality was a way of constituting norms in various domains including families, public parks and streets, schools, jails, workplaces, and the government itself. This, I argue, was part of a process whereby ideals of American identity were anxiously defined through selective inclusions and exclusions intent on maintaining clear-cut gender distinctions, racial separatism, limited class mobility, and heterosexual reproduction.

WHY FOCUS ON SCIENCE AND MEDICINE?

Tracing the history of medical and scientific ideas about homosexuality reveals how specific episodes, assumptions, and modes of inquiry are shaped by and, in turn, influence the social relations, cultural context, and political debates surrounding and infusing them. In general terms, scientific inquiry, though reputed to be the pursuit of universal truths, is always embedded within historically specific conditions. And scientific knowledge is always authored by specific individuals and groups, who are situated in a variety of ways in relation to political, material, personal, and cultural interests. However, while the doctrines and professions of science and medicine have come to be particularly powerful in the modern world, they neither dictate nor simply reflect these interests. Instead what one finds are resonances and interconnections, as well as occasional disjunctures, between scientific observations and historically specific social and political agendas. This is especially the case when it comes to the morally laden subject of homosexuality.

What is remarkable about scientific and medical commentary on homosexuality is that, from its inception, this commentary has been interventionist. That is, efforts on the part of scientists and physicians to understand homosexuality and to discover its causes have always been linked to larger agendas concerned with what ought to be done not just about homosexuality but about the sexual and social phenomena to which it has been attributed. Expert commentary on homosexuality, much of which approaches homosexuality as a modern problem, thus offers a privileged window for analyzing broader cultural anxieties about the changes wrought by modernity. Contemplating homosexuality as a particular effect of modernity licensed an array of judgments and a host of penetrating observations and interventions, seemingly circumscribed in their attention to sexual inversion and deviance, but whose reach far exceeded such narrow territory. Studies which putatively focus on homosexuality reveal broader concerns about the meaning of sexuality in modern times. Hence they have detectable subtexts that signal worries about the precariousness of masculinity, the specter of feminism, the rise of urban sexual subcultures, the instability of marriage and the family, and the dangers of class-crossing and race-mixing.

Critics often dismiss the scientific study of homosexuality (and, indeed, sexuality in general) as "pseudo-science," chock full of prejudices and preconceptions. The charge is abetted by the very dense and broad terrain encompassed by modern definitions of sexuality. Human sexuality, as it has been imagined in and out of science, encompasses not just bodily factors but emotions and other subjective phenomena whose reduction to objective, quantifiable elements comes at a serious cost, whether it be the act of "de-humanizing" sexual affection or that of imposing upon sexuality more obvious moral judgments than are usually acknowledged in other areas of scientific inquiry. Many who accuse sexology of being "pseudo-scientific" would like to maintain a *cordon sanitaire* around "value-free" or "objective" science. A common tactic for doing so is to set aside the affective nature of sexuality in favor of measuring body fluids, anatomical characteristics, sexual response cycles, and the like, as if these were purely scientific matters that are distinct from moral agendas or from the social practices that inform what will count as scientific phenomena worthy of study. At times, advocates of "value-free" science enter a covert pact with others who are repulsed by what appear to be moralistic prejudices in medical commentary about homosexuality. Together, they readily dispense with many of the medico-scientific studies of homosexuality by calling them a load of speculative bunk. But such an assessment overlooks not only the significant power and broader cultural influence of scientific and medical proclamations about homosexuality. It also ignores how studies of homosexuality have been situated in history and how their purveyors function within the acceptable scientific parameters of their time. This is as true for contemporary scientific inquiries and discussions about homosexuality as it is for those in the past. By closely examining the production of scientific and medical facts and placing them in context, I demonstrate how they cannot simply be relegated to "pseudo-science," even though they may appear ludicrous in hindsight. Scientific facts about homosexuality, including those concerning the specifics of biology and anatomy, were produced via certain accepted presuppositions and gained truth-value because, like all scientific facts, they made sense to their authors and audiences and were intelligible within the cultural and historical framework of their origin.

Scientific and medical discourses on homosexuality encompass variously situated knowledges structured by different disciplinary precepts and methods as well as by different conditions of possibility. If their purveyors share anything, it is a primary belief that scientific inquiry can establish truth and be inherently useful to humankind. But this framing ethos has permitted substantial divergences, conflicts, and transformations in theories and methods used for explaining homosexuality. The majority used scientific authority in efforts to control, eradicate, and prevent homosexuality while a smaller number deployed science to argue for social tolerance of homosexuality. Though some authorities dissented from the prevalent idea that homosexuality is a pathological condition, even they agreed that this anomaly must be explained and accounted for. Furthermore, in many cases, scientific facts produced about homosexuality had political consequences that were unintended by their producers. In any case, what we find in the history of modern discourse on homosexuality are scientists and physicians undisguised in their efforts to offer remedies for social problems believed to be signaled and exacerbated by homosexuality, whether they condoned or condemned it.

WHY AN *AMERICAN* OBSESSION?

I have titled this book *An American Obsession* in order to zero in on features of culture, politics, and identity formation in the United States that have contributed to making homosexuality symbolically central here. I am not arguing that an obsession with homosexuality is unique to the United States. Indeed, as subsequent chapters make clear, American scientists and doctors borrowed many of their notions from European authorities who themselves were motivated to investigate homosexuality because of the larger cultural preoccupations with sexual dissenters in their own national contexts. But what I want to stress is how the treatment of homosexuality in the United States was shaped by particular aspects of this culture. Hence, we will be examining how the histories of racism, sexism, and anti-foreigner nativism played out in efforts to manage homosexuality and social diversity in general. As we shall see, such efforts frequently involved the invoca- tion of principles of democracy, individualism, and assimilation, prin- ciples that were often in tension with one another.

The matter of claiming to promote democracy and equality while also confronting vastly diverse and seemingly "unruly" populations vexed American authorities during the period we will explore. To this end, scientific research was often interwoven with efforts to identify and police troublesome individuals and groups, homosexuals being pronounced among these. These efforts oscillated between seemingly opposing strategies. On the one hand, some authorities promoted the segregation of socioeconomic classes and races, assuming that homo- sexuality resulted from the breakdown of social distinctions in these domains. On the other hand, some advocated techniques aimed at as- similating individuals and groups into a larger American "melting pot." Under the latter formation, conformity was promoted through a combination of administrative governing tactics and extragovern- mental moral education, including popularized advice-giving by be- havioral scientists and physicians. In turn, desires to conform were to be internalized in the individual and became a sign of one's patriotic commitment to the nation.

Another distinguishing feature of the American obsession with ho- moscxuality concerns a complex dialectical tension between a tradi- tion of Puritanism that valorized hard work, self-improvement, and sexual restraint on the one hand, and an expanding consumerism that promoted pleasure-seeking and self-fulfillment through hedonism on the other. These two cultural forces, operating in obvious tension with one another in the American context, contributed to theories about the causality of homosexuality as well as to strategies proposed to contend with it. Some believed that moral rigidity and sexual repression actually caused homosexuality and other "modern nervous disorders." Others blamed the boundless pursuit of pleasure, unleashed by consumer capitalism and urban anonymity, for the growing preponderance of homosexuality and other moral perversions. In either case, a common prescription was to encourage the individual to gain some kind of control or balance over his or her desires, and to direct them toward meaningful moral and psychological fulfillment.

In contrast to European writings on homosexuality, the American valorization of individualism and identity is evident in much of the writing by physicians and scientists in the United States. Thus, in order to comprehend the particular character of the American obsession with homosexuality, one must take into account how the cultural veneration of individualism contributed both to authorities' pronouncements on homosexuality and to the self-perceptions of those who were labeled homosexuals. As we shall see, among the prominent spokespeople in both groups, homosexuality was taken to be more than merely a set of behaviors or bodily gestures, but as a central feature of identity for those who engaged in it. Though some European authorities had similar ideas, Americans privileged individual identity to a significantly greater degree, regarding it as the principal site for uncovering the causes of homosexuality and for intervening and guiding the individual toward a more harmonious balance with social norms. Hence, whereas European authorities, especially in the early years of this history, cast homosexuals in somewhat sympathetic terms as creatures suffering from a pathological lack of individual will who should thus not be blamed for their behavior, Americans were initially more inclined to punish those who exhibited an unwillingness or inability to control their desires. As subsequent chapters demonstrate, the American cultural ethos of perfectionism and self-improvement functioned throughout this history to structure etiological theories, treatment strategies, and prevention campaigns. And, importantly, this ethos introduced a key idea that has contributed to making homosexuality a veritable American obsession today: the notion that sexuality is a fundamental component of one's identity—a component subject to improvement or debasement, depending principally upon one's will power and upon the company one keeps.

Notwithstanding the cherished American ideal of privacy (which, after all, remains a privilege largely limited to the middle and upper classes), many efforts to control homosexuality were aimed at modifying the behavior of the individual by encouraging "adjustment" to a host of middle-class ideals. These generally involved striving for "normality," moderation, and sexual discretion, all of which were presumed to be abetted by diligent work and productivity. Lasciviousness came to be associated with the excesses of consumer capitalism and functioned to cast as menacing renegades those who lived for pleasure, those who refused to be discreet, and those who disregarded work, either in terms of engaging in productive labor or moral self-improvement. In this way, homosexual men and women in economically and socially disempowered groups, including people of color, poor native-born whites, and impoverished foreigners, bore the brunt of many of the punitive campaigns against homosexuality, since they were often presumed to be lazy, lust-driven, and morally primitive.

MODERNITY, SEXUALITY, AND SUBJECTIVITY

My focus in this book is on modern American society, and thus some discussion of my use of *modernity* is warranted. I am using the term to invoke a historical period distinguished by particular material transformations, including the expansion of industrialized production and massive urbanization, the emergence of consumer capitalism, the proliferation of scientific disciplines and technology, and the rise of technocratic administrative governing. Related to these historical developments, the term modernity connotes a way of thinking that privileged several key notions. Paramount among these is the notion of progress, an idea cherished by moderns according to which "advanced" civilizations are imagined to be moving ever-forward, and "civilized" humans are engaged in an ongoing process of gaining a more complete understanding and control of the world's resources. This adherence to progress opposes regression and primitivism and is closely related to deep cultural investments in science and technology. Cast in contrast to magic, superstition, and backward-looking folk traditions, science, during the modern period, was taken to be self-refining, reasonably predictive, and liberatory. Touted as the superior method for understanding the world, empirical science became institutionalized in remarkable ways. Although it often incorporated religious and juridical precepts about homosexuality, science was capable of disguising these under a rubric of impartiality and objectivity. Thus it became the most legitimate avenue for uncovering the mysteries of sexuality and for gaining epistemological, if not also modern moral, control over homosexuality.

To paraphrase Foucault, modernity marks a moment when humans in the Western world turned the sciences on themselves. With a pronounced interest in enlightenment and advancement, modern authorities sought to analyze what constituted the human being, to delineate its various types, and to predict its behavior. Modernity, then, is distinguished not only by the human subject becoming the object of scientific inquiry but also by a broad cultural fascination with the self and its complexities. What is striking about the modern scientific study of sexuality is its palpable investment in unearthing what Foucault referred to as secrets of the self. In addition to being assumed to be a property of the body and an effect of particular social milieux, homosexuality was understood to be a enigmatic essence or force rooted deeply in the complicated domain of the psyche. Thus a general preoccupation with understanding human behavior was closely related to understanding the self and identifying what were taken to be its aberrant forms and expressions. In the modern framework, science was elevated to the task of uncovering these aberrations as a way of making the self and its sexual complexities systematically intelligible.

Broadly speaking, I attempt to extend and particularize Foucault's theoretical framing of sexuality and his understanding of the discursive production of "peripheral" sexualities by examining the scientific and medical study of homosexuality in the United States. Foucault speaks of sexuality as a modern historical construct or what he refers to as "an especially dense transfer point" through which power and a range of new knowledges and practices circulate. In this way of thinking, sexuality is neither a bodily drive to be repressed or liberated, nor a furtive reality, nor an obscure domain to be uncovered. Instead, it is a "great surface network" produced through discourses and practices that subject bodies and lives to increasingly detailed forms of inspection. "Our epoch," writes Foucault, "has initiated sexual heterogeneities." And it has done so through the proliferation and implantation of perversions and, importantly, through a dedication to speak of sex *ad infinitum,* while exploiting it as a secret. Thus discourses on sexuality constitute an elaborate regulatory apparatus whereby "the love that dare not speak its name" has been compelled, in fact, to keep the words coming, to expose interior secrets, to pose for close examination, to demonstrate perverse gestures, to do anything but shut up. Of course, this apparatus policed statements, screened out certain utterances, welcomed some speakers, refused others, and produced not one but many silences.[2]

Drawing on Foucault's broad outline of the deployment of sexuality, I trace specific ways that homosexuality—under its various aliases of contrary sexual instinct, sex inversion, sex perversion, and sex variance—was disseminated and implanted in various locations. I look at how the implantation of homosexuality impinged upon the sexuality of a fictive and changing group (variously called "normal," "unafflicted," and "heterosexual") and at how the dissemination of perversion allowed distress about homosexuality to channel other anxieties and interests in the United States. Homosexuality, like other perversions of the normal, has incited immense speculation, intricate corrective procedures, and penetrating therapeutic interventions in a fashion that bears down on sexual dissenters but which also imposes prescriptions and demands on the "unafflicted" by way of warning the "general population" of the dangerous proximity of perversion. I take from Foucault the admonition that homosexuality, along with a host of other perversions, was produced as an object of expert scrutiny not on a principle of inhibition but instead as part of a larger inciting and multiplying process that intensified power and pleasure and constituted modern society "in actual fact and directly perverse."[3]

This incitement process, licensed by the putatively taboo nature of homosexuality, implanted perversions not only within specific individuals but within American society itself at many levels, from the recesses of psyches and bodies to families, schools, clinics, and all the way to the halls of Congress. The process was largely enacted by a general consensus, shared across a range of commentators, that something should be done about homosexuality—that it should be located, explored, accounted for, and, somehow, contained. The very act of describing those who engaged in homosexuality as inherently diseased and then decrying their ubiquitous presence and contagiousness ensured the proliferation of discourse on sexuality through an obsessive interest in its perverse manifestations. I chart the dynamics of this process through particular episodes when homosexuality incited acute interest and anxiety. And I focus on homosexuality because it has incited remarkable volumes of discourse and, indeed, has signaled a broad range of sexual perversions and social transgressions. Moreover, over the history I trace, homosexuality has become a particularly powerful grounding point for the development of identities formulated around dissenting sexual desires and practices. Thus an analysis of how this came to be so allows us to see how the modern implantation of perversions produced subject-positions from which troublesome dissenters intervened in knowledge being produced about them.

As methods for analyzing this history, I rely on aspects of discourse analysis and genealogical analysis as Foucault outlined them in his larger project of understanding the nexus of power-knowledge. For Foucault, power and knowledge "directly imply one another." In his words, "there is no power relation without the correlative constitution of a field of knowledge, nor any knowledge that does not presuppose and constitute at the same time power relations."[4] The matrices of power-knowledge are established in discourse which, as Foucault defines it, is a broad network of converging, conflicting, and intervalidating enunciations delimited by conventions which include certain interlocutors and allow certain utterances while excluding others. Discourses weave together institutional bases, qualified participants, and contingently intelligible modes of claiming truth.[5]

Discourse analysis, as Foucault conceived it, recognizes the materiality of discourse and appreciates its effects on the constitution of the subjects and objects of knowledge through a conceptualization of power which sees power not as a possession acquired, seized, or shared but as "exercised from innumerable points, in the interplay of nonegalitarian and mobile relations." From this perspective, power inheres in relationships, rather than being a force or entity exterior to them, and is effected and exercised at local and micro-levels. For my purposes, discourse analysis is useful for tracing how authority on the subject of homosexuality is staged and for locating the concatenation of discursive moves that produce "common knowledge" concerning it or a set of accepted truths that envelope a range of authors and agents in a field ostensibly focused on homosexuality but vastly exceeding it. In other words, to perform a discursive analysis of scientific and medical commentary on homosexuality involves seeing science and medicine as particular avenues of truth-production whose salience must be attributed neither to internal consistencies within these fields (for there are few) nor to their tendency to express the economic, political, and social interests of a ruling class (which they sometimes but never only do). Instead, analyzing these discourses reveals presuppositions, conflicts, and peculiar recombinations within particular circles of interlocutors at particular moments when power relations and anxieties are acutely palpable.

In the chapters that follow, I draw on Foucault's method to analyze power as it is effected in and through discourse on homosexuality and to trace the insidious effects of a tendency on the part of doctors and scientists to describe homosexuality as somehow anomalous. At the same time, I attempt to show how discourses about homosexuality engendered various forms of resistance, especially on the part of those toward whom so much suspicious scrutiny was directed. This latter point I link to *variant subjectivity* which is forged in the relay between questions posed by probing inquiries and responses produced by research subjects and patients. Many of the sources I analyze reveal historical actors asking what I call *questions of the self,* questions, we might say, of modern homosexual identity by which the subject must account for herself as an anomaly: "Who am I?" "How did I come to be this way?" "How and why am I different?" "Is there something wrong with me?" These instances of self-interrogation are often embedded in published psychiatric case histories and statistical surveys which allow the historian to watch the complex interplay between authorities and homosexuals as both attempted to make sense of diverse and culturally minoritized forms of desire.

The history I present here is indebted to several main areas of scholarship and analytical formations that have made a book of this sort possible. The project has been informed by biographical and historical work that documents the lives of lesbians, gay men, and transgendered people and that traces the emergence of their identities, communities, subcultural practices, and political organizations.[6] This work has allowed me to appreciate that the experiences of homosexual and transgendered people far exceed the grasp of most scientists and physicians who have produced commentary about them. Within much of the scientific and medical commentary, homosexuals and gender transgressors themselves are often little more than phantasms, whose subjectivities, desires, and experiences are *profoundly* reduced to stereotypical constructs. I am grateful that there are other texts that allow us to see what is missing in these stereotypes and that prevent us from assuming that medical and scientific classifications represent anything approximating the totality or diversity of homosexual subjectivities and histories. Rather than producing a history of homosexuality and sex inversion from the discrete vantage points of homosexuals and transgendered individuals, I focus primarily on how scientists and doctors imagined them. And, more specifically, I focus on how authorities structured many of the terms and conditions according to which sexual dissenters—myself included—have been constrained to exist. To be sure, our lives have been deeply affected by scientific and medical appraisals. At various moments, our perspectives have been influential in shaping the views and research of experts. What I try to do in this book is to trace the contours and intricacies of dominant discourses in relation to which we have been and still are compelled, daily, to make sense of ourselves.

Although most existing historical analyses have focused on either male homosexuality or lesbianism, I consider them together mainly because scientific discourse on homosexuality emanated from studies of both. In addition, I note experts' interest in the phenomenon of sex inversion exhibited by individuals who passed between or blurred the normative distinctions between male and female, some of whom did not engage in homosexual relations. Thus I examine scientific constructions of three phenomena—sex inversion, lesbianism, and male homosexuality—precisely because, in the early sexological writings, authorities relied on these constructions to group together a panoply of sexual dissenters as members of a "third" or "intermediate" sex—between male and female—who exhibited "contrary sexual instinct." They have been classified under various names (the homosexual, the invert, the pervert, the variant), which have been modified often, but not always, by a preceding adjective (male or female). At other times, the males and females of these anomalous types have been considered by experts to be clearly distinct from one another, representing different kinds of disorders and posing different types of danger to the rest of the population. To make sense of this, it is necessary to understand how assumptions about sex (i.e., maleness and femaleness) and gender (masculinity and femininity) infuse commentary on homosexuality, and to understand how lesbians and homosexual men are situated differently by and in relation to this commentary.[7]

In his own analysis of the discursive construction of the homosexual, Foucault wrote that, through the modern production of discourses on sexuality, "homosexuality appeared as one of the forms of sexuality when it was transposed from the practice of sodomy onto a kind of interior androgyny, a hermaphrodism of the soul. The sodomite had been a temporary aberration; the homosexual was now a species."[8] Such a transition from defining homosexuality in terms of habitual sins regardless of who practiced them to declaring it an essence in particular individuals was related to a new form of persecution that sought not to exclude aberrant sexualities but to "strew reality with them and incorporate them into the individual."[9] But, as an illustration of his postulate that "where there is power, there is resistance," Foucault noted that discourses on homosexuality produced "a starting point for an opposing strategy." The construction of homosexuality as a diseased essence was deeply tied to exercising control over it. But this construction engendered a "reverse discourse" whereby homosexuality spoke on its own behalf and demanded legitimacy, relying on the same categories and terms that pronounced it to be pathological.[10]

Foucault has been accused by ungenerous critics of granting too much power to physicians and scientists. They arrive at this accusation through misreading Foucault to have said that homosexuals were literally invented by authorities and had no sense of a distinct identity prior to being labeled as such. Those who rely on Foucault's general theoretical framework to analyze homosexuality have also been charged with maintaining a dogma of medicalization that disregards the many ways that homosexuals in history led rich and complex lives prior to, during, and after the time when doctors labeled them as members of a perverse species. It was not Foucault's intention to say that those who engage in homosexuality then or now owe their existence to experts, nor that their lives can be summarized by medical classifications. He was, however, interested in how the classification of homosexuality as a medical condition created a new kind of identity that, though severely limiting, could be a site from which to produce a "reverse discourse." In other words, he was interested in understanding how homosexuals, subjected as they are to intense social opprobrium, speak on their own behalf by appropriating aspects of the very discourse that named them as inherently pathological.

Having said that, I believe it is of considerable significance that individuals who recognized "contrary sexual instinct" in themselves were among the initiators of early scientific discourse on the subject, rather than being merely respondents thereto. Furthermore, they have been crucial collaborators in the elaboration of this discourse at various moments in the history I present. Foucault's semantical intimation is that the experts spoke first and then homosexuals appropriated, or "reversed," the discourse. This is quite simply not the case. The implantation and dissemination of perversions of which Foucault speaks occurred through the participation of many who recognized their own desires as aberrations in the framework of their times. This led them to write texts no less speculative than those written by bona fide experts and to correspond with doctors, whom they beseeched for examinations and consultations, and, most importantly, for help and support in protecting them from hostile police harassment and fierce social prejudice. So, to correct a rather consequential effect of Foucault's choice of the word "reverse," the scientific and medical construction of homosexuality was and is a collaborative process involving sexual dissenters who appraised science and medicine as enlightened, unbiased, and potentially benevolent avenues for producing knowledge about homosexuality. Moreover, they believed that this knowledge could be put to use as a defense against moral condemnation and legal punishments. However, it is quite clear, as the following chapters show, that this collaboration was episodic rather than constant, that it was seldom harmonious, and that it was nearly always nonegalitarian. To put it another way, the dissenters who appealed to science for help and upon whom inquiring experts fixed their attention got the short end of the stick.

Sources for tracing variant subjectivity vary in their discursive form and effects, and thus they require the discourse analyst to work in a supple fashion, taking account both of the manifest language of any given text and of the silences or gaps that are structured by the context in which this language is produced. Texts in which homosexuals speak in the first-person often reveal power relays between experts and deviant subjects, especially when the words of the latter obviously clash with those of the former. Those which render the subjects as mute objects require an analysis that considers how the text itself is an effect of power relations of the larger context out of which the text is generated. Neither type of text necessarily corresponds to greater or lesser toleration of homosexuality by the experts who wrote them. My point is that they require different analytical strategies for tracing the formation of variant subjectivity.

Medical case histories frequently render the patient a mute object. Generally written in a third-person register, they offer little direct evidence of the patients' perspectives. This is especially common in cases involving individuals who are poor or incarcerated or who, in some other clear way, belong to a lower social status than the expert. But even in cases involving white middle-class homosexual men, medical and textual objectification is not uncommon. Because of the common omission of their perspectives in medical texts, it is easy to assume that patients were wholly controlled by the experts. On the other hand, in texts featuring first-person accounts of homosexuals, it is tempting to assume that patients exercised more power in relation to the experts who scrutinized them. Neither assumption is adequate. In fact, the total suppression of patients' perspectives can be read as a sign of the physician's effort to gain control over unruly individuals.

And, in many published psychiatric cases, homosexuals' perspectives and self-perceptions, when not omitted altogether, were often appropriated to underscore experts' pronouncements of pathology and danger.

A slightly different problem presents itself in analyzing published reports of statistical surveys. In these, the starkness of numbers can disguise how specific power relations between experts and their research interviewees shaped the research. By contrast to most medical case histories, which tended to pathologize homosexuality, these sources often show it in a positive light by virtue of its common statistical occurrence in society. Thus, I am not suggesting that the mere presence of first-person narration by homosexuals is, by definition, liberatory, nor that its absence means the subjects were docile or compliant. Instead, I am arguing that all the texts I analyze have power relations embedded within them, some more obviously than others. Thus, as an aspect of genealogical analysis, I am interested in analyzing texts in context in order to trace how certain ideas about homosexuality came to be taken for granted. One way to do so is to identify, where possible, the effects of power between experts and their patients or research subjects, effects that are most obvious where those identified as aberrant yield evidence of resistant or alternative ways of conceptualizing homosexuality.

On the whole, cultural proscriptions on homosexuality authored and promoted by experts were imposed more forcefully on economically and socially disempowered people, including, notably, poor whites and people of color. By contrast, experts generally showed greater sympathy toward middle-class, white, native-born homosexuals, and their perspectives were often valued. In turn, middle-class homosexuals were generally more enticed by the liberatory promises of scientific inquiry and, to some extent, their sexual subjectivities bear the marks of ongoing engagement with the opinions of experts. Those who had little reason to trust medicine or science, in many instances, were actually more resistant to experts' proclamations or, at the very least, not so spellbound by them. Their alienation from experts, together with experts' apparent lack of respect for them, may have allowed these people more room to imagine their homosexualities in a different light and to seek other avenues for understanding and defending their desires than through science. Though it warrants more study, my research suggests that scientific definitions of homosexuality were incorporated most prominently in personal reflections by middle-class homosexuals than they were by people of color, poor people, and many women. That members of these lower-status groups had medicine and science to thank for pronouncing them inherently inferior may account for why they were not as inclined to engage scientific thinking about homosexuality nor to conceptualize their own identities and practices in its limited terms. Hence, a thorough analysis of variant subjectivity would require expanding the scope of sources beyond scientific texts and institutions to consider subcultural practices, argot, and entertainment forms they would allow us to specify the particular effects of scientific discourse on homosexual subjectivities, rather than assume this discourse was universally influential. But my contribution here is to lay out the effects of science and medicine in contributing to our dominant notions of homosexuality and thus to the identities generated in relationship to these.

EFFECTIVE HISTORY

In a critical reconsideration of Nietzsche's work, Foucault appropriated the idea of genealogy to make sense of conditions of possibility that give rise to ideas that come to be taken for granted. In contrast to the ideal of historical narrative which fixes events and actors into a seamless story of the past, Foucault conceptualized *effective history* as a way of thinking genealogically. By effective history, he was not suggesting a more efficient or instrumentally useful kind of history, as the term's translation into English suggests. To the contrary, he thought about genealogy as a process which takes stock of effects, or, in other words, of "the accidents, the minute deviations—or conversely, the complete reversals—the errors, the false appraisals, and the faulty calculations that gave birth to those things that continue to have value for us."[11] Genealogical method "refuses the certainty of absolutes" and involves what Foucault called "historical sense"—a strategic awareness of points of emergence or conditions of possibility existing at particular historical moments in the formation of the notions that comprise discourses. The genealogical method identifies critical junctures before an idea gains the status of an implicit presupposition, or before it simply "goes without saying." It enables one to locate how an idea won out over other ideas with which it was in conflict. Effects are like shrapnel in a discursive battle. They are not to be forged into a seamless rendering of the past but remain as evidence of the violence of hegemonic discourses. They are traces of the unremitting and carefully crafted terms of hegemonic accounts which structure conditions of truth and cast other ideas and actors as invalid.

To be a historian of effects, as I imagine myself to be, involves exposing the points at which certain ideas came to be accepted as truthful and analyzing what conditions made their ascent to the status of truth possible. The assumption that homosexuality is related to a deep-rooted essence, whether benign or deleterious, persists, but it is an idea with a point of origin and a complex history. Locating the various factors which solidified such an idea is the focus of the first three chapters of this book. In these chapters I trace the emergence of forces, practices, ideas, and actors that constituted the homosexual—in both its male and female form—as an anomalous creature requiring scientific and medical explanation. I begin chapter 1 by examining classificatory practices in science, undertaken in the wake of democratic revolutions in Europe, which formed the broad epistemological foundation upon which homosexuals, along with a host of social and sexual dissidents, came to be regarded as distinct and inferior types of human beings. In chapter 2 I examine the early medicalization of homosexuality, starting around 1864, and review the foundational theories of homosexual causality, developed primarily in Europe. These etiological theories reveal various epistemological stakes as well as competing ideological and professional interests which operated in the claiming of homosexuality as a medical matter and in the naming of homosexuals as distinct from the general population. Chapter 3 then examines how etiological theories were borrowed, elaborated upon, and applied in the United States starting around 1880. In this chapter, I trace how scientific and medical commentary on homosexuality functioned in the United States as a vehicle for expressing conservative anxieties not only about gender and sexuality but about the management of diverse populations congregating in cities during a time of dramatic social change. I discuss the various ways that homosexuals were classified as degenerates and associated with "primitive" peoples in the context of larger agendas concerned with moral purity, eugenics, racial segregation, and social engineering.

In the next two chapters I examine how homosexuality came to be regarded as an index or symptom of what might be wrong with modern heterosexuality, starting in the 1920s. Chapter 4 examines the emergence of scientific surveys of sexual behavior in the United States. These studies, undertaken in the spirit of solving social problems through scientific research, revealed that homosexuality was practiced among seemingly normal people and thus could be a sign of larger problems that might be remedied through better sex education and loosening constraints on sexuality in general. Though much less condemnatory toward homosexuality than early authorities had been, researchers regarded it as a threat to the private realm of matrimony and the family and used its presence to diagnose heterosexuality as endangered but restorable through expert intervention. In chapter 5 I analyze various discipline-specific considerations of sex differences which came to the fore primarily in the 1930s, when scientific research and commentary on the relative and changing nature of masculinity and femininity emanated from endocrinology, psychology, and cultural anthropology. Authorities in these three fields conceptualized sex differences in terms of degrees on a continuum in a manner that highlighted the fluid and malleable nature of distinctions between male and female. In doing so, they paid particular attention to sexual inversion as an interesting manifestation of the fluidity of sex. But even as research from this period indicated that all human beings were scattered across a single sex continuum with characteristics often associated with the opposite sex, this did not result in a consensus that "inverts" were normal. I argue that the outcome was quite to the contrary: the focus on inversion, across these various disciplines, functioned as a means for positing, by contradistinction, what would count as proper manhood and womanhood in the midst of considerable transformations in gender roles and sexual relations in the United States.

In chapters 6 and 7 I turn to a multidisciplinary study of "sex variants" undertaken during the late 1930s in New York City, which investigated the backgrounds, sexual experiences, social attitudes, and bodies of a group of lesbians and homosexual men who volunteered as research subjects. The study, unprecedented in conceptual scope and size, brought to light the experiences and perceptions of self-identified homosexuals. But my analysis focuses on the complex power dynamics and conflicts between, on the one hand, the subjects, who participated mainly in the hopes of using science to engender greater social acceptance of homosexuality, and, on the other hand, the experts, who diagnosed them, again and again, as sexually maladjusted "by-products of civilization." By examining the techniques and discursive maneuvers of the study, I attempt to show how the scientific study of sex variants functioned as an alibi for constructing modern norms of gender as well as of sexual desire, behavior, and identity. However, the study is significant not only for its inclusion of the thoughts and perceptions of self-avowed lesbians and gay men, but for the ways that it conceptualized sex differences and sexual orientations on a continuum rather than as mutually exclusive binary oppositions. This shift from earlier ways of thinking about sex and sexuality contributed to a growing suspicion that sex inversion and homosexuality were far more prevalent and were, in fact, becoming a pronounced threat to social order in the United States.

In chapter 8, I explore aspects of the larger historical context of New York in the 1930s in order to account for why sex variant subjects may have been inclined to see science as benevolent, at least in relative terms. With the crash of the stock market came efforts on the part of the municipal government in New York to crack down on characters who were associated with the reckless hedonism of the Roaring Twenties and whom many believed were to blame for the Depression. Chief among them were homosexual men. I examine the policing of male homosexuality in relation to gender trouble occasioned by the Great Depression and flavored by a sex crime panic that gripped the city in the second half of the decade. Municipal efforts to stem a purported tendency among homosexual men to roam city streets and prey upon innocents led to the involvement of forensic psychiatrists in the development of a special diversion program that targeted homosexual men for psychiatric rehabilitation. I analyze the perspectives of these psychiatrists who intervened in the harsh punishment of gay men and offered what many believed was a benevolent alternative. Compared to the brutality of the law, they seemed to offer sympathy and concern. This, in part, accounts for the willingness of sex variant men and women to see scientific authorities as possible allies. Yet even as progressive psychiatrists suggested that sex crime statutes ought to be reformed to distinguish between violent offenders and those who engaged in consensual homosexuality, they were neither able to effectively counter the anti-homosexual hysteria fomented by the sensationalistic journalism of the day nor did they abandon the notion that homosexuals were fundamentally maladjusted.

The remaining chapters examine developments and debates among experts in relation to broader cultural concerns over the purported increase of homosexuality in America following World War II. In chapter 9 I examine the impact of Alfred Kinsey's research, which reported that homosexual behavior was relatively common among adult men and women and which used these findings to argue for greater tolerance of homosexuality and the reform of laws prohibiting it. Kinsey's work drew fire from a host of scientists and physicians, but psychoanalysts were by far Kinsey's most vociferous critics. They protested that homosexuality was neither normal nor natural but evidence of diseased personalities. In this context, I consider how debates between Kinsey and his psychoanalytic detractors highlight differing concerns not only about the meaning of homosexuality in a period of Cold War paranoia and xenophobia but about the validity of objective statistical methods versus subjective psychiatric case studies for assessing the value or danger of homosexuality in the population.

Chapter 10 takes a closer look at acute manifestations of post-war paranoia about homosexuality by analyzing how, through the writing of psychiatrists, the family became a locus of vigilant surveillance in efforts to ward off the dangers imposed upon innocent children through the purportedly pathological behavior of parents, or through salacious and suggestive popular entertainment, or, worse, through the predations of psychopathic sex criminals who accosted children in public places. Psychoanalytic opinions, echoed in sensationalistic media reports, paradoxically idealized the nuclear family while describing it as a perilous site that, in many cases, bred homosexuality and thus required expert intervention. At the same time, psychoanalytic ideas also reinforced the popular notion that homosexuals were pedophilic sex criminals bent on corrupting the youth of America. As childhood vulnerability became a metaphor for the nation's vulnerability at the hands of evil, invisible forces, homosexuality became a central symbol of the dangers that threatened both the public sphere and the private domain of the family upon which the integrity of the nation was presumed to be based.

In chapter 11 I explore how notions propounded by psychoanalysts manifested themselves in an intermingling of Cold War homophobia and anti-communism that grew to colossal proportions and reached all the way to the Congress and the White House. Psychoanalytic assessments of homosexuals as psychopathic, untrustworthy, and cunning in their behavior were incorporated into government crusades to purge them from employment on the grounds that their voracious and indiscriminate sexual desires made them part of an international conspiracy and would cause them to consort with opportunistic Soviet agents, spill national secrets, and bring the nation to its knees. Chapter 12 examines the rise of homosexual rights organizations that opposed psychoanalytic theories and championed Kinsey's research. Finally, the epilogue reflects on the nature of scientific and medical commentary on homosexuality in relation to a broad and organized movement for gay and lesbian liberation. I conclude with a consideration of the legacy of etiological theories of homosexuality and note the political context of debates concerning recent research, authored by openly gay scientists, purporting to have discovered neuroanatomical and genetic markers for homosexuality.

Over a century ago, Nietzsche warned of dangerous tendencies to regard history as either heroic, quaint, or an account of past mistakes to be overcome. He decried what he called monumental, antiquarian, and critical approaches to history, for each dwelt on that past in a manner that distanced the past from the present. Each approach, he believed, tamed the past and thus obstructed human action. In *The Use and Abuse of History*, he wrote:

> A historical phenomenon, completely understood and reduced to an item of knowledge, is, in relation to the man who knows it, dead; for he has found out its madness, its injustice, its blind passion, and especially the earthly darkened horizon that was the source of its power for history. This power has now become, for him who has recognized it, powerless; not yet, perhaps for him who is alive.

Nietzsche championed the human "who is alive" and believed such a creature was rare. He lamented that many of his contemporaries had lost sight of the dynamic nature of being and had become servants to banal trivialities in their own time, blinded to the many possibilities for human agency in the past and the present. "We do need history," he wrote, "but quite differently from the jaded idlers in the garden of knowledge, however grandly they may look down on our rude and unpicturesque requirements. In other words, we need it for life and action, not as a convenient way to avoid life and action, or to excuse a selfish life and a cowardly or base action." In his ideal, "we would serve history only so far as it serves life."[12] Building on Nietzsche's critique of history, Hayden White has referred to the burden of the historian as "the special task of inducing in people an awareness that their present condition was always in part a product of specifically human choices, which could therefore be changed or altered by further human action in precisely that degree." History thus has the capacity to sensitize people "to the dynamic elements in every achieved present" and can reveal the inevitability of change. In doing so, the historian can contribute to the release of the present from the past "without ire or resentment."[13] I have attempted, in assembling this history, to alert readers to the dynamic and contingent nature of the past and the present. If there is such a thing as a "useable past" in the pages that follow, my hope is that readers comprehend the violence committed against sexual dissenters via discourses that officially proclaim them inferior, defective, and maladjusted. Moreover, I hope that they comprehend how this violence deforms the lives of even the "normal" and "unafflicted."

MODERNITY AND THE VEXING PRESENCE OF HOMOSEXUALS

> If man were deprived of sexual distinction and the nobler enjoy-
> ments arising therefrom, all poetry and probably all moral ten-
> dency would be eliminated from his life. . . . The sublimest vir-
> tues, even the sacrifices of the self, may spring from sexual life,
> which, however, on account of its sensual power, may easily
> degenerate into the lowest passion and basest vice.[1]
> —*Richard von Krafft-Ebing (1886)*

When they first appeared in the late nineteenth century, scientific writings on homosexuality offered meditations on the complex nature of sexuality in modernity and especially on the myriad social disruptions and cultural transformations with which modernity came to be associated. The originators of scientific discourse on sexual perversion suspected that the emergence of a distinct type of person— variously known as the invert, pervert, or homosexual—was a sign that modern life had deeply disrupted the natural order of things. Thus ensued debates over whether this creature was fundamentally dangerous, merely pathetic, or a brilliantly evolved hallmark of advanced civilization.

Reports of homosexuality in modern cities raised several questions. What caused homosexuality? What factors contributed to its purported prevalence? Was it a holdover of primitive instincts usually found only in "uncivilized" groups? Or was it a particular effect of modern life? If so, was it a symptom of regression to a perverse state that marked the end point of advanced civilizations? Or was it a positive sign of cultural evolution whose appearance challenged the superstitions of a repressive age? In any case, what, if anything, should be done about it? In their answers to these questions, physicians and scientists gained substantial authority in shaping public discourse about homosexuality. These self-appointed promoters of public health cast homosexuality as an anomalous, pathological condition and suggested that it was a perplexing byproduct of modernity. Their reasoning grew out of important developments in the larger history of science and medicine that provided discursive and methodological frameworks for producing a set of plausible fictions, including the idea that the homosexual was a distinctly modern, yet atavistic, creature.

Historically rooted scientific thinking about race and sex structured debates about the etiology of homosexuality. By surveying important features of racial and sexual science and by noting the cultural contexts out of which they emerged, one can begin to make sense of how homosexuality grew to be nothing short of a cultural obsession in industrialized societies and especially in the United States.

THE PROBLEM OF HUMAN DIVERSITY

To trace the scientific and medical construction of the homosexual, I begin earlier than this character's actual debut in the late nineteenth century and focus instead on relevant events from the turn of the eighteenth to the nineteenth century. This was a moment when somatic and psychical distinctions between human beings captured the imagination of scientific experts, with an unprecedented intensity, especially if one uses as a measure the sheer volume of encyclopedic texts dedicated to pondering the nature and significance of human diversity. This historical moment was marked as well by the proliferation of scientific disciplines focused primarily on rationally codifying distinctions between humans. Notably, scientific fascination with classifying human beings intensified in tandem with the political revolutions against monarchical rule that marked the emergence of modern nation states in Europe and the United States, governed not through the divine right of noble families but through the principles of equality and democratic consent. In spite of lofty ideals, the problem of distributing power democratically and of rationalizing limited political enfranchisement to certain groups plagued the nation states and civil societies of France, Germany, Britain, and the United States. In the United States, the cherished revolutionary doctrines of democratic equality and inalienable rights were legally undermined through the exclusion of large numbers of people from the right to vote, including women, slaves, and all others who were restricted from owning property.

The history of scientific thinking on the subject of human diversity during this period is deeply tied to the era's political transformations, whereby differences between people were much more than matters of curiosity. Scientific inquiries on the subject were situated in the context of a larger set of debates not only about who was different and how they were different, but also about what would count as the ideal standard against which a panoply of Others, at home and abroad, would be measured. Such questions, as we shall see, even when phrased in scientific terms, resonated with political anxieties specific to democratic nations concerning the principles of equality, inalienable rights, and majority rule. Attenuations of universal human rights and institutionalized elitism were rationalized, in part, through the deployment of scientific reasoning that pronounced certain individuals and groups as uncivilized and thus unworthy of self-governing. However, when considering the specific permutations of scientific discourse and institution-building during this period, it is important to bear in mind that the scientific quest to classify variations among humans was neither politically innocent, on the one hand, nor merely a respectable front for hypocrisy, on the other. In other words, science was not obviously partisan, but instead became a privileged discursive field within which broader political questions about human diversity were debated.

From this perspective, the presentation, later in the nineteenth century, of etiological theories of homosexuality was bound up with issues of epistemological and social control. For at the heart of early scientific discourses about sexual perversion were interests in understanding how and to what extent these modern manifestations of sexual instinct signaled the erosion of cherished social divisions. The specter of modernity both haunted and propelled what was, from the beginning, a scientific discourse marked by profound ambivalence about the possibilities and liabilities of progress.

CLASSIFYING HUMANS AND OTHERS

During the eighteenth and nineteenth centuries, emergent disciplines within the life sciences were greatly attentive to developing systematic classificatory outlines for understanding the material world and humans' place in it.[2] Initially, taxonomies elaborated by scientists ordered human diversity according to two principal logics of difference which, together, laid the foundation upon which the major etiological frameworks of homosexuality were based. One of these logics of difference concerned *race*, a term then used to encompass phenotypic, as well as ethnic, national, and cultural differences within the overall human species. And the second concerned *sex*, principally defined in terms of the difference between male and female. In constructing classifications by which to sort human beings, studies using these logics focused on perceived variations in both anatomy and behavior, assuming the features and desires of the body to be inextricably bound to moral character. Let us take a closer look at the general contours of each of these logics, before proceeding to how they came to bear on the classification of homosexuality.

Racial Science

Eighteenth century natural historians dedicated enormous energy to constructing taxonomic schema whereby, in addition to plants and animals, varieties of human beings were ordered according to particular structures, functions, and distinguishing characteristics. Their work was animated by a longer Western tradition of ambivalent fascination with the oddities and eccentricities of "primitives," "savages," and "aboriginals."[3] Such ambivalent sentiments can be traced to the European Renaissance and what history textbooks refer to as the "Age of Discovery," when the noblemen of Europe took great pride in assembling "cabinets of curiosity" to display wonders of the world retrieved by discoverers.[4] Fascination and repulsion with the Other was commonly expressed in writings by fifteenth- and sixteenth-century European voyagers to the "New World," slave traders, authors of adventure tales, Christian missionaries, and later, Orientalist scholars and European colonists.[5]

By the eighteenth century, collecting the "wonders of the world" had become more than an aristocratic amusement. Natural historians systematically classified elements of the world on the basis of observing similarities and differences between types of things.[6] In addition, they ordered European and non–European peoples according to racial categories through a variety of schemes which covertly addressed coterminous political questions concerning the faculty of self-governing. Speculations about climate, character, and morphological differences between types of people served as evidence for arguing over who was civilized enough to be granted human rights and to be free from enslavement and domination. Thus early modern scientific inquiries about human diversity provided an important framework for structuring subsequent debates about whether homosexuals lacked the moral integrity to merit the full privileges of democratic citizenship. Though their formal rights to vote were never overtly challenged, homosexuals, to the extent that they were characterized as atavistic, were likened to "primitive" races, and thus their capacity for self-governing was seriously questioned.

Prior to the nineteenth century, "primitive man" was often idealized by European philosophers in benign and even romantically fond terms. Philosophical treatises advocating democracy deployed the idea of the "noble savage" as a basis for arguing that the democratic social contract was rooted in man's origins and supported by natural law. Jean-Jacques Rousseau, for example, imagined the noble savage to be an innocent being who offered evidence of man's origins in a state of nature, unmolested by others and dwelling peacefully in uncultivated lands.[7] However, once encroached upon by others, the noble savage could no longer live in isolated peace and thus needed to establish a pact of mutual self-protection with others, which was taken to be the natural basis for democratic social order. The noble savage in these texts was presented in a generally positive light, a humble creature from whom civilization evolved.

In contrast to earlier, Rousseauian notions of the noble savage, much of the scientific writing of the nineteenth century presented much less hospitable stereotypes of "primitive" and unruly peoples.[8] This is especially pronounced in scientific depictions of Africans. In evangelical missionary writings, Africans were characterized as wild heathens whose blackness signified blighted souls. These texts, together with travelers' tales of savage and perverse Africans, resonated with nineteenth-century scientific discourse in a fashion that, to a large extent, relegated the noble savage to an oxymoronic figure. Nineteenth-century scientists, building on natural historians' project of distinguishing between "primitive" and "civilized" human groups, frequently noted the former as intrinsically inferior, backward, and even, in some cases, as inherently diseased.[9]

Comparative anatomy and anthropology emerged as academic fields seeking to categorize human differences primarily through a rubric of *race* which was overtly hostile to "primitives" on the grounds that these groups were at a lower stage of evolutionary development than Europeans. Experts in these fields tended to classify human groups in hierarchical order, privileging modern European nations and the men who led them as superior by virtue of their higher levels of rationality, morality, cultural refinement, and technological development. Thus, in many cases, anatomists and anthropologists relied on a standard represented by European men of propertied classes— a group to which they belonged—to describe "primitives" as lacking in these essential qualities due to innate deficiencies and a tendency toward unruliness and sexual perversion.[10]

With increasing intensity as the nineteenth century progressed, scientists in these disciplines, along with like-minded physicians, applied a similar logic to classify an array of "defective" types within

Western Europe and the United States, whose resistance to being civilized was noted as a sign of innate depravity and disease. Like primitives, they exhibited atavistic desires and thus signaled a process of biological and cultural regression. Pronounced among those labeled as inherently atavistic were people who dissented from the regimes of discipline and productivity required by industrial capitalism. Thus, during the second half of the nineteenth century, the bodies and behaviors of prostitutes, thieves, vagabonds, and the "feebleminded" were examined, measured, and classified as evolutionary throw-backs or degenerates driven primarily by innate and hereditary defects to misbehave.[11] What they were presumed to share with other atavistic groups, including people of non-European origins and animals, were biologically innate and inherited characteristics that placed them at a lower rank in the order of human beings. Starting in the 1860s, characters manifesting *contrary sexual instinct* were added to a growing catalogue of defective types.

Sexual Science

Intersecting with the development of scientific knowledge aimed at identifying and measuring racial differences was a science focused upon sex and sexuality. As Michel Foucault notes, sexuality, in spite of pretensions about its unspeakability, expanded during the eighteenth and nineteenth centuries, saturating the discursive and social relations of modern societies. Rather than being a natural instinct or a domain to which power is applied, sexuality became what Foucault calls "an especially dense transfer point" and a "great surface network" through which power and a range of new knowledges circulated. The historical and cultural dynamics which produced sexuality as such radically transformed notions of the self, the sexes, the family, the body, and life itself.[12] Discourse on sex, carrying with it taboos and prohibitions, in fact ensured, over the last two centuries, "the solidification and implantation of an entire sexual mosaic."[13] And through a putatively objective approach to sex, *scientia sexualis*, a "science of evasions," emerged.[14]

The scientific construction of homosexuality occurred through broad and intricately interwoven discourses and practices circulating through positivist sciences, bureaucratic governing, and modern regimes of discipline. Together these produced a broad field (or "surface network") of sexuality by first delineating its anomalous embodiments and expressions. Through elaborately evasive strategies, *scientia sexualis* busily constructed deviant types as a means by which to produce an elliptical residuum of "normal" sexuality.

To understand the emergence of the particular problem homosexuality represented, one must add to Foucault's radical theorization of sexuality a consideration of the central and powerful organization of a particular sex/gender system characteristic of the historical and cultural context we are examining.[15] A number of key assumptions constituted this system and structured a sexual science particularly intent on maintaining that men and women belonged to mutually exclusive categories.[16] First, it was assumed that there were two and only two sexes among humans. A second tenet was that these sexes—male and female—were fundamentally different and, at best, complementary halves of a whole that culminated in heterosexual reproduction. And, third, this sex/gender system held that the two sexes were arranged in a hierarchical order with males being positioned as superior to females, thanks to their inherent superiority in the domains of reason, intelligence, and moral fortitude.

In this two-sex system, the sexes were not different in *degree*, as they had been in the ancient Aristotelian and Galenic models, but in *kind*.[17] Woman's primary role in reproduction was the basis upon which she was decreed to lack reason and other faculties necessary to function in the public spheres of commerce and democratic governing. Thus, disciplinary methods from natural history, comparative anatomy, anthropology, gynecology, and psychiatry intersected during the nineteenth century not only to classify race and class differences among humans but to construct hierarchical schemes along the axis of sex.[18]

Primitivism and Perversion

Racial and sexual science converged in a most remarkable fashion through nineteenth-century male scientists' obsessive fascination with the "primitive" female. This fascination manifested itself initially in scientific efforts to penetrate the terra incognita of African women's bodies, but subsequently entailed similarly detailed examinations of the bodies of "perverse" women in "civilized" societies, including women who desired or had sexual relations with other women.[19] Scientific explorations of "perverse" bodies paralleled and anatomically localized the concurrent scientific projects of penetrating and mapping the "Dark Continent" of Africa and of shedding light on the shadowy underworlds of homosexual perversion in Western metropolitan centers. According to this logic, promiscuity and unruliness characterized the mysterious territories of lascivious bodies and wild geographies. Such specters licensed scientists and physicians to become intrepid explorers as well as fitting authorities to cast light on the dark domains of perversion, in and out of Africa.[20] Indeed, Georges Cuvier, the father of comparative anatomy who is remembered for his dissections of the "Hottentot Venus," devised techniques that were adopted by British and American gynecologists seeking to further establish differences between "civilized" and "primitive" peoples by inspecting women's genitals.[21] Using the logic that genitals would reveal a group's lascivious nature, they examined African and Native American women living in the U.S. and Britain as well as white working-class European women who were deemed to be "hypersexual," including prostitutes, nymphomaniacs, and lesbians.[22] Scientists anxiously scrutinized the bodies of male "perverts" as well, based on a similar assumption that they were inherently atavistic. But their focus on women's bodies was significantly more pronounced. This had much to do with the general framing tenets of the Victorian sex/gender system.

A predilection among European men of science to associate "savage" and unbridled lust with the genitals of geographically far-flung types of disreputable women and men reveals the intersecting logics of race, class, and sex that aimed at controlling heterosexual masculinity and femininity close to home. Such an interest was at the foundations of a Victorian sex/gender system that counted on the idea of middle-class women's innate passionlessness and domestication to keep the naturally lustful appetites of bourgeois men in check. The hypersexuality of lower-class men was taken as a sign of the primeval lust that gentlemen had learned to control through the civilizing process, but which lay just below the surface and required vigilant discipline and true virility to hold at bay. Scientific claims that European gentlemen had larger brain sizes than both their female counterparts and savage men appeared around the same time that scientists noted the extraordinarily large penises of primitive men. Thus, what European gentlemen had lost in terms of genital endowment, evolution compensated in their superior capacity to think. These claims were consonant with Victorian ideals of masculinity according to which civilized virility was expressed through self-assured rationality rather than furtive promiscuity or excessive sentimentality. In this light, homosexual men were imagined as embodying the worst of both savages and women; while they were insatiable in their sexual pursuits and frivolously emotional, they lacked the modesty of bourgeois women and the primal strength of savage men.

By highlighting the innate promiscuity of "savage" women, Victorian era science reinforced notions of respectable femininity that quite literally domesticated bourgeois women and maintained sexual double-standards for men and women. Authorities demonized women who resisted middle-class domestication. This group included not only "primitive" women in general but also lesbians, prostitutes, and "nymphomaniacs," who were regarded as having stronger sex drives, akin to those of men. At its more insidious level, the line dividing the morally superior bourgeois lady of the house from women associated with sexual perversion provided a way of ensuring male control over the public domains of commerce, education, science, and governing, at home and abroad. These sexist motivations became increasingly evident in later medical and scientific writing on lesbianism in which male authorities warned of the dangers of mannish sex drives, feminist sympathies, and other forces they believed encouraged women to behave like men and to refuse to be proper wives and mothers.

THE SCIENTIFIC CONSTRUCTION OF HOMOSEXUALITY

In this broader context marked by the elaboration of racial and sexual science, the subject of *homosexuality* was approached simultaneously as a mystery to be solved and a social problem to be managed. Those manifesting this perverse instinct were described as *contrary* primarily because they defied the expectations and conventions of a sex/gender regime that not only presumed the mutual exclusivity of the two sexes but also held that these sexes were naturally organized into reproductive heterosexual couplings. Legal rules requiring individuals to be designated as either male or female were part of a larger apparatus that was manifest also in the sanctioning of heterosexual marriages, with man-made laws understood as civilized conventions ensuring what nature intended.[23] Homosexuals were contrary to nature according to the two cross-cutting axes of sexuality and gender: not only were they attracted to members of the "same" sex, but they were presumed, on these grounds, to be inverted, with bodies, conduct, attitudes, tastes, and personalities characteristic of the "opposite" sex. According to this logic, for a woman to desire a woman sexually, she must have some male characteristics, and for a man to desire a man he must be, in some way, female. Thus gender and sexuality were collapsed in the earliest writing on homosexuality, firmly rooted as it was in the key assumptions of the prevailing two-sex system. Further-more, drawing on the logic of racial science, inverts, by combining the worst features of both sexes, represented a dangerous mixture of hypersexuality associated with masculinity and irrationality associated with femininity.

During the second half of the nineteenth century, physicians labeled many forms of social deviance as innately rooted diseases, through a process that complemented the early scientific classification of non-European peoples as biologically and morally inferior. This trend resulted in the labeling of the kleptomaniac, the neurasthenic, the hysteric, the nymphomaniac, the alcoholic, and the psychopath as constitutionally tainted classes of people. The homosexual officially joined their ranks in 1869, in the midst of a great deal of speculation about the body's role in expressing inverted sex characteristics and deviant sexual desires, when the German physician, Karl Westphal, wrote that *contrary sexual feeling* was rooted in the individual's constitution.[24] By positing this creature as belonging to a particular subspecies of human, Westphal, like most of the early authorities on homosexuality, used a principal classificatory logic of racial science. In other words, the racial logics at play in the initial naming of the homosexual as a distinct type involved more than merely drawing an analogy between homosexuals and racial Others, or, for that matter, between the concepts of sexuality and race. Indeed, the homosexual was viewed as having many of the same characteristics that distinguished "primitive" races from their "advanced" European heterosexual counterparts, namely degeneracy, atavism, regression, and hypersexuality. In this respect, race functioned as both an *analogous* and *synonymous* rubric for conceptualizing sexuality in its deviant homosexual form.

Evolutionary theories, which came to the fore by the middle of the nineteenth century through the publication of Charles Darwin's *On the Origin of Species*, contributed to the scientific construction of homosexuality by speculating on the *temporal* and *developmental* nature of distinctions across and within species.[25] By imagining nature as dynamic, evolutionary theories explained variations among living beings as outcomes of adaptations and reproductive patterns necessary to ensure survival. And, importantly, evolutionists attributed to nature a grand, though sometimes idiosyncratic, logic that could result in the appearance of anomalous characteristics and beings whose emergence was tied to fluctuating forces of natural selection. Because natural selection was bound up with dynamics of mating, reproduction, and survival, evolutionary theorists focused much of their attention on sexuality to explain species' progress and regress. To the extent that homosexuality was viewed as anti-reproductive, it engendered a host of theories designed to explain why nature would give rise to beings who appeared to defy imperatives of species' survival. In the view of some evolutionists, the prevalence of homosexuality in the modern world suggested a potentially dangerous turn toward extinction, while others argued that the special talents of homosexuals in the arts, music, and literature proved that, through evolution, nature had produced certain individuals whose contributions to the human race were as important as having children and even made them immortal.

During a period marked by rapid social transformations, large-scale population migrations across national borders and into cities, and close encounters between wide varieties of people, authorities invoked ideas about biological and social evolution to support a variety of political positions concerning whether interactions between social and natural forces were propitious or deleterious.[26] "Social Darwinists" used evolutionary theory to claim that social hierarchies of race, class, and sex merely reflected a natural order.[27] Many among them warned of the dangerous effects of demographic intermingling in modern life and urged scientific interventions in human reproduction to ensure the births of "fit" offspring. Some appropriated evolutionary theory to explain homosexuality as a form of hereditary degeneracy and a sign of regression, attributable to the disruption of an imagined natural order caused by modern stresses and contaminations. Others used the idea of evolution to argue that homosexuals were "nature's gifts" whose accidental existence was auspicious. In either case, homosexuality was regarded as one of several discernible hallmarks of modern cultural advancement.

Many about whom physicians and scientists wrote belonged to an increasingly discernible community of like-minded people, visible mainly through their dissent from norms that structured the two-sex system.[28] As we shall see, while experts invented technical terms by which to classify such dissenters, they did so by relying to a significant degree on ideas generated within a growing subculture whose members offered medical authorities stories of their experiences, including their suffering. Importantly, the original language of inversion emanated from the writings of Karl Heinrich Ulrichs, a German lawyer whose meditations on his own dissent from gender and sexual norms provided a foundation for theorizing sexual attractions among rather than between the two sexes. It is quite clear that the individuals to whom the diagnostic labels of invert, pervert, and homosexual were attached did not owe their existence to those labels. Nevertheless, the discourse produced about their bodies and desires had extremely powerful and lasting effects, enough to lead many to believe they were, in fact, somatically and psychologically distinct from the rest of the population.

The scientific practice of classifying social deviants in terms of innate deficiencies emerged not out of some isolated or merely coincidental discovery by scientists; the belief that moral character and psychical features were fundamentally tied to biology emerged in response to a number of significant historical events. Growing out of a context of heightened European colonial interests in subjugating non-European peoples to an inferior status, this belief intensified with the rapid social and material transformations of the late nineteenth century and informed the process of cataloging a growing number of deviant types. Classifying them as inherently inferior occurred in the context of public debate over who would enjoy the privileges of legal and economic enfranchisement in a newly reconfigured and changing public sphere.

    Conflicts were especially acute in the United States, where white racist reactions against newly freed slaves, hostility among industrial capitalists toward an increasingly resistant proletariat, nativist fears about disorderly immigrants, and backlashes against feminist agitation for the vote took many forms, including scientific research aimed at demonstrating that social inequality was merely a matter of biology and nature. Those experiencing contrary sexual instinct were described as threats, first and foremost, to the social order of the sexes and thus to the sanctity of the reproductive unit of the heterosexual family. But of no less concern was the noted tendency of these anomalous people to transgress established racial and class boundaries, threatening to erode the moral and social distinctions upon which a civilized society was presumed to be ordered. Their defiance of sexual and racial order, especially when expressed among the otherwise "civilized" classes, was, in the view of most early scientific commentators, a sign of a deeply rooted disorder. Thus it logically followed that physicians, whose professional niche was in the treatment of disorders, would become the primary authorities to analyze and treat this problem. Before turning to their particular role in shaping American cultural responses to homosexuality, let us first consider the broad context and theoretical contours of early medical discourse on the subject. For though it originated primarily in Western Europe, this discourse provided a foundation upon which American doctors and scientists formulated ideas and recommendations for handling the strangely modern phenomenon of homosexuality in a manner that contributed to making it an obsession in American culture.

2   MEDICALIZING HOMOSEXUALITY

Congenital sexual inversion occurs only in predisposed and tainted individuals, as a partial manifestation of a defect evidenced by anatomical or functional abnormalities, or by both. The case becomes clearer and the diagnosis more certain if the individual, in character and disposition, seems to correspond entirely with his sexual peculiarity.[1]
—*Richard von Krafft-Ebing (1886)*

Popular conception makes definite assumptions concerning the nature and qualities of sexual instinct. It is supposed to be absent during childhood and to commence about the time of and in connection with the maturing process of puberty; it is assumed that it manifests itself in irresistible attractions exerted by one sex upon the other, and that its aim is sexual union or at least such actions as would lead to that union. But we have every reason to see in these assumptions a very untrustworthy picture of reality.[2]
—*Sigmund Freud (1905)*

THE ASCENT OF MEDICAL AUTHORITY

For several centuries, official disapproval of homosexual acts stemmed primarily from Judeo-Christian religious doctrine upon which secular laws proscribing "offenses against nature" were based.[3] Religion and law constituted the principal authoritative discourses through which homosexuality was understood. This changed with the emergence, in the nineteenth century, of a medical approach to the subject. To be sure, religious and juridical characterizations of homosexuality were by no means wholly supplanted by this new approach. But they were significantly modified, and this had much to do with the way physicians positioned themselves as scientific authorities uniquely suited to solving problems confronting the modern world. By proclaiming homosexuality an urgent medical matter, they asserted themselves as authorities with special knowledge for treating it. Thus, by the end of the nineteenth century, they were to become the leading purveyors of knowledge about the topic. But what specific factors account for their ascent? First, doctors' expertise concerning the body gave them authority to comment on the causality, prevalence, and treatment of any socially deviant behavior that they could plausibly link to heredity or to bodily processes. Indeed, at the heart of many early studies of homosexuality was a fascination with the body. Physicians territorialized bodies and treated them as sources of evidence of perversion by studying their structural characteristics, motions, and habits. Bodies thus became sites of phantasmatic projections on the part of both the physicians studying them and, to a significant degree, the subjects who inhabited them. While medical experts debated whether homosexuality was innate or acquired, the terms of their early debates were circumscribed to a great degree around *how*, not *if*, the body gave rise to homosexual desire and sexual inversion. Even those who argued that homosexuality was psychogenic (i.e., the product of developmental psychological processes) saw the body's drives as instrumental in directing certain individuals toward homosexuality.

Through techniques of clinical surveillance and diagnosis, homosexual bodies, as they were imagined by physicians, were objects to be measured, zones to be mapped, and texts to be interpreted. For, in the view of many experts from this period, both the surfaces of perverse bodies and their dark interiors contained the secrets of abnormal desire. The phantasmatic homosexual body, like savage bodies, became a text of telltale signs by which to measure moral character and the effects of civilization.

In contrast to other modes of scientific inquiry, medicine provided an intimate proximity between the doctor and the patient. This, too, enhanced doctors' authority on homosexuality because they seemed to be able to elicit patients' deeply harbored secrets. Alienists and neurologists, the most prominent authorities on homosexuality, believed that bodily examinations, together with the telling words of inverts themselves, offered a more complete picture. Such a trend led to greater reliance on patients' narrative accounts of homosexuality, especially among psychoanalysts. But the body remained central even after some declared homosexuality to be psychogenic in origin. Then it became a site not for discerning hereditary features per se but for tracing the afflicted individual's anomalous psychosexual development through analyzing, in minute detail, how the patient reacted psychologically to the body's anatomy and drives.

Doctors' authority on the subject of homosexuality was further enhanced by their professional affiliation with the exalted domains of healing and science. Insofar as medicine was seen as both humane and rational, its practitioners offered an enlightened way to understand and manage the problem. They decried backward, superstitious, and cruel punishments visited upon homosexuals in favor of modern and beneficent methods. Thus, some homosexual men and women beseeched doctors to make sense of their unusual desires and to defend them against criminal charges and religious intolerance. But faith in the healing power of medicine was certainly not limited to this group. Many who opposed homosexuality thought modern medicine would yield the most reliable knowledge, and in so doing, be useful in ridding modern society of the problem. The growing trust in medicine, held by a wide range of people, was tied to the belief that its practitioners were rational, truthful, and objective, while also caring and compassionate.

The particular authority granted to physicians also stemmed from the professionalization of medicine. Previously, the field had been disorganized, consisting of minimally trained practitioners whose treatment methods were haphazard. Those who advocated professionalization sought to make medicine more systematic, and, to this end, they advocated specialized medical training. Medical specialization led to increasingly technical languages which gave medicine a more disciplined and scientific valence.

In the final decades of the nineteenth century, the medical profession grew in status, size, and credibility, abetted by important breakthroughs in the management of contagious disease and the establishment of professional standards of medical training and practice. American and European physicians enjoyed the growing benefits of scientific authority and its peculiarly modern purchase on the truth. By the turn of the century, the profession consisted almost entirely of affluent white men, as most medical schools excluded women students and very rarely were men of color admitted. Thus, when one speaks of European and American medicine during this period, one speaks not only of science but of a profession largely dominated by ruling-class men who distanced themselves from nonprofessional healers.[4]

ETIOLOGICAL FRAMEWORKS

Beginning in the 1860s, Western European physicians developed the first medical interpretations of homosexuality. Their frameworks were then appropriated and amplified by American doctors and scientists. Among these European authorities, there were three main groups, each of which commented, to varying degrees, on the *constitutional* basis of homosexuality. The term *constitution* generally referred to an ensemble of elements and drives of the body, although authorities disagreed as to whether these were innate and hereditary or the product of social conditions and psychogenic processes.

A first group of authors—including, most notably, Karl Heinrich Ulrichs and Magnus Hirschfeld—interpreted homosexuality in a *naturalistic* manner. The naturalists perceived homosexuality to be a benign but inborn anomaly, linked to an organic congenital predisposition or to other evolutionary factors.[5] Homosexuality, to them, was a condition of inborn *sexual inversion*, which caused homosexuals to be neither truly male nor truly female but to have characteristics of the opposite sex. A second group—including Richard von Krafft-Ebing, Jean-Martin Charcot, and Valentin Magnan, all writing in the 1880s—consisted of *degenerationists*. They considered homosexuals to suffer from an inborn constitutional defect that manifested itself in sex inverted characteristics and in overall degeneracy.[6] Although they differed significantly in their appraisal of homosexuality, both naturalists and degenerationists believed one's constitution was comprised of what we would now distinguish as biological and psychological attributes, including moral and intellectual qualities. All of these elements were thought to be deeply reflective of each other and embedded in the body.

At the beginning of the twentieth century, Sigmund Freud called into question the idea that homosexuality was inborn and inherited. In contrast to both naturalists and degenerationists, Freud and his fellow *psychogenists* generally regarded homosexuality as a psychogenically caused outcome of early childhood experiences. They considered homosexuality to be a *perversion of the sex drive* away from the normal object of desire (i.e., the opposite sex) toward a substitute object, including someone of the same sex.

SEXUAL INVERSION AND THE THIRD SEX

In 1864, Karl Heinrich Ulrichs, a man without formal training in science or medicine, was the first to come up with a scientific theory of homosexuality.[7] Ulrichs regarded homosexuality as an inborn benign anomaly and posited the notion of a third sex in order to explain its existence. His writings gave rise to the paradigm of sexual inversion which structured most nineteenth-century scientific theories of homosexuality. Ulrichs's ideas also posited that homosexuality was an attribute of a particular type of person, marked by the paradoxical presence of characteristics of both sexes.

An early advocate of homosexual rights, Ulrichs was spurred to activism after being barred in 1854 from practicing law for engaging in homosexual acts. He believed that a scientific approach to the subject would be emancipatory. For if homosexuality was inborn and benign, it ought not be socially condemned or legally punished. He wrote at length on the subject of "man-manly love," producing twelve volumes between the years of 1863 and 1865, initially using the pseudonym *Numa Numantis* to protect himself from further social opprobrium. He was interested in literature on hermaphroditism, and he borrowed both from Plato and from the French novelist Theophile Gautier the notion of a third sex to describe beings having both male and female qualities.[8] Ulrichs portrayed male homosexuals, or *Urnings,* as people with male bodies and female psyches. In his view, sexual attraction to men was fundamentally female in nature and sexual attraction to women was male. Thus, homosexuals were psychical hermaphrodites, having bodies that seemed to be normal but psyches that were inverted.

To explain this anomaly, Ulrichs posited two types of "germs" *(Keim),* one determining the development of sexual organs and the other the direction of sexual drive. He reasoned that since males and females were undifferentiated in the embryonic stages of life, a particular germ determined whether the sexual organs would develop into male or female genitals. A separate germ determined the direction of the sexual drive. Ulrichs believed that these two determining agents were usually in harmony. But in rare cases, they functioned in a contrary relationship to one another, leading to a being who was neither truly male nor truly female but who belonged to a third sex. Ulrichs focused most of his attention on male Urnings but later suggested the existence of a "fourth sex" consisting of those with female bodies and male psyches. *Uranians,* as he referred to lesbians, resulted from the same process. But, for the most part, the nomenclature of a "fourth sex" receded from discourse, as the third sex, between male and female, came to stand for both homosexual men and lesbians.[9]

Ulrichs's idea was embraced by self-identified homosexuals of the time.[10] In 1868, the German-Hungarian nobleman and writer Karoly Maria Benkert wrote Ulrichs a letter discussing the idea of *homosexuality,* a neologism he invented to describe the general phenomena Ulrichs had begun to theorize.[11] Benkert, who went by the pseudonym of Kertbeny, was less interested in the causes of homosexuality than in repealing the laws that made its practice illegal. But he urged scientific inquiry into homosexuality as a way of winning its general acceptance on the grounds that it was an inborn anomaly.

Ulrichs's notion of a "third sex" was embraced heartily by physicians as well. In the first published medical article on homosexuality, Karl Westphal used Ulrichs's general ideas to interpret the case of a girl who preferred to dress in boys' clothing and who acquired sexual satisfaction with other girls. Westphal concluded that her abnormality was congenital and thus should not be prosecuted by the police.[12] In the beginning, Ulrichs regarded Westphal and other physicians as allies in his cause, but he gradually grew disenchanted by their diagnoses of inversion and homosexuality as forms of disease.

HOMOSEXUALITY AND NERVOUS DEGENERATION

Many scientific authorities who speculated about the causes of homosexuality classified it as a manifestation of a diseased nervous system. They believed the nervous system was vulnerable to pressures of modern life. The German psychiatrist Richard von Krafft-Ebing was the most prominent purveyor of this etiological theory. In his famous *Psychopathia Sexualis*, first published in 1886 and expanded in numerous editions, Krafft-Ebing wrote: "The medical investigator is driven to the conclusion that this manifestation of modern life [homosexuality] stands in relation to the predominating nervous condition of later generations, in that it begets defective individuals, excites the sexual instinct, leads to sexual abuse, and, with continuance of lasciviousness associated with diminished sexual power, induces sexual acts."[13] Krafft-Ebing's reasoning here echoed Lamarckian notions of evolution: pressures of modern life caused pathological enervation whereby predisposed individuals passed on the acquired condition of nervousness to subsequent generations.

Krafft-Ebing's interest in homosexuality stemmed from his experience in asylum-based psychiatry. The tendency among physicians at the time was to regard the nonprocreative sexual behaviors of their patients as signs of mental disorder. As his career progressed, Krafft-Ebing moved into forensic psychiatry, dealing with crimes that were presumed to have underlying medical causes. He intended *Psychopathia Sexualis* to be a reference text for lawyers and doctors who discussed sexual crimes in court. Over the course of his career, Krafft-Ebing relabeled many cases of perversion as diseases, noting that they were deeply rooted disorders, hereditary in nature and beyond the control of the afflicted. On this basis he argued that sufferers of such diseases ought to be treated medically rather than punished or jailed, because their perverse behavior was motivated by a pathological weakness of will, not by conscious volition. Thus, for many who believed themselves so afflicted, Krafft-Ebing appeared to offer a benevolent alternative to legal punishment. Indeed, many wrote letters to him describing their lives and seeking his counsel, often objecting to his characterization of homosexuality as unhealthy.[14]

But Krafft-Ebing, like Westphal, used Ulrichs's ideas against the author's intentions by claiming that sexual inversion was troubling evidence that homosexuals were arrested at a more primitive stage of evolutionary development than normal (i.e., heterosexual) people. To support this, he first asserted that those inclined toward homosexual perversion would have what he called *bisexual* or hermaphroditic traits, and he noted that hermaphroditism was characteristic of lower life forms from which humans had evolved. Thus he reasoned that humans, under unfavorable hereditary conditions, regressed to anatomical or psychological hermaphroditism.

To Krafft-Ebing, hermaphroditism in an individual was the sign of a lagging evolutionary process because, as the logic followed, the lesser the distinction between masculine and feminine traits in any one person, the lower the individual on the evolutionary scale. Individuals who displayed what were taken to be sexually ambiguous traits—whether these be anatomical or behavioral—were seen as atavistic, as suffering from a form of evolutionary regression. Conversely, sexual dimorphism and monogamous procreative heterosexuality were taken to be indicators of evolutionary progress and maturity. Homosexual inverts, because they blurred the boundaries between the sexes—either as masculine women or effeminate men—were regarded as either "unfinished" specimens of stunted evolutionary growth (a status they shared with savages) or as evidence of regression similar to inborn criminality. Thus, degenerationists such as Krafft-Ebing posited the invert in mainly negative terms, as "uncivilized," lacking the ability to repress primitive and immoral instincts that human progress had otherwise eliminated.

Krafft-Ebing conceptualized those afflicted with contrary sexual instinct as living signs of modern nervous degeneracy. These creatures suffered from an underlying nervous disorder that often manifested itself in physical stigmata as well as in sexually inverted personality traits.[15] Among homosexuals, Krafft-Ebing claimed to find skull dimensions, postures, gestures, and mannerisms that set them apart from normal people, and he concluded that homosexual degeneration originated in the brain and nervous system, where he believed the damage was most pronounced. He conceded that the genital anatomy of inverts was neither hermaphroditic nor unique, but he stressed that the sexual responses of inverts revealed symptoms of nervous disease. A disturbed nervous system, according to his impressions, negatively affected the function of the genitals and reproductive organs. He argued that this damage was not visible in organic tissue but only perceptible through scrutinizing the invert's behavior, a claim that authorized detailed observations of afflicted individuals. He further warned that neuroses "awakened and maintained by masturbation" could result in extreme cases of *neurasthenia sexualis,* which caused afflicted men to ejaculate spontaneously and experience "abnormal feelings of lustful pleasure." It also inclined them further toward homosexual liaisons.[16]

Krafft-Ebing was quite convinced that contrary sexual instinct was an unfavorable and degenerate condition, a belief that came to overshadow the naturalist perspective of Ulrichs. In developing his etiological theories on the matter, he was influenced by the evolutionary ideas of Charles Darwin and the hereditarian precepts of the French alienist Benedict Auguste Morel. Morel attributed mental disorders to hereditary factors and believed that degeneration worsened over the course of subsequent generations.[17] Krafft-Ebing drew on Morel's idea of degeneration and added that modern civilization led to ever greater levels of inherited nervousness.

For Krafft-Ebing, the homosexual's tainted body was not only a necessary precondition for the expression of homosexuality; it also inclined the individual toward even more degenerate acts and moral dissipation. Homosexuality was only one of an array of signs, albeit among the strongest, of defective heredity. Those so afflicted inherited some degree of neuropathic taint which could manifest itself in a number of other biologically based deviations including neurasthenia, eccentricity, imbecility, and even artistic brilliance. The ancestors and relatives of homosexuals were assumed to be degenerates and neurotics who passed on their defects to successive generations with cumulative intensity.

Krafft-Ebing was concerned with stemming homosexuality in general, and, to this end, he posited a distinction between *sickly perversion* and *immoral perversity.* Sickly perversion was caused by a constitutionally based pathological drive toward committing perverse acts. By contrast, immoral perversity referred to the practice of homosexuality itself when it occurred under unusual circumstances among individuals who were otherwise neither tainted nor sexually inverted in their identity or sex role. What distinguished cases of immoral perversity from sickly perversion was the individual's ability to exercise will.

Krafft-Ebing's approach, like that of many forensic psychiatrists during this period, was to argue that *true inverts*, or those who suffered from sickly perversion, were also afflicted with pathologies of the will. This malady was linked to the condition of abulia. Abulia, as conceptualized in the mid-nineteenth century, was marked by a lack of healthy will caused by an innate defect. An individual so afflicted was driven to commit certain acts. Abulics, including homosexuals in Krafft-Ebing's appropriation of the idea, often expressed inordinate passion and lacked the qualities of a healthy will that could mediate between impulse and inhibition. The abulic homosexual's malady was a characterological disorder rooted in a tainted constitution. Thus, Krafft-Ebing argued, they should be pitied rather than punished, so long as they "remain within the limits which are set for the activity of their sexual instinct."[18]

Krafft-Ebing's distinction between perversion and perversity was commonly adopted by other physicians, and it allowed for various conflicting proposals for controlling homosexual behavior. On the one hand, the distinction could be used to excuse casual or occasional homosexual behavior among those who seemed to be otherwise normal, including sex-segregated school children, soldiers, and college students. On the other hand, it could be used to punish this behavior, if, as Krafft-Ebing believed, immoral perversity was a willful act, as it was when practiced by offensive but neurologically untainted adults. At the same time, the idea of sickly perversion, while it might function to allay a jail sentence, underscored the notion that those who suffered from it were inherently defective. Sickly perversion, Krafft-Ebing noted, was common among *true inverts* and could not be corrected. By contrast, those who developed an unseemly habit of homosexuality as a result of "unfavorable conditions" but who were manly men or womanly women were regarded as redeemable. This suggests that, in Krafft-Ebing's view, sex inversion was more grave than homosexual behavior per se.

Krafft-Ebing's distinction between perversion and perversity echoed the inherent class biases of degenerationist theory. Degenerationists suggested that acts of perversion committed by individuals from middle-class backgrounds were symptoms of a medical malady tied to a weakness of will. On these grounds, they deserved compassion rather than punishment. On the other hand, when acts of perversion were committed by "primitives" or those of the "lower classes," degenerationists generally regarded these acts as willfully performed and the actors as personally culpable and punishable. At the same time, some degenerationists conceded that lower-class "defectives" lacked the will power to control their actions. Such pronouncements legitimized the incarceration of poor and socially disenfranchised homosexuals in state asylums, thus effectively subjecting them to punishment under the guise of medical supervision.

In general, conceptualizing homosexuality as a form of constitutional degeneracy generated two different frameworks, both of which attributed it, in part, to the stresses of modern life. The first of these considered homosexuality as a sign of the loss of adaptive ability.[19] This line of reasoning posited that degeneration, of which perverted individuals were both signifiers and sufferers, was caused by an exhaustion of the nervous system due to inordinate cultural constraints and stress. It regarded the nervous functions as the highest and most complex bodily system. When these functions were broken down by stress, the individual, and, by implication, the civilization itself, underwent a process of regression, signified by a lack of differentiation between the categories of male and female and of savage and civilized. This debilitation of the nervous system allowed primitive instincts to run free, manifesting themselves in insatiable sexual appetites and promiscuity. In cases involving homosexuality, nervous exhaustion thus led to the emergence of a morphologically undifferentiated class of defective individuals who were neither clearly male nor female, and who were hypersexual.

A second set of explanations linking homosexuality with constitutional degeneracy involved a Spencerian notion of overspecialization resulting from modern progress and civilization itself.[20] According to this reasoning, as the human species became more complex—and those of European origin were seen to be the most complex—less energy was available to be spent on reproduction. Homosexuals, whose numbers were thought to be increasing, through their presumed refusal to procreate represented a pathological response to the demands of modern civilization. They signified cultural complexity taken to the point of elected sterility. The alleged preponderance of homosexuality among childless intelligent women and artistic men of the upper classes was supporting evidence that this contrary sexual instinct was a troublesome side-effect of European cultural refinement.[21]

By the late nineteenth century, those exhibiting contrary sexual instinct came to symbolize sterility, mental instability, and moral decadence in the most prominent medical writing on the subject. Psychiatric discourse combined conservative sexual mores with scientific opinion in the exaltation of heterosexual marriage and reproduction. Among the degenerationists, masturbation and homosexuality were condemned for contaminating and exhausting the source of noble sentiments that would otherwise develop as a part of normal sexual instincts and culminate in the birth of healthy children. For example, Krafft-Ebing believed that masturbation could induce neurasthenia which, in tainted individuals, could deteriorate further into homosexual perversion. As compulsive nonreproductive practices, both forms of self-pollution, especially when practiced by men, drained the body of its vitality and left no offspring to show for it. Ultimately the ongoing practice of both perversions led to a point of no return, leaving the "youthful sinner" with an excessive sex drive but in a state of "psychical impotence" which made an adjustment to heterosexual relations impossible.[22]

HAVELOCK ELLIS AND CONGENITAL PREDISPOSITION

The British sexologist Havelock Ellis concurred with Krafft-Ebing that homosexuals suffered from arrested development.[23] However, in Ellis's view, inverted sexual instinct grew not necessarily out of hereditary defect but out of a predisposition developed in an individual's early embryonic life, similar to the conditions under which other congenital defects such as idiocy, criminality, and genius were believed to originate.[24] Those with such a congenital predisposition were susceptible to becoming inverts in adulthood, but some could be spared this fate if, in childhood, they were subjected to healthy routines which fostered heterosexuality and proper gender identification.[25]

Ellis, who co-authored the first edition of his famous *Sexual Inversion* with the British homosexual John Addington Symonds, strongly opposed viewing homosexuality as a vice. Ellis sought to reform what he thought were archaic attitudes toward sexuality, and he advocated what he believed was an enlightened approach to homosexuality. He corresponded extensively with British homosexual activist Edward Carpenter and was seen by many homosexuals, men especially, as an important and sympathetic ally.[26] To Ellis, homosexuality was the result of a congenital organic variation. Like color-blindness, which deprived a person of the ability to distinguish between certain colors, the invert lacked the ability to see and feel normal emotional desires toward the opposite sex. Ellis believed that "strictly speaking, the invert is degenerate; he has fallen away from the genus." But he disliked the term degenerate because he believed its meaning had become vulgarized and vague, and thus unfit for scientific use. Although in his view all inverts had some form of congenital predisposition to homosexuality, he claimed that "inversion is rare in the profoundly degenerate."[27]

In many respects, Ellis had a much more charitable approach than Krafft-Ebing, at least when it came to appraising male homosexuality. *Sexual Inversion* included the first-person biographical accounts of thirty-three homosexual men, all of them educated professionals, who underscored Ellis's congenital explanation and claimed to be of sound pedigree and in good health. In contrast to Krafft-Ebing, Ellis stressed the moral fortitude of homosexual men and noted their superior artistic abilities and intelligence. He dispelled many of the negative stereotypes surrounding male homosexuality, such as the notions that homosexual men were innately promiscuous, misogynist, and effeminate. But Ellis did not extend the same charitable understanding to lesbians. To the contrary, he emphasized their mannishness and their tendencies toward predation, while criticizing their feminist beliefs as pathological.

However, in other respects, Ellis's thinking was quite progressive. For example, he placed inverts on a continuum with heterosexual men and women, noting that sexual differentiation was a matter of degree and that all humans were constitutionally bisexual. In his view, each sex possessed recessive characteristics of the opposite sex. Thus inverts were merely statistically rare variants rather than a wholly separate subspecies, as some degenerationists had suggested. Furthermore, he sought to legitimize a range of tabooed sexualities by emphasizing their close relationship to normal sexual practices.[28]

However, even though he claimed to do otherwise, many of Ellis's ideas defaulted to prevailing assumptions that linked homosexuality with pathology. The tone of many of his detailed descriptions underscored the notion that homosexuality was an unfavorable condition that might be avoided if congenitally predisposed children were protected from unhealthy conditions. By the time he began writing about homosexuality near the turn of the century, the idea that homosexuals suffered from a weakened will was widely embraced. Ellis built upon it to explain adult homosexuality by tracing it to sexual precocity in children. As he explained, initially, human sexual instinct was neither specialized in a homosexual nor a heterosexual direction. However, in constitutionally predisposed children who suffered from defects of will, sexual instinct could be steered down the wrong path. This most often occurred when such a child was subjected to unhygienic circumstances, including attending sex-segregated schools or being exposed to sexually aggressive adult inverts. He warned parents, as other writers had, about the dangers of perverse household servants who drew unwitting children into perversion, suggesting that individuals of the lower-classes had a proclivity toward preying on the innocents of the bourgeoisie.

Ellis added the dimension of arrested development to his theory of congenital predisposition. Sexually precocious children were especially vulnerable to becoming homosexuals in adulthood because, as a result of expending sexual energy at a young age, their development would be arrested. If the body's development was stalled, then its sexual energy remained feeble and was more likely to go either toward masturbation or toward homosexual relationships because in these situations "there is no definite act to be accomplished."[29] In Ellis's view, subsequent pathological symptoms stemmed from an individual's lack of balance between inhibition and impulse. This he linked both to congenital taint and to the unhealthy pressures of modern society that activated a predisposition to perversion.

Like Krafft-Ebing, Ellis believed that homosexuals had aberrantly strong sexual drives, again, emanating from defects of will. In his view, many tended to have irritable "sexual centers" which disturbed the interlocking system of the brain, nerves, reproductive organs, and genitals. Irritations of this sort manifested themselves in promiscuity, but also in patterns of self-sacrifice and intense affection. He surmised that male homosexuals' main problem was neither impotence nor indifference but an abnormally directed libido.

Although he emphasized that homosexuality in most cases was due to a congenital predisposition, Ellis granted that it could be acquired by individuals who, when subjected to unhygienic conditions, would begin to engage it in habitually and, as a result, become weakened and morally dissolute. In Ellis's view, many of the conditions that could trigger such a downward trend were those associated with a lower-class social milieu. He noted congenital perversion was common among the "lower races and classes" who regarded it "with considerable indifference," a factor he believed might account for "the prevalence of homosexuality among criminals." Thus, when considering its presence among "the uncultured man of civilization" and the "savage," Ellis suggested that homosexuality was most likely due to congenital abnormalities which were triggered by the generally degraded environment in which these "lower classes" lived.[30] As for individuals of higher social standing, he warned that, if drawn down into the unsavory environment occupied by the lower classes, they too may suffer its debasing effects, whether or not they had congenital predispositions toward perversion. Hence Ellis placed greater onus on the lower classes for producing what he saw as a growing epidemic of homosexuality. Although he generally argued against the association of homosexuality with degeneracy and pathology, Ellis discussed the subject in terms that often defied this claim. In comparison to other naturalists, especially Magnus Hirschfeld, much of his commentary on homosexuality construed it primarily in terms of an abnormality rather than a purely benign variation.

HIRSCHFELD AND BENIGN VARIATION

In 1896, the same year that Ellis published his first edition of *Sexual Inversion*, the German physician and homosexual rights advocate Magnus Hirschfeld offered a manifestly positive appraisal of homosexuals.[31] Following Ulrichs, he believed that homosexuals were rare but natural variants, and like Krafft-Ebing, he believed that homosexual desire was impelled by something other than free will. But Hirschfeld, a homosexual himself, substantially modified the ideas of these thinkers through large-scale comprehensive sex research surveying thousands of people, including other self-proclaimed homosexuals. Most importantly, he countered the prevailing idea that homosexuality was a symptom of constitutional degeneracy. Furthermore, Hirschfeld emphasized that the principal disorders suffered by homosexuals were those caused by the ridicule and contempt heaped upon them by an intolerant society.

In 1895, Hirschfeld organized a movement for homosexual emancipation, following the highly publicized trial that found Oscar Wilde guilty of gross indecency for his affair with the son of a British nobleman. In 1896, Hirschfeld organized the Scientific-Humanitarian Committee, the world's first homosexual rights organization. Its name captured Hirschfeld's strong belief that science could allay suffering through an enlightened approach to understanding sexual anomalies. Science, for Hirschfeld, should enhance humanity rather than exist as a socially detached and value-neutral field. The Scientific-Humanitarian Committee's primary goal was to repeal Paragraph 175 of the Prussian legal code, which outlawed consensual sexual contact between adult men. But gradually the committee's efforts extended to a larger campaign to change popular attitudes.[32]

In 1894, Hirschfeld met the Italian anthropologists Paolo Mantegazza and Cesare Lombroso and was impressed by their ideas about sexuality and especially by Lombroso's methods for large-scale studies of criminals, prostitutes, and geniuses.[33] He was interested in adapting Lombroso's techniques to study the constitutional features of variant individuals, including homosexuals. In 1919, Hirschfeld founded the Institut für Sexualwissenschaft in Berlin, the first of its sort dedicated to studying the array of anomalous conditions associated with sex and sexuality. Over the course of his career, he conducted physical examinations and interpreted the biographical questionnaires of tens of thousands of people who visited his institute. Hirschfeld's scientific investigations supported his ethos of sexual pluralism by revealing the anatomical and psychosexual variations among human beings.

Hirschfeld was drawn to evolutionary theory and was interested in the natural occurrence of variations in sexual dimorphism. In particular he was compelled by Darwin's idea of the indispensability of natural variation in evolutionary processes. He likened homosexuality to hermaphroditism and referred to it, in 1896, as a "congenital impediment of evolution."[34] In 1914, he clarified that homosexuality was a natural variation similar to eye color or handedness. "Homosexuality is neither a disease nor degeneracy," he wrote, "but rather represents a piece of the natural order, a sexual variation like numerous, analogous sexual modifications in the animal and plant kingdoms."[35] Without question, this placed him at odds with many of his contemporaries who associated homosexuality with pathology and morbid degeneracy, and who charged Hirschfeld with denigrating objective science through his "propagandistic" aims.[36]

Drawn to monism, Hirschfeld had a deep reverence for nature, and he regarded its beauty and logic as endangered by precepts of the modern world which sought to tame instincts and repress nature's true design. His monism also led him to criticize the Judeo-Christian separation of mind and body. Seeing the two as harmonious and mutually influential, Hirschfeld postulated that sexual desire emanated primarily from the central nervous system, which, in homosexuals, combined male and female qualities. This desire manifested itself not only in genital sensations but in the overall personality and character of homosexuals. Although Ulrichs's idea of the third sex had greatly influenced him, by 1904 Hirschfeld abandoned the term because it

lumped a wide range of sexual intermediates, including physical hermaphrodites, into a single scientifically imprecise category. His research on gradations between individuals allowed him to identify homosexuality as one of many sexual anomalies, each of which had its
own particular characteristics.

Around 1912 Hirschfeld advanced the view that normal and abnormal sexual desires resulted from innate constitutional factors, which
were influenced by the glands of internal secretion, later named hormones. He was drawn to the new scientific field of endocrinology to
investigate sexual intermediacy and variations in genital anatomy in
psychology, and in sex drive. Hirschfeld was among the very first scientific writers to claim that all people had qualities of the other sex,
and he argued, contrary to Krafft-Ebing, that similarities between the
sexes increased rather than decreased with evolution. Presaging what
would later be taken for granted, he offered the radical insight that
each individual was comprised of a variety of qualities, making the
pure female and the pure male merely abstract concepts seldom found
among actual people. His research showed that homosexuals tended
to have psychological and physical traces of the other sex. On this
basis he argued against treatments to "cure" homosexuality, saying it
would be undesirable to disrupt the harmony between an individual's
physical features and the orientation of his or her sex drive. For a
lesbian to be a "pure female" or a homosexual man to be a "pure man"
would be, in Hirschfeld's words, "something discordant, mon-
strous."[37]

Hirschfeld's notion of homosexuality as a natural variation was
echoed by the German physician Otto Weininger, who observed that
while in all cases of inversion "there is invariably an anatomical ap-
proximation to the opposite sex, . . . it is not generally recognized that
sexual inverts may be otherwise perfectly healthy, and with regard to
other matters quite normal."[38] But, for the most part, the naturalist
perspective was overshadowed by a consensus among most physicians
that inversion and homosexuality were, by definition, troublesome
disorders. This consensus was elaborated in new directions by emerging psychogenic theories.

PSYCHOANALYSIS AND PSYCHOGENIC THEORIES
OF HOMOSEXUALITY

Growing evidence that many homosexual men and women were neither apparently sexually inverted nor congenitally degenerate spurred

the development of psychogenic theories. Their proponents were mainly psychoanalysts who understood homosexuality not in terms of a hereditary or congenital defect that manifested itself in sexual inversion but as *perversions* of the normal sex drive caused by the stresses and strains of psychosexual development.[39]

Psychoanalysis offered several ideas that radically countered prevailing etiological theories. First, it postulated that since individuals were essentially bisexual (i.e., oriented originally toward neither sex in particular), homosexuality was a stage in normal childhood development, passed through by all individuals during the course of the Oedipus complex. This idea undermined a prevalent notion that homosexuality was a behavior or disposition confined to only particular types of people. In other words, an individual was neither naturally nor inevitably destined toward heterosexuality or homosexuality, but gravitated toward these various outcomes through complicated psychosexual developmental processes. This notion also presumed that individuals might retain some aspect of the homosexual stage and manifest it in their adult life, even to the benefit of society. Freud, for example, noted that a certain degree of sublimated homoeroticism played a valuable role in adult social relationships, including those comprising fraternal civic and military institutions.[40]

A second and related psychoanalytic innovation was the notion of *latent homosexuality*. According to this idea, homosexual tendencies may not manifest themselves in overt homosexual relations but underlie and motivate a wide range of psychological conflicts, even in individuals who engage exclusively in sexual relations with the opposite sex. Latent homosexuality arose from a child's difficulty in adjusting to the psychosexual demands of maturation. Thus psychoanalysts believed it was important to consider how homosexuality might be operating in the neurotic behavior of heterosexuals.

Thirdly, psychoanalysts noted that psychopathological symptoms in general were neither rare nor were they only exhibited by those diagnosed as neurotic or insane, but instead occurred in the daily-life situations of nearly everyone. In other words, psychopathology was intrinsic to psychosexual development since maturation, by definition, involved traumatic processes of repression.[41] The population, taken as a whole, revealed gradations of pathology along a continuum from the relatively "adjusted" to the fully insane. Thus Freud and other psychoanalysts suggested that homosexuality in adulthood was perhaps no more pathological than the wide range of perversions, aggressions, and neurotic desires commonly expressed in heterosexual relations.[42]

Fourthly, psychoanalysts were inclined to see homosexuality and a growing number of perversions of the normal sex drive as the result of stresses of modern life. Without question, their theories reflected preconceived notions that the individual's healthy adjustment to normative gender roles and monogamous reproductive heterosexuality were favorable. But psychoanalysts did not assume proper gender identification and healthy heterosexuality were inevitable outcomes of a "natural" process. Instead these were regarded as triumphs against mounting odds. They could be achieved through psychoanalytic treatment administered to the many who had difficulty adapting to cultural norms.

Finally, by focusing on the bourgeois nuclear family as the primary context in which psychosexual development occurred, psychoanalysts fueled a growing cultural anxiety that sexual perversions might not originate in the social milieux of lower or primitive classes but in fact were primarily incubated by the middle-class family itself. Each of these innovations allowed psychoanalysts to argue that homosexuality was far more pervasive than prevailing theories had suggested. This, in turn, broadened psychoanalysts' authority to speak about a broad range of pressing social concerns, including homosexuality. Although they denaturalized heterosexuality and construed neuroses to be commonplace, psychoanalysts at the same time offered a new language and method for consolidating the equation between homosexuality and pathology.

Freud, in particular, persisted in arguing that existing theories did not adequately account for the wide range of homosexual tendencies among his patients. He repeatedly criticized the notion that homosexuality would be visible in physical stigmata of the body. In most of his writings, homosexual tendencies represented arrested psychosexual development that might result from a vague underlying biological component that predisposed certain individuals toward it. But he stressed that this biological component was neither clear nor sufficient for separating out homosexuals as a group with a special nature. Nor did he equate all homosexuality with inversion.[43]

Freud's focus on the body mainly concerned how homosexual tendencies were related to psychological fixations on particular anatomical parts of the body (i.e., the penis, clitoris, vagina, anus, and breasts) that occurred through the psycho-cultural taming of the id and the circumscription of the maturing child's erogenous zones. He mapped the child's development through stages by which its body's polymorphous pleasures gradually became focused first at the oral stage, then the anal stage, and finally the phallic stage. Each of these stages corresponded to the particularly intensified pleasures of the mouth, anus, and genitals around which the child progressively experienced limitations of its essential drives in accordance with cultural norms requiring the child to separate from its mother and become a mature individual. Referring to male homosexuals in particular, Freud noted that "in the inversion types it can be ascertained that they are altogether controlled by an archaic constitution and by primitive psychic mechanisms. The importance of the *narcissistic object selection* and the *clinging* to the erotic significance of the *anal* zone seem to be their most essential characteristics." He noted, however, that "one gains nothing by separating the most extreme inversion types from the others on the basis of such constitutional peculiarities. What is found in the latter as seemingly an adequate determinate [of inversion] can also be demonstrated only in lesser force, in the constitution of transitional types, and in manifestly normal persons."[44]

In Freud's reworking of the term constitutional disposition, he stressed the innate drives, or instincts, of the body which constituted the *libido*.[45] He was most compelled by how these drives were directed in particular ways as a result of the conflicts between an individual's experiences of boundless infantile pleasure and the subsequent cultural imperative that the child's desires be disciplined to achieve maturity. He suggested that the intense sexual repression characteristic of bourgeois Victorian society led to a perversion of the body's inherent sex drive away from its normal aim and object, as expressed in heterosexual reproduction, toward fantasies and practices involving substitute objects.[46]

Freud's important distinction between *sexual aim* and *sexual object* unsettled the prevailing idea that homosexuality was principally tied to sex inversion. As he defined them, *sexual aim* was "the aim toward which the instinct strives" and *sexual object* denoted "the person from whom the sexual attraction emanates."[47] In other words, an individual's *sexual aim* consisted of his or her preferred mode of sexual behavior, including whether the individual preferred to take a passive or active role in sexual encounters or preferred specific acts such as oral or anal sex. This was distinguished analytically from *sexual object choice*, which denoted the process by which an individual formed and expressed desire toward particular objects, or partners.

In Freud's framework, the normal object of sexual desire was a member of the opposite sex. He included homosexual object choice among the problematic deviations signalling a perversion of the normal sex drive away from normal objects toward substitute objects. On these grounds he argued that earlier definitions of hereditary and congenital inversion had collapsed these two dynamics by defining "true" homosexuality in terms of sex-inverted somatic and psychological characteristics from which it was inferred that homosexuality emanated. Freud developed his framework in part to account for why many homosexual men exhibited "the most perfect psychic manliness" and even sought partners with pronounced "feminine" qualities (i.e., young men and effeminate male prostitutes) though they themselves "retained the psychic character of virility."[48]

Freud was especially interested in what he called *sexual instincts*, which he believed were channeled by the individual's sexual aim. He argued that modern society placed far too much emphasis on judging individuals by the choice of their object, assuming they were normal so long as they directed their instincts toward the correct object. Citing the ancients who had "extolled the instinct and were ready to ennoble through it even an inferior object," Freud lamented the modern privileging of objects as the grounds for determining what is normal and what is not. Instead, he argued that greater attention should be paid by physicians to the sexual instinct, "which is the essential and constant element" about which judgments as to normality and pathology should be made. He went on to say that "no uniformity of sexual aim can be attributed to inversion," noting that among homosexual men, some desired anal intercourse, others preferred masturbation, and others engaged in oral intercourse. Thus, he concluded that "the sexual instinct is probably entirely independent of its object." In making this argument, Freud reiterated that among apparently normal people, perversions of the sexual instinct were also present, manifesting in fixations on animals, children, or fetishistic items such as leather, fur, or perfume.[49]

Homosexuality, as Freud theorized it, was endemic to the Oedipus complex through which the child must negotiate the processes of differentiating from its primary love object (the mother) and come to terms with the incest taboo forbidding it to possess its mother or father. For the boy child, the desire for his mother was coupled with a desire to eliminate or "kill" his father. Once the child saw that his mother "lacked" a penis, and normally concluded that she had been castrated, his own fear of castration made him fearful of his father's retribution. As a way to avoid castration, the child might seek to take the place of his mother in an effort to attract his father's affection rather than his hostility. This, Freud noted, would be a normal course of events for the boy reaching maturity through the Oedipus crisis. However, in situations of arrested development or regression, brought on by excessive fear or an inability to navigate the perilous path resolving the castration and Oedipus complexes, the male would commonly resort to homosexuality in adulthood.[50] For the girl child, Freud noted that homosexuality was even more pronounced in the normal stages of development since the primary love object from which the child was to separate was also a female. In what Freud admitted was a more complex process of resolving the Oedipus and castration complexes, girls began in a homosexual relation with their mothers, before having to separate in order ultimately to identify with their mothers and attract the affections of the father.[51]

Freud maintained that homosexuality only became a neurotic personality disturbance in the event that the adult individual could not adequately (i.e., without neuroses) mature to the cultural demands of sexual repression and heterosexual reproduction. From his own observations, Freud believed that many who showed homosexual tendencies contributed a great deal to society and, far from being degenerate, were of high moral and intellectual standing. He stressed this when referring to male homosexuality, but, as we shall see, he was not nearly so positive about female homosexuality. In either case, though, he was concerned about the emotional well-being of those who suffered difficulties adjusting to the demands of psychosexual maturation of the sort required by modern "civilized" societies.[52] Thus he generally saw homosexuality in adults as a symptom of arrested development and thwarted maturity, two generally unfavorable conditions that posed a threat to the future of modern life.

Overall, Freud's theories suggested that homosexuality, like other perversions, was inferior to heterosexual relations geared toward reproduction. Sexual pleasure not ultimately oriented toward reproduction represented immaturity to him. Furthermore, he noted that homosexuality was often linked to narcissism, and thus that it interfered with an individual's maturation process whereby the drives of the body would be directed toward an appropriate sexual object.

In contrast to Krafft-Ebing's idea that homosexuals were evolutionary throwbacks, for Freud, they were quintessentially modern—indeed, symptoms of advanced civilization itself. But he too likened homosexuality to a form of atavism that threatened cultural advancement. He did so by warning that modern pressures caused homosexuals to be trapped at an immature stage of psychosexual development, with fixations that were infantile and primitive. To flesh out his concern, he offered an elaborate critique of sexual repression characteristic of modern societies and cautioned that these societies might be undergoing cultural, if not hereditary, regression due to intensifying pressures that obstructed individuals' psychosexual maturation. He worried that homosexuality, like other conditions of arrested development, threatened cultural progress. Indeed, he argued that modern society would benefit from overcoming the intense sexual repression characteristic of Victorian mores. In his view, repression, though necessary in some degree for cultural advancement, had actually engendered neuroses in modern society.

In his 1908 essay on civilized sexual morality and modern nervousness, Freud expressed his concern by drawing parallels between stages of psychosexual development and cultural evolution. The essay denigrated both homosexuals and sexually permissive "primitive" societies on the grounds of their immaturity. The logic here was based on Freud's characterization of "primitive" societies and neurotic homosexuals as infantile, and "modern" societies and reproductive heterosexuals as mature. This scheme conformed to a larger teleological inclination of European men to regard sexual sublimation as necessary for the advancement of civilization and to regard the nuclear family as the primary institution for insuring both proper sexual sublimation and survival of the species.[53] Freud, like many of his contemporaries, generally assumed that modern societies were superior to others as evidenced by their more sophisticated institutions and aesthetic tastes, which developed through the sublimation of primitive sexual drives. Monogamous heterosexuality geared toward reproduction provided the means for this sublimation while also guaranteeing the birth of legitimate offspring. By contrast, neither primitive societies nor homosexuals adequately sublimated sexual drives toward the two important interlocking goals of species survival and cultural refinement.

Models of cultural evolution that underpinned this way of thinking generally posited a linear progression of civilization whereby small-scale cultures were classified as "primitive" and promiscuous in infantilizing and condescending terms. Conversely, bourgeois European societies (to which the purveyors of such models belonged) were revered. In Freud's view, though modern societies may be vexed by the effects of excessive sexual repression, they were still superior to other cultures. Likewise, though heterosexuals commonly showed signs of neuroses, modern matrimonial reproductive heterosexuality was elevated well above perversions of the proper sexual aim and object. In sum, even though Freud sharply criticized hereditarian assumptions and did not believe homosexuals could be "cured," he generally worried that the growing prevalence of homosexuality, like other neurotic perversions, threatened cultural progress.

THE CONUNDRUM OF FEMALE HOMOSEXUALITY

Anxiety over the perceived erosion of traditional sex roles, unleashed by modern developments, manifested itself in the scientific theories of lesbianism. Nineteenth-century bourgeois notions of proper manhood presumed that men, by nature, would be active, aggressive, and independent, while women were passive, meek, and dependent. Toward the end of the century, these prescriptive norms were unsettled not only by feminist agitation but by social and economic forces that expanded women's involvement beyond the household. Industrialization and the expansion of new career possibilities for women had a transformative effect on gender relations, engendering, among other things, a backlash against the notion of women's autonomy from men. Starting around 1890, a growing number of middle-class women entered college and took employment in the expanding professional sectors of teaching, secretarial, nursing, and social work. Meanwhile, working-class women entered the industrial work force at an unprecedented rate. Although women's wages were significantly lower than men's, paid employment for both working-class and middle-class women granted them some financial independence and mobility beyond the confines of marriage and the family. In this context, the figure of the New Woman began to appear in popular commentary as well as medical writing. Broadly speaking, she was described as a modern-minded, sexually desiring woman, cast in contrast to the chaste and modest lady of the household idealized during the Victorian era. Medical writings from this period of transition indicate a growing preoccupation with the consequences of women's greater presence in the public sphere. Indeed, in this context, physicians found female homosexuality in particular a puzzling problem requiring modified etiological theories that increasingly revealed an uneasiness about women's independence from men.

In much of the medical writing on homosexuality, female sexual inversion was generally subsumed in discussions of male inversion as the other side of the coin, so to speak. But some physicians asserted that lesbianism was less prevalent and dangerous than homosexuality in men. Nevertheless, female sex inversion was regarded as no less a sign of constitutional abnormality, even if its social consequences were perceived as less dire. What was more pronounced in these writings were the shortcomings of men whose excessive sexual appetites were offensive and drove women into protective sex-segregated environments and toward relationships with other women. The implication, then, was that most lesbianism would disappear if men were more sensitive to women.

In writings from the late nineteenth and early twentieth centuries, lesbians were generally described as innately less lustful and promiscuous than their male counterparts. For example, Krafft-Ebing granted that women had strong friendships but, like many men of his time, he believed that sexual relations between them were neither as powerful nor as threatening to the social order as male homosexuality. In his view, because women lacked penises and had weak sex drives, they suffered neither from impotency nor from excessive sexual needs, and so were spared the temptation to take relief in homosexuality. Furthermore, he noted, "the majority of female urnings do not act in obedience to an innate impulse, but they are developed under conditions analogous to those which produce the urning by cultivation." Their "forbidden friendships" flourished in settings such as girls schools, nunneries, and prisons, where the mere absence of males drew them together. In addition, brothels, where women developed "repugnance for the most disgusting and perverse acts which men perform on prostitutes," were "hot-beds of Lesbian love." The cultivated vice of lesbianism thus gradually led to "acquired antipathic sexual instinct."[54] While Krafft-Ebing believed that "true" female inversion existed in some cases, the majority of lesbians were drawn into perversion because of the absence or misdeeds of men.

The Swiss neurologist August Forel, writing in 1905, commented in his influential work, *The Sexual Question*, that it was difficult to distinguish between the normal expression of sentiments between women and those originating in "hereditary disposition to inversion." While "nymphomaniac inverts," whose sex drive exceeded that of normal men, were "not very common," Forel noted that "sapphism acquired by seduction or habit" was not rare. But neither was it as threatening to the health of the individual as the "pure inversion" of some women or of male homosexuality, because women commonly experienced a "vague sensual pleasure" from "sentiments of exalted sympathy" which may grow out of love for other women. By contrast, sexual relations among men were devoid of love, and thus they were primitive, debased, and pathological in Forel's view. Like Krafft-Ebing, he generally construed lesbianism as a form of "mutual onanism" that was continuous with natural female affections. Nonetheless some lesbians posed dangers to otherwise "normal" women who, because of their natural tendency toward "monogamous love," would cling to a "pure invert" if the latter had been successful in seducing her.[55]

Forel relied upon a gender distinction when contrasting the constitutionally tainted "pure female invert" and the impressionable "normal" woman, noting that over time, a sexual relationship between these two types would become "pathological" for the "normal" woman:

> The pure female invert feels like a man. The idea of coitus with men is repugnant to her. She apes the habits, manners, and clothes of men. Female inverts have been known to wear men's uniforms and perform military service for years, and even behave as heroes, their sex sometimes only being discovered after their death. . . . A female invert, dressed as a young man, succeeded in winning the love of a normal girl and was formally betrothed to her. Soon afterward the woman was unmasked, arrested, and sent to an asylum, where she was made to put on women's clothes. But the young girl who had been deceived continued to be amorous and visited her 'lover,' who embraced her before everyone. . . . I took the young girl aside and expressed my astonishment at seeing her continue to have any regard for the sham 'young man' who had deceived her. Her reply was characteristic of a woman: 'Ah! you see, doctor, I love him, and I cannot help it!' . . . This is how it happens that a normal woman, systematically seduced by an invert, may become madly in love with her and commit sexual excesses with her for years, without being herself essentially pathological. The case only becomes really pathological when it is definitely fixed by long habit; a thing which easily occurs in woman owing to the constant and monogamous nature of her love.[56]

For Forel, as for many other physicians who commented on lesbianism, sexual relations between women were interpreted according to a two-sex model whereby the seducer was cast as fundamentally masculine by virtue of her manly taste in clothing, her desire to be virile, and her predatory pursuit of the passive (i.e., feminine) woman. Relying on this gender model, Forel warned that masculine women were a danger to impressionable young women whom they seduced. His suggestion for avoiding such an outcome was twofold: pure female inverts should be forbidden contact with young feminine women, and feminine women, since they were innately passive yet prone to excessive sentiment, should be steered toward men.

As political campaigns for women's rights intensified around the turn of the century, medical discourse warning of the dangers of lesbianism increased. Although it had previously been seen as less menacing than male homosexuality, lesbianism incited authorities on sexuality to voice more condemnatory opinions. Feminist arguments stressing similarities between the sexes were countered by scientific arguments to the contrary that tended to pathologize women who sought equality and rights. Lesbians were an easy target and were stereotyped as betrayers of the natural order of the sexes. In much of this writing, the constitutionally tainted female invert was the worst of all women offenders.

Havelock Ellis was particularly agitated by the subject of lesbianism. The subject compelled him in part because his own wife, Edith Lees, was a lesbian. Writing at the time of the emergence of the independent-minded New Woman, Ellis warned that homosexuality among women was increasing with the march of modern progress and feminism. In his view, middle-class women's growing autonomy from men and marriage was as likely to foster homosexuality as was the nervous strain men experienced in the face of intensifying business competition. Recapitulating a Victorian notion, Ellis explained that most women tended to be heterosexual because they were generally passive: their bodies and personalities lacked the variations common among men, making them naturally susceptible to sexual advances and normally unlikely to initiate any sexual encounters. But like Forel, Ellis believed those with abnormal instincts had predatory tendencies along with an array of other masculine physical characteristics, and he feared that this type of woman was becoming more common.

In his view, mannish women tended to exploit more impressionable young women, seeking affection from those toward whom men felt indifference. The unfortunate recipients of such attention were "womanly women" who were described as weak willed, and some among them lacked the fitness for child-bearing. Like normal women, they were naturally seduced by masculine people, whether the seducers be "normal" men or sexually inverted women. Were it not for being constitutionally tainted, these womanly women would be spared the temptation to succumb to an invert's advances. Steering them toward heterosexuality from an early age was thus advisable as a way to circumvent a future of lesbianism.

Ellis also warned of increasing rates of incidental lesbianism among otherwise normal women, precipitated by the unusual conditions of modern factory work and the entertainment industry. He observed that concentrated work places fostered perversion, citing lace makers and seamstresses, who commonly engaged in lesbian practices. Cooped up together in close, hot quarters, factory girls talked about sex to a point of intense arousal which could be relieved only through masturbation. This "vague form of homosexuality" occurred when, in the summer, some girls wore no underwear and worked with their naked legs crossed while other girls inspected them. As Ellis reported it, the heat of the midday led to sensual stimulation which led to mutual masturbation among the aroused women. Similarly, actresses, chorus girls, and ballet dancers grew excited about performing as they waited in the wings and in crowded dressing rooms. Ellis suggested that the mere presence of women in close proximity to each other could trigger a state of nervous exhilaration which would culminate in a sexual frenzy of lesbianism. But these women could be restored to normalcy once removed from such arousing circumstances.[57]

By the early twentieth century, modern women's sexual desires were foregrounded in medical explanations of lesbianism. Hirschfeld made alliances with German lesbian feminists and used his research on lesbians to further feminist political claims for women's sexual emancipation. But he was exceptional in this regard. Most other authorities disparaged lesbianism especially when it was linked to feminism. As Ellis put it, "acquired antipathic sexual instinct" was growing more common among women as a result of their forays into feminism and out of the confines of the domestic sphere. A solution to this problem was to protect otherwise normal women by sheltering them from the deleterious effects of modern life.

Freud's assessment of lesbianism was more complicated than Ellis's but no more charitable. His main commentary on the subject focused on the troubling and protracted dynamics of the castration complex in females. He noted that during the castration complex, girls normally believed that their "castration" was a form of punishment for something they did wrong. Thus guilt became the underlying emotion of femininity, manifesting itself in masochism among extreme cases. In normal cases, when girls realized they were "castrated" and could neither have their mothers nor replace them in order to have their fathers, they transferred these needs by seeking companionship with other men and by gradually ascending to the apex of maturity exemplified in heterosexual marriage and the birth of children.[58] In Freud's view, having a baby was the ultimate experience that quelled the woman's longstanding sense of lacking a penis. He distinguished this from cases of penis envy, common in many cases of latent and overt lesbianism, where the girl was arrested at an earlier stage marked by clitoral fixation and a strong resistance to accepting the terms of castration that constitute the basis of normal femininity.

Freud linked penis envy to what he called the "masculinity complex," wherein the girl resented her inferior status in relation to boys. Instead of experiencing guilt in relation to "castration," those suffering from a masculinity complex believed that they had been punished unjustly. This led to a reaction of bitterness which Freud believed was at the root of the masculinity complex.[59] In some cases of penis envy, the daughter could not overcome her frustration about not having a penis and developed hostility toward her father and, by extension, toward all men.[60] Freud noted that such a condition often manifested itself in an adult proclivity toward feminist political sentiments, an outcome he regarded as decidedly unfavorable.

Freud believed that a sufferer of the masculinity complex might also become an overt lesbian as the result of a frustrated attempt at gaining her father's affections: when it became clear to her that she could not interrupt the sexual intimacies of her parents, as in the event of the birth of a new sibling, the girl turned away from her father and all men and turned her affections toward her mother or replacements thereof, having been, in Freud's terms, "changed into a man."[61] This line of reasoning influenced much of the subsequent psychoanalytic writing on lesbianism, which interpreted female homosexual relationships as attempts to reproduce a mother-daughter relationship in the wake of a girl's envy or disappointment with her father.[62]

Freud opined that a girl's desire for revenge, upon realizing she has been "castrated," may also manifest itself in resentment toward her mother, whose own presumed castration was the cause of the daughter's dread. As a consequence, she may be drawn toward sadistic relations with other women in order to avenge this initial wrong, taking as her object a character resembling her mother against whom she can express aggression. In other cases, those who experienced a lack of original love from their mothers may manifest latent lesbianism in fickle or conflicted relations with men, frequently associated in Freud's thinking with paranoia.[63]

Whereas Freud's emphasis on distinguishing sexual aim from sexual object allowed him to make sense of "manly" homosexual men, he noted that "inversion of character can be expected with more regularity only in female inverts." He wrote in 1905 that "the conditions in the woman are more definite; here the active inverts show with special frequency the somatic and psychic characteristics of man and desire femininity in their sexual object; though even here greater variation will be found on more intimate investigation."[64] Freud reiterated this idea in 1920, when he reported a case of homosexuality in a woman. He described his patient as suffering from a "masculinity complex" arising from her envy of the penis of her younger brother, whose liberties and privileges exceeded her own. This envy resulted in her wanting to assume the role of man, marked both by her pursuit of another woman and her sympathies toward feminism. Freud deduced her "masculinity complex" from her object choice of another woman, emphasizing that her sexual perversion was linked not only to her object of desire but more fundamentally to her desire to be a man. Thus, while he believed it possible to conceptualize male homosexuals as conforming to the expectations of their sex (i.e., being the active partner in pursuit of sex with other men), the young woman who experienced lesbian desire wanted to be "changed into a man." That is, her object of desire signaled the perversion of her sexual aim, in Freud's reasoning. This contradiction in his thinking suggests that Freud could not imagine sexual activity without the presence of a masculine character who would be motivated by the want of a phallus to pursue feminine objects. Echoing earlier authorities on sexual inversion with whom he otherwise voiced great differences of opinion, Freud thus construed female homosexual object choice as, by definition, a pathological manifestation of masculinity.

THE LASTING EFFECTS OF MEDICALIZATION

As the nineteenth century ended, homosexual acts, previously spoken about in terms either of sin or crime, were recast in medical and scientific terms and came to be associated with particular types of people. This shift was facilitated by larger epistemological and cultural developments that privileged scientific medicine as an avenue for contending with social problems. The most pronounced scientific legacy from the initial medical writings was the idea that the homosexual was an inherently distinct type of person. But as the century turned, new ways of conceptualizing homosexuality, specifically those proposed by Hirschfeld, Ellis, and Freud, opened up the possibility of alternative approaches to the question of the etiology and embodiment of homosexuality that would rival, if not wholly supplant, the original constitutional theories of degeneracy and inversion. As Hirschfeld's ideas evolved, he suggested that all individuals were on a continuum between the abstract poles of pure maleness and pure femaleness. Ellis argued the same. In addition, Hirschfeld moved toward a model of sexual variations that was far more nuanced than Krafft-Ebing's scheme, which continued to posit, even through the many editions of his *Psychopathia Sexualis,* a fundamental difference between homosexuals and heterosexuals that was rooted in the body.

As we have seen, Freud claimed that homosexuality was much more common than previously believed and argued that it could not be discerned simply by examining bodies. He and his psychoanalytic colleagues also contended that the binary distinction between homosexuality and heterosexuality was no more stable than that between masculinity and femininity. Whereas Krafft-Ebing's model of the tainted invert had presumed these dividing lines were clear, Freud's notions offered a more complex picture by showing that all individuals pass through a homosexual stage in early life and by introducing the idea of a latent homosexuality that, in many cases, animated the psyches of those otherwise presumed to be heterosexual. Yet by defining homosexuality principally as a psychosexual disturbance, psychoanalysts including Freud, contributed to a science of evasions that cast the so-called overt homosexual as a pathological being in contrast to a characteristically vague notion of the normal population.

Medical inquiry from the period we have surveyed so far was regarded by both its purveyors and by self-identified homosexuals as benevolent in comparison to religious condemnation and criminal punishment. Moreover, it was significantly shaped by the perspectives and contributions of homosexuals. Ulrichs and Kertbeny introduced pioneering concepts that formed the foundation of scientific discourse on homosexuality. And scores of others corresponded with physicians, offering accounts of their experiences in the hope that they would be accepted as anomalies and nature's gifts. Although many of these correspondents criticized medical opinions that declared them to be pathological, they saw physicians as sympathetic allies in a larger struggle to change prevailing attitudes and to reform laws that were used to prosecute homosexuals.[65] Indeed, though it would be reductive to assume that they owe their existence to medical discourse, many homosexual men and women, especially those who were educated, were drawn toward it and constructed identities in relation to the authoritative knowledge being produced about them. But, as we shall see, viewing scientific medicine as a refuge proved to have enormous consequences for those who were named, or who identified themselves as, homosexuals.

The process by which homosexuality was medicalized led to certain outcomes that were to have lasting and oppressive effects. This process, despite of the intentions of physicians such Hirschfeld, ultimately implanted in Western culture the idea that homosexuality was pathological, that it was exacerbated by conditions of modern life, and that it ideally ought to be prevented. Once the problem of homosexuality moved from being considered first and foremost a punishable moral offense to becoming a medical matter, initial appeals for decriminalization and social acceptance were increasingly overshadowed by pitying condescension and aggressive medical interventions. In the face of this, Hirschfeld's naturalist paradigm continued to be appealing to homosexual men and women to the extent that it regarded them as anomalies and not, by definition, pathological. Although many of its later purveyors were explicitly hostile to homosexuals, psychoanalytic approaches during the early years of the twentieth century succeeded in broadening the definition and scope of homosexuality in a manner that engendered a complex mixture of sympathy and pity toward homosexuals. While most psychoanalysts were charitable toward the naturalist paradigm than degenerationists had been, their imperative to regard homosexuality as an affliction in need of psychotherapy offended many naturalists. At the same time, psychoanalysis offered a new language for thinking about homosexuality which appealed to some homosexuals as intriguing and compassionate.

Even though the lasting idea that emerged out of the medicalization process was that homosexuality was a form of pathology, the various etiological theories encompassed by this process could be deployed to various political ends. Hereditary and congenital theories, as much as they could be used to argue that homosexuality was a form of biological and moral degeneracy, could also be used to argue that it was simply a natural occurrence in the population, deserving acceptance or compassion rather than punishment or "cure." Such a claim was articulated with significant force by Magnus Hirschfeld and his followers throughout Europe and the United States. One can find evidence of this in the meditations of many homosexual writers from the period. Following in Ulrichs's footsteps, British writer Edward Carpenter thought of himself as a member of an intermediate sex endowed by nature with special insights and abilities.[66] And in 1899, lesbian poet Natalie Barney wrote "I consider myself without shame: albinos aren't reproached for having pink eyes and whitish hair. Why should they hold it against me for being a lesbian? It's a question of Nature. My queerness isn't a vice, isn't deliberate, and harms no one."[67]

As I have suggested, medical and scientific discourses about homosexuality, from their inception, were situated in relation to cultural anxieties about protecting and managing modern democratic societies from disturbing incursions, inversions, and perversions. A goal of safeguarding the fictive "normal population" from the dangers of modernity lurked, in varying degrees of intensity, across the major etiological paradigms we have surveyed. Even Hirschfeld's more nuanced model for understanding sexual variations was used to argue that homosexuality ought to be tolerated on the grounds that it was primarily inborn and thus not contagious. Similar claims were asserted on the basis of the work of Krafft-Ebing and Ellis, although this was a trickier undertaking since they both emphasized the pathological nature of homosexuality and hinted that it could be activated by deleterious social factors. Freud, whose psychoanalytic ideas in the beginning placed him at the margins of the psychiatric profession, rciterated that homosexuality was pathological and, although not casually contagious, was likely to increase as a result of the forms of sexual repression common to modern society.

In hindsight, it may appear that medical writing about homosexuality from the 1860s to 1920s was, on the whole, speculative and far from scientifically credible. We may be tempted to question its authority or to dismiss its ideas altogether as ludicrous. We could, for example, note that the main theories of causality were hardly based on sound scientific evidence since they counted either on anecdotally reported psychiatric cases or on the subjective accounts of homosexual men and women who corresponded with doctors. And we could say that, for the most part, medical authorities neglected to devise sound hypotheses or to conduct empirically sound studies measuring a properly constituted research population against a control population. In addition, we could also be tempted to disclaim this work as lacking objectivity since several of the principal concepts that organized the whole discourse were contributed by self-interested lay people such as Ulrichs and Kertbeny, rather than by objective and credentialed scientists. Would that not discredit the work and indicate that it was inherently biased from its very inception? On the basis of these considerations, we could perhaps declare the whole enterprise to be pseudo-scientific and we could presume that any reasonable person, either then or now, would regard ideas from this period as nonsense. However, to do so would be to ignore several important factors.

First of all, the physicians we have surveyed were respected authorities within the medical professions of Germany, Britain, France, and the United States. Although each faced opposition to their work, the majority of this opposition came not from their peers within the medical or scientific professions but from sexually conservative critics outside the professions. What they wrote was generally regarded as scientifically valid, and their methods closely resembled those of other physicians of their time. Secondly, although they aligned themselves with the powerful discourse of science, physicians during this period, whether they were writing about sexual perversion or any other form of anomalous or pathological phenomena, based their claims primarily on individual cases of patients whom they encountered in clinical practice. That is, medical knowledge was generated on the basis of observations of ailing individuals who were examined usually on a case-by-case basis, rather than as part of a systematically devised study. Thus if one were dismiss ideas about homosexuality because they were derived from such individually based observations, one would have to do the same for most medical knowledge of the time. Finally, and perhaps most importantly, the main medical approaches to homosexuality from this early period were, by and large, accepted not only by other scientists but also by growing numbers of laypeople as the truth about homosexuality. Their ideas, like other ideas that come to be accepted as facts, made sense to a large number of people within the cultural and historical context of their time. And, furthermore, these notions took root and formed a discursive field within which a century's worth of debate was to occur. To declare them as pseudo-scientific would be expedient and even accurate, if we were to use a current definition of appropriate scientific method.[68] But these ideas were not only accepted for their time. As we shall see, many continue to be regarded as viable to this day.

The main etiological paradigms from this early period shared two key assumptions that homosexuality was deeply rooted in the individual and was, in some significant way, related to family life—either due to inherited biological factors or to psychological factors encountered in early childhood. Families, whether perceived as genetic units or as the origin point of psychosexual development, carried a great deal of responsibility for producing homosexuality in all of the major etiological models. By assuming that homosexuality was a deeply rooted condition, authors of these various paradigms shared the idea that homosexuality was not within the will of the individual to control easily. Thus, while this notion was part of the defense of homosexuals advanced by all three schools against criminal punishment, it left a legacy of attributing to homosexuality a lack of control. Rather than being a positive choice, it was seen as driven by instinct and by constraints that militated against the homosexual's adjustment to norms of modern society.

Debates on the matter of etiology emanating from Europe illustrate a growing skepticism about the idea that homosexuality was hereditary and a confusion over how to classify and evaluate homosexuality when practiced by those who manifested no apparent signs of sex inversion. What motivated the effort to identify and analyze the discrete features and causes of homosexuality was never only a matter of detached scientific inquiry. The idea that perversion was becoming more prevalent as a result of modern conditions propelled this effort through an implicit assumption that homosexuality was ultimately undesirable and ought to be controlled.

At stake in theories of causation in the context of the United States were larger moral and, indeed, political concerns over whether homosexuality could be prevented, eliminated, or, at the very least, contained. Social conflicts during this period were particularly pronounced as a consequence of rapid urbanization and remarkable demographic diversity. These conditions animated much speculation about the disturbing social effects of homosexuality, highlighting especially how it signaled dangerous modern transgressions of cherished boundaries dividing races, social classes, and sexes. European etiological theories were shaped by, and in turn, shaped how homosexuality was imagined by scientific and medical authorities in the United States. They also figured into social reform policies that brought sexuality, primarily by way of marking its aberrations, to the center of public debates about managing the extraordinary changes wrought by modernity in what was seen, for better or worse, as the most modern nation of all.

3 THE UNITED STATES OF PERVERSION

Homosexual Boundary Transgressions of Sex, Class, and Race

There is in every community of any size a colony of sexual perverts; they are usually known to each other, are likely to congre-
gate together. At times they operate in accordance with some definite and concerted plan in quest of [a] subject wherewith to
gratify their abnormal sexual impulses.[1]
—*Dr. G. Frank Lydston (1889)*

Male negroes masquerading in women's garb and carousing and
dancing with white men is the latest St. Louis record of neurotic
and psychopathic sexual perversion. . . . These perverted creatures appear to be features of million-peopled cities.[2]
—*Dr. Charles Hughes (1907)*

The female possessed of the masculine idea of independence . . .
and that disgusting anti-social being, the female sexual pervert,
are simply different degrees of the same class—degenerates.
These unsightly and subnormal beings are the victims of poor
mating.[3]
—*Dr. William Howard (1900)*

A form of perversion that is well known among workers in reform
schools and institutions for delinquent girls, is that of love-making
between the white and colored girls. . . . An interesting feature of
these love episodes is found in the many superstitious practices, especially among the colored when they wish to win the love of a
white girl. . . . These practices, some of so coarse a nature that
they cannot be written down, seem to be part of a system, for system it must be called, so thoroughly ingrained it is in school life.[4]
—*Psychologist Margaret Otis (1913)*

Although the foundational etiological theories of homosexuality
were developed primarily by European physicians, they were
elaborated upon by American doctors in a fashion that highlights particular political dynamics in American culture during the decades
surrounding the turn of the century. Like their European counterparts, American physicians drew connections between nervousness
and moral corruption that pointed to a number of deleterious modern
developments believed to engender homosexuality and to allow it to

flourish. They worried that inversion and homosexual perversion signaled a general trend toward the erosion of distinctions between men and women. And they were concerned that inverts and perverts proliferated as a consequence of changing relations between the races and classes.

Indeed, much of the medical writing on homosexuality in the United States reflected a conservative reaction to modern life, perhaps not surprisingly since most physicians were themselves members of a social strata that had a stake in maintaining clear and hierarchical class, race, and sex distinctions. They construed challenges to this order as part and parcel of moral and evolutionary regression. Thus, embedded within early medical case reports of homosexuality were authors' fears concerning the dangerous effects of people of various ethnicities, nationalities, and social classes mingling together. Likewise, their commentary on lesbianism emphasized the dangers posed by women's increasing interest in equality, independence, and pleasure—qualities taken to be signs that virtuous femininity would soon disappear and, along with it, men's prerogative over women. A concern for preserving the purity of superior genetic stock operated subtextually in much of the early medical commentary on homosexuality: by focusing on the dangers of sexual perversions and the distressing erosion of traditional sex roles, America doctors expressed attitudes that bolstered racist, sexist, and bourgeois reproductive agendas. Theories of degeneration were particularly accommodating to their political perspectives.

This chapter closely examines etiological theories of homosexuality as they were developed and applied by American doctors from around 1880 through roughly 1920. As we shall see, medical commentary on homosexuality from this period provides a privileged window for analyzing larger political concerns and conflicts over the proper management of diversity in the United States.

LICENSE TO SPEAK THE UNSPEAKABLE

In contrast to Europeans such as Krafft-Ebing and Ellis, who wrote at length about perversion and published multiple editions of encyclopedic texts on the subject, American doctors tended to register their commentary through reporting on individual cases scattered throughout various psychiatric and medical journals. Because the topics of "inversion" and "sex perversion" were regarded as unspeakable in respectable company and dangerously corrupting to the public,

American doctors claimed a kind of reluctance to write about them. By emphasizing the depravity of homosexuality and by likening it to mental derangement and criminality, they constructed the homosexual as an innately distinct type of human being sharing characteristics with other uncivilized or degenerate types. That many of the reported medical cases involved impoverished and disempowered patients implicitly underlined the prevailing presumption that lustful perversion was commonly found in the lower classes.

Although many American physicians were reticent to speak openly about sexual perversions, their reticence took the form of regularly recited warnings to audiences that what they were about to talk about was really quite unspeakable. This staged modesty was coupled with an explicit sense of urgency that the problem of "sex perversion" needed to be addressed. Thus, while frequently acknowledging the odious nature of the subject, American doctors actually licensed rather than repressed detailed discussions of homosexuality. At the same time they insisted that these discussions be limited to audiences comprised of qualified experts. If discussed openly with the general public, the problem, they believed, would only increase. This conceit functioned to underscore the idea that homosexuality had a dangerously alluring and contagious quality. Claiming that their knowledge was objectively scientific and adequately discreet, physicians elevated it above other, less reputable avenues of popular knowledge about homosexuality, including erotic fiction and popular entertainment. Thus, they constructed boundaries around what should be thought and said about homosexuality in the service of policing and eliminating it. In their hands, homosexuality became a particularly powerful symbol against which a broad array of standards of normalcy were generated.

Writing about sexuality in any manner other than strictly proscribing it was discouraged in the United States. Authors met with publishers' refusals, censorship, public criticism, and even prosecution on obscenity charges. Such circumstances narrowly circumscribed what could be said about sexuality, let alone homosexuality, who could legitimately say it, and in what sorts of publications their ideas could be presented. In 1914, for example, Margaret Sanger was charged with obscenity under the Comstock Law for distributing *The Woman Rebel,* her journal that argued for birth control and that challenged working women to think for themselves.[5] Even scientific discussions of heterosexual intercourse were considered off-limits. In 1899, Denslow Lewis presented a paper entitled "Hygiene of the Sexual Act" at the annual meeting of the American Medical Association. Howard Kelly, a gynecologist at Johns Hopkins University, objected, stating that the "discussion of the subject is attended with filth and we besmirch ourselves by discussing it in public." The *Journal of the American Medical Association* refused to publish it for the same reasons.[6]

Similarly, in his 1887 review of Ellis's *Sexual Inversion*, William Noyes protested "against the appearance of such a work as this in a library (series) intended primarily for popular reading." Noyes continued, "Even Krafft-Ebing, although writing solely for the profession, has been severely and justly criticized for [the] unnecessary emphasis and importance he has given this subject by his articles on the perversions of the sexual sense, and nothing but harm can follow if popular literature is to suffer a similar deluge." Noyes complained that publicizing nonprocreative sexual activity was of little value to anyone but perverts. He recommended that it was better not to mention the subject at all since nothing could be done to eliminate it.[7]

Noyes's sentiments were echoed in a 1902 review of the first German edition of Havelock Ellis's *Sexual Inversion*, when another reviewer credited Ellis for his efforts but complained that the author was too inclined to fill his books "with the pornographic imaginings of perverted minds rather than cold facts, and the data which are collected are seemingly of little value." The reviewer concluded that it was doubtful that any practical results could come from works of this sort.[8]

THE HOMOSEXUAL DEGENERATE IN AMERICA

Nineteenth-century American physicians tended to classify many expressions of sexuality that contradicted strict standards of heterosexual monogamous matrimony as diseased. Indeed, the overwhelming majority of published medical cases equated "sex perversion" with lunacy. By doing so, physicians posited a strict delineation between perverted degenerates and the population of normal people who were presumed to be free of hereditary taint, who exercised sexual restraint, and who engaged in sex primarily for the purposes of reproduction. But physicians, while always assuming the existence of normalcy, seldom supported their conception of it with any concrete evidence. Instead they delineated a growing number of perversions as a way of asserting, indirectly, their view of what would count was natural and normal sexuality.

In medical discourse from the time, sex perversion was a broad and elastic term, frequently deployed as a synonym for inversion, homosexuality, and a range of nonreproductive sexualities, including those labeled as voyeurism, sadism, masochism, fetishism, exhibitionism, and bestiality. But of all these perversions, physicians and those whom they influenced voiced particular worry about the dangers of homosexuality, which they closely tied to sex inversion and which they claimed involved extreme expressions of the other perversions. Their pronounced anxiety about inversion and homosexuality can be accounted for on several grounds. First, inversion signaled the alarming effacement of gender distinctions upon which social order (i.e., male dominance) had been based. And, secondly, homosexuality further affronted the two-sex system according to which men and women, as opposites, were thought to be naturally attracted to one another. Thus, particularly when it came to lesbianism, physicians were upset that it violated Nature's plan, whereby women would be dependent on men. But conventions regarding gender and sexuality were not the only matters upset by the purported increase of "sex perversion." As we shall see, inversion and homosexuality were construed as dangerous forces that threatened to break down social boundaries between races and classes.

For the most part, medical discourse reflected dominant conventions of the time. Physicians' implicit definition of normalcy corresponded to middle-class Victorian ideals according to which women were to be chaste beacons of morality for the family and men were to be the breadwinners and protectors. Boys were to be disciplined and educated to become productive citizens, while girls were encouraged to become helpmates to future husbands and children. Large families with working mothers, fathers, and children living in congested quarters, common among the working class and the poor, were viewed as lacking discipline and moral virtue. Authorities generally held these families culpable for morally and genetically inferior offspring. When upper- and middle-class men and women consorted with these types, their actions not only signaled a degenerating social order but were taken as evidence of accelerated moral chaos.

The degenerationist assumption that perversion was tied to primitive lust confirmed American physicians' idea that homosexuality was concentrated among working-class and poor people who, by nature, were less controlled in their sexual desires than normal middle-class people. To a great degree, physicians couched their contempt for the lower classes in medical diagnoses that pathologized any sexual behavior not centered around heterosexual reproduction within the context of state-sanctioned marriage.

Occasionally doctors suggested that perversion and degeneracy were also common among the decadent rich. What the lower-class degenerate shared with his ruling-class counterpart was an innate propensity for perversion, the former because he had never adequately become civilized in the first place, and the latter because he suffered from decadence and regression. Although they stood at opposite ends of the social ladder, "perverts" from these two classes, especially when brought together, comprised a dangerous brew of vice and moral dissolution. Whereas the lower classes were blamed for spreading perversion through promiscuity, animalistic lust, and the birth of defective offspring, the slothful and hedonistic rich, with appetites for pornography and orgiastic bacchanals, were also imagined as culprits of moral decline. As such, the middle class was portrayed as imperiled by evil forces from both ends of the social hierarchy. They deserved vigilant protection to fortify the will to stave off defilement.

In contrast to most European physicians who studied homosexuality, their American counterparts were not particularly motivated to decriminalize it. Even as they readily classified it as a form of inborn insanity, American doctors showed little of the pity and compassion conveyed by Krafft-Ebing, for example, who stressed that inverts and perverts should be pitied, not punished, for their inborn weakness of will. Instead American doctors believed that homosexuals showed a lack of will-power which, although it may be a sign of innate defectiveness, was not excusable on those grounds. The dominant ethos of American individualism, with its privileging of will-power and self-improvement, helps to account for American physicians' initial intolerance toward homosexuality. Nineteenth-century American doctors tended to embrace American hegemonic ideals of upward mobility and social adjustment, which they believed would be best achieved through the individual's moral tenacity and dedication to hard work. Placing great emphasis on maintaining social order, these authorities implicitly valorized individual self-determination but only to the extent that its expression conformed to other dominant social ideals. In addition, the fact that many of the initial medical reports in the United States focused on homosexuality in economically and socially marginal groups may account for why American doctors were not inclined to relax legal punishments for homosexuality, since the accused (or afflicted) belonged to a lower social strata commonly associated with general lawlessness and disorder.

The tendency among European medical authorities to argue for decriminalization was based upon the notion, stemming originally from Schopenhauer's ideas, that disorders of the will, including homosexuality, were primarily medical maladies.[9] In other words, they believed that tossing an afflicted individual in prison without any medical diagnosis or care ran counter to ameliorating the problem. In this way, they sought to control homosexuality through medical regulation. American physicians adopted this argument significantly later, and even then they tended to argue for medical treatment as part and parcel of criminal prosecution for "sex offenses" such as sodomy, indecent exposure, gross indecency and the like. To the extent that libertarian notions of guarding the privacy and liberty of individuals operated in the United States, these were extended only to the afflicted of the middle and upper classes. Meanwhile, those in the lower strata were still assumed to be engaging primarily in criminal behavior, although physicians stressed that this behavior was the result of an underlying disease. Such sentiments led American physicians to advocate invasive medical procedures and to declare, in purple prose, their revulsion toward homosexuals.[10]

In one of the first reported American medical cases, the psychologist G. Alder Blumer focused on a patient with "perverted sexual instinct," whom he classified as insane with epileptic tendencies.[11] The doctor endorsed the patient's incarceration on the grounds that he was a danger to society. Seven years later, in 1889, Dr. G. Frank Lydston of Chicago opined that sexual perversity was linked to defects of either the brain or the genitalia, with many cases showing evidence of congenitally misdirected impulses which led to insanity. Lydston stressed the dangers of masturbation and linked homosexuality to the "overt stimulation of sexual sensibility and the receptive sexual centers, incidental to sexual excesses and masturbation."[12] Such defects, he noted, were common among primitive types. He recommended a procedure to cauterize the nerves of afflicted patients to stem their perverse impulses. In addition, he believed that the extirpation of the ovaries and clitoridectomy would solve the problem of lesbianism. Lydston's claim that surgical treatments could successfully eliminate homosexuality remained unsupported by any reliable scientific evidence, but his grossly invasive experiments reveal the level of hostility toward homosexuality among certain physicians associated with the degenerationist paradigm.[13]

In 1894, a Chicago physician and professor of psychiatry, James G. Kiernan, dispelled the common assumption that homosexuality was more common in males than females and echoed the notion that perversion was clearly a sign of insanity. Kiernan was most peeved by the use of medical diagnoses to defend homosexuals in court cases such as that of Alice Mitchell, which I discuss a bit later in this chapter. Instead, he urged other physicians to join him in suppressing public knowledge of perversion and to work toward curing patients by fortifying their weakened wills. Providing them with sympathy only confounded the problem. His words convey the typically punitive attitude common among American physicians writing on the subject in the late nineteenth century:

> There is entirely too much sympathy wasted on these patients, since sympathy to them is as poisonous as to the hysteric whose mental state is very similar. Insistence on the morbidity of the pervert ideas and prohibition of sexual literature as in the sexual neurasthenic together with allied psychical therapy and anaphrodisiac methods cannot but benefit. These patients, like the hysteric, will not "will" to be cured while they are subjects of sympathy.[14]

Kiernan's idea of medically eliminating sexual perversions was shared by other American authorities. Most believed that incarcerating them in asylums and subjecting them to experimental surgeries were effective control strategies. In this respect, homosexual asylum patients were treated very much like others who were diagnosed as insane or feebleminded, the overwhelming majority of whom were socially and economically disadvantaged people.

A trend toward performing surgical castrations to eliminate homosexuality emerged in the 1880s. In the middle of that decade, F. Hoyt Pilcher, head of the Kansas State Home for the Feebleminded, ordered the castration of four boys and fourteen girls without legal permission. Pilcher, who was attacked by opponents of sterilization, defended his action by stating that castration would prevent "excessive masturbation and pervert sexual acts."[15] Similarly, in 1893, Dr. F. E. Daniel of Austin, Texas, wrote that sexual perversion, alcoholism, insanity, and criminality were transmitted by heredity. He asserted that such signs of degeneracy were common among "the lower classes, especially negroes," and recommended castration as a remedy. The doctor warned that blacks were hypersexual and prone to commit rape as well as homosexual sodomy. His solution to these problems was to eliminate them at their root by surgically sterilizing African American men. However, Daniel did not believe "castration" (i.e., excising the clitoris) was necessary in perverse white women because they were innately "passive." Nevertheless, he advocated sterilizing them as a way to prevent the birth of defective children.[16]

In 1899, Dr. Harry Clay Sharp of the Indiana Reformatory instituted a program also aimed at preventing the spread of sexual perversion by sterilizing inmates who showed evidence of hereditary defects. Sharp rationalized his program on medical, moral, and economic grounds, stressing that defective individuals cost the society money and degraded the overall gene stock by reproducing at higher rates than normal people. Arguing against surgical castration because of its disturbing effects on the individual, Sharp instead promoted simple and efficient sterilization by vasectomy:

> There is no longer any questioning of the fact that the degenerate class is increasing out of all proportion to the increase of the general population. . . . [This class] includes most of the insane, the epileptic, the imbecile, the idiotic, the sexual perverts; many of the confirmed inebriates, prostitutes, tramps and criminals, as well as the habitual paupers found in our county poor asylums; also many of the children in our orphan homes.

Dr. Sharp performed the procedure on 236 cases with no "unfavorable symptoms," but instead discovered "sunny dispositions" among his patients.[17] Consonant with the increasing popularity of the eugenics movement in the United States, castration and sterilization procedures were used not only as experimental techniques to stem homosexual sex drive but to prevent the birth of defective offspring.[18]

Starting in 1907, several states began to pass statutes legalizing eugenic sterilization procedures, with Indiana being the first. By 1917, fifteen other states had such laws, and by 1931 the total came to thirty. All the laws passed by 1921 and many that were passed later were applied to "sexual perverts," and some states listed "moral degenerates" as appropriate candidates for sterilization. This latter group included homosexuals, prostitutes, drug addicts, and syphilitics. According to conservative estimates, by 1931 just over 12,000 operations had been performed in the United States. Although it is difficult to ascertain how many of these operations involved patients who were homosexual, those diagnosed with "insanity" accounted for the overwhelming number of cases. They were sterilized at a rate of two to one compared to those classified as "feebleminded," and at a much higher rate of frequency than epileptics or common criminals. Most sterilizations were performed on indigent men and women in asylums, state hospitals, and prisons. The general assumption among psychiatrists who dealt with poor people was that homosexuality was a form of insanity. No doubt the recommendations of doctors such as Pilcher, Daniel, and Sharp to sterilize homosexual people were heeded by others, as difficult as it is to discern how many cases were performed specifically on these grounds.

HOMOSEXUAL INSANITY IN ITS FEMALE FORM

The idea that homosexuality was, by definition, a form of insanity was underscored in several stunning medical cases of female sexual inversion reported in the 1880s and 1890s. These cases emphasized the extraordinary power of masculine women to drive otherwise normal women to ruin. Male doctors offered copious details of these women in a manner that revealed a combination of fascination, amusement, and revulsion. In 1883, Dr. P. M. Wise of the Willard Asylum for the Insane in New York State described a patient, one Lucy Ann Slater, alias Rev. Joseph Lobdell, whose voice "was coarse and her features masculine."[19] The patient was a 56-year-old widow and a "declared vagrant." She had earned a meager living by passing as a man and by performing menial labor.[20]

The doctor noted that "her excitement was of an erotic nature and her sexual inclination was perverted," a fact demonstrated by the unrestrained and "lewd" advances she made toward the female asylum attendants. After an ill-fated marriage to a man, "Joe" (as the doctor referred to Slater in the report), who had been a tomboy, "followed her inclination to indulge in masculine vocations most freely; donned male attire, spending much of the time in the woods with a rifle, and became so expert in its use that she was renowned throughout the country as the 'Female Hunter of Long Eddy.'"

The case of Lucy Ann Slater, as Wise told it, highlighted the dangers caused by the association of an unmistakable "pervert" of low-class origins with a "young woman of good education," whom Joe had become attached to "upon returning from several years out West, living and trapping among the Indians." Joe met her in an alms-house, after the recently abandoned wife had been left destitute by her husband. What struck Wise as significant was that this most unusual attraction occurred when the poor, abandoned woman was weak and susceptible to the perverse attentions Joe offered her:

The attachment seemed to be mutual and, strange as it may seem, led to their leaving their temporary home to commence life in the woods in the relation of man and wife. The unsexed woman assumed the name of Joseph Lobdell and the pair lived in this relation for the subsequent decade. . . . An incident occurred in 1876 to interrupt the quiet monotony of this Lesbian Love. "Joe" and her assumed wife made a visit to a neighboring village, ten miles distant, where "he" was recognized, was arrested as a vagrant and lodged in jail.

Joe's arrest occurred at the impetus of his wife's uncle, for whom Joe worked. The uncle, suspecting Joe was a woman, claimed to be incensed when his suspicion was confirmed, and immediately called the police, who made the arrest. Much to Wise's amazement, Joe's wife, taken under the spell of Joe's strange ways, bailed him out of jail after four months, and they lived together for another three years "until Joe had a maniacal attack" and was hence placed in the asylum under Wise's care.

Wise concluded his summary of Joe Lobdell's case by noting that the patient was a "victim of a distressing mono-delusional form of insanity. It is reasonable," he concluded, "to consider true sexual perversion as always a pathological condition and a peculiar manifestation of insanity." Joe's wife's involvement apparently warranted little comment except the suggestion that Joe's diseased and predatory nature led this hapless woman into tragic moral dissolution. The doctor's report emphasized that such an unfortunate turn of events was common when a female invert from a lower strata encountered a temporarily troubled woman of higher standing. Thus he urged the protection of such women from the predations of insane inverts. In spite of the doctor's sentiments, sensationalistic newsreporting of the case also portrayed the wife as "crazy."[21]

In 1896, Allan McLane Hamilton, a consulting physician to the Manhattan State Hospital and member of the New York Neurological Society, echoed P. M. Wise's distinction between innately degenerate masculine women and their hapless feminine prey. He stressed that in most cases of homosexuality, there is "an active and a passive agent, the former being usually a neurotic or degenerate, who is a sexual pervert, and whose life is pretty well given up to the gratification of his or her unnatural appetites."[22] Hamilton described the female version of this as someone who is masculine, or "if she presented none of the 'characteristics' of the male, was a subject of pelvic disorders, with scanty menstruation, and was more or less hysterical or insane." In addition, she tended to lack the ordinary modesty typical of women. By contrast, the "passive agent was, as a rule, decidedly feminine, with little power of resistance, usually sentimental or unnecessarily prudish." Hamilton mentioned that often the "unnatural attachment" between these two types was not premeditated but began as a casual relationship and degenerated over time.

To illustrate, Hamilton recounted the case of an affluent feminine women who seemed to have come under the powerful influence of a masculine woman. Their relationship, as Hamilton described it, was one of extortion on the part of the masculine female doctor who initially treated the other woman as a patient but eventually began scheming to get control of the wealth of the younger woman. The facts, even as he reported them, suggest that the younger woman was acting with full volition in offering money and other gifts to the doctor. But Hamilton read it all as the result of a degenerate and evil influence of the older predatory woman over the "passive" one. Hamilton's proclivity to read lesbian relationships through gender distinctions that demonized the mannish woman was typical by the end of the nineteenth century, and it revealed a growing tendency on the part of male doctors toward pathologizing female masculinity as a particularly grotesque form of degeneracy. Although they frequently showed disdain for effeminate men, many physicians, including Hamilton, were far more vicious in their attacks on masculine women which, incidentally, were written during the ascent of a powerful feminist movement seeking women's rights and equality with men.

In 1892, the most widely publicized case of homosexual insanity was reported, involving "lust murder" perpetrated by a deranged female.[23] Adding to the scandal and sensationalism already surrounding perversion, the case concerned a girl with tendencies not only toward masculinity but toward deadly violence. A young Memphis woman named Alice Mitchell fatally slashed Freda Ward, who had been the object of her increasingly desperate affection, after Freda's relatives discovered tokens of love given to her by Alice and demanded that the two not see each other again. Driven by red-hot rage and jealousy over Freda's impending marriage to a young male suitor, Alice had taken Freda's life in a most unladylike way. Mitchell was decreed insane by a Memphis court, on the advice of psychiatric authorities, who attributed her insanity to an inborn mental derangement which she inherited from her mother. The psychiatrist explained that Alice's defectiveness expressed itself in her preference for masculine hobbies as well as in her passionate and violent love for Freda Ward. Alice was fully lacking in feminine virtue and manifested unrestrained masculine lust. Her attorneys had introduced the plea of insanity to defend Alice against the charge of first-degree murder, referring to her sexual inversion as evidence thereof. This was precisely what upset James Kiernan whom, you will recall, decried the tactic of using medical diagnoses to defend and garner sympathy for homosexuality, despite the fact that the Mitchell case did anything but yield such results.

The news of the Mitchell case brought the subject of lesbianism to the attention of thousands of Americans. It also interested physicians around the United States and in Europe, including Krafft-Ebing, who included it in subsequent editions of *Psychopathia Sexualis*. Although Alice Mitchell was from a prosperous and reputable family in Memphis, her insanity and inversion were regarded by psychiatrists as one and the same. Both were signs of degeneration presumed to have passed down to her. Like others diagnosed as insane, Mitchell represented an atavistic and primitive disposition that defied civilized behavior and that manifested itself in an innate propensity to lust, immorality, and criminality. The fact that she behaved like an uncivilized man was itself evidence of her lunacy.

Many of the cases of female inversion and sex perversion included comments on the physical features of patients. In particular, the genitals of lesbians were often examined by psychiatrists with the help of gynecologists who applied their skills and knowledge of female anatomy to discern any characteristics that might indicate homosexuality. Their research methods were strikingly similar to those used initially by comparative anatomists to examine the genitals of the "Hottentot Venus" and by criminal anthropologists to discern the atavistic qualities of prostitutes and nymphomaniacs. It was believed that these women would show signs of innate immodesty and primitive evolutionary development.[24]

For example, the case of Lucy Ann Slater/Joseph Lobdell included Wise's inspection of Slater's genitals to determine characteristics that might distinguish "true inverts" from "normal" women. Quite specifically, Wise wanted to confirm Slater's own assertion that s/he was endowed with an elongated clitoris that satisfied the wife quite nicely. Indeed, the doctor noted that he was "unable to discover any abnormalities of the genitals, except an enlarged clitoris." This he took to be physical evidence of the patient's innate proclivity toward mannishness as well as hypersexuality, since Slater had been accused of making unwanted sexual overtures toward asylum nurses.

Although cases involving lesbians were among the most graphic and detailed in American medical writing from the nineteenth century, instances of homosexuality in "primitive" cultural groups were reported in equally sensationalistic language. In 1882, Dr. William A. Hammond reported the existence of *mujerados* among the Pueblo peoples in New Mexico. Mujerados were effeminized males who performed tasks traditionally done by women and who were regarded within the tribe to have special metaphysical powers. Hammond described the mujerados' "pederastic ceremonies which form so important a part of their religious performances" and noted that the these creatures were highly esteemed within the tribe. At the same time, he compared the mujerado to the "disease of the Scythians," noting that the customs of Pueblos, like those of the ancient Scythians, had given rise to pathological inverts.[25] In 1889, A. B. Holder, a Memphis physician who studied the Absaroke [i.e., Crow] Indians of Montana, discovered the *bote* (translated as "not man, not woman").[26] The *bote* was a biological male who performed acts of fellatio on men, wore a squaw's dress, and did female-designated tasks. Holder described the bote as disgusting, full of "perverted lust . . . whose tolerance I attribute not to any respect in which he is held, but to the debased standard of the people among whom he lives." Holder then went on to compare the perverse homosexual of the white race not to Hammond's highly esteemed invert (the mujerado) but to "his more disgusting cousin," the *bote*, who was depraved by perverse passion. By discovering pathological inversion and homosexuality in "primitive" societies, physicians and anthropologists argued that these practices were signs of evolutionary regression when they appeared in "civilized" societies. The logic worked in reverse as well: ethnocentric European American observers of Native American peoples deployed psychiatric labels from "civilized" societies to describe the culturally sanctioned roles and actions of the transgendered *berdache* in terms of mental infirmity. For example, as late as 1925, anthropologist Alfred Louis Kroeber reported cases of cross-dressing and transvestism among Native Americans of California and concluded they were psychologically abnormal and homosexual.[27] Thus, in either primitive or civilized societies, homosexuality was confirming evidence of atavistic insanity.

AMERICAN CITIES: HOTBEDS OF HOMOSEXUAL MISCEGENATION

That homosexuality was presumed to flourish in cities, where traditional boundaries separating the races and classes were dissolving, led many physicians to speculate on how city life might be hastening a trend toward moral and genetic degeneration. Their hunch was that cities attracted defective types who, in turn, spread their "moral insanity" by congregating with other defective types or with otherwise normal people whose moral integrity was compromised by the hedonism and anonymity of urban life. Starting in the 1880s, it became common for medical authorities on both sides of the Atlantic Ocean to allude to American cities as remarkable sites of ruptured traditions, licentious consumption, and cultural "miscegenation"—factors they regarded as primary generators of sexual perversion.[28] In their view, the nervousness underlying homosexuality was exacerbated by the dense geographic space of the metropolis, which brought diverse peoples into greater proximity to one another and tempted them with endless invitations to improvident self-gratification.[29] Indeed, in 1886, Krafft-Ebing noted that "large cities are hotbeds in which neuroses and low morality are bred; consider the history of Babylon, Nineveh, Rome, and the mysteries of modern metropolitan life."[30] Although Krafft-Ebing traced the origins to ancient Babylon, like other sexologists he was particularly concerned that the modern city had increased the dangers exponentially. American physicians' ideas about sexual perversion and city life were shaped by and contributed to conservative sentiments about maintaining order in the face of profoundly changing, diverse, and often antagonistic urban populations. Many of their ideas resonated with reactionary "social purity" campaigns that emerged in the second half of the nineteenth century.

Around this time, social patterns in the United States were changing significantly, and along with these changes came new ideas and habits that conservatives viewed as threatening to the nation's moral integrity. As a result of the Industrial Revolution, a significant portion of the population had become nomadic or relocated to fast-growing cities. Cultural, ethnic, and religious groups, which previously had little to do with one another, were brought together in the same schools, work-places, and neighborhoods. Massive waves of immigration added to the cultural heterogeneity of urban centers. Value systems were altered with the increased mobility, anonymity, and demographic mixing of the time. Individuals learned that the values and attitudes they had previously accepted were not necessarily shared by neighbors and co-workers. As a result, many experienced life as more complex and, in some ways, more permissive. New choices and options were available, but they were accompanied by problems wrought by massive economic and demographic changes. The perceived increase of unemployment, vagrancy, extramarital pregnancies, marital desertion, and alcoholism alarmed especially those who had a stake in social stability and preserving some semblance of order upon which their own privileges, as native-born middle-class Americans, were based. It was largely from this group that social purity crusades emanated, attracting men and women to the cause by emphasizing the dangers unleashed by the loss of traditions and the decline of moral standards.

Beginning around 1870, social purity campaigns emerged with the goal of ridding society of a host of evil forces seen to be fostered by modern city life. The movement reflected the notions from evangelical Christianity that God punishes sinners, that sin is contagious, and that innocents should be protected. The movement's activists focused especially on rescue work to save "fallen women" and to protect children from vice and disease. Their most celebrated causes included the prohibition of alcohol, campaigns against prostitution, and organized opposition to pornography. While they believed in social uplift, many strongly adhered to the idea that certain individuals and groups were inherently degenerate and beyond the pale of rehabilitation. Their ideas influenced the first generation of American physicians writing about homosexuality.

Drawing its main support from pro–nativist, middle-class men and women, the social purity movement tended to associate degeneracy with the lower socioeconomic classes, including immigrant laborers as well as impoverished American-born blacks and whites. But social purifiers were just as alarmed by the evil influences of libertine writers, artists, and intellectuals whom they associated with the moral decadence common among the idle and gluttonous rich. The specter of the vile rich consorting with the wretched underclasses in rituals of debauchery greatly exercised social purity activists.

In general, social purity activists idealized sexual continence. In their view, sex perversions represented both a satanic force and a dangerous bodily affliction. Along with prostitution, pornography, and, later, birth control, "sex perversion" became a key target of campaigns launched by self-proclaimed guardians of virtue. Under the leadership of Anthony Comstock, this loose-knit network of local groups gained a national foothold in 1873 when Congress passed the Comstock Act, signed by President Ulysses S. Grant, "to restrict the trade and circulation of obscene literature and articles of immoral use."[31] As an amendment to the U.S. Postal Code, the act outlawed the production and availability of contraceptives and pornographic materials, regarding both as encouraging perverse sexual behavior. Comstock, who headed the extra-governmental New York Society for the Prevention of Vice, supervised the enforcement of the law as an unpaid U.S. postal inspector in New York City. His intent to restrict the public discussion about sexuality was instrumental in preventing texts by Krafft-Ebing and Havelock Ellis from being available to lay-readers in the United States.

Social purifiers argued for moral reform by focusing heavily on fighting bawdy entertainment.[32] Homosexuality was attacked on similar grounds, as a form of vice brought on by hedonism, race- and class-mixing, and the degradation of heterosexual virtue by a strange affinity between degenerate underclasses and amoral "bohemian" elites. It required direct and vigilant public intervention to prevent its spread. To that end, Comstock and his supporters sought to ban books by homosexual authors or authors whose books included homosexual themes, to raid and close down establishments where lesbians and gay men gathered, and to bring a halt to entertainment involving cross-dressing, including "pansy acts" and drag masquerade balls.[33]

In contrast to a later generation of physicians who distanced themselves from moral crusades in favor of a "rational" and "progressive" approach to sexuality, nineteenth-century physicians were closely allied with social purity forces in their attitudes and rhetoric. And the discursive traffic moved in the opposite direction as well: moral crusaders relied upon the medical condemnation of homosexuality in their campaigns to eradicate perversion from cities. In the early 1880s, the American physician George Beard, writing on nervous exhaustion and its relationship to modern life, argued that neurasthenia and sexual perversion were unfortunate outcomes of progress.[34] He tied nervousness to the dizzying growth of industry, the overcrowding of American cities, and the dissolution of moral fortitude and cultural traditions caused by these abrupt developments. Beard's work was accepted widely among European and American doctors, who concurred that fast-growing cities engendered nervousness and led to moral corruption, promiscuity, and unbridled lust. Medical opinions of this sort were invoked by social purity activists in their campaigns against homosexual vice in the cities.

The moralistic reaction to homosexual vice was fueled by rumors, at home and abroad, that American cities fostered perversion and were resorts for sex perverts. In the 1880s, European medical texts suggested as much. For example, in their 1889 handbook of forensic medicine, the German doctors J. L. Caspar and Carl Liman included the account of a German homosexual man, who, upon visiting the United States in 1871, reported that homosexuality was "more ordinary" in America than in Germany. By his own account, the visitor was "able to indulge his passions more openly, with less fear of punishment," having been "always immediately recognized as a member of the [homosexual] confraternity."[35] In 1906, the German physician Paul Näcke, writing in the *Archiv für Kriminal-Anthropologie*, suggested that "degenerate Urnings" from Germany were emigrating to American cities, where perversion was more prevalent. He wrote that "among the multitude of inferior individuals who cross the ocean year in and year out, there are probably more homosexuals than others, because there are probably more degenerate and inferior specimens of humanity among them than in the ranks of the heterosexuals."[36] To the chagrin of American authorities, European physicians believed that the United States offered a refuge for degenerates to indulge their depraved desires.

In the 1915 edition of *Sexual Inversion*, Havelock Ellis reiterated that the modern American metropolis was giving rise to an elaborate and menacing homosexual subculture by quoting the words of an American correspondent:

> The great prevalence of sexual inversion in American cities is shown by the wide knowledge of its existence. Ninety-nine normal men out of a hundred have been accosted on the streets by inverts, or have among their acquaintances men whom they know to be sexually inverted. Everyone has seen inverts and knows what they are. The public attitude toward them is generally a negative one—indifference, amusement, contempt. The world of sexual inverts is, indeed, a large one in any American city, and it is a community distinctly organized.[37]

Ellis's American correspondent—if we are to disregard conceit—was simply stating the obvious, reporting what he believed most urban-dwelling Americans already knew by 1915. In his assessment, the nation's cities were nearly overrun with the "sexually inverted" who habitually harassed "normal men." Despite the contempt with which they were met, these creatures inhabited cities and belonged to a strange world of their own making. As many others before him had detected, the candid observer reported an open secret that was typically obvious and obtuse at once: inverts were everywhere but their "distinctly organized" world and their peculiar desires remained mysterious. Such news was remarkable enough to find its way into Ellis's scientific text. Indeed, Ellis sought not to verify the correspondent's alarming impression but readily incorporated it in his argument for rational scientific inquiry into the disturbing changes wrought by modern urban life.

Well before Näcke and Ellis made their remarks, American physicians were clearly dismayed that the United States had earned a reputation as a breeding ground for sexual vice. They responded to such suggestions with alarm and vociferously countered them by condemning perversion. It was, in fact, true that by the 1890s homosexual subcultures had begun to flourish in New York, Chicago, Washington, D.C., Boston, San Francisco, and other American cities. American doctors reacted by decrying their existence and urging medical colleagues and city officials to take action to stem the problem. In 1894, New York psychiatrist Allan McLane Hamilton warned of the growing presence of male "sexual perverts" and lesbians in America's cities, echoing a similar observation made by G. Frank Lydston in 1889 that homosexuals sought each other out in cities in order to satisfy their abnormal desires. Lydston beseeched other physicians to pay attention to this problem and offer their assistance to lawmakers seeking to bring it under control.[38]

While granting that vice-ridden cities could exacerbate degeneracy, physicians generally held that individuals engaging in perversion were biologically predisposed to do so. Under morally upstanding circumstances, a predisposition to homosexuality could be held at bay. But pressures of modern life undermined moral constraints, activated pathological tendencies, and led to bad breeding, thus allowing tainted individuals to produce innately perverse offspring. Lacking morality, they expressed their perversions more openly and dragged the constitutionally unfit down with them into an underworld of decadence and moral dissolution. The reasoning here followed a Lamarckian view that, by engaging in perversion of whatever sort, individuals could acquire a predisposition to perversity that would then be passed down to offspring. Presumably, if morally upstanding circumstances prevailed, homosexuality would be minimized, but, logically speaking, that should have a paradoxical effect: those with the predisposition would marry and have children who would also have the predisposition. However, in morally depraved circumstances, the predisposition to homosexuality would be activated: the predisposed would not marry and presumably would not have children, insofar as their sexual activities were limited to persons of the same sex. But doctors were aware that many who engaged in homosexuality also had heterosexual relations that resulted in the birth of children, and this worried them. Furthermore, physicians believed that perversions of all sorts would appear, in one form or another, in subsequent generations. For example, in families where the father was a promiscuous womanizer, or the grandmother was nymphomaniacal, or the great-grandfather was an alcoholic, offspring stood a good chance of being inherently predisposed to perversion. Thus degenerationists cited the vices of previous generations to explain the presence of homosexuality when it appeared in descendants. What was inherited was a predisposition to engage in immoral acts of various sorts, and hence one recommendation for eliminating homosexuality was to sterilize degenerate individuals, whether they actually engaged in homosexuality or not, to prevent such an outcome in later generations. Even when their focus was primarily on homosexuality, American doctors working within a degenerationist framework were setting boundaries around what would count as healthy heterosexuality through recommendations to prevent breeding among the innately perverse.

In much of the medical and anti-vice commentary, the city was described as unleashing the inherent lasciviousness of the lower classes that older traditions had kept in check. While physicians never referenced such things explicitly, one can surmise that the hallowed traditions included those which bolstered racial segregation and class stratification and which allowed for face-to-face moral shaming of nonconforming individuals in small towns and rural settings. Earlier practices of moral policing were undermined by the migration of many men and women into cities. Calls for a return to a time before the proliferation of vice were often coupled with commentary emphasizing the unrestrained passion and promiscuity of African Americans. Medical case reports of homosexuality involving black people implied that middle-class white people would be debauched if they came into proximity with African Americans. The fact that some white lesbians and homosexual men sought the company of their kind among African Americans was given as evidence of their moral debasement and of the rampant spread of degeneracy.

Fears of miscegenation were expressed in commentary by moral reformers as well as by certain physicians and scientists around this time. They dreaded the coming of a "mongrel race" and believed that increasing numbers of black and brown people were slipping across the color line and "passing" into whiteness, thus tainting the purity of the superior white race. A growing phobia about racial passing and the alleged disappearance of outward signs of racial difference paralleled a panic that inverts and perverts were everywhere but becoming more difficult to distinguish by physical characteristics.

Moreover, this panic focused heavily on the frightening specter of white and black "perverts" congregating in bizarre sexual rituals involving cross-dressing and clandestine orgies. Alongside fears of "interbreeding" by heterosexuals, some of the same racist anti-miscegenation logic was applied to homosexuals: contact of an "unnatural" sort would corrupt the population and lead to irreparable social disorder.[39]

Dread of this sort was evident in the writing of Dr. Irving C. Rosse, professor of nervous diseases at Georgetown University. In 1892, Rosse read an influential but meandering paper at a meeting of the Medical Society of Virginia about "Perversion of the Genesic [procreative] Instinct."[40] In it, he warned of the rampant perversion and "sexual crime" in the nation's capital, and he noted that "both white and black were represented among these moral hermaphrodites, but the majority of them were negroes."[41] The specter of white and black men engaging in sex with one another was, he thought, an indication of the depths to which perverts would stoop. He believed that contact with black "sexual criminals" would worsen the moral derangement of white men and further degrade the white race.

Homosexuality, Rosse believed, was common among African American men. To support this he cited a "vadoux" [voodoo] society in New Orleans and an "androgynous band of negroes" in Washington, D.C., who engaged in strange masquerade parties that culminated in nights of unbridled carnality.[42] The connection he drew between African Americans and homosexuality was underpinned by Rosse's assumption that perversion was an expression of primitive instincts evident in animals and which culminated in "sexual crimes." Sexual crime, by Rosse's definition, included any sexual activity other than "normal coitus," but the most disturbing manifestation was homosexuality. Linking such violations to "the biological beginnings of crime as observed in curious instances of criminality in animals," Rosse enunciated what was clearly a tendency among American doctors to see homosexuality as an innate characteristic in tainted individuals which was both atavistic and animalistic.[43]

To ground his argument, Rosse reported anecdotal evidence gathered on the serendipitous occasion of his taking refuge from the rain while visiting the Washington Zoological Gardens. There he found two male elephants, "Dunk" and "Gold Dust," whom he witnessed "entwining their probesces together in a caressing way," each having "simultaneous erection of the penis," and completing the act "by one animal opening and allowing the other to tickle the roof of his mouth with his proboscis."[44] Although a seemingly harmless and even tender encounter between the two beasts, Rosse construed such unnatural lust as evidence of the primitive origins of vice in human males. Among the most detrimental effects of the "nameless crime that moves in the dark" were syphilis and overall moral degradation. Such problems were most pronounced in cities, he noted.

Rosse was particularly alarmed by the growing prevalence of perversion afflicting Washington, D.C. where both lesbianism and male homosexuality posed threats of spreading everything from abject moral turpitude to venereal diseases. He was especially unsettled by black and white men engaging in homosexual acts "under the very shadow of the White House." Referencing the arrest of eighteen men in Lafayette Square, Rosse asserted that such events presaged the dangers that lay before the people of America. "I take it for granted," he stated, "that what is true of Washington as regards sexual matters applies more or less to other American large cities."[45]

Rosse was not alone in drawing a connection between "primitive" peoples and the sexual perversion that seemed to be growing in cities as a result of the decline of traditional boundaries separating whites from blacks and the middle class from the working class and poor. One year later, Charles Hughes, an alienist practicing in St. Louis, alerted other physicians about "orgies of lascivious debauchery" known to their participants as "drag dances." Commonly held in the nation's capital and in cities like New York, these spectacles were carried on by "colored erotopaths," who gathered annually, providing entertainment for each other and for similarly perverse whites. The participants belonged to secret societies and engaged in elaborate rituals known only to other members. They represented a bizarre cult that mocked all respectability by violating the conventional color line and inverting the sexes:

> In this sable performance of sexual perversion all of these men are lasciviously dressed in womanly attire, short sleeves, low-necked dresses and the usual ballroom decorations and ornaments of women, feathered and ribboned head-dresses, garters, frills, flowers, ruffles, etc., and deport themselves as women. Standing or seated on a pedestal, but accessible to all the rest, is the naked queen (a male), whose phallic member, decorated with a ribbon, is subject to the gaze and osculations in turn, of all the members of this lecherous gang of sexual perverts and phallic fornicators.[46]

Hughes was especially exercised by two key factors. The first was the proximity of these underworld degenerates to the seat of the nation's power in Washington, D.C. And the second was that their bizarre gatherings brought together men from different social classes whose degeneracy manifested itself in a dangerous blend of male lasciviousness and female vanity. Hughes wrote: "Among those who annually assemble in this strange libidinous display are cooks, barbers, waiters and other employees of Washington families, some even higher in the social scale—some being employed as subordinates in the Government departments."[47] Fearing the degenerate outcome of unnatural mixtures of white and black men, Hughes warned that erotopathy was infectious and had the power to compromise not only the health of individuals but the vitality of the nation.

Hughes reiterated his warning in 1907, with an additional admonition that "negro perverts" masquerading in women's garb at "miscegenation dances" were corrupting the city of St. Louis. In a detailed description of their debauchery, Hughes noted that these men drove their masters' cars to a levee dive and dance hall, gowned as women, to attend "miscegenation dances" where some had been recently arrested and then bailed out by a white man. White men frequented their "handsomely furnished levee resort," where "scores of west end butlers, cooks, and chauffeurs" met. The doctor went on to state, rather inelegantly, that "social reverse complexion homosexual affinities are rarer than non reverse color affinities," but it appeared that American cities were fostering interracial homosexual encounters at an alarming rate. "The reverse erotopath"—Hughes's arcane term for the sex invert—was, in his view, a common feature of large cities, and he endorsed police vigilance to bring this creature "into the light." Otherwise, "homosexual miscegenation," like "cliteromania" [nymphomania] and "satyric imperative propulsion" [male hypersexuality], was bound to proliferate and further corrupt the morals of American city-dwellers.[48]

Throughout this period, American physicians habitually characterized homosexuality as emanating from elements and forces outside the native-born white population. In a letter to Magnus Hirschfeld dated 1911, a homosexual man from Colorado wrote that it had become a common practice among American authorities to blame "one or the other ethnic group for homosexuality." The correspondent, a professor, continued: "A criminologist from the Southern states recently stated that male prostitution first spread into his area of the country with the immigration of the Italian 'Vergazzi'; and one often hears Americans claim that the yellow-skinned population is strongly given to homosexuality."[49]

Blaming foreigners and the lower classes for perversion had proven convenient for social purity activists and nineteenth-century physicians who had stakes in upholding class and racial distinctions upon which their prestige and privilege were based. But the picture grew a bit more complicated in light of the "New Woman," a figure largely implicating middle-class women, who symbolized women's desire for independence, fulfillment, and equality with men. New women were neither typically foreigners nor easily classified as primitive degenerates in the way that indigent and working-class lesbians were. They tended to come from reputable families and aspired to educational and professional achievements championed by the middle class. That they seemed to be politically feisty and have a proclivity to form sexual relationships with other women alarmed conservatives, including a fair number of male doctors. In their view, the New Woman's political goals, along with her purported inclination toward lesbianism, pointed to a violation of the boundary between the sexes, and this was taken to be a sign that she was mentally disturbed.

THE NEW WOMAN AND HER EVIL TWIN

Around the turn of the century, opponents of feminism used the sexual inversion paradigm to pathologize agitation for women's opportunities in education, employment, and politics. It was not uncommon to find antifeminist doctors diagnosing women's desire for equality with men as an expression of mannishness and, therefore, a symptom of an underlying disorder. In addition, many sought to discredit feminism by linking it with lesbianism, which, thanks to sensationalistic accounts of the Mitchell case in 1892, had become associated in the public's mind with insanity and destruction. Thus, as the New Woman gained public recognition, so did the demonic figure of the mannish lesbian.[50] By the accounts of reactionary male physicians, they were evil twins who needed to be reformed or eliminated altogether. Other medical commentators were more hospitable toward the New [heterosexual] Woman, but their praise of her sexual and social liberation was often at the expense of lesbians, who were described as pathological man-haters. So long as the modern heterosexual woman was happy and cooperative in the intimate company of men, she was the good version of the modern woman. The misanthropic lesbian was another story. She was generally categorized among the bad seeds of modernity. These two different perspectives—one that lumped the New Woman and the lesbian together and the other that used the lesbian as a foil to police the sexuality of heterosexual women—were evident in much of the medical writing about lesbianism occurring between middle-class women around the turn of the century.

One New York physician, William Lee Howard, was of the evil twins school of thought. In 1900, he warned that women seeking the "masculine idea" of independence were just as degenerate as "that disgusting anti-social being, the female sexual pervert." To make matters worse, he exclaimed, "emancipated" mothers created effeminate boys and masculine girls, giving rise to generations of tainted citizens. Howard's attack was aimed directly against the New Woman, whose child was to be pitied:

> If [the child] could be taken away from its environments, kept from the misguidance of an unwilling mother, nurtured, tutored, and directed along the sex line Nature has struggled to give it, often would the child be true to its latent normal instincts and grow to respected womanhood or manhood. Unfortunate it is that this development does not take place. The weak, plastic, developing cells of the brain are twisted, distorted, and a perverted psychic growth promoted by the false examples and teachings of a discontented mother. These are the conditions which have been prolific in producing the antisocial "new woman" and the disgusting effeminate male, both typical examples of the physiological degenerate.[51]

Howard warned that the degenerate class consisting of feminists and female sex perverts clamors for women's higher education and freedom, and "demands all the prerogative of the man." These hysterical "female androids" formed sects and societies, "superciliously flaunting health laws and hygienic regulations" and "shout[ing] their incomprehensible jargon" without any knowledge of science or medicine.

In short, for Howard, the New Woman was no better than the lesbian, and possibly even worse since she would have "unsexed" children. A menace to civilization, she produced mental and physical monstrosities. Howard compared the New Woman to the degenerate lesbian to emphasize the absolutely despicable nature of both. But embedded in his vicious attack was the idea that a child might triumph over degeneracy if given a better environment in which to mature. Howard's logic reveals how notions of innate degeneracy were tempered by reformist thinking, a trend that became more common beginning around the turn of the century.

In 1914, another New York physician, L. Pierce Clark, stressed the particularly threatening nature of female sex inversion, noting that "the homosexual woman leads an active, energetic life—is enterprising, aggressive, adventurous, and at times brutal and regardless. In general she is cold-blooded."[52] Clark's conclusion was that lesbians posed a more disruptive threat to traditional sex roles than did homosexual men, whom he described as meek. By contrast, lesbians, due to their zeal to live and act like men, posed a more pressing problem. That same year Dr. Herbert Claiborne, writing ostensibly about excessive hair growth in women, related lesbianism and pathological sex inversion to feminism and women's participation in business.[53] Both doctors spoke with contempt toward women who sought equality with men.

The purported prevalence of lesbian relationships among middle-class women piqued doctors' curiosity, and it led some to question the sex inversion paradigm that had dominated scientific thinking about lesbianism. In 1913, the physician Douglas McMurtrie was alarmed that, in many lesbian relationships, masculine and feminine roles were occasionally reversed or avoided altogether. This puzzled the doctor and led him to suggest that many cases of lesbianism could not be explained in terms of constitutional inversion. He turned his attention to the curious motivations of "feminine" women to pursue lesbian relationships. Rather than seeing them as hapless and passive victims of mannish inverts, he viewed feminine lesbians as just as guilty of vice and perversion as mannish women. McMurtrie found it disturbing that they displaced men entirely either by taking masculine women as their partners or by shunning any connection to masculinity in their erotic lives.[54]

Other physicians during this period were particularly concerned that middle-class women were rejecting marriage and motherhood in favor of spending their lives with other women. These women were described as suffering from arrested psychosexual development. Although they had been exalted a decade or so earlier, affectionate relationships between middle-class women began to be regarded as pathological refusals to mature. This trend in thinking among physicians, bearing the influences of psychoanalytic ideas, reflected what historian George Chauncey has called a "heterosexual counterrevolution" when male commentators sought to place heterosexuality on a stronger, "modern" footing, while bringing women back into a subordinate companionship with men. Through the demonization of lesbianism, the New Woman was duly warned of the importance of keeping a good rapport with men and she was encouraged to marry and find fulfillment through motherhood. Lesbians, in turn, were scapegoated in a larger ideological campaign aimed at undermining women's aspirations for erotic, legal, and economic autonomy.[55]

But it was not only women's subordination to men that was at stake in the heterosexual counterrevolution of the time, which, it should be said, was concerned primarily with ensuring a particular kind of heterosexuality. It consisted of "hygienic" reproduction among middle-class white men and women, in contrast to the heterosexuality engaged in by the degenerates. Concerns over the purported increase of homosexuality among middle-class women emerged around the same time that conservative American men began issuing dire warnings that the lower classes, immigrants, and people of color were outpacing middle-class whites in reproducing children. In this context, middle-class white women were targeted by pro-natalist and pro-nativist campaigns to marry and have children as part of their duty to the nation.[56] Manifesting itself in adamant demands that women grow up and overcome the irritating tendency to challenge men's authority, the backlash against feminism and lesbianism was deeply interwoven with eugenical reproductive agendas as well.

HOMOSEXUAL PERVERSION AND "RACE SUICIDE"

In 1901, the political commentator Edward A. Ross coined the term "race suicide" to refer to the declining birth rate of "Old American" stock, especially when compared to immigrants who were blamed for militant labor unrest and other affronts to the social order.[57] Old American stock generally referred to middle-class American-born people of European origins, and more specifically to upper-class Anglo-Saxon Protestants. In 1905, President Theodore Roosevelt, speaking at the annual meeting of the National Congress of Mothers, invoked Ross's term to admonish white women of respectable origins to reproduce. Warning that recent immigrants, along with poor and working-class people, were "swamping" the nation with defective offspring, Roosevelt elevated the obligation of motherhood to a patriotic duty. "Race suicide," he charged, was being committed by genetically superior women who neglected or refused to give birth to a sufficient number of children. Roosevelt's invocation of the term placed the onus on the New Woman, whose interest in higher education and paid professional employment distracted her from the important task of motherhood.[58]

Roosevelt's admonition echoed ideas of the eugenics movement in the United States, which was particularly diverse and strong by 1905.

Eugenical doctrine was based on the assumption that the processes of natural selection theorized by Charles Darwin were thwarted or contaminated under the conditions of modern life, and thus required intervention to correct the imbalances caused by deviations from Nature's design. These deviations were thought to manifest themselves in the growing number of feebleminded, insane, and perverse people cropping up everywhere from isolated rural hollers to the neighborhoods of modern cities. Central to the eugenics movement was an interest in alleviating social problems by regulating birth rates. This was articulated through two main approaches, one which encouraged the "fit" to reproduce at a greater rate, and the other which discouraged or aimed to prevent the "unfit" from having children.

Although some eugenicists explicitly opposed making distinctions between the "fit" and the "unfit" on the grounds of class and race, the more vocal and politically successful proponents of eugenics generally assumed that the inherently degenerate were concentrated among the poor while the "fit" demonstrated their superiority through prosperity. The "fit" were not only biologically superior but also morally so. Thus, the leading eugenicists were concerned with regulating and maintaining boundaries between racial groups and socioeconomic classes, and they viewed intermarriage as tantamount to poisoning a future generation. The main purveyors and proponents of eugenics in the United States were affluent and educated European-American men of "native born" stock who were joined by a newly emerging professional class of scientists and physicians interested in the power of manipulating rates of reproduction for the sake of eliminating problems of poverty, crime, unemployment, and social unrest. Politically conservative "Old American" men such as Charles Davenport, Harry Laughlin, Roswell Johnson, G. S. Gosney, Paul Popenoe, Henry Goddard, and Lothrop Stoddard controlled most of the laboratories and centers for eugenics research and policy, and their political activism resulted in state laws permitting compulsory sterilization of asylum patients. But eugenics as an idea appealed to a rather broad range of Americans, including some feminists, Jews, homosexuals, and people of color. Liberals, socialists, anarchists, and women's rights advocates were drawn to eugenics for its utopian promise to alleviate social ills through modern scientific management of rates of reproduction. It appealed to leftists who favored a social or collective vision over that of the individual, thus authorizing the suspension of certain individuals' rights to have children if they were unfit. Although left-leaning eugenicists were less inclined toward the assumptions held by political conservatives that the races, sexes, and classes were arranged, by nature, in hierarchical order, many believed that qualities such as intelligence, personality, and behavior were based on hereditary factors, and that proper breeding could optimize the best of these traits. Thus, they shared with the more conservative eugenicists the idea that society could benefit from foresightful regulation of reproduction.[59]

Eugenics activists transformed the act of procreation into a moral as much as a biological matter. Promoting hygienic reproduction involved eliminating deleterious "germ plasm" and "cacogenic" elements from the gene pool. Thus, as we have seen, sexual perversion, regarded as a hereditary defect, was targeted for eradication. This mentality had given rise to the castration and sterilization of male and female "sex perverts" in the 1890s. But in the early years of the twentieth century, certain middle-class men and women of Old American stock who engaged in homosexuality were targeted instead for social rehabilitation through Progressive reform strategies, some of which responded directly to Roosevelt's appeal to end race suicide. Thus, the eugenics movement engendered contradictory responses to middle-class people who engaged in homosexuality.

On the one hand, some argued that homosexuals, since they might be inherently defective, did a service to the greater society by not reproducing. This approach believed that homosexuals should not be encouraged to marry or have children.[60] On the other hand, others thought that, if homosexuals could be recuperated and reformed— that is, kept away from degenerate influences and encouraged to become good fathers and mothers—perhaps they could help to stem the process of moral degradation visited upon the nation by swarms of truly defective people. Of greatest concern were middle-class women whose sympathies to feminism and affection for other women were causing them to stray from healthy adult lives as wives and mothers. They were the primary focus of campaigns to right the demographic imbalance between the healthy and the infirm, the decent and the degenerate. Although not explicitly singled out the way middle-class lesbians were, middle-class homosexual men were also among the "maladjusted" whom reformers targeted for rehabilitation under the rubric of mental hygiene that emerged in the first decade of the twentieth century. In the meantime, perverts from the lower-classes were generally considered to be beyond the pale of rehabilitation.

But the lines demarcating class and those discerning ethnic groups ("races") were not so easy to draw. Intermarriage between ethnic groups was becoming more common, and people from very different backgrounds were settling into adjacent neighborhoods and encountering each other in schools, civic organizations, and workplaces. The image of the American "melting pot" offered a way of thinking about social diversity that accommodated the upward mobility and cultural heterogeneity of generations of children born to parents of different religious, national, and ethnic origins. The economic and political ascent of ethnic groups such as the Irish, Italians, and Germans in cities like New York altered municipal power structures and testified to the virtues of cultural assimilation. In the meantime, the more progressive daughters and sons of Old American parents joined with children of immigrants and professionally trained emigres from Europe to champion a host of social reforms that, rather than harking back to older traditions, looked forward optimistically to the challenges of modern life.

REFORMING THE HOMOSEXUAL

Around the beginning of the twentieth century, when homosexuality seemed to be increasing among middle-class men and women, progressive reformers proposed new strategies for stemming the problem. These were aimed primarily at rehabilitating middle-class individuals and at helping them to overcome psychological "maladjustment." Reformers' efforts were supported by a significant shift in theories about the cause of homosexuality. Several prominent American psychiatrists noted that many cases of homosexuality resulted not from hereditary taint but from unfortunate conditions and circumstances that interfered with individuals' psychosexual maturation. Influenced by psychogenic theories advanced by European psychoanalysts, they proposed interventionist methods to prevent homosexuality from taking root in childhood and to control it among adults. Although the new rehabilitative model did not wholly supplant degenerationist thinking and in fact maintained the assumption that inversion and homosexual perversion were more pronounced in the lower classes, it viewed individuals on a scale whereby some who showed signs of maladjustment might be rehabilitated if they received proper guidance and encouragement. A common recommendation was for homosexuals to simply abstain from sex and be removed from environments that encouraged perversion. The population targeted for such strategies consisted mainly of middle-class individuals, while homosexuals of lower social and economic strata continued to be associated with deeply-rooted disease. Whereas middle-class homosexuals might be reformed, the rest were generally regarded as beyond redemption and as living evidence of the degraded milieux from which the middle class needed protection.

In 1895, Havelock Ellis, whose initial articles on homosexuality were first published in American medical journals, recommended abstinence as the only viable way to control homosexuality. He articulated this by focusing on lesbianism, which he found particularly disturbing. Dismayed that social acceptance of affection between women only made the matter worse, Ellis wrote: "By a wholesome and prolonged course of physical and mental hygiene the patient may be enabled to overcome the morbid fears and suspicions which have sometimes been fostered by excessive sympathy and coddling, and the mind may thus indirectly be brought into a tonic condition of self-control. The inversion will not thus be removed but it may be rendered comparatively harmless, both to the patient herself and to those who surround her."[61] Ellis, whose wife had intense love affairs with women, advised lesbians against marrying men and encouraged other doctors to give the same advice, stating that it caused undue suffering for the husband and could lead to defective offspring. His admonition to self-control was particularly welcomed by American doctors who valued the idea of self-improvement and who believed that exerting will-power was a viable way for individuals to bring their perverse tendencies under control. Ellis thought that a disciplinary regimen of work and dedication to civic activities would allay homosexuality. The principles of productivity and self-sacrifice were central to physical and mental hygiene as he imagined it.

Although Ellis maintained that homosexuality stemmed from a congenital predisposition, a growing number of American doctors entertained psychogenic explanations and proposed aversion therapies to overcome and eliminate homosexuality. For example, in 1899, Dr. John D. Quackenbos of Columbia University presented a paper at the New Hampshire Medical Society meeting in which he claimed to have developed a kind of "moral anaesthesia" to cure nymphomania, kleptomania, and "unnatural passion for persons of the same sex." The initial treatment consisted of hypnotizing the patient to strip him or her of "abnormal feeling" and to encourage "a natural desire for the opposite sex." In a second session, the patient, under hypnosis again, would be warned of the "moral, mental, and financial ruin" of "unnatural lust" and then offered depictions of marriage as the "greatest human happiness." This early form of aversion therapy was directed at building up the patient's ability to refrain from homosexuality, and Quackenbos claimed success in many cases.[62]

Psychogenic theories of homosexuality were compatible with the ethos of social amelioration that was popular around the turn of the century. At that time, a loose-knit group of academically trained physicians, lawmakers, social workers, and social scientists promoted the idea that the social environment could be manipulated or altered to ameliorate a host of problems. They looked to the future with both concern and optimism, believing that problems such as homosexuality could be prevented and eliminated through a combination of scientific expertise, social engineering, and the fortitude of the individual. Their thinking was consonant with cultural ideals championing productive work and self-improvement of the sort expressed by conservative-minded medical commentators. But what distinguished the ameliorationists was their embrace of the notions of progressive change, cultural assimilation, and "adjustment," rather than a return to traditions that adhered to static classifications and valued the separation of groups.

Believing that expertise was necessary for confronting the many challenges of modern life, social reformers promoted scientific approaches to the study of sexuality and advocated sex education in order to prevent venereal disease and unwanted pregnancies and to foster harmonious and hygienic marriages.[63] Their agenda on sexuality betrayed a bit of prudery around the subject of homosexuality, which they tended to speak of euphemistically as sexual "maladjustment." But the term suggested the possibility of improvement to achieve adjustment, rather than the hopeless impossibility of ever overcoming the "inborn defect" or "degeneracy" of perversion. The idea of achieving sexual maturity and adjusting to social norms echoed a self-proclaimed "progressive" approach to contending with social diversity—one that valued social progress and harmony, rather than stasis or conflict. This approach also opposed reactionary extragovernmental moral crusades and favored modern scientific rationality, through coordination with an expanding administrative state apparatus.

The idiom of adjustment was a crucial part of the new language of expert management during this period, and it found its way into psychiatric terminology as well. Adjustment in everything from family psychology to corporate management came to stand for the finely regulated balanced between the individual and his or her environment. Those resisting regimes of management, consciously or not, were characterized as maladjusted in relation to the general population and to their environment. Behavioral experts devised therapeutic interventions to bring the maladjusted into a better fit with what was being constituted as the normal environment of modern life. They measured standards and noted deviations across a range of sectors, from industry to health to political participation.

Social engineering focused on calculating human activities and manipulating people and environments, and it was initially developed in the context of industrial management to enhance levels of productivity and efficiency in the workplace. Its popularity grew enormously, and social engineering methods were applied to domains as sentimentally laden as marriage and the family, where scientific reformers applied criteria of efficiency, psychological harmony, and hygiene to propose solutions to rising rates of divorce and lowered birth rates among middle-class couples. Ideas from social engineering influenced psychiatrists in their efforts to encourage sexually maladjusted men and women to adjust to heterosexuality and to adapt themselves to the proper sex roles upon which it was based.[64]

Metric thinking was part of an overall trend toward discerning norms and controlling deviations that was promoted by behavioral experts and progressive reformers. It was used to diagnose psychological problems during a time when psychiatry was expanding beyond the treatment of the patently insane in asylums toward remedying conflicts confronting normal people. Psychiatrists became concerned with ensuring what they called the mental hygiene of the general population, acknowledging that modern life brought with it many stresses and challenges. In 1909, the National Committee for Mental Hygiene formed in New York City with the aims of preventing psychological problems and of improving the care and treatment of those suffering from mental diseases. The psychiatrists who joined the Committee's ranks and published articles in its quarterly journal, *Mental Hygiene*, were progressive-minded reformers who believed that the majority of psychological problems had important social dimensions. Among the more pressing were homosexuality and sexual activities that interfered with matrimonial reproduction.[65]

By 1909, psychoanalysis transformed and broadened the scientific terms for thinking about homosexuality and began to make its mark on select psychiatrists in the United States who were associated with the mental hygiene movement.[66] Most American medical authorities writing about homosexuality around this time were less sanguine about the purely psychogenic perspective of psychoanalysts, having invested quite significantly in hereditarian theories which underpinned widely accepted ideas from the eugenics movement. However, under the influence of psychoanalytic theories, a few of the more prominent psychiatrists in the United States began to consider homosexuality through what came to be referred to as a *psychobiological* approach.

This approach was described by its purveyors as an alternative to narrow biological determinism, on the one hand, and to overly speculative and anti-somaticist psychoanalysis, on the other. It sought to consider the interdependent influences of the mind, the body, and the external social environment in what was described as a holistic and dynamic perspective. Earlier constitutional models from the nineteenth century had presumed a unity of the individual's body, mind, moral character, and social status. By contrast, psychobiology was a neologism that made sense only after the intervention of psychoanalysis, which had discerned the psychological and the biological as two distinct realms, and focused on the former, assuming it to be more definitive than the latter in causes of homosexuality.

The psychobiological framework accommodated the notion that homosexuality could be inborn in some cases, an idea refuted by most psychoanalysts. At the same time, it stressed the importance of individual agency and free will to overcome adversity—ideas that had been undercut by the strict hereditary determinism of degenerationists. These features made it a particularly attractive approach in the United States, where it was developed to explain the mutually influential relationships between biological, psychological, and social phenomena that could both explain modern perversions and help bring them under control.

The term psychobiology was coined by the Swiss émigré psychiatrist Adolf Meyer, who was one of the founders of the mental hygiene movement in the United States and who served on the National Committee for Mental Hygiene for many years. Meyer's psychobiological framework epitomized the new ameliorative approach to homosexuality. Meyer was above all a pragmatist. He was intrigued by Freud's psychoanalytic method but believed psychoanalysis placed too much emphasis on the mysteries of the unconscious and focused too much on analyzing patients rather than remedying their problems. Moreover, Meyer thought Freud's emphasis on sexuality was extreme, bordering on the distasteful.[67]

Although trained as a neurologist, Meyer came to believe that many mental illnesses could not be explained in simple organic terms.

Instead, he believed that problems such as homosexuality were rooted in emotional and interpersonal problems emanating from difficulties presented by the individual's environment. His pragmatic psychobiological approach borrowed methods from psychoanalysis, neurology, and behavioral science to determine what constituted the individual's overall *personality*, which Meyer defined as the integration of organic, psychological, and social functions of an individual.[68] He emphasized the holistic nature of the individual, placing considerable emphasis on the importance of the ego. The ego, Meyer believed, was structured through a process of development in which an individual's psychical development interacted with the drives and organs of the body through complex actions and reactions. The ego thus consisted of a blend of psychological and biological phenomena. The primary conflict for the individual was in negotiating tensions between this psychobiologically developed ego and aspects of the larger social environment.

In Meyer's view, among the dangers that threatened the healthy integration of the ego and the social adjustment of the individual was the menace of sexuality run amok, taking various forms including sexual perversion. As a response to what he perceived as the sexual libertinism of psychoanalysis, Meyer remarked that sexual continence should not be viewed as a cause of psychiatric problems, as Freud and others had suggested.[69] Although he spoke of it in generally dispassionate tones, Meyer believed "sexual maladjustment" was a troublesome outcome of modern pressures, related to both psychological and organic factors. Practically speaking, he believed the main problem concerning homosexuals was their inability to conform to social conventions. His goal was not so much to divine the specific causes of their disorder but to bring those who manifested it into greater harmony with their environment and to ameliorate the environmental conditions that gave rise to homosexuality. He believed that, through pragmatic therapy, some might be able to abandon their perverse ways by either practicing abstinence or by becoming adjusted and fulfilled heterosexuals.

Adolf Meyer's privileging of the conscious mind and the notions of amelioration and adjustment resonated with American cultural ideals of individualism, self-sufficiency, and social mobility, whereby distinct selves fashioned their lives in relative harmony with their surroundings, striving to achieve goals of health, prosperity, and happiness. In contrast to strict hereditarians and to psychoanalysts who believed adult sexuality could not easily be changed, Meyer considered individuals malleable and spontaneous in their actions and reactions, capable of overcoming hardships rather than doomed to misery because of genetic defects or childhood psychosexual traumas.[70] He valued the individual and applauded the fact that the only common trait of humanity was that each individual was different from all others. But, like many social reformers of his time, Meyer also valorized conformity for the sake of social harmony.[71]

Although Meyer privileged the power of conscious will to overcome adversity and to exercise moral fortitude, he also acknowledged that homosexuality was deeply rooted and should be treated as an affliction. In turn, he considered healthy heterosexuality a triumphant achievement rather than an inevitable outcome. Thus, rather than assuming psychosexual problems were only suffered by the patently insane, Meyer's ameliorative model of mental hygiene maintained that heterosexuals also faced psychological difficulties in adjusting to modern demands. This notion propelled the expansion of psychiatry into the mainstream of society and, in turn, contributed to the growing influence of psychiatrists in American life.

Although Meyer and many American psychiatrists writing in the first two decades of the twentieth century were critical of psychoanalysis, a few were convinced that homosexuality was psychogenic in origin and believed that psychoanalysis was a useful method for assisting patients in coming to terms with their homosexual orientation. In 1913, psychoanalyst Abraham Brill of Columbia University recommended what he called "adjustment" therapy. Brill, another European émigré, studied under Freud in Vienna and consulted with Hirschfeld, from whom he derived many of his ideas about homosexuality. He reported that after seeing forty-nine homosexual patients during the course of ten years, he was "convinced that a great injustice is done to a large class of human beings [homosexuals], most of whom are far from being the degenerates they are commonly believed to be." He acknowledged there might be some congenital inverts but stated that none of his patients fit that profile. Most were "perfectly contented with their lot," and did not want anyone to interfere with their personalities. He harshly denounced "bladder washing," "rectal massage," castration, and other quack remedies, arguing instead that psychotherapy was the only effective means for dealing with those who were in need of help to cope with their condition. In his view, curing patients did not consist of eliminating their homosexuality but of helping them to cope with or even get rid of mental problems (i.e. psychosis and impotence). And, like Freud, he warned that psychosexual problems were not uncommon among heterosexuals.[72]

Brill's relatively sympathetic perspective remained that of a minority in the United States during this period. By comparison to nineteenth-century attitudes toward homosexuals, Meyer too seemed sympathetic. But the mental hygienic view was basically that homosexuality should be overcome; and the virtue of adjustment therapy, as it was conceived by Meyer, was that it furthered the goal of ensuring mental health through social conformity. Brill, on the other hand, advocated a more generous approach, having been influenced by Hirschfeld's version of adjustment therapy. As Hirschfeld conceived this (or what he also referred to as "adaptation" therapy), the patient would be encouraged to accept his or her homosexuality as a natural and viable sexual orientation.[73] The doctor's role was to put the patient's mind at ease by explaining that homosexuality was an innate drive and not inherently a misfortune. In contrast to Meyer, Hirschfeld believed that psychological and social adjustment involved giving up the "depressing attempts at sexual relations with the opposite sex" and the whole "idea of marriage," since it only created further tragedy. Therapy should involve advice on jobs, families, marriages, and relationships that could help the patient. But, he stressed, coping with problems in any of these areas did not require eliminating the individual's homosexuality. He strongly believed that "regular, intensive work, whether manual or intellectual" was "the most important condition for the patient's well-being." This model of therapy was consonant with the naturalist paradigm Hirschfeld had developed from Karl Ulrichs's original ideas.

The naturalist paradigm was, for the most part, rejected by American physicians during this period. It was not until the late 1920s and 1930s that a few doctors were willing to suggest that homosexuality was a benign variation that should be tolerated, some having been influenced by the writings of Radclyffe Hall and Edward Carpenter.[74] The American degenerationists of the nineteenth century, while they believed that homosexuality was inborn, were not at all inclined to accept it as a natural and harmless variation. And the ameliorationists associated with the mental hygiene movement generally believed that homosexuality was the result of poor psychological development rather than an accident, auspicious or otherwise, of nature. In spite of physicians' refusal to entertain it, the naturalist paradigm offered consolation to lesbians and homosexual men in the United States who were able to read some of Hirschfeld's work and who were audience members during his American lecture tour in 1905.

Hirschfeld had made an earlier trip to the United States in 1893, during which he gathered information about homosexuality in several major cities, including New York, Boston, Philadelphia, Chicago, Denver, and San Francisco. He spoke informally with male prostitutes, sailors, and heterosexual transvestites and concluded that while "homosexual life in the United States is somewhat more hidden than in the United Kingdom," this was not to due to an absence of homosexuals but to the Puritan influences that kept them out of public view. Visitors from Philadelphia and Boston assured him that, although it was not apparent on first glance, there was "an awful lot going on within private circles in these centers of Quakerism and Puritanism." Hirschfeld found more obvious signs of homosexual subcultures on the streets of New York, Chicago, and San Francisco. The professor from Colorado with whom he corresponded informed Hirschfeld of the substantial number of homosexual men and women living in Denver and provided details about their preferred meeting places and social networks.[75] When Hirschfeld came to America again in 1905, he lectured on behalf of the German Scientific-Humanitarian Committee and drew audiences ranging from around twenty to over a hundred people in many of these same cities. Homosexual men and women, along with others who saw themselves as sexual anomalies of the sort Hirschfeld was studying in Germany, were in attendance as well as physicians, clergymen, and lawyers.

In 1906, Otto Spengler, one of the Scientific-Humanitarian Committee's directors, gave a lecture on sexual intermediates at the German Scientific Society in New York. Spengler wrote to Hirschfeld that "the debate was very lively" and that it had included ministers, doctors, and lawyers. He continued: "You can deduce the inflexibility of the people from this incident; after the topic had been illuminated from all sides, a lawyer stood up and maintained . . . that homosexuals belong in prison. This shows plainly what educational efforts are still required here, where such educated people are so stupid."[76] In 1907, another Committee member, Dr. Georg Merzbach, toured the United States and lectured on homosexuality before the New York Society of Medical Jurisprudence. Merzbach reported to Hirschfeld that his lecture "made a truly sensational impression upon a select audience which, considering the circumstances in this country, was extraordinarily large." He noted that the distinguished doctors, legal scholars, and clergymen who attended asked questions ranging from "naive" to "quite intelligent," including "Can homosexuality be eradicated by castration? Doesn't homosexuality lead ultimately to paranoia or other psychoses? Can homosexuals have children?" But Merzbach also stated that some "spoke out against the penalization of [consensual] homosexual acts." He concluded that "now we have had this singular success in the very country where bigotry and prudishness are truly at home."[77]

Because of their interest in reforming dominant attitudes about homosexuality, Spengler and Merzbach highlighted the professionals in their audiences. But it is also clear homosexual laypeople were in attendance and found the lectures extremely important. For example, following Merzbach's 1907 lecture tour, the Scientific-Humanitarian Committee received an anonymous letter from a "Uranian" in Boston who wrote:

> I'm always delighted to hear about even the smallest success you have in vanquishing deep-rooted prejudices. And here in the United States we really need this kind of activity. In the face of Anglo-American hypocrisy, however, there is no present chance that any man of science would have enough wisdom and courage to remove the veil which covers homosexuality in this country. And how many homosexuals I have come to know![78]

A number of American homosexuals incorporated ideas advanced by Hirschfeld in their published works.

In 1908, the pseudonymous Xavier Mayne (Edward I. Prime Stevenson), commended the idea of adjustment therapy which allowed homosexuals to accept their sexual orientation as natural and worthy of respect. Mayne criticized the prevailing scientific equation of the "intersexual" with moral viciousness, degeneracy, and criminality. "Can we 'cure' Nature?" he asked. "Can we make the leopard change his spots?" "The shame of a gross blunder," he observed, "falls to the psychiater [sic] who promises a 'cure' of what is not a disease." In Mayne's view, the psychiatrist should give sympathy, moral encouragement, and self-respect to the homosexuals who seek help. Homosexuals should be urged to make the most of themselves "before God and man," but this meant affirming their sexual orientation rather than repressing it. Mayne looked forward to a time when "coming generations will redeem a present-day and ignorant intolerance of [homosexual] impulses." The homosexual presaged a superior, more evolved and enlightened moment. In this respect, Mayne combined the embrace of progress voiced by ameliorationists and of natural evolutionary variation supported by Hirschfeld.[79]

Likewise, in 1918, Earl Lind (Ralph Werther, a.k.a. Jennie June), who described himself as an "androgyne" and lived an illustrious life as a male-to-female cross-dresser, argued that since homosexuality was a congenital condition, it was not contagious and posed no harm to others. On these grounds he advocated the abolition of laws prohibiting it and an end to the social condemnation of it.[80] Several years later, in 1924, a small group of homosexual men established the short-lived Society for Human Rights in Chicago, one of the first known groups of its sort in the United States. The society stated that its purpose was

> to promote and to protect the interests of people who by reasons of mental and physical abnormalities are abused and hindered in the legal pursuit of happiness which is guaranteed them by the Declaration of Independence, and to combat the public prejudices against them by dissemination of facts according to modern science among intellectuals of mature age. The Society stands only for law and order; it is in harmony with any and all general laws insofar as they protect the rights of others, and does in no manner recommend any acts in violation of present laws nor advocate any matter inimical to the public welfare.[81]

The group deployed a naturalist argument but, like many seemingly sympathetic physicians, used the word abnormalities to refer to homosexuality, thus underscoring a popular association between homosexuality and innate disorders.

The society received its primary support from what founding member Henry Gerber referred to as "poor people." Its national officers included Al Meininger, "an indigent laundry queen," Henry Gerber, a postal employee, Ralph, a railway worker, and John T. Graves, a street preacher "who earned his room and board by preaching brotherly love to small groups of Negroes."[82] Shortly after its establishment, these men were rounded up, their property was seized, and they were charged by the Chicago police with disorderly conduct and trafficking in obscene materials. Although the judge dismissed the charges on the grounds of a lack of evidence, Gerber and several other members lost their jobs and the society disbanded. As Gerber put it, "the parting jibe of the detective was 'What was the idea of the Society for Human Rights anyway? Was it to give you birds the legal right to rape every boy on the street?'" The Chicago policeman cared little about whether homosexuality was innate or psychogenically caused. He, like many other Americans at the time, believed that homosexuals were violent, unruly people.

THE PERSISTENCE OF RACIALIST THINKING ABOUT
HOMOSEXUALITY

It would be a mistake to assume that the assimilationist attitudes promoted by reformers led them to abandon racial and socioeconomic
class hierarchies, especially when it came to the subject of homosexuality. The kind of assimilationism implied in the dominant version
of adjustment therapy neither assumed that homosexuals should be
tolerated nor that those of a lower strata were readily redeemable. It
is true, however, that many of the professional purveyors of social reform were émigrés and women who had personal and political stakes
in promoting an assimilationist perspective in general. But the melting pot, as it was generally imagined, had its limits. Even after the
shift to ameliorative strategies that emphasized the environmental
causes of homosexuality, American psychiatrists and psychologists
presumed sex perversions emanated from degenerate milieux—a euphemistic term used to refer to the poor and disenfranchised. If their
bodies were no longer the cause of perversion, their families and social environs were viewed as far from hygienic.

Racial distinctions were commonly noted in writings by reform-
minded psychiatrists and psychologists well into the twentieth century. Homosexual relationships between black and white people were
often a source of seemingly benign curiosity to experts, but their interpretations and proposed interventions were not without significant
racist undertones. For example, in 1913, the psychologist Margaret
Otis, reporting on "A Perversion Not Commonly Noted," discussed
"love-making between the white and colored girls," where "the
difference in color, in this case, takes the place of difference in sex,
and ardent love-affairs arise between white and colored girls in
schools where both races are housed together."[83] In spite of racial segregation in one institution, Otis noted that "the separation seemed
to enhance the value of the loved one, and that she was to a degree
inaccessible, added to her charms." After explaining the phenomenon
that some disdainful white girls called "nigger-loving," Otis remarked
that intercepted notes sent between African American and white inmates showed "the expression of a passionate love of low order" and
"many coarse expressions are used and the animal instinct is seen to
be paramount." She described superstitious practices among the "colored" girls which were a crucial part of the "system" of wooing white
girls in school life but noted that white girls also initiated the affairs
in some cases.

Otis's tone suggested this perversion was an undesirable outcome of reform school life, even though, in some cases, "the love is very real and seems almost ennobling." A most disturbing aspect of this phenomenon from Otis's point of view was that the white girls "indulging in this love for the colored have, perhaps, the most highly developed intellectual ability of any girls of the school." Although she ruled out mental defectiveness as a cause of the white girl's activities, Otis suggested that contact with African American girls had degraded them and led them into the depths of deeper perversion. Similar concerns arose at the Albion Reformatory for Girls in New York, where officials were disturbed by relationships between black and white inmates. At Albion and many other reformatories and prisons, inmates were racially segregated in the interest of maintaining order but often with the implicit understanding that white women would otherwise be drawn into deeper trouble through contact and lesbian relationships with women of color.[84]

An article appearing in 1929 reported a similar pattern to the one Otis outlined, noting the intense passions exchanged by African American and white women inmates. Psychiatrist Charles A. Ford, a member of the Ohio Bureau of Juvenile Research, distinguished between "temporary or pseudo inversion," resulting from the sex-segregation in prisons, and "pathological" homosexuality of the sort Krafft-Ebing and Ellis reported earlier. Ford's account resembled an ethnographic report of a foreign tribe, as he carefully described the cross-racial courtship rituals and affectionate attachments among female inmates, noting that they were the result of "artificial conditions" common in girls' schools and convents. Sadly, he noted, official attempts to interrupt the surreptitious passing of love notes and the exchange of treasured tokens were practically ineffectual, as passionate attachments and jealousy escalated among female inmates.

Ford assessed these relationships as abnormal and suggested that such strange interracial intimacies, some of which involved "mutual masturbation" and "cunnilinctus," were the result of particular unhygienic conditions giving rise to ritualized practices, "friendships," and "husband-wife" relationships that were actually sublimations of heterosexuality which functioned to make prison life bearable. Interestingly, relationships forged across the racial barriers of residential segregation seemed to him more durable, and he suggested that racial difference had taken the place of sexual difference in the artificial environment of the girls' prison. The phenomenon disturbed him, but he recommended that prison officials ignore rather than punish those involved since they tended to be women who liked to break rules and would only gain satisfaction from being reprimanded. Instead, they should be given tiring but interesting tasks and other "socially acceptable sublimations" that could allay their tendencies toward perversion. Although less overtly judgmental than Otis or officials at the Albion Reformatory, Ford voiced a typically reformist interest in discouraging homosexuality, especially when it involved interracial couplings, believing that race-mixing thwarted the rehabilitation of white girls and women.[85]

From 1880 to 1920, homosexuality was appraised by American physicians as a troubling effect of modernity that posed a threat to the nation's welfare. Efforts on their part to address homosexuality as a psychological and social problem resulted in several key developments, unfolding across a sequence of social and political transformations. First, nineteenth-century American physicians gained public legitimacy by defining homosexuality as a form of madness, thus arrogating the subject to the domain of medicine. They differed, however, from their European counterparts in their more overt denunciation of homosexuality, choosing to argue for punishment and condemnation in most cases rather than pity or acceptance. By associating homosexuality with the lower classes, they stressed that it was separate from normal middle-class life and thus were able to underscore a larger segregationist perspective that regarded the blurring of classes, races, and sex roles as inimical to the nation. Such a perspective served their own professional interests and asserted their superior status in the context of changing social relations and cultural mores.

Secondly, by distinguishing themselves from superstitious and overtly moralistic condemnations of homosexuality, members of a second generation of commentators on homosexuality positioned themselves as purveyors of rational and enlightened discourse and thus augmented medical and scientific authority to produce broader cultural meanings about homosexuality in the context of progressive social amelioration that meshed with the larger interests of an assimilationist agenda. But by assuming that homosexuality was the product of unhygienic social milieux, progressive reformers echoed sentiments of their predecessors that inversion and perversion were concentrated in the lower strata of society. The presence of these maladies in the middle and upper classes, rather than being regarded as signs of cultural advancement or refined evolution as European naturalists had suggested, were taken as evidence of a kind of dangerous infection caused by contact with bad environments made worse by rising rates of bad breeding.

Finally, by claiming homosexuality was the result of modern conditions that could be remedied, American physicians in the 1910s began to bring the subject of homosexuality into public discourse, using it to define, by contradistinction, what it meant to be a healthy, well-adjusted citizen. Their ameliorationist model was useful for encouraging middle-class individuals to come to terms with living in the modern world where social distinctions were being redrawn and sexual pleasure in its own right was beginning to acquire a value it had not previously enjoyed. In a new world of dizzying pressures and possibilities, strategies for ensuring the mental hygiene of the population were not as explicitly tied to eugenical agendas as was the degenerationist model, but were aimed more broadly at engendering social conformity and discipline as a way to minimize unhealthy influences and to contain the bad milieux from which they emanated. Although shrouded in the language of "sexual maladjustment," homosexuality was identified in seemingly normal people more than it had ever been before.

Thus, over the course of these four decades, American medical commentators shifted from a strong adherence to degenerationist and segregationist thinking to a framework that emphasized the individual's ability to control his or her homosexual tendencies as a condition of assimilating into modern society. Although quite pronounced in the earlier years, distinctions along the axes of race, class, and gender were not dissolved by the shift to an ethos of social rehabilitation. To the contrary, they were used to define what would count as normal standards to which individuals should conform for the sake of social harmony and order. Likewise, while sex roles for men and women changed, clear-cut distinctions between the sexes continued to be a gauge of normalcy. As it appeared that homosexual subcultures were growing in cities and attracting middle-class men and women, the new recuperative model of sexual adjustment stressed psychogenic and sociogenic causes of homosexuality and advocated strategies to bring afflicted individuals into conformity with a modern version of hetcrosexual companionship.

In the same years that American physicians began to write about the dangers of inversion and sex perversion, culturally heterogenous sexual subcultures emerged and grew in American cities, comprised of dissidents from the prevailing two-sex system upon which compulsory matrimonial heterosexuality was based. Homosexual men and women of various races and classes, along with other sexual dissenters and bohemian iconoclasts, developed elaborate vernaculars of speech, style, and entertainment that allowed them to recognize one another while at the same time be shielded against direct crackdowns by vigilante groups and the police. Indeed, American doctors did not give birth to the homosexual, nor did their European counterparts. But together they produced a set of categories and a technical language for speaking about the invert and sex pervert as inferior types who dwelt in the shadowy margins of society. Doctors' assessments rhymed with middle-class sentiments denouncing forces that unleashed sexuality and disrupted the delineation of sexes, races, and classes. As doctors elaborated upon typological models, sexual subcultures in American cities, while far from being free of race and class hierarchies, brought people of diverse backgrounds together in search of others like themselves, making homosexuality a ground for staking cultural identities and an increasingly visible part of American urban culture.

Progressive ameliorationists, voicing some of the same sexual prudishness of their predecessors, were concerned about the emergence of homosexual subcultures and advocated cleansing cities of vice and disease. Sex perversion, along with prostitution, gambling, and alcoholism, was targeted as an unseemly phenomenon that made the city unlivable for decent people. In 1911, a report of the Chicago Vice Commission, created as part of the progressive reformers' agenda, referred to homosexuality as among the worst social ills afflicting the city.[86] Around the same time, the New York Society for the Suppression of Vice, headed by Anthony Comstock, capitalized on the mood of municipal reform initiated by progressives to step up its campaign to rid New York City of homosexual perversion. Although tensions ensued between Comstock and progressive reformers, who opposed his vigilante tactics, the police appreciated Comstock's support and it was not until around 1920 that philanthropic groups who funded some of his activities diverted their support to reformers who worked closely with municipal officials to carry out prevention and intervention efforts in accordance with the law. The move to a more "rational" approach to dealing with vice and perversion involved the building of formal alliances between physicians, scientists, and governing officials. In some important ways, these new networks of expertise loosened the constraints on discourse about sexuality at a time when public interest in the private affairs of individuals was escalating and expanding.

By 1920, hygienic heterosexuality was no longer regarded as an inevitable outcome of "natural" development. Instead, it came to be regarded as a triumph over the psychosexual and "cacogenic" pressures wrought by modern life. A growing scientific interest in childhood development, stimulated by Freud's theories of infantile sexuality and psychosexual maturation, led to strategies aimed at ensuring children's proper development. The family thus became a site of social engineering as a generation of newly trained behavioral scientists advised men and women to pick suitable mates and instructed parents to provide appropriate role models and to intervene in cases of children who seemed to be straying from the normal course of development toward heterosexuality.

Even as doctors during this period generally maintained that homosexuality was a topic unsuitable for public audiences, increasing references to homosexuality, although often coded in double-entre and surreptitiously couched in popular entertainment, filled the public sphere. That homosexuality seemed to be gaining popularity enough to attract increasing numbers of men and women across a broad strata of urban society continued to intrigue modern-minded reformers. In the 1920s, the subject was approached in a slightly new way, thanks in part to the introduction of psychogenic theories and to the apparent prevalence of homosexuality among seemingly "normal" people. During that decade, for the first time in the United States, homosexuality was approached by a few key researchers as a telling variation of "normal" sexuality. As we shall see, homosexuality functioned as a diagnostic indicator of how sexuality in general was changing, away from a model of strict restraint toward a model that valorized fulfillment and pleasure.

PROGRESSIVE SCIENCE IN SEARCH OF SEXUAL NORMALITY

Beginning in the 1920s, scientific sex reformers were especially interested in matters concerning the health and well-being of the modern heterosexual procreative family. What is significant about research from this period is that, through the scientific exploration of nonreproductive sexual desires and practices, a modern idealized reproductive family was constructed, often, but not always, in contradistinction to two undesirable phenomena. Reformers deemed it favorable, on the one hand, to the excessive repression associated with Victorianism and, on the other, to sexual perversity associated with the ills of modernity. This new form of the family was to accommodate hygienic reproduction without sacrificing the sexual pleasure of either husband or wife. Thus experts turned their attention to the study of what was considered normal behavior. In so doing, sexuality came to encompass a broader range of activities consisting of increasingly specified elements, linked in crucial ways to normative definitions of masculinity and femininity, and delineated along axes of class and race.

Reformers used a mixture of quantitative surveys and clinical case histories to advocate, in pragmatic terms, the adjustment of normal, healthy individuals to a changing environment. These methods emerged during a time when larger cultural transformations in modern American life brought sexuality and sexual behavior to the fore as a crucial part of being. Sex was not only an instinct leading to reproduction. It was recast as a domain of pleasure and, indeed, as an essential part of being where the secrets of the self lie waiting to manifest themselves in love or, in the disturbed individual, in acts of perversion. Sex came to mean more than a bond between lovers; thanks to Freud, it was imagined to be the very basis upon which individuals and cultures were built. In this context, the domain of sexual behavior became a site of scientific scrutiny and of intervention in campaigns to ensure the nation's integrity through the promotion of social and mental hygiene.

As a modern ethic of sexual reciprocity and companionship between partners emerged, scientific sex researchers of the 1920s turned their attention to the question of what exactly constituted "normal" sexual behavior. Their assumption that sexual pleasure was a crucial aspect of happiness and health for both men and women led them to explore aspects of sexuality that signified enlightened pleasure rather than mere matrimonial duty or procreative obligation. Sexual behavior not geared specifically toward reproduction, including homosexuality, provided, on the one hand, a way of measuring the importance of sexual pleasure in its own right, and on the other, of prescribing new norms of behavior that encouraged sexual pleasure in the form of the companionate heterosexual marriage.

Empirically derived evidence suggesting that lesbianism and male homosexuality were practiced by seemingly normal people contributed to a growing concern that heterosexuality itself was endangered. In this context experts concerned with reform in the areas of social and mental hygiene debated, though often indirectly, whether or not homosexuality posed a particular danger to the larger social order. By tracing the processes by which "normal" sexuality emerged as an object of scientific investigation, this chapter explores how the delineation of homosexual variation assisted in the establishment of new norms that were aligned to changing relations between men and women, especially in the middle class.

MARITAL HYGIENE

In the 1920s, the problem of "marital hygiene" came to the fore. This new scientistic rubric denoted the conditions by which couples could achieve happiness in marriage. Sex surveys from this period were concerned first and foremost with the nature and significance of sexual and emotional compatibility between partners, and, significantly, the most prominent surveys focused on the dispositions, complaints, and attitudes mainly of women, both single and married.[1] To be sure, heterosexuality was presumed to be the norm, but, because the researchers who undertook these surveys valued sexual satisfaction, they were less inclined to demonize masturbation, homosexuality, or other forms of sexual behavior that appeared to pose no inherent harm in their view when practiced in moderation. Their ideas represented a much more progressive and tolerant view of extramarital sexuality when compared to much of the popular commentary on marriage during the 1920s.

Katharine Bement Davis, Robert Latou Dickinson, and Gilbert V.

Hamilton—three noteworthy scientific sex reformers analyzed in this chapter—promoted sexual pleasure as a cornerstone for the modern marriage that could be enjoyed by husbands and wives alike. In addition, they argued for rational sex education and women's sexual rights, including access to safe and legal contraception. One of the main avenues to ensure sexual enlightenment, they believed, was to offer a scientific view of sexual behavior as it was commonly practiced. Carefully gathered data would not only reveal the problems that resulted from a lack of adequate knowledge of sex and birth control but would also make clear that repressing sexuality caused much more harm than good. Thus they used scientific methods to call into question the older Victorian model that posited men as sexually driven and women as passionless. They believed that such archaic notions contributed to sexual dissatisfaction and marital unhappiness. Inclined toward what they saw as the need for a "modernization" of sex roles, the researchers used science to argue for social reform that would liberate both women and men. And, with this perspective, they regarded homosexuality—especially when practiced by women—with much greater tolerance than did most American physicians and anti-vice moralists.

Importantly, both Davis and Dickinson saw single women, including lesbians, as key sources of information for determining what made women happy. Lesbianism was seen in this context as a symptom of a larger problem with heterosexuality, although, especially for Davis, it was not assumed to be pathological. This approach to thinking about lesbianism was different from that of other commentators during the same decade. To understand what made scientific sex reformers such as Davis, Dickinson, and Hamilton important, their ideas should be appreciated in the context of the overtly hostile commentary about lesbianism that was also generated out of concern for the future of modern marriage.

IDEALS OF MODERN MARRIAGE AND THE BACKLASH AGAINST LESBIANISM

During the 1920s, a number of progressively minded people wrote popular books that stressed that modern life required a new form of marriage—and that offered advice on how to achieve it. Their books were targeted at a popular audience primarily of middle-class women and men, as well as lawyers and physicians who encountered patients with marital problems. They enjoyed a wide readership.

The authors of such books suggested that modern marriage should be based upon elective affinities between two partners whose personalities and strengths complemented one another. Cast in contradistinction to marriages of the Victorian period, the modern marriage was to consist of a man and a woman who were companions rather than strangers. In 1927, the term *companionate marriage* was coined in a work by the same name. Its authors, Wainwright Evans and Ben Lindsey, a Denver family court judge, advocated reforms in marriage law that could accommodate their modern model of marriage, including legalized birth control and the right to divorce by mutual consent for childless couples.[2] Their book enjoyed an enthusiastic reception. It was serialized in *Redbook* magazine.

Lindsey and Evans invoked scientific rationality to argue that companionate marriage was the appropriate form of intimacy for the modern day that would ensure the birth of healthy offspring. They described men and women as very different types of people, but as people whose complementarity was essential and good. The authors were careful to note that marriage and childbearing were cornerstones of the health of society, with the potential to rid society of the ills of promiscuity, demoralization, and vice. They argued that birth control and divorce should be made available to the "poor and socially unfit, who need it most," and they looked forward to a time when American society "would breed its geniuses intensively."[3] As Lisa Duggan has noted, "legalization of companionate marriage involved not only 'freedom' and liberalization of repressive sexual mores but an enforcement of a new pattern of gender hierarchy based on love, heterosexual marriage, and reproduction (for the eugenically 'fit')."[4] Lindsey and Evans's promotion of modern heterosexuality included an unfavorable depiction of lesbianism. Indeed, they quoted at length a "respected churchman" who, as others had done, drew a connection between feminism and lesbianism by noting that both were threats to the future well-being of women and to the institutions of marriage and the family:

> I know women who have never married, and who ought to—who need marriage badly. They have the notion that they have sublimated all the sex they've got in feminist careers. . . . They miss the companionship, the human elements, of marriage; and they lose heavily by that. . . . I've concluded that many of these people who think that they have

sublimated their sex impulses into something they call 'higher' have really translated them into perversions and disorders and a general inability to love, think, and feel right. The psychoanalysts call that 'introversion,' I believe.[5]

Lindsey and Evans relied on the quotation to reiterate that women's dissent from marriage was deleterious and to warn that the rise of lesbianism was a pathological symptom to be treated.

A Dutch physician, Th. H. Van de Velde, advocated similar ideas in his widely read *Ideal Marriage: Its Physiology and Technique* (1926), which argued for marriage between companions as the natural and optimal form of matrimony. "Sex," Van de Velde asserted, was "the foundation of marriage"; knowledge about it would ensure the happiness of a marriage. In his view, several factors underpinned a happy marriage. These were the right choice of partner, the physical fitness of the partners, and a vigorous and harmonious sex life. Addressing an audience of medical professionals and married men in his book, Van de Velde urged that marriage be saved from forces which sought to degrade and eliminate it, including high rates of divorce, increasing incompatibility between men and women, and "the many voices [who] have clamored for its destruction." Though Van de Velde did not specify to whom these voices belonged, it is likely that he was referring to socialist critics of marriage with whom he was otherwise was sympathetic.[6]

In a sequel entitled *Sexual Tensions in Marriage* (1928), Van de Velde summarized psychological theories to show that hostility between the partners was endemic to marriage, but he argued that this hostility could be controlled and happiness achieved.[7] The book included a chapter about the essential differences between men and women, in which Van de Velde argued that women who resisted marriage were disturbed. He also appraised feminism as having a "more or less unfavorable influence on the foundations of marriage, and on the mental disposition in many marriages."[8] He noted that, among the "fanatical men-women" who were drawn to feminism and to resist marriage on political principle, there were some who did so due to "a homosexual disposition, or disturbance of the inner secretion." But as for the other fanatical men-women, he asked "Is there really one . . . who . . . if honest, will not admit that she would like to be feminine and exclusively feminine (or at one time wished to be) and would have been only too glad to have seen a 'real' man in her life?"[9] Van de Velde's comment suggests that, while he believed that innately inverted females were fixed as such, he also believed that many women were disguising their natural femininity and desire for "real" men by consorting with one another in the service of feminism. Van de Velde, who acknowledged that feminism had "arisen for the most obvious and justifiable reasons," ultimately belittled it, along with women's intimacies with one another, as pathological symptoms. He believed that, in many cases, these symptoms could be eliminated through a modern, scientifically informed approach to sexual relations—one that took into account the fundamentally different physiologies and dispositions of men and women. These notions echoed what Lindsey and Evans had proposed in their book: enforcing heterosexual marriage and proper gender roles were antidotes to deleterious modern developments, including the rise of lesbianism among women who were not inherently defective.

Floyd Dell, a socialist writer, also promoted companionate marriage. He condemned antiquated patriarchal conventions but at the same time denigrated male homosexuality and lesbianism. The latter was the result of "ideological overcompensations" by feminists in their development of theories of female independence and by free lovers in their embrace of sex as amusement. Dell advocated monogamous marriage and families and decried the ills of promiscuity, frigidity, and homosexuality that made people lead "tormented and frustrated lives." Marriage was to be sexually fulfilling but at the ultimate cost of sacrificing female autonomy.[10]

Importantly, books by politically progressive male authors extolling the virtues of companionate marriage were written in the wake of the ratification of the nineteenth amendment granting women the right to vote in 1920. They appropriated aspects of feminist and leftist critiques of traditional marriage, but they reinforced notions of male superiority and female subordination even as they invoked the rhetoric of equality between the sexes.[11] Most significantly, they drew a distinction between the normal modern woman and women whose proclivities toward self-indulgence manifested themselves in a resistance to wifely and maternal duties and to men in general. In spite of an increase in marriage rates and a drop in the age at marriage during the 1920s, unmarried women, childless women, and lesbians became the targets of intensified ideological attacks on women's independence from men who accused them of straying from what were seen to be appropriate feminine duties.[12]

The normal modern woman was confident and pleasure-seeking rather than modest and prudish, but she was to be feminine and decidedly oriented toward men for companionship, love, and sexual fulfillment. She enjoyed heterosexual courtship and married out of preference, not duty.

This image fit well with the companionate marriage model. Heterosexuality in this model was pleasurable and natural, as contrasted to the deviance and pathology represented by spinsterhood, lesbianism, and frigidity. In much of the commentary on modern marriage, the ideal woman was described in contradistinction both to her sexually repressed nineteenth-century counterpart and to the mannish lesbian. But it should be noted that, during the 1920s, the proponents of companionate marriage had a generally positive outlook on modern life and that they valued the modern trend toward overcoming sexually repressive attitudes. By contrast, more conservative types continued, as they had earlier, to regard modern life as full of danger, especially because it seemed to them to be destroying the natural order of the sexes and to be unleashing perverse sexualities. Modern trends did so, they believed, by tempting men and women to flout social conventions, to engage in sexual relations outside of marriage, and to mingle with disreputable characters in hedonistic pursuits. Conservatives saw all of these factors as contributing to the rising incidence of homosexuality. Indeed, in their view, the specter of the mannish lesbian loomed as a hazard whose pathology manifested itself in the desire to usurp the position of men, turning natural and social order upside down. Sensationalistic tales of her seducing young and hapless women made their way into popular journalism as well as some of the medical writing of the time.[13]

In the context of this pejorative commentary, the work of scientific sex reformers stands out as far more tolerant toward lesbianism. This may be in part because the key experts in the field were either single women or progressively minded men who employed women assistants to help them in conducting their research. The crucial influence of Katharine Bement Davis in defining the field of sex research opened up the possibility of countering or, at the very least, questioning the overtly antifeminist commentary of other authors.

KATHARINE BEMENT DAVIS AND THE SEX LIVES OF NORMAL WOMEN

The first substantial American research on normal sexual experiences was undertaken in 1920 by Katharine Bement Davis, who conducted a study of "factors in the sex lives of twenty-two hundred women," published eponymously in 1929.[14] Davis's study occurred in the wake of several key historical developments affecting women. In the two decades leading up to 1920, many women entered the paid work force. A significant number of middle-class women acquired college educations as a result of the opening of women's colleges and the expansion of universities to include more female students. During the 1920s, across various socioeconomic strata, birth rates continued to go down, as they had been for a century,[15] and, while the median age of marriage dropped (to 26 for men, 24 for women),[16] divorce rates went up. Premarital sexual activity increased, and women who first became sexually active in the 1920s reported engaging in sexual "petting" and sexual intercourse at earlier ages and at greater rates than had their mothers' generation.[17] These demographic realities, together with the public visibility of broad-based support for women's rights, made the matters of women's sexuality and of what made women happy a public concern, inspiring anxiety among some and optimism among others.

In 1913, a record number of 30,000 marched for women's suffrage in New York City, and for the next seven years feminist agitation was strong. Middle-class women's sexual satisfaction came to the fore as a matter of public interest in the context of feminist activism that called into question the institution of marriage itself. As "free lovers" and feminists argued that marriage was a vestige of barbaric patriarchy that confined women to a subordinate role, conservatives sought to reinforce the family as the principal site of instilling morality upon which, they believed, the fate of the nation was based.

Across a broad political spectrum, the modern woman was a puzzle to solve. What were her desires and ambitions? And how might they reflect the changes wrought by modern life? A handful of progressive reformers, including a substantial number of college-educated women, seized the moment to explore an aspect of women's lives that had been veiled behind the cloak of civilized sexual morality: zeroing in on middle-class women's sexuality, they sought to shed the light of scientific inquiry on women's happiness as one approach to understanding how intimate relations could be achieved successfully. This was the context out of which Davis's study of normal female sexuality grew.

Davis had a distinguished but unusual career. Born in 1860 to a New England family, she was part of the wave of middle-class women who attended college as higher education expanded for women following the Civil War. After graduating from Vassar in 1892, she supported herself by teaching chemistry part-time at a seminary in Brooklyn Heights and at Columbia University, and in the following year she was appointed director of the New York state exhibit for the Chicago World's Fair, where she helped design a model workingman's home that was to be healthy and economical. On the basis of the exhibit's success she was offered a social work position in Philadelphia, where she designed urban housing and oversaw the renovation of tenements.

Impressed by her 1893 visit to the newly opened University of Chicago, Davis returned there to be among the first women to study political economy and sociology. Her advisor, Thorstein Veblen, encouraged her to focus on empirical research and, like other graduate students in the department, to investigate social problems using empirical methods. She received her Ph.D. in 1900 at the age of forty, after successfully completing a dissertation that was a comparative analysis of "causes affecting the standard of living and wages" among Bohemian agricultural workers who remained in Europe and among those who came to the United States. Upon graduation, Davis's career took a sharp turn when she was offered a job as superintendent of the new Reformatory for Women at Bedford, New York, which began her life as an influential penologist.[18]

Davis was among a generation of prison reformers who sought effective forms of rehabilitation for women inmates. She believed that many women got into trouble because of a lack of opportunities, and that inmates would benefit from learning practical knowledge and life skills as well as trades that would allow them to be self-sufficient. In her efforts at rehabilitation, Davis set up a program to identify different types of offenders, whereby hardened inmates could be separated from those she believed could be reformed. A pamphlet she wrote on the subject was noticed in 1911 by John D. Rockefeller, Jr., whose interest in social reform and fighting corruption had led him in 1910 to chair a grand jury charged with investigating white slavery in New York City.

In 1911, after the mayor refused to follow the recommendation of the grand jury to set up a commission to study laws relating to prostitution, Rockefeller decided to do so himself by establishing the Bureau of Social Hygiene. Katharine Bement Davis, along with Rockefeller's friends Paul Warbur and Starr Murphy, was chosen for the advisory board. Impressed by Davis's work at Bedford Hills, Rockefeller acquired land next to the reformatory and established the Laboratory of Social Hygiene in 1912, which Davis directed. Many of the incarcerated women in Bedford Hills were serving time for prostitution, so Davis believed they would be an ideal population to study in order to understand what drew women into committing such crimes.[19]

As a result of her successful accomplishments at Bedford Hills, in 1914 Mayor John P. Mitchell appointed Davis Commissioner of Corrections for New York City, making her the first woman in the city's history to occupy a cabinet position. She carried her innovative ideas about reform and rehabilitation into the job, causing controversy among some who believed that running prisons was a man's job. Her proposals for probation, indeterminate sentences, and parole were partially successful, and in 1915 she was appointed to chair a newly created Parole Commission. During her tenure she quelled a prison riot on Riker's Island and survived a state investigation of the city's prison system. When Mitchell was ousted from office in 1917, Davis lost her job and became the general secretary of the Bureau of Social Hygiene, which dedicated itself to the "study, prevention, and amelioration of those social conditions, crimes and diseases which, adversely, affect the well being of society."

The Bureau focused its main efforts on promoting responsible and scientifically sound sex education, preventing venereal disease, stemming prostitution, and, under Davis's direction, surveying sexuality through empirical methods. Davis initiated her research on women's sexual experiences in 1920 with funds from the Bureau, whose earlier studies were focused on prostitution.[20] The idea, promoted first by Max Exner of the American Social Hygiene Association, who believed Davis was ideally suited to carry it out, was simply to learn more about the sex lives of normal women as a way of understanding sexuality more generally.[21] The subject of women's satisfaction, sexual or otherwise, was at the center of public discourse in 1920, the same year that the century-long struggle for women's suffrage culminated in Congress's ratifying the nineteenth amendment.

Davis, at the age of sixty, agreed to coordinate the research under an initial plan to survey five thousand women in an effort she later described as "put[ting] sex on the scientific map."[22] In the spirit of deploying science to assist in understanding social behavior, Davis introduced the study as growing out of "the need for more adequate data as to both the physical and the mental facts of the sex life of the normal individual . . . generally recognized by psychologists, psychiatrists, and students among medical men, as well as those whose interests lie in the practical fields of social hygiene."[23] An advocate of research and public education about sex, Davis wanted "to bring about more satisfactory adjustments of the sexual relationship," and she lamented the fact that "except on the pathological side, sex is scientifically an unexplored country."[24] Her interest, then, was in studying the "normal" woman, whom she defined (acknowledging the difficulty of the term) as a woman who was "capable of adjusting satisfactorily to her social group."[25] Thus Davis and her female colleagues who helped conduct the research distinguished both their techniques and their findings from clinical psychiatric histories of sexuality; their study merely reported data on sexual experiences without offering judgments or interpretations of the findings. They simply reiterated that the study was intended to generate data upon which educational programs could be based.

The team of female researchers, most of whom were either M.D.s or Ph.D.s in psychology, first decided to study married women. Drawing subjects from published membership lists of women's clubs and alumnae registers around the United States, the researchers received initial responses from one-third of the ten thousand married women they contacted. An eight-page mailed questionnaire covering the subject's general background from childhood and adolescence through marriage was completed by 1,073 respondents, from which researchers drew the first one thousand. In a second phase of the study, the questionnaire was refined and expanded to twelve pages and sent to unmarried women, drawn from college alumnae records, who had been out of college for at least five years. The response among single women was somewhat greater than the married women—out of 10,000 contacts, 1,200 were selected as subjects. But the general enthusiasm for the survey was apparent among respondents; on the whole, they took great care in answering the questionnaire thoroughly. In some cases, respondents used additional pages to write fuller responses.

The survey was designed to guarantee the anonymity of the subjects, and responses were numbered consecutively as they were received. To the criticism that only those who were abnormal would answer such a questionnaire on sex practices, Davis replied frankly that her subjects were "sane and sensible" women whose only interest was in contributing to a field where great study was needed. The subject population was homogenous, consisting entirely of middle-class (i.e., educated) white women, and this, Davis cautioned, meant that other groups must be studied before any general application of the results is tried.[26]

The topics covered in Davis's research set a standard for future sex surveys of the century. They were organized into chapters beginning with responses to questions on birth control, general and sex factors related to happiness, "auto-erotic" practices, periodicity of sexual desire, and homosexuality. For Davis and researcher Marie Kopp, who composed the chapters on lesbianism in the published study, affectionate and sexual relations between women were significant and substantial. In contrast to existing clinical cases on homosexuality, the authors give no indication that there was anything particularly pathological about these experiences, nor did they ask any questions about physiological or anatomical factors that might be correlated to lesbianism.

An interesting choice by Davis and her team was to include in their survey of homosexuality a category of experiences involving "intense emotional relations with other women," which did not include "overt" sexual relations. They placed this alongside categories for "homosexual feeling without overt practices" and "homosexual feeling with overt practices." By using these distinctions without implying any moral judgments, and by incorporating all of them in relation to the general subject of homosexuality, the researchers indicated that they conceptualized lesbianism to be on a continuum of variations in women's intimate relations with one another. This stood in stark contrast to the psychiatric tradition that tended to delineate more sharply between normal women and constitutionally distinct lesbians, the latter being pathological on the grounds of their desire for other women and their mannishness. No such intimations of pathology, inversion, or constitutional difference were made in the Davis study. Indeed, in broaching the subject of homosexuality as broadly as they did, the researchers assumed that most women had close female friendships and relationships that shaped factors in their sex lives generally. This assumption is perhaps illuminated by the fact that several of the researchers, including Davis herself, were unmarried women with strong and lasting ties to other women. Like the majority of their research subjects, they gave no indication that they were suffering from any unhappiness as a result.[27]

Davis believed that lesbianism was more widespread than Krafft-Ebing, Havelock Ellis, or Freud suspected. Indeed, her study found that over one-half of the unmarried women experienced intense emotional relations at some time or other with women, and over one-quarter reported that the relationship was "carried to the point of overt homosexual expression." Among those single women classified as having overt homosexual experiences (317 of the 1,200), about one-third engaged in sex play with other girls in pre-adolescence. This distinguished them slightly from women classified as IER ("intense emotional relations with other women" without overt experience, other than kissing and hugging). Women with a history of IER tended to have attachments that intensified during college but that tapered off afterwards.

Davis pointed out that this evidence indicated the inaccuracy of pathologizing stereotypes of women's emotional involvements with one another. Of those who had overt homosexual relations, most reported experiences with only one woman (63.1 percent), while smaller numbers had them with two women (17.9 percent) or with "several" women (13.8 percent), thus dispelling the prejudice that lesbianism and promiscuity were related. Some in the overt group believed these relationships prevented them from marrying, but an overwhelming majority voiced no regrets about this. The evidence shed light on how developments in childhood may shape later experiences and revealed that the college "crush" was common and did not seem to interfere with future happiness.

Davis noted a few additional factors. It appeared that a majority of women with strong attachments to other women, whether emotional or overtly sexual, went into social work careers. Those who went to women's colleges tended to have a slightly higher percentage of attachments, sexual or emotional, to other women, compared to graduates of co-ed colleges. And rates of happiness and life success were the same among women who had homosexual relations and those who formed intense emotional relations without engaging in overt practices, thus dispelling the idea that lesbian sex led to misery.[28] Finally, masturbation was found to be more common in the group that indulged in overt practices. Davis's general perspective on the topics of masturbation and homosexuality was that both were more commonly practiced among "normal" women than most commentators acknowledged, and that the dangers of both had been exaggerated. This position, in addition to removing much of the stigma associated with both acts, implicitly validated the notion of women's sexual satisfaction independent of men.[29]

The picture of homosexuality among married women was slightly different, but the percentages were still substantial. Among the 1,000 married women Davis studied, nearly one-third (306 women) had intense emotional relations with other women before marrying, of which a little less than half (140) had homosexual relations with overt sexual practices (including "mutual masturbation, contact of genital organs, or other physical expressions generally recognized as sexual in character").[30] As the findings from the unmarried women indicated, married women with histories of homosexual relationships indulged in masturbation in significantly higher numbers. Again, a college education seemed to make a difference: of the married women admitting to emotional attachments to women, with or without overt sexual relations, a higher percentage were college graduates. The percentage was even higher among those admitting to overt homosexual relations before marriage.[31]

Echoing the data on unmarried women, overt homosexual relations between women had no effect on their general health. Nor did a history of any of the forms of intense emotional relations between women, sexual or not, have an effect upon the happiness of women in subsequent marriages to men. Some significant differences between unmarried and married women with regard to homosexuality were noted: of those women reporting some kind of homosexual attachment, many more of the single women engaged in homosexual play as children (27.5 percent of singles v. 16.5 percent of marrieds), and many more married women reported dropping homosexual play after adolescence (65.5 percent compared to 48.2 percent of the singles). The data suggested a stronger commitment to homosexuality for those who experienced it from a young age, although Davis commented minimally on this point to say that this information could help in the development of sex education for younger children, but again she gave no indication that homosexuality was undesirable.

Although few in number, some married women reported homosexual relations *during* marriage, a fact that raised some interesting considerations as to the flexibility of modern marriage. One half of these eighteen women said it had no effect on their marriage, positive or negative. Among the other nine, one said it was carried on with the "advice and consent" of her husband while another reported that it almost wrecked her marriage. Only four out of the whole group reported homosexual attachments to have a negative effect on the marriage, while the remaining fourteen did not, suggesting either that husbands were not threatened or that they were plainly unaware of these affairs between women. Several features were noticeable among this group of eighteen wives, namely comparatively *higher* percentages of childlessness (one-third had no children), gainful employment after marriage, worse health before and after marriage, greater recall of sexual experiences from childhood and of homosexual experiences before marriage, and higher rates of sexual intercourse after marriage. They had a markedly *lower* percentage of good health before marriage, change for the better after marriage, sex instruction in childhood from a responsible source, and happiness in marriage. In the author's words, "Here, then, are 18 women, of decidedly erotic tendencies, more than a third of them childless, physically less fit than the average of the entire group, who experienced intense emotional relations with other women after marriage. . . . Those married women who go out into the world to work, like those who go to college, are more apt to form such attachments."[32] Davis hinted that these women's unhappiness might result from a conflict between their homosexual desires and their decision to conform to heterosexual marriage.

Among the Davis study's most important conclusions, cited by subsequent sex researchers for whom Davis's work provided a template, was that homoerotic and autoerotic experiences were common in the lives of a high percentage of normal women. Contrary to superstitions and traditions that claimed otherwise, these women were able to make adequate and satisfactory adjustments to life, most achieved some distinction in their professional fields, and an outstanding percentage of the married women were happily married. Those among the single and married women classified as highly erotic seemed to be most happy and socially adjusted; they were also those who received sex education from "responsible sources" (well-adjusted mothers and school teachers), which supported Davis's original interest in promoting sex education in society. Thus, Davis concluded that sexual satisfaction depended on knowledge rather than ignorance and prudery and that it was an important factor in the well-being of normal women.[33]

The publisher of *Factors* introduced the book slowly and conservatively "in order to avoid undesirable publicity," heeding the author's and the Bureau of Social Hygiene's requests to market the book in a fashion that would underscore its scientific character and prevent it from being marred by any association with pornography. Even so, the first print run of two thousand copies was nearly exhausted within one year of its publication, and an additional thousand copies were printed. Davis and her research team went to great effort to establish the book's reputation as a legitimate scientific text by limiting its distribution to academics, social workers, and physicians.[34] Although its publisher, Harper and Brothers, received many requests to have the book translated into foreign languages, they declined, after consulting with the BSH. The worry was that self-elected translators were not sufficiently scientifically motivated and might take liberties with the book's content.[35] Davis also worried that conservative moral crusaders would accuse her and the BSH of fomenting salacious desires among the American public. Others, including Havelock Ellis, had been accused of as much. The decision to forgo mass distribution was probably wise. In the same year *Factors* was published, a New York City magistrate ruled Radclyffe Hall's *Well of Loneliness* obscene on the grounds that it exposed the public to untoward ideas about lesbianism.[36]

Davis's study, completed around her seventieth birthday, established a standard that influenced many subsequent sex surveys. Her choice of topics became staples of other studies, especially birth control, masturbation, homosexuality, degrees of happiness in relationships, and the opinions and attitudes of subjects. Thus Davis succeeded in broadening the field of what would count as "factors in the sex lives of normal women." Her research on homosexuality, in the context of broader social and sexual factors, though not often acknowledged among psychiatrists and other physicians writing on homosexuality, influenced the perceptions of many social scientists working in the area of social reform. It introduced the notion, without moral judgment, that homosexuality between women, like masturbation, signified the importance of emotional intimacy and sexual pleasure in women's lives.

THE COMMITTEE ON RESEARCH IN PROBLEMS OF SEX

Davis's study grew out of efforts to promote scientific sex research undertaken in 1920 by a small group of reformers associated with social hygiene organizations. In that year, Earl T. Zinn, a psychology graduate student at Clark University hired by the American Social Hygiene Association, proposed a series of research projects that were reviewed by ASHA educational director Max Exner and Katharine Davis. Davis and her colleagues at the Bureau of Social Hygiene were persuaded of the value of large-scale research on sex, but they believed it would be wise to have an independent and scientifically legitimate organization undertake such a project rather than have the policy-oriented Bureau be its sponsor. Hence, the Bureau and its benefactor, John D. Rockefeller, Jr., approached the National Research Council (NRC) to set up a special committee focused on sex research.[37]

The National Research Council was originally established in 1916 by the National Academy of Science as a preparedness move to coordinate research funding during World War I. It was financed by the Engineering Foundation, a private philanthropy established by engineer-reformers to promote scientific research for industry.[38] Rockefeller had supported many NRC projects, and in 1921 the NRC accepted the Bureau's request to sponsor a conference, coordinated by Zinn, to consider the systematic study of all aspects of human sexuality in its biological, social, and psychological dimensions. Among the special topics covered would be masturbation, intercourse, prostitution, venereal disease, marital happiness, family planning, sex education, and "aberrations."[39] The conference was officially associated with the NRC but funded by Rockefeller money through the Bureau of Social Hygiene. The Bureau was lucky to have the support of comparative psychologist Robert Yerkes, a paid officer of the NRC, who sought sponsorship for the proposal from the newly created Division of Anthropology and Psychology. The Division declined on the grounds that sex-related projects were beyond its purview. Yerkes then turned to the Division of Medical Sciences, where he also encountered resistance to research on sex; he was nonetheless able to persuade a new chair to support the proposal in late 1921.

At its first conference in 1921, the twelve participants established the Committee on Research in Problems of Sex (CRPS) to be part of the NRC's Division of Medical Sciences. The CRPS' original committee members were Robert Yerkes, Katharine Bement Davis, William F. Ogburn, physiologist Walter B. Cannon, biologist E. G. Conklin, endocrinologist Frank R. Lillie, psychiatrist and mental hygiene advocate Thomas W. Salmon, and anthropologist Clark Wissler. Earl Zinn was its director. From its inception in 1921 until 1933, all of the funding for CRPS, totaling $670,000, came from Rockefeller money through the Bureau of Social Hygiene. The CRPS's mission was to promote scientific research on sex in the areas of physiology, psychology, anthropology, and sociology. It argued that systematic research was sorely needed and had been unfortunately impeded due to the shame and taboos surrounding sex.[40] Among its initially proposed topics were sex and internal secretions (hormonal studies), sex habits of primitive peoples, variations in sexual satisfaction, differential birth rates among various peoples, and the physiological and psychological effects of masturbation. No explicit mention was made of homosexuality, a topic that had aroused public anxiety as a result of highly publicized anti-vice campaigns in several major U.S. cities.

The topic was scrupulously avoided in original documents stating the Committee's goals. Indeed, in spite of its proposed focus to include research on social and psychological factors of human sexual behavior, the CRPS, especially during its first years of existence, restricted its funding to biological and physiological studies with a special emphasis on nonhuman populations. This was partly a strategic decision to acquire scientific legitimacy, based upon the assumption that laboratory studies dealing with discrete body fluids or with the isolated reflexes and mating habits of rodents and monkeys were less subjective and less prone to scandal than those involving human sexual behavior. Underlying this preference was the disciplinary placement of the CRPS within the Medical Sciences Division of the NRC, which exercised considerable influence on which proposals would be accepted. In a 1928 CRPS file memorandum, Dr. Vernon Kellogg of the Division emphasized that research on sex sponsored by the Division should be related to "human biology" rather than focus on "primarily sociological" matters. Kellogg believed that the Division was not adequately prepared to judge the merits of research on human psychological and social behavior except when it was directly related to biological factors.[41] Ironically, although homosexuality had been discussed much more by medical doctors than by biological or social scientists up to that point, physicians associated with the NRC were not inclined to support research on it. This, coupled with the fact that influential committee members from fields such as physiology and nonhuman behavioral research tended to fund projects in their own disciplines, meant that proposals for sociological or psychological studies of human homosexuality tended to be rejected.[42]

Indeed, proposals concerned with human behavior were generally rejected ostensibly on the grounds that they had little to do with advancing medical knowledge, but they more often were avoided because they were regarded as lacking scientific rigor. Committee members were very concerned that sex research not be construed to be in any way speculative or geared toward popular audiences, lest it be associated with pornography by hostile critics. The few CRPS-funded projects involving human behavior tended to be focused more centrally on gender than on sexual behavior per se, and were undertaken by experts whose reputations were secured on the basis of research in areas unrelated to sex, as in the case of the psychologist Lewis Terman and, later, the zoologist Alfred Kinsey.

GILBERT V. HAMILTON AND *RESEARCH IN MARRIAGE*

In 1929, the same year that Davis's work was published, the psychiatrist Gilbert V. Hamilton published *A Research in Marriage*, which surveyed one hundred married men and one hundred married women, some married to one another, from among the middle-class professionals he encountered in New York City. Hamilton's training in both clinical psychiatry and psychology made him well positioned to undertake sex research. But his proposal for funding, while recommended by the CRPS, was rejected by the NRC on the grounds that his research fell outside the rubric of medical science and did not appear to be sufficiently scientific.[43] He turned to the Bureau of Social Hygiene, headed by Katharine Davis, which supported his research. It commenced in 1924, with the CRPS assuming an advisory role.

While Hamilton stated clearly that he was interested in how normal people felt about marriage and sex, his concern was to understand "marital maladjustment." He opened his book with several main questions: Was marriage itself a flawed institution that annihilated love and passion? If so, could this account for the high rates of divorce and marital unhappiness? Or were marriages failing because of the psychological weaknesses of husbands and wives that were exacerbated by modern life? Hamilton's first two questions bore the influence of an anarchist critique of marriage advanced by "free lovers" who described it as a vestige of patriarchal barbarism. Hamilton entertained this idea briefly, but he proceeded with the assumption that marriage was the primary institution of human sexual affinity and thus he was interested in determining how it might work to the benefit and happiness of the parties concerned. His hunch, borne out in his findings, was that psychological conditioning in early life made a big difference in whether individuals would be capable of achieving and maintaining marital happiness; those who were frightened or sexually inhibited and those who were psychologically immature would suffer greater dissatisfaction in adulthood. What is striking about Hamilton's study is the emphasis he placed on sexual pleasure, particularly that of women, as the key factor in successful marriages. In a reversal of Victorian wisdom about the presence of passion in men and its absence in women, Hamilton found that "women tolerate sexual inadequacy in husbands less well than men tolerate it in their wives," and that a woman's greater capacity for orgasm, governed as much by psychological as by physical factors, was a gage of her overall health and happiness.[44]

In conducting his study, Hamilton followed the psychobiological tradition introduced by his mentor, Adolf Meyer, who privileged the conscious mind and stressed the importance of considering the "whole person" in terms of his or her integration of mind, body, and environment. Although influenced by Freud's ideas about the importance of childhood events shaping the individual's psychosexual disposition in adulthood, Hamilton, like other American psychiatrists and psychologists with whom he studied, was openly skeptical about Freud's "speculative" method and his granting so much significance to the Unconscious. Hamilton was interested in gathering data about conscious thoughts, memories, fantasies, and experiences, believing that a carefully constructed survey questionnaire could illuminate these in a more scientific fashion than Freudian psychoanalysis. In contrast to Davis's use of written questionnaires and concern for the anonymity of the respondents, Hamilton believed it was important to interview subjects face-to-face so that the examiner could take stock of the range of answers and accompanying physical and temperamental responses.

Hamilton admitted that his subject sample, gathered by a "snowball" technique, was socially homogeneous. Most interviewees lived in New York City, were under the age of forty, and were above average in intelligence and "cultural attainment." Though concerned that his sample was too homogenous, Hamilton believed that studying this group could offer an important first step in understanding why so many seemingly adjusted people had unhappy experiences in marriage. One of the key ways he went about exploring this was to ask questions about "variations" in their sex acts, including masturbation, homosexuality, and achieving pleasure through inflicting pain.

As in Davis's study, which he relied on for devising his interview questionnaire, Hamilton asked questions about marital satisfaction, familial relationships, love affairs prior to marriage, and attitudes and opinions of subjects regarding sex. But Hamilton's work was concerned primarily with charting developmental factors from childhood that gave rise to adult "maladjustments." Whereas Davis explicitly intended to generate data upon which to base sex education, Hamilton, also a proponent of sex education, sought to draw together the insights of psychiatry and psychology in order to enhance the clinical practice of helping patients. Like Davis, he presumed that data on nonprocreative forms of sexual behavior, mainly homosexuality and masturbation, were germane to understanding how to make heterosexuality work in modern life.

His comparative research on the sexuality of humans and nonhuman primates, undertaken under the guidance of his mentor, Robert Yerkes, led Hamilton to define sexual behavior in terms of a range of activities he called "sex play," pleasurable gestures which satisfied the biological, psychological, and social needs of individuals and social groups. To wit, he defined masturbation as a pleasure-oriented activity practiced either separate from or complementary to copulation, and he noted that not only was it a very common practice but was often beneficial. After observing homosexuality among apes, Hamilton was led to consider the meaning and significance of homosexuality in the larger ensemble of social and sexual relations within primate species. He demonstrated that homosexuality was natural in animals and a stage in the development of mature heterosexuality: "Success in moving from a homosexual to a heterosexual stage was due to the animal's ability to manipulate its environment."[45] Thus he implied that homosexuality was superseded if an individual was able to adjust to its environment in a way that enabled it to fulfill its reproductive instinct. His thoughts on homosexuality from comparative "infrahuman" research shed light on why he approached the subject not as if it were a behavior practiced only by degenerate types or a sign of inherent constitutional defect, but rather as a socially conditioned phenomenon, albeit primarily a psychopathological one, that occurred under particular circumstances. He believed it could offer hints to the larger organization of sex and pleasure even among "normal" people, but he generally saw it as a symptom of psychological unhappiness and, in many cases, of arrested psychosexual development.

Hamilton did not believe that homosexuality was negative in every instance. But, echoing psychoanalytic reasoning, he regarded homosexuality as a manifestation of the overzealous enforcement of incest taboos in childhood that caused heterosexuality to be the source of fear and anxiety. Hamilton's comparative study of sexual behavior in apes and humans led him to conclude that males engaged in homosexuality more readily than females and often used it as a mode of expressing aggression and dominance. He found among human males that homosexuality was associated with paranoia and anxiety, whereas among women he found a "less potent" tendency to inhibit homosexual urges. To support this, he cited schoolgirl crushes as well as "the effusive demonstrations of affection which adult women lavish upon one another," and the "greater frequency of female than male homosexual marriages." He also noted the discomfort of some of the married men he interviewed when they were asked about homosexuality; this he took to suggest that heterosexual men who were anxious about homosexuality may themselves be suffering from a pathological effect of sexual repression. In making these observations, Hamilton implied that homosexuality per se was not as much a problem as the aggressive and phobic reactions to it.[46]

Hamilton also noted some women's pronounced fear of heterosexuality, especially those who had been originally instructed about sex from either their fathers or older brothers or who, in childhood, suffered sexual assault by an older man. Hamilton found it significant that two wives that he classified as "overt homosexuals" had been subject to this kind of abuse as children. This, for him, was a lamentable situation and one which led him to urge men to be more sensitive and respectful toward women and to seek consensual relations with women who were their peers.[47]

Whereas Davis had refrained from evaluating homosexuality, Hamilton generally perceived lesbianism and male homosexuality as symptoms of the crisis in relations between the sexes. Thus, in his view homosexuality was not the expression of inherently deviant types, but a sexual behavior that seemingly normal people might adopt as an alternative to an undesirable version of heterosexuality. Thus, for him, the elimination of problems that resulted in homosexuality was part and parcel of a larger effort to restore happiness and stability to heterosexual relations.

Hamilton's questions were shaped by psychoanalytic perspectives. In this formulation, homosexual activity and masturbation resulted from a child's inhibition toward heterosexuality instilled at an early age by a strong taboo against incest. But his subjects' responses indicated something quite different. Hamilton's research revealed that seventeen of the men he surveyed and twenty-six of the women reported "indulging in homosexual episodes since the 18th year," with all cases involving "mutual stimulation of sex organs."[48] Compared to those who did not engage in homosexuality, those who did tended to masturbate and to have premarital heterosexual intercourse at greater rates. Furthermore, Hamilton found that a substantial number of unhappy marriages were correlated to general sexual inhibitions, leading him to conclude that engaging in masturbation and other forms of nonprocreative sexual relations, including homosexuality, may actually make a man or woman better suited to marriage, so long as the marriage could provide them sexual satisfaction.

Because Hamilton was interested in marital maladjustment and many of his subjects (21 percent) sought psychiatric help before participating in the study, it came as no surprise when he found high levels of unhappiness in marriage. In spite of his insistence that his subjects were basically normal, other experts criticized his work for having included such a large number of "maladjusted" people. Indeed, Hamilton, like Freud himself, sought to redefine the term normal: both were intent upon showing that seemingly normal people suffered from serious damage done to them in childhood. For Hamilton, demographic trends and clinical experience supported his assumption that the institution of marriage was in trouble. Thus he was keen to pass his insights along to the general public by writing columns for women's magazines and by releasing a more readable version of his study in *What's Wrong with Marriage: A Study of Two Hundred Husbands and Wives*, which he co-authored with journalist Kenneth MacGowan.[49] These gestures disturbed Rockefeller and others at the Bureau of Social Hygiene, who insisted that Hamilton remove any mention of the BSH's endorsement from all publications about the research. The Bureau feared a backlash by some of its conservative benefactors and worried that its own legitimacy would be undermined by Hamilton's appeal to a popular (either prurient or overly impressionable) audience.[50] For his part, although Hamilton wanted to reach wide audiences, he did not assume that public exposure would reduce his work to the status of pornography. That the BSH and the CRPS went to considerable effort to distance themselves from Hamilton's popularizing efforts attests not only to the social stigma surrounding sex research on humans in the 1920s but also to the anxiety felt among experts in the field that to avoid moral reproach one would have to balance "science" with discretion, the way Davis succeeded in doing.[51]

But like Davis, Hamilton expanded the notion of what would count as normal sexual behavior and placed special emphasis on the centrality of sexual satisfaction to ensure not only the success of marriages but also the health and well-being of the individual, male or female. That homosexuality was among the practices of otherwise normal people created less of a stir than one might imagine, given the otherwise pathological connotations of the subject in most psychiatric accounts of homosexuality. In his discussion of homosexuality, Hamilton regarded it not in terms of sex inversion nor did he single out specific types of people as homosexual by nature. Instead, given his specific purposes regarding marriage, homosexuality was simply one of many variations that could, but not always did, obstruct an individual's achievement of mature heterosexual adjustment.

THE DICKINSON/BEAM STUDIES: RETROSPECTIVE OBJECTIVITY

Two other significant studies of "normal" women's sex behavior from this period were those compiled by Robert Latou Dickinson and Lura Beam. Based on case records from Dickinson's nearly half-century of gynecological practice, *A Thousand Marriages* and *The Single Woman* offered detailed information about the health and sex lives of some 2,078 women who at one time or another were Dickinson's patients.[52] The volumes were prepared and written in collaboration with Dickinson by Lura Beam, whose background in applied psychology and education suited her to the task. They were part of a publication series established by the Committee on Maternal Health, founded in 1923 and headquartered in New York City.

The Committee's board of directors was comprised primarily of physicians, many of whom were associated with social hygiene organizations.[53] It was dedicated to two main efforts: first, to studying "the actual sex life and endowment of socially normal persons as revealed in medical case histories," and, second, to studying the "control of fertility by such methods as contraception, sterilization, therapeutic abortion and prevention and relief of involuntary sterilization" (the latter being a euphemism for the physical and psychological barriers to conception on either the wife's or husband's part, including "frigidity" and impotence as well as infertility).[54] Dickinson was made the Honorary Secretary of the Committee, and, upon his retirement from full-time clinical practice at the age of sixty-three, he gave the Committee all his books and notes. These included the thousands of histories, spanning the years 1895 to 1924, that were later interpreted in *A Thousand Marriages* and *The Single Woman*.

Dickinson is remembered most by historians for his efforts to legalize contraception. Indeed, he urged the forming of the Committee on Maternal Health as a body that could lend professional credibility to the birth control movement. Dickinson felt that the grassroots activism of Margaret Sanger and Emma Goldman was too radical and not respectable enough to convince other doctors and lawmakers of the merits of birth control.[55] In 1916 he voiced strong opposition to the unscientific nature of the birth control movement and urged his medical colleagues to professionalize it. In order to gain respectability, he recommended that a group of doctors be brought together to study contraception in order to assess its effectiveness and safety.[56]

This would be an organization devoted to empirical research, not a distribution center for birth control, as Sanger's clinic was characterized. On this basis, Dickinson gained the support of a small number of doctors and received initial funding from several society ladies.[57] In 1930, the Committee changed its name to the National Committee on Maternal Health and shifted from doing primarily clinical research to publishing reports and handbooks for doctors on contraception and sex anatomy, funded by money from the Rockefeller-supported Bureau of Social Hygiene.[58]

Many Maternal Health Committee members and supporters, including Dickinson, had institutional ties to eugenics organizations, and, by 1935, the Committee articulated an explicit goal of bringing birth control to poor women, who were seen to be most in need of contraception.[59] The Committee argued that these women, for their own good and that of the "race," should be taught "the birth control habit." In 1930, Gertrude Streges, an outspoken member of the Committee, urged that it help stop "the propagation of defective and substandard types in general."[60] Streges's comment may sound politically conservative to our ears, but such sentiments were echoed by many liberal advocates of birth control as well as some on the Left, including Margaret Sanger. Dickinson, who thought of himself as a modern man and believed that sexual fulfillment was essential, argued that the lot of women and of society as a whole would be improved if their fertility could be controlled. He sympathized with poor women who could not afford to care for their children and believed they would be well served by having birth control and sterilization available to them. He, like others on the Committee, assumed that contraception and sex education would contribute to ensuring happiness in marriage. They believed that the open discussion of sexual desire and behavior, including variations previously cloaked in taboo and shame, represented an enlightened approach that would ease the discomfort and suffering experienced by previous generations of women.

Dickinson decried the sort of Victorian prudery embraced by Anthony Comstock, and he passionately criticized religious dogma in favor of a more enlightened model of scientific management of sexual matters. Dickinson was a liberal Episcopalian of New England Yankee stock. He was married to Sarah Truslow Dickinson, a charter member of the Brooklyn Auxiliary of the New York Committee of Fourteen, an anti-vice organization dedicated to eradicating prostitution and commercial vice.[61] Dickinson believed that physicians should participate in making the city a more inhabitable place and in ameliorating the difficulties patients experienced under the stressful conditions of modern life. In this respect, he cautiously advocated schemes for regulating prostitution that involved registering and detaining women as a means for controlling venereal disease.[62] But he dedicated his greatest efforts to assisting "normal" women not only in the treatment of gynecological problems but in achieving happiness in marriage, an institution he believed was the most superior human relationship. Rising rates of divorce and the prevalence of unmarried women concerned Dickinson as it had Hamilton. Thus, making modern marriages work to the satisfaction of both partners would not only restore the institution but bring order to a changing world.

What distinguished Dickinson from most gynecologists of his time was a strong belief in the role of the doctor to encourage sexual happiness in women, a factor Dickinson believed was key to the success of marriages. In his gynecological practice, Dickinson took into account issues of birth control, female sexual satisfaction, masturbation, "frigidity," and lesbianism, especially as these related to matters of marriage.[63] He sought to relieve "maladjusted" and inhibited women, focusing particular attention on dynamics that caused certain women to resist men, including everything from a fear of pregnancy to a prolonged attachment to other women. He saw himself as a spiritual advisor to women. Doctors, he believed, were "the new ecclesiastics," since medicine had gained authority over religion on matters of sexuality. In 1908, he suggested that physicians in the modern world serve as clergymen and confessors for members of the "saintly half of the race" who needed direct, intimate, and gentle guidance in dealing with their medical problems.[64] Throughout his career he urged obstetricians and gynecologists to overcome modesty and act as sex counselors to their patients by incorporating a broader psychological and sociological understanding of gynecology, an ethic endorsed by Havelock Ellis in his preface to *A Thousand Marriages*.[65] While this sensitivity can be seen as a positive shift from doctors treating women as silent objects or neglecting them altogether, Dickinson's notion of concern and attention brought with it the effect of greater clinical penetration into women's lives and bodies.

While mainly dedicated to middle-class, American-born white women, Dickinson's gynecological practice included the treatment of poor and working-class women, on whom he tested experimental and controversial techniques, often without their fully informed consent.[66] Though these cases were not included in *The Single Woman* and *A Thousand Marriages*, they illustrate aspects of Dickinson's broader preoccupation with the female body that manifested itself in his clinical studies of middle-class women's sexuality as well. Dickinson has been credited for his "daring innovations" of depicting women's genitals at a time when local gynecological exams were rare, but many of his techniques pushed the ethical boundaries of their time as well as ours.[67] Unbeknownst to many women, Dickinson used them as experimental subjects in his massive collections of case histories on gynecological health and disease. His interest in women's sexual satisfaction led him to develop some extraordinary examination techniques, including making copious illustrations of women's genitals as well as, in some instances, stimulating women sexually as a way of gaining knowledge about their sexual response cycles. Dickinson's hands-on approach bordered on scandalous and would have been attacked were it not for the fact that his most radical techniques were practiced on working-class women who, because they were patients in public clinics, were inclined to think that receiving medical care was contingent upon their compliance to the doctor's wishes.

Whether or not this was in fact true, Dickinson took advantage of his working-class patients' obedience in order to investigate women's sexual responses. For example, in an 1883 experiment using domestic servants employed by well-to-do New York households, he wanted to demonstrate that the vaginal muscles play a significant role in securing the penis close to the os of the uterus in order to discount a prevalent theory that the uterus was responsible for ingesting sperm. To do this he first needed to demonstrate how the vagina gripped the penis in intercourse, and to do so he greased a wax dildoe and inserted it into the relaxed vaginas of his patients. The women were then told to contract their vaginal muscles firmly, which left an impression on the dildoe and indicated the strength of the levator ani muscle, confirming his hypothesis.[68]

But Dickinson did not confine these techniques to working-class women. Some forty years later, in 1933, he performed another stimulating experiment, this time on a group of middle-class women, to chart the effects of orgasm. In order to observe the action of the "favinal lining" and cervix during what Dickinson believed was an orgasm, he inserted a glass tube resembling an erect penis into the patient's vagina, stimulated it, and then looked down into it to discover whether she indeed experienced physiological changes.[69] Sexually stimulating his patients in examinations was a common practice about which Dickinson had few qualms, noting only that "to avoid criticism, a nurse or attendant is advisable though not essential."[70] Hoping to gain knowledge about female sexual responses and to treat women for "frigidity," he timed nipple erections, measured the "dusky flush" of women's labia, and was among the first to use electrical vibrators to teach patients how to climax. Signs and rates of arousal, he opined, could shed light on other physical or psychological factors relevant to a patient's case. He frequently commented on the excitation certain patients experienced before, during, and after examinations, which he stated was commonly perceptible in cases involving excessive masturbation, nymphomania, or lesbianism.[71] On occasion, Dickinson noted when female patients seemed more aroused by female gynecologists than by male, a factor indicating the patient's possible tendency toward lesbianism.

Surprisingly, Dickinson was never rebuked by other doctors for these practices, nor is there evidence that women whom he examined complained, though the only remaining documentation of these women comes through Dickinson's own writings and recollections.[72] His case records indicate that many of his patients returned regularly to be examined, including some whom he had sexually stimulated, so we cannot assume that all of his patients found this objectionable. In fact, this might indicate that his rapport with these patients was good. However, we should also remember that it is likely that many of his patients visited Dickinson primarily in order to receive birth control devices. The law required that they only be administered by a licensed physician and only when deemed medically necessary, as in cases when pregnancy might endanger a woman's life or in cases when a woman or her partner had a venereal disease. It remained illegal to prescribe or distribute birth control in cases not clearly involving medical necessity until late 1936, when Judge Augustus Hand of the New York Supreme Court overturned the Comstock Law and allowed doctors to prescribe birth control devices without regard to disease.[73]

In any case, it is important to note that during exams the patients' arousal was mainly in the eye of the beholder, as it was Dickinson's perception gleaned not from women's verbal admissions but from examining their genitals that led him to assume they were excited. But in other matters, he relied on patients' reports of physical symptoms to gain information about their sex lives. He cautioned that it was important to listen carefully to patients' complaints and cryptic asides, and to scrutinize these as signs of psychological problems concerning marital incompatibility and sexual frustration.

The doctor was a master of clinical scrutiny, placing great emphasis on accuracy and comprehensive detail in recording his patients' visits. He hoped to make gynecology more humane by taking careful stock of the patient's complaints and more scientific by recording in exacting and standardized detail any significant features of her case.[74] Fancying himself both artist and scientist, he called his method "medical natural history" to capture both an aesthetic and accurate depiction of his observations.[75] He signed every sketch, a practice that led one commentator to call him a cross between Havelock Ellis and Leonardo da Vinci.[76] It was his belief that a skilled observer could discern aspects of a patient's emotional life and her sexual history by studying her genitals.

While in most cases he sketched his observations of women patients, in his later years Dickinson incorporated photography, hazarding another ethical violation. Realizing that patients may be a little put off by the idea of being photographed during a pelvic exam, he concealed a camera in a flower pot, strategically angled to the examining table. Without the patient knowing, he could press a hidden foot pedal and the camera would secretly take a picture. The doctor defended such actions against critics by saying that, when dealing with patients who were deeply inhibited, such surreptitious techniques were the only way to determine important aspects of hymens and other genital structures, which assisted in making diagnoses and preventing future problems.[77]

Dickinson recommended still other dubious examination techniques. For example, using a finger penetration test, he believed one could determine whether a woman had experienced coitus. If her hymen would admit no more than one adult digit in its full length, she was an "anatomic virgin." Penetration by two whole fingers meant that she frequently had coitus. If four fingers or a whole hand went in, this suggested "prolonged manualization." In cases of women who were regular patients, however, Dickinson acknowledged that the admission of several fingers could be a sign of prolonged gynecological treatment.

He was enthusiastic about the role of the doctor in preparing women for heterosexual intercourse, reproduction, and contraception. He advocated the idea of the marriage clinic, which in its earliest incarnation in Germany encouraged lay people to consult experts in order to solve their sexual and reproductive problems.[78] Impressed by the German clinics he visited in the 1920s, Dickinson urged experts to disseminate sex information especially to their female patients through what he called preventive gynecology.[79] This innovation consisted of giving routine gynecological examinations and consultation to brides-to-be before they officially announced their engagements. In these sessions, besides providing counseling on what to expect in sexual relations, the doctor inspected the woman's hymen and, if necessary, dilated or ruptured it in order to facilitate post-wedding intercourse. Thus the doctor was placed in a crucial role of delivering his female patients to another man, her husband. As part of this initiation to marriage, Dickinson urged practitioners to advise patients about contraception and require them to return after three weeks of marriage in order to be fitted with a diaphragm.[80] Dickinson spoke of marriage as a psychological and spiritual union between husband and wife, and he privileged women's physical conditions with the power to make or break a marriage. Hence, it was the future wife and mother who should be examined. In a very few cases, the gynecologist met with male partners who were briefly counselled in a separate meeting, fully clothed, and who were given no physical exam.

Dickinson's interest in preventive gynecology and marriage counseling inspired him to analyze the nearly 5,200 gynecological cases he had collected between 1895 and 1924, the year he retired from regular practice. The cases were of women born between about 1870 and 1905. The earliest of them came of age during the Victorian period in decades following the Civil War, years marked by the expansion of industrial capitalism and the rapid growth of cities, but also years in which women were generally thought to be passive and passionless and when sexual issues were shrouded in silence. The cohort of more recent cases included women born at the beginning of the twentieth century when gender relations changed significantly, the idea of women's independence and equality was debated openly, and matters related to sexuality, though putatively still taboo, were the source of growing interest and public conversation. Both *A Thousand Marriages* and *The Single Woman* were intended to present the "actual sex life and endowment of normal persons as revealed in medical case histories" by paying special attention to the "cost and meaning of the conflicts between biological functioning and social adaption."[81] *A Thousand Marriages*, published in 1931, surveyed the details of success or failure in the sexual adjustment of 1,098 married women. *The Single Woman*, published three years later, addressed the question of what caused women to remain single by reporting on the conditions and experiences of 1,078 single women. Subjects for both volumes were mostly educated urban women who, in the case of the married women were homemakers, mothers of one or two children, and wives of professional men who had consulted Dickinson on problems with childbirth and various pelvic disorders. The single women were mainly educated, native-born white U.S. citizens who supported themselves financially. Like the married women, they visited the doctor for gynecological problems and to acquire information about birth control.

The Dickinson/Beam studies, prepared with financial support from the Bureau of Social Hygiene, differed from the previously conducted surveys of Davis and Hamilton in several ways. First, they were longitudinal in nature; that is, many patients included in the studies were seen by Dickinson over many years, affording him the opportunity to witness their progress and to note how changes in their lives affected women's mental and physical health. This also allowed Dickinson to observe how historical transformations in social mores influenced his patients attitudes about sexuality. He found that his earlier patients tended to be far more repressed in talking about sex and suffered greater problems because of their reticence to visit the doctor, compared to later patients who were more open about sexuality, came more often for checkups, and were described as modern in their outlook. Higher incidences of masturbation, homosexuality, and divorce were found among his later group of patients, suggesting that the previous code of morals was giving way to new tendencies that could be endangering the institution of marriage. Furthermore, that many middle-class women in this later generation returned to visit the doctor regularly suggests that his clinical manner and hands-on techniques were not as off-putting as we might assume.

Secondly, the Dickinson/Beam studies differed from Davis's and Hamilton's studies because they involved physical examinations, an aspect that Dickinson believed made his findings more thorough. A gynecological inspection would bring to light aspects of women's sex lives that they were inclined to avoid in conversations with the doctor. Concretely, Dickinson believed that the condition of a woman's genitals could indicate the variety of sexual practices she might have experienced. Most specifically, "the hymen, the vulva, and vagina are believed . . . to document sex practice to a degree sufficient to give clues about both auto-eroticism and coitus."[82] What Dickinson saw on the examining table could either serve to corroborate or cast doubt on the patient's narrative, as in cases where the doctor suspected she was either avoiding a subject or lying.[83]

In a friendly criticism of the studies by Davis and Hamilton, Dickinson stressed that, especially in the case of female sexuality, even if a woman did talk, her conscious mind alone could not reveal all the important aspects operating in sexual satisfaction and incompatibility.[84] Instead, her body must also be studied, since it could provide an index of emotional or psychological conditions. The female body, observed through the experts' gaze, could function as a master text, revealing what was otherwise hidden in the unconscious mind or cloaked in taboo.[85] Accordingly, Dickinson believed that solving a physical problem could almost guarantee that a psychological problem would, in turn, dissolve. However, in this entire framework of medicalizing marital compatibility, Dickinson was only interested in women's bodies; men's bodies were never brought under his clinical gaze even though, presumably, they were the other half of the puzzle of heterosexual compatibility.

Finally, the Dickinson/Beam studies differed from Hamilton and Davis because they were based upon the admittedly subjective point of view of a practitioner.[86] Rather than relying on a standardized questionnaire to which subjects responded, anonymously or by interview, the cases Dickinson and Beam analyzed were drawn from actual medical practice and the insights of a single practitioner. Indeed, Dickinson labored to standardize his method of examination and treatment, but he believed that information about sex was complex and required that the doctor listen carefully to the patient rather than pose preestablished, and thus often irrelevant, questions to her. His role as a sympathetic and compassionate practitioner earned him the trust and confidence of his patients, he said, which helped him in understanding sexual experiences in a larger context. Havelock Ellis, in his introduction to *A Thousand Marriages,* endorsed Dickinson's work on these grounds, noting especially that superstition and shame were the cause of much unhappiness among women who, prevented from learning about sex, often experienced their relationships with men as alienating. Ellis believed that the task of helping to forge happy companionships among men and women was best placed in the hands of a medically trained and compassionate expert.

In the volume on married women, Beam and Dickinson reported findings on masturbation, orgasm, attitudes toward husbands, hobbies, and habits. A survey of these topics led the authors to conclude that many unhappy marriages were due to sexual problems stemming from male insensitivity, lack of sexual experimentation, female frigidity, and fear of pregnancy. Furthermore, they stressed that, contrary to popular misconceptions, all women had not only the capacity but the need for sexual satisfaction. Hence, men should learn something about their wives' desires, and physicians ought to assist female patients in learning better sex techniques and birth control methods.

Although the authors mention that behavior not directly related to procreation was crucial to women's sexual satisfaction, their remarks were mainly limited to the subject of masturbation, which they noted was even more common among married than among single women.

Beam and Dickinson said very little about homosexuality among the married women. Their commentary was limited to an analysis of several cases concerning husbands', not wives' homosexuality. The husbands pursued other men and refused to have intercourse with their wives, thus causing a problem in their marriages.[87] The volume on single women yielded information about female homosexuality. Importantly, none of Dickinson's patients came to him specifically for problems related to homosexuality; instead, it was during the course of examinations for other matters that the subject emerged. This led him to speculate, in retrospect, that his few cases vastly underrepresented the much greater prevalence of lesbian experiences among American women. Among the group of 1,078 single women he surveyed, twenty-eight showed evidence of homosexual experiences, eighteen by their own admission and ten based on physical evidence gleaned by the doctor from anatomical and psychological observations. Their median age was twenty-six, and one-third had attended college. Although the overwhelming majority were white women, one was described as "a colored woman, full African type, very dark," but other than this remark no specific mention is made of her case.[88]

Several key factors distinguish Dickinson's cases from those more commonly found in the medical literature of the time. First, Dickinson emphasized that in the overwhelming majority of these cases, homosexual experiences had been transitory, often occurring during developmental stages in young adulthood or in sex-segregated environments such as college. Hence he and Beam noted that to speak in terms of a constitutionally specific type of woman who engaged in homosexuality was inappropriate for understanding the vast majority of women who at one time or another engaged in lesbian relationships.[89] Indeed, they noted that among these twenty-eight women there was "no evidence of maleness of feeling or attitude," none were employed in "especially masculine" occupations, most were exceptionally attractive, "[none wore] either exotically feminine or smartly masculine clothes," and "four continued to wear their hair long during the vogue for short hair," a set of findings that defied many of the stereotypes surrounding lesbianism at the time.[90] Although some were noted for their eccentricities, their "manners appeared adopted [*sic*] to those of the age or period, neither rigid nor free."[91] On the whole they were described as healthy and valuable members of their communities, caring for the welfare of others and supporting themselves and family members and friends during times of difficulty.

Patients' responses to questions Dickinson asked about their homosexual relations defied the inversion paradigm, since when asked "whether she or the other person took the male part, she [the subject] always answered that it was not she and the typical reply was that they did not think of it that way."[92] The doctor summarized the most common practices as "mutual masturbation" and "imitative coitus." Evidence from physical examinations indicated the common appearance of protruding labia minora among women who engaged in homosexuality, features that were also present among women who masturbated. Although some reported being disturbed by the social repercussions of their relationships with other women, all reported sexual satisfaction and emotional fulfillment. In spite of the authors' mostly positive appraisal of these women, without doubt they believed that lesbian experiences, if persistent or excessive, were negative because they could impede marriage or could make a woman resistant to intimacy with men. Dickinson was especially worried that women who achieved emotional and sexual satisfaction in lesbian relationships may defer or decline marriage. Evidence of the sexual dissatisfaction among many married women underscored his concern that men's lack of knowledge and sexual clumsiness accounted at least in part for the fact that many women were remaining single. Lesbianism, Dickinson feared, might be more an indication of men's incompetence than a sign of women's inherent deviancy.

In concluding, Dickinson reassured readers by noting that, on the whole, homosexual experiences among women were seldom lasting and thus, like masturbation when done in moderation, were not inherently sinful or permanently damaging. That many of Dickinson's patients went on to marry or to have relationships with men was encouraging, he believed. True to her public demeanor, his co-author, Lura Beam, did not divulge her own lesbianism as she analyzed Dickinson's cases in writing.[93] But it would appear that both authors took a position that practicing lesbianism did not make one an invert nor did it condemn one to a state of irreparable disease. In fact, it was their belief that lesbianism, as Hamilton had implied, resulted from a crisis in heterosexuality caused by men's insensitivity to women or by women's lack of the knowledge of sex they needed to mature into happy marriages. Thus, lesbianism could be read as a symptom that could assist doctors like Dickinson in shoring up the institution of marriage by making men more aware of what it took to make women happy. In the end, the authors sounded a tone of dismay when describing the separation of love and sex their heterosexual cases suggested. This, coupled with a "trend toward individualism" among both single and unhappy married women, were cited as causes for the crises in marriage.[94]

THE CONTINUUM OF VARIANCE

The 1920s marked an important shift in popular and scientific thinking about sexuality. In contrast to the repressive morality promoted by Anthony Comstock, modern-minded commentators and scientific sex reformers conceptualized sexual desire and pleasure as healthy and necessary for women's and men's happiness, especially in the context of marriage. Antifeminist authors used this new way of thinking to argue that the ideal modern marriage should bind men and women together as complementary partners for the sake not only of happiness but also of eugenic reproduction. Even as they preferred the language of variance and maladjustment to sin and vice, many modern-minded commentators on sexuality shared moral assumptions embraced by anti-vice agitators about the importance of eugenically sound heterosexual marriage and middle-class family life as cornerstones of a healthy society.

However, sex researchers such as Davis, Hamilton, and Dickinson were interested in broadening what would count as permissible behavior in a fashion that especially took women's sexual satisfaction into consideration. Suspecting that prudery and sexual repression were to blame for many social ills, Davis, Hamilton, and Dickinson were prompted to study sexuality with the hope that this knowledge would shed light on how modern women and men could enjoy, rather than suffer, the changes signaled by modern life. To this end, they focused on "normal" sex practices among women who seemed rather average, and they approached sex as an aspect of the putatively private realm of relationships and marriage. But by publishing their findings, the researchers made the private sex lives of normal women, and by extension men, public so that others could compare themselves to the norms presented. Explicit data on the sex lives of normal people were offered as useful for remedying common problems of marital incompatibility and sexual dissatisfaction. In this context, lesbianism became a significant index of what women might be lacking in their heterosexual relations and marriages to men.

Davis, Hamilton, and Dickinson positioned themselves as dispassionate practitioners of objectivity and science. Though they were actively involved in reform organizations, they claimed a nonpartisan status as experts interested only in discovering scientific truths. Through this ethical stance of claiming to be expressly modern, rational, and scientifically enlightened, they sought to distance themselves not only from pornographic connotations but also from earlier superstitious and overtly moralistic approaches to sexuality. Approaching sexuality in "sociological" terms, they took into consideration a vast array of individual personality traits, behaviors, gestures, and desires previously not overtly associated with sex. They relied on empirical methods and statistical analysis as a way of identifying and mapping normalcy and thus dramatically changed the way that sexuality would be thought about in decades to come. Their methods contrasted to the clinical case history model in which abnormal individuals would be studied in a manner that assumed an a priori definition of the normal. Surveyists instead used methods to calculate, in metric terms, frequencies, intensities, norms, and deviations that characterized the range of practices and experiences that actually made up the normal American. This represented a self-conscious move to a discourse of what *is* rather than what ought to be. The former would be established through scientifically-sound empirical observations, in contradistinction to the latter, which was a vestige of the moralistic and anti-objective vigilance campaigns against which progressive science staged itself.

Significantly, research on "normal" sexuality from this period was centered in New York City, which, by the 1920s, was home to a flourishing gay and lesbian subculture comprised of men and women from vastly different backgrounds and socio-economic strata. Though certainly not openly sanctioned, the subculture provided entertainment to prominent New Yorkers who attended "drag" masquerade pageants, "pansy acts," and theatrical plays dealing with homosexuality. Popular perceptions that homosexuality was growing more attractive and prevalent in the city may account for why the subject was on the minds of the noteworthy researchers we have considered in this chapter. In addition to taking up the question of the New Woman's desires, New Yorkers Davis, Hamilton, and Dickinson were also intrigued about what attracted increasing numbers of seemingly normal men and women to homosexuality.[95]

Rather than regarding homosexuality as always pathological, Davis in particular initiated a turn in the United States toward viewing it as a variation of normal sexual behavior. Hamilton and Dickinson concurred but suggested that it was a sign of immaturity in some cases. However, they were inclined to view homosexuality more as an indication of what might be wrong with heterosexuality than to focus on homosexuality as inherently pathological. The new sex researchers' tolerance toward homosexuality undoubtedly had much to do with the fact that a majority of the subject populations surveyed were native-born, middle-class, white women and men. By contrast, American medical reports of homosexuality from the 1880s through the 1920s tended to be based upon cases of economically and socially marginalized individuals. Thus, in medical writing, defining homosexuality as a form of pathology went hand-in-hand with ruling-class assumptions that poor and working-class people, people of color, and disadvantaged immigrants were generally inclined toward sexual perversion. This discourse generally emphasized a distinct difference between homosexuals and heterosexuals, and did so by stressing the links between sexual perversion, sexual inversion, and the lower classes. When incidences of homosexuality came to light in surveys of "normal" Americans, its equation with pathology was far less pronounced. Researchers said almost nothing about incidents of homosexuality outside the middle class, choosing instead to place a primary emphasis on recuperating eugenically sound matrimonial heterosexuality. Though seemingly charitable, this did little to disturb the culturally embedded assumption that perversion was more common and more menacing among the underclasses.

Nevertheless, the new focus on sexual variations in "normal" people introduced significant changes in how homosexuality, as well as a host of other behaviors, was conceptualized. The idea of *variance* formed the central logic of sociological research aimed at ensuring social and mental hygiene in the population. Statistical studies from this period deployed the model of a continuum across which a wide variety of phenomena and behavior could be mapped and qualitative distinctions made. An emphasis on statistical variation signaled a new model for thinking about difference based on empirical observations and statistical calculations rather than on a notion of fixed and mutually exclusive categories. It manifested itself in studies of sexuality, but also in the work of those concerned with noting racial, class, and ethnic differences. In many respects, statistical methods articulated well with modern bureaucratic management with its reliance upon standardized record keeping, quantification of costs and benefits, calculation of risks, and assessments of individual and group behavior.

Not surprisingly, some of the same techniques used to study the intimate aspects of sexual behavior were used to classify all kinds of human behavior, from rates of productivity to voting patterns to consumption habits. And, at an uneasy moment in U.S. history marked by tensions over who and what would be included in the "melting pot" of the nation, quantification techniques were used to redraw the boundaries between permissible and impermissible behavior, often in a manner that classified working-class people and people of color as deviant rather than as mere "variations" in the population. Studying the "normal," whether researchers intended it to be so or not, was thus part of a larger transformation whereby distinctions were reconfigured according to a logic of assimilation, but one which, nevertheless, continued to involve selective inclusions. The norm, while a mutable construct, was, after all, a means for marking the deviant and thus could be used to mobilize methods for bringing the deviant into conformity with the majority or for further marginalizing such a character in the interest of maintaining majoritarian social order.

New scientific approaches aimed at establishing statistical norms had the effect, however, of making norms more contingent and fluid. This had two important consequences. First, using the model of the continuum opened up possibilities for further scientific research to quantify more elements with greater exactitude, in hopes of drawing ever more fine and accurate lines between what appeared to be common and what was unusual. And, secondly, because variance was based on a somewhat flexible understanding of norms and deviations, it actually in many instances fueled the level of anxiety over drawing boundaries between types of people and determining with some certainty what would count as normal, healthy behavior.

In many respects, continuum models seemed more benevolent than early degenerationist medical models that presumed a binary opposition between homosexuals who were essentially diseased and heterosexuals who were not. However, by seeking to measure variance, continuum models subsequently licensed a range of practices of observation, counting, and classifying in efforts to characterize the nature of homosexuality. In turn, the procedures which brought to light the variant, produced, by contradistinction, what would count as the normal. In other words, norms were neither fixed nor constant but were statistical constructs produced in relation to that which was named as either variant or pathologically deviant. As a result, the category of the normal, like that of the variant, was fundamentally contingent and relational, making it somewhat precarious and, in some people's view, subject to undesirable corruptions as a result of contact with deviance. In an attempt to stabilize this relationship between the normal and the variant, the commonly used terms of "adjustment," "conformity," and "balance" performed a certain regulatory function whereby the variant was made subordinate to the normal through the idiom of "fitting in." The inventions of sex variance and of modern hygienic heterosexuality thus became powerful elements through which an elaborate regulatory apparatus was constructed, with scientists playing a central role in its implementation.

But this regulatory apparatus was neither consciously dictated nor wholly controlled by the researchers involved. Indeed, it produced many unforeseen effects. With the publication of sex research from the late 1920s and early 1930s, variant sexual behavior grew to be a source of popular fascination and official concern in light of data indicating that homosexuality may be more prevalent among Americans that previously imagined. Significant revelations offered by sex researchers during this period called into question the cherished distinction between heterosexuals and homosexuals. In some respects, this functioned to normalize variations. By doing so it served to lessen the stigma attached to homosexuality at least among certain social classes wherein it was seen as transitory and thus relatively benign. But, on the other hand, it provided opponents of homosexuality with the impetus to "fix" it once again by equating statistical variance to disease. As we shall see in the next chapter, this paradoxical oscillation between normalizing and pathologizing homosexuality occurred in the midst of worries over the dissolution of another cherished binary opposition upon which so many assumptions about sex were based— that of the distinction between masculinity and femininity.

5   FLUID SEXES

During the 1930s, scientists in the fields of endocrinology, cultural anthropology, and psychology focused their attention on the nature of sex differences between men and women. In so doing, they substantially influenced how homosexuality would be studied by subsequent researchers in the United States. Their interests in pursuing the subject of sex differences varied. But taken together, their work signals a broader cultural concern at the time for understanding the nature of gender relations in modern society. How were differences between the sexes conceptualized by experts in these fields? How and to what ends did research on sex differences make use of the subject of homosexuality? What were the implications of research on sex differences for conceptualizing homosexuality in new terms? And how did research in these various fields shape future inquiries into homosexuality?

In my attempt to answer these questions, I will argue that, across the fields of endocrinology, cultural anthropology, and psychology, the subject of homosexuality had a spectral presence and functioned as a means for positing what constituted proper manhood and womanhood in advanced societies. To the extent that homosexuals were assumed to combine elements of both sexes, they were invoked in efforts to delineate, by contradistinction, what would count as proper femininity in women and proper masculinity in men.

THE IDEA OF A SEX CONTINUUM

Prior to the publication of the sex research discussed in the previous chapter, most American medical and scientific authorities clung to a clearly dichotomized two-sex model as a way of understanding sex differences in general and homosexuality in particular. To review the two-sex model briefly, it rested on a number of key assumptions: first, that males and females were fundamentally different in their anatomies, physiological functions, sexual desires, aptitudes, and characters; second, that men were naturally sexually aggressive and women naturally passive; third, that sexual attraction naturally occurred be-

159

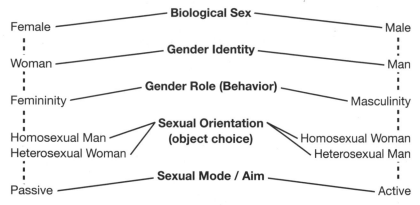

Figure 1. Assumptions about sex and gender. After Birke, *Women, Feminism and Biology* (1986), 72. © 1986 by Lynda Birke.

tween opposites (thus making same-sex attractions conceivable only if one of the partners was understood to be sexually inverted); and fourth, that those who harbored or expressed homosexual desire belonged to a third sex, between the normal categories of male and female, and were consequently inverted not only in biological constitution but in general comportment and sexual behavior. Thus, lesbians were presumed to be mannish and sexually aggressive and homosexual men to be effeminate and passive. Evidence to the contrary—manifested in homosexual desire among individuals who appeared to conform to the normal characteristics for their sex—caused problems for authorities who attempted to conceptualize homosexuality in terms of the inversion model.

The vocabulary and conceptual framework of the inversion model collapsed sex roles, sexual aim, and sexual object choice onto a principal dichotomy between biological males and females. Hence, homosexual desire and gender deviation were seen as consequences, rather than causes, of biological sex inversion. Lynda I. A. Birke offers a useful mapping of the chain of dichotomized associations that were undifferentiated in most of the early scientific and medical writing on homosexuality. As figure 1 indicates, these ideas were based upon a first premise that privileged a fundamental distinction between male and female. Birke's scheme allows us to see, in retrospect, where male homosexuality and lesbianism were situated with regard to the assumption that they would, in almost every respect, have characteristics normally found in the opposite sex. That is, for example, the "true" male homosexual would be similar to the heterosexual woman, expressing feminine behavior and preferring the "passive" or "receptive" position in sexual relations. The "true" lesbian would be similar in comportment and desire to the heterosexual man, with masculine bodily traits and personality, and preferring the "active" role in sexual relations.

By the early 1930s, several scientific developments, including those discussed in chapter 4, raised serious doubts about the value of this strictly dichotomized model for explaining the vast array of variations in sex anatomy, gender roles, and sexual practice in the human population. This was not the first time such doubts were raised. Ulrichs, Hirschfeld, Ellis, and Freud suggested that humans were fundamentally bisexual and that each individual would have features of the other sex, to one degree or another. This led them to argue that it would be best to think of individuals on a sex continuum.[1] But their opinions on this point lacked the kind of concrete scientific evidence that was to come to the fore in the 1920s and 1930s. During that time, in addition to the work of such as Katharine Davis, significant contributions to a sex continuum model came from research in endocrinology, cultural anthropology, and psychology. Discoveries and insights from these fields resonated with changing cultural norms concerning gender and would later be incorporated in subsequent studies of homosexuality.

Endocrinology

In the early years of the twentieth century, researchers in the emerging field of endocrinology generally concurred that males were hormonally distinct from females. But during the 1920s new findings challenged this notion. A revolutionary shift occurred in 1927, when a research group at the University of Amsterdam reported that female sex hormones were present in the testes and urine of "normal, healthy" men.[2] In 1931, a German gynecologist complemented this finding by reporting the presence of male sex hormones in normal females.[3] Several years later in 1934, while conducting hormonal studies of horses, the German gynecologist Bernhard Zondek discovered "very large quantities of oestrogenic hormone in the urine of the stallion."[4]

Scientists described Zondek's "unexpected observation" as "a strange and apparently anomalous discovery," a "paradoxical finding."[5] Their choice of words reveals how wedded researchers had been to the notion of a mutually exclusive and even hormonally antagonistic relationship between the sexes. But by the mid-1930s, the discovery of estrogen and progesterone in normal males and testosterone and other androgens in normal females prompted researchers to explore the functions and determinations of "male" and "female" hormones in normal anatomical development and physiology. Many believed this research would, in turn, provide clues about anatomical anomalies and homosexuality.

By the mid-1930s, endocrinologists confirmed that the sexes were organized according to a fluid system of internal secretions that could be influenced by factors within and outside the body. To make sense of this fluidity, researchers developed methods for studying the physiological basis of sex differences and sexual behavior, deploying a continuum model for conceptualizing degrees of maleness and femaleness in individuals and among groups. Thus, while maintaining a fundamental distinction between the nominal categories of male and female, endocrinologists began to understand individuals as scattered across a physiological spectrum with normal males concentrated on one side and normal females on the other.[6]

Endocrinology grew significantly during this time, as Zondek's "paradoxical finding" of 1934 inspired other scientists to develop hormone research as a means of determining with greater precision what exactly differentiated males from females. Physiologists working in the field of endocrinology devoted particular attention to clinical cases presenting anomalous anatomical characteristics and sexually aberrant behavior. Studying anomalous cases became one of the key ways of ascertaining general knowledge about normal sex differences, and it formed a foundation upon which ideas about normal sexual attractions between "opposite" sexes were based.

As hormonal research advanced, many researchers assumed that homosexuality was tied in some deep way to physiological dysfunctions that resulted in sex inversion. This led them to conduct hormonal experiments as a way of altering sexual behavior and "curing" or "correcting" homosexuality. With the advent of synthesized hormones, clinicians began to treat homosexuals with hormones of the "opposite" sex in efforts to change their sexual orientation. In 1938, a small study conducted by a general practitioner in Los Angeles reported that homosexuality was curable by hormonal replacement therapy.[7] But just two years later, a study of the role of hormones in homosexual personality development found no conclusive findings in this regard.[8] In 1941, two American doctors described the "organotherapy" performed on a 46-year-old African American man who was incarcerated as a mental patient for nearly twenty years. The experimenters reported that "no influence upon the behavior or the personality of the patient could be detected."[9] Three years later, another study, co-authored by Roswell Johnson, a proponent of applied eugenics, reported "an actual intensification of the homosexual drive."[10] Despite research that proved inconclusive, scientists continued to search for the physiological origins of homosexuality and to administer experimental therapies.[11]

Anthropological Studies of Sex Variance

Around the same time that endocrinologists sought to determine sex differences in terms of a physiological continuum, writing by anthropologists associated with the emergent Culture and Personality school of thought posited a cultural continuum for understanding cross-cultural variations in the expression of sex roles and behaviors. Beginning in the 1930s, their ideas about sex influenced scientists, public policy makers, and the educated public by focusing specifically on cultural and historical factors that gave rise to conventions regarding gender and sexuality. Debates about the relative determinations of biological versus environmental or psychological factors (known popularly as the nature/nurture debate) had occurred among anthropologists and psychologists since the turn of the century. In the 1930s, those arguing against biological determinism began to gain significant ground. Franz Boas was a key figure in moving anthropology away from earlier models of social evolution that presumed that cultural practices emanated from biological determinants.

Boas's influential work gave rise to a trend within American anthropology toward cultural relativism. Boas was a pioneering critic of biological determinism, and he privileged the contingent and culture-bound meanings given to key aspects of human life among discrete groups.[12] In challenging the prevailing evolutionary paradigm, he developed the method of *historical particularism*, which focused on the specificity and integrity of individual cultures, thus countering the comparative method by which evolutionists presumed a linear conception of history and placed all human groups on a single scale of development from the primitive to the civilized. Boas's approach regarded all surviving groups as evolved but in different ways, and it argued against the ethnocentricity of evolutionary anthropologists who viewed non-European peoples as less evolved.

Students of Boas extended his method further by noting patterns of culture and comparing systems of kinship, exchange, language, political organization, and religious rituals. These comparisons allowed them to show what was specific to advanced industrialized cultures and what was shared across seemingly disparate cultures.[13] Several of Boas's most prominent women students went on to examine specifically the roles ascribed to the sexes and the range of permissible and taboo sexual behavior practiced in specific cultures. The Culture and Personality school, with which Boas's students Ruth Benedict and Margaret Mead were associated, emerged principally in the United States during the 1930s as an elaboration of the kind of cultural relativism initiated by Boas. Spanning the social sciences, it combined elements of anthropology, psychology, and sociology to investigate the particular cultural dynamics that gave rise to certain types of personality, starting from the assumption that the personality was shaped fundamentally by culture and that specific cultures imposed a unique "psychological set" on their members.[14]

The study of sex roles and sexual behavior was key to this subdiscipline. Researchers, greatly influenced by Freud, applied psychoanalytical principles to ethnographic material gathered from both "primitive" and "civilized" cultures. The main argument that unified theorists of this school was that personality types were created through a process of socialization that was contingent upon varying cultural conventions. Thus they stressed the fundamental importance of cultural factors experienced during the developmental stages of infancy, childhood, and adolescence.

In 1928 and 1930, Margaret Mead published what were to become classic texts in cultural anthropology. In *Coming of Age in Samoa* and *Growing Up in New Guinea,* she explored children's psychological development in two "primitive" societies, making the point that American norms regarding sex roles, sexual identity, and sexual behavior were, though no more or less meaningful, just as contingent as those emanating from Samoa or New Guinea.[15] In the mid-1930s, Mead returned from fieldwork in the South Pacific to work as a curator at the American Museum of Natural History in New York, and she became an influential authority on cross-cultural comparisons of gender and sexuality. She lectured frequently on cultural variations in sex roles and sexual behavior, noting their implications for life in complex societies like the United States.

In 1935, Mead published another famous comparative study, *Sex and Temperament in Three Primitive Societies.*[16] Through her analysis of three different New Guinea tribes, she illustrated that biological factors were distinctly secondary to psychological ones in determining what she called *masculine* and *feminine* temperaments. Mead found that among the Arapesh, males and females both exhibited a single temperament pattern, corresponding to femininity in modern Occidental cultures, while among the Mundugumors, both males and females exhibited a pattern corresponding to masculinity as commonly defined in the modern West. And among the Tchambuli, both masculine and feminine patterns were exhibited but reversed in relation to the sexes: Tchambuli males approximated what Americans would call the feminine and females the masculine. On the basis of these findings, Mead remarked that temperament was modifiable and variable across cultures. Furthermore, nurture, not nature, gave rise to these differences, even in the domain of sex. Mead's comparative method, popularized in subsequent magazine columns, elaborated Boas's historical particularism by situating sex in the larger dynamics and social organization of a culture.[17]

Mead posited a continuum model for analyzing the diversity of appropriate sex roles in various cultural contexts. She placed human groups as well as individuals on a spectrum of masculinity and femininity according to how various cultures interpreted "natural" (i.e. anatomical) distinctions between the sexes. Comparing her findings from the South Pacific with what she called "complex" societies like the United States, Mead noted that in every culture, the sexes were distinguished as opposites and that cultural systems operated to structure and enforce that opposition.[18] But, she cautioned, since definitions of "masculinity" and "femininity" varied from culture to culture, and since there was no natural dictate as to how the sexes should be organized, there should be greater tolerance of variations. She criticized what she viewed as a common practice of condemning individuals who deviated from given cultural norms.[19]

Referring to her own society, Mead argued that no one was exclusively "masculine" or "feminine." Instead she believed that people were situated in a range, so that a strong woman may be located closer to a prize fighter than a sensitive "Caspar Milquetoast" would be. To underscore the point, Mead pointed out that, according to endocrinology, "each sex depends for full functioning upon both male and female hormones."[20] But, in Mead's view, a woman's "masculinity" was not necessarily a sign of lesbianism or sexual inversion. It merely indicated that some physiological or constitutional qualities we call "masculine" were present in some women, and the inverse was true in some men. As she put it, "it may well be that we could disabuse our minds of the habits of lumping all males together and all females together and worrying about the beards of the one and the breasts of the other, and look instead for males and females of different types."[21]

While theorizing about sex roles, Mead explored the significance of "the deviant" in the final section of *Sex and Temperament*. The deviant, in her terms, was "any individual who because of innate disposition or accident of early training, or through the contradictory influences of a heterogeneous cultural situation, has been culturally disenfranchised, the individual to whom the major emphases of his society seem nonsensical, unreal, untenable, or downright wrong."[22] Mead was disturbed that, in modern Western society, deviant individuals were lumped together under the heading of "neurotic," a category she believed obscured important differences between types of deviants and overlooked valuable human qualities among them. She preferred to distinguish between those who are physiologically weak or "defective" and the "cultural deviant" who is at odds with the values of his or her society but whose difference from the norm may be culturally beneficial.

Mead further argued that societies which assign personality types according to sex "pave the way for a kind of maladjustment of the worst order."[23] Extending her critique to the stigmatization of homosexuals, she continued, "in addition to, or aside from, the pain of being born into a culture whose acknowledged ends he can never make his own, many a man has now the added misery of being disturbed, in his psycho-sexual life."[24] She went on to say that if men were not punished for expressing certain "feminine" traits, there would perhaps be less homosexuality. Here her thinking was consonant with theorists of sexual adjustment from Freud to Meyer to Gilbert V. Hamilton: homosexuality was the sign of an individual's maladjustment to modern pressures. Whereas individual cases may not be wholly "cured," the phenomenon of homosexuality might be eliminated by tolerating greater variation in sex roles as well as by allaying modern stresses that compelled people to conform to harsh conventions.

Like many of her contemporaries, Mead's ambivalence about homosexuality resulted in contradictory theories about its cause as well as its cultural significance. She, too, assumed that it was a problem deriving from sex role inversion rather than a matter of sexual object choice, which could be expressed by someone who appeared to act appropriately for his or her sex. But, like several of her intellectual contemporaries including Freud, Mead believed that "cultural deviants"—including some homosexuals—could offer something of great value to the culture in which they lived since they were clearly independent-minded and not simply following the lulling drumbeat of social conformity.[25]

Overall, Mead's cross-cultural analysis invited a more tolerant approach to understanding homosexuality by calling into question what was "normal" and what was "deviant" based on the diversity of human cultural expression. She was critical of the strictly dichotomized organization of the sexes in American society, believing that it exacerbated problems of personality and social adjustment and stigmatized those who were really only slightly different under the clinical designation of "neurotic" and "psychopathological." It was her goal to loosen the rigidity of sex roles in American society so that boys and girls would be able to express a broader range of behaviors. However, she never let go of the notion that the men and women were fundamentally different, irreducible and complementary, advocating that each sex should be given "its due" and that heterosexuality was the optimal arrangement.[26] Thus Mead's ideas attest to the durability of binary logic surrounding the subject of sex even in the promising field of cultural anthropology. Her thinking invited a later generation of anthropologists to delineate the domains of gender and sexuality, though she, too, lacked a language which would have allowed her to speak of these domains as analytically distinct.[27]

In addition to Mead, a number of other anthropologists contributed to the reconceptualization of gender norms through their fascination with sex-role inversion in other societies. They were particularly interested in examining the socially sanctioned roles for feminine males and masculine females common in many Native American Indian cultures. The result was a burgeoning literature on the *berdache*, a character whose cultural role and identity was the inverse of his or her sex anatomy. In contrast to earlier studies which condemned the *berdache* and the *bote* as evidence of a culture's degeneracy and inferiority, the trend among anthropologists in the 1930s was to approach these examples of inversion with moral detachment. They noted the ways that various societies accommodated sex inversion and even developed social conventions and institutions to perpetuate it.[28]

Cultural anthropologists' writings from the 1930s, when cited in debates about social hygiene and public policy, were often used to make arguments against the criminal punishment of homosexuals. But this more tolerant view ran counter to a prevailing assumption that homosexuality in modern societies was a pathological condition not only afflicting certain individuals but also signaling a society's deeper problems.

Psychological Testing and Psychometry

During this same period, a first generation of academically trained psychologists turned their attention to the topic of sex differences. By deploying recently developed standardized testing techniques, they hoped to understand the relationship between sex and personality. Psychometricians, as they were called, emphasized the virtues of scientifically controlled data gathering and statistical quantification. They described their methods as complementary, if not also superior, to the subjective methods of psychoanalysis and clinical psychiatry for ascertaining knowledge about normal psychological phenomena. Using the logic of reductivist science, psychometry offered a way to isolate, control, and compare factors related to personality development across a range of individuals.

In the case of sex research, psychometry offered what individual clinical histories could not by revealing correlations, norms, averages, and rates of prevalence of particular behaviors within a larger population. Its practitioners believed that psychometry gave a broader, more accurate picture of personality factors distinguishing men and women and could bring to light significant deviations, including sex-role inversion and homosexuality. Psychometry's leading proponents carefully positioned themselves as objective scientists and claimed that psychometric data on sex roles and homosexuality could assist in social engineering efforts to predict, intervene, and eliminate undesirable patterns of deviation.

Lewis Terman, a psychologist at Stanford University, undertook the most ambitious psychometric surveys involving sex roles and homosexuality. Following his earlier research on intelligence testing and gifted children, Terman, who studied the works of Krafft-Ebing, Ellis, and Freud, turned his attention to investigating what he called "sex correlated" aspects of personality development.[29] Terman hypothesized that a child's sex had an important influence on his or her overall development. His research, begun in 1925, was the first major project on human psychology funded by the National Research Council's Committee on Research of Problems of Sex, which had up to that point focused mainly on biological research and animal studies.[30]

In 1927, Terman was joined by his former graduate research assistant, Catherine Cox Miles, and in 1936 their work culminated in the publication of *Sex and Personality: Studies in Masculinity and Femininity*, which reported the findings of over fifteen years of personality differences between girls and boys, and men and women.[31] Having determined in earlier research that intelligence levels were equal between the sexes, Terman and Miles were interested in exploring personality traits as they related to sex differences in instinct, emotion, sentiments, interests, attitudes, and behavior. In doing so, they devised a continuum model with extreme masculinity at one pole and extreme femininity at the other. Terman and Miles used this model to situate individuals according to a broad range of traits they believed were correlated fundamentally to sex, or what we would now call gender. They tested a variety of standardized questions and kept only those to which men and women gave different answers. On the basis of this empirical research, they showed that most men had traits and interests that placed them on the side of masculinity and most women on the side of femininity.

In *Sex and Personality,* Terman and Miles introduced what would soon become the broadly administered Masculinity and Femininity Test, a seven-part diagnostic tool.[32] The "M–F test" was used by a number of researchers and employers from its inception through the 1950s. One shaving cream company required its executives to take the test, while physicians and scientists used it in inquiries regarding homosexuality, delinquency, and paranoia.[33] Referred to officially as the Attitude Interest Analysis Survey, its name was designed to ensure objectivity by concealing the test's purpose from its takers. The survey included a standardized questionnaire for acquiring general information about the test-taker, followed by multiple-choice questions covering emotional and ethical attitudes, interests, and opinions. Among the wide variety of questions posed, subjects were asked to choose, from a multiple-choice selection, what books they preferred to read, what kind of people they admired, what historical events they found significant, and what hobbies they cultivated. In addition, the M–F test included stimulus tests involving word association and ink blots. Scores from the seven components were added together to give the overall masculinity and femininity rating of the test-taker.

The research instrument consisted of questions and possible answers believed to be universally applicable, regardless of specific cultural, socioeconomic class, or age differences among test-takers. Upon close inspection, it is clear, however, that the test was filled with racial and class biases, to say nothing of the gender stereotypes upon which it was constructed. For example, in the Emotional and Ethical

Attitudes portion, where subjects were asked to indicate the nature and degree of emotion they felt in response to words or phrases, "Negroes," along with Burglars and Lightening, were listed among frequent sources of fear.[34]

Based on testing a pilot group of white middle–class adolescents and teenagers, norms for boys and girls were statistically determined. The boys' most frequent responses were classified and counted as "masculine" (worth one positive point) and the girls' as "feminine" (worth one negative point). Choices selected equally by boys and girls were designated "neutral" (worth zero). An individual's F score was subtracted from his or her M score to obtain the total M-F score. For a male to have a high masculinity score was akin to having an above-average intelligence quotient: both were desirable signs of merit and superior adjustment. Similarly, a female with a high femininity score was appraised as normal, even though the test was weighted to give masculine points for answering more sophisticated questions correctly. Hence the test itself was biased in a manner that regarded knowledgeable females as abnormal.[35]

Terman believed that the M-F test, like the I. Q. tests he developed earlier, would be useful to efforts of social improvement.[36] It established gender norms concerning behavior and attitudes that corresponded to stages of normal development, and it determined deviations that might warrant some kind of expert or parental intervention. Terman and Miles had far-reaching ambitions for the test, noting that it could be used "in investigations of the relationship of masculinity and femininity of temperament to body build, metabolic and other physiological factors, excess or deficiency of gonadal and other hormone stimulation, and homosexual behavior, and to such environmental influences as parent-child attachments, number and sex of siblings, sex of teachers, type of education, marital compatibility, and choice of friends or of occupations. . . . In short, the measurement of M-F differences will make it possible greatly to expand our knowledge of the causes which produce them."[37] The test was thus a means to gather data about the differences between typical men and women and to note undesirable trends which social engineering could correct. The authors recommended its use in practical settings such as schools and employment agencies to assist in properly placing individuals according to their interests and needs. Most importantly, the test had a prescriptive agenda, as it was used most often to identify individuals who deviated from norms, and thus it especially signaled homosexual inversion.

Homosexuality was integral to the development of the M-F test: Terman and Miles relied on data obtained from male and female homosexuals to design and validate the test. Here we find an interesting instance of how focusing on "deviant" characters became a means for constituting norms in relation to which the larger population would be measured. The continuum model Terman and Miles used assumed that true male and female homosexuals would be in the middle between normal masculinity and femininity, having personality traits and tastes of the opposite sex. Thus lesbians and gay men were imagined to be in an intermediary position, a notion harking back to the "contrary sex instinct" described in nineteenth-century medical writing. But Terman and Miles also speculated that some homosexuals were normal with respect to gender-specific personality traits. Thus, to analyze this phenomenon, Terman and Miles, with the help of Terman's graduate student E. Lowell Kelly, devised a Sexual Inversion Scale specifically for measuring degrees of masculinity and femininity among homosexuals. It was premised on a dichotomy between "active male homosexuals," who were presumed to be more typically masculine, and "passive male homosexuals" presumed to be more feminine.

To test their hypothesis about gender and personality differences between active and passive homosexuals, the Terman team conducted a study focusing on 134 male homosexuals in San Francisco, some of whom were serving prison sentences for sodomy. They initially classified subjects as either passive or active based upon interviews conducted by an army psychiatrist and Kelly. In contrast to the range of questions regarding gender characteristics encompassed by the M-F test, these initial interviews focused specifically on the subjects' sexual experiences. Thus it is clear that, when studying individuals whom they assumed were members of a homosexual subculture, the researchers privileged sexual behavior as a primary indicator of underlying personality characteristics related either to activity or passivity. That is, for the purpose of labeling each subject as either active or passive, the researchers initially narrowed the range of how gender differences would be measured by focusing specifically on the roles the men took in homosexual encounters as if these were more salient, for example, than the books these men enjoyed or their preferred hobbies. This focus on sexual role reveals how researchers in the 1930s continued to conflate one's preferred role in sexual encounters (i.e., passive or active) with one's overall gender identification (i.e., masculine or feminine).

The initial interviews indicated that seventy-seven of the men played the "female role" (i.e., were receptive) in fellatio or sodomy and thus were classified as passive, while forty-six "active" homosexuals "played the male role in the copulatory act." Eleven prisoners suspected to be homosexual but for whom no information was available as to their role in sexual relations were classified as "doubtful."[38] Once this classification was made, individuals in the two larger groups were given M-F tests.

Test results showed that the passive homosexuals had significantly higher femininity scores, exceeding even those of athletically-inclined women college students. On this basis, Terman and Miles came up with a composite picture of the passive male homosexual's personality. He was fastidious, preoccupied with domestic affairs, preferred feminine occupations, and liked sentimental movies and romantic literature. He did not enjoy aggressive leadership, energetic activity, warfare, adventure, outdoor sports, science, or mechanical things. He was introverted, psychoneurotic, lax in ethical standards, generally lazy, socially maladjusted, nervous, worrisome, anxious, and excessively "sex conscious."[39] In short, the passive male homosexual "takes advantage of every opportunity to make his behavior as much as possible like that of a woman," adopting a "queen" name, mincing as he walks, and engaging in behavior "that often seems exaggerated and ridiculous." Rather than mere affectation, this character's "true inversion" was the outcome of developmental anomalies either in early psychological conditioning or in his biochemistry, and it thus was more fixed than that of the "active" homosexuals.[40]

By contrast, the average M-F scores of active homosexuals were decidedly masculine, exceeding the rate of a comparable group of heterosexual soldiers. However, a few who tested high in femininity were deemed to have been misclassified "passives." The contrasting data between the passive and active homosexuals, the researchers noted, "present a true dichotomy of personality."[41] On the basis of their findings, Terman and Miles distinguished between true *inverts* (i.e., *passive*, feminine homosexuals) and situational or circumstantial *perverts* who were *active* and masculine but who were generally attracted to feminine men, reprising select aspects of an older dichotomy between constitutional inverts and situational perverts posited by Krafft-Ebing, Ellis, and other early sexologists.

A physical examination was administered to determine whether there were constitutional differences that distinguished passive homosexual men from active homosexual and normal men, in part because Terman and Miles were interested in weighing the evidence between "nature" and "nurture" as to the causes of types of homosexuality. Among the passives, examiners found that they were not significantly different from normal army or college men, but they did notice two fairly distinct body types: the small, slender type and the large, fat, voluptuous type. None had defects of the genital organs, but many showed scant distribution of facial and pubic hair, features the researchers suggested might signal certain endocrine disturbances. The research team did not examine the bodies of active homosexuals and offered no specific reason for this oversight. Terman asserted, however, that these men's bodies were probably typically masculine, by which he meant that they were likely to be hairy and muscular, with narrow hips and broad shoulders. The oversight is striking, for what it might indicate about the "active" men's possible unwillingness to be inspected (for which there is no documented evidence but which may have been a factor). Terman's unsupported assertion also signals how his team, having classified these men as having a preponderance of masculine traits, felt confident in assuming, rather than proving, that their bodies showed no apparent signs of sex inversion. These were, after all, men who scored high in masculinity and who took the active role in sexual encounters. In other words, their gender dispositions and their chosen sexual roles made them normal even if their choice of sexual object—other men—did not. In general, Terman was not particularly interested in exploring homosexual object choice as a category that was distinct from gender. What most compelled him was the idea that sexually inverted homosexuals might provide illuminating evidence for understanding sex differences in general.

In their further efforts to develop a Sexual Inversion scale, Terman and Miles turned to women and hypothesized a similar dichotomy between "active" and "passive" types. Initially, they lacked data about lesbians. As a dubious alternative, they studied incarcerated female juvenile delinquents whom they divided into masculine and feminine groups for the sake of developing the Sexual Inversion scale. However, in contrast to the male prison subjects, these girls were initially classified according to degrees of femininity and masculinity in their general behavior and not according to information about their preferred sexual practices. From this we might assume that the researchers saw gender deviance as the central defining feature of lesbianism, and sexual deviance as a secondary characteristic. Or, perhaps because their subject sample did not consist of lesbians per se, the research team refrained from asking inmates about sexual experiences involving other women. It may have been that the reform school officials were not keen to have researchers plant suggestive ideas in inmates' impressionable minds. Or perhaps the researchers were less clear as to what sexual activities between women should be classified as passive and which active. In any case, no explanation was given for why they changed the protocols they had used earlier in the classification of male homosexuals.

Comparing scores of the incarcerated girls to those of a small group of eighteen lesbian volunteers, the researchers simply reversed the hypothesis they had applied to male homosexuals. In other words, they speculated that *passive* lesbians were perverse under certain sex-segregated circumstances such as jails and boarding schools and that *active* or *"mutual"* lesbians were true inverts, with masculine personality traits. Thus, Terman and Miles hypothesized a distinction reminiscent of Krafft-Ebing's contrast between inverts and perverts, emphasizing gender traits as the basis for distinguishing types of lesbians. According to their hypothesis, the invert exhibited inappropriate gender behavior due to deeply rooted pathological factors, while the passive lesbian showed appropriate gender characteristics but turned to homosexual perversity because of unfortunate circumstances or merely transitory curiosity. However, their hypothesis was troubled when, on the whole, the M-F test scores of the group of lesbians indicated a high level of femininity among them.[42] Nevertheless, Terman and Miles persisted in their assumption that the true lesbian was aggressive and mannish.

While Terman and his associates were expressly inconclusive as to the cause of homosexuality, they emphasized that inversion probably resulted from early developmental processes, either caused by psychological or constitutional disturbances.[43] Thus, gender atypicality was the defining feature of true homosexuality, and it warranted greater scientific attention. In their own words, Terman and Miles admitted that the M-F test "does not measure homosexuality, as that term is commonly used, but it does measure, roughly, degrees of inversion of the sex temperament, and it is probably from inverts in this sense that homosexuals are chiefly recruited."[44]

Recommending modes of prevention, the researchers suggested that those who were "potential homosexuals" might be identified through M-F tests administered early enough to correct this "defect of personality." Others deviating from gender norms could also benefit from the test, including those who may later experience unhappy marriages and "other difficulties of adjustment." Indeed, Terman and

Miles's subsequent research on personality factors in marital happiness showed that happily married women tested more feminine than women who were unhappily married or divorced, while divorced men tended to be more feminine than men who were happily married.[45] Thus, to be able to detect deviations early in a child's life would help clinicians to treat them, and it would thus prepare them for adult adjustments to gender-dichotomized heterosexual marriage.[46]

Terman and Miles's continuum model itself allowed for greater fluidity in conceptualizing sex differences, especially compared to the more rigid two-sex model that presumed normal men and women belonged to mutually exclusive categories. But, in spite of this, Terman stressed that the sexes were mainly distinct from one another and that sex-typed behaviors were fundamental, universal, and stable components of the self. In his words, sex-related traits were "not to be thought of as lending to [the personality] merely superficial coloring and flavor; rather, they are one of a small number of cores around which the structure of personality gradually takes shape."[47] Nevertheless, Terman's continuum model suggested that distinctions between masculinity and femininity were not always so clear cut. This was especially apparent when one observed individual cases. By measuring sex differences in terms of norms and averages on a single continuum, the model brought to light cases where traits and interests common to one sex were present in an individual of the other sex. And the model indicated that even "normal" men and women evidenced degrees of inversion.

THE IMPLICATIONS OF RESEARCH ON SEX DIFFERENCES

By the second half of the 1930s, the conceptual insights and methodological innovations from new scientific research on sex differences brought to the United States many of the hypotheses Magnus Hirschfeld had developed in Berlin. His hypothesis that human beings were naturally scattered across a sex continuum was confirmed by hormonal research. Although Hirschfeld had suggested as much at least a decade earlier, American researchers presented evidence to show that masculinity and femininity were abstract and changing categories rather than the expressed essences of an underlying biological difference between men and women. This new evidence helped to make sense of the changing gender roles of men and women in American society, which had been transformed by women's inclusion in the voting polity, their increasing participation in the paid and professional work forces, and their advancements in education. Sex continuum models came to the fore as material conditions placed women on a more equal footing with men than they had been in the past. Research that posited modern gender and sexual norms in some respects undermined many of the assumptions of the two-sex model. But even while differences between men and women were reconceptualized as matters of degree and not kind, the sex continuum models that were developed in the 1930s had not abandoned the notion that men were in significant ways superior to women and that heterosexuality was superior to homosexuality. This had certainly not been Hirschfeld's intention.

With the advent of sex continuum models, differences between the sexes, even as they were reinscribed along fluid spectra, remained mapped in a dichotomous arrangement that suited the general norm of male dominance and female subordination upon which heterosexual marriage and reproductive families were based. Homosexuality became an index for making important distinctions in the constitution of new gender and sexual norms. As in the earlier inversion model, homosexuals were imagined as intermediate creatures situated between normal males and normal females. But the crucial difference in models generated by research from the 1930s was that even normal men and women were discovered to have qualities and characteristics previously associated only with the "opposite" sex. By signifying a middle position between the poles of masculinity and femininity, homosexuals were situated conceptually in greater proximity to the norm than earlier models of inversion had permitted. For if the difference between the sexes was a matter of degree and not kind, then the homosexual could be conceptualized as sharing many qualities with the rest of the population. But, as we shall see, such news did not alter the popular perception that homosexuals belonged to a distinguishable and pathological group, set apart from the normal healthy population. A case can be made, as I do over the course of the following chapters, that conceiving of homosexuals as similar to heterosexuals worried many people. This worry led to renewed efforts to determine and police the difference between, on the one hand, heterosexuals who were deemed to express normal gender characteristics and sexual desire and, on the other hand, those who were assessed as abnormal because they showed "sex variant" tendencies.

None of the insights advanced by the researchers we have surveyed in this chapter were as nonjudgmental about homosexuality as Katharine Davis had been. Endocrinologists persisted in thinking that homosexuals had physiological defects. And the very framework, methods, and conclusions of psychometricians indicated that they saw homosexuals as inferior and defective. Cultural anthropologists came the closest to offering a neutral appraisal. They did so by suggesting that sexual orientation was malleable and that homosexuality, as it was understood in modern societies, may have been the result of inordinately strict customs and beliefs. In other words, the problem lay with the cultural system that encouraged people to deviate from proper sexual desires and to pursue inferior substitutions. Mead's opinion that homosexuals could offer something positive to society by resisting rigid conformity was exceptional compared to the otherwise negative assessments of homosexuality by researchers who analyzed sex differences. But even she voiced reservations about homosexuality and advocated heterosexuality as the best of all possible orientations.

The new conceptualization of sex differences had significant implications for future research on homosexuality. Endocrinologists would continue to do studies to measure and, in some cases, to alter the hormonal levels of androgens and estrogen in homosexuals. Anthropological methods would be used for studying the customs and argot of homosexual subcultures. And the Terman and Miles M-F test would be used as a way to gauge levels of masculinity and femininity among homosexual men and women. All of these techniques were brought together in the most ambitious study of "sex variance" ever undertaken in the United States, an episode to which we now turn.

6 THE COMMITTEE FOR THE STUDY OF SEX VARIANTS

Observing a Subculture of Homosexuality in the 1930s

In 1935, a scientific study of homosexuality, unprecedented in scope and ambition in the United States, was undertaken in New York City. During the spring of that year, the newly formed Committee for the Study of Sex Variants convened for the first time with the broad and formidable aim "to undertake, support and promote investigations and scientific research touching upon and embracing the clinical, psychological, and sociological aspects of variations from normal sex behavior . . . through laboratory research and clinical study."[1] In the spirit of solving social problems through scientific knowledge, the Committee gathered a panoply of experts to acquire information about the practices of a homosexual population believed to be growing in size in the urban context of New York. For the first time in the nation's history, a multidisciplinary group of physicians and scientists seized the opportunity to interrogate and inspect self-avowed homosexual men and women who volunteered to take part in an investigation of "sex variance."

The Committee's founders conceived the problem of homosexuality broadly. Among those who volunteered to pursue research on sex variance were psychiatrists, gynecologists, surgeons, radiologists, physiologists, neurologists, clinical psychologists, an urban sociologist, a physical anthropologist, and a commissioner of the New York City Department of Correction. They made use of new methods offered by endocrinology, psychometric testing, x-ray imaging, photography, and psychoanalysis to study those who varied from norms of gender and sexuality. The coordination of these various specialists and techniques was considered crucial to the Committee's goal of learning more about homosexuality. More specifically, the Committee sought to establish the distinguishing characterological and physical qualities of the "sex variant," their preferred term for homosexuals, through an elaborate series of observations.

As we have seen, during the 1920s and 1930s in the United States, an array of scientific studies were launched to analyze sex differences and sexual behavior that took into consideration homosexuality. But the efforts of the Committee for the Study of Sex Variants reveal, on a large scale, the production of a particular kind of being against which the sex roles and sexuality of the "normal" population was, in turn, constituted. Moreover, never before in the United States had self-avowed lesbians and gay men participated to such a great degree as voluntary subjects of scientific study. While it was unlikely to have been their intention, the candid accounts of these "sex variants" contributed to the scientific establishment of new sexual norms as well as new strategies for ensuring the vitality of heterosexuality.

Reviewing the Committee's broad and multidisciplinary research brings to light key developments germane to the scientific study of homosexuality in the late 1930s. Researchers associated with the Committee, by deploying a variety of discipline-specific techniques, broadened the definition of homosexuality by putting it on a continuum with heterosexuality. The adoption of a continuum suggested that sex variance was far more prevalent than previously believed, while at the same time assuming it was, by definition, a manifestation of sexual maladjustment. In addition, the study was flexible enough to allow its subjects to give rich accounts of their experiences, since researchers were immensely curious about homosexuality and believed that, by focusing on it, they could also figure out what might be wrong with heterosexuality. In the Committee's view, heterosexuality seemed to be imperiled as a result of inordinate modern pressures and cultural taboos that gave rise to "substitute activities," the most common of which seemed to be homosexuality. Researchers wanted to know what sex variants had to say for themselves, believing their impressions and histories would offer useful clues as to the causes of sex variance. Their participation thus unleashed vivid accounts of homosexuals' self-perceptions and sexual experiences not yet presented in American medical texts. But, given the pressure to develop prophylactic and remedial measures, researchers did not interpret subjects' accounts as evidence of benign variation but combed them for indications of the psychological, biological, and social factors that seemed to be interfering with proper sexual adjustment. Thus, as we shall see, the scientific study of sex variants ultimately functioned as an occasion for constructing modern norms of gender, sexual desire, behavior, and identity.

THE FRAMEWORK OF SEX VARIANCE

Several assumptions framed the research conducted under the auspices of the Committee for the Study of Sex Variants (CSSV). First, the Committee claimed a modern and enlightened perspective by approaching the subject as a scientific inquiry into human variance. They agreed that scientific intervention and social engineering would be the best way to manage what they called sex variance. In fact, the psychiatrist George Henry, who supervised the Committee's major research project, remarked that sex variance was more common than most believed and for this reason prejudice and ignorance must be countered through scientific research: "If we could thus divide humans into two groups and if the sex variant were a rare individual, we might spare ourselves unpleasant contemplation by remaining oblivious of the few who deviate from our standards. As a matter of fact the sex variant is not an uncommon person and he is found in all classes in society."[2]

Following from ideas advanced in the 1930s by Bernhard Zondek, Margaret Mead, and Lewis Terman, the CSSV focused not on variations concerning sexual behavior per se but on variations across a spectrum or continuum between pure masculinity and pure femininity. As Henry put it, "there is little scientific basis for precise classification of humans as male and female. Masculinity and femininity are quantitative and qualitative variations. These variations are registered in structural, physiological and psychological attributes which are peculiar to each individual. Regardless of the sex, a person gives expression to masculine or feminine traits in accordance with his innate tendencies to maleness or femaleness and in proportion to the opportunities for expression of these tendencies."[3]

The Committee thus proposed that naturally most men were clustered around the masculine pole and most women around the feminine, but no woman was one hundred percent feminine, nor was any man one hundred percent masculine. In other words, pure masculinity and pure femininity were abstractions, and qualities generally associated with the opposite sex could be found in many individuals. These ideas were supported by recent endocrinological research that indicated significant hormonal similarities between males and females, by psychological research that revealed sex variance in personalities among those who seemed to be anatomically normal, and by anthropological research that suggested that sex roles were culturally contingent and varied from one society to another.

Significantly, neither the Committee's vocabulary nor its conceptual framework distinguished between the analytical categories of *sex, gender,* and *sexuality.* In other words, the Committee conflated *sex*—the biological or anatomical "raw material" differentiating males and females—and *gender*—the system by which a culture makes this raw material meaningful by distinguishing masculinity from femininity in the construction of subjects we call men and women. And the Committee conflated both of these with *sexuality*—the domain encompassing an individual's desires, preferred practices, and object choice or orientation. In other words, while the Sex Variant Committee understood that human beings were scattered across a continuum between masculinity and femininity, it assumed that an individual's anatomy, general behavior, and sexual aim and orientation were deeply enmeshed in the formation of "sex."

As with earlier third sex models, the Committee's conflation of sex, gender, and sexuality manifested itself in the primary assumption that homosexual desire and behavior stemmed from psychical and anatomical sex inversion. Sex variants were seen as falling between the two poles of masculinity and femininity, exhibiting physical, behavioral, and attitudinal characteristics common to the opposite sex. In other words, homosexuals were to be found in the intermediary zone at the middle of the sex continuum. Not only would they exhibit somatic traits of the other sex, but they would invert what we would call, in contemporary analytic terms, their proper gender role, and together these characteristics gave rise to variant sex practices. The assumption, then, was that homosexual men appeared and acted "effeminate," while lesbians were "masculine" and "aggressive." Adhering to this model made it difficult for researchers to explain homosexual object choice in cases where inversion was not apparent. And, symptomatically, they largely overlooked individuals who evinced inversion but whose sexual orientation was heterosexual.

The Committee's preferred term, sex variance, suggested a move away from the mutually exclusive categories of the two-sex model toward a more fluid paradigm that was based on statistical averages. Indeed, by positing a continuum rather than a binary categorical distinction, the Committee advanced a notion of variance which blurred the lines of demarcation upon which most existing models of sexual inversion were based.[4] But by constituting a category of individuals labeled "sex variants," the Committee repeated a common typologizing move based, again, on assumptions about what constituted normal sex anatomy, gender comportment, and sexual practices.[5] The variance model was premised on the notion that the abstract categories of masculinity and femininity were inherently distinct. And although sex differences were seen in terms of degrees, the model rested on a conservative foundation that presumed maleness and femaleness were underlying essences. Individuals with sufficient degrees of each for their sex were deemed normal. Furthermore, heterosexuality was taken to be the norm while sexual attraction between the same or very similar individuals (i.e., homosexuality) was at the very least aberrant, if not entirely inconceivable. In other words, the CSSV assumed that sexual activity between two people required a polarity of "masculinity" and "femininity," even when the partners were of the same sex. Thus they could not understand sex between two equally "masculine" men or two equally "feminine" women and instead strove to classify one partner as relatively more masculine and the other as relatively more feminine. However, at the same time, they had difficulty making sense of masculine homosexual men and feminine lesbians since, according to their definition of the sex variant as an intermediate being, the manly homosexual and the womanly lesbian were oxymoronic figures. To contend with this contradiction, the researchers noted relative differences in degrees of masculinity and femininity in seemingly alike partners and noted that, compared to normal men and women, both partners were in the middle of the sex continuum.

THE BIRTH OF THE COMMITTEE

In 1935, at the age of seventy-four, Robert Latou Dickinson, a gynecologist and outspoken enthusiast for sex research and education, heard about the work of a lesbian journalist named Jan Gay, whose interest in the scientific study of homosexuality had taken her to Magnus Hirschfeld's Institut für Sexualwissenschaft in Berlin. Dickinson encountered cases of lesbianism among his gynecological patients and was very interested in the phenomenon. Like Havelock Ellis, whom he deeply admired, Dickinson believed that the stability and future of modern heterosexual marriage and reproduction were potentially threatened by women's sexual dissatisfaction with men. Indeed, many of Dickinson's patients who complained of such dissatisfaction also showed what the doctor believed were physical signs of masturbation and lesbianism. This spurred his interest in investigating the appeal of "variant" sexuality to what appeared to be a growing number of women. When Dickinson heard of Jan Gay's preliminary interviews of European and American lesbians, he enthusiastically sought to form a scientific committee that would expand and deepen Gay's initial investigation.

Beginning in 1933, Dickinson and the pediatrician Josephine Hemenway Kenyon tried unsuccessfully to get the Committee on Maternal Health (CMH) to sponsor a study of "sexual inversion" under the guidance of Jan Gay and a young gay man named Thomas Painter, a graduate of Union Theological Seminary who was interested in scientific research on homosexuality. The CMH had already been mired in controversy after moral conservatives charged that it was a front for the birth control movement. Taking on a controversial subject like homosexuality seemed utterly imprudent in the view of many of its members. The CMH's official reason for rejecting the proposal was that it was too far afield of the committee's express goals. Undeterred, Dickinson contacted other colleagues in order to assemble a new committee devoted specifically to studying homosexuality.[6] In January 1935, he sent a letter to six prominent physicians and scientists, requesting their participation in an organizing committee for the study of homosexuality.[7] Dickinson suggested that the committee's initial research should be centered in New York City, since Gay's preliminary study had included many "sex variants" living there and also because the city was full of experts suited to the task of furthering her research.

Jan Gay's involvement with the CSSV was crucial in many ways, but most significantly, she was effective in recruiting self-avowed homosexual men and women to be studied. By the age of thirty, Gay had interviewed some three hundred lesbians she met in Paris, London, Berlin, and New York. Born in 1902 to American parents in Leipzig, Germany, Gay began her career as a reporter in 1922 for the *Chicago Examiner*. She wrote several children's books as well as *On Going Naked*, a European travelogue advocating nudism which caused a scandal in the United States during the early 1930s.[8] Before her writing career began, she changed her last name from Goldberg to Gay, and she lived for many years with her lover, an artist who went by the name of Zhenya Gay and who illustrated all of Jan's books. She belonged to a world of bohemians who were interested in art, literature, and science, especially as modern developments in these areas elucidated aspects of the psyche and identity. Her special interest in homosexuality led her to devote nearly five years to reading scientific and popular literature on the subject at the New York Academy of

Medicine, the British Museum, the Bodleian Library at Oxford University, the Bibliothèque Nationale in Paris, and Hirschfeld's Institut für Sexualwissenschaft in Berlin.[9]

Hirschfeld's influence on Jan Gay was clear. Like him, she venerated nature for its beauty and its evolutionary variations, sentiments she expressed in her studies of nudist subcultures around the world which she described as in harmony with nature and more evolved than the sexually repressive societies that condemned them. And she, too, believed that scientific explanations of sex variance would engender greater tolerance toward lesbians and homosexual men. At a very practical level, Gay's interviews were based on survey methods developed earlier by Hirschfeld to analyze variations in "sex instinct."[10] But Hirschfeld himself had no direct involvement in the CSSV research. In 1933, just two years prior to the founding of the Committee for the Study of Sex Variants, Hirschfeld's Institut für Sexualwissenschaft was destroyed by marauding Nazi students who believed it was a center of immoral and degenerate thinking. Even though the Sex Variant Committee's principal study was based on the very same tenets as Hirschfeld's institute, he is not mentioned nor is there any reference to the destruction of his institute either in the Committee's main publication, *Sex Variants*, or in archival material about the study. Hirschfeld, deeply demoralized, died in exile in Paris in 1935, the year the CSSV was founded.

Gay prepared a manuscript based on notes from interviews she conducted and on her library research. Around 1935, it was tentatively accepted by a London publisher, and she went to work verifying her initial research, which had been based on assumptions, observations, and a review of existing scientific and medical literature on homosexuality. Robert Dickinson read the manuscript and became interested in undertaking thorough research on the subject of homosexuality. He was intrigued by Gay's work but believed that the study of homosexuality ought to involve trained experts. Furthermore, Dickinson thought that because of its controversial subject matter, a committee assembled to study homosexuality needed to acquire legitimacy by including particularly prominent scientists and physicians. Dickinson's efforts were largely successful on this score; his initial organizational meeting included the distinguished psychiatrists Adolf Meyer of the Henry Phipps Clinic at Johns Hopkins University, Clarence O. Cheney of Columbia University Medical School, and Edward A. Strecker of the University of Pennsylvania. In addition, notable psychologists Lewis M. Terman of Stanford University and Carney

Landis of Columbia University School of Medicine were included, as well as Columbia University anatomist Earle T. Engle and New York pediatrician Josephine Kenyon.

At an initial meeting, the gathered experts agreed that, because of the multifaceted nature of homosexuality, additional outstanding experts should be included. Among those invited to join were psychologists Catherine Cox Miles (Stanford), Robert Yerkes (Yale University), and Karl S. Lashley (Harvard). The invited psychiatrists were Eugen Kahn (Yale University), Harold D. Palmer (Penn), Robert W. Laidlaw (Columbia), George W. Henry (Cornell), Marion Kenworthy, and Karl M. Bowman (Bellevue Hospital). Social psychologist Dorothy Swaine Thomas and sociologist Maurice R. Davie, both of Yale University, were invited as well as Harvard anthropologist Earnest A. Hooton. Endocrinologist Philip E. Smith from Columbia University and New York City Corrections Commissioner Austin H. MacCormick, who served under Mayor La Guardia, rounded out the list.

All but Yerkes accepted the initial invitation.[11] Yerkes, then head of the Rockefeller-funded Committee for Research on Problems of Sex, had been stung by earlier controversy over Gilbert V. Hamilton's qualitative sex research in the 1920s, and he perhaps felt that formal affiliation with a committee focusing on the taboo subject of homosexuality would compromise his own authority and that of his committee. His official response was that the work of the CSSV "lay outside the scope of the National Research Council." He nevertheless approved of the Committee's efforts in general.[12] Although only a few of the CSSV executive committee members actually conducted research under its auspices, they oversaw several research projects and, more importantly, gave the study of homosexuality more legitimacy than it had previously enjoyed in the United States.

In spite of the participation of esteemed experts, the Committee was largely unsuccessful in its appeals for financial support from established scientific funding sources and charitable organizations. Although the Committee's name shielded it from some criticism by disguising the subject of homosexuality under the term sex variance, its focus made it too controversial to support. Grant applications to Yerkes' Committee for Research on Problems of Sex were routinely rejected, as were applications to the Commonwealth Foundation and the New York Foundation.[13] The CSSV met a similar fate in additional efforts to get money from the newly renamed National Committee on Maternal Health. In late 1935, Dr. Raymond Squire, the

Executive Secretary of the NCMH, reported that certain members of his committee "would not wish to feel that the two committees were directly associated in any way." Initial donations to the Sex Variant Committee were paid through the NCMH, whose lawyer subsequently strongly recommended against routing contributions and payments to the Sex Variant Committee through it, both because this arrangement made the NCMH potentially liable for its debts and obligations and he feared that its focus on homosexuality would alienate the NCMH's supporters.[14]

CSSV members regarded the lack of support from charitable foundations and science funding agencies as evidence of the taboo surrounding homosexuality, which contributed to the dangerous ignorance they sought to eliminate.[15] To overcome the lack of funding, in late 1935, Robert Dickinson came up with the idea that the Committee "find wealthy homosexuals who would be interested in our work," and in 1941, George Henry reported that the Committee's extensive research on sex variants was made possible by an anonymous "private citizen, a man of outstanding breadth of vision and filled with enthusiasm for scientific research."[16] All told, the cash donations amounted to a mere $7,500, which was spent entirely on the Committee's major endeavor, the study supervised by Henry and presented in *Sex Variants: A Study of Homosexual Patterns*.[17] The Committee depended entirely on the volunteer work of many clinicians and researchers, and on small anonymous donations which came from wealthy homosexuals who welcomed scientific study. For these donors, not only was science a possible defense against club-wielding policemen and impassioned anti-homosexual moralists, but it also offered a seemingly sympathetic and objective way for homosexuals to understand themselves. That Jan Gay and Thomas Painter were involved in the initial stages of the research lent it credibility in the eyes of other lesbians and gay men.

CENTERING THE STUDY IN NEW YORK

Through the formation of the Committee for the Study of Sex Variants, a web of expertise was woven together, drawing in professionals who represented various disciplines, universities, clinics, hospitals, and municipal offices. While their affiliations extended to institutions along the northeast seaboard and California, the Committee was concentrated in New York City and was shaped by the city's particular history and context. Since the turn of the century, particular problems faced by the city inspired newly trained physicians, scientists, and social scientists to design and implement ameliorative reforms intended to improve the standard of living among New Yorkers. Modern initiatives in social engineering, mental hygiene, and public health placed scientific expertise at the center of social reform. Aggressive attempts to institutionalize these innovations were undertaken in New York, where a mixture of private philanthropic and municipal and state support led to a broad social welfare system that counted on the involvement of university-trained professionals to carry out its goals.

By the 1930s, many scientific reformers had taken positions in leading academic, medical, and governmental institutions based in New York. Columbia University attracted leading academics and students in the social sciences who were interested in applying scientific methods to study social problems. Medical schools associated with Cornell, Columbia, and New York University operated in conjunction with large public hospitals in the city.[18] During these same years, reform-minded city officials promoted the idea of scientific management as an antidote to the corruption they associated with Tammany Hall and its vestiges in Jimmy Walker's mayoral regime of the 1920s. Researchers from leading universities on the East Coast used New York City as a field site for studying the dynamics of the American "melting pot."

The CSSV was comprised of progressive men and women interested in contending with social problems through scientific study and intervention. A majority were American-born Protestants from the northeastern and midwestern United States whose academic training in the sciences and medicine was completed around the turn of the century. Many came to New York City and were members of a newly professionalized class trained to assist individuals in adjusting to the conditions of modern urban life. They were joined by similarly inclined European émigrés whose training particularly in psychiatry and psychoanalysis substantially influenced American ideas about homosexuality.

While some believed that sex variance was related to hereditary and congenital factors, others focused on family and parental relations as contributing causes. Having been influenced by psychogenic theories, several CSSV members were particularly interested in the dynamics of childhood development. Three of the four women on the committee—Thomas, Kenyon, and Kenworthy—had expertise in this area. Their combined knowledge of pediatrics and child psychology was central to the larger inquiry. Dickinson also recruited specialists in the closely related fields of obstetrics and gynecology, whose expertise was encompassed under the rubric of maternal and child health. Gynecologists, he believed, could also assist in determining any distinguishing features of female sex variants, including genital or reproductive abnormalities, as well as signs of homosexual "sex play" on the genitals.

Biologists and physiologists were included in the inquiry for their knowledge of endocrinology and the bodily processes of sex differentiation. Urologists specializing in disorders of the male reproductive system were enlisted to study any apparent genital anomalies among the male subjects. Experts in constitutional medicine, associated with the Constitutional Clinic at Columbia Presbyterian Hospital, assisted in classifying and measuring the physique types of sex variants in efforts to correlate body form with behavior and personality traits.[19] Practitioners of constitutional medicine were advised by Harvard anthropologist Earnest Hooton, famous for his anthropometric studies of "race mixture" and the physique types of criminals.[20] Social psychologists and sociologists with expertise in the psychological effects of migration and urbanization were recruited in hopes that they could offer insights about social conditions that might be contributing to the purported rise of sex variance.[21] Thus, all of the major etiological theories of homosexuality were taken into consideration in the Committee's overall interest of determining causes and advising on preventive and remedial methods that would alleviate sexual maladjustment.

In addition to being a center of scientific expertise, New York City had a lively gay subculture, especially in Greenwich Village and Harlem. This made the city an opportune place for conducting research on homosexuality. In the decade leading up to the Committee's founding, the Village had become an epicenter for the growing fascination with psychoanalysis and sexuality, and it was where eccentricity, free expression, and opposition to social inhibitions were elevated to the level of art. Poets, writers, artists, and social critics in both the Village and in Harlem, during its Renaissance, explored ideas about sexuality, subjectivity, and modern culture in art, music, and literature. During the "Roaring Twenties," a growing number of tearooms, cafeterias, bookstores, speakeasies, and cabarets catered to a largely bohemian clientele which included lesbians and homosexual men. In addition, certain streets, parks, and waterfronts around the city were known among gay men as cruising spots. "Pansy acts" and "drag balls" provided entertainment to large numbers of New Yorkers, regardless of their sexual orientation. Broadway plays, movies, and novels dealing with homosexual themes and characters attracted significant audiences and critical attention. By the 1920s, gossip columnists hinted humorously about the gay adventures of prominent New Yorkers, using double-entendre and coded references to wink at readers in the know. As George Chauncey has noted, on the whole, New Yorkers were relatively tolerant or oblivious to homosexuality during the 1910s and 1920s. By contrast, during the 1930s, a more overt repulsion and hostility toward homosexuality was expressed in print as well as in the activities of municipal policing officials.[22]

Following the highly publicized trial in 1929 charging Radclyffe Hall with obscenity for writing *The Well of Loneliness*, lurid and morbid stories of homosexuality filled the tabloid press and became common in cheap, popular fiction.[23] During these same years, anti-homosexual attitudes among conservative moral reformers and a growing number of middle-class New Yorkers were validated by the actions of various municipal agencies aimed at protecting property values and ridding the city of disorderly behavior. Mayor Fiorello La Guardia's platform of reform targeted municipal corruption, vice, and immorality as inimical forces facing New Yorkers. As part of his campaign to clean up the city, LaGuardia ordered police crackdowns on public displays of homosexuality, which encompassed not only sexual relations but also cross-dressing in public or in unlicensed entertainment venues.

As the devastating effects of the Great Depression plagued New York City, anti-homosexual moralists fueled homophobia by casting homosexuality as a symbol of the immoral excesses of the Roaring Twenties that led to the stock market crash of 1929. Homosexuals, seen as flamboyant and indulgent, were scapegoated as menaces to public hygiene and morality. As a result of this prejudice and La Guardia's aggressive policing campaigns, increased arrests for homosexual-related activities, generally classified as sex crimes, fueled the dual perceptions that homosexuality was actually increasing and that it represented something as horrific as rape, lust murder, and sexual assaults on children.[24]

Growing contempt expressed toward homosexuality in the 1930s shaped the work of the CSSV in a number of indirect ways. Although most committee members opposed the hysteria whipped up by anti-vice reactionaries, their expertise on homosexuality was actually augmented by the increased public vigilance against homosexuality. Independent of the CSSV, several of its leading members had been asked by Mayor La Guardia to look into the social and psychological dynamics contributing to rising rates of sex offenses, which encompassed consensual homosexuality. Karl Bowman, as head of the Psychiatric Division of Bellevue Hospital, coordinated a pilot program to test and treat sex offenders for underlying psychiatric problems. Bowman worked on this issue with Austin MacCormick, who brought to the Sex Variant Committee his credentials and expertise as a reform-minded prison official. Bowman and MacCormick were liberals who advocated sex education for children and adults and believed that the problem of sex offenses could be remedied by rational scientific study and individual psychotherapy rather than regular criminal punishment. But they also acknowledged the public dangers of homosexuality. Along with MacCormick and Bowman, psychiatrist George Henry worked on the La Guardia initiative to expand the purview of forensic psychiatry, a point to which I will return in chapter 8.

The authority of these men on the subject of homosexuality stemmed, to a substantial degree, from their involvement with sex offender rehabilitation plans authorized by the mayor. In very practical terms, their research was facilitated by having access to involuntary research subjects who filled the jails and prisons at higher rates as a result of La Guardia's mandate to apprehend suspected homosexuals. Although they generally regarded homosexuality as psychopathological—a notion they confirmed by pointing to men who were repeatedly in trouble with the law—Bowman, MacCormick, and Henry speculated that sex variance might be remedied by loosening strict social constraints on sexuality in general and by teaching the population about sex in rational ways to avoid the occurrence of what they referred to as unhealthy and immature substitutive sexual behaviors. They were able to assume a position of benevolence by distinguishing themselves from vigilantes, while at the same time operating within a medical model that defined homosexuality as pathological and potentially menacing. They approached it as a telling sign of the flaws of a sexually repressive society which mystified and so idealized matrimonial heterosexuality that many took refuge in sex variance.

Although homosexuality was talked about more openly in New York during the 1930s than it had been previously, popular and police attitudes toward it tended to be more vicious and condemnatory than they had been in the 1920s. Gay life, as a result of this backlash, became more secretive and segregated. What European homosexual rights activists Karl Ulrichs and Magnus Hirschfeld had experienced decades earlier, gay men and lesbians became acutely aware of in New

York during the 1930s: public hostility toward them, abetted by pejorative depictions in the media as well as by concerted police crackdowns and criminal prosecution for obscenity and sex offenses, led many gay and lesbian New Yorkers to see science as a promising means to defend themselves against intensified malevolence. This accounts, in part, for why over one hundred men and women offered themselves as research subjects to the Committee for the Study of Sex Variants, although they received no monetary support or direct benefits for doing so.

THE SEX VARIANT STUDY

Early in 1935, the CSSV identified several studies it wanted to sponsor, though only one came to fruition.[25] This was an augmented version of Jan Gay's initial interviews, which were to be supplemented by a more thorough inquiry into subjects' heredity as well as an array of physical exams.[26] Drawing from her approximately 300 case records, Gay acquired the consent of fifty women who agreed to the examinations.[27] Under the guidance of the CSSV, Gay's study was expanded to include men.

By May 1935, George Henry agreed to take primary responsibility for supervising the expanded research. Henry, then a psychiatrist on the staff of the Payne-Whitney Psychiatric Clinic of New York Hospital, submitted a proposal to the Clinic requesting the use of some of its offices and examining rooms.[28] To persuade Clinic officials of the need for support, his request stressed the medical value of the study in a fashion that underscored the equation of homosexuality with pathology: "Since homosexuality is a form of arrested psychosexual development which seriously interferes with reproduction and leads to personality conflicts often ending in mental illness and many other forms of tragedy, its causes, methods of prevention and the ways in which those already distorted may be aided in achieving a socially acceptable adjustment should be studied with the greatest care."[29] After being assured by Henry that the subjects of the study—whom he described as "well educated" and "socially prominent"—would behave respectably, the Department of Psychiatry at Payne-Whitney Clinic agreed to allow examinations to occur but only during designated hours several evenings a week and on the weekends for the summer months of 1935.[30] The Clinic explicitly stated that it would assume no costs. Eleven doctors from major hospitals in New York City donated their time and labor to the project.[31]

In his public pronouncements of the study's purpose, George Henry made clear that its multidisciplinary research went beyond a neutral quest for knowledge. Rather, he stressed that information gathered from this extensive study was to assist doctors and scientists in identifying and treating patients who suffered from "sexual maladjustment." Moreover, this research would go toward preventing the spread of sex variance through the "general population." In this way, according to Henry, doctors had the duty and capacity to play a crucial role in ensuring the mental and moral health of the community.

Reciting what had become a common refrain among advocates of sexual enlightenment, George Henry, speaking for the Committee, believed that medical and scientific research brought a modern perspective to a problem that superstitious biases, vigilance campaigns, and criminal punishment had exacerbated. It was far better to treat the problem of homosexuality in a humane fashion, making it visible through a wide range of probing techniques. Science would bring what was hidden into the light of clinical research. True to the tradition of progressive reform, this visibility, the Committee believed, promised greater human welfare through knowledge. Thus, in boldly announcing itself to the medical and scientific community, the Committee reiterated a call to discourse. Following the initiative of European sexologists, the Sex Variant Committee sought to wrest the taboo subject of homosexuality from the tyranny of silence. Thus, the Committee was concerned with acquiring as much data as possible, favoring a frank and explicit approach, thorough in its clinical gaze, and not squeamish about sexual details. This led to mobilizing an army of experts to do more and greater listening, watching, counting, classifying, and describing—with the hope of consolidating a range of behaviors and characteristics into a composite picture of the sex variant.

The Subjects

Prior to any examinations, Jan Gay agreed to obtain preliminary information from potential research subjects and to explain the nature of the study to them. While Gay recruited mainly female subjects, Thomas Painter contacted men.[32] Those willing to participate gave Gay and Painter an account of their personal and family histories from which the researchers could discern key aspects of this population, including their "nationalities," occupations, socio-economic backgrounds, and any information deemed relevant to their homosexuality. Subjects of the study ranged in age from twenty to sixty-four.

SAMPLE FAMILY CHART

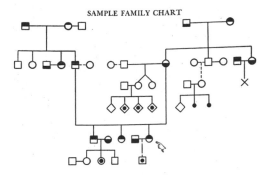

KEY TO SYMBOLS IN FAMILY CHART

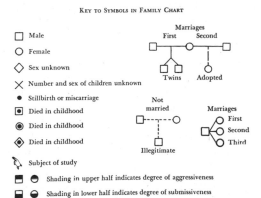

Figure 2. Sample family chart. From Henry, *Sex Variants* (1948 ed.), xxiii.

Many were born in the United States. A substantial number had immigrant parents and were of Italian, Irish, English, Scottish, German, Russian, or Eastern European descent. Included among the subjects were also one African-American man and four African-American women. Information about the ancestry and genealogy of each subject was regarded as central to the inquiry, as researchers entertained the notion that sex variance might be hereditary and the product of mismatched or maladjusted parents. To this end, a pedigree chart was constructed for each subject; it appeared at the beginning of each case history referencing relatives whose characteristics or behavior might have contributed to the subject's maladjustment (see figs. 2 and 3). Thus, for example, incidents of alcoholism, promiscuity, epilepsy, mental retardation, divorce, bisexuality, and artistic tendencies among relatives were highlighted.[33]

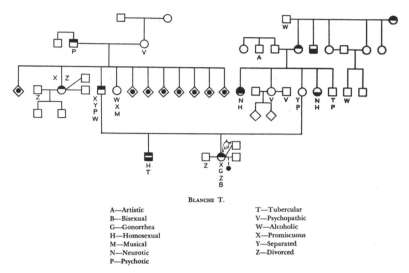

Figure 3. Pedigree chart of Blanche T. From Henry, *Sex Variants* (1948 ed.), 683.

Many of the subjects had been married or had had sexual relations with the opposite sex, and several had children. They preferred homosexual relations, with the exception of three of the male subjects who were included in the study not because they had homosexual experiences but because they preferred to cross-dress as women. The inclusion of these heterosexual transvestites in the study indicates how its theoretical paradigm emphasized gender variance over homosexual object choice as a guiding principle. However, among the sex variant women, there were no such exceptions; all of them had experienced sex with other women and none were selected solely on the basis of their variance from gender conventions, although the experts claimed to find significant degrees of masculinity in each case.

What made the vast majority of the subjects suitable for the study was their own admission of engaging in homosexual sex. Hence, they could function as human specimens to reveal any unique characteristics which researchers could attribute to either lesbianism or male homosexuality. Breaching a key tenet of scientific method, the researchers failed to assemble a control group of heterosexuals against which to compare sex variant individuals. This oversight was perhaps a result of the practical difficulty of recruiting heterosexuals, though no mention was made of this in any of the archival or published materials about the study. At the very least it can be seen as evidence of a glaring blind spot on the part of researchers who assumed that heterosexuality was the norm requiring no particular definition, measurement, or explanation.

In contrast to most existing research on homosexuality, the Sex Variant study included an equal number of male and female sex variants. Previous studies undertaken in the United States had focused on one or the other. CSSV researchers believed that male and female sex variants represented an intermediary sex, sharing similar characteristics of inversion, and this belief inclined them toward studying both lesbians and gay men. But practically speaking, the main reason the study included as many lesbians as homosexual male subjects was because Jan Gay was able to persuade women to be involved. During the 1930s, the familiar avenues used to gather research subjects for studies of homosexuality favored the study of men. In addition to psychiatric patients, experts mainly drew subjects from among prison inmates arrested for homosexual offenses, patients of venereal disease clinics, and individuals expelled from the military. With the exception of psychiatric cases, lesbians were seldom included in these groups. Thus, Jan Gay's connection to the lesbian scene largely accounts for how researchers, who would not otherwise have had easy access to lesbians, were able to examine them, along with homosexual men, in the study.

On the whole, the female subjects differed from the males in several key ways. They tended to have longer lasting romantic involvements with fewer lovers than the men. And they tended to articulate more explicit connections between the oppression of homosexuals and that experienced by other groups, including women, people of color, and political activists on the left. Compared to the men, fewer of them had experienced direct conflicts with the police and a significantly greater number had lovers who were also interviewed in the study.

The Regimen of Data Gathering

The search for signs of homosexuality took the subjects through an assembly line of examinations. First, each subject was given an extensive psychiatric interview. Second, the subjects were given the Masculinity and Femininity Test (i.e., Attitude Interest Analysis Survey), developed by Terman and Miles (see ch. 5).[34] Third, subjects were given a series of general physical exams and tests, including skeletal x-rays, pelvic and physique measurements, metabolism tests, and hormonal assays. Finally the women were given thorough genital examinations which were depicted in minutely detailed sketches and which appeared in a graphic appendix entitled "The Gynecology of Homosexuality." In several cases, male subjects' genitals were measured, their anal sphincters tested for elasticity, and the viscosity of their semen observed, but nowhere near as much attention was paid to them as to the women in this regard, and no visual representations were made of their genitals.[35]

Drawing on both psychiatric interviews and physical examinations, the study was based on correlating the subjects' narrative accounts of their lives with body measurements in order to get a comprehensive picture of sex variance and to develop methods for identifying homosexuals that other physicians might find useful. Therefore, techniques to produce visible differences through anthropometric measurements, drawings, photographs, and x-rays constituted the scopic regime which were compared to the subjects' autobiographical interviews. The imperative to survey bodies was fueled by a kind of scientific scopophilia: the pleasures of viewing were deeply tied both to a positivist quest for the truth in physical evidence and to a desire to read the body for indications of sexual practice. But the importance given to the subjects' own stories indicates that researchers believed the body alone could not provide adequate information about the causes and defining characteristics of homosexuality.

One-third of the subjects allowed photographs to be taken of them in the nude. The photographs were explicitly intended to supplement other physical data and to act as diagnostic instruments for correlating body form with behavior. But since no note was made of which individual was being photographed, no correlations could be made between an individual subject's personality characteristics and his or her specific body. The result, instead, was the construction of a typical or generic sex variant body. To protect their identities, photographed subjects' faces were intentionally wiped out (fig. 4), a technique which had the effect of further rendering them as specimens or objects. Moreover, the photographs were encoded as morbid by their stark presentation at the end of the published findings, where they recall the images of bodies commonly featured in medical textbooks. Thus, their very composition as well as their presentation in the scopic regime invite the viewer to look for and find pathology in much the same way that photographs of prostitutes and criminals were read for signs of atavism and sexual lasciviousness by earlier anthropologists and physicians.[36]

Grouped together with the frontally photographed bodies were

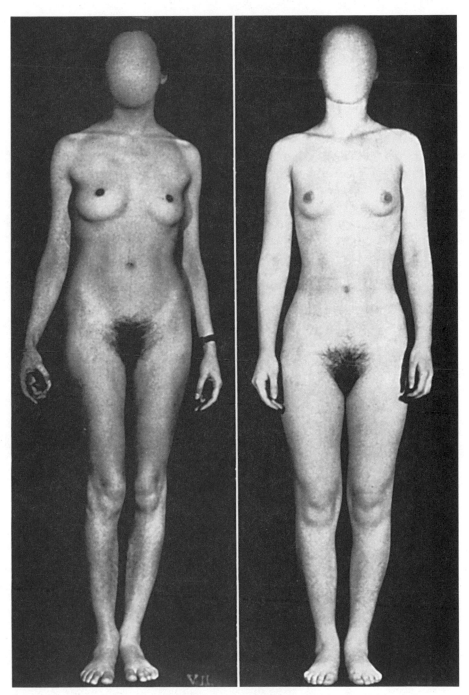

Figure 4. Photos of women. From Henry, *Sex Variants* (1941 ed.), 1044.

several uncanny images that were presented without explanation. While all but two of the photographed subjects appear naked in the text, one picture of a male subject features him in the standard posture but wearing women's underwear (fig. 5). In addition, a rather bizarre triptych features another male subject, adorned in a wig of ring curls and posed in a flowing gown which evokes neoclassical theatrical performance and statuary (figs. 6, 7, 8). In these images, Sappho meets Salome through the semi-clothed subject, who was apparently offered the option of presenting an image that was not conventionally clinical. It remained uncaptioned and thus suggests that such interpretive displays offered some kind of useful scientific evidence. Given the study's express purpose of using photographs to correlate physique with behavior and given that existing physique studies generally relied on naked bodies in order to examine their dimensions unobscured by clothing, the inclusion of clothed and dramatically posed characters is peculiar. Apparently both naked and adorned subjects were regarded as useful in the larger endeavor. At the very least, the inclusion of both types of images suggests that the Sex Variant researchers were as much interested in presenting not just the bare dimensions of subjects' pelves and torso–leg ratios but also the fetishes and dramatic personifications adopted by subjects. This is one of several instances in the text where researchers reveal a confusion over the boundary between inborn characteristics of physique and biology and culturally acquired aspects of clothing, comportment, and attitude.

Each published case history groups extensive text of personal interviews with data from physical examinations. The effect is a contrast between complex autobiographical meditations and reductive notations recording measurements of everything from leg bones to skulls, chests, and body hair distribution.

STORIES GENITALS TELL

In addition to featuring extensive autobiographical material, to which we will turn in the next chapter, another remarkable aspect of the Sex Variant study was its inclusion of detailed graphic representations of female genitalia. As we noted in chapter 4, Robert Dickinson believed that a woman's genitals offered evidence not only of innate deviance but also of deviant sexual experiences. Dickinson wanted to examine sex variant women to see what their genitals might reveal. He was aided by Dr. L. Mary Moench, who conducted the gynecological

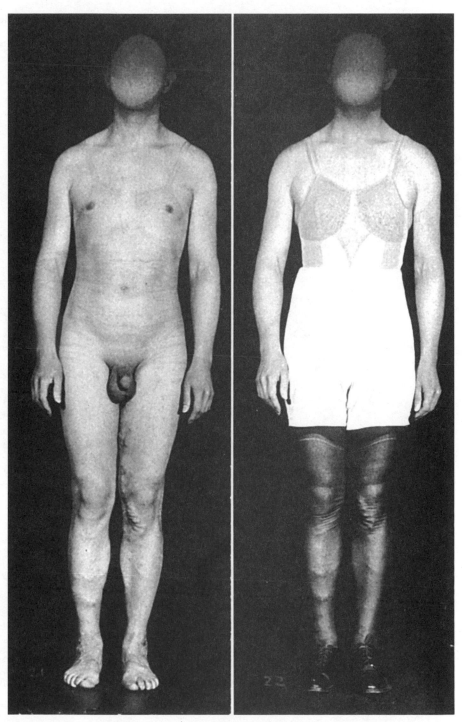

Figure 5. Photos of man in women's underwear. From Henry, *Sex Variants* (1941 ed.), 1053.

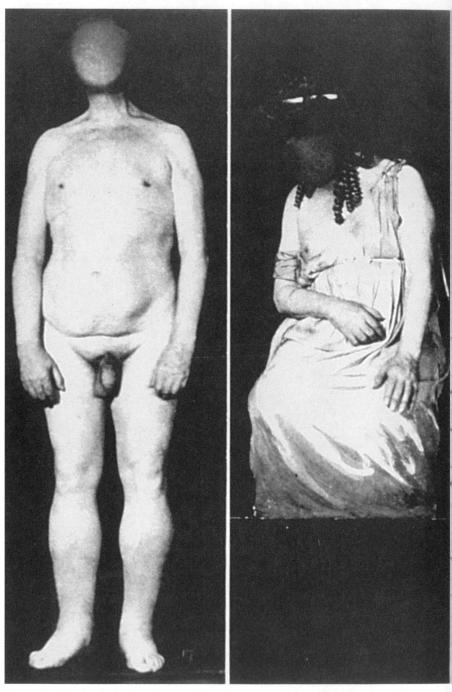

Figure 6. Dual panel photo in tryptich series. From Henry, *Sex Variants* (1941 ed.), 1054.

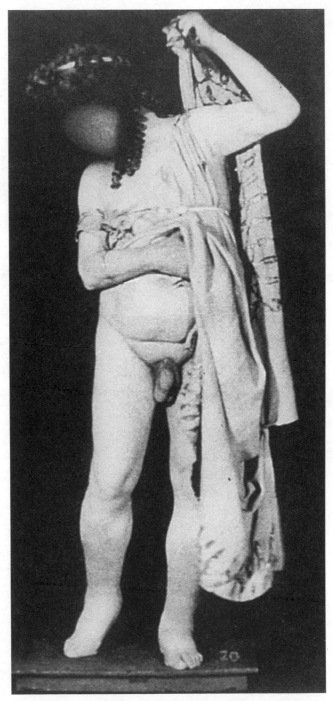

Figure 7. No. 2 of tryptich series. From Henry, *Sex Variants* (1941 ed.),
1055.

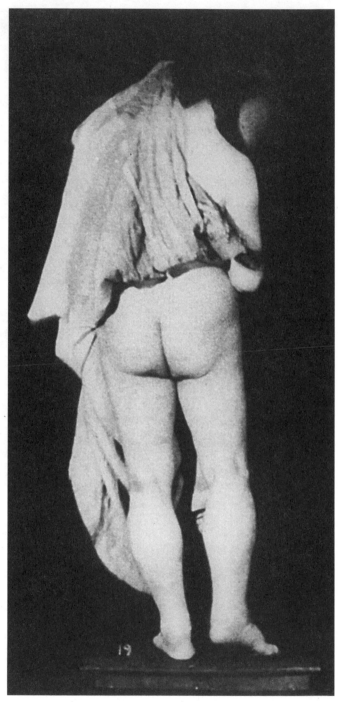

Figure 8. No. 3 of tryptich series. From Henry, *Sex Variants* (1941 ed.), 1056.

examinations of "all but the most vigorous, assertive women" who refused to be examined. All traces of modesty fell by the wayside in the pursuit of accuracy. Dickinson encouraged Moench to measure genital parts using a small ruler and her fingers. Vaginal penetration was measured in terms of the number of fingers the examiner could fit into the subject, thus making the doctor's own body a crucial part of the research. Moench then placed a small glass plate on the vulva, outlining the external genitals upon it in soft crayon, which she then traced on the subject's record sheet. These line tracings were later annotated and enhanced by Dickinson, who noted remarkable or distinguishing features.

Dickinson was intent upon achieving exactitude. In his *Human Sex Anatomy* (1933), he had produced highly detailed sketches of female genitals.[37] Dickinson's sketches illustrate how scientific practices of close observation and detailed recording bolstered the authority of the study's scopic regime. One drawing included Dickinson's careful notation of specific measurements and his recording of the duration of one subject's nipple erection at 70 seconds (fig. 9). Part of his intense focus on detail involved the segmenting of the subject into component parts or zones which could be deciphered. This reconfiguration of the body into territories highlighting breasts, vaginas, clitorises, and labia was itself a powerful act of interpretation on Dickinson's part. He and Dr. Moench assumed that markings in these highly scrutinized areas would reveal what distinguished sex variant women, and thus genitals became indices of moral character.

The gynecological exams gave rise to the wildest speculation about lesbian anatomy and experiences. Regardless of the absence of a heterosexual control group, ten typical characteristics of lesbians were established which, it was assumed, distinguished their genitals from those of "normal women." The typical female sex variant had a larger than average vulva, longer labia majora, protruding labia minora, a large and wrinkled prepuce, a "notably erectile" clitoris, an elastic and insensitive hymen, a distensible vagina, a small uterus, and erectile nipples. The list bore a remarkable resemblance to that assembled by Dickinson's friend and advocate Havelock Ellis several decades earlier.[38]

Dickinson drew a composite sketch of a "normal" woman's vulva that contrasted it to that of a typical sex variant. The terms used to describe lesbians' genitals connoted extraordinary size and hypersexuality. Pejorative adjectives such as wrinkled, thickened, and protruding connoted excess and literally marked the subjects as pathological,

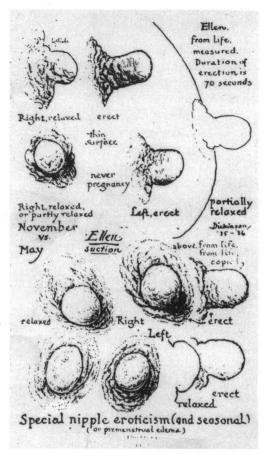

Figure 9. Nipple erection. From Henry, *Sex Variants* (1948 ed.), 1122.

while the normal unmarked female was represented in unmodified terms (fig. 10). Sketches isolating particular genital parts featured the unusual characteristics of particular subjects, and images were captioned with subjects' names and any significant qualities. In one sketch the doctor attempted to represent the action of the clitoris in its so-called "excursions" up and down. Elongated clitorises were noted in several of the African American women as well as some of the white women, perhaps because a few of them boasted about how their lovers really liked them for the fact. Some gynecological sketches noted the race of the subject ("negress") next to what was seen to be an unusually long clitoris (fig. 11), recalling the lesbian counterpart to the stereotypical savage with an unusually long penis. Here, as in

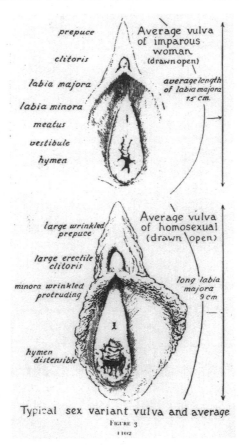

Figure 10. Typical vs. Average vulva. From Henry, *Sex Variants* (1948 ed.), 1122.

other representations combining racial difference and sexual deviance, we find a link in the medical imagination between blackness and hypersexuality, this time through a clinical reading of lesbian masculinity in female genitals.

Dickinson was quite convinced that, like nymphomaniacs, sex variant women on the whole showed evidence of greater sexual excitability, especially when being examined by a female gynecologist.[39] He suggested that an examining doctor might be able to detect a woman's perversion by watching the way she conducted herself during the examination. A habitual rhythmic swing of the hips, unnecessary exposure or exhibitionism, and restless behavior on the examining table could tell the doctor much about his patient even before he had a

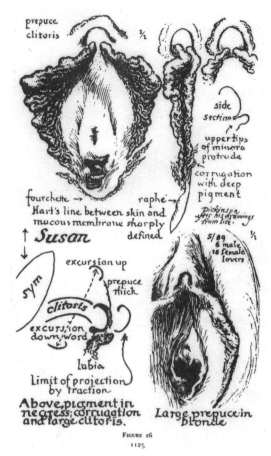

Figure 11. Sketches of "Susan's excursions." From Henry, *Sex Variants* (1948 ed.), 1125.

chance to examine her genitals. Other more minute indications included "marked vulvar hypertrophies," clitoral erections, free mucous discharge, or general signs of vaginal congestion. He warned practitioners to be especially on the lookout for signs of arousal, which could "serve to check up on the statements of the patient, being important chiefly where sexual excitability or response is flatly denied."[40]

In his final report, Dickinson asserted that, for the gynecological exam, the most clear indications of female sex variance were not constitutional or innate hereditary deficiencies but instead those characteristics resulting from what he called "female-to-female sex play"

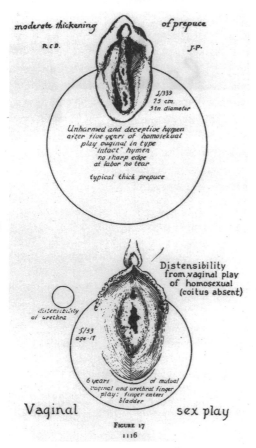

Figure 12. Vaginal sex play. From Henry, *Sex Variants* (1948 ed.), 1116.

(fig. 12). Thus, Dickinson clinically decoded the genital zones of the female body as evidence of a subject's behavior, experiences, and sexual desires, and not necessarily her genetic or congenital makeup. He paid special attention to what he called the "hypertrophy" of the prepuce and the size of the clitoris, characteristics which he asserted were primarily produced by masturbation or homosexuality. Meticulously measuring clitorises and labia, he surmised that variant "sex play" was typically focused on "digital and oral caresses." This was supported by his earlier assertion that the clearest correlation between genital characteristics and experience occurred in cases where he suspected the patient masturbated or engaged in "traction, pressure, or friction."[41]

Dickinson concluded that all of the gynecological findings could be the result of a strong sex urge plus anything from "self-friction" to homosexual or heterosexual sex play. In other words, all of the typical characteristics of female sex variants could result, in fact, from any sex practices other than exclusive heterosexual intercourse in the missionary position. And this is precisely where the logic of the gynecological examinations began to unravel. Elsewhere in his earlier writing, Dickinson had encouraged men to stimulate their partner's clitoris as a remedy for frigidity or sexual frustration (fig. 13).[42] For example, in 1928, he outlined instructions to be given to men who were entering marriages: a man should be aware of his wife's need for "certain preliminaries" to vaginal intercourse:

> Her zones are three: the mental, the surface erogenous area, and the vaginal. . . . The mental zone is stimulated by loving words and an atmosphere of tenderness. The second zone calls for the kiss or deep kiss, the breast caress or nipple excitation, and the vulvar contacts. The third, or vaginal, zone may not become aroused until she has passed through the two preliminary phases of feeling. It is therefore essential that the man should understand the need for special attention to these zones, and specially to the clitoris and other parts of the vulva, during the early weeks and months [of marriage] in order that adequate stimulation and complete climax may be effected. . . . The two-fold preliminaries outlined, and the attempt to lead up to an orgasm with her, may take a considerable time at first, but with training, all comes right. She may also require two or three minor orgasms to his one, to discharge the battery, and to this possibility his attention should be drawn. She may be slow at first, so that ten, fifteen or even twenty minutes will be required. If he cannot wait within, she must learn to reach a quicker climax, and he to wait for her, until the harmonious adjustment has been made.[43]

Several years later in the Sex Variant study, he regarded evidence of clitoral stimulation to be a reliable sign of lesbianism. Many of the female subjects Dickinson examined had extensive sexual experiences with men, making it a tenuous exercise to delineate physical features that could be definitively attributed to lesbian relations. In reality, what he thought were remarkable characteristics distinguishing lesbians from heterosexual women could actually have been put there by a male partner, a female partner, or the woman herself through masturbation. Dickinson appeared unaware of this contradiction in his own thinking between his advice to heterosexual men and what he presented as evidence of lesbian relations.

Although Dickinson did not admit it, over the course of the Sex Variant research, a woman's genitals had become less reliable as

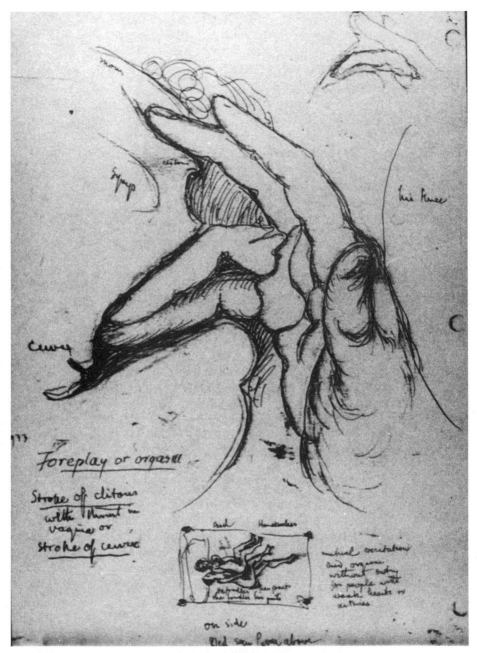

Figure 13. Dickinson sketch of manual stimulation. Courtesy of the Francis A. Countway Library of Medicine, Harvard Medical School.

evidence of her lesbianism, especially if one were to take into account the fact that heterosexual relations and masturbation could just as well have left the physical traces attributed by Dickinson to lesbianism. By themselves, these traces were not absolute evidence of the crucial distinguishing factor of lesbianism—that is, the sexual object choice of a woman for another woman. However, through rendering lesbians' genitals as pathological, the doctor's findings implicitly posited a normal woman who was not only heterosexual but who also masturbated in respectable moderation and whose sexuality revolved around intercourse with her husband, primarily for the purposes of reproduction. Clearly, the normal woman was no less of a scientific construct than was the lesbian.

RESULTS OF THE PHYSICAL EXAMINATIONS

The researchers interpreted the data from the various physical examinations in a manner that reiterated aspects of the earlier constitutional and congenital theories of homosexuality. They concluded that, as a group, both male and female subjects displayed physical characteristics of sexual inversion. For the women this meant the common deficiency of fat in the shoulders and abdomen, dense skulls, firm muscles, excess hair on the face, chest, back, and lower extremities, a tendency toward "masculine" distribution of pubic hair, a low-pitched voice and either excessively developed or underdeveloped breasts. The women's muscles were described as small and firm but angular with "masculine contours."[44] The male subjects showed the inverse pattern, with higher-pitched voices and a general lack of muscle tone. In addition, aspects of general comportment, such as a tendency to swagger or to walk with a mincing gait, were regarded as features commonly found among female and male sex variants respectively. The researchers claimed that these characteristics were observed when all the subjects were taken statistically as a group, but in many cases they strained to find more than one or two of these qualities in individual subjects. Therefore, in an attempt to draw a composite sex variant body, variations among subjects were homogenized in favor of a stereotypical construction of sexual inversion.

The long-standing idea that homosexuals suffered from constitutional nervousness and arrested development lived on in the Sex Variant study's methods and conclusions. In summarizing the vast interview and examination data, George Henry concluded that the sex variant was indeed a distinct type, and a "by-product of civilization" who was unable to adjust to modern society's high standards requiring adults to establish and maintain a home for the proper rearing of children.[45] Echoing a persistent stereotype, Henry referred to the sex variant as immature in sexual adjustment, and he noted that this was obvious in both the psychological and somatic domains. Sex variants had inherited constitutional deficiencies, troubled family relations, and a lack of social opportunities for heterosexual development. By stating this conclusion, Henry acknowledged that both constitutional and environmental factors contributed to homosexuality.

Aggressiveness, independence, sympathies to feminism (also referred to as "sex bitterness"), and the rejection of wifely and motherly duties were listed as attitudinal signs of masculinity common among lesbians. Promiscuity, compulsiveness, and petulance were recognized as typical qualities of sex variant men. Effeminate uncles, domineering grandmothers, spinster aunts, alcoholic mothers, suicidal siblings, tubercular fathers, and even artistic cousins were taken to be indicators that the germ of homosexuality could, like other manifestations of degeneracy, be inherited. Henry credited the family with a dual, if ambiguous, function of, on the one hand, passing down hereditary traits that could contribute to sex variance, and, on the other hand, producing the environment where patterns of deviant behavior could be replicated by offspring who became sex variants. By defining the family's contribution in this dual way, the study simultaneously recapitulated nineteenth-century degencrationist explanations for homosexuality, while equally stressing the significance of environmental and psychogenic factors.

At the level of the body many other indicators of sex variance were discovered. While acknowledging that the physical examinations yielded no conclusive evidence for determining whether a person was a sex variant, Dickinson and Henry noted certain recognizable morphological patterns common to both male and female sex variants. The common presence of broad shoulders and narrow hips in both the female and male subjects was described as "an immature form of skeletal development," and it was taken as evidence that sex variants were at a lower stage of evolutionary development marked by a lesser degree of sexual dimorphism. Noting the accompanying condition of psychosexual immaturity among subjects, the researchers combined evolutionary theories of innate atavism with the psychoanalytic notion that homosexuality was a condition of arrested psychosexual development. In this formulation, refined civilization and heterosexuality were coupled as desirable outcomes requiring some degree of expert scientific intervention in the biological realm of reproduction and in the social or psychological realm of parenting.

Purported evidence of immaturity was gleaned from the gynecological examinations as well. On the one hand, Dickinson remarked that the common presence of an "infantile vulva" and the small uterus were signs of constitutional immaturity or arrested evolution in many lesbians. But while coital pain reported by many sex variant women was seen as a sign of arrested sexual development, Dickinson suggested that this could just as well be a sign of psychological immaturity. Thus a finding of infantilism in the somatic realm was again coupled with a psychoanalytic construction of lesbianism as a stage of arrested sexual development, characterized by a fixation on clitoral pleasure and by the failure to attain the maturity that welcomed vaginal intercourse, childbearing, and motherhood.

HOW RELIABLE WAS THE BODY?

After summarizing the data from the physical examinations and noting that there were significant exceptions to general somatic patterns, Henry and Dickinson concluded that the more "pronounced deficiencies" of the sex variant were psychological rather than physical, and thus that the psyche offered better information concerning who was prone to sex variance, compared to the contradictory and complex evidence of individuals' bodies. Thus, even though Henry continued to endorse the project of looking for signs of sex variance on and in the body, he emphasized that doctors should conduct careful interviews with each patient in order to locate the possible indications of sex variance. Bodies alone would not always reveal innate or distinct features. But, after talking with a patient, the body might be approached in a new way and interpreted to correlate certain characteristics with the patient's own narrative. While the examiner could search for physical patterns connoting innate sexual inversion or constitutional immaturity, he should be advised to look carefully for any indications of perverse practices. In other words, the body did not merely reveal innate features, but was capable of disclosing the marks of its environment and its sexual history. Even then it would not speak entirely for itself, but it could be a grounding point for the narratives of the person to which it belonged.

By the end, both Dickinson and Henry realized that one could not determine whether an individual was a sex variant or not merely by looking at his or her body. Over the course of the research, the goal of establishing a typical or composite homosexual body had been compromised, if not altogether thwarted, by contradictory evidence and exceptions to the study's assumptions. Furthermore, Henry asserted that a great many heterosexuals had constitutional deficiencies, so it was impossible to discern sexual orientation on this basis alone. Since human beings mated "irrationally"—that is, on the basis of desire rather than eugenical efficacy—there were many kinds of constitutional weaknesses throughout the population, and not all of them were concentrated among sex variants, Henry warned.

However, even as the notion of constitutional deficiency was slightly revised to include psychogenic factors, the body became anything but extraneous or obsolete in the clinical study of homosexuality. Instead, as the gynecological examinations show, it became a source of scientific knowledge about deviant practices. Rather than merely revealing congenital or hereditary defects, it came to be seen in terms of surfaces or zones where experiences and behaviors left their marks. Having exhausted the possibility of determining a distinctly sex variant skeleton, pelvis, complexion, or pattern of hair distribution, experts were urged to turn to the body instead for stories about behavior and desire.

In his conclusion, Henry continued to believe it a worthy undertaking to survey the general population in order to identify statistical patterns of sexual variance. At best, however, the typical sex variant could be little more than a statistical construct. The regime of examinations made it apparent that about the only thing sex variants had in common was what Henry called a lack of adjustment to adult heterosexual modes of sexuality. There was so much variety among these people that Henry recommended doctors study each case of sex variance for its particular form and content.

In addressing the issue of how to categorize people, Henry declared that elements of each individual should be studied for their relative degrees of masculinity and femininity. An individual's placement on the sex variance spectrum depended on statistical calculations for each element, which could then be regarded as indices of that person's overall constitutional development and sexual preference. For example, a man's firm muscles and forceful enunciation were taken as signs not only of his masculinity but also his presumed heterosexuality. The same traits in a woman were signs of her masculinity which implied she was a lesbian. But clearly, some subjects had contradictory qualities, with shoulders that might place them in a normal range for their sex but vocal intonations or hair distribution that placed them closer to the average for the opposite sex and thus closer to homosexuality. Contradictions of this sort made it difficult to draw any clear lines either between individuals, or between groups of people. Clearly, the broader implication of this variance model for all men and women was that the line between the sexes could no longer be drawn sharply, nor, by logical extension, could the line between heterosexuals and homosexuals. An important consequence of this was the growing concern in the late 1930s and 1940s that people with homosexual desires may be everywhere and may be difficult to detect.

IMPERILED HETEROSEXUALITY

The paradigm of the CSSV researchers caused them to go to great lengths to tether homosexual orientation to gender and sex inversion. This tendency revealed that the Committee was as interested in demarcating norms of masculinity and femininity as it was in comprehending the distinct qualities that pertained to sexual attractions between women or between men. By focusing on the former, researchers generally believed they were accounting for the latter. In the end, the CSSV's conclusions indicate that remedying the problem of sex role inversion was part and parcel of a larger effort to place heterosexuality (i.e., sexual adjustment) back on a stronger footing. Thus, the sex roles of heterosexual men and women were implicated in this inquiry, given the presumption that a lack of healthy differentiation between males and females in the overall population was contributing to the problem of sexual maladjustment.

The Sex Variant study was thus as much an effort to construct and maintain hygienic heterosexuality as it was to investigate homosexuality. Its conclusions implied that heterosexuality was neither a natural nor guaranteed system but an endangered cultural institution requiring the commitment and effort of individuals and families, and the ongoing intervention of scientific experts. Since their research had indicated that there may not be an innately distinct homosexual body, experts shifted their focus to thinking about sex variance as a product of one's environment and conditioning. Not surprisingly, the family was identified as a site for engineering mental hygiene, and Henry recommended that parents provide proper gender roles for their children.

He strongly urged that to prevent or control sex variance, "all childhood and adolescent emotional attachments must be scrutinized."[46] His conclusion, based on amassing the case histories of eighty sex variant subjects, was that homosexuality began to take hold in childhood and that, once in its clutches, a person would find it increasingly difficult to overcome. Thus, adult observation and guidance of children was crucial to detecting and preventing sex variance at an early age. This careful watching could be done by doctors and other experts, but it would be best to start with parental vigilance. The doctor noted that "there is no adequate substitute for well-adjusted parents. The supervision of the psychosexual development and conduct of children is one of the greatest responsibilities of parenthood. Servants, siblings and other relatives as well as friends often contribute to the psychosexual distortion of children."

Clearly, this strategy of monitoring the children required parents to conform to gender and sexual norms, and it turned the family into a site of surveillance and behavior modification. The ideal domestic setting Henry imagined was clearly based on a model of the nuclear family; extended kinship groupings common among many immigrant and African American families were not effective, in Henry's view, for carrying out the kind of close scrutiny and intervention he advised.

From Henry's perspective, children were to model appropriate sex roles based on watching their parents. He advised that mothers should teach their girls how to perform domestic duties such as cooking and sewing, and boys should learn mechanics and home maintenance from their fathers. Beyond merely instructing children in these ways, mothers and fathers were to display and perform the appropriate attitudes, gestures, habits, preferences, occupations, and hobbies for their respective sexes. In other words, sex roles were regarded as cultural information imparted by the repetitive performance of sex roles by parents.[47] Incentives and discipline were to be designed by parents to reinforce an imitative mode of learning gender. Through advancing a relatively crude behaviorist model, Henry believed that parents would play a crucial role in discouraging sex variance. And by recommending a binary system of sex roles and responsibilities, he reinforced the hierarchical status of men and women in a nuclear family setting, with men heading the household and women carrying on the subordinate duties of social reproduction in the family.

Henry warned that some parents may be starting with a disadvantage if their child had greater levels of masculinity or femininity than were appropriate. Noting that "well-adjusted adult men and women usually have been predominantly male or female from early childhood," Henry commented that "a sissy or tomboy begins his or her psychosexual development with a handicap."[48] If a child exhibited handicaps of this sort, it was the duty of parents to discourage rather than to indulge them, no matter how amusing these eccentricities might be. Similarly, parents should not have—or at least not show— a preference for the sex of a child prior to birth. If they did, the preference would probably manifest itself in later life and negatively influence the child's sexuality in adulthood.

According to Henry, boys seemed to be "more vulnerable to distortion in psychosexual development than the female."[49] Masculine tendencies were therefore to be encouraged in boys and femininity discouraged. He stressed that it was important to dampen rough-and-tumble play and pugnacity in little girls, but boys who acted like sissies were far more likely to become sex variants and thus should be the target of aggressive parental intervention. The road to manhood, in Henry's view, was a perilous one, and masculinity, the more fundamentally valued of the two poles of gender, was difficult to achieve. Femininity, by contrast, was much easier, and in fact was a common pitfall for weak boys.

A few rare children manifested extreme signs of sex variance very early in life, and Henry warned parents that it may be undesirable to steer them toward the "conventional sex pattern." In other words, these children may represent the more acute forms of nature's "byproducts," and, therefore, because it would violate their fundamental nature to force them to be conventional, they should be tolerated. Still others who were in the danger zone, at risk for becoming adult sex variants, should not be pressured overtly one way or another because this may cause a reaction formation which would obstruct a process of adjustment. In the absence of a theory to account for the many different kinds of people who engaged in homosexuality, Henry fell back on a rather simple notion that children who were vulnerable to becoming sex variants need only be encouraged to act in a fashion appropriate to their sex. Given that he also recommended that children who showed clear signs of extreme sex inversion should be tolerated, Henry sent a mixed message to parents. At the very least he implied that parents, with the help of experts, would be able to discern the rare extreme cases from children who were at risk for becoming sex variants but who would conform to proper sex adjustment if steered in the right direction. Given also that Henry believed that sex variance or inversion among adults led to such outcomes in their children, his faith in parents' ability to identify and correct these problems in their offspring was based on rather shaky logic.

Interestingly, Henry never warned parents to be on guard for same-sex sexual activities. While he cautioned against what he called "sex segregation" and encouraged the lifting of restrictions against heterosexual associations in childhood, adolescence, and young adulthood, he said nothing about parents watching for homosexual play or exploration. To dispense with the possibilities of sex variance, parents and society as a whole were to enforce norms of masculinity and femininity and things would generally fall into place.

Henry acknowledged that sex education was also important. This was especially necessary for children of parents who were themselves maladjusted. Henry observed that many of the sex variant subjects he interviewed were confused about sex and maintained what he regarded as superstitious beliefs, especially about heterosexual reproduction, which inhibited them from approaching the opposite sex. In keeping with the idea that sex could be rationally understood, Henry and the CSSV endorsed the frank discussion of sexuality to prepare children for their future lives as reproducing men and women. They recommended starting the process of education in infancy and continuing "until the person is well adjusted to his sex pattern." Although Henry offered no details about the form and content of this education, the doctor advocated candid and ongoing instruction rather than giving children a single course on hygiene which, he noted, often added to the fear surrounding sex rather than allaying it.

As an instrument of social intervention, the Sex Variant study sought to construct and stabilize a system for guaranteeing social order by focusing on the imperative of proper reproduction. Implicit in the study's methods and conclusions was the idea that heterosexuality was itself in trouble, having become adulterated by men and women of mixed national origins and social statuses reproducing defective children in unhygienic environments. Decades after eugenicists had begun to warn that white middle-class heterosexuality was threatened by various "unhygienic" trends, including miscegenation, homosexuality, prostitution, and overpopulation among the poor, the Sex Variant research of the 1930s reiterated many of the same notions. According to this vision, the crucial unit of civilized adulthood was specifically the middle-class white companionate heterosexual marriage which took account of the virtues of pleasure but guided them toward responsible and genetically sound reproduction. That so many of the subjects seemed to come from ethnically mixed parentage and were the products of unstable households led Henry and his colleagues to underscore the need to overcome "irrational" breeding practices among heterosexuals. In his own words, "As long as sex mating continues to be irrational, constitutionally predisposed sex variants are to be expected."[50]

Even though he concluded that sex variance was a form of psychosexual maladjustment, Henry believed that experiences of homosexual men and women offered clues about what might be wrong with heterosexuality. His thinking in this regard echoed insights brought to light by Katharine Bement Davis, G. V. Hamilton, and Robert Dickinson and Lura Beam. In particular, many sex variants offered a model of greater emotional and sexual satisfaction compared to heterosexuals: "the sex variant is more likely to continue with the romantic aspects of affectionate unions and he or she makes full use of erogenous areas which, through ignorance or indifference, are often neglected by heterosexuals."[51] But what sex variants lacked that heterosexuals should strive for was the ability to choose mates rationally based on what would be best for the entire society and for future generations.

This rationality was to include sexual pleasure. In case after case, female sex variants commented on the pleasures of sex with other women that they seldom, if ever, experienced with men. Sex variant men also reported a high level of sexual satisfaction, a matter that was explained away, in part, by stressing their proclivity toward promiscuity and sexual pursuits at the expense of lasting relationships. Overall, Henry and his colleagues were less anxious about what homosexual men's sexual satisfaction connoted for heterosexuality compared to that reported by lesbians. The female subjects' sexual autonomy from men was interesting to researchers who believed it indicated a problem in heterosexual men's behavior. An underlying assumption was that if men were more sensitive to women's sexual and emotional needs, fewer women would take refuge in lesbian relationships. Thus, using sex variance as a diagnostic instrument to discover the general problems of sexual maladjustment involved discovering that among the many obstacles to heterosexual maturity was the fact that many men behaved badly. This revelation contrasted significantly with the elaboration of psychoanalytic notions in the decade after the Second World War, when the onus shifted to women's inadequate maternal behavior as the principle cause of homosexuality in their sons and daughters.

Henry implied that sex variance was seductive. Assuming that the number of sex variants in society was increasing, he warned that, without intervention, more people would be converted or seduced into homosexuality. He cautioned that the longer one engaged in "substitutive activity," the more narrow one's chances of maturing to heterosexuality. Homosexuality was a sexually pleasurable but treacherous trap which attracted the weak, while healthy heterosexuality represented a difficult and hard-won success achieved by those who had the strength to attain it. Henry stressed the happiness promised by heterosexual marriage, which he strongly believed would be a better alternative to the bewitching appeal of homosexuality. He advocated affectionate unions between men and women in which "excessive aggressiveness" and "marked passivity" were replaced by greater parity and companionship. In his view of a new, more rational heterosexuality, harmony and balance would allay irrational desires of passion and lust as well as the imbalances created by overly rigid sex roles. These were the important lessons learned from studying sex variants and taking note of the appeal of love between members of the same sex.

George Henry's conclusions may leave the impression that the CSSV study ultimately functioned to contain homosexuality once again, primarily by means of construing it as an unfavorable consequence of modern developments. But as we shall see, the study also provided a means for sex variant subjects to engage in the terms of how homosexuality was being imagined—to speak through and against many of the existing assumptions about them. What did such an ambitious and probing study offer them? Why did they agree to speak to doctors and to allow themselves to be scrutinized so closely? What were their express motivations and hopes? And what consequences, intended and unintended, were unleashed by these unusual people when asked in great detail about what made them different? These are the questions to which we turn next.

A striking aspect of the Sex Variant study was the willing participation of sex variant men and women who offered George Henry
and his collaborators rich accounts of their lives. Henry characterized
the subjects as mostly "members of the professional classes" and
emphasized that this made them more reliable and trustworthy. In
reality, many worked only occasional odd jobs which brought them
few financial resources, and quite of few had been devastated by the
economic catastrophe of the Great Depression. Several of the women
were close to destitute, and a few of the men were street hustlers eking
out a meager existence made more difficult by Mayor Fiorello La
Guardia's anti-vice campaigns. For some of the subjects, marginal
employment was a choice that allowed them to pursue other interests
in the arts and in leftist political causes. Henry's emphasis on their
respectability was, in part, a rhetorical strategy for ensuring his readers of the veracity of the published study, but he just as often stressed
their "maladjustments" when he appealed to Payne-Whitney Clinic
and other medical institutions for support.

For the most part, the subjects were members of an urban bohemian subculture, and many inhabited downtown neighborhoods. In
interviews, they spoke frequently about meeting other lesbians and
gay men in their travels abroad and at parties and nightclubs around
Greenwich Village, Harlem, and Midtown. Many were part of lively
theatrical and artistic worlds, and they knew each other as friends or
lovers. Their accounts reveal a sense of the rich cultural life of New
York City during the zenith of a modernist outlook which inflected
their interests in self-analysis, in artistic, literary, and political hetero-
doxy, and in scientific inquiry. Many were especially curious about
Freudian psychoanalysis, and they used its jargon and concepts to
describe themselves and speculate on their conditions. At the same
time, many regarded their homosexuality to be the result of "nature"
and not of psychogenic factors.

Out of the hundreds of men and women who were contacted for
the study, ultimately about one hundred were selected and agreed to

submit to the extensive physical and psychological examinations. The histories of forty men and forty women believed to be the most informative cases were selected for inclusion in Henry's *Sex Variants*. Subjects were given pseudonyms in order to protect their true identities, and these names were often denotative of the subject's ethnicity, an aspect that was particularly foregrounded in cases such as that of "Moses" and "Jacob," two Jewish sex variants, and "Rafael" and "Jose," two Cuban sex variants. The case histories of lovers and close friends were cross-referenced in order to highlight any significant features of relationships. The cases presented in *Sex Variants* were arranged according to the extent to which subjects deviated from heterosexual adjustment. The first were bisexuals, or those who "approximated heterosexual adjustment," followed by homosexuals, and finally narcissistic types, which included "those who show eccentricities in psychosexual behavior." Homosexuals and narcissists were deemed to pose the greatest challenges for recuperation and adjustment. Henry admitted that these designations were somewhat arbitrary, but that they "afford[ed] a grouping which should be useful to the reader."[1] They bore only the slightest resemblance to the delineations laid out by Freud and other psychoanalysts for classifying various kinds of arrested psychosexual development linked to homosexuality.

There seems to have been no explicitly coercive force compelling the subjects to participate in the study, nor was any money paid to them. A few viewed the study as an opportunity for general medical consultation and requested blood, urine, and venereal disease tests, though it appears that none received clinical treatment. According to Henry, "most of them welcomed an opportunity to participate in a scientific and medical study of their development and of their problems. Through this study they hope for a better understanding of their maladjustments and as a consequence a more tolerant attitude of society toward them."[2] Because the term *variance* offered an interpretive fluidity and openness, it was appealing to so-called sex variants themselves, especially when compared to the more rigid belief that sexual inverts or homosexuals were of an entirely different and inferior order.[3] Clearly the subjects had many different motivations for participating, but what is striking from the perspective of the present is that they were generally willing to be placed under intense and penetrating observation that many of us today would find utterly intrusive and perhaps even ghoulish.

VARIANT SUBJECTIVITY

The published volumes include over a thousand pages of edited psychiatric interviews featuring the subjects' stories about their family backgrounds, childhood sexual experiences, adult desires, perceptions of their bodies, and opinions about the prejudice they suffered. The interview format closely resembled that of Hirschfeld's written psychobiological questionnaire, but the responses were all the more lively, and occasionally contentious, as a consequence of emerging out of conversations with the psychiatrist.[4] Henry conducted the majority of the interviews, with some assistance from August Witzel of Brooklyn State Hospital, but both doctors asked a common set of questions. They encouraged subjects to narrate their experiences freely, as these accounts were to be an important source of psychological and cultural data.

Henry reasoned that since the interview method was interactive, it allowed the psychiatrist to steer the course of the inquiry, which was especially useful in cases where the subject misunderstood or could not fully comprehend a question. In addition, the free association method was beneficial not only for establishing a good therapeutic rapport between the doctor and the subject; it also helped to maximize the amount of factual information the researchers could acquire from the subject's testimony. Henry believed that it allowed the subject to speak openly without fear of prohibition or judgment since the doctor "showed no reaction to what was divulged other than interest."[5] "To preserve the language of the subject as well as the facts relating to his development," the doctor kept a verbatim shorthand record of these responses which he later edited "to make a connected history."[6] Although Jan Gay's initial questions formed the foundation of the study, the experts controlled the terms of the psychiatric interviews and wrote the final conclusions of each case and of the study. And it is important to note that the texts of the psychiatric interviews represent George Henry's editorial decisions, which were themselves structured by his general assumption that homosexuality was pathological. While the published interviews approximate what subjects' actually said, Henry's efforts to "make a connected history" were acts of interpretation that highlight the fact that we, as readers, are only able to know the subjects through the doctors' solicitation, translation, and organization of their words.

The eighty cases in *Sex Variants* reveal complex aspects of homosexual identities as they were being forged in urban America during the first half of the twentieth century. The autobiographical accounts are structured broadly around modern questions of the self, including not only the generic question of who am I, but also the question of how did I come to be this way? How and why am I different? Is there something wrong with me? Am I a danger to myself or others? Such questions have been central to the construction of modern homosexual identity, strongly influenced as it has been by scientific and medical discourses. Evidence of a particular kind of subjectivity—one which we could call *variant subjectivity*—becomes evident from the ways that subjects addressed these broad questions through their responses to the particular interrogatories of the researchers.[7]

In what follows, I trace instances of the interplay between, on the one hand, medical experts intent upon identifying symptoms and prescribing remedies and, on the other, the men and women who resisted such reductions even as they were drawn to scientific inquiry in hopes that it would be liberating. Foucault has written of a "reverse discourse" by which "homosexuality began to speak in its own behalf, to demand that its legitimacy or 'naturality' be acknowledged, often in the same vocabulary, using the same categories by which it was medically disqualified."[8] My notion of *variant subjectivity* derives from Foucault the idea that sex variants made use of medical characterizations of themselves in a variety of ways, some dissonant and some consonant with the assumption that homosexuals were abnormal. But I do not assume that, in expressing their variant subjectivity, the subjects merely "reversed" medical discourse. For one thing, the subjects spoke in a language that had multiple sites of origin and enunciation, including, importantly, the subcultural practices they shared as dissenters from normative regimes of sex, gender, and sexuality. For another, they understood medical discourse as a powerful mode for understanding themselves and for achieving some measure of dignity and respect. Moreover, they, like previous generations of sex dissenters, played a significant role, whether intentionally or not, in shaping the terms according to which homosexuality would be understood.

The interviews published in *Sex Variants* feature homosexual subjects who were not merely docile victims. They were, instead, agents engaged in their own investigations of how they came to desire others of the same sex. A close reading of the subjects' accounts and the doctor's appropriations of them reveals the subjects' articulation of their variant subjectivity. We can find instances, even when the doctor was not specifically opposing the subjects, when the men and women interviewed spoke back against a larger discursive formation emanating from the intermingling of the pathologization of homosexuality and anti-homosexual sentiments present in popular discourse by the middle of the 1930s.

From the very outset of the study, both the researchers and the subjects were curious about the significance and meaning of homosexuality in the broader society. But the two groups had quite different stakes and occupied very different positions in what appeared to be a shared field of inquiry. The experts initially claimed a disinterested concern for acquiring greater scientific knowledge about sex variance, while the subjects approached the study often with very personal stakes, as an avenue of self-enunciation and a forum to engender public toleration. The regime of interrogation and examinations reinforced the different positions of these two groups, the one being occupied by putatively objective experts and the other by their subjects whose first-person accounts allowed them to be cast as partial, and moreover, as afflicted.

Considering the CSSV's opening premise and Henry's general conclusion that homosexuality was fundamentally a sign of pathological maladjustment, it is important to note that the sex variant subjects were situated on an uneven playing field. Add to this the fact that, in the view of the larger society, scientifically trained experts were superior, neutral, and objective in their understanding of the nature of homosexuality, compared to homosexuals themselves. In other words, the relays to which we will turn in a moment—those occurring between the interrogating expert and the subjects—took place in a nonegalitarian discursive and social context. If we grant that the Sex Variant study was a collaboration of sorts, it must be said that this collaboration involved two distinguishable sets of players, the experts and the sex variant subjects. The former enjoyed greater authority and legitimacy to produce truths about sex variance than the latter. Though power was not concentrated exclusively on the side of the experts, they had the final word in summarizing each case, which uniformly consisted of denoting the underlying pathology of the subject.

It is useful to consider Foucault's conceptualization of power here. Power, he noted, is not a possession to be seized, held, or shared. Instead, Foucault spoke of power as "exercised from innumerable points, in the interplay of nonegalitarian and mobile relations." Power inheres in relations and is effected at micro-levels. It effects—that is, it constructs—players in a given discursive field, rather than being a force which they wield. In the relays which follow, I explore how exchanges between the expert and the sex variants are relations of power. In each instance, neither the doctor nor the subject holds power, nor do they simply share power; instead power circulates between them. It does so in a manner that indicates at certain moments antagonism and at others conciliation. Moreover, the collaborative interrogation of sex variance that occurred between the subjects and the expert functioned in multifaceted ways to render sex variance as complex and not, without some effort on the part of Henry, reducible to pathology. As we shall see, the very tendency on Henry's part to make this kind of reduction is detectable from the manner in which the interviews unfolded.

The researchers' posture of assuming scientific neutrality allowed them to veil their own psychological and personal stakes, but their assessments evince some very telling prejudices, blind spots, and anxieties. The sex variants were invited to respond to a set of questions, but their accounts were annotated in a manner that clearly underscored the doctors' equation of homosexuality with pathological immaturity. Indeed, the interviews were presented as patients' case histories and supplemented with data from physical examinations that stressed abnormalities and evidence of sex inversion. At the same time, subjects clearly functioned as ethnographic informants imparting information about a shadowy subculture. The study, which included a lengthy glossary of homosexual slang, was as much an ethnography as it was a medical text.[9]

The edited versions of the case histories occasionally reveal tensions between the experts and the subjects. Working with the text of the interviews, one can locate various dynamics of conflict and compliance where variant subjectivity is articulated. In many of these same moments, it is possible to witness a pronounced uneasiness in the doctor which tends to precipitate his effort to restore order by applying medical diagnoses to the subject. In what follows, I refer to these instances as *relays* to highlight exchanges of power and to analyze unsettling tensions between the subject and the doctor, while both parties are ensconced in a discursive process of accounting for sex variance. As we shall see, the texts of the interviews reveal the constraints imposed on the subjects by the equation of homosexuality with pathology. But they also reveal the possibilities offered by such an open inquiry to counter or strategically appropriate assumptions about the pathological nature of homosexuality.

Relay 1: Desire in Excess/Mountains of Lesbian Flesh

Each of the published case histories began with the doctor's "general impression" in which the interviewer summarized his initial survey of the subject, noting any unusual signs which might be related to "sex variance." He frequently noted aggression, excessive size, masculine gait, and forcefulness in the female subjects and weakness, insecurity, flamboyance, and mincing gait in the male subjects. While these were taken as signs of sex inversion, the doctor was perplexed when subjects or their lovers boasted about these anomalies and excesses or displayed them with a flourish. In addition, he was not always sure of what to make of the subjects' descriptions of their lovers as both "feminine" and "aggressive," or "masculine" and "sensitive" since these couplings were, according to existing logic, internally contradictory. This point was evident in an interplay between the psychiatrist and two white women, Ursula W., an accomplished violinist and composer, and Frieda S., a sculptor:

> *[Doctor's] general impression:* Ursula is a short, stocky woman of thirty-two who heaves broad shoulders as she swaggers into a room. After expressing her regret that she had agreed to participate in this study, she gradually . . . talked easily and freely. She was much interested in the various examinations and asked many questions. Much of the time she had her arms akimbo with her hands resting on her hips. Her hands were in almost constant motion and there were tic-like movements of the fingers. She smoked one cigarette after another, stopping every now and then to hitch up her dress as though she were wearing trousers. (808)[10]

Elsewhere in the volume the doctor offered his impression of Frieda, Ursula's lover:

> *[Doctor's] general impression:* Frieda is a small woman of twenty-eight whose long black hair is graying. She has the pallor, softness, and the general timidity in bearing of an oriental woman. . . . Frieda's artistic productions have attracted attention because they are so masculine. For many years her work was believed to be that of a man. (700)

When readers return to Ursula's case history, they find her waxing expansive about her desire for Frieda, and doing so by appropriating the terms "femininity" and "aggressiveness" which she might have detected the doctor would use in his attempt to make sense of lesbian desire. With teasing aplomb, Ursula talked about femininity and virility as if they were perfectly compatible:

I found Frieda, the grandest person in the world. She's tiny and very feminine, a fine artist, very virile and aggressive, my equal in aggressiveness and not at all possessive. . . . Love is a form of madness—every part of the body becomes beautiful—caressing and kissing all parts of the body. This is the greatest love of my life. . . . My sex life has never caused me any regrets. I'm very much richer by it. I feel it has stimulated me and my imagination and increased my creative powers. (814–15)

Ursula refused the standard opposition between femininity and aggressiveness. In addition, she was aware that researchers were very curious about how lesbians had sex. Hence, in responding to the direct question of how she experienced pleasure, Ursula spoke not about genitals but instead territorialized the lesbian body as capable of polymorphous desires and satisfaction. To amplify the mystique, she narrated her lesbian desire in relation to creative powers, explicitly negating tragic or pathological definitions of homosexuality.

Meanwhile, Frieda offered an account of her attraction to Ursula that emphasized her desire for mannishness and that reveled in Ursula's excessiveness. In what appears to be a playful anticipation of the curious doctor's disbelief, Frieda produced a hyperbolic description of her lover:

At twenty-six I found Ursula, a woman I am actually in love with. . . . According to [my friends] she is a big, bold, mannish, fat woman who heaves into a room like a locomotive under full steam. . . . To me this force, this energy, this bigness and boldness are tremendously attractive. My admiration for bulk is such that I really enjoy getting into bed with this mountain of flesh. . . . She is 100 percent masculine, both mentally and physically. . . . I am convinced I will never again be interested in a man. I'm sure I would like to spend the rest of my life with Ursula. (706–707)

Mountain of flesh indeed. Unapologetically, Frieda claimed her love of mannishness and bigness in women in a manner that seemed to both address and counter the conventional presumption that desires of this sort were pathological.

Indeed, in his closing summary of Frieda's case, the doctor pathologized her desire for Ursula by using her own words to reduce it to an obsession:

Having thus disposed of men there was nothing left [for Frieda] but the conquest of virile women, of those who had the force, strength and bulk she lacked. . . . She had developed a strange obsession for flesh. Ursula, a big, bold, mannish, fat woman, has satisfied her desires. (710)

Here, in a rather typical fashion, the doctor countered both Frieda's and Ursula's confidence and desires by casting them as pathological symptoms. In so doing, he revealed his limited ability to comprehend lesbian desire, and, moreover, proved to be impervious to the subjects' humorous hyperbole.

Relay 2: A Compound Riddle of Femininity

Several of the male subjects embraced the role of "woman." This meant not only cross-dressing but often taking the "passive" (i.e., receptive) role in anal sodomy or the "active" role in fellatio. According to their own subcultural formulations, many sex variant men associated these acts with the "feminine" role in sex. Thus, for example, Antonio L. (Tony) and Daniel O.'L., two drag queens, explicitly disclaimed their masculinity by appropriating the feminine position. These two friends, who worked the streets together as transvestite prostitutes and went to "drag" masquerade balls together, expressed their desires to play feminine roles:

> [Tony]: I would like to be a girl. Being like this ain't getting me nowheres. Being a girl I would be more satisfied. I like to wear girl's clothes and at home I regularly wear complete female attire. In sex I act as a woman. I want to be the woman. (422)

> [Daniel]: . . . Soon after coming to New York I began to dress up as a girl. I went to a masquerade ball with another boy who dressed as a girl. At the ball the fellows asked us to dance with them. I like to dance with men if the other fellow leads. I have no trouble following. It comes natural. . . . Men about forty or fifty years old used to pick us up on the streets or in saloons. They usually wanted sodomy. I didn't like them but just did it because I needed the money. Occasionally one of these men would want me to play the active role but I never cared for it very much. There is much more pleasure from passive relations and I never cared for a person who did the same things I did. (432)

George Henry described the friendship between Tony and Daniel:

> Over a period of several years Tony has been associated with Daniel, a young man with long eyelashes and girlish complexion. Tony has publicly championed Daniel and, whenever there was any question of insult or fight, Tony presented himself immediately for 'her' protection. As they sat at cafe tables or appeared at costume balls they were a somewhat ludicrously contrasting pair. Daniel set off an evening dress with such authenticity that Tony, with his bulging muscles in chiffon sleeves and with his torso threatening dress seams, was in comparison a cheap travesty. (423–24)

Henry assumed that, by taking up feminine roles, Tony and Daniel suffered from self-degradation and self-humiliation. That both men had resigned any hope of being masculine was a clear sign of their psychopathology. In his summary of each case, Henry stressed their abjection, despite the fact that both men, while acknowledging the hardships of living as prostitutes, also spoke of the pleasures they experienced. Daniel told the doctor, "When I go to bed with this man I'm living with we lie face to face, kiss and embrace and get excited. Then I lie face down or sometimes I put a pillow under my hips and hold my legs up. This gives me more pleasure because we can kiss and embrace. It's more like being a woman. . . . I am contented this way" (434–35). And Tony recounted that "I like old men. I like them because they admire my body and because they give me presents and pay me well" (419). Henry concluded Tony's case by noting that "with dissipation and with neglect of his physique Tony is gradually getting flabby and unattractive. He is being displaced by younger men. He has now practically resigned all claims to masculinity. He would like to be a girl; he acts and dresses as a woman; in the sex act he is a woman" (424). And about Daniel, Henry remarked:

> He is dutiful and submissive; even in his sexual embraces he approximates a woman as closely as possible. . . . The probabilities are that he will in a few years need help. He is now dependent in large part upon his physical charms and these will soon fade. As he becomes less and less attractive his promiscuity will be with those on a lower and lower social scale. His physical deterioration may be hastened by venereal disease. (437–38)

In short, like women, their happiness depended on their ability to attract men. While this was normal for women, for men it was, in Henry's view, absolutely not. Henry worried that Tony and Daniel combined the promiscuity common among men and the weakness of will and excessive vanity common among women. This, coupled with the fact that they were part of a lower class milieu characterized by loose morals, made Tony and Daniel a danger to themselves but also, Henry suggested, perhaps a danger to the larger society which would be degraded by unbridled immorality and by rising rates of venereal disease.

Relay 3: The Mincing Gait

George Henry commented in detail on the demeanor and comportment of the most effeminate male subjects. In these passages, Henry's uneasiness is unparalleled in his description of the female subjects, from whom the psychiatrist seemed to enjoy a greater sense of his own psychological distance. By contrast, when introducing several of the effeminate men to the readers, Henry's discomfort was pronounced when he noted how these subjects trailed behind him in a "mincing gait" on their way to the interviewing room.

The demeanor of Percival G., a forty-six year old former matinee idol, provoked Henry to comment at length on the subject's mannerisms:

> On seeing him in action no one would have any doubt as to why he has been called a sissy and the discerning would now recognize him as an 'aunty.' He talks in a chatty, gossipy manner with a soft, high-pitched voice which has a suave, syrupy quality. While talking he holds against his upper lip an extended index finger, an affected gesture of delicacy in exposing the mouth. The superlatives, 'terrific,' 'tremendous,' and 'horrible,' as well as the expletives, 'Oh my God' and 'Oh my dear' characterize his speech. His clothing and his posture are accentuated by theatrical details and his gait includes enough girlish movement of the hips to give him a decided 'swish.' (477)

Henry noted that Percival exercised his own rather unnerving powers of observation, which were difficult for the doctor to interpret: "His glances also suggest the sly, scrutinizing habits of homosexual men who study other men without disclosing their particular interests" (477). The doctor found himself in the rather confusing predicament of suspecting he was the object of male desire, a situation which placed him in the position women most often occupy. Hence, he was made the invert by the desiring, if ambiguous, male gaze.

There is a tone of uneasiness in Henry's description of Victor R., a male prostitute who ran a small-scale prostitution ring. In introducing Victor, Henry noted that "[Victor] speaks with a high-pitched voice and snivels as he talks. In his posture and gait he seems uncertain. He walks two feet behind the physician. In general he gives the impression of not only being a passive victim of circumstances but also a defeated person" (440). Victor ran a male "house of assignation," which was no more than a fixed-up tenement apartment in midtown Manhattan. Rather than conducting the interviews at Payne-Whitney Clinic, Henry, assisted by his fieldworker, conducted several interviews at Victor's "headquarters," ostensibly because Victor was very busy and erratic and could not be counted on to meet his appointments at Payne-Whitney. The unusual interview arrangement allowed the researchers to observe Victor's home and daily habits, the details of which became central to the doctor's description of Victor as a typically effeminate male homosexual.

Like Percival, Victor's features and facial expressions, as well as his living and working accommodations, were read by Henry as an index of his maladjusted personality:

> The kitchen was furnished in tenement elegance with new linoleum on the floor, an icebox and brightly painted kitchen table and chairs. Victor was proud of his establishment. He considered it to be one of the better of its class. . . . A glimpse of Victor's usual environment may serve as a background for the personality characteristics which are peculiar to him. Victor is now twenty-three years old. He has a weak, girlish face with an embarrassed smile that shows his teeth and makes him appear to have low average intelligence. His curly dark brown hair through its disarray gives him a distinctly feminine appearance. His skin is pasty and sallow. His mouth is small and his chin is pointed. (438–40)

A tone of class condescension is evident in Henry's description of Victor's abode, which is interwoven with a pitying portrayal of Victor's dissolute character.

But in contrast to Henry's impression that Victor was a defeated person, Victor described himself as a man who really enjoyed dressing in women's clothing and teasing fellows sexually. He talked about his homosexuality and line of work in a matter-of-fact tone, acknowledging the difficulties of social stigma while at the same time saying he had no regrets. This outlook, together with his livelihood, earned him the distinction of a "by-product of civilization" in Henry's opinion. But in spite of his judgments about Victor, Henry knew this man was an important informant who, in the course of telling his own life story, gave Henry an elaborate picture of the world of male prostitution in New York City. When asked about it, Victor described the details of how he ran his business:

> I furnish male prostitutes to my clients. I have eight or ten boys working for me. They average twenty years of age and they are tall, strong, and heavily built. Few of them are homosexual and they have relations with men in order to earn money. I get the boys by cruising Riverside Drive, Forty-second Street, the parks and the cafes. . . . Frequently such boys blackmail or threaten their clients to get money. I try to get a more honorable class of boys. Many of my clients have been coming to me for several years. They return to me because they know my boys can be trusted and because I have frequent changes and always some new boys. . . . All kinds of sex are available at my place but the more

frequent calls are for active fellatio and passive sodomy. Occasionally there are men who simply want to caress the body of a beautiful young boy and once in a while there is a call for a boy to beat a client. (445)

Victor distinguished his handsome boys from "homosexuals" (i.e., effeminate men) based on the fact that the former engaged in these activities primarily for money and otherwise could pass as straight men. In the subcultural parlance, there were a variety of terms for distinguishing types of men who engaged in homosexuality. Gender was the primary means of making distinctions (i.e., masculine versus effeminate men), but socioeconomic class and age differences also figured in the denotation of a variety of sex variant identities. For example, young working-class prostitutes who were masculine were not necessarily seen as "homosexual" but merely as hustlers, not to be mistaken for sex inverts. Their middle-class clients were frequently assumed to be "homosexuals" (i.e., gender inverts or sometimes manly men who sought "rough trade" hustlers for transitory sexual pleasure). Effeminate types in the world of male prostitution were called "fairies" or "drag queens" and were assumed to be exhibitionistic and the most pronounced culprits of indiscreet public sex. Thus, Victor's subculture shared with dominant discourses the idea that effeminate "homosexuals" were notably deviant while those who practiced homosexual sex but were masculine in comportment belonged to a different (and more "normal") class of men. The latter were less despised largely because they repudiated the connection between femininity and male homosexuality in favor of valorizing masculinity. The denigration of femininity played out in prestige systems within Victor's subculture, reflecting the sexist devaluation of women in the broader society.

Following Victor's account of his social milieu, Henry concluded the case by interjecting a warning about the dangers posed by this world to the welfare and safety of the larger society:

Victor's autobiography is a typical account of the way in which a boy may drift into a life of male prostitution. Poverty, subnormal intelligence, and low moral standards are common factors in the transition to male prostitution just as they are in female prostitution. Victor's subsequent homosexual career is typical of the male prostitute in any large urban community. Periodic raids by the police do little more than shift the scene of his action temporarily. When the authorities close one homosexual rendezvous another springs up overnight and word of its location is passed from one client to another. . . . The menace to society comes chiefly through the seduction of adolescent boys who are often thereafter drawn into male prostitution, and from the spread of venereal disease which is about as common among male as among female prostitutes. Society has thus far devised no effective measures to protect itself from this menace. (450)

While Henry used Victor's story to sound this alarm, Victor stressed that he was providing a vital service which was in demand. This same point was emphasized by Peter R., a self-avowed opportunistic fashion model who slept with men and women in order to enjoy certain privileges, including cash. Victor, Daniel, and Peter frankly stated that they served all kinds of men, including those who were married, had children, and appeared perfectly normal. This information fueled Henry's worries that homosexuality had invaded the mainstream and thus represented a growing threat to the innocent and to society as a whole.

Relay 4: Homosex Made Explicit

The subjects' candid stories of sexual encounters exposed readers of Henry's *Sex Variants*—many of them curious but secretive homosexuals and bisexuals—to the experiences of homosexual drag queens as well as "rough trade" prostitutes working the streets of New York. Henry's case studies may have underscored popular fears, but they also brought many obscure aspects of gay and lesbian life into the light of greater visibility. The subjects' accounts also gave rise to another unintended effect of the text: *Sex Variants,* though published by the medical branch of Harper and Row and aimed at an audience of trained experts, was read by the general public and offered the possibility of one-handed reading for many who found explicit discussions of sex intriguing and titillating. Indeed, for several generations of lesbians and gay men, the book has functioned not only to provide reassuring evidence that there are and have been others like themselves, but it also has been a source of erotica, offering engrossing and pleasurable reading.[11]

Indeed, a major portion of the interviews involved subjects' descriptions of their sexual desires. They were asked to explain in detail what kinds of sex practices and partners they preferred. In this section of the interviews, tensions between the doctor and interviewees were more intricate and embedded in pathologizing discourse, as subjects spoke back in anticipation of the doctor's desire to define the normal and the abnormal at their expense. In these instances, many narrated their homosexual desire in detail, being campy and jocular as well as introspective. In response to questions about passion and pleasure, some seized the opportunity to be iconoclastic or scandalous, offering tales of group sex, bisexuality, promiscuity, prostitution, intergenerational love affairs, and sexual relations with married men and women.

For example, Reginald M., a thirty-five-year-old businessman, described "mass sex" in graphic terms to the inquiring psychiatrist:

> Several times in the last two years I've indulged in mass sex. . . . Those participating are in a large circle, a daisy chain, on the floor unless the host provides mattresses and sheets. Generally they start with sixty-nine but any form of sexual relationship may be practiced and sometimes both sexes are observing or participating. (398)

To which the doctor responded in his summary: "[Reginald] requires maximum stimuli to obtain satisfaction. . . . He has had his fun; sex is now little more than a compulsive act. He is bitterly disillusioned" (402).

Henry characterized Reginald as defensive, defiant, selfish, and hardened as a result of his promiscuous sexual experiences. The great detail with which Reginald recounted his sexual encounters not only gave the doctor the impression that the man was ruthless but that he was typical of a group of homosexual men who roamed the streets in search of sex. Reginald anticipated a reaction from the doctor:

> I've had homosexual relations six or eight times a week. I know that sounds astounding, Doctor, but that continues up to the present moment. . . . At times I pick up men on the streets and in the theater but mostly at bars. A queer person can almost instinctively sense another. At a bar it is simple. You have a few drinks, look over the crowd, see someone you like and then buy him a drink. (397–98)

In his account, Reginald spoke freely about his many affairs and described the ways homosexual men recognized each other in public amidst the flow of oblivious heterosexuals:

> On the streets all queer people look at every man that passes. One look is enough. They keep on walking and then look in a window. If a man is interested he will stop and look back. No normal man will turn to look at another. (398)

Reginald acknowledged that this ability to recognize another homosexual man was linked to a survival tactic. When he was in the company of his family or professional colleagues, he was "on guard all the time lest something should be revealed. I watch every gesture and manner of speech" (399). He also admitted to feelings of disgust at

himself because he could not overcome his "abnormality," and beseeched the doctor to tell him "How do I stand in your eyes? How
much do I reveal to the average man. That's what interests me." At
the same time, about his homosexuality he said that "I have no desire
to change my tastes. If I had to do it over again I would be the
same" (399).

Reginald concluded the interview by explaining that his biggest
problems were linked to a colossal misfortune he experienced in the
stock market crash, which left him penniless with a sense that the
future looked empty. Nevertheless, Henry appropriated Reginald's
feelings about the business failure to describe the inevitable sadness
caused by homosexuality:

> Reginald's affairs seem to have been carried out in a spirit of bravado
> and to have been largely for physical satisfaction. Sometimes he felt
> disgusted with himself but there is no evidence that he made any effort
> to change. He wished to be bold and wicked, to compensate for the
> insecurity which had troubled him from childhood. Reginald correctly
> visualized his future—it looks empty. There is no affection in connec-
> tion with his relationships and even if he could maintain himself in
> comfort he would have little incentive [without having a family].
> (401–402)

Many of the male subjects, in describing positions and sexual activities they enjoyed or were willing to do, distinguished between certain
acts according to the level of intimacy they felt with their partner.
Some men, like Daniel, performed fellatio and allowed themselves to
be penetrated only when they had strong affection for their partners.
Otherwise, mutual masturbation, penetrating another man, or getting
fellated were ways of maintaining emotional distance, and sometimes,
of enacting psychological control over a partner.

Graphic stories about childhood sexual experimentation are a pronounced feature of many of the case histories. Henry's questions
placed particular emphasis on this topic mainly because he, like many
other psychiatrists of his time, believed that homosexuality could be
the result of perverse experiences in childhood. A few of the female
sex variants reported lesbian experiences with schoolmates, girlfriends, and even sisters prior to adulthood. And among the male
cases, explicit descriptions of early homosexual play are practically a
staple. Reginald offered this tale of his precocious homosexuality:

> When I was about seven I started a friendship with a boy which lasted
> twelve years. Within a year we were practicing mutual masturbation

and had other sexual relations, lying down side by side. He was a year older and probably took the initiative at first but later on I did. At ten we were practicing mutual fellatio three times a week. A third boy two years older joined us when I was twelve, still in knee pants. . . . We had many masturbation parties and used to line up to see who could shoot semen the farthest. The three of us continued these parties three or four times a week for about four years. (395)

In medical discourse as well as popular lore, masturbation and homosexuality were often linked as forms of perversion which weakened men's constitutions and minds. This idea persisted well into the 1930s and appeared in some of the subjects' accounts. For example, Rafael G., described by Henry as a twenty-three-year-old handsome Spaniard, recounted stories about early sexual experiences which he believed were responsible for his sense of dissipation:

From the age of twelve until nineteen I practiced masturbation twice a day. I stopped because it was making me sick. I looked very bad. I read in a book that it was very bad—that it would make you go crazy or have tuberculosis. I was troubled about this because masturbation is my preference. The more I do it the less I am interested in other forms of sex. . . . At sixteen I practiced sodomy for the first time. I was with the Boy Scouts in the country. One boy would pretend to be asleep and the others performed sodomy. I enjoyed it. This boy liked it that way. . . . Only one of my brothers participated. He said it was all right to take the active role. (387)

Antonio's story of being seduced by an older man also stoked Henry's fear that homosexuality was caused by predatory adult men corrupting young boys for life. However, in Antonio's own account, he described the early experiences with "Dirty Bill" in terms of sexual excitement rather than of trauma:

When I was nine an old man on a boat would have me come down to see the boat. I didn't know anything about the queer life then. Every time he would have me down there he would kiss me and feel my body and my behind. I used to go down to the boat and shut the door. This boy told that he saw this man kiss me. That day I played with his privates. I used to call him "Dirty Bill." When I was naked with him there was a thrill to me as much as to him. He just went between my legs, face to face. . . . Since then I have liked old men. (419)

The experience of having sexual contact with adult men left very different impressions on the female sex variant subjects compared to those of most of the male subjects. Antonio's sense of thrill about being seduced by an older man was certainly not present in the stories told by the female subjects molested against their will by older men. Similarly, Walter R., a black man whose maternal grandmother was a slave, hated the childhood experience of being raped frequently by an older English man under whose charge he was placed because Walter's mother could not afford to care for the boy. In Walter's case and those of many of the female subjects, episodes of childhood sexual trauma were compounded by deeply rooted social inequalities based on race and gender which separated them from their molesters. Henry, while sometimes sympathetic to those who experienced abuse in childhood, used this information to emphasize the tragedy of their homosexuality, affording survivors little room to appreciate their adult homosexual desires as in any way positive. Instead, these desires were frequently regarded as symptoms of maladjustment and Henry, like many other authorities, associated them closely with child abuse: both were unhealthy outcomes of immature psychosexual development and were seen as directly contributing to one another.

Even in the face of Henry's tendency to pathologize homosexuality, many subjects described their sexual preferences as healthy for them, thus countering the notion that heterosexuality was preferable for everyone. As if to warn the doctor that she had no intention of being "cured" or reformed out of lesbianism, Myrtle, a black vaudevillian, traced her precocious desires, embracing them as inborn and crucial to her health and well-being:

> I can't remember when I wasn't interested in women. When I was six I used to stand on the fence and look admiringly at all the women who passed. Even earlier than that I had a lively curiosity about the bodies of little girls. When I was eight I tried to have sex with a little girl. I've played with little girls since I was big enough to raise a hand to pat them and I ain't never gonna stop! . . . Titty calms me. If I can't have it every day I get evil. (778, 782)

Prompted by the doctor to give graphic details of their sex lives, subjects also described innovative sexual positions and fetish items they used. Rose S., a thirty-five-year-old Jewish businesswoman, told of enjoying penetration with sex toys her lovers designed and crafted especially for her. Besides having a candle that could be bent so that it could penetrate both Rose and her lover at the same time, another lover gave her the gift of a homemade dildo:

> It was made out of a rubber hose and a condom was used over it. She painted it to look like a penis, the color of the skin. It took a genius to make it look as much like a man's organ as it did. (929)

In summarizing her case, Henry opined that Rose "tried to enhance her masculinity through an artificial penis," and he expressed concern over a common tendency among some female sex variants to appropriate the phallus and thus render heterosexual men dispensable. Rose told him that "since the first affair with a woman I have wanted to be a man in order to give more pleasure to women. I like the thought of being able to seduce women and to penetrate them and of doing all the things that men do" (929). At the same time, she explained that "I have gradually broken down the antagonism to men and I have grown to enjoy a man's body. I've learned to enjoy men sexually. I never thought I could do that" (929). She had engaged in menage-a-trois with several married couples, and she credited one of the husbands for teaching her to appreciate men sexually. About this couple she said: "They are respectable people and have two lovely children. I've had invitations from others like them. There are so many women in New York who want to know about it. I don't know why" (930). This admission earned Rose the diagnosis of narcissism with rebellious tendencies.

Relay 5: Playing Roles and Confusing Binary Oppositions

Subjects often described how their relationships were shaped by emotional and sexual role playing. For example, Irene, a middle-aged businesswoman, recounted the ecstasy of sex with a lesbian lover whom she could treat as her "son" by day but at whose passionate mercy she would be by night. Borrowing the notion of a "maternal complex" from psychoanalysis, she offered a subversive spin on the family romance:

> A girl twenty-eight years old wished herself on me. . . . For a year she wore boys' clothes and I introduced her as my son. That satisfied my maternal complex. She was powerful and aggressive as far as sex was concerned but in everything else she was completely childish. At night she was a giant and in the day a little child. . . . She was an insatiable little wench and I was burned up most of the time. I wanted so much to play with this youngster that I didn't care whether I worked or not. We stayed in bed for two or three days at a time, repeating our sex play. I never before knew what real sex excitement was. . . . I never knew that anybody could set up a current of electricity such as this girl did in me. And I loved her little soft hand as well as her mouth. (757)

Henry picked up on Irene's suggestion that her desire for this young woman was a form of maternal passion when he concluded her case with these lines: "In her love affairs, she has arrived at a compromise.

Emotionally she has taken over some of the functions of both her father and her mother. She has a daughter and a son and a lover combined in one person, a person with whom she can, in sex orgies, disregard convention" (760). From the doctor's point of view, Irene's main motivation in love and sex was summed up as immature defiance, a diagnosis that emptied out the pleasure and passion of her love affairs with women and contradicted Irene's own claim of happiness.

In the framework of the study, the terms active and passive generally corresponded to masculinity and femininity. However, again and again the subjects deployed these terms and altered their meanings. In many instances, they described their sexual preferences not only in terms of homosexual partner choice but in terms of the role or position they most enjoyed. Hence, their explicit narratives of sex introduced possibilities unforeseen by the doctors. Subjects often expressed a fluid or contextually specific desire to be passive one moment and active the next. This fluidity confused the doctors who had not adequately separated the complexities of gender from those of sexual object choice or sexual role.

For example, Rowena K., a married woman who told of having an ongoing affair with a woman in another town where she took her daughter to weekly tap dancing lessons, explained: "We have mutual mouth relations. We do sixty-nine or take turns, whoever wants to go first. I get pleasure in the active relationship but more in the passive" (736).

Alberta I., another artist, redefined the terms active and passive in describing herself as someone who was both male and female. This dual identity allowed her to be active, experiencing sexual desire for women the way men do, but having women's superior ability to extend sexual relations for hours:

> I'm active, I'm a very active lover, and I wouldn't dream of being passive. I have no inhibitions about any activity in love. I can stop an orgasm whenever I want to. If I let myself go I can finish in two minutes or I can wait hours. I can realize the physical experience of being a man. I can look at a woman exactly as a man does. I'm really both. I can understand a man better than most women. I feel so much like a man that I don't understand how a woman falls in love with a woman. (861–63)

Interestingly, in this statement Alberta refused the possibility of homosexuality—or more precisely, of sex between two people of the same gender. When she had sex with a woman, she did not imagine herself to be a woman. Hence, she posited a model of heterosexuality in which the partners continued to identify as gender opposites even if they anatomically belonged to the same sex.

Alberta used the term "feminine" in an ambivalent fashion when she described a woman whose beauty nearly overwhelmed her:

> When I was twenty-four I went to a New Year's party and was very bored until very suddenly I saw a woman who simply made me feel faint she was so beautiful. She was thirty-five and had black hair. She looked like a very beautiful cat. She was feminine in a very strong way, not elaborately feminine, not a pretty sort of girl. She was too independent to be feminine. (863)

Henry, rather than addressing Alberta's complex commentary on gender roles, reduced her desire to lust for control of women from whom she acquired artistic inspiration.

Rose's interview also revealed a fluidity of gender identifications and erotic roles. When having sex with other women, Rose imagined herself to embody powerful aspects of both female and male sexuality by having the capacity to give birth while also being able to enjoy the pleasures of vaginal penetration without the presence of a man. Her account highlighted the fantasy of appropriating the phallus from men and allowing it to circulate between women:

> In my relations with [this woman] I pretended I was a man and that I had a penis which penetrated the other woman. She pretended that also. . . . With her body against mine and the clitoris against clitoris the feeling that we were men was much more exciting than the finger. We talked about having babies and giving a woman a baby. That's a common fantasy. (928)

By simulating a male-to-male sexual encounter, Rose's homosexual fantasy radically subverted conventions of gender and heterosexuality: she and her lover were two lesbians pretending they were men engaged in a newly recombinant tribadism. And in the next breath, male homosexuality was followed by the "common fantasy" of female-to-female impregnation. Thus, through her erotic fantasies, Rose disturbed the conventional alignments of the two-sex system out of which the earlier figure of the sex invert had emerged. By contrast, Rose's desires and her bodily fantasies were eccentric and pointed to the inadequacy of equating lesbianism with inversion.

Though she may not have been totally conscious of this, Rose's experiences signaled a dangerous psychosexual chaos, in Henry's view. The doctor summarized her case at length, foregrounding her psychopathic impulses which led her to desert her husband and child for a married woman and to demonstrate her envy of men by cutting off her hair, putting on a tailored suit, and pretending she was a man in sex. According to Henry, her psychological problems were registered in her rebelliousness, her envy of men, and her desire to seduce a young virtuous girl the way she had been seduced. By contrast, as she reported it,

> There have been moments when I have thought it would be very lovely to take a young virtuous girl and seduce her. I've always had a vision of a young girl, aged sixteen, just budding, just awakening to things. I don't think I would ever do it but I think it would be lovely. . . . Just now I feel I would like to be more like a man and have normal sex. You just feel grand and go out and accomplish things. (932)

This finally led Henry to reiterate again the potential threat sex variants posed to innocent children. The danger was compounded by Rose's aspirations to masculinity, he noted.

Henry was also disturbed by another aspect of several sex variants' accounts, that involving sadomasochism. He prompted the subjects to talk about this in the context of describing the roles they tended to adopt in relationships. Henry used evidence of sadomasochistic desires to underscore the psychopathological nature of homosexuality, despite claims by subjects that they engaged in sexual power plays consensually and found them pleasurable. Susan, for example, gave a detailed account of how she became aroused by the experience of giving and receiving pain:

> I like to be hurt, both mentally and physically. One girl I lived with I used to allow her to beat me and pull my hair and be very brutal to me. I liked it. It aroused me sexually. This was the girl I lived with for five years. . . . I'm still very proud of my life. This woman enjoyed beating me. She is very sadistic. Her mother understood and used to come in and say, "You will kill each other" but we liked it and we didn't want to be disturbed. We would pull the draperies down, break the glasses and the lamps, take the tubes from the radio and smash them all on the floor and then sit down and laugh about it—just to excite ourselves. Then we would have sex relations. This would happen very often. I was always very submissive. I was afraid I would hurt her breasts. She enjoyed it. She would bite, use her fists, pull hair, pull it out by the roots. She would hit me with anything she had in her hand, a glass or anything. She struck me with a violin bow and broke it in half. . . . She used to lock me in a closet for at least ten minutes until I would scream and try to knock the door down. I didn't like it while I was in there but I thought it was very thrilling after I was let out—I

was sexually aroused. She wouldn't be angry anymore and we would have sex. She knew it would arouse me and that I wanted it. She wouldn't allow me to go. (914–15)

Henry concluded that Susan was carrying childhood trauma into adulthood. Her enjoyment of playing these power games with her lover and, moreover, her consent to do so were read by Henry as signs of pathology originating in her relationships with her parents. In his terse conclusion, he stated: "[Susan's] homosexuality represents a desire to possess mother, a fusion of the sado-masochistic tendencies in the family and an identification with the father." (918)

Relay 6: Girls on Top

The most remarkable instances of confrontation between the female subjects and the doctor occurred when the subject claimed, as many of them did, that she could do anything a man could do but better. This is particularly highlighted in lesbians' descriptions of their deft love-making techniques and their remarkable genitals. They are discernable because they stir in the doctors a mixture of anxiety, curiosity, and doubt. Myrtle, the black vaudevillian, claimed:

As I started going with women [my clitoris] enlarged itself. [It] enlarges when I get steamed up. . . . I insert my clitoris in the vagina just like the penis of a man. . . . Women enjoy it so much they leave their husbands. My clitoris natural is two inches long. Enlarged it's three inches and the thickness of a little finger. I think it's grown half an inch in the past year. I'll have to get a jock strap if it gets much more. . . . While a woman is going down on me I visualize myself as a man and I talk as if I was a man. I say, "Ain't that a good dick? O baby, ain't that good." (783)

Myrtle's playful tone offers evidence of a kind of resistant counterpoint to the clinical jargon of the experts. Though her intent may not have been simply to scandalize the doctor, Myrtle's vernacular language and humor, coming from a seasoned performer, may account for why Henry seemed particularly unsettled by her appropriation of the penis in her sexual fantasies. The doctor countered her claims by noting, with doubt, that "with her enlarged clitoris, she says she is able to produce orgasms in other women" (777).

Myrtle's self-proclaimed sexual endowment, which she described with glee in the interview, led gynecologists to exam her body carefully. She was one of the few subjects whom the doctors physically stimulated in order to measure the nature and intensity of her sexual response first to the male doctor and then to the female doctor. According to Robert Dickinson, Myrtle registered almost no response to his examination but showed a strong response to Mary Moench's inspection, manifesting "a nipple erection, dusky flush of the vagina, and clitoral erection from 10 x 8 millimeters at the beginning of the exam to 25 x 9 millimeters as the exam progressed." Aside from what this might tell us about Myrtle's sexual disposition, it most certainly reveals the power of her own narrative to incite fascination and to direct the experts' examination protocols.

Henry believed that "Myrtle's rapport with other women is typical of many homosexual negro women," by which he meant that she was generally hypersexual and masculine by nature. Henry and his assistants tended to refer to the African American subjects as promiscuous, reprising the long-standing stereotype of the licentious and well-endowed savage, a highly fetishized figure in modern European cultures. This fetishistic stereotype was a source of power for subjects such as Susan, another African American woman who astounded the doctors when she vividly described her "erect" clitoris which apparently was the talk of the town among her lesbian lovers:

> [My first lover] would lie on top and rub the clitoris. Her clitoris was not well developed but mine was—about one inch—twice as much as the average. When I realized what it was all about I thought I should take the active part. . . . It's more pleasure and more complete when I'm taking the active part. I like girls who have lots of experience. It saves a lot of trouble. I like girls who are naturally that way, not curiosity-seekers. Some of them are white. I have no preference. The relations last longer when I'm active. Usually it's about twenty minutes but if the other girl wants to stop I do, to prolong the period before the orgasm. I think they are fond of me because of my large clitoris. I think that's the chief reason. They comment upon it. They whisper among themselves. They say, "She has the largest clitoris." (913–14)

As in Myrtle's case, Susan's descriptions of how much her girlfriends admired and enjoyed her clitoris influenced the gynecologists in their summary of her exam. Dickinson, echoing Henry's skepticism that Susan was exaggerating when she said her clitoris could penetrate her lovers, went to some effort to explain that a clitoris could never truly take the place of a penis:

> She declares the clitoris enlarged is three inches, though it actually can be drawn out but 1 1/2 inches. . . . Such a clitoris permits entry, not into the vagina, but into the shallow funnel or elliptical groove of the spread vulva, thus resembling nonpenetrating or vulvar coitus. There

is a bit of discrepancy here, in that the finger is employed for clitoris friction while lying above. (1096)

Dickinson's anxiety manifested itself in a case of literal-mindedness intent upon showing that the clitoris could not do what penises do, in spite of what Susan proudly claimed. However, if we believe Susan and especially her reports of whispering admirers, her lovemaking abilities were more than a mere sleight of hand. The general uneasiness incited by accounts such as Susan's led Robert Dickinson to produce a series of illustrations indicating that tribadism ("clitoris pressure between women") was less effective in satisfying women than was "normal" heterosexual vaginal intercourse (figs. 14, 15).

Both Myrtle and Susan, through their claims about the power of the clitoris, wrested the power of the phallus from the penis. This was accomplished by appropriating the popular belief that both black men and women were unusually well-endowed and sexually more desirable. Each of these women, perhaps knowing what would shock the male doctors, presented them with the specter of the woman who threatened to render men sexually dispensable.

Marian J., a black nightclub performer, especially piqued Henry's curiosity when she spoke of how marvelous she made her lovers feel and how her reputation as a gifted lover was well established among lesbians in New York City:

> I became so expert in lingual caresses that I was noted in theatrical circles and in the fringe of polite society for my excellence. . . . Sometimes I put my tongue in the vagina to increase the sexual excitement. A friend of mine who has a reputation as a good cook says I can do more with my tongue than she can with her pots and pans. (726)

In the course of her interview, Marian described an exciting life spent performing in clubs and cabarets in the United States and Europe. By her own telling, for thirteen years prior to the Bolshevik Revolution she lived in Russia, enjoying popularity among the "livelier members of Czar Nicholas' court" (724). Then when the Revolution occurred, she fled on a train headed for Siberia. During the trip she met a Russian millionaire and his wife who persuaded her to go to Japan with them. Marian seduced the wife, who had not been satisfied sexually by her husband, and had sex with her once a day for two years without the husband knowing. Henry referred to this story to warn readers that women like Marian had particular power over other women whose husbands had not satisfied them.

In Marian's case, the doctor was impressed by her tales of numer-

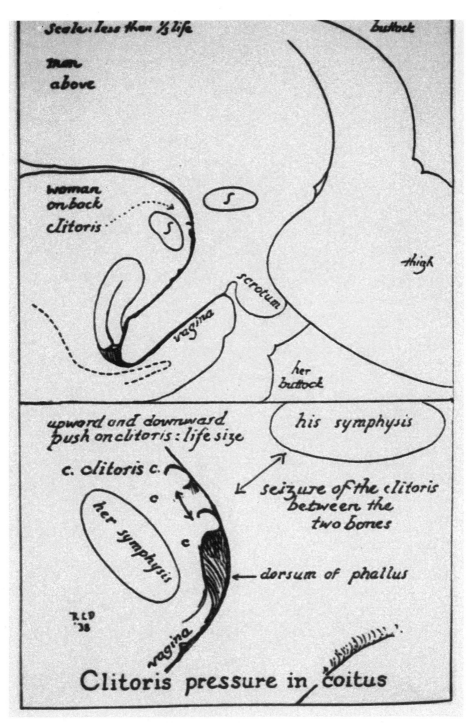

Figure 14. Clitoris pressure in coitus. From Henry, *Sex Variants* (1948 ed.), 1128.

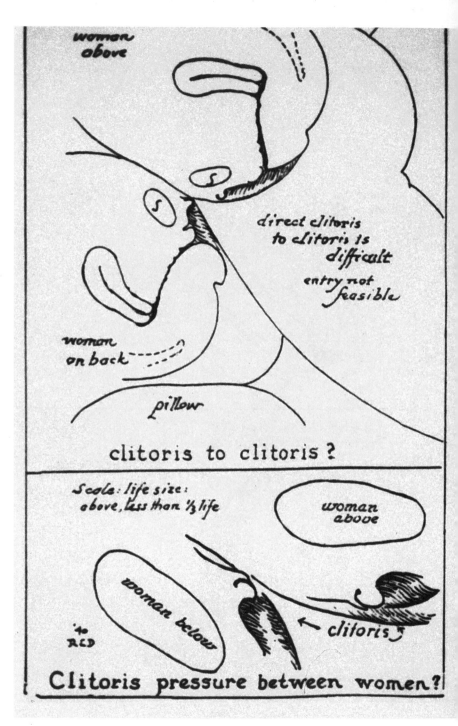

Figure 15. Clitoris pressure between women? From Henry, *Sex Variants* (1948 ed.), 1129.

ous love affairs with both men and women, and he relied on assumptions about race and gender to describe her. He remarked that her "well-developed breasts and hips" were features of the "gentle mammy," but these contrasted with her "distinctly masculine attributes," which made her seem strong and attractive to women. He went on say that Marian's "promiscuous" bisexuality was evidence of the dangers of race mixing:

> With several generations of illegitimate children of negro and white bloods and with an admixture of Indian, the chances that Marian would have lived in accordance with convention probably were few. (728)

Here we find evidence of Henry's underlying agenda concerning eugenics and the maintenance of race purity. To Henry, Marian was a byproduct of civilization in that she represented the intermingling of races and the accompanying moral anarchy wrought by the effacement of race, sex, and class distinctions. Hence, Henry echoed the concerns of a previous generation of medical commentators on homosexuality, citing Marian's case as an unfortunate outcome of dyshygienic breeding. But by her own telling, Marian's life was rich and rewarding precisely because she was not constrained by old-fashioned conventions.

Relay 7: Out of Bounds

Sex variant subjects were self-consciously unconventional in a variety of ways. Many were openly critical of matrimonial heterosexuality and embraced "free love" as a positive alternative to moralistic constraints imposed by monogamy and marriage. About half of the subjects were actively bisexual, although they preferred sexual relations with members of their own sex. Hence, neither the subcultural nor the medico-scientific discourses defined the sex variant as necessarily exclusively homosexual. In fact, the boundaries of sexual identity were not so clearly drawn along the lines of exclusive sexual orientation as we might presently conceptualize them in light of the lesbian and gay liberation movements beginning in the 1960s. While many of the subjects described themselves in terms of being "naturally" different from heterosexuals, their lives were intricately interwoven with heterosexuals in their families, jobs, and social circles. Yet at the same time, many embraced a sense of belonging to a subculture with distinct characteristics and alternative values.

Olga R., a "short, chunky woman of twenty-eight" who grew up on the Lower East Side and was raised by her Jewish mother after her

English father ran off, described the situation of lesbians among urban bohemians quite frankly:

> Usually a girl stays only a year or two in this environment. She is enchanted by the easy morals, its cafe life and the camaraderie of third rate artists and writers who lend a facile explanation to the idleness paramount there. I have stayed there a dozen years, a landmark in all the well-known speakeasies, especially those frequented by women. During that time I have been everybody's and anybody's girl. (978)

Henry frequently equated the lifestyle of free love to promiscuity, suggesting that homosexual desire was voracious, selfish, flippant, irresponsible, and, ultimately, likely to doom the individual to disappointment and abjection. To the psychiatrist, promiscuity, first and foremost, symbolized an immature refusal on the part of the subjects to settle down and take on the responsibilities of adulthood—that is, stable marriage for the purposes of reproduction. Their resistance to enter the social contract of heterosexual marriage and monogamy was pathologized as a fixation or retardation preventing maturity. Because of this bias, Henry was unable to comprehend that many of the subjects actually enjoyed having a variety of sexual relationships, including some which separated romance and sexual satisfaction. They found these relationships perfectly suitable to modern life. Henry, on the other hand, viewed them as evidence of moral decline and danger.

Henry construed Olga's bisexuality as expressive of licentiousness and childishness since it appeared to him to represent a lack of commitment. Her brazen disclosures seemed to anticipate this prejudice as she extolled the virtues of freedom, reciprocity, and intimacy in sex:

> My bedfellows are ever changing and there is alternating attraction to men and women. I'm completely and thoroughly bisexual and I hope I never have to make a choice. Sex is always mutual, a coming together of two people. It's not a question of initiative or that one is more active than the other. I like to make people happy and most of the time I find sex a very important thing in my relation with people. (978)

The doctor used some of her own words to summarize Olga's case, but he underscored the connection between her bisexuality and a selfish habit of laziness and debauchery, qualities that he believed were common in the sex variant subculture:

> [Olga] has had ever changing bedfellows, casual and serious affairs with women, and affairs with men who mean little more to her than

drinking companions. . . . Olga frankly acknowledges that she is totally lacking in worldly ambition and is content to play the role of nurse to down-at-heel writers. She likes to make people happy and to accomplish this she is ready to participate in any form of sex play. . . . Too lazy to work and too content to sit around and drink, to have an easy living however it may be got, Olga is certain she wants to remain bisexual. She has been the lover of women of distinction and she has been everybody's and anybody's girl. . . . Homosexuality is a result of futile search for affection. Identification with mother leads to promiscuity and disillusionment. (981–82)

Henry's summary elided Olga's appreciation of mutual feeling of love between two people regardless of their sex and assessed her desire for freedom in negative terms, which allowed him to conclude her case with the prognosis that she inevitably would be disappointed. In broad strokes, he used Olga's case, among many others, to proclaim the milieux of sex variants to be pathetic and morally dissolute.

Bisexuality among male subjects was also alarming to the doctor. Indeed, many described their affairs with men and women, including lesbians. For example, Peter, described as a tall, handsome blonde with hoodlum tendencies and a criminal record for theft and prostitution, remarked:

> For the past four years I've been having sex with both men and women. I like to have a sex party with a man every now and then. I have little desire for active sodomy and I'm never passive. . . . The only woman I ever had go down on me was an actress now in Hollywood. That's all she wanted. I've had affairs with dykes, had normal sex with them. I don't imagine they got as much of a kick out of it as I did. . . . I've had affairs with a prominent lawyer, an osteopath, with a physician in New York, and with a prominent buyer for a big house on Fifth Avenue. I've also had affairs with several actors and movie stars. (472)

Henry summarized Peter's case by interpreting his affairs as signs of an underlying psychopathology, manifesting itself in criminality: "Just as Peter found no place for himself in his home, he has been unable, as he wandered about aimlessly, to attach himself to any person or place. He indulges in pleasures wherever he can find them. . . . Most of his traveling is a manifestation of an inability to adjust to an orderly mode of living" (476). To Henry, Peter was a rogue who posed a threat to the stability of marriage and the family. Peter asserted a very different summary of his own view: "I have no feeling that homosexual relations are abnormal. I just take them as a matter of course" (474).

Relay 8: Stigma and Danger

Several subjects spoke of the need to conceal their homosexuality—
and of the damaging consequences of being found out. For example,
Daniel remarked:

> I've got in trouble with the police a couple of times. When I first came
> to New York a man at the movies put my hand on his penis. He was a
> large man and older than I was. After a while he said he was going to
> take me some place—the police station. . . . I've often worried about
> my relations with men. I thought I might be sick—that my blood
> might be bad. I was afraid I might have syphilis because I was with
> so many people. I was always afraid to go to a doctor. I never took
> precautions. . . . I'm nervous about a lot of things. Sometimes I get
> nervous on the street. I think something is going to happen to me. I
> just think somebody is going to beat me up or do something to me.
> (433)

Daniel's strategy for dealing with homophobia was to isolate himself
from heterosexuals. He reported: "I have no contact with heterosexual people. I wouldn't feel comfortable with them and I would rather
be with people of my own type. . . . Sometimes I talk with Lesbians
about my sex relations and sometimes they tell me about their relations with women and the different types they like. I don't like to talk
to normal girls because they don't understand" (434–35).

Rafael echoed Daniel's sentiments, stating that "I'm very unhappy
with conventional people. They would hate me if they knew my actual
mode of life. I go with girls now just to conceal my homosexuality"
(389). Irving, a thirty-year-old fashion designer from Paris, also commented on the psychological and physical dangers caused by the
stigma attached to homosexuality. In addition to leading him to con-
template suicide, he told of being raped and blackmailed by men who
seduced him and left him feeling "utterly disgusting." It was not until
he "began to break away from . . . old associations, from the whole
life of lying and fighting against [himself]" that Irving achieved some
kind of happiness. But this happiness was based on keeping his homosexuality concealed from his "conventional" friends (338).

Peter, whose nomadic life included a series of experiences of police
harassment, recounted: "Detectives have picked me up time and time
again and wanted to have an affair with me for their own pleasure. In
certain cities most of the police are queer. I got fifteen days in one
city for vagrancy but really because I wouldn't have anything to do
with the police" (474).

Max N., a thirty-year-old Jewish man, spoke of the dangers of consorting with the hustlers in Times Square and Central Park. "They have sex for money or to get a chance to rob someone. They feel sure that no charge will be made against them because the victim doesn't want to run the risk of being involving in homosexual scandal" (410). Max's platonic marriage of convenience to a lesbian who held public office ended when his homosexuality was exposed. Henry concluded the case by saying that when sex became "merely a form of pleasure," Max no longer regarded homosexual relations as abnormal. Such an outcome worried the doctor that more men and women would resort to invert marriages as a way to cover up and justify their homosexuality.

Leo S., a twenty-six-year-old white man from the South who had affairs with African American men, described being arrested and charged with sex crimes and the murder of a boy "out West," while roaming a public park one evening with a black lover. The police punched him in the face several times and held him for twelve hours before he confessed to having affairs with the black man, who was charged with another murder. Leo was bailed out of jail by another "colored boy" with whom he felt for the first time that he was monogamous. Appropriating the parlance of adjustment theory, Leo stated: "I felt I was getting out of the promiscuous class. I was glad I was getting nearer the normal curve"(364). Leo's sister, Bertha, the only family member who knew about his homosexuality, paid a visit to Henry for advice on how to help Leo overcome his homosexuality. Although she had many homosexual male friends, she was concerned about his health and stability. The doctor commented that Bertha appeared to be "a bisexual person with strong masochistic tendencies" and is "unconventional enough to qualify as a confidential companion for him"(368). In summarizing Leo's case, the doctor made reference to Leo's proclivity toward associating with black men as a sign of his self-destruction:

> A growing sense of inadequacy and of failure so magnified his fundamental feeling of insecurity that he has come to feel most at ease in the companionship of negroes. Even at this level he gropes for something more conventional. . . . Leo still has hopes of thus re-establishing himself in society but in the meantime he is continuing his friendships with negroes. (369)

Clearly, in the doctor's view, Leo's attachment to African American men was evidence of his moral and social dissolution.

In many of the cases where subjects pointed to homophobia as the primary cause of their suffering, Henry, while more sympathetic than many of his day, nonetheless used the speakers' testimony to emphasize the tragic and unhealthy nature of homosexuality. The onus was placed on the sex variant to conform to social conventions rather than on society to rid itself of homophobic intolerance. Henry criticized police brutality but in general endorsed the goal of removing overt displays of homosexuality from public spaces. The message was that men harassed by the police would be spared their suffering if only they dedicated themselves to controlling their sexual desires and to living more orderly, productive lives.

Relay 9: Female Sexual Dissatisfaction

Several subjects specifically voiced their revulsion or distaste for the opposite sex. This pattern was much more common among the female than the male subjects. For example, Irene remarked:

> Every time I had sex with a man I would sit up and tell him how lousy he was. . . . I really have a desire to inflict pain upon [men]. I've had to compete with them and they have never played fair with me. (756–57)

Henry concluded that Irene's "heterosexual adjustment failed because of [her] rebellious attitude toward men (father). Homosexuality provides [an] outlet for [her] masculine drive" (761).

Betty E., a thirty-five-year-old woman of German ancestry whom the doctor described as having "tantalizing and somewhat sad eyes that suggest a Mona Lisa smile contrast[ed] with hard lines about the mouth," commented that her husband was sexually inadequate compared with her women lovers. This led the doctor to conclude that "as a husband he was a complete failure. Betty had already known many female lovers who were experienced in the art of love. Her husband was a steady, plodding person with no imagination and no technique and he was unable to satisfy her" (960). Attributing lesbianism in many cases to the failures of men, Henry relied on cases such as Betty's to suggest in his conclusions that if men were more sexually adept there would be fewer lesbians.

Charlotte N., a twenty-seven-year-old daughter of Russian Jewish immigrants whose lover, Nora, also participated in the study, described how Nora seduced her:

> I didn't know she was a Lesbian. She kissed me and hugged me and used her hand. She got me very passionate. I told her to stop. . . . Finally she used her mouth. It didn't bother me. It was rather surprising but I didn't realize what it was at that particular moment. She just

slipped down in bed. I had an orgasm and it seemed to be greater than any I had with my husband. (586)

She then went on to describe her preference for Nora over her sexually inadequate husband:

> My husband is still fond of me but he isn't able to satisfy me physically. He really wants to. The moment he is near me he has an orgasm. . . . If I were in love with my husband I think I would prefer being with him. It's more exciting with this woman and it lasts two or three times as long. She is so tender, affectionate and attentive. It's a longing I have had and she seems to fulfill that greatly. I feel more protected with her than with my husband. My husband is masculine but he's happy-go-lucky. (588)

Henry used Charlotte's case as an example of how women's dissatisfaction in heterosexual marriage could leave an otherwise normal woman open to perverse persuasion. He summarized her case as follows:

> Failure on the part of her husband to satisfy her desires seems to have been the chief cause for Charlotte's retreat to her own sex. . . . Quite innocently Charlotte accepted the companionship of some girls she met through her husband's family. She was cordially received and their friendship was soon expressed by affectionate caresses. Finally a few drinks removed the inhibitions. Charlotte had been neglected by her husband and she was therefore susceptible to passionate embraces. Moreover, the caresses of her Lesbian partner were so effective that the climax was greater than Charlotte had experienced with her husband. (590)

Thus, Henry, rather than countering their claims, occasionally used women's sexual dissatisfaction with men to suggest, as Robert Dickinson had in *A Thousand Marriages* and *The Single Woman,* that one way to prevent lesbianism was to teach heterosexual men how to be better lovers. In this way, the Sex Variant study was geared toward repairing heterosexual relations as much as it was toward eliminating homosexuality.

Relay 10: New Marriages

Some subjects voiced the desire to have children and to enjoy the respect and social acceptance extended to "normal" people, but at the same time they did not want to repress their homosexuality. Many envisioned new forms of marriage that would be more liberating than those of their parents. For example, Rebecca, a twenty-five-year-old "boyishly feminine" Jewish woman, did not believe that marriage ought to preclude the possibility of continuing affairs with women: "My present notion of an ideal solution is to marry a man who will make a good husband and from time to time take women as lovers" (969). As a counterpoint to Rebecca's forthright intention to have her cake and eat it too, Dr. Henry classified her desire as not only masculine but extremely narcissistic and, thus, profoundly immature. In a gesture that removed Rebecca's agency, Henry recast her desire to have the best of both worlds as a pathological conflict originating from an unresolved Oedipus complex:

> Her inherent masculine tendencies were in constant conflict with [her father's] wishes and with her own ideal of herself as a feminine beauty. The conflict was a factor in her bisexuality. . . . In none of her subsequent affairs with men has she got beyond infatuation and a desire to be physically satisfied. She ventured with men because she felt it was a duty, a duty to assure herself that she was feminine. (971)

Sometimes lesbians and homosexual men married each other as a result of pressures placed upon them by families and heterosexual friends. But they also used marriage as a strategy for ensuring mutual support and companionship without having to give up homosexuality. This was the case among several of the sex variant subjects who reported having nonsexual companionships with the opposite sex in self-conscious defiance of the possessive trappings of traditional marriage. In some cases, these marriages evolved into sexual relationships when both partners felt liberated from the expectations implied in heterosexual monogamy.

Donald H. found himself in such an arrangement. He was a forty-year-old man from a wealthy family whose inheritance permitted him to lead an unconventional life. He described his marriages to two lesbians, explaining that these arrangements allowed him to feel some degree of stability while also enjoying occasional sexual affairs with other men. Because of the freedom from compulsory heterosexuality within the marriage, he and his second wife, who was in love with another woman, actually developed a fulfilling sexual relationship but not one which prevented them from seeing their other lovers:

> I was sent to my present wife to solicit her help in business. . . . She was very tall and had a beautiful figure but her face was not good looking. . . . The first thing that struck me was that she probably was a Lesbian. One day we were drinking and talking. She was divorced and we were talking about remarrying. She said she didn't think she wanted

to get married again. I said I didn't either. Then she said, "There's a kind of loneliness that comes when you're not married." I said, "I know there is." She said, "Let's get married." I agreed. . . . The next day I told her I didn't know whether I was impotent. She said her first marriage had killed any desire for sex. That was a great relief for me. We agreed to get married on a purely conventional basis and announced our engagement. The fact that she made no demands made me more passionate. . . . We are still deeply in love. . . . She knows I love David but she doesn't have much notion of what goes on. (34)

Henry and his colleagues were uneasy about sex variants using the institution of heterosexual marriage this way. They were concerned that marriages involving sex variants would lead to more biological and social degeneration because if constitutional factors did not taint the offspring, an unconventional home environment certainly would. Even where there were no children involved, Henry believed that these marriages would denigrate the value of matrimony and thus lead to sexual license and moral decline.

As evidence of the powerful legacy of degenerationist ideas, some of the subjects appropriated notions from eugenics to defend their refusal to procreate. For example, Antonio explained: "I don't want to get married but I have thought of children. I can just imagine what they would look like. I'm afraid they might be nothing but bitches, fairies, or dykes" (422). Similarly, Olga, described by the doctor as having "an exotic charm that is lost on close inspection," stated "I've no desire to have children. I believe in heredity too much and I don't think I would make any better mother than my mother did. Besides I have never met anyone I would want to be the father of my child" (978). Though hereditarian discourse could be deployed to counter compulsory heterosexuality, it also underscored the dominant notion that homosexuality was pathological. This is characteristic of the process of variant subject formation, whereby those marked as anomalous or pathological make use of available discourses to account for themselves sometimes in a fashion that wins them latitude in one direction while also reiterating a constraining premise of inferiority.

Relay 11: A Natural Desire to Embrace Homosexuality

Many of the subjects agreed to participate in the study in hopes that it would foster a greater understanding and tolerance of homosexuality. In an anticipatory fashion, they were prepared to defend their homosexuality in a variety of ways. Some invoked "nature" and "instinct" to explain their homosexual desires. Walter commented: "I have no regrets. [My homosexuality] is as natural as I live"(289). Similarly, Gabriel stated: "I realize I'm different from the majority and yet I don't think I'm unique. I have been drawn to men as far back as I can remember but I have always felt normal and I have never wished to be different. The fact that a homosexual still gets a jail sentence is the damnedest social problem in the world" (326). Archibald T., a fastidious twenty-nine year old who sold fine fabrics, told the doctor that "a homosexual should be looked upon as just another example of nature and not as a freak" (300). He wanted respect and dignity and even mentioned that he would like to be "cured" if possible. But, in the same breath, he noted the special contributions of homosexuals to society: "Some of the homosexuals I have known have a sensitiveness that usually doesn't go with the average normal. There is a certain understanding that goes with it [homosexuality] and I would regret to lose that" (300).

Mae C., who was uneasy about participating in the study for fear that her neighbors would discover her lesbianism, nevertheless described her first lesbian love affair as totally natural: "Like two innocent children we became lovers. Neither of us knew anything about it. It was just nature. We were very much in love with each other. We slept together, kissed and embraced and rubbed our bodies together. I would have an orgasm and enjoy it. Before long I was taking the initiative, kissing her breasts and her clitoris" (577).

Olga, too, invoked nature and instinct when describing her first lesbian sexual experience: "I had an affair with a woman, an old school friend. She was three or four years older and was a practiced Lesbian. We had liked each other for about a year and I was just beginning to become aware of homosexuality and to realize that she was a Lesbian. One night I spent the night with her and she initiated me in the postures and gestures of love between women. She began by masturbating me. The experience was different from that with a man although it never occurred to me to compare them. Then I began to use my hand and my mouth and seduced her. I did it by instinct. She was a boyish thing and I liked to make love to her" (977).

Other subjects argued the merits of homosexuality as a kind of liberation from oppressive conventions, emphasizing how it has allowed them to be more creative and independent minded. For example, Frieda announced to the doctor that "the usual distinction between normal and abnormal is baseless. I rebel against the narrow code of the world, the one that points a maligning finger at two people whose pattern of life does not accord with ordinary standards" (772). Virginia K. remarked that "homosexual women have a certain masculine attitude about the way they think. They are not apt to be so hysterical and self-seeking in a feminine way. They are not always playing a cagey game to get somebody. That's what I dislike about the female attitude. I think they have much more sense of honor than a man has. They are always generous. I've always liked them because they are apt to do things that are creative. They seem to live more interesting lives than the average heterosexual woman. They seem to keep alive longer. They don't get into ruts" (772).

APPROPRIATING SEXOLOGY

In some cases, certain well-known sexological texts played a big part in the subjects' understandings of themselves, for better or worse. Rather than wholeheartedly embracing sexology, subjects tended to be ambivalent about the ideas published by Krafft-Ebing in *Psychopathia Sexualis,* Havelock Ellis in *Sexual Inversion,* and Radclyffe Hall in *The Well of Loneliness.* Taken with a grain of salt by many of the subjects, sexology texts circulated among lesbians and gay men, providing them with limited tools of self-interrogation from within the framework of science and medicine. Many explicitly countered pejorative characterizations of homosexuality made by Krafft-Ebing, but few opposed scientific authority per se. Donald H., for example, talked about reading the work of Magnus Hirschfeld and Havelock Ellis on homosexuality, and he credited them with doing "a lot of good and a lot of harm." He continued: "The old books are devoted to the abnormal. I think there should be a more intelligent attitude" (37).

In fact, many subjects, while opposing everyday homophobic prejudice as well as laws which criminalized homosexuality, echoed medical ideas that assumed homosexuality was pathological. For example, when Nora M. confessed her love of women to a homosexual friend and co-worker, Salvatore N., he gave her a copy of *Psychopathia Sexualis.* Up until that point, Nora, a thirty-year-old businesswoman, was unaware that what she was feeling for other women was pathological. She continued to go out on dates but "the enlightenment made me feel discouraged and that there was something wrong with me." Clearly, the exposure to Krafft-Ebing's fatalistic assessment of sexual inversion created great conflicts in Nora because just after reading it she tried to have intercourse with another male friend and vomited, unable to go through with it. But when asked by Henry what caused her to be a lesbian, she responded with ideas borrowed from sexology:

> I still wonder why I feel and act toward women as I do. It might be some form of human life in evolution. I'm neither masculine nor feminine except that I am masculine in my attitude toward women. . . . The more I see of homosexuals the more I disapprove of them. They seem incapable of leading normal lives. (852)

Nora believed that the greater promise of sexology was to explore all forms of sexuality, even those of "normal" people, and to break down the distinction between homosexuals and heterosexuals as part and parcel of lifting the constraints imposed by heterosexual marriage:

> I want to understand the normal mind as well as my own. I want to know how women who like men feel about life. I don't want to change my mode of living. Even if I were not a homosexual I wouldn't want to marry. I have no desire to have a home or family. I don't want to be deprived of my freedom. (852)

Henry summarized her case by interpreting her actions as rebellious, perverse, and self-destructive, owing in large part to her psychopathological parents who "should not have married":

> In spite of the fact that Nora appears to have adult female genitals, it is unlikely in view of her background and her animosity toward men that she could make a heterosexual adjustment. . . . The platonic friendship which she has had with Salvatore is a caricature of the fairly satisfactory relations often realized between a masculine woman and an effeminate man. . . . Her Lesbian activities give her only temporary pleasure and they are now in large part compulsive. . . . To Nora the future is uncertain and she expresses her apprehension in fears that she is going insane or that she is going to commit suicide. (854–55)

Other subjects were clearly affected by sexological ideas that gave rise to internal conflicts. Will G., one of the male subjects credited for bringing many of his friends and acquaintances into the study, was very curious about psychiatric and psychoanalytic theories of homosexuality. Will had been in psychoanalysis but said that he was not "cured." He was very interested in what the doctor thought of him. In an effort to make Henry's job easier, he prepared a long list detailing his sexual desires. In spite of this obsequiousness, Will fired off a sarcastic remark about the ineptitude of doctors whom he credited for his homosexuality:

> [By 16] I had come to the conclusion that I was homosexual and I told my father I wanted to be psychoanalyzed. He sent me to one of the

leading neurologists in the city. I think I owe my homosexuality to this neurologist. He pooh-poohed it because I had hair up to my navel. . . . [For years] I went on with the feeling that I wasn't homosexual because the doctor said I couldn't be. I did nothing about it and kept on being more and more homosexual. (376–77)

Will continued: "I keenly resent homosexuals and being classed with them."

Other subjects were clearly unhappy about being homosexual. For example, Reginald confessed to Henry that "sometimes I was quite disgusted with myself. I was quite in love with a girl in my home town . . . and I was puzzled over how I could have such a deep love for this girl and still keep on with the abnormal" (396).

Several of the male subjects remarked that, after reading about the possibility, they wished they could be castrated and become women. Moses I., a married thirty-eight-year-old with "distinct Semitic features," stated: "I hope against hope for the impossible, that perhaps in time my genitals will become so useless that I must be castrated. They could operate on my pituitary gland and give me an ovarian extract. In time I could assume the role of woman and follow the inclinations I have bottled up for so long in my heart of hearts—to do nursing, looking after children. . . . I would prefer to have my penis removed and a vagina made surgically" (540–41).

Rudolph von H., a sixty-four-year-old transvestite who was reported to have undergone an "American Steinach operation" (hormonal castration), had met Hirschfeld in Berlin: "Hirschfeld claimed that I was an inverted Lesbian, that I would attract men but would rather have women fondle me. In Berlin I was a member of a club of Lesbians. They tolerated transvestites dressed as women. I felt quite at home" (495). Rudolph, whom Henry portrayed as decrepit and pathetic, loved to cross-dress and was proud to be in a long line of transvestites: "I'm crazy for taffeta. Hirschfeld published some letters of Richard Wagner in regard to dress fetishism. Wagner spent enormous sums for brocades. I have a photo which shows him in complete feminine dress. That was his mania" (492). Reminiscing about his earlier years, he went on: "I liked to go places in formal dress. . . . I went to a great many masquerades as a woman. Koenigin Louise was a type that impressed me very favorably and the outcome of my trial to portray her was marvelous" (493).

Moses, Rudolph, and Howard, the only primarily heterosexual cases in the Sex Variant study, were included because of their apparent sex inversion as signified by cross-dressing. Today they would be considered transgendered people whose primary identification is in crossing gender lines rather than in homosexual object choice. Moses fantasized about being with men, but in these scenarios he imagined himself as a woman. Rudolph, the oldest subject in the study, had sex with a man only once or twice and did not find it to be very "pleasant." His overwhelming desire was to dress and act like a woman, but he wanted to do so in sexual relations with more aggressive females. He described how he would have been able to maintain his marriage if only his wife had agreed to take the dominant position in sexual relations.

Howard N. was a heterosexual transvestite who never had sex with another man but who, over the course of the interviews, expressed some curiosity in doing so. His greatest passion was for wearing women's undergarments and dresses. Howard reluctantly described his experience to the doctor:

> I wore my first wife's clothing with her knowledge. She was not altogether approving. I wore her girdle and stockings, just fooling in the evening, perhaps preparing for bed or for love making. It was done just as a matter of gaiety. It was not an obsession. (515)

Howard, described as a scholarly looking man whose friends regarded him as a pest, also preferred socializing with lesbians rather than with heterosexuals, whom he disparaged for their sexual repression. He narrated his affinity for lesbians as a relief from the centrality of genitals in typical heterosexual relations:

> I like homosexual women because with the heterosexual there is no opportunity to be free in conversation. In this country heterosexuals are dirty minded or strait-laced. I'm not given to talking about sex. I might talk about love in the sense of giving the entire personality. I'm not interested in the sexual act per se. It amazes me to hear men and women talk about sex as an end. What I want is contact with another person but not contact with the genitals. I want an intimate understanding and a relationship of soul to soul. (518)

Howard had several outbursts against Henry, whom he regarded as detached and unforthcoming: "You sit there and listen and offer nothing of yourself. It's like talking into a dictaphone. I have been fairly frank but there are things I have not told you. Whether I will or not I don't know. It seems probable that I won't" (500). Henry analyzed Howard's resistance thusly:

> With each succeeding interview it was evident that he was irritable and easily offended and that he demanded much attention. Occasionally

he complained bitterly but briefly that the physician was too cold and scientific. . . . It is evident that he wants to establish a personal relationship with the physician. (500, 518)

Howard, who was simultaneously tortured and ecstatic when he wore his girdle, stockings, and the dress his "frigid" wife made for him, explained that his perversions disappeared momentarily when he was finally able to be sexually satisfied by a French prostitute. He was driven to talk at length about his fetishes for rosary beads, corsets, children's diapers, and young men dressed in feminine clothes. His pleasures made him "nervous" and even hostile, but he justified them as a response to being so deeply misunderstood by everyone.

A few subjects came out with downright vicious statements about homosexuality. The most malevolent of these was made by Gene S., a "handsome boy of twenty-five years old" whose artwork was exhibited at one of the top New York galleries. After telling stories about being teased as a child for being a sissy and recounting many sexual and love affairs with other men, Gene concluded his interview by saying:

> I don't like [pansies] and I don't begrudge normal people their feelings against homosexuals. I don't think it's too good a plan to have homosexuality too much accepted because it gives pansies too much chance. I think the police should stamp it out. That is what Hitler is doing. (254–55)

The subjects were not immune to self-loathing, having internalized discourses that equated homosexuality and pathology. But many blamed the difficulties of being homosexual on the hostile social environment. In a plea for compassion, Virginia explained:

> There are homosexuals who are not perverted and they can be in love with each other. . . . The homosexual should have the same position in society as the so-called normal person has. They wouldn't then be all running around to dives and getting persecuted. They wouldn't be so sorry for themselves. They wouldn't be so queer or fight people who didn't understand. They wouldn't have to be hiding more than fifty percent of the time. I think they wouldn't be so mannish or on the defensive about things. (772)

Similarly, Ellen T., who had a tempestuous affair with a French countess, stated:

> I feel it is important not to be hypocritical and not to be persecuted. The causes should be relieved. Homosexuals are likely to turn out to

be antisocial, disruptive people purely because of the attitude which
society takes toward them. It is easy for them to be bitter and antisocial
and very easy for them to turn into sadists and fascists because they
have been so mistreated. (795)

This prompted Henry to conclude:

[Ellen's] bitterness is now projected on society: if she were a stronger
person she would "come out in the open and raise hell" about the attitude toward homosexuality. At present Ellen is an ardent reformer but
if Marvel [her girlfriend] should fail her she might turn out to be one
of those "antisocial, disruptive people," a sadist or a fascist. (797–98)

In this move, the doctor appropriated Ellen's antihomophobic social
critique as evidence of her psychopathology, going so far as to suggest
that her political convictions were a cover for mental illness. In an
astounding move, Henry misconstrued Ellen's words, suggesting that
she was on the brink of becoming a sadist or fascist rather than considering how her analysis of homophobia might be useful for remedying the political and psychological problems brought on by hostility
toward homosexuality.

The psychiatric interviews allowed the sex variants to appropriate
some of the experts' questions to account for themselves in terms that
resisted a common tendency toward pathologizing homosexuality.
Even the limited possibilities of self-articulation offered by the interviews gave subjects the means to represent their desires in terms
which challenged some of the basic assumptions about homosexuality.
They variously appropriated, subverted, accommodated, and resisted
aspects of the prevailing discourse about homosexuality, and in so doing provide evidence of variant subjectivity.

From a historical point of view, the interviews can be seen as textual effects of a discursive formation that approached homosexuality
as a problem to be solved. In the end, the experts reinscribed it as
pathological. But the subjects' words offer rich documentation of the
contest between variant subjects and the many assumptions about
homosexuality that made their lives difficult. These people were
never merely docile victims. They deployed interventionist strategies
within and against a medico-scientific discourse in relation to which
they—with humor, anger, excess, irony, and sometimes abjection—
addressed questions of the self which complicated the determined interrogation of the experts. Their interviews reveal that they could not,

without considerable prejudice, be reduced to being sick or harmful individuals. Furthermore, what we find is that the medical discourse itself, independent of the intentions of either the experts or the subjects, offered a variety of means for interpreting sex variance that exceeded the control of its speakers. In other words, this discourse was multifaceted, internally complex, and not particularly stable. It was pliable enough to offer a means for subjects' self-interrogation while also being a vehicle for experts to pronounce homosexuality once again as aberrant and socially unfavorable.

By reducing the subjects' narratives to symptoms of their pathologies, George Henry's summarizing comments inadvertently revealed how clumsy it was to draw up a set of typologies which encompassed the diversity of experiences he encountered among these eighty very different people. The complexity of the subjects' stories made the subsequent reporting of data from physical examinations, focused as they were on stark quantitative measurements, seem inadequate not only because they revealed as many exceptions as rules about features that could distinguish sex variants but also because numbers seem so obviously arid and reductive compared to the depth and range of the subjects' first-hand accounts.

The probing work of the CSSV contributed to making homosexuality a matter of growing public fascination. In their own historical context, the psychiatric interviews unleashed explicit narratives of lesbian sex and homosexuality between men the likes of which had not yet been heard and which were not fully comprehended by the researchers. Although George Henry and the Committee for the Study of Sex Variants intended *Sex Variants* as a medical textbook with limited distribution, it became a rich source of information about how lesbians and gay men lived, including graphic accounts of their sexual relationships, stories about their relationships with their families and friends, and explanations of how they negotiated difficulties of living "the gay life." Just as Krafft-Ebing's catalogue of sexual perversions had circulated among this literate and curious group of subjects, George Henry's *Sex Variants*, even though it was full of the doctors' attempts to define homosexuality as pathological, was a book with many subversive possibilities. The volume's obsessive attention to erotic details was legitimated under the rubric of science, and thus *Sex Variants* can be seen as an artifact of what Foucault described as the implantation of perversions characteristic of modern society. Among its many effects, the volume brought aspects of the lives of lesbians and homosexual men into greater visibility, while providing the grounds for elaborating an increasingly militant reverse discourse among its homosexual readership.

THE SEX VARIANT STUDY AND ITS IMPACT ON HOMOSEXUALS

Thanks to Jan Gay and Thomas Painter, a group of collaborating physicians and researchers were able to take a very close look at members of homosexual subcultures in New York City. But Gay and Painter, as well as other homosexuals who participated in the Sex Variant study, were ultimately at cross-purposes with the experts. Although both groups favored decriminalization, sex variants sought social toleration while the experts who studied them continued to construe homosexuality as pathological, a move that significantly broadened their authority to set the terms for how homosexuality would be regarded by the general population. By proclaiming it a form of maladjustment and offering themselves as suitable experts to prevent this problem, psychiatrists in particular became the principal purveyors of mainstream knowledge about homosexuality. Indeed, as the research of the CSSV progressed, both Gay and Painter were marginalized, especially when it came to interpreting findings and making recommendations about the treatment of homosexuals. After relying on Gay and Painter to secure the cooperation of eighty sex variant men and women, the scientifically credentialed researchers ultimately took control of the project and excluded Gay and Painter as unqualified to draw conclusions about homosexuality. Thomas Painter's privately funded research on male prostitution was deemed by the CSSV to be "impressionistic" and thus it was never published. Nevertheless, in the late 1940s, Alfred Kinsey credited Painter's work for providing important evidence of the variety of men who engaged in homosexual relations, whether they identified themselves as homosexuals or not.[12] In the end, Jan Gay was dismayed by the CSSV's insistence that homosexuality was an inferior and pathological form of sexuality.[13] This negative assessment of homosexuality was, in part, responsible for a growing alienation and disaffection between lesbians and homosexual men on the one hand and psychiatrists on the other.

The Sex Variant study succeeded to some extent in bringing the subject of homosexuality out into the open, but the effects of this exposure were quite mixed. George Henry's larger goal was to assist sex variants in adjusting to social norms through psychotherapy. While this seemed more humane than subjecting them to castrations, psychosurgery, shock treatments, and incarceration, the Sex Variant study extended the reach of psychiatry deeper into the lives of lesbians and homosexual men and added to the public perception that they posed a threat to society. Rather than accept them as either benign variations of nature or essentially capable of being healthy and happy, the study ultimately licensed even more penetrating scrutiny, internalized homophobia, and prejudice against homosexuality, whether it initially intended to do so or not.

George Henry's recommendation of adjustment therapy stressed the individual's coming to terms with homosexual desires in a manner that would alleviate neuroses and suffering. But this was to be achieved through conformity and self-control. He strongly urged that homosexuals be discreet in their behavior and sexual pursuits. What most seemed to disturb him was the flamboyant and "exhibitionistic" behavior of many of the more "extreme" sex variant cases. Cross-dressing "fairies" and "rough trade" hustlers and wolves were much more troublesome in his view than the "orderly" homosexuals. It would seem that their shameless public displays of perversion, along with their ruthless extortion and blackmail schemes, posed far greater social problems than those of the meek and circumspect orderly types. But Henry's compassion for orderly homosexuals was quite conditional: if they chose to make themselves vulnerable (i.e., if they had affairs with men or women below their social station), he tended to hold them culpable for their misfortune. While he was clearly at times fazed by the mannish behavior and "rebelliousness" of some lesbians, they seemed to pose less of a threat to society in his view. The fact that most conducted their affairs in private seemed to be a sign of greater prudence than men whose sexual desires took them into the public streets and parks. But he had no greater affection for women with "masculine" aspirations who preyed upon impressionable women and sought to usurp men's positions in business and the professions, as well as in bedrooms.

Henry's prejudice against men and women who, from his point of view, showed little interest in changing their behavior and little regard for law and social conventions led to his closing recommendations that officials, including the police and doctors, should label and isolate disorderly homosexuals. Speaking of child molestation, Henry warned:

Recent publications have left the impression that any homosexual may become a public menace as he grows older because of tendencies to attack children. There is no evidence which indicates that homosexuals harbor such potentialities [to, as they grow older, attack children] any more than any other group of men. . . . If a man is attracted to adults he will continue to be thus attracted. A man who is conspicuously attracted to children merits continual observation and psychiatric investigation. (ix)

But Henry also cautioned that there was indeed a subset of homosexuals who preyed upon children, and he urged that they be identified as soon as possible. His recommendations for treating them involved indeterminate sentences and psychotherapy rather than regular imprisonment. Though he hoped to allay public hysteria, Henry's particular focus on the homosexual child molester, to which he devoted considerable attention in his summarizing comments, underscored the notion that public displays of homosexuality in whatever form were dangerous to the larger society, and especially to innocent children who might witness them. At the same time, by suggesting that families were at fault for creating homosexuals, Henry implied that mothers, as the primary care-takers of children, had an special responsibility to raise them correctly. These two main lines of reasoning—one that focused on the menace of homosexuals in public and the other that harped on the psychosexual damage caused by mothers—intensified in the following decades as homophobia grew to be nothing short of a national affliction.

Though Henry appreciated that many of the problems faced by sex variants were due to the intolerance they experienced, he believed that hygienic heterosexuality was, by far, superior to homosexuality. This placed the onus on lesbians and homosexual men to conform to heterosexuality and the sex roles that underpinned it. Though cloaked in more benevolent terms than anti-homosexual vigilantism, George Henry and the CSSV in the end assessed homosexuality as far from a benign variation and as a decidedly undesirable outcome of modern developments. Thus, while pity replaced contempt, the CSSV's reiteration of homosexuality as pathology seriously undermined the subjects' goals of promoting social toleration.

In retrospect, the Sex Variant study may strike readers today as an immensely invasive inquiry to which a group of hapless and unenlightened homosexuals submitted. However, as I have argued, the study promised to shed benevolent light on the subject of sex variance. It appealed to men and women who believed that rational scientific inquiry might spare them from social oppression, public harassment, and private pain. It gave them an opportunity to reflect on their lives, to engage in self-inquiry, and to appropriate or counter dominant assumptions about them. Their willingness to participate in the study had much to do with specific circumstances occurring in New York City at the time. Understood in its particular historical and cultural context, the study appeared to offer a refuge from renewed public contempt. Many of the men and women involved in the study had witnessed first-hand the damaging effects of public hysteria about homosexuality. Many had been victims of police crackdowns, extortion schemes, and harassment by neighbors, co-workers, and family members. What factors account for a renewed wave of homophobia in New York during the 1930s? What role did progressive scientists and physicians play in this context? What historical circumstances may have made physicians seem more sympathetic especially to homosexuals, compared, for example, to common prejudices and to the threat of criminal punishment? And what made their ideas seem strategically useful to homosexuals? We can find answers to these questions by examining the larger context in which the Sex Variant study occurred.

8   POLICING HOMOSEXUALITY

Several key historical events account for why homosexual men and women in New York City would have found rational scientific inquiry an appealing alternative to the other ways homosexuality was being dealt with in the 1930s. The decade was marked by a public backlash against homosexuals of significant proportions. Lesbians and homosexual men were subjected to aggressive police raids on gay establishments, to increased arrests for "homosexual offenses," and to elaborate extortion schemes. Subjects of the Sex Variant study reported being expelled from jobs, evicted from their homes, and threatened by violence. Their accounts underscore the oppressive effects of homophobia and indicate that hostility toward homosexuality was on the rise.

The backlash against homosexuality during the 1930s was fueled, in a general sense, by social turmoil and public anxiety stemming from the stock market crash of 1929 and the onset of the Great Depression. Homosexuality, already generally regarded by many as a sign of sickness and social degeneracy, came to be associated with the reckless hedonism of the Roaring Twenties that many believed had plunged the nation into the Great Depression.

In addition, the decade was marked by gender trouble. Normative understandings of the proper sex roles for men and women had been called into question by social and economic transformations beginning around the end of the nineteenth century. By the 1930s, in the wake of women's formal political enfranchisement, questions about the differences between men and women animated popular and scientific interest. As we saw in chapter five, scientific authorities were interested in making sense of sex differences, and their research, when placed in the historical context of the 1930s, can be read as an implicit commentary on changing gender relations, including those wrought by the specific conditions of the Depression. As we shall see, broad concerns about gender relations and about masculinity in particular inflected the backlash against homosexuals in a manner that expressly demonized male inversion but also in a fashion that mobilized the image of the homosexual deviant to posit norms according to which the rest of the population ought to live.

Before examining these contextual factors in greater detail, let me mention one other key development occurring in New York City that sheds light on why homosexuals might have been drawn to authorities who appeared to be sympathetic to their plight. Toward the latter half of the decade, the general public, spurred by news of an alleged increase of sex crimes in the city, responded favorably to the mayor's efforts to cleanse the city of unsavory elements. Near the top of his list of targets was anyone whose behavior could be construed as an open expression of homosexuality. Such behavior included not only the public solicitation of sexual relations but also "loitering" in areas known to be frequented by homosexuals and even cross-dressing in public. Economically and socially disadvantaged homosexual men experienced the impact of this stepped-up police vigilance directly. But the backlash had a chilling effect on other gay men as well as lesbians who witnessed the intensification of public contempt for homosexuality stoked not only by the police but by the popular press.

When progressive physicians were brought into policy discussions aimed at stemming sex crimes, they generally argued against harsh criminal punishments for homosexual activities taking place between consenting adults. Furthermore, as we shall see, some even suggested the sex crime statutes ought to be reformed in the interest of aiding homosexual offenders to overcome their maladjustments. While they agreed that public displays of homosexuality were wrong, they argued that such actions could be most effectively discouraged not by criminal punishment but by psychotherapeutic interventions that would inculcate a sense of discretion and self-control among homosexual men who would then be spared the humiliation of being arrested or subjected to blackmail schemes. Such an approach seemed more sympathetic toward homosexuals, compared to facing a stiff jail sentence to be spent in the company of violent criminals. Now let us focus on the details of the developments I have outlined so far.

CLEANING UP THE CITY

Arrests for homosexual activities had been steadily increasing since the late 1920s. The majority of these cases involved men, but a few notable cases of disorderly conduct among lesbians also occurred, including that of Eve Kotchever, who went by the biblically derived pseudonym, Eve Addams. In 1926, Addams, who owned a Village tea-room catering to lesbians, was charged with "disorderly conduct" after being entrapped by an undercover female police officer toward whom Addams allegedly made homosexual advances. She haplessly gave the disguised officer a copy of her manuscript, *Lesbian Love*, was promptly arrested, and had her manuscript confiscated as "obscene" material. Addams was sentenced to a year in the workhouse but was deported in December 1926.[1]

Following the stock market crash of 1929, public opinion in New York City turned against the excessive consumption and recreation of the "Roaring Twenties," which were associated with a host of vices, including sexual promiscuity and homosexuality.[2] Gambling, drunken vagrancy, prostitution, and "sex perversion" were singled out as ills that brought on the Great Depression. City authorities promised to prosecute these crimes, and one of the main means for doing so was through the strict regulation of cabaret and liquor licensing.

In 1931, the New York City police department were given jurisdiction over cabaret licensing. Rules prohibiting "sex perversion" were used to pressure establishments from allowing "pansy acts." Speakeasies and other places that served alcohol did so clandestinely during these years and, unlike "cabarets," did not officially feature musical acts or dancing, leaving them relatively unaffected by these regulations. Once Prohibition was repealed in 1933, the same rules were used to prevent establishments from acquiring liquor licenses that featured pansy acts or even allowed the presence of patrons assumed to be gay. The regulation of liquor licenses became a powerful tool for police harassment and entrapment in places patronized by gay men and lesbians. Paradoxically, the repeal of Prohibition, which initially decriminalized many of the haunts where gay men and lesbians mingled during the 1920s, actually intensified the policing of homosexuality through a whole new set of regulations and laws. Technically, many of the arrests involving homosexuality during this period were classified as sex offenses, thus confirming a popular perception that gay men and lesbians represented a majority of violent sex offenders when their "crimes" were often simply acts of congregating in public places.[3]

Police crackdowns on homosexual men's cruising spots had occurred from time to time beginning in the early 1920s. In 1923, the New York state legislature passed a law specifically prohibiting homosexual "lewdness," which encompassed public cruising. The law fortified existing laws used to prevent men from soliciting or having sex in public. By the early 1930s, Mayor Jimmy Walker recognized the political power of vigilance groups that had organized vast cross-sections of the city's population in extra-governmental campaigns against prostitution and other vices, including sex perversion. Walker railed against vice, even though his own reputation was far from pristine; indeed, his mayoral term ended prematurely in 1932, when he abandoned the office and fled the country to evade larceny charges.[4] During the 1920s, Walker had taken a hands-off approach to the city's drag balls, mainly because many influential and affluent New Yorkers had been in attendance. In 1931, when it was politically expedient to do so, Walker's police force cracked down on "pansies" in certain parts of town, patrolling the waterfront, city parks, and streets where they were reputed to gather.

Following the repeal of Prohibition in 1933, Mayor Fiorello La Guardia assured voters of his intentions to clean up the city, and to prevent alcohol consumption from falling back into the hands of low-life bar owners. Shortly after taking office, La Guardia launched an aggressive campaign to crack down on homosexual men's cruising spots, including bars, and ordered police to round up any drag queens between Fourteenth and Seventy-Second Streets. Several years later, in preparation for the 1939 World's Fair, his police force again cracked down on men assumed to be homosexual, especially in Times Square and other tourist attractions, as part of his campaign to make New York vice-free for both its residents and its visitors. Growing public disdain toward homosexuals led police to increase arrests and judges to mete out harsher sentences than those served by other offenders.[5] By 1937, hundreds of men were brought into the criminal justice system on charges related to homosexuality.

PUBLIC PANIC AND THE WAR ON THE SEX OFFENDER

In 1937, in the wake of sensationalistically reported sex crimes against children, FBI director J. Edgar Hoover declared "War on the Sex Criminal," singling out the "sex fiend" as "the most loathsome of all the vast army of crime," a character who "has become a sinister threat to the safety of American childhood and womanhood."[6] Citizens' groups in major cities across the country lashed out against accused child molesters and called on public officials to do whatever it took to eliminate sex crimes. As an incited public argued for everything from castration to the suspension of parole for sex offenders, psychiatrists and their few allies among law enforcement officials urged that a rational, scientific approach to the problem was warranted.

Much of the popular reporting about sex crimes reinforced an existing notion that homosexuals were, by definition, child molesters. This idea was abetted by the common assumption that homosexuals were trapped at an arrested stage in development which led them to prey upon innocent children to satisfy their perverse desires. In addition to this assumption, arrests for consensual homosexual acts by adult men were increasing in New York City. This inflated the statistics on sex crimes and led members of the public, mistakenly, to believe that violent sex crimes in general were on the rise. Since all homosexual acts were against the law and most were classified as "sex offenses," homosexual men were lumped together in the public imagination with violent offenders, rapists, and child molesters. Homosexuals became easy scapegoats in the context of public hysteria over sex crimes against children that were fueled by the popular press.

The growing worry over sex crimes was not confined to New York. During the second half of the 1930s, in response to public outcry about sex crimes, five states passed laws specifying "sexual psychopathy" as a criminal motivation. These laws, passed in California, Ohio, Minnesota, Michigan, and Illinois, focused on the figure of the sexual psychopath, an individual defined as having uncontrolled and often violent sexual desires arising from a fundamentally psychopathic personality. While several states passed laws during the 1920s that were based on psychopathic theories of disease,[7] the new laws from the second half of the 1930s were aimed at prosecuting psychopaths who were deemed to be sexually motivated in their crimes. Estelle Freedman argues persuasively that this addition of new laws was related to the social stresses of the Great Depression, which led to an intensified focus on male sexual deviance.[8] In Freedman's view, popular commentary, psychiatric discourse, and lawmaking about sex offenders had the particular effect of demonizing homosexual men to the extent that they were presumed to be, by definition, child molesters. She argues that the war on the sex criminal, proclaimed by Hoover in 1937, provided the means for reconstituting sexual boundaries in modern America in a manner that increased homophobic attitudes. The sexual psychopath laws, Freedman argues, intensified the public's focus on sex crimes and this, in turn, functioned to increase public hostility toward anyone suspected of or arrested for "sex offenses," even if their acts were consensual and nonviolent. Sexual psychopath laws were rarely used to prosecute men arrested for homosexual acts, the majority of whom were charged under existing laws that classified homosexual acts as misdemeanors or felonies. But an important consequence of the far-reaching public concern about sex crimes was that socially disturbing but consensual behaviors, including homosexuality, became subject to greater scrutiny, regulation, and prosecution.[9]

Let us consider the historical emergence of the sexual psychopath and how his emergence relates to larger anxieties of the period and to the scapegoating of male homosexuality. The figure of the sexual psychopath became the focus of psychiatric authorities at a time when men's traditional economic and social roles were eroding. High unemployment rates and economic devastation wrought by the Great Depression displaced many men from their traditional position as family breadwinners.[10] As social relations and families were radically disrupted, the figure of the sexual psychopath, imagined as a drifter or shiftless man cut loose from family ties, symbolized the dangers threatening innocent citizens in the streets, schoolyards, and parks. Thus, the specter of anarchy and social collapse occasioned by the crash of the economy was projected onto several deviant types who were associated with the hedonism and sexual excesses of the Roaring Twenties. Urban bohemians, "pansies," and boot-legging "slummers" were scapegoated as culprits of the Depression. As George Chauncey has noted, moral conservatives were relatively successful in whipping up popular hostility toward these three groups by claiming that each contributed to the reckless self-indulgence that culminated in the Depression. According to Chauncey, "some worried that the cultural developments of the late Prohibition period had somehow contributed to the Depression by replacing a productionist ethic with a consumerist one, a regard for traditional American moral values for the flaunting of illicit desires."[11]

To be sure, this was not the first time that hedonism and male lust had become a matter of public concern or lawmaking. Proponents of the legalization of prostitution in the second half of the nineteenth century had claimed that men's normal sexual desire exceeded that of their passionless wives, making state-regulated prostitution a preferable outlet to rape or failed marriages.[12] In addition, African American men as well as working-class and immigrant men were frequently described, in both popular and psychiatric discourses, as having excessive lust which knew no rational bounds. Racist beliefs that black men were atavistic creatures with voracious sex drives provided the rationale for laws and public vigilance campaigns against interracial intimacy from the era of Jim Crow well into the twentieth century.[13] But what distinguished the sexual psychopath's urges from earlier expressions of male lust was that this new character's uncontrolled desires were not only abnormal but diseased. Psychiatrists took a central role in diagnosing sexual psychopathy and recommending policing mechanisms for bringing it under control.

In the midst of increasing public anxiety over the erosion of traditional male roles, two seemingly contradictory types of men became the focus of new sex crimes legislation, including the sexual psychopath laws, and psychiatric discourse. These were the effeminate homosexual, a man lacking in masculinity, and the hypermasculine sexual predator. The latter category included pedophiles, rapists, and "active" masculine homosexual men. Both types were described as maladjusted characters whose psychological immaturity led them to prey upon the innocent. Curiously, whereas most existing statutes against sexual assault had specified the protection of women, sexual psychopath laws and psychiatric discourse from the 1930s placed much greater emphasis on protecting the innocence of children. They did little in the way of prosecuting violent crimes against women and did practically nothing to prosecute coercive incest committed by male relatives against children in their families.

As Freedman notes, this shift indexes women's changing roles and was part of a backlash against feminist claims for greater sexual and social freedom for women. An unfortunate outcome of changing perceptions of femininity starting with the New Woman was that women were seen as desiring creatures, and thus culpable in many instances for their own sexual victimization. While working-class women, women of color, and especially prostitutes had been treated in this fashion historically, by the 1930s even white middle-class women were increasingly viewed as sexually savvy and manipulative. Their involvement and interest in extramarital sexual relations actually made them more vulnerable to charges that they had invited the advances of men whom they accused of rape. Middle-class heterosexual women no longer held the crucial position of modesty and innocence against which nineteenth-century sexual aberrations were defined; this position was ceded, by the 1930s, to children but, it should be added, not to children whose violators were members of their own families. Rates of prosecution for forcible incest had been very low and did not increase with the addition of new laws against sex crimes. This suggests that the public's greatest concern was on policing public spaces where children were assumed to face the greatest danger, rather than on providing greater means for protecting them from assaults within the private sphere of the family.

According to much of the psychiatric discourse on sex offenses, what the two demonized figures of maladjusted masculinity had in common was their fundamental inability to mature to the stage of healthy, heterosexual intimacy with adult women. Instead, they gravitated toward objects that would substitute for normal heterosexual objects, whether the substitute was a child or another man, or they committed "immature" acts such as voyeurism, exhibitionism, or oral sodomy that substituted for normal heterosexual intercourse. As psychoanalytic theories infused discussions about the proper legal treatment of offenders, the theory that offenders were psychologically immature led to a general assumption that sex offenses were pathological compensations for individual inadequacies that were rooted in childhood psychosexual maldevelopment. This, it was believed, prevented men from having normal relations with women. Among these inadequacies were impotence and premature ejaculation as well as offenders' anxieties about having small penises, or their general fears of women. Psychosexual immaturity was measured against the ideal endpoint of a healthy maturation process: adult reproductive heterosexuality, comprised of complementary male and female partners, preferably sealed in a bond of marriage.

So what became a common association between child molesters and homosexuals had its roots in the psychoanalytic idea that both types were arrested in their psychosexual development.[14] A disturbing effect of this theoretical emphasis was that men's rape or assault of women was seldom commented upon in psychiatric diagnoses of sexual psychopathy. In fact in much of the discourse on sex offenses, the rape of women was deemed closer to normal relations than homosexuality, since the perpetrator's sex object was normal, and his aim, though excessive, conformed to a basic gender ideology that positioned man as active agent and woman as receptive object.[15]

FORENSIC PSYCHIATRY AND THE NEW YORK COMMITTEE FOR THE STUDY OF SEX CRIMES

Responding to the public outcry about sex crimes, the New York State legislature in 1937 requested the help of psychiatrists to control and prevent sex crimes and thereby advanced the field of forensic psychiatry in dramatic ways. Responding to the public's concern, Mayor La

Guardia appointed a Committee for the Study of Sex Crimes, consisting of psychiatrists, lawyers, and criminologists. The committee recommended that sex offenders be subject to psychiatric observation and given indeterminate sentences, preferably to be served in secure medical facilities, where they would be examined and treated by psychiatrists until they were deemed rehabilitated.

Officials in New York City took a particular interest in addressing the problem of the sex offender. In 1937, La Guardia established a unique arrangement between the court system and psychiatrists with the help of his Commissioner of Crime Austin H. MacCormick. The plan resembled an idea first advanced in 1914 by Katharine Bement Davis, who argued for prisoner rehabilitation rather than crude incarceration and punishment. It also borrowed ideas from a resolution passed in 1929 by the American Bar Association to make psychiatric exams routine before parole was granted in cases involving psychopathy, sexual or otherwise. Following this resolution and a recommendation by the Committee for the Study of Sex Crimes, La Guardia initiated a plan whereby accused sex offenders and other felony defendants before the New York City Court of General Sessions could be ordered to undergo psychiatric appraisal.[16]

New York State statutes against sex crimes defined a sex offender as a person who "commits adultery, commits rape, commits incest, engages in sex practices with a minor, exposes himself indecently, or engages in perverse sex practices with beast, bird, or man."[17] Men arrested for homosexual activities were generally included under the last two categories. The court system in New York distinguished between felonies and misdemeanors, the former being tried by the Court of General Sessions and the latter by the Magistrates' Court. In addition to screening the accused, all those found guilty of a felony, including consensual sodomy, were remanded by the probation bureau of the Court of General Sessions for psychiatric investigation at Bellevue Hospital, where a report was assembled to assist the judge in making the appropriate sentence. In most cases, the convicted felon served prison time and could be given an indeterminate sentence with release contingent upon a psychiatrist's approval.[18] Those accused of misdemeanors, including "homosexual disorderly conduct," were punished by either a fine or a short sentence in a city penitentiary or workhouse. But in cases involving homosexuality, the judge had the discretion to refer the case for prosecution to the higher courts and the grand jury could decide to indict the defendant for felonious sodomy. Although psychiatric referrals were made across the range of sex offenders, the cases involving children or homosexuality between adults were the main focus of reports in psychiatric journals from the period. Coercive child abuse and consensual homosexuality were thus highlighted as the two most menacing offenses.[19]

Arrests for all types of sex offenses increased considerably in New York City during the last half of the 1930s. During 1936 alone, 500 convicted sex offenders were sent to Riker's Island, of which 175 had been charged with various offenses involving homosexuality and the remainder with offenses ranging from indecent exposure to pedophilia and rape. Following two highly publicized murders of children in the borough of Queens, twice as many men were charged with sex offenses from August 1 through September 1937 as were during the same period in 1936, largely because of stepped-up police vigilance and the agitation of panicked citizens.[20]

The perception among many psychiatrists that homosexuality was fundamentally psychopathic made those arrested for homosexual offenses a readily available population upon which to try out various kinds of psychiatric intervention. While some men were able to serve short sentences or pay fines and be released, a significant number lacked the resources to acquire adequate legal representation. Those who faced felony charges for sodomy included a fair number of what psychiatrist George Henry referred to as "underprivileged" homosexuals, lacking the educational and economic resources of their more "socially adjusted" counterparts.[21] Police harassment of "homosexual hoodlums" and "exhibitionistic fairies" was part and parcel of the mayor's public relations campaign that especially targeted working-class and impoverished men, including a significant number of African Americans and Caribbean immigrants.

In spite of subsequent evidence debunking the notion that homosexual offenders were recidivists, the more economically disadvantaged among them were subject to indeterminate sentencing as much in the interests of keeping them off the streets as of rehabilitating them.[22] In addition, many lacked the financial resources to pay for defense lawyers. La Guardia's anti-homosexual crackdowns, along with the psychiatric commentary that underpinned them, increased class tensions within the gay subculture of New York City, and established what amounted to a class distinction between those who were "socially adjusted"—that is, discreet in their sexual assignations and gender comportment—and those who were classified as "delinquent." In the latter category were placed those seen to pose a greater danger to the public by using city thoroughfares and parks as rendezvous spots for male prostitution and sexual trysts. Their legal fate was similar to that of female prostitutes, who during this same period were also scapegoated for engendering vice and venereal disease in the city.[23] The flamboyant display of cross-gender "exhibitionism" among "fairies" dressed in drag and the treacherous acts of lewdness and extortion among the "homosexual hoodlums" were described by George Henry both as psychopathic symptoms and public nuisances. Thus, psychiatry and policy-making were coupled in New York City's response to the sex offender.

"THE CHALLENGE OF SEX OFFENDERS"

The subject of homosexuality was addressed at a 1937 symposium on "The Challenge of Sex Offenders" held in New York at the Twenty-eighth Annual meeting of the National Committee for Mental Hygiene. The Committee's sponsorship of such a symposium was in keeping with its history of lending scientific expertise to remedy problems of modern life. From its inception, the movement for mental hygiene focused on the prevention of psychological problems which had important social dimensions, including mental deficiency, criminality, psychoneuroses, war-related traumas, epilepsy, alcoholism, family and marital unhappiness, and homosexuality and other "perversions."

The National Committee for Mental Hygiene, consisting mainly of psychiatrists, coordinated interdisciplinary research on these topics nationwide and offered advice to schools, industries, and prisons on dealing with the mentally disturbed. In addition, it promoted legislation to treat mental illness more effectively, and it developed programs to ensure mental hygiene in the general population through public education. The mental hygiene movement contributed to the expansion of psychiatry into the mainstream of public discourse and policy-making by focusing on common psychological problems.[24] But policy-minded psychiatrists also positioned themselves as experts in the treatment of grossly aberrant and socially threatening disorders as well. Thus, it was fitting that by the late 1930s, leading psychiatrists associated with mental hygiene would be commenting on the perceived increase of sex criminals in New York City. Interestingly, they did so by suggesting that sex offenders and "normal" people had much more in common than was generally believed. Echoing a Freudian tenet, they announced that everyone had sexual and psychological problems, but that what distinguished normal people was their ability to control their primitive urges.[25]

Three of the speakers at the 1937 symposium were members of the Committee for the Study of Sex Variants, though no mention was made of this in the symposium proceedings. Edward Strecker, Karl Bowman, and Austin MacCormick were concerned about the potential social problems caused by homosexuality, but they were opposed to the persecution of homosexuals and they questioned the value of prosecuting men for engaging in consensual homosexual acts with other adults. They cautioned that sensationalistic reports had exaggerated the incidence of sex crimes. But they agreed that something needed to be done about the problem. Each authority reiterated that rational and dispassionate scientific approaches to the problem were superior to harsh legal punishment or public hysteria. Psychiatrist Edward Strecker opened the session by stating the proposition that contemporary American social taboos and a lack of proper sex education, rather than preventing the problem, were significant factors contributing to sex offenses. Without denying that the public should be protected from sex criminals, Strecker called for a more liberal consideration of the matter, stating that "there is a very close relationship between so-called normal sex and abnormal sex."[26]

Strecker noted that cross-cultural evidence of different sex customs revealed that the American system of taboos and laws was not only arbitrary but may even engender the psychological repression that gave rise to sexual maladjustment. His bottom line was that ignorance and moral contradictions were largely to blame not only for the offenses perpetrated by maladjusted individuals but also for the social condemnation and harsh punishment that prevented those classified as sex offenders from maturing to healthy adult heterosexuality. In his comments, Strecker problematized the existing state of knowledge about sex crimes by drawing upon two boundary disputes simultaneously being debated within anthropology and endocrinology: that between the categories of "normal" and "abnormal" sex customs, and that between the categories of "male" and "female": "In the present state of our knowledge, the exact differences between the male and the female sex hormone cannot be determined with any certainty, so alike are they in their chemical structures. That is an index of our abysmal ignorance concerning this problem."[27]

New York City Commissioner of Crime Austin MacCormick commented that recidivism rates for sex offenders were alarmingly high and that psychiatric treatment, medical castrations, and proper sex education were possible remedies to the problem.[28] Karl M. Bowman, director of the psychiatric division of Bellevue Hospital, followed by advocating a holistic approach to understanding not only sex crimes but sexuality in general. "Any attempt," he noted, "to study sex behavior apart from the personality of the individual and the culture in which he lives, can be of little value."[29] Repeating what had become a commonplace among forensic psychiatrists dating back to the nineteenth century, Bowman stated that one should focus not on the crime but on the personality and environment of the criminal, a job best left to psychiatrists.[30]

In an effort to quell the public hysteria about sex offenses, Bowman reiterated Strecker's comments that "there is no general agreement as to what constitutes normal behavior. Different cultures have entirely different standards and customs."[31] He drew upon recent research in cultural anthropology, including the work of Bronislaw Malinowski and Margaret Mead, to argue that sex offenses were not the product of biological instinct, but arose from cultural systems that repressed and deformed the expression of healthy sexuality.[32] Bowman credited Malinowski and Freud for demonstrating that, contrary to popular belief, children were naturally sexual beings.[33] Thus, extreme repression of children's sexuality may be unhealthy and public hysteria to protect the innocent may be misguided if it further intensified irrational restrictions.

Without condoning sex offenders, Bowman went on to note that humans were relatively plastic beings who adapted to the conventions and restrictions of their cultures. A high level of sexual repression together with double standards and contradictions in social mores, he argued, may give rise to sexual maladjustment resulting in sex offenses. A society that punishes "peeping Toms" and "exhibitionists," while encouraging people to watch salacious motion pictures and paying strippers to dance in nightclubs, was a breeding ground for maladjustments. "Our own culture," he continued, "is very repressive, inconsistent, and divided on some phases of the subject [of sex]. Such a cultural attitude makes for greater conflict and difficulty in adjustment of the sex instinct."[34]

Specifically addressing the subject of homosexuality, Bowman questioned existing constitutional and biological theories, quoting a favorite passage from Bernhard Zondek's finding that "the testicle of the stallion contains over 500 times as much female hormone as the ovary of the sexually mature mare."[35] "Certainly no one would think of the stallion as homosexual," Bowman observed. Marshaling evidence from Mead's study in Samoa, he continued by remarking that the definitions of masculine and feminine vary across cultures, thus making studies which assume an equivalence between homosexuals and sex inversion deeply problematic.[36] In sum, Bowman argued that sex offenders, whether they be homosexual or heterosexual, differed from normal people not so much in constitutional traits but in their inability to control impulses otherwise restrained by normal people. In his words, "there is a deep-rooted sexual problem in most normal persons, but the individual is able to carry on in spite of this. We do not find that the neurotic necessarily has any greater sex problem than the normal individual. Often he is merely unable to adapt himself so well to the stresses and strains imposed by such a problem."[37]

In this gesture, Bowman noted the tenuous and culturally contingent nature of normality and implied that homosexual offenders and "normal people" were divided by a thin line, subject to changes and disturbances in the cultural system. The civilized sexual morality that Freud had noted to be a cause of modern nervousness was, in Bowman's view, also an impediment to treating and preventing sex offenders. But he departed from Freud's thesis in *Civilization and Its Discontents*, by noting that excessive sexual repression in "primitive" societies indicated that repression itself was not a prerequisite for the advancement of civilization but could in fact be an impediment to true enlightenment and healthy social order.

In light of the growing public hysteria about sex crimes, the participants at the 1937 symposium sought to establish a rational approach to the subject. They were concerned that the media was whipping up irrational fear and that the police and judges would act capriciously in prosecuting men who were not responsible for crimes against children. Their intervention to stop this hysteria offers another clue as to why the subjects of the sex variant study would turn to them with trust. At the same time, their scientific quest to learn more about homosexuality continued to be rooted in a general assumption that homosexuality was a sign of maladjustment that deserved careful attention.

TREATING THE HOMOSEXUAL OFFENDER

The problem of homosexual offenders led forensic psychiatrists in New York City to investigate and weigh causal factors in the hopes that homosexuality could be controlled and eliminated. George Henry played an important role in such investigations. His studies of homosexual mental patients, "overt homosexuals," and "underprivi-leged homosexuals" formed the basis for assumptions about what motivated certain individuals to commit homosexual acts that were against the law. He opposed the idea of throwing people in jail but believed the some were seriously maladjusted and could pose a danger to themselves and to the rest of society. He believed that in order to establish proper prevention and treatment methods, scientists would need to discern the specific factors that led to the kinds of gross mal-adjustment that threatened public safety.

In earlier studies published in 1934, Henry had explored the psy-chogenic and constitutional factors that related homosexuality to per-sonality disorders among 250 adult mental patients, 228 of whom were homosexuals (123 male and 105 female).[38] He concluded that psychoses in male and female homosexuals were more intense than among heterosexuals and that they suffered from paranoia and schizo-phrenia as a result of early life traumas. But he noted that, while psychogenic factors were influential, the psychosexual differences between heterosexuals and homosexuals depended also on consti-tutional deviations obvious in homosexuals. The males, he noted, tended to have "boyish form," longer legs, and relatively narrow hips, indicating delayed gonadal development with compensatory pituitary activity. These traits, along with the feminine carrying angle of the pelvis, "suggest that structurally the homosexual male has remained nearer the species type rather than progressing to the highly differ-entiated adult masculine form." In reference to the female patients, he noted that "skeletal immaturity in the female homosexuals is most evident in the high percentage of contracted pelves."[39] The muscula-ture of the homosexuals compared to the heterosexuals also suggested that the former are closer to the species type: the men were reported to have excess fat and feminine contours and the women had deficient fat, firm muscles, and masculine contours. Henry noted, "assuming that there are constitutional differences, such as have been mentioned, between homosexual and heterosexual individuals, it is not surprising that their psychosexual behavior should also be different."[40]

In 1937, Henry reiterated these general conclusions, this time re-porting on one hundred "socially well adjusted men and women whose preferred form of libidinous gratification is homosexual and who regularly experience pleasure from homosexual relations."[41] Out of this group, eighty were ultimately selected for inclusion in *Sex Variants*. Although these people were, in Henry's view, not as seriously disturbed as were his mental patients, he noted that their interviews indicated that "well adjusted overt homosexuals are rare."[42] In his summary to the 1937 article on psychogenic factors in overt homosexuality, published in the *American Journal of Psychiatry*, Henry concluded that a large proportion of homosexuals appear to be predisposed by constitution and environment and many drift into homosexual adjustment because of obstacles to heterosexuality. Furthermore he noted that many of these cases could have been prevented; "prevention involves eugenics as well as the mental hygiene of the predisposed individual and his family."[43] Dr. E. E. Mayer of the Pittsburgh Municipal Mental Health Clinic commented on Henry's report by noting that Henry "has rightfully emphasized the importance of psychogenic factors." However, he continued, "there is no practical aspect in considering homosexuality from the standpoint of a biological defect, or of misdirected hormone activity, or of residuals of primitive cults inherent in certain individuals."[44]

It appears that Henry took Mayer's comment to heart as he proceeded, in the following year, to publish an article on the "social factors in the case histories of one hundred underprivileged homosexuals" (see note 18). But even in this study, though his emphasis shifted toward focusing on social factors, Henry continued to believe that certain men were constitutionally predisposed to homosexuality. His logic resembled that advanced by Havelock Ellis, who had argued that true homosexuals had a particular constitutional predisposition but that this predisposition could be overcome or could remain dormant if such individuals did not experience a triggering episode or were not subjected to unhealthy milieux. Henry, like Ellis, thought that loose morals and a disregard for the law were common among the lower classes and that these elements, combined with poverty, activated a constitutional predisposition to homosexuality and exacerbated the maladjustments suffered by homosexual men.

In his 1938 study of "underprivileged homosexuals," Henry reviewed probation records and employed an undercover research assistant to gather incidental information about a homosexual underworld within which he believed criminal behavior was endemic. Statistics on convictions in New York City revealed that the majority of those arrested for all sex crimes were white native-born American men.[45] Nevertheless, Henry believed that "invariably these men were found to come from recent immigrant stock," and that they tended to lack formal education and have difficulty holding down jobs. Furthermore, "they came from depressed districts. . . . They made no constructive use of the overabundance of leisure. The cheap movies, the pool room, the street-corner gang, and the underworld enterprisings furnish the boundaries of the sex offender's social life."[46]

Henry concluded that excessive sexual impulses and a general tendency toward criminality led these men to commit offenses as expressions of hereditary taint ("a poor biological start") and socially conditioned psychopathic personalities.[47] Poor parental relations, lack of education, and poverty were primary contributing factors in their maladjustment. In the homosexual underworld, Henry observed, even the economically disadvantaged but "orderly homosexual" slipped into deeper moral and psychological corruption as a result of their uncontrollable impulses to solicit sex in public places. These men were forced into blackmail and extortion by opportunistic "rough trade" and predatory "wolves," men whose appearance and demeanor were unmistakably masculine, who tended to assume the "active" sexual role, and who were loathe to admit they were homosexual. The presence of these various types of homosexuals scattered across a continuum of both gender and sexual roles led Henry to question the inversion paradigm, as Terman had done several years earlier. But he continued to believe that the majority of homosexuals were constitutionally predisposed to have difficulty conforming to normal sex roles and to achieve psychosexual maturity.

Biological theories regarding homosexuality and sex offenders were countered emphatically in 1939 in a pair of articles in the *American Journal of Orthopsychiatry* by New York psychiatrist Joseph Wortis and anthropologist Ruth Benedict. Wortis and Benedict noted that sex offenses resulted not from biological instinct but from social and cultural factors that deprived men of opportunities to mature into law abiding citizens.[48] Wortis was persuaded by Benedict's culturalist approach and commented that "the argument that only congenital psychopaths can become sexually depraved, because sexual depravity is a sign of constitutional psychopathy, amounts to little more than a more technical expression of the spontaneous distaste generally felt toward sexual perversions."[49]

Referencing her own studies of Native American Plains Indian tribes, Benedict supplemented Wortis's ideas. She observed that in societies with "certain political arrangements, rules of distribution of property, [and] certain familial structures," sex offenses such as rape, bestiality, and corrupting the morals of minors were nonexistent, "since every adult has opportunity for sex expression among his own age-group, girl children are married at puberty and there are freely accessible means for changing sex partners."[50] Noting that "sexual perversions" existed in some tribes, Benedict described homosexuality as it was culturally sanctioned among the Dakota in the figure of the berdache, a "passive homosexual" who assumed the role of woman, cross-dressing and marrying other men. Those designated as such, while ridiculed behind their backs, were regarded with high esteem as the best wives because they excelled in both men's and women's tasks.

Benedict used the example to question the constitutional etiology of homosexuality, stating that the berdache was physiologically indistinguishable from other men and acquired his position as a result of balking at the masculine role during adolescent training for the "warpath." A neighboring tribe, the Ojibwa, had no distinctly male and female roles and consequently no berdaches. Comparing these cultures with one another and with modern metropolitan societies, Benedict argued that sexual orientation was plastic, that social factors gave rise to homosexuality, and that homosexuality, which could be beneficial to the overall functioning of a culture, arose only in contexts where there were strictly enforced distinctions between femininity and masculinity.[51]

Benedict, like Bowman and Strecker, stressed that the intensity of sexual repression in the United States was to blame for psychosexual maladjustments among its citizens. She argued that classifying consensual homosexual acts as sex crimes was evidence of the acute sexual repression that in fact fostered the very thing it sought to eliminate. That is, by requiring the strict adherence to gender roles and by placing taboos on premarital and extramarital heterosexuality, modern society had engendered reactions that resulted in substitutive sexualities. She did not believe that these reactions were by definition neurotic symptoms nor did she think they were necessarily bad. She was careful to distinguish between violent sexual assaults and consensual acts, noting that while both might be responses to sexual repression, the latter were positive and the former ought to be prosecuted. Though she never mentioned her own lesbianism in discussions of homosexuality, Benedict was clearly more tolerant toward homosexuals than the moral conservatives who advocated intensified police surveillance, increased arrests, and harsher punishments for those who committed homosexual acts. And, through her emphasis on the plasticity of gender and sexual roles, she questioned the idea that homosexuality resulted from constitutional or inborn factors. In so doing she was one of a growing number of authorities who suggested that the distinction between heterosexuals and homosexuals, like that between masculinity and femininity, was culturally produced and thus contingent and subject to change. She also was among the few of her time to state that homosexuality in and of itself was not a sign of pathology.

Clearly, scientific research on sex roles and homosexuality had an impact on discussions of public policy for dealing with the homosexual offender. And although psychiatrists generally believed that homosexuality was a pathological condition, many began to think of it on a continuum of sex variations, involving biological, psychological, and cultural factors. Placing it in a cultural context, as Wortis and Benedict did, revealed a need to reform both the sex offender himself and the society out of which he emerged. Such a task was multidisciplinary in scope, but psychiatrists positioned themselves as the key authorities for assessing and treating the problem. Out of their efforts would emerge new insights into what should constitute modern and enlightened norms in gender relations and sexual mores. The subject of homosexuality, highlighted among other sexual aberrations, became a vehicle for pronouncing and positing new norms, couched mainly in contradistinction to homosexuality, and applicable to modern men and women of the "normal" population.

THE LIMITS OF PROGRESSIVE INTERVENTIONS

In general, the social scientists and physicians discussed so far in this chapter contributed to the articulation of an optimistic and interventionist approach to social problems. Like those responsible for the implementation of the New Deal, these writers were confident that enlightened public policy could reduce if not cure many social ills. In their eyes, the cornerstone of such policies was rational scientific inquiry. On the basis of their research, they offered an interpretation of antisocial activities that attributed such activities to psycho-social maladjustment. George Henry persisted in believing that constitutional factors played a role in causing homosexual delinquency, but he, like others, began to focus more on the psychogenic and environmental factors that gave rise to homosexuality. In the area of sexual offenses, the moral a reader could draw from the works of Mead, Benedict, Strecker, and Bowman was that the difference between the offender and the "normal" person lies not in the nature of the offender's sexuality but rather in the offender's failure to channel his or her behavior into socially acceptable forms of expression. And the conclusion, for public policy, that such a reader could draw is that the cure to the problem of sexual offense lies in readjustment: in most cases, the adjustment of the person to society, so that the person no longer gives offense; and in some cases, the readjustment of society, so that the "normal" population no longer takes offense. The reader would also understand that the site of such readjustments of individuals ought to be the clinic, or for serious cases the mental hospital, rather than the prison.

However, in spite of the intentions of progressive authorities, their interventions did little to counter popular prejudices that regarded the homosexual as a distinct and dangerous type of person commonly associated with lower-class social milieux. In a grossly apparent way, sensationalistic reporting characterized the homosexual in a manner that portrayed the public sphere as endangered by a sick and licentious underworld. At the same time that New York's commissioner of corrections Austin MacCormick was working with Bowman and Henry to develop the diversion program, the rank-and-file policemen of New York City were aggressively carrying out orders to crack down on homosexuals. Their actions were fueled by La Guardia's response to the public outcry over sex crimes. Regardless of experts' admonitions to the contrary, police arrests of homosexuals increased dramatically during the second half of the decade. Through the intertwined actions of the police and sensationalistic journalists, the "normal" public was encouraged to regard homosexuality as threatening and repugnant. Clearly, George Henry had a more sympathetic and pitying attitude toward homosexuals than did many of the police on Mayor La Guardia's force. But he too believed that the public indiscretions of overt homosexuals were unsavory and that they required official intervention. His observation that homosexual offenses grew out of the general disorder of the underclasses both reflected and further fueled the disproportionate arrests of men who were legally, socially, and economically disadvantaged.

Reactions against the homosexual *qua* sex offender were displacements of larger fears about social and economic upheaval occasioned by the Depression, by the changing nature of women's and men's roles leading up to it, and by rising tensions within heterogeneous urban populations. Casting the homosexual as a danger to public safety became a powerful means for establishing a new version of distinctions between male and female, heterosexual and homosexual, and normal and abnormal sexualities. Progressive social scientists and physicians stressed that sex differences existed on a single continuum. Some, such as Mead and Benedict, suggested that the same could be said of sexual orientation: that homosexuality and heterosexuality existed on a single continuum, that the definition and manifestations of each were culturally constructed, and that therefore they were subject to change. These notions accommodated new ways of thinking about masculinity and femininity and about sexual roles and sexual orientation. But, again, they did little in practical terms to put an end to the idea that homosexuals could and should be readily distinguishable from heterosexuals. To the contrary, LaGuardia's new plan to divert homosexual offenders into psychotherapeutic examinations required that they be identified and isolated from other men. This may have been for their safety as much as for any other reason, but the policy was also based upon an assumption that homosexuals ought to be singled out for special investigation. Progressives such as Bowman and Henry believed that this would allow them to get to the root causes of homosexual maladjustment and that it would help their patients to bring indiscreet sexual impulses under control.

Karl Bowman, however, noted in 1937 that "when we try to study such problems as homosexuality, we find ourselves lost at once in a tremendous mass of contradictory studies, and the problem seems to become hopelessly involved."[52] Indeed in the second half of the 1930s, theories about the cause of homosexuality ranged from hereditary and constitutional explanations to those emphasizing social conditioning and psychosexual development. But the general scientific and medical consensus was that homosexuality, when expressed publicly or "overtly," was not only socially undesirable but psychopathic. There were, however, differing opinions as to whether laws were the most effective means for dissuading homosexual behavior.

Because arrests for homosexual offenses generally involved consenting adults, psychiatrist Joseph Wortis questioned whether a reform of the New York state sex crime statutes was warranted to distinguish consensual from nonconsensual acts. He argued that homosexuality in some situations ought to be regarded, like adultery, as perhaps socially undesirable but not as grounds for criminal prosecution. Wortis, like many other forensic psychiatrists, believed that criminal punishment of coercive sex offenders without psychiatric treatment was useless. He argued for reform in social attitudes toward homosexuality, believing that sexual aberrations might wither away if moral contradictions were eliminated and sex education were encouraged.

The best deterrents to perversity, Wortis argued, were consistently applied social taboos, together with sexual enlightenment that encouraged heterosexual adjustment. Such an approach would increase the "uneasy conscience of perverts" so as to help them control their impulses. Judges, doctors, and parents should work "not merely to protect individuals, but also to perpetuate and strengthen the normal sexual traditions of our society."[53] Hence, even arguments suggesting the decriminalization of homosexuality reinforced the idea that it was an undesirable outcome of psychopathology. But, importantly, the solution of applying moral pressure to stem the rise of homosexuality was not confined to the targeting of homosexuals. Instead it was part of a broader agenda for prescribing norms that would apply to the entire society.

During the social upheaval of the Depression, homosexuality came to associated again with criminality, uncontrollable urges, psychopathic personalities, and a proclivity toward violating the innocent. Against a specter of menacing lust in the public sphere, the companionate marriage and stable nuclear family itself had a spectral presence in much of the scientific discourse on sexuality during the 1930s. Its invocation in scientific and popular commentary grew out of delineations of sex variance and homosexual offenses and, as such, was assumed to be the necessary foundation of social order and economic recovery for modern America.

Most authorities who adopted a self-proclaimed rational approach to the problem of homosexuality in the 1930s made clear that their ideas should not be mistaken for condoning it. Among the experts we have surveyed, Benedict was the only exception, and even she was careful to distance herself from openly advocating homosexuality. However, through their contributions to policy-making about sex offenders, reformers urged lawmakers and citizens alike to understand homosexuality through a seemingly benevolent lens, as a pathological condition requiring the expertise and guidance of scientifically trained experts. Thus, the presence of sex variance and homosexuality in modern societies provided a rationale for further inquiry to determine its particular causes and manifestations. We have seen some of the consequences of this rationale in our survey of the Sex Variant study of the same period.

Bowman, like Wortis, respected the suggestions offered by Mead, Malinowski, and Benedict that extreme sexual repression actually engendered homosexuality. Nevertheless, laws that criminalized consensual homosexuality remained in force. In the context of heightened public fear about sex crimes, there was little hope that legal reforms to decriminalize homosexuality would be accepted. Bowman and his colleagues who sought to counter the fears of the public instead advocated what they thought was a reasonable middle course: subjecting men convicted of homosexual offenses to psychiatric observations and treatment. Bowman would wait another decade and a half to propose that homosexual acts among adults should be decriminalized. His action was prompted by the tremendous impact of research conducted by a zoologist turned human sex researcher, to which we will soon return.

PSYCHOANALYTIC AND BEHAVIORISTIC APPROACHES TO HOMOSEXUALITY

By the early 1940s, subtle suggestions to reform laws and attitudes about homosexuality were drowned out by fear and loathing toward homosexuals, despite the express aims of people like Henry, Wortis, Benedict, and Bowman. This loathing was abetted, though not directly intentionally, by the assumptions of some psychoanalysts and behavioral psychologists who believed that homosexuality was due to psychogenic and environmental factors.

Psychoanalysis, which began gaining influence in American psychiatry during the 1930s, shaped the discussion of homosexuality by rejecting the idea of a congenital or hereditarian basis and by exploring familial relations that seemed to engender it. In many of the psychoanalytic writings of the time, sex inversion (or what we would call gender inversion) was tied not to endocrine or genetic factors but to children's difficulties in identifying properly with either the mother or father. According to this view, the overarching factor in homosexuality was not biological but familial; parents of the same sex as the psychosexually disturbed child were described as unstable, abusive, or absent while those of the opposite sex were either dominant or over-solicitous. Authors stated that such circumstances led children to identify with the parent or parent-substitute who represented strength, affection or security. Boys in these family scenarios tended to identify with the mother and girls with the father.[54]

Initially, psychoanalytically inclined doctors in the United States, writing in the 1910s, appeared to be more sympathetic toward homosexuals and suggested, as Freud did, that no one escaped childhood psychosexual trauma and thus that neuroses were common even among those with heterosexual orientations in adulthood. But in the 1930s and 1940s, some American psychoanalysts grew more hostile toward homosexuals and tended to blame them, rather than society, for their neuroses. They were influenced by a similar trend among some European psychoanalysts.

In 1930, the Viennese psychoanalyst Wilhelm Stekel attacked Hirschfeld's "propaganda" in an American psychoanalytic journal, saying that it "produce[d] homosexuality" by "removing these people from all sense of responsibility, thus blocking possibilities of reform."[55] In his argument for curing homosexuality, Stekel asserted that he had never met a "truly happy homosexual." Writing specifically about male homosexuals, he vehemently opposed both hereditary etiology and models of congenital inversion, arguing instead that homosexuals were incapable of real love. He opined that they feared love and dreaded women, sentiments which were rooted in sadism. Stekel emphasized that male homosexuality resulted from pathological families with strong mothers and weak fathers. This idea was to become a truism among American psychoanalysts by the middle of the twentieth century, who elaborated on it by suggesting that families with strong fathers and weak mothers could also result in homosexual children.

Stekel further noted that the homosexual was afflicted by a kind of psychological atavism, and he explained the preponderance of homosexuality among artists and writers as a manifestation of hypertrophied ego, of which a most pronounced symptom was pathological rebelliousness. In his view, most homosexuals quit or evaded psychoanalysis and pretended to be happy but were really miserable. He believed adamantly that homosexuality could be overcome and accused Hirschfeld of leading patients to believe that they could "neither be changed nor cured"; the patients then "cling to their illness because they either derive erotic thrills from it or through it." In what would appear to be a strange twist, Stekel opposed criminal sanctions against homosexuality, not for reasons of tolerance but on the grounds that it only created self-pitying martyrs. A growing number of American psychoanalysts echoed Stekel's sentiments by openly condemning homosexuality on similar grounds.[56]

In a popular advice book by W. Beran Wolfe, published in 1935, the author used psychoanalytic ideas to place the onus of psychopathology on the individual rather than on an intolerant society. To make his point, Wolfe attacked Radclyffe Hall's *Well of Loneliness:*

> Homosexuality is not, as is popularly supposed, a product of pre-natal influences, of congenital predispositions, or of hereditary taint.... Any girl with the usual homosexual tendencies of adolescence may be led to believe that she is condemned and dedicated to a life of homo-

sexuality reading such pseudo–scientific hocus–pocus. . . . When the smoke screen of misinformation about homosexuality is cleared, sexual inversion will unmask itself as a flight from the reality of mature heterosexual relations. As in every other neurosis, the victim attempts to camouflage the real nature of his evasion by setting up a plausible exoneration and exculpation. The most common homosexual argument makes heredity the scapegoat for sexual deviation. The fact that there is no single shred of biological or medical evidence for this view does not deter the average homosexual from pointing mournfully to the idea that his feeling for the opposite sex is congenitally abnormal.[57]

You will recall that in 1929, six years before Wolfe wrote *A Woman's Best Years,* Radclyffe Hall's *Well of Loneliness* was banned for featuring a female invert as its central character and for making the claim that inversion, though anomalous, was natural and thus ought to be tolerated. Wolfe's text, appearing in the year the CSSV initially formed, indicates a hostile attitude toward homosexuality among some of the American popularizers of psychoanalysis, if not also among psychoanalysts themselves.

In 1935, Karl Menninger exclaimed that "homosexuality is never silent, it always expresses itself in everybody's personality in some way or other." But for Menninger, as for other American psychoanalysts, an individual's mental health inhered in his or her ability to repress or sublimate overt homosexual behaviors and thus to adjust to the cultural context in which heterosexuality was the undisputed norm.[58] Thus, ideas about overcoming homosexuality through will-power and therapy, advanced by Adolf Meyer several decades earlier, persisted. By contrast Freud, in his famous 1935 letter to an American mother, stated that homosexuality "is assuredly no advantage, but it is nothing to be classified as an illness; we consider it to be a variation of sexual development. . . . It is a great injustice to consider homosexuality as a crime and cruel, too."[59] He assured the mother that he would be unable to transform her son into a heterosexual, but that analysis could certainly help him to adjust to his situation and to ameliorate the unhappiness or conflicts he might suffer.

The Viennese emigre psychoanalyst Abraham Brill, who had translated many of Freud's works into English for American audiences, revised his earlier sympathetic sentiments by emphasizing the deep-rooted pathology of homosexuality. In 1940 he wrote:

> That even so-called classical inverts are not entirely free from some paranoid traits is quite obvious on even superficial observation. Having encountered hundreds of homosexuals, some of whom were prominent

in artistic, philanthropic and other fields, I have never found one who, on closer observation, did not show paranoid traits. They are all over-suspicious, "shadowy," and mistrustful. Most of them are unreliable, intriguing, picayune and impetuous. . . . I have felt for years that this behavior was engendered by our civilization, where homosexuals are treated as outcasts. However I am convinced that this is only partially true. Most of these traits are due to anal-sadistic fixations and regressions.[60]

As hereditarian and congenital theories declined in the 1940s, psycho-analysts were among the more openly hostile critics of homosexuality within the medical profession. Though Henry and his colleagues had construed sex variants to be deeply troubled and assumed many suffered from sexual maladjustments that could not be fully over-come, they were more sympathetic in general toward homosexuals than many psychoanalysts writing at the time. But the research of the CSSV was part of an overall trend toward greater psychiatric inter-vention and medical surveillance of homosexuality that came to the fore around the middle of the century and grew more powerful in the 1950s and 1960s.

Other psychiatrists in the United States refuted hereditarian and congenital etiological theories in the interests of establishing thera-peutic techniques they believed could assist homosexuals in gaining control over their impulses. For example, in 1937, Joseph Wortis re-futed existing research that claimed homosexuals had a distinct body build. He found psychogenic explanations much more convincing since they could account for the wide variety of homosexual men and women and did not repeat the common mistake of assuming homo-sexuality was part and parcel of sex inversion. In 1939, Hyman Bara-hal, who conducted his own study of constitutional factors under the auspices of the New York Psychiatric Institute, concluded that "there is little evidence that homosexuality is an organic or endocrinologi-cal condition."[61]

In subsequent years, there were a few exceptions to this trend to-ward rejecting hereditarian explanations. In 1945, the military psychi-atrists Herbert Greenspan and John D. Campbell reiterated the con-stitutional etiology of homosexuality. They specifically repudiated the notion that "bad" environments and undue maternal attachments caused homosexuality. Surprisingly, compared to many psychiatrists writing at the time, Greenspan and Campbell showed a remarkable sympathy for male homosexuals, distinguishing them from stereo-types that lumped homosexuals with neurotics, schizophrenics, and psychopaths. They noted that the "true homosexual" personality type was inverted (i.e., effeminate) as well as "'pseudo-sophisticated,' artistic, intelligent, productive, and even charitable and peaceable. . . . The true or latent homosexual does not rebel at his environment, but rather succumbs to the biological course laid out for him by nature. Further, the homosexual is capable of the deep warmth of emotional expression and human attachments that are so lacking in the usually cold and indifferent schizoid."[62] This led the authors to conclude with an argument against criminal penalties for homosexuality in favor of a psychotherapeutic approach that was "humane" and "understanding." In their words, "we are gradually coming to the realization that the homosexual suffers from a regrettable sexual anomaly, but otherwise is a normal, productive individual, who is neither a burden nor a detriment to society."[63] This perspective was largely overshadowed by 1945, especially among military psychiatrists who had linked the homosexual personality type with paranoia, schizophrenia, and pathological perversion and thus classified homosexuals as unfit to fight.[64]

In contrast to Greenspan and Campbell, a growing number of physicians and psychologists were interested in developing techniques to avert homosexuality in their patients. These included nausea-inducing aversion therapies, electroshock treatments, castrations, and lobotomies, all of which became much more common in the late 1930s and 1940s. In the framework of such treatments, the body remained key to ideas about homosexual etiology and behavior, but for psychiatrists inclined toward behavioral modification through stimulus interventions, it was conceptualized as a site where complex factors of conditioning could be manipulated. Thus, in contrast to being fixed by hereditary or congenital taint, behaviorists viewed the body as a register of the individual's psychosexual conditioning. In short, it was akin to a *tabula rasa* upon which experiences left their mark and aversion therapies could effect a reorientation.

Maverick psychiatrist Louis Max of New York University reasoned that homosexuality could be eliminated by interrupting or reconditioning a neurotic homosexual's desires. In 1935, he administered electric shocks to a young man whose homosexual behavior tended to occur following contact with a fetishistic stimulus. The aversion treatment was meant to "disconnect the emotional aura from this stimulus by means of electric shock, applied in conjunction with the presentation of the stimulus under laboratory conditions." Max reported that low shocks were ineffective, but "intensities higher than those usually employed on human subjects in other studies definitely diminished the emotional value of the stimulus for days after each experimental period." His patient claimed that four months after the end of the experiment he had lost "that terrible neurosis . . . not completely but 95% of the way."[65]

Other behavioral aversion studies continued to be developed in the late 1930s. In 1937, Atlanta doctor Newdigate Owensby experimented on male and female homosexuals using convulsive shock induced by Metrazol, a chemical stimulant. Owensby claimed success in administering the drug to induce seven to ten grand mal seizures per patient, thus eliminating all homosexual desires in a number of them. Concerned about the apparent increase of homosexuality in the United States, Owensby believed that this technique could benefit the nation as well as those who were willing "to make a sacrifice . . . to become sexually normal people."[66]

By comparison to techniques of this sort, the psychotherapeutic treatments suggested by progressive doctors, including those involved in the Sex Variant research, appear all the more enlightened. The Sex Variant study's approach to the body was not so plainly invasive nor was the study specifically intent upon altering the sexual orientation of its subjects. Furthermore, the study and the progressive psychiatrists who were summoned to respond to the alleged increase of sex crimes during the late 1930s seemed to offer a positive alternative to harsh criminal punishment, social condemnation, and ghoulish aversion experiments. When one imagines the public cry to eliminate all sex offenders and the zealous efforts of police and anti-vice agitators to apprehend all who were suspected of being homosexual, it is not surprising that sex variants would turn to authorities whom they believed were sympathetic and who might protect them from such hostility.

But in the years following the Sex Variant study, the faith many lesbians and homosexual men had invested in medical inquiry diminished. While many remained hopeful that physicians could be helpful and compassionate, a growing number began to see the pitfalls of relying on psychiatric models for understanding themselves and for making meager bids for social tolerance. They became aware of the limits of toleration when it was based on condescension and pity. Their disaffection amplified as psychoanalytic ideas gained greater influence in the United States. And as invasive aversion therapies became more widespread, many homosexuals came to regard these as graphic illustrations of physicians' and psychologists' hostility toward them. But faith in science per se was not abandoned, especially when a scientist named Alfred Kinsey came along to produce quantitative and massive evidence that homosexuality was a natural and common occurrence, even in the "general population." As we shall see, these findings led to pronounced political and professional tensions between purveyors of medical models for understanding homosexuality and Kinsey, who advanced a continuum model that would radically undermine the equation of homosexuality with pathology and that moved beyond pity and condescension toward arguments for homosexual rights.

9   DISEASE OR WAY OF LIFE?

Rarely has man been more cruel against man than in the condemnation and punishment of those accused of the so-called sexual perversion. . . . The penalties have included imprisonment, torture, the loss of life or limb, banishment, blackmail, social ostracism, the loss of social prestige, renunciation by friends and families, the loss of position in school or in business, severe penalties meted out for convictions of men serving in the armed forces, public condemnation by emotionally insecure and vindictive judges on the bench, and the torture endured by those who live in perpetual fear that their nonconformant sexual behavior will be exposed to public view. These are the penalties which have been imposed on and against persons who have done no damage to the property or physical bodies of others, but who have failed to adhere to the mandated custom. Such cruelties have not often been matched, except in religious and racial persecutions. . . . The judge who is considering the case of the male who has been arrested for homosexual activity, should keep in mind that nearly 40 percent of all other males in the town could be arrested at some time in their lives for similar activity, and that 20 to 30 percent of the unmarried males in that town could have been arrested for homosexual activity that had taken place within that same year.[1]
—*Alfred Kinsey (1948)*

Kinsey's erroneous conclusions pertaining to homosexuality will be politically and propagandistically used against the United States abroad, stigmatizing the nation as a whole in a whisper campaign, especially since there are no comparable statistics available for other countries.[2]
—*Edmund Bergler (1948)*

By the mid-1940s, most scientific authorities agreed that homosexuality resulted from a mixture of psychological factors and social conditioning and that also it could not be detected merely by examining the bodies of those suspected to be homosexual. Many continued to entertain the idea that homosexuality arose from underlying physiological processes related to hormones and that it might be hereditary in some cases, but they acknowledged that bodily factors could not be isolated from social factors. Following widespread revelations about the horrors of Nazi medicine, which had sullied the reputation of hereditarian and biological explanations for human behavior, the pendulum swung toward psycho- and sociogenic arguments that privileged "nurture" over "nature" as the origin of behavioral variations such as homosexuality. Alfred Kinsey's work radically shifted the way homosexuality was regarded since he not only called into question the idea that homosexual behavior was an epiphenomenon of specific biological conditions. More importantly, he deferred the question of causality in favor of exploring the significance of homosexual variation as a social phenomenon that he believed might reveal something about the human animal and about modern culture in general.

In 1941, the same year that George Henry conceded it was impossible to determine with any certainty the physical features that distinguished homosexuals from the "general" population, Kinsey published a highly influential article criticizing research on androgen and estrogen levels in the urine of male homosexuals. He noted a number of the study's methodological problems, including the small size of the subject sample and the inconsistencies in obtaining and measuring hormones among subjects. But Kinsey saved his greatest criticism for the study's unqualified use of the categories "homosexual" and its putative opposite, "normal," to classify individuals:

> More basic than any error brought out in the analysis of the above data is the assumption that homosexuality and heterosexuality are two mutually exclusive phenomena emanating from fundamentally and, at least in some cases, inherently different types of individuals. Any classification of individuals as 'homosexuals' or 'normals' (= heterosexuals) carries that implication. It is the popular assumption and the current psychiatric assumption, and the basis for such attempts as have been made to find hormonal explanations for these divergences in human behavior.[3]

Though targeted at a particular study, Kinsey's critique applied to the vast majority of the existing research on homosexuality. Taking issue with the "long-standing and widespread popular opinion that homosexual behavior depends on some inherent abnormality," Kinsey believed that most research on the subject encouraged this notion by relying on vague and simplistic definitions of homosexuality. Moreover, he implied that homosexuality ought not be regarded as an abnormality at all but instead as a naturally occurring variation in behavior.[4]

Kinsey, whose scientific credentials were well established, was particularly well situated to launch such a critique. He had been trained in zoology and spent the early portion of his career studying the behavior and morphology of gall wasps before turning in the late 1930s to study human sexual behavior. As a result of his training, Kinsey insisted on careful methods of classification and investigation. The researcher, he argued, must thoroughly investigate all relevant factors that might distinguish one individual from another rather than presume inherent differences based on unquestioned cultural assumptions. Kinsey believed that most extant research on homosexuality was careless and speculative on this score. And he was particularly critical of declarations made by psychiatrists who were satisfied to base their theories on very small numbers of ailing patients. Kinsey's methodological rigor led him in the 1941 article to reiterate that no causal relationship between anatomy and sexual history could be demonstrated without a knowledge first, of the full range of human sexual variation, and secondly, of the frequency with which each kind of sexual variation occurs in the population. "Until we know the nature of the gross behavior [of homosexuality] itself, no hormonal or other explanation is likely to fit the actuality."[5]

Kinsey based his famous studies of human sexual behavior on these very methodological principles by surveying a substantial number of people whom he believed represented a cross-section of the population. His interest in sexual behavior began in 1938 when he was chosen as the faculty coordinator at Indiana University of a newly established interdisciplinary marriage course in which Kinsey lectured on biology and invited guest faculty to cover various approaches to studying sex. In the summer of that year, he began collecting histories from his students and then moved on to include interviews from outside the university to vary his sampling. He was met with a conservative backlash which resulted in his removal from the marriage course in 1940. Regarding this more as a challenge than a defeat, Kinsey persisted in his research, believing, like other sex researchers who preceded him, that scientific knowledge about sexuality could alleviate problems caused by socially sanctioned forms of repression. In 1941, he received his first grant from the Rockefeller-funded Committee for Research in Problems of Sex to devote his efforts to a massive study of sexual behavior that culminated in the publication of his best-selling volumes, *Sexual Behavior in the Human Male* and *Sexual Behavior in the Human Female.*[6]

Kinsey undertook his research under the auspices of the newly established Institute for Sex Research at Indiana University. He was joined by assistants Wardell Pomeroy, Paul Gebhard, and Clyde Martin in conducting face-to-face interviews concerning the erotic histories and behavior of over 11,000 Americans (5,300 men and 5,940 women). Kinsey recruited subjects by word of mouth as well as through a variety of institutions including gay bars, schools, prisons, private clubs, YMCA groups, professional associations, colleges, hospitals, and medical clinics around the United States. Kinsey's team traveled to rural areas, small and medium–sized towns, suburbs, and large cities to conduct interviews. They sought a representative sample of average Americans in terms of "race–cultural group," geographic origin, religious affiliation, age, occupational class, educational level, and marital status. They interviewed subjects from posh locales, middle- and working–class neighborhoods, and city slums. Nearly all of the individuals analyzed in the published study were white, and Kinsey regretted not having enough histories of "Negroes" to include in his analysis. But his preliminary data from African American men indicated that "Negro and white patterns for comparable social levels are close if not identical."[7]

In sessions that lasted about two hours, each subject was asked between 300 and 500 questions, prepared ahead of time, though not strictly standardized. The team was not particularly interested in their interviewees' psychological motivations to behave as they did, and they generally assumed that subjects were telling the truth in reporting their histories.[8] They focused on "sexual outlet," or orgasm, as a way to measure sexual activity by analyzing the frequency of orgasm through six outlets: masturbation, nocturnal emissions, heterosexual petting, sexual intercourse, homosexual activity, and sexual contact with animals. Interview questions largely pertained to how, at what level of frequency, and under what circumstances subjects achieved orgasms or experienced erotic arousal from these various outlets.

Among the most publicized findings of the male study, published in 1948, was the surprisingly high rate of homosexual behavior among American men. Thirty-seven percent of the men surveyed reported at least one homosexual experience to orgasm after puberty, a slightly smaller number than the fifty percent who had homosexual experiences prior to puberty. Twenty-five percent had occasional homosexual experiences for at least three years between the ages of sixteen and fifty-five. Ten percent were exclusively homosexual for a period of at least three years between these same ages.[9] The data showed that homosexuality occurred in every age group, in every social class, in all occupations and in all regions of the United States, whether rural or urban.[10] Kinsey believed these statistics gave an accurate picture of the percentages of homosexuality in the overall population of American men.

Kinsey defined male homosexual behavior as when "one or both parties in the relation have come to ejaculation as a result of stimulation provided by another male."[11] His interview data led him to devise a seven-point scale for analyzing variations along a continuum from exclusive heterosexuality to exclusive homosexuality. Those who had no homosexual experiences were placed at the zero degree, those who engaged exclusively in homosexual relations at the sixth degree, and those who had a mixture of homosexual and heterosexual encounters at the various degrees in between. In doing so he showed that the heterosexual category was no more clear-cut than the homosexual category posited in most existing scientific and medical research. Kinsey's figures indicated that only half of the total population of men surveyed were exclusively heterosexual all their lives, while four percent were exclusively homosexual all their lives. A substantial forty-six percent of men had some combination of hetero- and homosexual experiences in their adult lives, a figure that shattered prevailing scientific and psychiatric beliefs.

His findings were highly publicized, and the news was rather shocking to many laypeople and medical authorities alike who believed that homosexuals were fundamentally pathological, sexually inverted, and belonged to small, physically distinguishable group. But couched in the larger context of his research, which reported substantial rates of pre- and extramarital relations as well as masturbation among American men, Kinsey's findings on homosexuality were regarded by many readers as just one facet of a larger revelation that moral taboos against sexual variations were commonly disregarded in real life. In fact, public opinion polls showed that his studies met with approval among a vast majority of Americans.[12] On the other hand, the news about homosexuality alarmed those of Kinsey's readers who were unsettled by the prospect that perverts were all around—in their neighborhoods, teaching in their children's schools, playing golf at their country clubs, singing in their church choirs, and perhaps even making policy at the highest levels of government. As we shall see, these fears were stoked by anti-homosexual government officials during the wave of domestic repression retrospectively coined McCarthyism. Nothing could have been further from Kinsey's own intentions.

Kinsey's study of female sexual behavior, published in 1953, reported a much lower incidence of female homosexuality than had the male study. Nevertheless, the numbers were still significant: of the nearly 6,000 women interviewed, twenty-eight percent had "recognized erotic responses to the same sex" and about twenty percent reported some same-sex erotic experience, which included "casual" contacts that elicited an erotic response but not orgasm. Thirteen percent of women had at least one homosexual experience involving orgasm prior to the age of forty-five, while three percent had exclusively homosexual experiences. Compared to males, a much larger proportion of women reporting homosexual contact restricted their activities to a single partner or two. Furthermore, of the 142 women who had the most extensive homosexual experience, seventy-one percent reported that they had no regrets about it. They represented every social and economic level, from prostitutes to physicians. Some twenty-seven percent of them reported getting into trouble because of it, usually with parents and family members who refused to accept them once their homosexual experiences were made known.[13] Kinsey used this information to suggest that taboos against lesbianism were harmful and outdated.

Kinsey regarded data on lesbianism as crucial for supporting his hunch that there was no such thing as a strictly vaginal orgasm. He discovered that women who engaged in sexual relations with other women reported a significantly higher frequency of orgasm and suggested that this was perhaps due to their ability to understand each other's "physiologic responses" as well as the psychology of their own sex better than men might.[14] He believed that men had perpetuated the myth of vaginal orgasm and, by doing so, had projected their own sexual needs onto women.[15] Kinsey was influenced in his thinking on the matter by Robert Latou Dickinson, who had become an ardent supporter and a personal friend.

Both Dickinson and George Henry had arrived at similar conclusions in their earlier studies, which found that lesbians tended to enjoy a high level of sexual satisfaction with one another and that they derived erotic pleasure from a wide variety of emotional and physical stimuli. This led Dickinson and Henry to urge men to learn about women's bodies and even to emulate the "sex play" carried out by lesbians.[16] Similarly, in his 1953 study, Kinsey went so far as to suggest that women in heterosexual relationships may be "more likely to prefer techniques which are closer to those which are commonly utilized in homosexual relationships," including "generalized emotional stimulation," "physical stimulation of the whole body," and "stimulation

of the clitoris and the labia minora." Kinsey, a master of euphemism
when it came to problems of male sexual performance and men's in-
opportune loss of erection, also suggested that women prefer "stimulation which, after it has once begun, is followed through to orgasm
without the interruptions which males, depending to a greater degree
than most females do upon psychologic stimuli, often introduce into
their heterosexual relationship."[17]

Kinsey's studies were popular among many women who found in
him an advocate for their sexual pleasure. Likewise, the work appealed
to a wide variety of average Americans who saw it as liberating largely
because it confirmed what many anecdotally knew: that what people
were supposed to do and what they actually did sexually were often
very different. Kinsey's research also changed the way that homosexuality was conceptualized in mainstream society as well as among scientists. Just as the research obliterated the idea of a clear-cut homosexual type, it effectively erased the possibility of such a thing as a
distinctly homosexual body. Katharine Bement Davis had done so decades earlier but without the benefit of the widespread publicity Kinsey garnered. Like Davis, Kinsey's use of statistical survey methods
called into question the typologizing methods endemic to most constitutional studies and psychiatric studies of homosexuality, including
George Henry's *Sex Variants.* But in spite of their apparent differences, both the Sex Variant study from the 1930s and Kinsey's research of the 1940s represented a shift from early sexologists' assumption of mutually exclusive binary oppositions (male versus female and
heterosexual versus homosexual) to a statistically based continuum of
variance. Most constitutional studies, which had been grounded on
the binary scheme, privileged the body as a key source for revealing
homosexuality and used techniques of physical examination in order
to divide people into distinct categories based on certain features. Using different techniques, psychiatric studies in the United States also
presumed that homosexuals belonged to a distinct class, though
mainly in psychopathological than in biological terms.

By contrast, the variance continuum was based on identifying and
quantifying variable elements, using statistical analyses for understanding the distribution of a population across a continuum, not necessarily in clearly demarcated categories. The variance model, albeit
deployed in different ways by Henry and Kinsey, pierced the *cordon
sanitaire* that had marked a clear-cut difference between males and
females and between heterosexuals and homosexuals, respectively. By
doing so, statistically based continuum models allowed for the possi-

bility that aspects of variance were dispersed throughout the population. Having demonstrated this, Kinsey's studies engendered intense anxiety, registered in a wide variety of criticisms launched almost immediately by social scientists, psychoanalysts, clergymen, and journalists who variously charged that his research was scientifically flawed, amoral, and even politically dangerous, whether or not it reported the truth.

THE BACKLASH AGAINST KINSEY

Many liberal psychiatrists, clergy, and public officials applauded Kinsey's work for bringing sexuality out into the open where it could be discussed rationally. In addition, the public was fascinated by his research findings. Immediately following its publication in 1948, *Sexual Behavior of the Human Male* made it to the New York Times best-seller list, where it remained for nearly seven months. The book ultimately sold more than 250,000 copies. But during this same moment, Kinsey was confronted by a number of critics, ranging from mild and generally hospitable reviewers to vociferously hostile antagonists.

Some critics charged that he was subjective, opinionated, and partisan in his methods as well as in his analysis. This group included statisticians who offered primarily technical critiques detailing flaws and biases in Kinsey's subject sampling and statistical analysis while otherwise praising his overall effort of elucidating sexual behavior.[18] But others focused specifically on the moral implications of his research. In their view, contrary to being objective and scientific, Kinsey was invested in promoting an agenda that valorized the widespread practice of sexual perversions. These critics were especially irked by Kinsey's intimation that sexual activities that were commonly practiced ought to be regarded as natural and thus tolerated as normal, even if they were morally objectionable.

Among the first critiques of this sort to appear in print was a scathing article in the *American Journal of Psychiatry*, written by two sociologists who took issue with Kinsey's sampling methods. They charged that Kinsey's interviewees were not representative of average American men and that his findings of sexual variations, and specifically homosexuality, were inflated as a result of interviewing sordid types of people. Who else, the authors asked, but perverted individuals would speak openly to a researcher about their sexual behavior? The principal author, A. Hobbs, raised similar moralistic criticisms of Kinsey's volume on female sexual behavior when it was released in

1953. Upping the ante from his earlier attack, Hobbs, along with co-author W. Kephart, referred to the research as largely a product of Kinsey's "fantasy" and argued that it sullied the reputations of normal American women whose "capabilities for greater sexual restraint" ought to be cherished and protected instead of questioned and thus undermined.[19] Lewis Terman, though less vociferous, made a similar critique of *Sexual Behavior of the Human Male*, stating that in "numerous passages" Kinsey "recklessly worded and slanted evaluations . . . the slanting being often in the direction of implied preference for uninhibited sexual activity."[20]

Kinsey's findings on homosexuality provoked a major portion of the criticism he received. Anthropologist Ashley Montagu, a staunch proponent of social conditioning arguments, applauded Kinsey's efforts. But he believed it was unfortunate that Kinsey's data had been used to imply that homosexuality, because it was prevalent, should be accepted. Montagu hoped that Kinsey's data could help parents to learn about the factors leading to homosexuality so that it would "be reduced to the vanishing point."[21]

Another group of critics believed Kinsey's approach debased human sexuality by equating it with animalistic appetite, ignoring any moral, emotional, or psychological considerations. For example, Margaret Mead, with whom Kinsey had a running feud, complained that the research reflected and further promoted a trend in the U.S. toward "atomizing" sex as merely "excremental." Accusing Kinsey of reducing sex to a biological function of "outlet," Mead believed instead that it should be respected for its "sacramental" qualities. Furthermore, she charged that he took sex out of the context of interpersonal relationships and never once mentioned its relationship to love. In a rhetorical twist that stunned the crowd at a 1948 symposium on Kinsey's work sponsored by the American Social Hygiene Association, Mead accused Kinsey of being a puritan because he didn't dare to talk about emotions in relation to sex, avoided mentioning that it was fun and fulfilling, and reduced the body to a set of amoral appetites. Her greatest concern was that Kinsey's work and his ambitious publicity campaigns offered no guidelines especially for younger people for whom the trend toward "patternlessness" of human sexual behavior was destructive.[22] Though Mead was silent on the subject of homosexuality, she feared that Kinsey's research would encourage young people to disregard morality and engage willy-nilly in sexual relations that thwarted the "cementing" of healthy bonds of marriage and family upon which society's welfare and survival was based. Karl Men-

ninger similarly called Kinsey cold and "unhuman" in his methods
and assumptions, and lamented that the word love rarely appeared in
Kinsey's book. He feared that Kinsey's data would relieve the guilt of
those who "rightly should feel it."[23]

The psychiatrist O. Spurgeon English, on the other hand, applauded Kinsey, saying that his research could offer a way for people
to channel their capacities for love in a positive and enriching way.
But, contrary to Kinsey's intentions, English regarded the findings
on homosexuality as a call for social intervention to eliminate it. On
this matter, English wrote:

> To condemn homosexuality will never accomplish anything, but to ac-
> cept it and work for its elimination should help everybody. Its elimina-
> tion lies in finding the most healthy and wholesome expression of sex-
> uality for all, and that will come only when we are willing to cease
> being afraid of sex and learn to make it serve love as well as the aims
> of procreation.[24]

English believed that homosexuals should be pitied since they were
the symptoms of a society where true love was thwarted. Despite Kinsey's own hospitable respect for homosexuals, psychiatrists such as
English appropriated his research as a diagnostic tool which could
point to restoring the beauty and moral superiority of heterosexuality.
In a world where true love was allowed to flourish, homosexuality—
which was never more than false or transitory affection—would
wither away.

One of the most sensationalist moral denunciations of Kinsey's
work came in the form of a pamphlet-like book entitled *I Accuse Kinsey! Startling Exposé of Kinsey's Sex Reports,* assembled by evangelical
Christian radio minister E. J. Daniels. The book included a chapter
by Billy Graham, who decried Kinsey's volume on female sexual behavior for its role in further hastening the deterioration of America's
morals, intensifying distrust between spouses over fears of infidelity,
corrupting the virtues of womanhood, promoting degeneracy in the
form of pornography and perversion, and drawing the ire of a venge-
ful God. The tract also contained a chapter by Chicago gynecologist
William S. Kroger who, without supporting evidence, asserted that
Kinsey's data on women were flawed because "women won't tell you
the truth about their sex life even when they are paying you to find out
what's wrong with them." Kroger saw Kinsey's work as advocating
immorality and concluded by condemning Kinsey for leaving love out
of his study.[25]

THE ATTACKS BY PSYCHOANALYSTS

Among the psychoanalysts who commented on Kinsey's work in print, some appreciated his criticism of psychoanalytic data gathering and acknowledged that psychoanalytic views on homosexuality may be highly subjective and even moralistically dogmatic, in part because psychoanalysts' knowledge was based only on patients who come to them with psychological disturbances.[26] Lawrence Kubie, on the other hand, defended psychoanalysts against Kinsey's criticism, claiming that Kinsey unjustly accused all psychoanalysts of seeing homosexuality as abnormal and pathological.[27] But as a matter of fact, an overwhelming majority of psychoanalysts and even non-psychoanalytic psychiatrists *did* regard homosexuality as fundamentally pathological and the sign of a deeper disturbance of the personality. They differed, however, in their ideas about how and whether homosexuals could be cured of their disorder.

In fact, the harshest and most relentless attacks on Kinsey came from a handful of psychoanalytically inclined psychiatrists who criticized him on several main grounds. First, they charged that Kinsey's interviewing technique and his methods of analysis did not take into consideration the unconscious motivations of subjects to answer in the fashion that they did. Nor did the researchers take into consideration that many individuals were likely to repress or misrepresent, consciously or not, the nature of their sexual behavior. Secondly, they accused Kinsey of using the candid answers of selective research subjects to speculate on why they engaged in certain sexual practices, rather than simply letting the data speak for themselves. On this point, some psychoanalysts argued that, since Kinsey was not trained to understand psychological motivations, he had no business speculating on these matters.[28] For example, in his critique of Kinsey, Aron Krich remarked that "overt behavior is highly deceptive in its meaning except to the psychologically sophisticated."[29] On the other hand, others faulted Kinsey for not going far enough to analyze the psychological motivations of his data. Lawrence Kubie, who was more receptive to Kinsey's work than most psychoanalysts, went even further, calling for more "intensive individual physiologic, anatomic, psychiatric and social studies of individuals who would constitute a statistically adequate random sample of each form of sexual behavior."[30]

A third common criticism among psychoanalysts was that Kinsey's framework did not take into account the dynamic and changing nature of sexual experience.[31] Thus, it could not explore the psychosexual development of individuals as it affected their overt sexual experiences and, moreover, their responses to an interviewer. How an individual answered at one moment in her life might be very different from another moment, depending upon her psychological state at the time as well as on subsequent developments of both the conscious and unconscious mind. To the extent that homosexuality was regarded by many psychoanalysts as a transitory state, common in childhood and adolescence, and a latent feature of some personalities, Kinsey's one-time interview could not reveal the subsequent transitions of individuals in or out of "overt homosexuality" any more than it could unearth the motivations for such events. Hence, his statistics on the prevalence of homosexuality were misleading. Furthermore, since Kinsey's team focused only on the individual interviewee, acquiring no corroborating evidence from his or her partners, they overlooked the possible influences that sexual partners exerted on individuals' homosexual behavioral choices and orientations, especially those of younger, more impressionable men and women.

Finally, and most importantly, psychoanalytic critics argued, as Montagu and Mead had charged, that Kinsey's finding of the prevalence of certain variations in the population should not be grounds for arguing that these behaviors were natural or normal. Instead, many of these variations, and especially homosexuality, ought to be regarded as symptoms of underlying psychological disturbances and thus be treated as illnesses that could be cured.[32] The psychiatrist Edmund Bergler, Kinsey's most outspoken and tireless psychoanalytic critic, focused on this point in his ongoing attacks on Kinsey throughout the late 1940s and 1950s.

BERGLER'S CONTEMPT OF KINSEY

In 1937, upon leaving his job as assistant director of the Freud Clinic in Vienna, Bergler arrived in New York City and gradually became one of the most outspoken opponents of homosexuality. He insisted that it was a neurotic condition afflicting the whole personality of those who practiced it, and he undertook what would become a life-long assault on hereditarian and naturalist etiological theories as well as on the idea that homosexuality was an acceptable life-style. While still associated with the Vienna clinic, he blamed "homosexual propaganda" for scientists' accepting and promoting an hereditarian model. Echoing Wilhelm Stekel, Bergler saw this as misguided and instead advanced a psychogenic theory that identified masochistic guilt as the main cause of homosexuality.[33] Rejecting the sexual inversion paradigm and somatic arguments in general, he argued that the social and legal ostracism of homosexual "perverts" actually satisfied their unconscious pathological need to be punished for their guilty pleasures, an idea he reiterated many times throughout his publishing career until his death in 1962.

In his early writings on homosexuality, Bergler was far from sanguine about the prospects of curing individuals of homosexuality, noting that only the "small percentage" of those with this unconscious guilt could be changed by therapy. He stated that social opprobrium and legal punishment, in most homosexual cases, functioned to externalize the individual's fear of castration which stemmed from the incest taboo. This process of externalization entrenched homosexuality to the point where most afflicted individuals could not change. This led Bergler to charge that "normal" people who disdained homosexuality actually contributed to the problem and showed neurotic symptoms of their own, namely their vigilance about maintaining defense mechanisms against their own perversion.[34] But Bergler's tone changed, starting in 1942, when he launched an aggressive campaign to promote the idea that homosexuality, in the vast number of cases, was a curable neurotic disease.[35]

Bergler took particular aim at Kinsey and the homosexuals who embraced Kinsey's work. Immediately following the release of *Sexual Behavior in the Human Male,* he attacked Kinsey for exaggerating the number of male homosexuals in the population; most of Kinsey's interviews, he charged, were conducted in cities and involved subject populations who were no doubt perverse. But Bergler's biggest grievance concerned Kinsey's intimation that homosexuality was natural and normal and his finding that men who practiced homosexuality either predominantly or exclusively were, on the whole, quite happy and very unlikely to change their sexual orientation. Moreover, why should they, asked Kinsey, so long as they were doing no harm to anyone and seemed to be as happy as the next person? These sentiments enraged Bergler, who argued, to the contrary, that "homosexuality is a neurotic disease in which extremely severe and unavoidable self-damaging tendencies engulf the whole personality." But, he added, it was nonetheless "a therapeutically changeable subdivision of neurosis." And he announced with confidence that "the therapeutic pessimism of the past is gradually disappearing; *today, psychiatric-psychoanalytic treatment can cure homosexuality*" (emphasis in original).[36]

Kinsey's volumes, as well as their positive reception by homosexuals, spurred Bergler to advance his own ideas about homosexuality that can best be summarized as a "blame-the-victim" theory *par excellance.* His assertions were backed by little more than tautological statements and eccentric methods, including "clinical analyses" of such literary figures as Herman Melville, Tennessee Williams, Oscar Wilde, and Marcel Proust. Based on reading their works, Bergler found a common pattern of homosexual masochism, and he supported his method by stating that the homosexual author's writing "corresponds to the inner alibis that he presents to his accusing inner conscience."[37] He was hardly in the best position to criticize Kinsey for lacking sound objective methods: his own style consisted mainly of assembling fragmentary clinical anecdotes that supported the equation of homosexuality with morbid masochism.

Bergler both capitalized on and contributed to the rightward ideological trend toward homophobia that intensified during the Cold War. His speculations, even as they lacked logical coherence and empirically sound backing, were echoed in much of the rhetoric and theatrics of public officials during the rising tide of anti-homosexual and anti-communist domestic repression that came to the fore during the 1950s. The image of the defiant, impulsive, deceptive, and fundamentally disloyal homosexual, featured in Bergler's case histories, appeared very prominently in the McCarthyistic demonization of gay men and lesbians carried out in the U.S. Congress during the 1950s.

Though regarded by some psychoanalysts as a publicity-seeking hack, Bergler was never criticized or countered by them in print. His books on homosexuality, published in numerous paperback editions for popular audiences, were read widely and influenced a growing number of Americans who thought that homosexuality was, without question, a dreaded disease.[38] Indeed, many of his colleagues, though they differed slightly over theories of causality, concurred with Bergler that homosexuality could be cured.[39]

INJUSTICE COLLECTORS, FRANTIC FUGITIVES, AND PSYCHIC MASOCHISTS

Bergler laid out several key characteristics of the male homosexual, which he later extended to describe lesbians. First and foremost, the homosexual was an "injustice collector," a psychic masochist whose neurosis involved constantly creating situations in which he was humiliated, rejected, and defeated. This pathetic creature, who was trapped in the pre-Oedipal oral stage of development, unconsciously provoked disappointments, reacted with righteous indignation, and expressed self-pity in order to complete a cycle of masochism. Proust, for example, suffered from life-long asthma, which was a psychosomatic condition arising from his "unconscious wish to be choked by the image of the pre-Oedipal mother." The fact that the French author starved himself to death was evidence of a pronounced manifestation of injustice collecting and masochism.[40]

Given their inability to move beyond the oral stage, homosexuals, in Bergler's view, were mortally afraid of the opposite sex. They expressed this fear through hatred in futile attempts to ward off their own masochism. Bergler identified this dynamic in the fashion industry, which he argued was dominated by homosexual men whose hatred for women was reflected in clothing designs that punished women.[41] These "frantic fugitives" extended their hatred toward lovers and were typically prone to irrational jealousy, which functioned as a "hitching post for injustice collecting." Homosexuals were always on the prowl and craved danger, constantly seeking to be beaten, or arrested, or to contract venereal disease, all of which could satisfy their self-punishing desires. At the same time, the typical homosexual had a megalomaniacal outlook on life and thought he was superior to everyone else. To camouflage his deep inner depression, he referred to himself as "gay," but underneath experienced "free flowing malice." Homosexuals tended to misuse power, were highly cynical, and engaged in emotional blackmail toward other homosexuals. These very character traits confirmed that homosexuals ought not be employed in sensitive positions in the government.[42]

Following the publication of Kinsey's volume on female sexuality, Bergler began to write much more about lesbianism. In 1954, he wrote, with gynecologist William S. Kroger, a book attacking Kinsey's volume on female sexuality in which lesbians were singled out as particularly damaged and dangerous people.[43] Two years later, in *Homosexuality: Disease or Way of Life?* Bergler devoted a chapter to disputing Kinsey's statistics on female homosexuality. Bergler charged that, whereas Kinsey's male volume inflated the number of male homosexuals, his female volume vastly underestimated the real number of lesbians in the population. Referencing his own work on female frigidity among patients he treated in private practice in New York City, Bergler asserted that most women who engaged in lesbianism were married and thus disguised their homosexuality. They married for convenience but often remained sexually unresponsive to their husbands, causing much unhappiness among men. Though they manifested it differently, lesbians, like homosexual men, suffered from profound inner guilt. The lesbian, he claimed, suffered from a masochistic attachment to the mother: "Lesbianism is not 'woman's love for woman,' but the pseudolove of a masochistic woman, admitting to an inner alibi that she consciously does not understand. . . . The Lesbian is unconsciously in search of constant masochistic pleasure; she is therefore incapable of conscious happiness."[44]

The "inner conscience" of the lesbian vetoed any pleasure, including masochistic pleasure, and thus represented a defense mechanism of "pseudohatred and pseudoaggression" toward the mother that manifested itself in righteous indignation leading to self-defense and self-pity. Like the male homosexual, the lesbian was a "glutton for punishment" and exhibited pathological jealousy for the sake of masochistic injustice collecting. She was no more to be trusted with government secrets than her homosexual male counterpart.[45]

Bergler's therapeutic techniques for curing homosexuality consisted of provoking and mobilizing the homosexual's guilt through confrontational therapy in which the therapist meted out punishment as a way of drawing the patient's attention to his or her masochism. He openly reported what were clearly violations of professional ethics, including flouting patients' confidentiality by discussing their cases with other patients, and bullying patients, calling them liars and worthless human beings.[46] He insisted that those who were willing to overcome their pathetic and self-destructive masochism could be cured, and he gave as evidence of 'cure' the most minimal signs, including one female patient's simple report to have married a man with whom she was happy. On the other hand, any who insisted that they be accepted as homosexuals were simply asking for punishment, which was a confirming sign of their pathological immaturity.

Bergler previously had parceled out some of the blame to those who disdained homosexuality because they provided a rationale for homosexual "injustice collecting." But by the 1950s and especially following the emergence of homosexual rights organizations in the first half of that decade, he repeatedly blamed homosexuals for their own oppression, removing any blame from homophobic heterosexuals. Bergler's attacks on Kinsey were also clearly attacks on homosexual rights advocates. He believed that Kinsey radically thwarted the possibilities of curing homosexuality because his research supported the specious notion that homosexuality was an acceptable way of life. In effect, Kinsey, along with journalists who supported his research, were guilty of perpetrating a "conspiracy of silence" against which

Bergler intended a campaign that "will puncture the illusion that there is glamour in 'being different.'"[47] In Bergler's view, Kinsey did homosexuals a great disservice by leading them to believe they were not sick. He asserted that Kinsey's research would steer young men and women who were "borderline" cases toward embracing homosexuality rather than toward overcoming it before it took control of their lives. Parents deserved to hear the truth that homosexuality was a disease that could be cured in order to avoid their own further suffering as well as that of their children.

CONSEQUENCES OF THE BATTLE

Although it was not his intention, Kinsey's critique of studies linking homosexual behavior with constitutional or biological qualities actually opened up a space for the articulation of psychogenic explanations. Kinsey himself insisted that questions about the origins of homosexuality were of little significance, and he was especially dismayed when psychogenic explanations took an increasingly homophobic tone. Indeed much of American psychoanalytic writing during the postwar period shared a common goal of not merely preventing homosexuality but of curing individuals afflicted by it. While Bergler and other homophobic psychiatrists otherwise lambasted Kinsey for his refusal to admit that homosexuality was pathological, many were keen to do away with the idea of a distinctly homosexual body. Kinsey's research was widely interpreted as a confirmation that the majority of men and women who engaged in homosexual behavior were physically indistinguishable from others. Bergler concurred with Kinsey that homosexuality was not an attribute of innate biology, but he used this idea to advocate therapies to eliminate it. Bergler shared with other psychoanalysts the belief that they were best situated to intervene therapeutically. Thus, even though by 1950 the body became increasingly problematic as a source of evidence about deviance, scientific hope to contain or abolish this sexual pathology, once advanced by early constitutional studies, came to be promoted by homophobic psychoanalysts. And even though they abandoned the idea of the homosexual body in order to institute their own therapeutic interventions, these psychoanalysts adhered to the idea that the homosexual was a psychopathological type of person.[48]

Whereas he argued that homosexuals needed oppression to enact their cycle of masochism, Bergler contradicted himself by saying that Kinsey normalized and even glamorized homosexuality in a way that would recruit more people into homosexuality and lead the country into ruin.[49] In his 1948 critique, Bergler accused Kinsey of nothing short of anti-American and pro-homosexual propaganda, warning that, if Kinsey had his way, "every homosexual will receive tax-free an 'irrefutable,' 'statistical,' and 'scientific' argument for the maintenance and spread of his perversion without conscious guilt." Such a calamitous outcome would pale, though, in comparison to the damage Kinsey's research could do by undermining the status and power of the United States in the world. Bergler charged Kinsey with feeding into campaigns against the nation waged by hostile enemies abroad. Homosexual "injustice collectors," along with their advocate in Kinsey, would be crucial players in plots to sabotage the United States from within.[50]

Bergler's alarmist sentiments were echoed in a variety of highly charged and widely publicized discussions of the dangers posed by homosexuality in postwar America. Through increasingly anxious discourse on the subject, homosexuality was identified as a nothing short of a threat to the nation. As we shall see, this threat was said to emanate from three key domains: the domain of the family, where a lack of proper parental guidance gave rise to gender inversion and sexual maladjustment of future citizens; the domain of public parks and streets, where the infamous "sex offender" endangered the innocence of the nation's youth; and the domain of government employment, where "sex perverts," likened to communists, jeopardized the nation's security and its status as a leader of the "free world."

10 PARENTS, STRANGERS, AND OTHER DANGERS

> Homosexual perversion is not itself a fount of corrupting influ-
> ence, but only, as it were, the ineluctable consequence of a corro-
> sion which has already left its mark upon marriage and family life
> and, if not put in check, may ultimately undermine the social or-
> der and lead to sexual anarchy.[1]
> —*Episcopal Rev. D. S. Bailey (1955)*

PANIC IN THE FAMILY: PARENTAL SURVEILLANCE AS PROPHYLAXIS

Following the Second World War, the protection of young people was used as a rationale for implementing wide-ranging strategies of moral and sexual regulation. The idea of youthful innocence was mobilized by psychiatric authorities, lawmakers, and popular journalists in a broad campaign to set boundaries between normative and perverse sexuality. In an era when the nuclear family was valorized as a fundamental bastion of security in a dangerous world, psychologists and psychiatrists warned against the corrupting influences that lie in wait, outside the home, to prey on hapless youngsters. To counter these dangerous forces, parents were urged to inculcate in their children healthy and morally sound values that would lessen their vulnerability to such social ills as juvenile delinquency, teenage pregnancy, drugs, and sexual deviance. Thus the privilege of raising the next generation of American citizens was coupled with the responsibility of remaining vigilant in monitoring children's behavior, including, centrally, their adaptation to appropriate sex roles.

But not all parents were deemed psychologically equipped to raise their children to be fortified against the perversity that lay outside the family's door. In fact, rather than being havens in a perilous world, certain households seemed to breed homosexuality, or at least a susceptibility to it. Indeed, many psychiatrists believed that the problem originated at home. Hence, parents deserved the advice and guidance of experts who could assist them in raising their children to be sexually adjusted. During the late 1940s and 1950s, psychologists and psychiatrists wrote scores of books that offered advice on how to fulfill the parental duty of producing the next generation of Americans. An important topic in many of them was the prevention of homosexuality.

THE PERILOUS MOM

Borrowing freely from psychoanalysis, one very prominent line of thinking assumed that male homosexuality was the result of a wide range of problems caused specifically by mothers who cultivated unhealthy relationships with their sons. Even as World War Two was raging, psychiatry became intertwined with popular journalism on the subject of blaming mothers for the problems of the nation, including a purported increase of homosexuality. A particularly vicious attack was launched when a man of audaciously woman-hating opinions, wholly untrained in psychiatry, offered his thoughts on the subject of motherhood. In his 1942 bestseller, *Generation of Vipers*, the popular columnist Philip Wylie coined the term "momism" to describe the destructive tendency among the overwhelming majority of American mothers to stifle, dominate, and manipulate their children—particularly sons—into submission and crippling weakness.[2]

Wylie, a self-described "motherless" man, stressed the importance of American military might in earlier magazine columns warning of the threats of communism and fascism. But in *Generation of Vipers*, Wylie tied this militarist zeal to a vitriolic critique of mothers by drawing the character of the sexually frustrated, self-righteous, manipulative "mom" who dominated her husband, cultivated her son's dependence, and brought the nation's enemy, totalitarianism, literally home to roost. In Wylie's text, the family became the pit of hell for men and boys under the tyrannical dominion of pathological mothers. Mom's destructive power, for Wylie, was a horrid byproduct of civilization, brought on by women's pillage of men's money, their suffrage, and their subsequent capacity to "rape the men, not sexually, unfortunately, but morally." Women's voting patterns were to blame for an "all-time low in political scurviness, hoodlumism, . . . moral degeneration, civic corruption, . . . homosexuality, drunkenness, financial depression, chaos and war."[3] Besides causing internal decay, this disdained character, encompassing women of all social classes, hastened the nation's vulnerability to outside forces by way of destroying independent-minded males.

Several years after Wylie published *Generation of Vipers*, the psychiatrist Edward Strecker elaborated on the horrors of momism, this time giving the concept the luster of scientific truth. From the early years of his career in the 1910s, Strecker had been affiliated with the mental hygiene movement, which focused on preventing mental disturbances and encouraged individuals to "adjust" to the psychological demands of modern society. His early research, undertaken while a major in the U.S. Army Medical Corps during World War One, focused on shell shock as well as on the prevention of alcoholism and sex crimes. As professor of psychiatry at the University of Pennsylvania and psychiatric consultant to the Surgeon General of the Navy, Strecker authored textbooks and a number of popular books dealing with child psychiatry, morale, psychiatry and war, and the psychological perils of mass society, subjects that enjoyed popular appeal among middle-class audiences.[4] His tangential interest in the problem of homosexuality grew when in 1935 he joined the Committee for the Study of Sex Variants.

In the 1940s, Strecker offered scathing critiques of mothers in public lectures and in a regular column in the *Ladies Home Journal*.[5] These ventures led to two popular books on the menace of "moms," *Their Mother's Sons*, published in 1946, and *Their Mother's Daughters*, published ten years later with co-author Vincent Lathbury.[6] By his own account, Strecker was driven to write these books when he discovered that a substantial percentage of potential military recruits were rejected for "neuropsychiatric" reasons. He was convinced that the root cause of their problems could be traced back to bad maternal behavior. Strecker distinguished between *mothers*, who were good, and *moms*, who were bad, leaving the role of fathers in child-rearing unanalyzed, except to occasionally disparage Mom's counterpart, "Pop," an immature man lacking the masculine strength necessary to be a good citizen or effective parent.[7] Although the books were ostensibly manuals on child-rearing, they were filled with political commentary centered around Strecker's claim that the nation's weakness was due to bad mothering.

In Strecker's view, mothers "brought into the world the sturdy flesh, blood and sinew and activated it with the spirit of indominatable morale." They contributed good genes and good training and were not overbearing but "quiet in their diplomatic interventions," encouraging their children to make independent decisions. Moms, by contrast, prevented their children from maturing by keeping a tight hold on the "silver cord," the "emotional umbilical cord." The sons of moms failed to mature. Many were effeminate and homosexual as a result of their mother's desire to have a daughter or her untoward affections that caused sons to take flight from heterosexuality.[8] Some of moms' most immature and cowardly sons were those who went so far as to wear women's clothing to get out of military service.[9] Strecker reminded his readers that effeminacy barred many men from wartime recruitment and made them both a national burden and potential agents of sedition.[10]

Moms encouraged dependence and escapism, as did "mom surrogates," which included such far-flung things as psychoneuroses, alcoholism, mental hospitals, religion, social movements, fascism, communism, collective mob consciousness, national isolationism, labor unions, and even the army. Among the most repugnant "mom surrogates" was homosexuality, which drew young men into an underworld of secrecy and decadence and further stripped them of the will to think on their own. Mom herself invited both external and internal threats to run their calamitous course in the psyche, the family, the nation, and the world. And it was particularly her ability to thwart American individualism among her children that made mom, like communism, fascism, and homosexuality, an inimical force threatening to level all distinctions between people and render the world's population a mass, undifferentiated mob.

In Strecker's view, moms were also to blame for the lesbianism of a growing number of daughters. Some poisoned their daughters against heterosexuality by describing it as repulsive. Many expressed either too much or not enough affection toward their daughters, thus either thwarting maturation or triggering the daughters' neurotic quest to make up for a lack of love. Daughters distorted by demonic moms would most certainly either become wicked moms to a new generation or be so traumatized as to forego the basic instinct of motherhood in favor of corrupt and "biologically treasonous" lesbianism.

Lesbianism had close ties to feminism in Strecker's analysis. The former was an extreme version of the latter and both were rejections of femininity that resulted from a girl's unhealthy response to the Oedipus complex, whereby she refused to separate from her mother and developed a competitive and envious attitude toward her father whom the girl perceived as stealing her mother's love. The pathological mom, who fostered her daughter's prolonged attachment, contributed to the daughter's disturbed sentiments. The daughter's rejection of femininity, commonly coupled with the mother's rejection of her own femininity, prevented the daughter from becoming a healthy and happy heterosexual woman, locking the girl forever in a form of latent lesbianism. Strecker and Lathbury saw this rejection of femininity as tragic, noting that many women who aspired to success in business and professions were fundamentally unhappy, having renounced femininity, heterosexuality, and motherhood. This led the authors to claim that feminism was a pathological symptom posing as a political sensibility, brought on by the frustration or denial of essential maternal instincts.[11]

To Strecker and Lathbury, lesbianism signaled extreme pathological immaturity.[12] But moms not only induced lesbianism in their daughters; their own pathological behaviors were construed by Strecker and Lathbury as indications of latent lesbianism. Among the signs of this latency were a mother's bitterness about her maternal role and her resentment toward her husband or men in general. In other words, moms didn't just *make* lesbians; they *were* lesbians within a broad psychoanalytic construction of the term. Moreover, the most destructive moms were described as masculine, domineering, envious of men, and castrating, qualities they shared with the stereotypical mannish lesbian. The "biological treason" they committed violated norms of gender and sexuality and, by implication, were offenses against the institution of the family and the nation.

To solve the problem of momism, Strecker suggested revamping the entire social system, since in its present form it encouraged dependence and immaturity. First and foremost, the social prestige moms enjoyed must be taken away. Rather than being valorized through movies and popular media, moms should be condemned for the damage they do. As a matter of national security, they must be prevented from destroying the future citizenry. Second, expert intervention into parenting was crucial. Parents should be systematically educated on how to be good citizens and responsible role models, and classes should be developed to prepare boys for fatherhood and girls for motherhood. In Strecker's view, if parents—and especially mothers—failed to act appropriately for their sex, homosexuality would surely increase. Furthermore, the government should be on guard for "mothers' groups" that are fronts for breeding national disunity through their pacifist propaganda. By simultaneously arguing that child-rearing was the cornerstone of citizenship and that certain women were not good mothers, Strecker positioned psychiatrists as crucial experts for ensuring national security.

GUARDING THE INNOCENTS AT HOME

In contrast to Strecker, other psychiatrists warned that the greatest corrupting influences emanated from outside the family but could invade it and wreak havoc, especially if parents failed to be on guard against them. Chief among these bad influences were forms of popular entertainment that preyed upon youthful vulnerability. In 1954, Frederic Wertham, senior psychiatrist for the New York City Department of Hospitals from 1932–52, published *The Seduction of the Innocent* in which he railed against the perverse elements in American popular culture that threatened to tempt children into ruin.[13] Comic books, he charged, "stimulate children sexually," thwart the "free sexual [development] of children," and cause "sexual arousal which amounts to seduction."[14] With what Mary Louise Adams calls a "monkey-read monkey-do" theory of child development, Wertham took particular aim at the pernicious homoeroticism featured in comics such as Batman and Wonder Woman.[15]

Batman and Robin, for example, displayed an unsavory blend of superhero attractiveness and homoerotic attachment to one another that was certain to draw young male readers into homosexuality. Ensconced in decadent luxury and adorned in fey clothing, the Caped Crusader and his Boy Wonder were sure to lure impressionable boys into pathological behavior patterns that would "crop up later in adult life as perverse and neurotic tendencies."[16] Citing as evidence of their "Ganymede-Zeus type of love-relationship," Wertham noted:

> At home [Batman and Robin, aka Bruce and Dick] lead an idyllic life. . . . They live in sumptuous quarters, with beautiful flowers in large vases, and have a butler, Alfred. Batman is sometimes shown in a dressing gown. As they sit by the fireplace the young boy sometimes worries about his partner: "Something's wrong with Bruce. He hasn't been himself these past few days." It's like a wish dream of two homosexuals living together. Sometimes they are shown on a couch, Bruce reclining and Dick sitting next to him, jacket off, collar open, and his hand on his friend's arm.[17]

Wertham continued by pointing out that images of Batman and Robin emphasized "the genital region strictly" by frequently featuring the duo standing with their legs apart. These factors, combined with an absence of "decent, attractive, successful women" in Batman and Robin stories were solid evidence, in Wertham's view, of the dangerous homosexuality that permeated the comic strip. Similarly, Wonder Woman was an inappropriate model of femininity who exhibited cruel and "phallic" tendencies. Since Wertham assumed girls were even more impressionable than boys, Wonder Woman had the superpower to steer girls awry with her "psychologically unmistakable" lesbianism.[18]

Like many psychiatrists of the 1950s, Wertham emphasized the dangers facing children, but in reality his main focus of preventive intervention was on adolescents. Among many psychiatrists of the postwar period, the teenage years were regarded as a transitional stage between childhood and adulthood, imagined as a vulnerable moment when unsavory influences could corrupt the otherwise innocent or clean "blank slate" of the teenager. Disregarding the fact that many adolescents were already sexually active—if postwar statistics on teenage pregnancy are any indication at all—Wertham's rhetoric targeted popular entertainment and scapegoated particular groups of adults who were characterized as predatory and bent on corrupting the innocent.

Thus, while for Strecker, mothers, in their important role as the primary care-takers of children, were singled out for particular expert intervention and blame, Wertham warned that homosexual men were menacing strangers looming outside the family, who lured boys into perverse sexual acts in public toilets, alleyways, and parks.[19] At the same time, a host of other psychiatrists described "butch" lesbians who were fundamentally predatory, although their cunning predations were more likely to occur within a domestic setting through the psychological manipulation of hapless, innocent young women.[20] In a growing genre of exploitation novels and pulp nonfiction exposés of the time, authors similarly described lesbian relationships as pathological approximations of family relations between "husbands" and "wives," "mothers" and "daughters," and even in some relationships between "femme" mothers and "butch" sons. The predator was most often a masculine woman but could disguise this by appearing to be maternal.[21] To a great degree, both public and private spheres came to be regarded as equally endangered by dangerous trends that allowed male and female perversion to flourish.

PANIC IN THE STREETS: THE PROBLEM OF HOMOSEXUAL DELINQUENCY

Following the war, lesbian and gay subcultures became more visible in U.S. cities and became the focus of sensationalist journalism which added to the fear unleashed by Kinsey's research that homosexuals were operating more openly in public, taking over whole areas of cities, and recruiting young people into their ranks.[22] During this period, psychiatrists and like-minded policy-makers increasingly emphasized the dangers posed by mysterious seducers who roamed through public spaces in search of innocent and youthful sexual prey. The horrific specter of the pedophilic predator thus unleashed an intense wave of panic that led to stepped up police harassment and public vilification of homosexuals during the late 1940s and 1950s.[23] The postwar sex crime panic bore a striking resemblance to that which gripped New York and other cities in the United States during the late 1930s. As in the previous wave, highly publicized reports of atrocious crimes against children fueled public fears about the menace of the sex offender. And, although arrest records in California, for example, indicated that the vast majority of sex crimes perpetrated against children were committed by men against girls, the postwar panic, like its predecessor, especially targeted homosexual men as the principal menace threatening the nation's youth.[24] In many cases, police used the public demand for greater protection of children as a rationale for increased surveillance of all deviant behavior, whether it was violent or not. This point was made in a letter written by one homosexual man to another in the wake of the brutal murder of a young Chicago girl in 1946: "I suppose you read about the kidnapping and killing of the little girl in Chicago—I noticed tonight that they 'thought' (in their damn self-righteous way) that perhaps a pervert had done it and they rounded up all females [male homosexuals]— they blame us for everything and incidentally it is more and more in the limelight everyday—why they don't round us up and kill us I don't know."[25]

Several factors contributed to the popular misconception that sex offenders of children were homosexuals. First was the idea, emphasized by many psychoanalysts, that homosexuals were compulsive, obsessive, and uncontrolled in their impulses to acquire sexual satisfaction. Children and adolescents were easy targets for such rampant and impulsive desires. Furthermore, because homosexuality was described as a form of psychosexual immaturity, many believed that those who practiced it were likely to choose youthful partners with whom they would feel an affinity but over whom they could assume a position of dominance. Again, though statistics showed that sex crimes involving children tended to be committed by men against girls, the popular image of the sex offender was shaped by these psychoanalytic descriptions of male homosexuality.

A second factor pertained to newsmedia sensationalism that reported the sexual abuse and murder of children in the same stories featuring statistics on arrests of men who committed crimes related to homosexual acts involved consenting adults. Hence, media coverage of sex crimes, by mere suggestion, wove together pedophilia, child sexual abuse, and homosexuality. In New York City, New Jersey, and California, legislators responded to public pressure to enact more laws to punish any behavior that could be construed as homosexual. In some jurisdictions, a man's mere wink of the eye in a public park was grounds for arrest on charges of homosexual solicitation. In the early 1950s, the state assembly of California, in the wake of a highly publicized pair of child murders, increased the penalty for consensual sodomy between adult men from ten to twenty years in prison.[26]

Thirdly, Kinsey's findings on the prevalence of homosexual behavior among men contributed to a growing fear among many that such unspeakable acts were occurring right under the noses of the authorities. Although substantial statistics on adultery, masturbation, and bestiality caused concern among many of Kinsey's readers, no other "outlet" was as great a source of public anxiety as homosexual behavior. Media coverage of Kinsey's reports, occurring simultaneously with sensationalistic journalism about sex crimes, added to a growing panic that homosexuality was the source of sexual delinquency and the corruption of youngsters. Local vice squads in major cities around the United States interpreted this public concern as a green light for developing elaborate entrapment schemes in which men were accosted in gay bars and public toilets by undercover policemen who offered sexual relations and then arrested those who appeared to accept the proposition.

Finally, a growing climate of homophobia, stoked by Cold War xenophobia, was fueled by the specter of "strangers in our midst." A fear of dangerous conspiracies, secretive infiltration, and uncontrolled sexual perversion led to the passage of laws against sex offenders that painted a picture of the homosexual as a member of a clandestine underworld. FBI director J. Edgar Hoover, who in 1937 had declared a "War on the Sex Criminal" and identified the "sex fiend" as "a sinister threat to the safety of American childhood and womanhood," reiterated this rhetoric again in 1947. Testifying before Congress, Hoover stated that "the most rapidly increasing type of crime is that perpetrated by degenerate sex offenders."[27] During this same year, Hoover was busy exerting pressure on President Harry Truman and Congress to authorize massive investigations of communists and their treasonous and degenerate fellow-travelers throughout the country. The twin evils of sexual perversion and communism were to be countered by tactics of surveillance, arrest, and severe punishment. In Hoover's view, both made the country unsafe not only for children and young adults, but for all God fearing Americans. The sex crime panic of the time paralleled a backlash against the "pink menace" invoked in Congressional hearings and presidential executive orders to ferret out "sex perverts" from civilian government employment and the armed forces. Although in the discourse of these purges the term sex pervert encompassed a variety of unsavory characters, the most commonly named was the homosexual man. A similar dynamic occurred in the parlance of anti-sex crime legislation from the period, wherein the homosexual, by statutory definition, was a sex offender. Lesbians, though seldom mentioned explicitly as sex offenders, were lumped under the heading of "sex perverts" and were the target of an especially intense wave of expulsions of accused women from the military.[28]

As J. Edgar Hoover and a host of homophobic lawmakers and journalists stoked the public's fear of the homosexual offender, psychiatrists across the United States argued for legal reforms that would allow for psychiatric examinations and treatment of those convicted of sex crimes. Their proposals followed the general outline of Mayor La Guardia's plan adopted in New York City during the 1930s. Some even argued that homosexuals should be subjected to psychiatric treatment rather than be sent to regular prisons since, in their view, putting these men in sex-segregated environments might be more of a reward than a punishment. Though many believed that it would be ideal to sentence homosexual offenders to indeterminate periods in psychiatric wards until they were "cured," this strategy was criticized as a violation of due process by defense lawyers and as impractical by psychiatrists who believed homosexual orientation could not simply be eliminated. Also, as a practical matter, psychiatrists admitted that there were not enough psychiatric facilities to accommodate even the number of men convicted of violent sex offenses. In addition, a few of the leading forensic psychiatrists, including Karl Bowman, argued that those whose offenses did not involve youth or the use of force ought to be distinguished from violent sex offenders, and some even argued that consensual acts performed in private ought to be decriminalized altogether. But there was general agreement that most sex offenses resulted from psychological disturbances that psychiatrists were in the best position to assess and treat.

The postwar sex crime panics thus gave rise to legislative action that solidified psychiatrists' involvement in the criminal justice system. Between 1947 and 1955, twenty-one states and the District of Columbia passed new sexual psychopath laws, and six states funded psychiatric studies of sex offenders.[29] The most ambitious study took place in California, which had passed one of the first sexual psychopath laws in 1939. In 1949, the state assembly responded to public outcry about the murder and sexual abuse of two children by initiating a massive state investigation into sex crimes, led by psychiatrist Karl Bowman, then head of the newly opened Langley Porter Clinic affiliated with the University of California at San Francisco.

Before moving to California in the early 1940s to later become the state's Medical Superintendent in 1947, Bowman had headed the New York Magistrate Court's diversion program, whereby those accused of sex offenses were examined and treated by psychiatrists. Bowman, like George Henry with whom he was associated both through the Magistrate Court's diversion program and the Committee for the Study of Sex Variants, believed that imprisonment without psychiatric treatment merely worsened the problems afflicting most sex offenders and the society to which they posed a potential threat. Bowman's liberal attitude shaped his legislative activism and therapeutic recommendations in the postwar period, when he advised the governor and state legislature of California to reform and standardize its laws against sex offenses and to consider eliminating laws prohibiting sex between consenting adults.

Bowman and his research assistant, Bernice Engle, were influenced in their thinking by Kinsey, Margaret Mead, and two experts in animal sexual behavior, the psychologists Clelland Ford and Frank Beach. Arguing that many laws prohibiting particular sexual practices were arbitrary restrictions to uphold outdated taboos, Bowman and Engle suggested that scientific research on sexual behavior proved that many variations were natural and harmless. In fact, many of what were legally classified as sex offenses could be seen on a continuum with normal behavior. For example, exhibitionism was "a normal part of sexual foreplay," but when expressed in the extreme it was an obsessive-compulsive type of neurotic behavior that represented an aberrant displacement of sexual intercourse that could become a public nuisance or danger. Likewise, fetishism could be harmless in some cases but could lead to a serious type of sexual abnormality in which murder and mutilation could occur. The authors thus argued for a careful study of existing sex offender laws which would better distinguish normal and harmless variations from aberrant and dangerous ones.

On the subject of homosexuality, Bowman noted that there were various types and that "the majority of homosexuals are no particular menace to society." But he went on to caution that "a small number of them, like those who are heterosexual, will attempt to seduce or sexually assault others or try to initiate sex relations with small children. They are undesirable persons in the community." In spite of his more lenient tone, Bowman reiterated a popular assumption that associated forceful pedophilia with homosexuality by stating that homosexuals, because they commonly experience frustration and rejection, may turn to young people more often to satisfy their desires: "Some overt homosexuals, in their hunt for partners, may be attracted to latent ones who greatly fear any homosexual expression. Relations of this kind often end in atrocities that may be against children and youth."[30] Bowman and Engle believed that these cases should involve criminal punishment, but they argued in favor of applying moral, rather than legal, pressure to discourage homosexuality in most other cases.

Though generally more sympathetic, the authors echoed Edmund Bergler's reasoning that making homosexuality against the law and punishing it harshly only gave homosexuals a just grievance which allowed them to ignore the moral implications of their acts. A better way to deal with the problem would be to consider it a sin rather than a crime and to exert moral pressure on homosexuals to amend their ways. In some cases, Bowman and Engle believed "aversion therapy" might be useful for discouraging homosexuality through techniques designed to punish a patient's erotic responses to homosexual stimuli and reward his responses to heterosexual images.[31] But at the same time, Bowman and Engle recommended legal reforms to eliminate police entrapment and other violations of the first and fifth amendments to the Constitution and to ensure the right of privacy for consenting adults.[32]

Concerned about the damaging effects of the popular conflation of homosexuals and sex offenders of children, a handful of social scientists and other psychiatrists, including Alfred Kinsey and George Henry, cautioned that public panics over sex crimes greatly exaggerated the problem and, moreover, wrongly targeted homosexual men for sex crimes against children. Kinsey himself was a critic of laws that outlawed sexual relations practiced in private by consenting adults which caused no apparent harm to their participants. He pointed out that if existing laws were enforced, no less than ninety-five percent of adult men in the U.S. population would be paying fines or serving prison sentences on a regular basis. This proved the need for legal reform, since most laws restricting sexual acts were not only ineffective and archaic but were enforced selectively to scapegoat particular groups of people, most notably homosexuals.

In 1949, Kinsey, who had been conducting research on male and female sex offenders since 1939, testified before the newly formed California Subcommittee on Sex Crimes, on the request of his friend Karl Bowman. He called for legal reform that would limit sex offender laws to acts involving force, acts threatening the safety of children, and acts of a compulsive, repetitive nature which were a public nuisance. Kinsey concluded his testimony by asserting that homosexuality could not be eliminated through psychiatric therapy, and thus he made a general argument against subjecting those arrested for consensual acts to psychiatric treatment.[33]

George Henry had similar opinions on the matter of legal reform, and he especially argued that unduly harsh laws reinforced damaging social intolerance and led to blackmail and extortion schemes that drove many homosexual men deeper into a crime-ridden underworld. But, in contrast to Kinsey, Henry believed that psychiatric treatment of homosexual offenders was important in order to help them to "readjust" to social norms, even if it would not eliminate their homosexual urges altogether. Men charged with homosexually related offenses had been a concern of his since the late 1930s when he was involved in Mayor La Guardia's court diversion project in New York City. At that time, Henry and his assistant, Alfred Gross, published several articles analyzing the nature of the "homosexual delinquent" and of the conditions under which otherwise "orderly" middle-class men fell into ruin through extortion schemes of lower-class "exhibitionist fairies" and "rough trade" hustlers and "wolves."[34]

In 1940, Henry and Gross, addressing an audience of probation officers, argued for the necessity of social and legal reform to uplift individuals facing emotional and economic instability who tended to get in trouble with the law. In the spirit of liberal reform, the authors argued that greater educational, employment, and housing possibilities would help to make up for the broken homes and financial instability that plagued many homosexual men. Rather than imprisoning them, which would only exacerbate the problem of homosexuality, policies should be developed to help these men to overcome loneliness and to become productive and emotionally mature citizens. The authors advanced a similar argument in a 1951 article in *Pastoral Psychology*, aimed at an audience of clergymen, which urged them to counsel homosexuals toward greater social adjustment through sympathetic techniques geared to building individuals' self-esteem and helping them to mature psychologically.[35] Through the George W. Henry Foundation, established in New York City in 1948, Henry and Gross counseled homosexual parolees and other homosexual clients to achieve these assimilationist goals.[36]

Although Bowman and Henry were by no means marginal characters in legislative and legal deliberations about homosexual offenders, their liberal opinions were vastly overshadowed by growing public hysteria over the clandestine predations of morally degenerate and politically corrupt internal enemies. Psychoanalytic writing as well as sensationalistic journalism continued to reinforce the idea that homosexuality resulted from youthful seduction beginning in the family and continuing outside the domestic sphere. In the context of growing national hostility toward strangers and foreigners, childhood and adolescent vulnerability became a metaphor for the nation's vulnerability at the hands not only of terrifying and contagious carriers of immorality but also of creeping, voracious communists whose efforts to manipulate and dominate the United States would be successful if Americans were not vigilant in ferreting these characters out of hiding and punishing them for their evil and corrupt actions. Such attitudes were dramatized in the highly publicized Congressional antics of the McCarthy period, when it became obvious that homosexuality, despite the sympathies of liberal authorities such as Kinsey toward it, would become symbolically central as a figure against which proper patriotic citizenship was cast.

FEAR OF A WORLD CONSPIRACY

> By the very nature of their vice, [homosexuals] belong to a sinister, mysterious and efficient international. Welded together by the identity of their forbidden desires, of their strange, sad needs, habits, dangers, not to mention their fatuous vocabulary, members of this international constitute a worldwide conspiracy against society.
> —*Countess R. G. Waldeck* (Congressional Record, *May 1, 1952)*

The Cold War period was characterized by a large-scale tendency toward demonizing particular groups of people, largely through stereotyping them as inimical, in various ways, to national security. In Michael Rogin's survey of American political "demonology," he notes that the immigrant working-class labor militant had been the primary political demon and moral degenerate of the 1910s. It was against this demon that members of a native-born white middle class articulated an exclusivist discourse of American nationalism, couched in terms that assumed their own moral superiority. But, during the Cold War, the despised and menacing communist replaced the earlier demon, this time representing not only disorder and loss of restraint but also signifying control by a sophisticated alien order that was secretive, invisible, power-hungry, and profoundly dangerous. Cold War political demonology constructed the communist as having a diabolical desire to take over the world by tricking hapless and naive people into submitting to a totalitarian order in which all individuality was lost and every thought and action controlled by a dictatorial world power.[1]

To a significant degree, Cold War fears engendered by the specter of the communist demon signified a cultural dread of totalitarianism that had been articulated earlier in anticommunist "red scare" campaigns and again in wartime ideological campaigns against Nazi Germany.[2] After the Second World War, American's fear of fascism was transposed onto Russian and Chinese communism, a shift that can be traced to, among other things, the early warnings of the American charge d'affaires in Moscow, George F. Kennan, who in 1946 warned that the Soviets had a voracious geopolitical appetite aimed at taking over and destroying the free world. Kennan's admonitions were echoed several weeks later in a speech by former British prime minister Winston Churchill at Westminster College in Missouri. Churchill, accompanied by President Harry Truman, declared that Stalin had drawn an "Iron Curtain" across the totalitarian Eastern Bloc, separating it from the "free world," and behind which a devilish conspiracy to control the world was being concocted. These official proclamations, layered on top of long-standing anti–Soviet sentiments held by Republican isolationists, sparked widespread xenophobia which eventually reached colossal proportions and which fueled a broad movement to instill the fear of communism in every American man, woman, and child.[3]

In Kennan's view the Soviets were, by nature, secretive adherents to a "new fanatic faith, antithetical to our own, [which] seeks to impose its absolute authority over the rest of the world." Stalin personified the political psychopathology of the Soviet state, which manifested itself fundamentally in caprice, ruthless expansionism, paranoia, and deception. Kennan warned that Soviet leaders were intent on infiltrating labor, feminist, and civil rights organizations around the world and commandeering them for the purposes of expanding their influence and ultimately eradicating freedom and democracy. "World communism," he declared, "is like a malignant parasite which feeds only on diseased tissue. This is the point at which domestic and foreign policies meet. Every courageous and incisive measure to solve internal problems of our own society, to improve self-confidence, discipline, morale and community spirit of our own people, is a diplomatic victory over Moscow worth a thousand diplomatic notes and joint communiqués."[4]

Kennan's metaphors likening communism to a cancerous parasite and to neurosis evince the salience of medical and psychiatric language in articulating the goals of American nationalism during the Cold War. National security would depend on prophylaxis and mental hygiene, since communism was only contagious if it contacted a host that was weak enough to accommodate it. Though Kennan said nothing about homosexuality per se, Cold War ideologues who followed in his footsteps went on to proclaim that "sex perverts," because of their furtive and degenerate impulses and their susceptibility to blackmail, were perfect conduits for Soviet infiltration.[5]

Rogin argues that at the core of postwar political demonology was anxiety about the enormous and amorphous destructive potency of mass society and an all-powerful state. Paradoxically, these perceived dangers, exemplified by Nazism and Stalinist communism, provided the rationale for the rise of an elaborate national security state apparatus in the United States which was authorized to conduct extensive surveillance on any perceived enemies, including many of the nation's citizens. In addition, the mass media functioned as powerful channels for spreading anticommunist hysteria in a manner that militated against independent mindedness by repressing political dissent. Thus, the fear of totalitarianism actually led to the very outcomes anticommunists had decried.

With this in mind, Rogin further argues that political repression during this period had two dimensions, one manifest and the other latent. The first was the actual repression of perceived internal enemies through highly showcased government purges as well as through local citizens' witch hunts that targeted known communists as well as those identified within the increasingly broad categories of "fellow-travelers" and "security risks." But the second dimension of repression was submerged, taking on a latent or unconscious quality: anticommunist campaigns in the United States functioned to repress the reality that America's own state and popular mass psychology bore a striking resemblance to that which was regarded as most dangerous. Even as Stalin was admonished for his political purges and the Soviet regime was condemned for violating the civil rights of its citizens, the U.S. Congress, state governments, and law enforcement officials engaged in egregious violations of due process in their zeal to rid the nation of infectious, viral-like enemies.

These dual axes of repression manifested themselves in a series of displacements and projections during this period, whereby particular forms of sexually taboo behavior, though commonly practiced among average Americans, were attributed by conservative isolationists and anticommunists to external and evil forces outside the healthy mainstream of the nation. In the face of vast evidence that average Americans' actual sexual behavior greatly deviated from existing moral strictures, reactionaries launched a far-reaching ideological campaign which stressed a return to "traditions." These were little more than idealized fictions of a past when men and women had assumed vastly different roles, heterosexual intercourse was the one and only acceptable form of sexual expression, the nuclear family was the principal haven in a perilous world, and freedom was safeguarded by a strong and vigilant military and a robust capitalist economy.[6] Rather than resuscitating the actual past, moral conservatives and anticommunist liberals invented an idealized America that supported their moral and political agendas and projected a false consensus on the "mainstream" of the American population. Thus, social and political conformity, though decried as the hallmark of totalitarianism, was at the heart of the reactionary moral agenda that came to the fore during the Cold War.

In basic material ways, men and women during the postwar years were more alike than different in their rates of employment, their levels of education, and indeed, in their daily habits and roles. Yet conservatives insisted that men and women were inherently different. By nature, men were the breadwinners whose dominion over the household was respected by loyal and dutiful wives. Virile masculinity was associated with national fortitude, moral strength, and military might. Faithful and obedient wives symbolized ideal femininity.[7] Their tasks of nurturing children and keeping a haven-like household complemented their husbands' tasks of safeguarding the public sphere from external dangers. Thus, through healthy heterosexuality involving the two halves of nature's intended whole, the nation's future security could be ensured. Homosexuality, associated popularly with both gender inversion and sexual perversion, symbolized a dangerous affront to this idealized image of the perfect home and family. Not surprisingly, anyone who disturbed the foundations of the family and the gender roles that underpinned it came to be regarded as a threat to the nation's security.

A major reaction to the imagined fear of foreign infiltration by communists became manifest in an intense vigilance to protect the "domestic" sphere, a term used to denote both the family home and, in the parlance of international relations, the nation. The popular home bomb shelter literalized this connection. The dual meaning of the "domestic" which overlaid the home with the nation signaled the underlying dynamics of isolationism and xenophobia whereby the security and sanctity of home were seen as the basic foundations for national defense. In this context, personal behavior came to be regarded as deeply linked to political matters. During the Cold War, the nation's strengths and weaknesses were assessed primarily in terms of the moral disposition and psychological qualities of the nation's citizens.

Strikingly, morally conservative ideologues of the 1940s and 1950s elevated the domestic sphere of childrearing to a highly privileged domain since, in their view, it could either guarantee or thwart the moral development of future citizens. Though this was not the first time that motherhood was regarded as key to instilling patriotism in America's future citizenry, the ideological valorization of the home immediately following World War II created a special set of obligations for women which was pronounced in its intensity.[8] Indeed, the postwar "family boom" was part and parcel of a multifaceted ideological campaign to move women back into a position of subordination to men, as loyal wives and mothers. To make room in the job market for returning veterans, women were encouraged to return to the home, marry, and have children—duties that would restore American society and ensure the United States' status as a leader in international economic and military power.[9]

In postwar xenophobic ideological campaigns, from the halls of Congress to the studios of Hollywood, the clandestine, wily, communist infiltrator was fostered by a number of other dangerous characters. The demonic, controlling "mom" destroyed her son's independence through a pathological, voracious desire for him, making the son susceptible to hidden communist conspiracies.[10] In addition the sultry, two-faced vixen of postwar film noir threatened, through her crafty and feline ways, to seduce unwitting men into plots against the nation.[11] And homosexuals—both male and female—represented the repulsive bed-fellows, fellow-travelers, and dupes of the fiendish communist. Afflicted by a pathological weakness of will and tendencies toward impulsive behavior in their quest for sexual satiation, these creatures were regarded as weak links in the nation's chain of security.

Psychological metaphors played a big part in describing the dangers facing the nation from within and without. The totalitarian drive to control the will and mind of the American citizen was described as a form of psychopathology. The appropriate counterstrategy was to fortify the individual through fostering psychological independence and a healthy, self-determining will that could resist the cunning temptations served up by the nation's external and internal enemies. National security was figured through metaphors that crafted an isomorphic relationship between the healthy, robust, and sexually "adjusted" male citizen and the nation. The nymphomaniacal saboteur, the binding and controlling "mom," the male homosexual, and the lesbian were equally dangerous to the average man if he lacked the necessary will-power and vigilance to detect foreign manipulation. For Cold War era moral conservatives, military and diplomatic might and a strong system of surveillance were necessary at the national level as well, in order to resist the secret methods of infiltration deployed by communism. Everywhere loomed the totalitarian threat of brain washing and mind control. Both domestic and foreign policy became increasingly flavored with suspicion. For American Cold warriors, the insidious forces of evil required a national campaign of moral cleansing.

LOYALTY, SECURITY, AND THE HOMOSEXUAL CONSPIRATOR

The internal repression of the Cold War period made homosexuality into an American obsession primarily by unleashing far-reaching fear. National campaigns against communism and "sex perversion" became the ground for partisan battles between internationalists, concentrated among Democrats aligned with President Harry Truman, and isolationists, whose most staunch supporters were Republican congressmen with constituencies concentrated in the Midwest. Frustrated by the long-term Democratic control of the presidency under Franklin Roosevelt, Republican congressmen used the threat of communism to exert power and gain popular support for their isolationist agenda. They did so first by insinuating that Truman, and his predecessor, were soft on communism and had filled the State Department with men of questionable moral character whose loyalty to America was dubious. Truman tried to trump this insinuation by issuing Executive Order 9806 in late 1946, which established a Temporary Commission on Employee Loyalty charged with investigating security risks in the government. The Commission was comprised of representatives of various departments of the executive branch and the Civil Service Commission, and headed by A. Devitt Vanech, Special Assistant to Attorney General Tom Clark and close associate of J. Edgar Hoover. In March 1947 Truman again bowed to Republican pressure and issued Executive Order 9835, which authorized the attorney general to make a list of organizations he regarded as "totalitarian, Fascist, Communist, or subversive, or having adopted a policy of approving the commission of acts of force or violence to deny others their constitutional rights."[12] Membership as well as sympathetic association with such groups was considered grounds for investigation. In an effort to mobilize support for Marshall Plan legislation that would ensure that the U.S. would have considerable economic and political influence in Western Europe, Truman contributed to a growing fervor of anticommunism which inspired right-wing Republicans in their struggle to undo the New Deal and to weed out those of its policy-makers still occupying positions in various departments of the government.[13]

Over the next few years, a growing number of adamantly anticommunist congressmen, supported by J. Edgar Hoover, insisted that U.S. government employees and even prospective employees be investigated. They argued that the nation's secrets were not safe in the hands of communist sympathizers and "security risks" alleged to be concentrated in sensitive positions within the State Department and foreign service. Though Franklin Roosevelt had established loyalty and security procedures, Republicans and the FBI regarded them as ineffectual, especially in light of the imminent threat of Soviet infiltration. The Republican-controlled House Committee on Un-American Activities (HUAC), under the leadership of long-term opponent of the Soviet Union Martin Dies of Texas, had been busy since 1938 identifying left-wing federal employees and urging Roosevelt to dismiss them. He refused, largely on the grounds that HUAC's investigations had violated Constitutional rights to due process.

Following Roosevelt's death and the end of the war in 1945, anticommunist Congressmen increased the drive to implement more far-reaching loyalty oaths and internal security measures. By 1950, they benefited from the growing fears fueled by popular media campaigns which demonized communism. This gave them the necessary popular support and political clout to pass the Security Act of 1950, allowing investigations based on very little evidence and extending summary dismissal power to heads of "sensitive" government departments and agencies. The act also initiated a highly publicized Congressional attack on homosexuals, beginning with a unanimous vote in favor of a comprehensive study of the employment of "homosexuals and other moral perverts" in the federal government. Indeed, in his testimony before a senate appropriations committee in 1950, Undersecretary of State John Peurifoy stated that of the 91 employees dismissed for moral turpitude during 1949, the vast majority were homosexuals.[14] Starting in 1950, expulsion rates grew significantly.

The despised image of the effeminate male homosexual was symbolically central to an overall rightward shift among the nation's top lawmakers. During Roosevelt's time in office, Republican isolationists had developed a palpable contempt for the manner and privilege of Ivy League intellectuals, who tended to be concentrated in departments of the government focused on foreign policy. In their view, Roosevelt's staffmembers were friendly with the Soviets and other socialists in Europe, having spent the war years mingling with "Reds" in far-off lands. The stereotype of the FDR foreign policy specialist was a snobby, pro-communist pansy who gave communists exactly what they wanted—a stereotype that closely approximated that of the effeminate and effete homosexual.

The stereotype carried over into attacks on Truman's administration. His secretary of state, Dean Acheson, was described by Republican opponents as lacking the appropriate masculinity needed to stand strong against the communist threat. Even though Acheson himself was an ardent anticommunist, to detractors he was described as "the cookie-pushing, striped-pants diplomat" whose elitism was likened to effeminacy.[15] William F. Buckley, then on the faculty at Yale, chimed in by accusing Owen Lattimore, the "architect of the China tragedy," as "the first lady among American witches," replacing Alger Hiss in this position.[16] Virile masculinity and a strong national defense were coupled as the quintessence of patriotism. By contrast, gender ambiguity and especially effeminacy in men was evinced in anti-American sympathies. Together with sexual compulsivity, these traits were personified in the male homosexual.

Cold War homophobic purges were as much about gender transgression as about homosexuality per se. Arthur Schlesinger's *The Vital Center: The Politics of Freedom* (1949) warned against effeminacy in all areas of government policy-making, which he believed was increasing with the breakdown of clear distinctions between masculinity and femininity. The "vital center" was characterized by a "new virility," a crucial change from the "emasculated" ruling class of Henry Wallace's Progressive ranks.[17] In Schlesinger's words, communism was "something secret, sweaty, and furtive like nothing so much, in the phrase of one wise observer of modern Russia, as homosexuals in a boys' school."[18]

A journalist for the *New York Daily News*, reporting on the congressional elections of 1950, noted that a decisive issue in campaigns was the Republican charge that "the foreign policy of the United States, even before World War Two, was dominated by an all-powerful, supersecret inner circle of highly educated, socially highly placed sexual misfits in the State Department, all easy to blackmail, all susceptible to blandishments by homosexuals in foreign nations."[19] Such sentiments gained popular appeal. To fortify their senatorial campaigns, Everett Dirksen (R-Illinois) promised to remove "lavender lads" from the White House and Kenneth Wherry (R-Nebraska) warned of the dangers of sabotage posed by "a conspiracy of subversives and moral perverts in government establishments."[20] Dirksen and Wherry alleged that Joseph Stalin had seized a global roster of homosexuals from Adolf Hitler and planned to use it to conquer the world through blackmail and deception.

Initially, through presidential executive orders and congressional internal security legislation, "sex perverts" were classified primarily as reliability risks, prone to pressure from foreign agents. Toward the beginning of the purges, architects of internal security acknowledged that many homosexuals were not necessarily communist sympathizers per se. Nevertheless, due to their predilection for indiscreet sexual encounters, they lacked judgment and were hence vulnerable to blackmail and extortion. The famous case of Colonel Alfred Raedl, chief of Austro-Hungarian counterintelligence just prior to World War I, was often cited in congressional hearings on security risks. As the story went, Raedl, who had been an effective spy inside Russia, was "caught in the act of perversion" by the Russians who, knowing he was a homosexual, set a trap for him. Under the threat of exposure, he divulged secrets and destroyed intelligence reports on Russia, thus profoundly damaging the Austrian regime. As a consequence of Raedl's indiscretion, the Austrians had no accurate sense of Russia's intentions at the outbreak of World War I. He continued to give Austrian and Germany military plans to the Russians until his treasonous acts were discovered by the Austrian government, whereupon he committed suicide. The Raedl case was invoked often to explain the keen method by which Russians picked out homosexuals and forced them into blackmail. Raedl's moral weakness was to blame for Austria's impotence during the Great War. If such a calamitous compromise of national security could happen then, it could happen again.[21]

Congressional debates about homosexual security risks featured a mocking vernacular that further solidified a stereotype borrowed from medical discourse that homosexuals were audacious, frivolous, and generally unreliable. For example, "blabbermouths" and "briefcase losers" fell under a special heading of "reliability risks." The blabbermouth loved to talk and could easily be induced through alcohol or flattery to go on at length about his work. As the stereotype went, homosexuals were excessive talkers and narcissists. Overtaken by sexual desire for a Soviet espionage agent, the homosexual would throw down a couple of drinks and, in a typically flagrant, ostentatious manner, would blab about himself and, of course, about confidential matters of foreign policy. The "briefcase loser" was reckless and even contemptuous about security measures and would forgetfully or inadvertently leave secrets lying around. According to the original internal security provisions, loose habits, indiscretion, and mood swings typified homosexual men and, for these reasons, made them unsuitable for government employment.

The internal security measures also specified a second category of risks: those inclined toward intentional disloyalty. In contrast to reliability risks, "disloyal" employees exhibited a politically motivated desire to undermine American democracy. Initially, people who were, had previously been, or were likely to become communists were classified as disloyal and on these grounds summarily dismissed. This included "fellow travelers" or those sympathetic to communism. In the beginning, "sex perverts" were seen as basically unreliable. But as the security programs expanded by successive executive orders and congressional acts, homosexuals came to be seen not merely as bad security risks but as fundamentally disloyal, with behaviors, practices, and lives that were contrary to the American way of life.

Testimony surrounding the Security Act of 1950 marked the beginning of a shift from regarding homosexuals as reliability risks to seeing them as fundamentally disloyal. The act provided for the investigation of "the preparedness of authorities of the District of Columbia for protection of life and property against the threat to security inherent in the employment of such perverts by such departments and agencies." This special provision was the handiwork of Republican Representative A. L. Miller of Nebraska, who used the specter of "perversion" the way Joseph McCarthy used communism as a vehicle for building his political career. In 1950, Miller testified before Congress, announcing that he "would like to strip the fetid, stinking flesh off of this skeleton of homosexuality and tell my colleagues of the House some facts of nature." Among these facts were that Washington, D.C., happened to attract homosexuals, an assertion he supported with anecdotal evidence provided to him by the city's vice squad. Based on the reasoning that "birds of a feather flock together," Miller warned that homosexual employees expelled from one department of government would most likely seek employment in another, since Washington had become a mecca for the homosexual subculture. The pervert, he warned, led a secretive, pornographic life replete with a special vocabulary and private codes and signals:

> There are places in Washington where they gather for the purpose of sex orgies, where they worship at the cesspool and fleshpots of iniquity. . . . There are many types such as the necrophalia [sic], fettichism [sic], pygmalionism, fellatios, cunnilinguist, sodomatic, pederasty, saphism, sadism, and masochism. . . . Indeed, there are many methods

of practices among the homosexuals. You will find those people using the words such as, "He is a fish. He is a bulldicker [*sic*]. He is a mamma and he is a papa, punk, and pimp." Yes, in one of our prominent restaurants rug parties and sex orgies go on. Some of those people have been in the State Department, and I understand that some of them are now in other departments.[22]

Miller's suggestion that homosexuals were everywhere and especially in the daily traffic patterns of congressmen was a device used to heighten fear and mobilize support for increased vice squad raids as well as governmental purges. Furthermore, in Miller's view, perversion was not merely a ruse used by communists to manipulate homosexuals; Russians themselves were essentially perverts:

It is a known fact that homosexuality goes back to the Orientals, long before the time of Confucius; that the Russians are strong believers in homosexuality, and that those same people are able to get into the State Department and get somebody in their embrace, and once they are in their embrace, fearing blackmail, will make them go to any extent.[23]

Miller also warned that homosexual men were naturally prone to a kind of dangerous irrationality not unlike that of women, especially toward anyone who exposes their "nastiness":

Some of these people are dangerous. They will go to any limit. These homosexuals have strong emotions. They are not to be trusted and when blackmail threatens they are a dangerous group. . . . It is found that the cycle of these individuals' homosexual desires follow the cycle closely patterned to the menstrual period of women. There may be three or four days in each month that this homosexual's instincts break down and drive the individual into abnormal fields of sexual practice.[24]

Miller's testimony offered a crude rendition of conservative psychoanalyst Edmund Bergler's profile of the psychopathological homosexual. Typically, homosexual men exhibited extreme emotionality, which manifested itself in jealousy, dishonesty, neuroses, and instability, making them unreliable and prone to "indiscretions": "Male homosexuals will not share their fairy with anybody. His anger is unlimited for anyone who seeks to possess the object of his love. . . . The homosexual takes on many indiscretions. He has a tendency to lie and to lie on all occasions."[25]

A month before Miller offered his testimony, the Republican National Chairman, Guy Gabrielson, sent out a newsletter to 7,000 party members asserting that "sexual perverts who have infiltrated our Government in recent years" were "perhaps as dangerous as the actual Communists."[26] He noted the difficulties the press had with reporting on the "tragic angle" because of their respect for "the decency of their American audiences." A common rhetorical move by homophobic ideologues during this period was to stress the utter unmentionability of such a "dirty" and "nasty" thing as homosexuality. Emphasizing the mysteriousness of perverts and the strangeness of their sexual practices became a method used to prompt further investigation into the obscure world of homosexuals. Fear of the unknown thus played a big part in this strategy and also enabled copious and colorful speculations on the subject, even though Republicans such as Miller and Gabrielson constantly reminded their audiences of the unspeakability of the perversion. When asked to define homosexuality during a heated debate with a Missouri Democratic congressman, Michigan Republican Clare E. Hoffman replied: "The term needs no definition—I will not dirty my mouth by defining it."[27]

Congressman Cliff Clevenger (R-Ohio), argued that "the homosexual problem," like the loathsome disease of gonorrhea, needed to be "brought before the public and frankly discussed." Referring to the estimated 4,000 perverts alleged to be in the federal government, Clevenger asked with urgency "where are they? Who hired them? Do we have a cell of these perverts hiding in Government? Why are they not ferreted out and dismissed?"[28] The halls of Congress had become a theater for the performance of homophobic grandstanding, wherein no one dared defend homosexuality. By the end of hearings on the subject, a powerful consensus had been built, aimed at increasing political pressure on Truman and his cabinet to cleanse the government and, by extension, the U.S. society of sex perversion.

On April 24, 1950, Republican antagonists demanded that a Senate investigation into communist infiltration of the State Department be expanded to rid the federal payroll of sex perverts. With a sufficient amount of fear and intrigue aroused, a Senate Appropriations Subcommittee voted unanimously on May 19, 1950 for an investigation of alleged homosexuals in the executive branch. Senate floor leader Kenneth S. Wherry (R-Neb.) and Senator Lester Hill (D-Ala.) reported that about 3,500 perverts were employed in government agencies. Even though the Washington, D.C., vice squad admitted to fabricating these figures, they provided the rationale for the investigation.[29]

In June 1950, a subcommittee of the Senate Committee on Expenditures in the Executive Department was ordered to begin the investigation headed by Clyde R. Hoey (D-N.C.) and given $10,000 to do so. The investigatory hearings were closed to the public ostensibly to guard against harming innocent people who may be falsely accused, but the secrecy actually afforded informants more protection than the accused.

As the investigation was under way, in July 1950 the liberal journalist Max Lerner interviewed Kenneth Wherry in one of his regular columns in the *New York Post*. Lerner, who was one of the few openly critical columnists, asked the senator "whether the problem of homosexuals in the government was primarily a moral or a security problem," to which the senator replied that it was both. To Lerner's question of whether homosexuals and communists were closely related, Wherry answered, "You can't hardly separate homosexuals from subversives. . . . Mind you, I don't say every homosexual is a subversive, and I don't say every subversive is a homosexual. But a man of low morality is a menace in the government, whatever he is, and they are all tied up together. . . . There should be no people of that type working in any position in the government."[30]

Lerner's opposition to the government's investigation became clear as the interview proceeded. Citing Kinsey's finding of extensive homosexuality in the male population, he asked: "In light of these figures, Senator, are you aware of the task which the purge of all homosexuals from government jobs opens up?" Wherry replied: "Take this straight. I don't agree with the figures. I've read them all, but I don't agree with them. But regardless of the figures, I'll take the full responsibility for cleaning all of them out of the government." Lerner continued: "You must have a clear idea, Senator, of what a homosexual is. It is a problem that has been troubling psychiatrists and statisticians. Can you tell me what your idea is?" "Quite simple," answered the Senator. "A homosexual is a diseased man, an abnormal man." Lerner persisted: "Do you mean one who has made a habit of homosexuality? Would you include someone who, perhaps in his teens, had some homosexual relations and has never had them since? Would you include those who are capable of both kinds of relation, some who may even be raising families?" "You can handle it without requiring a definition," replied the senator. "I'm convinced in my own mind that any homosexual is a bad risk. . . . But look, Lerner, we're both Americans, aren't we? I say, let's get these fellows out of the government." Lerner protested: "We have to know what fellows we're talking about, Senator. That's just what is bothering many of us. What homosexuals are bad risks? How do you treat the others? Can they be helped? Would you, Senator, bring doctors and psychiatrists into the picture and make them part of the machinery for dealing with this problem?" "No," Wherry replied, "I don't think doctors are needed. We can handle this by rule of thumb."[31]

Indeed, Wherry's attitudes underscore the common assumptions held by members of Hoey's committee. They believed that there were thousands of homosexuals employed by the government and that suspected homosexuals should be removed from their jobs immediately and by any means necessary. On December 15, 1950, Hoey's investigative subcommittee published its report entitled "Employment of Homosexuals and Other Sex Perverts in the Government." The report firmly recommended that homosexuals should be "put out of government service and kept out."[32] According to the report, there were two grounds upon which homosexuals were to be excluded from government employment, both borrowed loosely from psychoanalytic notions of the sort Edmund Bergler was espousing. First, the homosexual's weakness for indulging in acts of perversion, his emotional instability, and his "corrosive influence" of seducing other employees made him unsuitable for employment. Secondly, because of the social stigma attached to sex perversion, the homosexual was a likely target of blackmail. Not only his persistent and powerful sex drive but also his tendency to talk about himself made the homosexual loose-lipped and weak enough to divulge secrets to Soviet spies.[33] The report acknowledged that there were no physical characteristics which positively identified the sex pervert. Instead, its authors ultimately relied on Kinsey's *Sexual Behavior in the Human Male* to warn that the problem of homosexuality was much greater than previously thought. The authors also encouraged the coordination of investigative and surveillance efforts among agencies in order to prevent the reentry of those previously dismissed on sexual perversion charges.

Hoey's committee cared little, if at all, about rehabilitating suspected homosexuals and could not be bothered with medical opinions. Its job was simply to remove homosexuals from positions where they could weaken the nation's security. That came to include any government job, not just those involving government secrets. Violations of due process were common, and those suspected of homosexuality were generally presumed to be guilty until proven otherwise. The taint of the accusation itself, given the climate of the time, was enough to ruin a career.

Between January 1, 1947 and November 1, 1950, 574 civilian federal employees were investigated on charges of sex perversion. Four hundred twenty resigned or were dismissed and 85 were cleared, with 69 cases pending. The greatest concentration was in the State Department, with 143 investigated, 121 dismissed or resigned, and ten cleared with twelve cases pending. Following the passage of the Security Act of 1950, the figures increased significantly and the popular press continued to print the numbers of employees who were dismissed or resigned on sexual perversion charges. Americans read of the federal efforts to weed out "bad elements" from government and witnessed harsh punishment for those who sexually and politically misbehaved. No doubt the reports had a chilling effect on the forty-six percent of American men who had reported their homosexual behavior to Kinsey in the mid-1940s.

To match the vigilance of the FBI and Congress, in 1951 Truman issued Executive Order 10241, which implemented a reasonable doubt standard that allowed official investigations of those who were "potentially" disloyal.[34] Increasingly, accusations of homosexual and communist tendencies became interchangeable—and damaging enough to lose presidential elections. In 1952, Democratic presidential candidate Adlai Stevenson was accused of homosexuality by a university athlete who was under arrest for fixing games. Stevenson's Republican opponents used this dubious allegation to maintain that Stevenson was soft on communists. The 1952 election was won by Republican Dwight Eisenhower, who campaigned on a heavily anti-communist platform that reiterated complaints about Democrats being soft on subversives and perverts. Three months after taking office in 1953, Eisenhower issued Executive Order 10450, which extended the summary dismissal power provided to heads of sensitive departments and agencies by the Security Act of 1950. EO 10450 gave the directors of *all* federal agencies and departments power to dismiss employees whom they believed were disloyal. The order explicitly mentioned character traits that should be evaluated for judging individuals' "fitness" for government employment; he or she was to be "reliable, trustworthy, of good conduct and character, and of complete and unswerving loyalty to the United States."[35]

Eisenhower's Executive Order 10450 was the first presidential order to explicitly mention sexual perversion. It listed sexual perversion, like "criminal, infamous, dishonest, immoral, or notoriously disgraceful conduct," as grounds for disbarment from federal employment. As a result of the order, 837 investigations of sex perversion took place between May 1953 and June 1955.[36] With strong support from Congress and with the FBI aggressively pursuing witnesses and conducting investigations, Eisenhower took several more steps to expand the repressive powers of his loyalty-security program.

On October 14, 1953, Eisenhower issued Executive Order 10491 authorizing the suspension of federal employees who relied on the Fifth Amendment during testimony before Congress investigating "alleged disloyalty or other misconduct."[37] Then on August 2, 1954, he issued Executive Order 10548 which authorized suspension of federal employees whose mental condition or illness might "cause significant defect in the [employee's] judgment or reliability."[38] Investigations ensured that evidence about informants would not be disclosed, thus providing no avenues for the accused to defend themselves against attacks. Such vague terms as "fitness" and "good character and conduct," along with allusions to mental conditions, allowed the loyalty-security apparatus enough flexibility to ensnare any employees deemed undesirable, regardless of whether they ever committed any acts of subversion. Evidence was not necessary to substantiate a charge of unfitness, since all investigatory files were sealed from the accused and anyone outside the investigatory apparatus. By 1954, a system existed whereby those who did not meet the rather vague standards of good, clean, American anticommunist living were subject to harassment and dismissal. Though homosexuals were certainly not the only ones who suffered from Eisenhower's expansive dragnet, his aggressive rhetoric and his singling out of homosexuals reinforced the assumption that these men and women were mentally ill and definitely not to be trusted.

SHADES OF RED AND PINK

As the loyalty and security apparatus expanded, homophobic commentary increasingly stressed the similarities between homosexuals and communists. This was part of a strategy to underscore that homosexuals were fundamentally disloyal to the nation rather than merely errant in their behavior. According to this conceptualization, homosexuals, like communists, were indistinguishable from the rest of the population; no identifying physical traits could be relied upon to set them apart. Both groups tried to appear "normal" in order to infiltrate government. Anticommunist and anti-homosexual ideologues described both communists and homosexuals as loyal to powers outside the morally acceptable realm of wholesome American life;

the communists answered to the Soviet Union and the perverts were controlled by their unnatural desires. Both groups corrupted the youth either through teaching in schools or by seducing and molesting them in streetcars and parks. Both were ubiquitous and their corruption was contagious.

Eventually, homosexuals and communists were no longer only imagined as parallel menaces but were considered to be one and the same. In 1952, the tabloid journalist Lee Mortimer wrote several sensationalistic exposés on the growing menace of homosexuality. Mortimer drew on material from the Hoey committee's report and from the results of the Kinsey study to describe homosexuality in the language of disease, infection, and contagion. Homosexuality, he wrote, was an epidemic spread by communists who wanted to infect and control the young. Working in secret cells and infiltrating the educational system, lesbians and homosexual men preyed on the innocent to destroy democracy.[39]

In 1952, an item appeared in the *Congressional Record* that illustrates, in purple prose, the rhetorical association between homosexuality and communism. The *Homosexual International,* a passionate treatise penned by "Countess R. G. Waldeck," drew parallels between the Communist International and a new global conspiracy of sex perversion. Describing the "Pink Decade," the countess warned of a dangerous affinity that was forming between homosexuals and communists, as both stood outside the boundaries of decency:

> Members of one conspiracy are prone to join another conspiracy. . . .
> Without being necessarily Marxist, [homosexuals] serve the ends of
> the Communist International in the name of their rebellion against the
> prejudices, standards, and ideals of the bourgeois world.[40]

By Countess Waldeck's telling, homosexuals were attracted to each other by their strange desires, and they disregarded national boundaries and class differences, effecting a dangerous fusion between the upper class and the proletariat. Like communists and Jews to whom other international conspiracies had been attributed, the homosexual had no loyalty to any nation. The countess provided a thumbnail sketch of Austrian diplomatic history, stating that the homosexuals were like a state within a state, occupying the core of the diplomatic circle and corrupting the goals and ideals of Austria through perverse subterfuge. Her story was reminiscent of anti-Semitic portrayals of Jews who, as ambassadors to European rulers, were suspected of

Janus-faced diplomacy that bespoke their allegiance to a secret order which had no loyalty toward the legitimate governing authorities in whose trust they were held.[41]

Waldeck described members of the "homosexual aristocracy" who discovered Marxism and were drawn to it out of a sense of guilt "concerning their forbidden desires and the hope to purge themselves of it by cooperating with the workers movement." Her depiction echoed Edmund Bergler's idea that homosexuals were fundamentally masochistic and suffered from profound and destructive guilt. She reprised a long-standing notion, articulated in medical commentary about homosexuality from the early decades of the twentieth century, that homosexuals were class-traitors who damaged the social structure by pursuing unseemly affiliations across class lines. In her formulation of this pathological tendency, wealthy homosexuals wanted to get closer to their proletarian brothers the way "some women take up bridge or golf or current affairs because it gives them a common interest with the men they love." The promise of a classless society, free from "bourgeois constraint," motivated them to seek unbridled sexual satisfaction and to form political organizations of their own, as they began to identify as an oppressed class. Thus the countess warned that the nascent movement for homosexual rights posed as great a danger to American society as communism.

She ventured further into the realm of psychology when describing the shared predilections of the twin evils of communism and homosexuality: both had a "passion for intrigue for intrigue's sake." And, like communism, the "homosexual auxiliary" was growing at an alarming rate, serving the Communist International by spreading immorality and sex inversion through popular entertainment:

> Probably no communist propaganda is intended by these comedians who, giggling and swishing and addressing each other by girl's names, invade the American home via the screen. But one can't help wondering what will become of a society whose children and youngsters are constantly exposed to the nauseating ambiguousness of their mannerisms, their poses, their jokes. The moral advantages for the Communist cause of getting the American home folks to absorb and applaud these indecent dance acts cannot be overrated.[42]

Finally, the countess, turning her attention to the matter of government security, asserted that homosexuals were inclined toward communist causes because of the "anti-social hostility and social promiscuity inherent in their vice." A proclivity toward masquerade and transvestism naturally drew homosexuals toward secret agent work, through which they would ultimately commit treason. Citing Theodore Reik's *Psychology of Sex Relations*, the countess theorized that "the fantasy of sex metamorphosis operating in most homosexual affairs which causes him to play the role of the other sex causes him also to enjoy any job which gives him the chance of playing a double role."[43] Thus, eliminating homosexuals from government positions was "only one phase of combatting the homosexual invasion of American life." The strategy of going after federal employees was the first step; rooting out perversion and "nauseating ambiguousness" in the rest of society was her ultimate goal.

THE IMPACT OF THE PURGE

In addition to the homophobic purge of civilians during these years, "perverts" were hunted and expelled from the military in increasing numbers. By the end of the 1940s, the armed forces, in contrast to their relatively lenient policy on the matter during wartime, were discharging about one hundred men and women per year on charges of homosexuality. In the 1950s, this rate rose to over 2,000 per year.[44] By 1957, a new program for indoctrinating navy personnel was established in the Crittendon Report, named for Captain S. H. Crittendon, who chaired the Navy's policy review board. The report called homosexuality "one of the very bad things in life . . . about which the majority of people know little or nothing. . . . Homosexuality is wrong, it is evil, and it is to be branded as such. . . . Homosexuality is an offense to all decent and law-abiding people, and it is not to be condoned on grounds of 'mental illness' any more than other crimes such as theft, homicide, or criminal assault."[45]

This hard-line attack led to the adoption of aggressive antihomosexual policies in all branches of the military to weed out gay men and lesbians. Women who sought guidance from psychiatrists, chaplains, and their superiors were reported and pressured to inform on one another. Without constitutional protections, men and women accused of homosexuality faced discharge hearings where rules of evidence as well as rights of examination and cross-examination and appeal were severely limited. In many cases, officials promised not to discharge (at least not dishonorably) accused men and women as long as they named names of others. Most often, after they named ex-lovers or friends, the accused and the accuser were expelled.

Focusing on the federal civil service and the armed forces allowed homophobic policy-makers to try out surveillance and purging techniques that were adopted subsequently by many local and state agencies around the country. It was possible to spread fear quickly among government employees. For the most part, national security provided an effective rationale for suspending constitutional protections to which others elsewhere were entitled. But many Americans in other sectors of employment felt the impact of the highly showcased purges, either directly by their employers' adoption of these dismissal procedures or indirectly by witnessing friends and neighbors face shame and humiliation.

In 1950, the FBI established connections with local police departments in an effort to prevent undesirables from acquiring government employment. This coordination allowed for intensified local investigations of homosexuals. Regional FBI officers developed extensive surveillance dossiers on scores of citizens. In many instances, information acquired through FBI surveillance techniques was provided to local government and private sector employers, who then fired suspected homosexuals. Harassment at the local level was further carried out by fearful co-workers and neighbors who were informed about alleged sex perverts operating in their vicinity.

Regional FBI officers coordinated with local vice squads in entrapment arrests and raids on gay and lesbian bars. During the early 1950s, over a thousand arrests per year were made in Washington, D.C., where undercover policemen cruised gay men and then offered to have sex. When the unwitting victim agreed to the offer, he was arrested and charged under sexual psychopath laws and other antivice ordinances which made public sex and homosexual solicitation illegal. Officially called "Resorts for Sex Perverts" by a member of the California assembly, bars provided space for gay men and lesbians to gather but were also targets used by rambunctious policemen who delighted in humiliating, harassing, and physically assaulting patrons. Bar raids were an effective way of identifying gay men and lesbians. Those who were arrested often had vice squad files which were then made available to the FBI and employers.

The number of bar raids went up considerably after the Congressional investigation of homosexuality occurred. On one night in September 1956, thirty-six lesbians went to jail after a raid on the Alamo Club in San Francisco. Sixty-four lesbians were arrested in one 1953 New Orleans raid. In 1955, 162 people were arrested in a bar raid in Baltimore. Often gay men were subjected to so-called VD inspections by police. Their names and addresses, along with the charges brought against them, were printed in local papers. Kinsey's Institute for Sex

Research reported the results of a survey showing that during the 1950s twenty percent of gay men had trouble with the police in their past.

In November 1955 three men in Boise, Idaho were arrested on charges of having sex with teenage boys. A large-scale public investigation was held over fifteen months, in which 1,400 local residents were called in to testify against their neighborhoods and co-workers. Following similar theatrics to those initiated earlier in the U.S. Congress, accusations of homosexuality and homosexual sympathizing became a very effective way for staging partisan political battles in Idaho's state capital as well as in other cities around the nation.[46] The nationwide escalation of fear and insecurity about sexuality did great damage not only to those who lost their jobs, were forced to flee, were jailed, or committed suicide; millions of Americans, regardless of their sexual orientations, suffered as their friendships were ruined and their families torn apart by allegations of homosexuality or the fear of them. Many gay people who were terrified ran for cover or stayed isolated in the closet. Many who were not gay but who were so accused and many who had gay friends or relatives suffered from the stigma attached to homosexuality. Any American who read the newspapers during this time would have witnessed the purges and would have learned that they should hide any homosexual desires they might have, that they should distance themselves from homosexuals, and that, to be safe, they should make it publicly clear that they too disdained homosexuality.

Kinsey was accused of aiding world communism by making homosexuality sound acceptable, and efforts were made to censor his work. These accusations account, in large part, for why the National Research Council's Committee for Research on Problems of Sex ceased funding his research in 1954. In 1953, the NRC's membership changed, as did the leadership of its funding source, the Rockefeller Foundation. The NRC leader, Dean Rusk, later John F. Kennedy's secretary of state, encountered forceful Republican opposition to Kinsey's research by congressional leaders who went after Kinsey, the NRC, and the Rockefeller Foundation, ostensibly for violations of tax-exemption laws. But their main aim was to showcase moral objections to Kinsey's research findings as a way of garnering support from like-minded constituents who responded favorably to the anti-homosexual antics of their representatives.

The congressional attack on Kinsey intensified in 1954. During that year, Republican Congressman B. Carroll Reece established a committee to investigate tax exempt foundations. The committee was handpicked by Reece. It heard the testimony of only twelve witnesses. A majority of the witnesses told Reece what he wanted to hear: that tax exempt foundations placed an undue burden on the American tax payer through the funding of dubious research. Reece, who would go on to chair the Republic National Committee, established the committee by taking advantage of criticism lodged against Kinsey. Harry Emerson Fosdick, head of Union Theological Seminary and brother of Raymond Fosdick, who headed the Rockefeller Foundation, was joined by Harold W. Dodds, president of Princeton University, in arguing that Kinsey's studies sanctioned immorality. Reece mobilized such criticisms of Kinsey to attack foundations by stressing that they funded unsavory research. The upshot of Reece's investigation was the end of Rockefeller Foundation funding for Kinsey. Though the foundation survived Reece's investigation, it bowed to political pressure and decided to award a major grant to the Union Theological Seminary. The foundation gave as the official reason for nonrenewal of Kinsey's research his failure to make a request, but, in fact, Kinsey continued to ask for money to no avail. Until his death in the summer of 1956, Kinsey's work was drastically curtailed. After suffering numerous attempts to obstruct his research, he was forced to rely on royalties from his published volumes as well as minor funding from Indiana University.[47]

Over the course of post-war backlash against "internal enemies," scores of careers were destroyed and thousands of people accused of sex perversion faced enormous economic and psychological hardships. Indeed, the pressure to be a good heterosexual citizen reached such magnificent proportions that it was felt even in the most uncanny places. The Cold War era hysteria about homosexuality had a damaging and enduring impact even on some of the very architects of homophobic and anticommunist witch hunts. One strategy used by their opponents was to discredit the witch hunters by charging that they were homosexual or in some other way sexually perverse. By the mid-1950s, rumors began to circulate about J. Edgar Hoover's sexuality as well as that of Joseph McCarthy's aide Roy Cohn.[48] FBI documents indicate that as early as 1943, agents under his direction believed that Hoover was "queer" and that his relationship with FBI official Clyde Tolson was homosexual in nature. Hoover attempted to suppress these rumors and kept his own private files on "derogatory information" that named the culprits of such gossip.[49] But rumors surfaced again in the 1950s, even as Hoover was publicly authorizing aggressive entrapment and investigation schemes undertaken by branch offices of the FBI. Roy Cohn, Joseph McCarthy's counsel and right-hand man, was instrumental in directing the 1954 investigations of homosexuality in the army. The rumor that Cohn was a homosexual was confirmed much later when he died of AIDS in 1986. The damaging power of homosexual allegations may account for the degree of vehemence with which anti-homosexual witch hunts were undertaken by men such as Hoover and Cohn. Fearing that their own homosexuality would be discovered, they made a public show of denouncing other homosexuals.

Even some of those most victimized by the witch hunts used the prevailing forms of repression against each other. During the 1950s, the Communist Party of the U.S.A. and other leftist groups encouraged gay men and lesbians to leave their organizations because of the security risks they posed. Many who had devoted years of energy to struggles on the Left were considered expendable and undesirable during times of heavy surveillance and government crackdowns. It was assumed that, if they were pressured, homosexuals would divulge secrets to the FBI. And, as we shall see in the chapter that follows, some homosexual rights organizations proposed loyalty oaths that required members to denounce communism as a condition of membership.

Anxiety about Communist subversion and sexual perversion occurred at a time when the threat of nuclear annihilation loomed large. Fear of such an overwhelming specter was, to a great degree, localized and turned inward onto the sphere of domestic politics in the United States. At the peak of this hysteria, many Americans were convinced that it probably was better to be dead than red . . . or pink. Many had learned, through witnessing highly publicized purges, that to be accused of subversion was about as good as being dead since it led not only to summary dismissals from jobs, to destroyed reputations, and, often, to permanent exile from communities but also, in many cases, to broken spirits, to depressing isolation, and to suicide.

As we have seen, an imperative to ensure "internal security" unleashed suspicion and paranoia on a grand scale. Orchestrated campaigns to hunt down and eliminate internal subversives were fueled by much talk of the threat of a totalitarian take-over and of a nuclear war with Russia. While military defense planners were plotting the face-off between the United States and Russia as a zero-sum game, spokespeople against internal subversion and the citizenry whom they influenced operated with a similar logic: internal enemies of whatever form were not to be tolerated. In a game of all or nothing, those named as even potentially dangerous were taken down by the expansive inquisitions authorized by national security.

To combat the purported totalitarianism and mass conformity demanded by the Soviet regime, the United States government vastly expanded its national security state, spied relentlessly on its citizens, insisted on a narrow definition of patriotism, violated its own Constitution, and demanded its citizens conform to strict standards of behavior. Personal behavior was overtly politicized: how one acted in terms of gender comportment and sexual desire counted as evidence for judging that person either to be loyal or seditious. Through the public tarring of homosexuals, deviation from gender ideals or any hint of homosexual desire became nothing less than acts of outright political disloyalty.

During the postwar decade, Alfred Kinsey's findings of widespread sexual variation in the population, in spite of his intentions, seemed to have fueled the fear and anxiety that homosexuality was everywhere and yet not so easily detectable. This perceived threat that homosexuality, like communism, was ubiquitous and yet hidden inspired a reaction-formation of widespread cultural disavowal and repulsion. Not surprisingly, great efforts were made to contain this threat through a resuscitated insistence that homosexuals were somehow a distinct group by virtue of their psychological motivations, their indiscretion, their inherent weakness of will, their tendency toward being manipulated by foreign powers, and their alleged disrespect for the common good of American morality and values. Yet during this same period, Kinsey's work opened up the possibility of imagining, for better or worse, the idea of a "homosexual revolution," a subject to which we turn next.

Those of us who are considered strange are not the sole property
of the medical profession and not a small segment of the total population to be walled off as an enclosed preserve for the hunting
psychiatrist. We who walk in shadow do know, perhaps, **something** about ourselves. We can read what the scholars have said
about us and some of that writing can be understood but much of
it is understood to be nonsense which has been adroitly camou-
flaged and in which we completely fail to recognize ourselves.[1]
—*J. D. Mercer (1959)*

The postwar period marked a watershed in the history of homosexuality in the United States. More obviously and on a grander scale
than ever before, homosexuality had become symbolically central in
American culture. The subject sparked heated public debate and
came to be a ground for articulating a wide range of political opinions
over the relationship of sexual behavior to freedom, democratic ideals,
and the future of the nation. Importantly, the putatively neutral research projects of medical and scientific authorities were central to
staking political claims about these matters. Psychoanalytic ideas in-
sisting that homosexuality was a morbid affliction aided moral conservatives in arguing that homosexuality was an evil and contagious
specter from which an idealized patriotic citizenry should be protected. By contrast, social scientific surveys that normalized homosexuality were championed by an emerging homophile movement and
led liberal Americans, during the decline of McCarthyism, to consider the possibility that homosexuality should be tolerated, if not actively endorsed.

SYMPATHETIC SCIENCE AND THE EMERGENCE OF THE HOMOPHILE MOVEMENT

As anti-homosexual hostility intensified during the 1950s, a growing
number of homosexual men and women, fed up with being harassed,
came together to form organizations to support one another and to
counter homophobic oppression.[2] In 1951, the Mattachine Society
was officially founded through the initial efforts of Henry Hay in Los
Angeles. Its early leadership consisted of gay men with leftist political

leanings, some of whom were members of the Communist Party U.S.A. Influenced by civil rights and social justice movements on the left, leaders of Mattachine thought of homosexuals as an oppressed minority and believed that marshalling support among sympathetic scientists and physicians could be an effective strategy for persuading the general public to accept homosexuality. As various chapters of Mattachine formed around the country, Hay incorporated the Mattachine Foundation in 1952 as a nonprofit organization focused on encouraging research into homosexuality and using results in educational campaigns to advance the rights of homosexuals. The organization published the *Mattachine Review*, a periodical featuring, among other things, news and commentary regarding scientific research about homosexuality.[3]

Four years later, the Daughters of Bilitis was formed in San Francisco, largely on the initiative of Del Martin and Phyllis Lyon, in order to respond to the particular needs of lesbians. The DOB originated with four couples. Of these eight women, four were blue-collar and four white-collar workers, one was a Filipina, one a Chicana, and two were Lesbian mothers.[4] Like the Mattachine Society, the DOB advocated scientific research and education about homosexuality as a strategy for combating homophobia in American society. Its publication, *The Ladder*, began in 1956, and, like the *Mattachine Review*, it featured columns about new scientific research as well as recruitment ads for possible research subjects who would participate in studies of the "adjusted" homosexual. DOB and Mattachine members saw research of the sort that Kinsey conducted as useful and important while they heavily criticized psychoanalytic opinions that equated homosexuality with disease. And increasingly, many argued that the subjective viewpoints of gay men and lesbians themselves should be taken more seriously by scientific and medical authorities.

Kinsey's political arguments against discrimination and for the decriminalization of homosexuality, together with his scientific evidence that homosexuality was widely practiced, inspired homosexual rights advocates in their organizing efforts.[5] That Kinsey avoided the question of causality allowed activists to do the same in making arguments for sexual diversity. Kinsey's continuum model offered a means for arguing that homosexuality was a normal part of American society and that those who engaged in it should be respected as a substantial and geographically far-flung minority. He was a sympathetic and powerful advocate, and his studies were frequently cited in homophile publications. Kinsey's work validated homosexuality through science in contrast to what many activists referred to as the "pseudoscience" of homophobic psychiatrists.

Increasingly, homophile activists regarded psychiatrists—even those who seemed sympathetic—as retrograde and oppressive because of their insistence that homosexuality was pathological and tragic. George Henry was cited by a columnist in the homophile magazine, *One*, as promoting an insidious form of prejudice that was disguised in benevolence.[6] True, Henry refuted the idea that homosexual orientation could be changed, and he advocated compassion toward those who suffered from homosexuality. But his adherence to a disease model encouraged pity and shame rather than respect. The columnist further noted that Henry's idea of successful social "adjustment" was based on homosexuals' ability to hide their sexuality in order to conform to oppressive social norms.[7] The column, entitled "The Case of the Well-Meaning Lyncher," was particularly critical of Henry's opposition to political organizations for the advancement of homosexual rights.[8] The author credited Henry with "highly humanitarian motives" but found some of his comments to reveal gross ignorance and "amateur science," as evidenced in the following statement by Henry:

> I have spoken of attempts of homosexuals to band themselves together in mutual protective leagues. Men interested in promoting such enterprises have come to us for counsel and possible support. It has been my consistent policy to refuse to countenance such societies, and I have pointed out the dangers lying in wait for those who operate them. . . . Lacking effective control, such groups inevitably deteriorate into places of assignation, . . . [due to a] lack of discipline and self-discipline.[9]

The columnist pointed out that Henry gave no details about homophile organizations and failed to consider their positive contributions toward alleviating prejudice. Furthermore, in a campy aside, the author noted that "Dr. Henry of all people should have known from his research that there were far more convenient 'places of assignation' to find than a homophile league could ever have hoped to offer."

By the mid-1950s, among homophile activists, the tide was turning against the condescending tone of Henry and other physicians who used the cases of troubled patients to oppose Mattachine and DOB. By contrast, these groups favored the work of scientists who surveyed non-patient populations to show that homosexuals could be happy, productive people. The movement's embrace of social science promoted two main points. First, it sought to argue that homosexuals were not, by definition, sick, stressing instead that homosexuals were average people, just like everyone else. Though a crucial rhetorical strategy, this emphasis valorized social conformity and, in effect, promoted the homogenization of differences among homosexuals into an ideal model of the "adjusted" homosexual. A consequence was that some homophile groups marginalized individuals whom they believed would damage the credibility of the movement. This included drag queens and butch women who, it was believed, confirmed the stereotypes that had further stigmatized homosexuals. Mattachine and DOB, as part of the larger campaign to gain public respect, encouraged their members to dress and behave in a fashion appropriate to their gender and to refrain from tactics that would alienate heterosexuals. Indeed both groups consisted mainly of white middle-class gay men and lesbians who were inclined to see the value in social conformity and who regarded science as a source of salvation for highlighting this conformity.

Also in the drive to gain social respectability and political credibility, in 1953 the gay men who founded Mattachine were pressured by other members of the society to refrain from leadership positions in the group because of their history with the left. New members who joined the group around this time were concerned about its connection with communism and proposed a loyalty oath be signed by all members. But despite these conservative tendencies on the part of some homophile activists, Mattachine and DOB were not entirely dominated by this kind of thinking. Their diverse members made informed strategic choices in efforts to counter homophobia and to gain public acceptance. Alongside public forums and conferences highlighting the affirmative opinions of experts, the groups used many other strategies to champion homosexual identity. They rightly identified that scientific authority would help them to turn popular opinion toward their favor. Who better than bona fide authorities were in the position to counter the long-standing assumptions that homosexuality was abnormal? A consequence of this strategy, however, was that, at times, broader claims for sexual and political diversity were submerged through the imperative to seem normal and adjusted.

Secondly, homophile activists' interest in scientifically generated statistical surveys was related to their arguing that homosexuals represented a minority, but a substantial one, worthy of respect for its social and cultural contributions. Scientific surveys became a strategy for visibility. In fact, the Daughters of Bilitis stated one of its foundational principles to be the gathering and dissemination of authoritative and reliable information about lesbians. For this they sought the expertise of sympathetic psychiatrists and social scientists. One of the most beloved scientists among homophile activists was UCLA psychologist Evelyn Hooker. In 1953, Hooker undertook studies of the male homosexual personality, drawing research subjects from among her friends in the Mattachine Society. Starting in 1957, she published articles disputing the disease model and presenting evidence of the adjusted homosexual male.[10] Hooker, who remained a lifelong supporter of the gay and lesbian rights movement, generously lent her scientific authority to the homophile struggle and presented her findings at professional meetings attended by psychologists, psychiatrists, physicians, clergymen, educators, and legislators. When she undertook her studies and even after they were published, most Americans, having been repeatedly told that homosexuality and mental illness were one and the same, were not particularly ready to accept her findings. In time and, in part, due to the careful promotion of her studies by homophile activists, Hooker was instrumental in changing the minds of some professionals and laypeople who would have otherwise continued to believe that there was no such thing as a normal, well-adjusted homosexual. As a result of her studies, a space was created for questioning the popular consensus, entrenched by postwar homophobia, that homosexuals were fundamentally diseased.

SUBJECTIVE COUNTERPOINTS TO HOMOPHOBIC MEDICINE

Many of the ideas of the homophile movement were articulated in Donald Webster Cory's *The Homosexual in America: A Subjective Approach*, published in 1951, the same year the Mattachine Society formed. The pseudonymous author frankly and sympathetically surveyed the problem of homosexuality from the point of view of a homosexual. This perspective, he believed, was "as essential as those of the psychiatrist, the jurist, or the churchman in arriving at any conclusions about homosexuality."[11] Cory argued for the advancement of civil rights of homosexuals and other minority groups. He warned that to do otherwise was to corrupt the idea of democracy and to fall into the trap of totalitarianism.

Drawing analogies from religious and racial discrimination especially suffered by Jews and blacks, Cory portrayed homosexuals as similarly victims of social oppression. Rather than advance a natural-ist perspective that grounded homosexuality in a bodily essence, Cory conceptualized homosexuality in terms of a social identity worthy of respect. He articulated this by offering a critique that argued that gen-der norms and the institution of heterosexuality were products of a crippling social system that caused undue suffering and injustice. In defense of homosexuality, he argued that, while not inborn, it was deeply rooted in certain individuals who could not simply assert their will to overcome it. Nor should they have to. They suffered a particu-lar form of oppression, one caused by the invisibility of their differ-ence which invited those afflicted to hide their true selves and move in the shadows of society, surrounded by shame and fear.

A good deal of Cory's book was devoted to surveying medical and scientific theories of homosexuality, and his ideas on the subject were rather contradictory. He criticized theories that rendered the homo-sexual entirely subject to bodily drives beyond his or her control, sin-gling out the idea of congenital homosexuality as well as inborn sexual inversion as problematic notions that further stigmatized homosexu-als while making heterosexuals think they were somehow flawless. Though sympathetic to how and why naturalist ideas were used by homosexuals as a defense against homophobic hostility, Cory pre-ferred to think of homosexuality not as an affliction but as an acquired attribute of character that could, if accepted, add to the wealth of di-versity in democratic societies. Thus, his book advanced what was to become a more common rhetorical position that staged homosexual rights not on a basis of biological difference but in terms of socially based arguments stressing that gay men and lesbians, like all other law-abiding members of society, possessed inalienable civil rights. While Cory criticized the psychoanalytic notion of arrested develop-ment, he suggested that homosexual desire was "implanted" in those who develop an unusually strong attachment for one parent, usually the mother, and then take flight from this due to the taboo against incest. The solution was one that had been offered by previous gener-ations of progressive thinkers: loosen the rigid constraints placed on sexuality, and everyone will find healthy fulfillment.

At times self-loathing, Cory candidly conveyed his painful desire to be normal, and he spoke of homosexual drives which tortured him. Anti-homosexual prejudice when internalized by homosexuals, he ar-gued, was one of the most tragic and painful aspects of being a homo-sexual in America. It also oppressed heterosexuals by giving them a false sense of superiority and by thus papering over the negative

effects of sexual repression on them as well. Cory argued that one of
the key ways to overcome the ills of sexual repression was to combat
prejudice. This could be done by homosexuals acknowledging their
sexuality publicly—speaking out openly and honestly—in order to
overcome oppressive attitudes that harmed everyone. In addition, he
added that though it was not the only avenue for change, science
could offer more accurate knowledge about homosexuals that would
encourage them to come out of hiding. This, in turn, would allow
heterosexuals to see that homosexuals were worthy people.[12]

In a similar vein, in 1959 J. D. Mercer completed *They Walk in
Shadows*, massive survey of homosexual topics across literature and
science in which Mercer reiterated many of the by-then established
arguments for the acceptance of homosexuality. Mercer dedicated the
book to Kinsey and his assistants, "who have pointed the way to the
study of human sexual behavior in the cool, clear light of investigative
science," and to Sir John Wolfenden for recommending changes in
sex laws "on a basis approaching equity, individual rights, and scientific facts."[13] Mercer announced himself as "a self-confessed and self-
accepting ambisexual who has struck a happy balance between his
own nature and the world at large."[14]

One of the most striking features of *They Walk in Shadows* is Mercer's insistence that one must go to the source of the experiences of
homosexuality—the homosexual himself—to counter the myths and
falsehoods which support social prejudice and harsh legal punishment. This idea of the authenticity of homosexual testimony came to
be a persistent theme in much of the "coming out" spirit of the gay
and lesbian rights movement that emerged around this time.

Mercer's book focused exclusively on male homosexuality. Much
of it is devoted to pondering etiological theories, and the author was
especially drawn to evolutionary arguments. Mercer brought Hirschfeld and Kinsey together by invoking a naturalist argument in which
homosexuality was assumed to be inborn while also stressing the wide
variation of desires and experiences within the otherwise "normal"
population. Having dismissed the disease model, Mercer's perspective straddled a difficult epistemological line between emphasizing a
fundamental difference between homosexuals and heterosexuals á la
Hirschfeld, on the one hand, and fundamental sameness between the
two á la Kinsey, on the other. This epistemological tension continued
through the expansion of the gay and lesbian movement in the 1960s
and in many respects continues to shape both scientific and political
debates about homosexuality to this day.

Mercer showed a troubling sexism when discussing the evolutionary origins of homosexuality in some individuals. Females, he remarked, are the more primitive and infantile version of the human species; males, in their anatomy, physiology, and disposition, are an improvement on this fundamental design. But he argued that males who are not fully differentiated are more accurately defined as infantile than feminine, a term he found disparaging. Whereas earlier gay writers had embraced femininity, Mercer and other gay men in the 1950s revealed a symptomatic repulsion toward it.[15] As a way of countering a common stereotype, Mercer emphasized that most gay men were not effeminate. But, in making this argument, he not only degraded those who were but also women in general. This attitude eventually led to rifts between gay men and lesbians. Lesbians, irritated by the arrogant and misogynist attitudes among many gay men, began to seriously doubt that masculinist scientific authority was an avenue for achieving their own liberation. Though many gay men were similarly skeptical, particularly of psychiatry, others, more often than lesbians, tended to advocate scientific theories, even some which were patently sexist.

QUESTIONING SCIENCE

It is possible to trace, beginning in the early 1960s, the emergence of a split between various chapters of the Mattachine Society and Daughters of Bilitis over the question of how important it was to have scientific studies conducted about homosexuality. Frank Kameny, a gay man and an astrophysicist who fought against the homosexual purges from the U.S. government during the 1950s, argued in the pages of the DOB publication, *The Ladder*, that spending so much time and energy on scientific and psychological research was a waste of time for homosexuals.[16] Kameny argued that most existing scientific studies lacked rigor and relied on an unsupported assertion that homosexuals were sick or defective. To counter this assertion, he insisted on a militant position that refused the notion that lesbians and gay men were sick, and he argued that it was time to fight for homosexual rights and for homosexuals to speak for themselves rather than taking the meek position of hoping that doctors and scientists would find homosexuals normal enough. The only scientific studies Kameny condoned were those that helped lesbians and homosexual men to understand their own worlds and lives better, not those which were meant to persuade the general public or other experts that homosexuals should be tolerated. Florence Conrad, chair of the DOB research committee, took a different position, arguing that lesbians and homosexual men needed to have their experiences translated by scientists so that other scientists and the lay public would listen with interest and be persuaded that being gay was acceptable. For Conrad, militant action would only allow scientists and the public to ignore and marginalize homosexuals. Instead, she recommended a careful course of cooperation. Conrad had a great deal of faith particularly in the virtues and possibilities of social scientific investigations.[17] But other lesbians, particularly those who came out through a process of feminist consciousness raising, were increasingly inclined to criticize male-dominated thought, including science, for its perpetuation of myths of male superiority.

Feminist sentiments of this sort, though not directly attacking science, were expressed in 1957 in two letters to *The Ladder*. The writer was the African American playwright and novelist Lorraine Hansberry, who signed the letter with the initials "L.H.N." for Lorraine Hansberry Nemiroff:

> I'm glad as heck that you exist. You are absolutely serious people and I feel that women, without wishing to foster any strict separatist notions, homo or hetero, indeed have a need for their own publications and organizations. Our problems, our experiences as women are profoundly unique as compared to the other half of the human race. Women, like other oppressed groups of one kind or another, have particularly had to pay a price for the second class status imposed on us for centuries created and sustained. Thus, I feel that *The Ladder* is a fine, elementary step in a rewarding direction.[18]

In a letter written several months later, Hansberry elaborated:

> I think it is about time that equipped women began to take on some of the ethical questions which a male-dominated culture has produced and dissect and analyze them quite to pieces in a serious fashion. It is time that "half the human race" had something to say about the nature of its existence. Otherwise—without revised basic thinking—the woman intellectual is likely to find herself trying to draw conclusions—moral conclusions—based on acceptance of a social moral superstructure which has never admitted to the equality of women and is therefore immoral itself. As per marriage, as per sexual practices, as per the rearing of children, etc. In this kind of work there may be women to emerge who will be able to formulate a new and possible concept that homosexual persecution and condemnation has at its roots not only social ignorance, but a philosophically active anti-

feminist dogma. But that is but a kernel of a speculative embryonic idea improperly introduced here.[19]

Without citing science in particular, Hansberry assailed the sexist nature of authoritative pronouncements about women, many of which can be traced to scientific discourse as well as to moral philosophy and other bastions of male-dominated thought. Mercer and the vast majority of homosexual men writing during this period were blind to such a critique as that raised by Hansberry. They paid little attention to how sexist presumptions about women were part and parcel of the homophobia suffered not just by lesbians but by gay men who continued to be viewed popularly and by most authorities as fundamentally effeminate. Hansberry's prescient remarks would be developed further by other women as the second-wave feminist movement emerged in the 1960s. But in the meantime, even as homophile activists and writers were attempting to challenge basic prejudice, they encountered yet another backlash, which, as we shall see, indulged a voyeuristic and largely disdainful popular interest in homosexuality.

HOMOPHOBIC CRITICS STRIKE BACK

Though Kinsey's work was useful in campaigns to gain homosexuals rights and respectability, it was also appropriated by others less sympathetic to the cause. A number of writers cashed in on the public fascination with homosexuality following the popularization of Kinsey's reports in a manner that perpetuated repulsive stereotypes while pretending to offer objective journalism on the subject. For example, in 1962, Jess Stearn published *The Sixth Man*, a pulp non-fiction book whose title referred to those who rated as exclusive homosexuals, or "Kinsey Sixes," on the famous homosexual-heterosexual continuum the scientist devised. Stearn offered a voyeuristic view of gay male life filled with salacious details and peppered with condescension and contempt. To give the book the luster of scientific credibility, he got George Henry's assistant, Alfred Gross, to write a laudatory preface, and he referenced interviews with Henry at length. Stearn wrote that, "like many students of contemporary Western culture, Dr. Henry feels that our civilization may be declining, somewhat as the Romans' did." Indeed, Henry's own words served Stearn's homophobic prejudice well:

> Homosexuality, with its lack of responsibility for the procreation of the species, is certainly a factor in that decline. . . . [Homosexuals]

never really attain the complete love which is possible only between men and women whose shared interests included the blessedness of children and grandchildren, which give a grand purpose to the sex relationship.[20]

Much of *The Sixth Man* is filled with accounts of conversations Stearn had with police authorities as well as with gay men he encountered in bars, social clubs, and show business. The intended audience was a general public fascinated but also repulsed by tales from the homosexual underworld.

Several years later Stearn published a companion volume on lesbians entitled *The Grapevine,* which was based in part on interviews with members of the Daughters of Bilitis.[21] The book exposed the lives, loves, and losses of lesbians. The Grapevine, an idiom Stearn appropriated from lesbian subculture, referred to the complex and tightly interwoven lives of bisexual and homosexual women. While not as overtly disdainful in tone as *The Sixth Man,* Stearn's assessment of lesbians and their subculture traded in titillating voyeurism and condescending dismissals of the value of relationships between women. Both of Stearn's books brought male homosexuality and lesbianism even more before the public's eye. His detailed descriptions of gay bars, bath houses, house parties, and political organizations no doubt were intriguing not only to curious, if queasy, heterosexuals but also to readers who found the homosexual world appealing and alluring. But without question the books painted a dreary picture of homosexual life-styles and generally emphasized, that despite this dreariness, the ranks of homosexual men and women were growing. Such notions continued, as they had in the past, to associate homosexuality with a lurid underworld that loomed in the midst of otherwise unwitting people. Stearn, like other sensationalistic journalists of the time, hinted that homophile activists were politically ambitious and wanted to expand their influence in the larger society.

In a more overt fashion, R.E.L. Masters sounded an alarmist tone that harped on the impending dangers posed by a power-hungry homosexual political constituency. In his 1962 pulp nonfiction book, *The Homosexual Revolution,* Masters offered a remarkable foreshadowing of what was to become later, in the 1990s, a wave of right-wing hysteria over the so-called "gay agenda" to take over government, industry, and civic institutions in the United States.[22] Based on interviews with homophile activists, attendance at their meetings, and reading their publications, Masters warned that "inverts" and homophiles were forming political organizations with an interest in winning public support and local electoral campaigns for promoting their "new society." Masters further warned that the homosexual revolution was abetted by Kinsey's findings that sexual perversions were commonplace in American society. While voicing condescending pity for inverts, the author's overall message was one of fear and loathing. He noted that inverts and homosexuals were seeking to influence American society through both overt and covert means, and, once they got going, little could stand in their way.

Dismissing analogies drawn by homophile activists to the civil rights struggles of "Negroes," Masters argued that homosexuality was not like race. Again the resonances to late 1990s right-wing attacks on antidiscrimination ordinances are remarkable. The author maintained that homosexuality was the product of circumstances and environment, not of inborn biological differences, and thus should not be protected as a matter of civil rights. To make such an analogy, homosexuals sullied the venerable and justified civil rights movement. Masters claimed that the oppression homosexuals experienced was due largely to their own inability to admit that homosexuality was a basically unhappy condition, marked by jealousy, alcoholism, promiscuity, and bitterness. Their secret world was not merely pitiful, though; it was politically menacing. Because homosexuals were no longer satisfied to stay hidden, the public sphere of politics would be destroyed by the pressures they would exert on politicians to adhere to their demands.

After stoking so much fear, Masters warned homosexuals that science, in which they had invested such great hopes, may actually come back to haunt them. If scientists could find a cure for homosexuality either through psychotherapy or through hormonal alterations, then homosexuals would be faced with the coercion to be cured or to be imprisoned:

> The homophile movement, the homosexual revolution, or whatever one wishes to call it, can only be based in the long run on the negative belief (or hope) that science is not going to be able to do anything to prevent or 'cure' sexual inversion. To the extent that homophiles are only striving for short-term goals of social acceptance or tolerance, this does not matter much. But the movement is also a kind of cult, with a mystique and the notion, stated or assumed, of inheriting the earth or of wrestling it away from the heterosexuals. Like the worm at the core of the apple, the uncertain future of the homosexual, the possibility that science may eliminate him and his kind once and for all, gnaws at

the heart of this dream. And the dream and the mystique, as sources of spiritual sustenance for many homosexuals, are of vital import. Therefore, there is dread, and the more intelligent and 'engaged' the individual homosexual, the more anxious he must be.[23]

Science, the friend of the homosexual revolutionaries, could in the end be as treasonous as homosexuals themselves. Masters' closing move was to annex science back to a moral agenda of compulsory heterosexuality, where its eminent reason would, in the end, prove homosexuality to be wrong and dispensable.

PSYCHOANALYSIS BEFORE AND AFTER STONEWALL

During the 1960s, psychoanalysts continued to claim that homosexuality was the result of particular and unfavorable conditioning experiences that should be overcome. In 1962, Irving Bieber, a psychoanalyst in New York, had argued that homosexuality resulted from negative experiences with the opposite sex, which were themselves engendered by the lack of a healthy resolution of the Oedipus complex.[24] According to Bieber's paradigm, homosexual men's inability to make a proper identification with the father resulted in arrested development, which played out in negative experiences with the opposite sex. Thus, Bieber claimed that homosexuals took flight from heterosexuality through a process of regression, a process that Bieber and many psychoanalysts of his time believed could be overcome through psychotherapy.

The psychiatrist Cornelia Wilbur collaborated with Bieber on his study of male homosexuals before going on to make similar claims about female homosexuality several years later. Wilbur, famous for her innovative regression therapy in the case of the multiple personalities of "Sybil," who became the subject of a popular book and a film, asserted that lesbians tended to have overbearing mothers and either detached or overly involved fathers. As a result, they were plagued by debilitating guilt over desires to gain their fathers' affection at the cost of losing their mothers' love. Lesbianism thus functioned as a defense mechanism against the fear of maternal hostility, and it resulted in feelings of loneliness and isolation toward siblings and parents. Chronic anxiety, ambivalence, an unrealistic longing for affection, instability, and transient relationships, common among lesbians, were signs of an underlying pathological condition. Adequate motivation on the part of the female patient, Wilbur believed, could result in the favorable outcome of a "reversion to exclusive heterosexual behavior."[25]

In 1968, psychoanalyst Charles Socarides reiterated Bieber's theoretical paradigm and therapeutic recommendations when he reported that his homosexual patients were profoundly grateful for the chance to change their condition. A year before the Stonewall Rebellion of 1969, Socarides voiced the same disdain for homosexuality as had Bergler and many other psychoanalysts who preceded him, and he specifically attacked the gay and lesbian rights movement and the idea that homosexuality may be a positive outcome:

> Homosexual circles or clubs consist of a "regrouping of outcasts." Homosexuality means an element of embarrassment and of aggressiveness toward normal human society. There is always a narcissistic element present and a more or less conscious and more or less supercompensated element of inferiority-anxiety. . . . The "solution" of homosexuality is always doomed to failure. . . . Homosexuality is based on the fear of the mother, the aggressive attack against the father, and is filled with aggression, destruction, and self-deceit. It is a masquerade of life in which certain psychic energies are neutralized and held in a somewhat quiescent state. However, the unconscious manifestations of hate, destructiveness, incest and fear are always threatening to break through. Instead of union, cooperation, solace, stimulation, enrichment, healthy challenge and fulfillment, there are only destruction, mutual defeat, exploitation of the partner and the self, oral-sadistic incorporation, aggressive onslaughts, attempts to alleviate anxiety and a pseudo-solution to the aggressive and libidinal urges which dominate and torment the individual.[26]

Ten years later, Socarides expanded upon these ideas and adamantly argued that homosexuality could be eliminated through psychoanalytic therapy. In his 600 page book, titled simply *Homosexuality*, Socarides offered a "systematized widely expanded, and vitally needed new section on the psychoanalytic therapy of homosexuality."[27] Homosexuality, he claimed, was a compensatory "neutralization" of psychical conflicts which may lead homosexuals to appear deceptively normal or without disease. Writing in the midst of a nationally prominent and vital movement for gay and lesbian liberation, Socarides warned that "homosexuality is unique in its capacity to use profound psychic conflicts and struggles to attain, for limited intervals, a pseudoequilibrium and pleasure reward (orgasm), often permitting the individual to function, however marginally and erratically."[28] Repeating verbatim his own sentences from the 1968 volume, Socarides accused homosexuals of regarding as "traitors" those who sought psychoanalytic treatment, thus casting gay and lesbian critics as a conspiratorial band of bullies. Socarides wholly refuted the notion of an innate or biological underpinning to homosexuality and reiterated that homosexual object choice was a "learned, acquired behavior." This set the stage for his proposal for "unlearning" or the "disacquisition" of homosexuality and the learning of heterosexuality. He felt that this was all the more urgent since the gay and lesbian rights movement had perpetrated the myth that homosexuals are proud and satisfied. What Edmund Bergler had accused Kinsey of two decades earlier, Socarides now held against homosexual activists: rather than restoring self-esteem to gay men and lesbians, the movement, Socarides claimed, had given them false hope and only isolated them further from normal and adjusted Americans.

GAY AND LESBIAN LIBERATION

Even as psychoanalysts and authors such as R.E.L. Masters attacked homosexual rights organizing, the movement was gathering steam and diversifying its tactics beyond appeals to scientific authority. In the early 1960s, gay and lesbian rights groups borrowed the strategies of direct-action street protests and picketing from the civil rights and free speech movements. They targeted federal and local governments for their discriminatory employment policies and police departments for their harassment and raids on gay bars and movement headquarters. Protesters emphasized the importance of homosexuals being visible after so many years of intimidation and shame. What the gay and lesbian rights movement shared with other grassroots progressive movements of the time was, among other things, a questioning of authority that foregrounded the violations of democracy and freedom carried out by a variety of institutions. Participants in the radical social movements of the 1960s had an affinity to leftist critiques of dominant ideology and of the social institutions that supported it. Oppressive attitudes would change only if the social institutions that underpinned them were radically transformed. Activists were no longer satisfied to argue for mere social tolerance but instead stressed in more militant tones that they deserved the privileges and respect granted to heterosexuals.

In 1973, after years of organizing within and around the psychiatric profession, gay and lesbian activists were successful in finally having the American Psychiatric Association remove homosexuality from its official manual of mental diseases.[29] The campaign highlighted psychiatrists' inhumane use of psychopharmaceuticals, lobotomy, psychoanalysis, and aversion therapy to eliminate homosexual desires in patients who, if freed from homophobic contempt, might be happy and valuable citizens. During this same time, activists broadened their strategies considerably by passing anti-discriminatory legislation and filing lawsuits against those violating the civil rights of individuals on the basis of sexual orientation. As the movement gained momentum, it began to rely much less on the validation of scientists and other authorities, compared to what it had done in the 1950s, and sought instead to affirm homosexuality not only through the election of supportive candidates but by organizing rallies and marches that made gay men and lesbians visible in the mainstream press more than they had ever been before. Gay and lesbian liberationists took the basic claim for rights a step further by arguing that sexual repression, rigid gender roles, and the institution of heterosexuality were damaging to everyone and ought to be eliminated. They took advantage of the rhetoric of the countercultural hippy movement and the broadening advocacy of sexual liberation to argue that homosexuals were everywhere and represented a positive alternative to the uptight conventions of "straight" sexuality. The emergent feminist movement of the 1970s offered a critique of male domination that lesbian-feminists extended to call into question the sexist bases of homophobia. A strong strain of anti-authoritarianism ran through the movements of the time, and, perhaps not surprisingly, both science and medicine— where they had previously enjoyed a particularly privileged position in positing meanings about homosexuality—were not nearly so central to claims for homosexual liberation.

Feminist ideas especially influenced lesbian activists to call into question a reliance on scientific authority to legitimate homosexuality. In 1972, Del Martin and Phyllis Lyon published *Lesbian/Woman*, which they described as a subjective account of lesbianism.[30] In their introduction, they explicitly set out to recuperate the experiences of lesbians from the distortions of most medical and scientific accounts. The authors foregrounded a feminist critique of male dominance and argued the merits of lesbianism as a positive refusal to accept male authority, specifically that of experts who had declared women inherently inferior to men. Martin and Lyon urged readers to question the authority of experts by noting the close relationship between medical contempt for lesbians and the sexist oppression of women. The authors claimed to offer an alternative by producing neither a true confession nor a scientific book but one that was written

from the subjective experience of lesbians themselves. They pointed
out, as Lorraine Hansberry had suggested earlier, that claims to objectivity and neutrality are often illusions or masks that conceal unex-
amined assumptions and partisan agendas. Lyon and Martin thus
affirmed their book as partisan and declared that it was time for lesbians to speak about themselves in their own terms.

The book did just that. Highlighting their own life stories and
those of others lesbians whom they knew from DOB, Lyon and Martin offered chapters on self image, sexuality and sex roles, lesbian
motherhood, growing up gay, and personal accounts of oppression.
Other chapters traced the history of the DOB and its various strategies to fight homophobic and sexist attitudes and to carve out a space
within the gay liberationist and feminist movements for the articulation of specifically lesbian concerns. Mixing anecdotes with political
analysis, they intended the book to dispel myths and to offer support
to women who loved women. But, while assuming the book would be
read by other lesbians, Lyon and Martin also addressed a larger audience in an appeal that went beyond mere toleration:

> These are your daughters, sisters, wives and mothers. They are real
> live people, not just characters in a book, and there are millions of
> them. They are ridiculed, hunted, raped, fired, put down, prayed over
> and spit upon. Hardly anywhere are they being supported—even by
> you who are so intimately bound to them. It is time you began to listen
> to them, and to your consciences and hearts. Millions of lives have
> been and are being destroyed by sheer nonsense, by politics and se-
> mantic games. It is time that you understood that. We Lesbians do not
> want your sympathy nor your pity; we want your love and respect. We
> are not looking for society's toleration, a "let live" policy which would
> simply relegate us to a second best kind of life; we want to partake of
> the richness of life and be a part of the mainstream of society. We are
> not looking for a minister who will take us into the fold as pitiable
> sinners to be "saved" by the grace of God; ours is a God of Love em-
> bracing all Creation. We Lesbians are not seeking changes in the law
> that will only protect us in the "privacy" of our bedrooms; we want
> our full citizenship with all its privileges and responsibilities. Nor do
> we see the value of counseling which will help us to "adjust" to our
> homosexuality only that we might better cope with the hazards of liv-
> ing in a heterosexual society; we want a society that will recognize and
> adjust to the diversity and the humanness of all its citizens.[31]

Lyon and Martin were careful to point out that the oppression of
lesbians was two-fold: as women, they were subjected to sexism and,
as homosexuals, to homophobia. In 1966, Shirley Willer, national

president of DOB, addressed this first aspect at the North American conference of Homophile Organizations held in San Francisco. Willer noted that "the Lesbian has agreed (with reservations) to join in common cause with the male homosexual, but her role in the homophile movement to date has largely been one of mediator between the male homosexual and society."[32] Willer's concern, echoed by Lyon and Martin, was that lesbians had devoted great energy to the struggle against police harassment of gay men but that few gay men had rallied to address the particular concerns of lesbians, including sex discrimination in jobs, the purge of lesbians from the military, and child custody battles involving lesbian mothers. Furthermore, most homosexual rights groups were dominated by men whose attitudes were chauvinistic.

At the same time, as Lyon and Martin also noted, DOB members faced homophobia and heterosexism within the women's movement, where they were referred to by Betty Friedan and others as the "Lavender Menace": a cadre of troublemakers who threatened to sully the credibility of the movement because of their alleged hostility toward men. Efforts by lesbians to get organizations such as the National Organization for Women to incorporate their concerns were ongoing through the 1970s. While many of the rank and file members of NOW were lesbians, the national leadership, under the influence of Friedan, was resistant to address these issues. "A Letter from Mary," written in 1970, responded to such attitudes in the women's movement and appealed to other feminists to confront their homophobia:

> We have all said in our leaflets, to our friends, in the screams in the night: what we want is equal, open, loving relationships where each person can see the other as an individual human being, not a member of some mythic group, where each person loves and wants the other instead of needing her for some quality he does not himself possess. So why when I affirm all this do you see me with strange eyes? Why when I love my sisters wholly do I make you uneasy? Why, if I talk of my feelings, do you look away or, if you listen, at the end relax as if to say "Well I guess you had to do that . . . it's probably very healthy that you brought your secret out into the open . . . but now that's over and we don't have to talk about it anymore." And, after that, every remark I make is filtered through the label "Lesbian." The irony of it all is that I probably never would have discovered my homosexuality without Women's Liberation. . . . The accusation of being a movement of Lesbians will always be powerful if we cannot say, "Being a Lesbian is good." Nothing short of that will suffice as an answer. . . . Women's

Liberation needs Lesbianism. Lesbians need Women's Liberation. We
are all sisters.[33]

The letter was quoted in *Lesbian/Woman* followed by Lyon and Martin's observation that "for those of us who recognize ourselves as
Woman as well as Lesbian, the emotional furor our presence has
wrought in the women's movement has been both comic and tragic."
But they were heartened by a vote at the 1971 national conference of
NOW that overwhelmingly approved resolutions stating that "a
woman has the right to her own sexuality and to choose her own lifestyle and that the oppression of Lesbians is a legitimate concern of
feminism."[34] In the final pages of *Lesbian/Woman*, Lyon and Martin
reflect on strategies used by lesbians and gay men to win respect, noting the limitations of earlier appeals for acceptance that, while significant for their times, were no longer adequate. In *The Well of Loneliness*, Radclyffe Hall had written: "You, God, in Whom we, the
outcast, believe; you, world, into which we are pitilessly born; you,
who have drained our cup to the dregs—we have asked for bread; will
you give us a stone? . . . Give us also the right to our existence."[35] To
this, Lyon and Martin responded:

> That was back in 1928. It was a plea. Today there are no pleas nor
> pleases—there are only demands. And they come not from the minor-
> ity of our population, but from the majority; not just from homosexu-
> als, but from women and from Blacks and all Third World peoples.
> The Great Society can only be as great as its people, and the people
> can only be as great as they know, appreciate, love, understand and
> express their diversity and individuality.[36]

By 1972, when *Lesbian/Woman* first appeared, Lyon and Martin had
been involved in coalition building among feminists, antiracist activists, anti-imperialist activists, and gay rights activists. Indeed,
Lesbian/Woman was published through the sponsorship of the Glide
Foundation in San Francisco, a grassroots and racially diverse organization that sponsored left-leaning civil rights activities. The foundation was affiliated with the Glide Memorial Church, which provided
meeting rooms for DOB events and for public forums that assembled
members of various movements to address racial and sexual oppression. The concluding passages of *Lesbian/Woman*, quoted above, show
the impact of coalition politics on Lyon and Martin as they linked
their vision of lesbian liberation to a broader movement for radical
social change. Their book indicates that by the 1970s the strategies of

lesbian and gay rights groups had shifted substantially away from a dependence on benevolent scientific and medical authority and toward a radical stance rooted in claims for social liberation.

A NEW DIAGNOSTIC CATEGORY

Besides opposing psychoanalysts' declarations, much of the critique of homophobic science and medicine from this period attacked the procedures aimed at altering the bodies of homosexuals. Yet even as these procedures were decried as dehumanizing, a small group of endocrinologists were busy conducting hormonal experiments on rodents and on nonhuman primates as part of a renewed attempt to determine the effects of hormones on sexual behavior, and especially to find a link between hormonal activity and homosexuality.[37] Scientists conducting these hormonal experiments conjectured, as they had in the past, that homosexual was a congenital condition that originated in the earliest stages of development and that arrested the natural maturation process of the male so that it behaved more like the *species type:* that is, more like a female. By contrast, female offspring, if showered by storms of androgens in the womb, would falsely mature beyond their primary status to develop masculine characteristics. Extrapolating from experiments on mice, in which males who were castrated at an early age tended to exhibit "female-typical" behavior (i.e. they presented themselves to be mounted), the scientist Gunter Dörner hypothesized that, as did the castrated mice, homosexual men had higher levels of estrogen and lower levels of testosterone than did heterosexual men.[38] Similarly, homosexual behavior in female mice was believed to be the result of higher levels of androgen in the mother's womb. Implicitly defining human homosexuality as a matter of gender inversion, Dörner assumed that the human analogue to the castrated, effeminized male mouse was the gay man. The idea that gay men commonly mount other men—mounting being the signifier of male-typical behavior in rats—was never reckoned with in these studies. In spite of this blind spot, these studies were aimed at establishing the cause of homosexuality as deficient biological makeup and at developing a "cure" through the alteration of hormones in gay men and lesbians. As in the past, homosexuality was viewed again through these studies as an unfavorable bodily condition linked primarily to gender disorders that should be eliminated.

Subsequently, a group of psychiatrists took a keen interest in this type of research as a way of accounting for "sissy boys" and tomboys.[39]

Many acknowledged that hormonal activity could be influenced by the environment and family relations. But, to a great degree, they biologized the process of psychosexual development to emphasize that sexual orientation is deeply embedded in the body from an early age—in other words, that it is the result, perhaps, of a genetic predisposition to hormonal anomalies or the outcome of maternal stress that subverted the processes by which male and female embryos normally develop. The underlying assumption in this work was that many gay men and lesbians were gender-inverted individuals whose bodies and dispositions distinguished them from normal people. This newer generation of research on gender inversion, occurring after the American Psychiatric Association removed homosexuality from its *Diagnostic and Statistical Manual,* delineated gender identity disorder as a particular affliction that might result from either psychological or biological causes. Studies of gender identity disorders did more than simply target homosexuality or homosexuals per se; they were aimed at diagnosing and possibly treating children who did not conform to proper gender roles of the two-sex model upon which normative heterosexuality was to be based.

As the movement for lesbian and gay liberation grew, biological research aimed at identifying and treating homosexuality was criticized by activists for its pretensions to explain complex human relations in biologically reductive terms. They were not alone in assailing biological determinism. During the 1970s and 1980s, feminists, leftists, and liberals decried attempts to explain social differences and inequalities in terms of biology. To a great degree, gay liberationists had no less disdain for scientific projects to discover the biological basis of homosexuality than they had for efforts to treat homosexuality as a mental disorder. In this context, gay and lesbian activists seldom articulated naturalist theories that grounded homosexuality in biology. While many stressed that sexual orientation was not simply chosen but was instead a deeply rooted in one's identity, they also advanced a social critique of homophobia. They argued for civil rights not because they were biologically distinct but because they were human beings living in a society that was unduly hostile toward the free and harmless expression of sexual desires. Thus, to the extent that they invoked scientific authority, activists tended to cite psychologists and sociologists who reiterated what Evelyn Hooker's research had shown earlier: that many homosexuals were happy and fulfilled especially when they were not subject to the damaging effects of homophobia.

THE POPULAR PERSISTENCE OF HOMOPHOBIA

Historians tend to date the end of McCarthyism to about 1957, when the domestic repression of the postwar period declined due largely to internal conflicts among Cold Warriors. Accusations of communism eventually became ludicrous, especially when hurled by anticommunists against each other. By 1960 McCarthy himself was portrayed as an opportunistic know-nothing in the popular press. Alongside "militant" civil rights activists, free speech advocates, antiwar protesters, and feminists, gay and lesbian activists further undermined the ethos of Cold War conformity. But, although public opinion gradually turned against the hysterical red-baiting that dominated most of the 1950s, anti-homosexual sentiments actually intensified as homosexuals "came out" into the public sphere as political actors.

Ideas sedimented by psychoanalytic discourse before and during the postwar period left lasting effects on a major portion of the American population. A 1965 Harris poll placed homosexuals third, behind communists and atheists, as groups most harmful to the nation.[40] In the same year, a sociological study showed that seventy-two percent of the 134 respondents believed that homosexuals were sexually abnormal, forty percent believed they were mentally ill, and twenty-nine percent assumed male homosexuals were effeminate.[41] Similar attitudes were discovered among San Franciscans in the following year: of the 353 polled, eighty-seven percent believed homosexuals were psychologically disturbed and sixty-nine percent believed they endangered children.[42] In 1966, a nationwide sample of 946 persons eighteen years or older found that one-third of the public believed homosexuality to be a social danger.[43] And in 1970, two-thirds of 373 respondents believed that homosexuality was a "sickness," thirty-eight percent that it was "dangerous," and about twenty percent believed that homosexuals were sex inverted and thus distinguishable from the "normal" population.[44]

These various polls from the 1960s reveal the tenacity of assumptions dating back to medical and scientific discourse from the early part of the century. In the latter half of the century, these assumptions were woven into overt political reactions against lesbians and gay men. Thus, homosexuality was not a mere curiosity in the margins of society but was seen as a national problem to be brought under control. Though Kinsey's studies had enormous impact on public discourse and contributed to lessening legal penalties for consensual homosexual sex in some jurisdictions, a large public opinion poll taken in the late 1960s revealed that anywhere from forty to eighty percent of the polled individuals tended to have a negative view of homosexuals and expressed their negative judgments in a wide variety of ways.[45] The survey reported that average Americans believed homosexuality was a curable sickness, although most doubted that gay men and lesbians would agree to being treated. Homosexual men were assumed to be child molesters, and half of those polled believed homosexuals tended to corrupt their fellow workers sexually. About the same percentage advocated laws that prohibited any form of homosexual contact, including activities between consenting adults in private. Nearly half believed that gay men and lesbians should not be allowed to form recreational or social groups. And an overwhelming majority reported that they would deny homosexuals the right to work at professions that carry authority and influence, including teaching, the ministry, the judiciary, the medical profession, and government service. Thus the surveyors concluded that, despite Kinsey's influence, "there exists in the United States a remarkably stable, conservative structure of public sexual morality."[46]

A more accurate assessment would be that conservative sexual morality was implanted, rather than preserved, by the emergence of homosexuality into public discourse and the open presence of gay men and lesbians in society. By the end of the 1970s, homosexuality was no longer a secret hiding out in grungy alleyways or, for that matter, in the deeper recesses of the psyches of disturbed individuals. Nor was its only mention tucked away in scientific journals or pornography. It had gone public in a big way, thanks not only to Kinsey's research but to the range of negative reactions and progressive appropriations he unleashed, both inside and outside of scientific circles.

To be sure, political activism by openly homosexual men and women during this period altered the terms of knowledge production about homosexuality. Rather than rely on the authority of heterosexual experts, texts and public protests growing out of this movement were aimed at generating alternatives to homophobic stereotypes by presenting homosexuality as a positive alternative to sexual repression and rigid gender roles. Though the majority of the mainstream population continued to associate homosexuality with pathology, gay and lesbian activism offered an alternative view, one that energized and inspired a growing number of men and women to come out of hiding and rally for their rights as legitimate members of the American body politic. What is striking about the foundational texts of the homophile and gay and lesbian liberation movements is that, as a way to offer affirming accounts of homosexuality, they engaged some of the same questions that animated scientific surveys and psychiatric case histories concerning homosexuality. In Martin and Lyon's *Lesbian/Woman* and Cory's *The Homosexual in America*, one can identify a similarity in the discursive structure of the subjects' self-descriptions and those of the earlier psychiatric interviews which were part of the Sex Variant study from the 1930s and which dated back even earlier to Hirschfeld's survey of the early years of the twentieth century. Again we find the articulation of questions of the self—"What am I?" "How did I come to be this way?" "How and why am I different?" "Is there something wrong with me?" Hence the discourses of gay rights and lesbian-feminism took on some of the same questions raised earlier by medical and scientific discourses that conflated homosexuality with pathology. This time, however, these questions provided the means for explicitly generating a counterdiscourse which replaced scientific authority with personal experiences in order to claim that homosexuality was healthy. The testimonies underscored that any pathology surrounding homosexuality was caused by homophobic social prejudice and misogynist hostility. But while these fueled a powerful social movement to affirm sexual diversity, they also incited a reaction formation from a variety of moral conservatives who, once they saw gay men and lesbians advocating their cause in public, manifested a phobia that was perceptible as early as a century before: that is, the fear that dissenters from heterosexuality and the two-sex model that underpinned it represented danger of potentially colossal proportions.

The idea that homosexuality was contagious, pathological, and possibly curable resonated with a significant majority of Americans who regarded the growing gay movement as further evidence of what psychoanalysts had been saying through the 1950s. Their persistence in seeing homosexuality as a form of curable illness caused considerable suffering, as Martin Duberman's memoir from the period documents in detail.[47] To a significant degree, the constant pressure to believe that individuals should overcome homosexuality was countered by a growing attitude among gay and lesbian rights activists that they should not have to change. Two main lines of argumentation were used to oppose the pressure to conform to heterosexuality, and these appear again in queer politics of the present. One argues the essential biological difference of homosexuals as a grounds for their acceptance. According to this view, homosexuals cannot change their orientation since it is given by nature and thus they deserve to be protected from discrimination. The other line of reasoning refuses or suspends an essentialist position and argues instead that homosexuality is a viable sexual orientation that should be respected, similarly to one's Constitutionally protected religious or political affiliation. Though not entirely incompatible, the tensions that arise from these two lines of argument live on today, a little over a hundred years after the first reported case of "contrary sexual instinct." We turn to these tensions now.

EPILOGUE

In 1973, Anne Koedt articulated a common tenet among radical lesbian feminists at that time:

> Basic to the position of radical feminism is the concept that biology is not destiny, and that male and female roles are learned—indeed that they are male political constructs that ensure power and superior status for men.[1]

Twenty years later, in March 1993, the gay journalist Chandler Burr, in a lead article in the *Atlantic Monthly,* asserted a different position, and one that runs counter to social constructivist and feminist critiques of biological determinism:

> Homosexuality's invitation to biology has been standing for years. Homosexuals have long maintained that sexual orientation, far from being a personal choice or lifestyle (as it is often called), is something neither chosen nor changeable; heterosexuals who have made their peace with homosexuals have often done so by accepting that premise. The very term 'sexual orientation,' which in the 1980s replaced 'sexual preference,' asserts the deeply rooted nature of sexual desire and love. It implies biology.[2]

What factors explain this obvious difference between Koedt's critique of biological determinism and Burr's more charitable assessment of it? Perhaps it would be useful to take a look at the larger context out of which new biological evidence of homosexuality was reported in the 1990s. This may help us to make sense of the shift from a critique of biological determinism prominent in 1973 to a powerful strand of gay rights politics in the final decade of the twentieth century.

It strikes me that there are several key cultural and political developments that have unfolded during the course of these decades that might shed light on the differences of perspective between Koedt and Burr. Let us begin by considering the rise of organized and aggressive anti-homosexual political campaigns launched during the 1970s by coalitions of fundamentalist Christians aligned with other right-wing constituencies. In the late 1970s, popular entertainer and former runner up to Miss America, Anita Bryant, denounced homosexuality as a wicked sin against God's will that was driving the United States into deep cultural ruin. Bryant's sentiments were echoed by New Right Christian televangelists, Jerry Falwell and Pat Robertson, who decried homosexuality as a sure sign of the nation's moral decline. In widely circulated media campaigns, right-wing Christians and their allies called for an end to "homosexual perversion," which they likened to satanism, adultery, and murder. In 1978, California state senator John Briggs authored a voter initiative which would have prevented openly gay men and women from teaching in public schools. Though his measure failed at the ballot box, the Briggs Initiative received substantial popular support among voters who were convinced that lesbians and gay men posed a threat to children. Briggs and his supporters invoked warmed-over stereotypes linking homosexuality with child molestation and stoked additional fear by claiming that the movement for gay rights proved that homosexual men and women would not be satisfied until they had limitless power. What better way to achieve this, Briggs asked, than stealing the hearts and minds of youth?

Similar fear tactics were used in other states and municipalities around the country where anti-gay activists linked homosexuality with child abuse and venereal disease in campaigns to rescind anti-discrimination ordinances, to bar homosexuals from various types of employment, and to deny child custody to openly gay fathers and lesbian mothers. By 1980, when Ronald Reagan took presidential office, the Christian New Right had successfully delivered millions of votes to the Republican Party through campaigns aimed at morally cleansing the nation. Alongside abortion, homosexuality was a fear-inspiring topic used very effectively by right-wingers to shore up a conservative ideal of the nuclear family as headed by a dominant husband, whose submissive wife and children served him so that he could better serve God. Homosexuality was described as a sinful and sick habit that attacked the family, children, the nation, and God's order.

Hate the sin, love the sinner. This is the catch-phrase of many ongoing right-wing Christian campaigns against homosexuality. Though homosexuality is imagined as tantamount to evil incarnate, those who engage in it are, in fundamentalist Christian discourse, ostensibly pitied and offered hope of redemption if only they would give up their wicked ways. While many anti-homosexual psychoanalysts might be loathe to acknowledge their likeness to fundamentalists such as Falwell and Robertson, what they share is a claim to care deeply for those who "suffer" from homosexuality. The answer for anti-homosexual authorities, be they religious or psychoanalytic, is to offer redemption for homosexuals, whether through psychotherapy or through submitting to God. In the face of this kind of pressure, it is not surprising that many gay men and lesbians take refuge in a naturalist position that claims that homosexuality is not a chosen sexual preference but is built into their bodies and thus cannot nor should it be changed or abandoned.

Indeed, the connections between anti-gay religious and secular arguments appear to be growing stronger these days. Charles Socarides, who during the massive expansion of the gay liberation movement in the 1970s argued that homosexuals should be cured, established the National Association for Research and Therapy of Homosexuality (NARTH) in 1992. He, along with Joseph Nicolosi, a psychologist based in Los Angeles, became involved in public legal and legislative debates about the implementation of a number of issues advanced by the movement for gay, lesbian, bisexual, and transgender rights. Both Socarides and Nicolosi are frequently quoted by anti-homosexual activists associated with the right-wing Family Research Council, as authorities who can show that (1) homosexuality is an undesirable psychological condition from which many of their patients suffer; (2) homosexuality is the result of pathological psychosexual development and not related to biological or innate factors; and (3) homosexuality can be eliminated and those afflicted by it "cured" under the proper therapeutic conditions (i.e., the patient has to want to change by recognizing the misery of his condition and must be committed to the therapeutic goals and techniques of the analyst).

Nicolosi is expressly political within the psychological profession as well as in the larger political landscape. In 1993, he wrote a lengthy position paper against Project 10, a proposed public high school program that would provide gay-positive curricular materials within a larger cultural diversity curriculum. Project 10 stipulated that gay-affirming counseling services would be available for students who experience same-sex attractions. Nicolosi opposed the project on a number of grounds, including that it would actually do harm to students and increase risks both to their mental and physical health (i.e., to AIDS). Nicolosi's paper was embraced by the Family Research Council, which distributed it widely in its efforts not only to oppose curricular reforms but to rescind state and municipal laws barring discrimination on the grounds of sexual orientation, to oppose gays and lesbians in the military, and to oppose legislative proposals for legal recognition of same-sex marriages and for the provision of domestic partnership benefits for partners of the same sex. In his two books, *Reparative Therapy of Male Homosexuality* and *Healing Homosexuality*, Nicolosi offers an "opposite" form of testimony to that presented in 1973, when the American Psychiatric Association, under pressure of "gay militants," removed homosexuality from the *Diagnostic and Statistical Manual (III)*.[3] His works include accounts of men who have tried to accept a gay identity but were dissatisfied and then benefited from psychotherapy to help free them from the "gender conflict" that lies behind most homosexuality. In Nicolosi's reasoning, homosexual men have a sense of incompleteness about their maleness, engendered in many cases by anxious and hovering mothers and by a failure of the child to internalize male gender-identity. Such men were often alienated from their male peers in childhood, which in turn led to "an eroticization of maleness."[4] In addition, Nicolosi notes that "gay couplings are known for their volatility and instability. Research consistently reveals great promiscuity and a strong emphasis on sexuality in gay relationships. Without the stabilizing element of the feminine influence, male couples have a great deal of difficulty maintaining monogamy." Furthermore, "gay relationships are also inherently troubled by the limitations of sexual sameness, making the sex act characteristically isolated and narcissistic through the necessity of 'my turn–your turn' sexual techniques." For Nicolosi, "there is not only an inherent anatomical unsuitability, but a psychological insufficiency that prevents a man from taking in another in the full and open way of heterosexual couples."[5]

Nicolosi maintains that reparative therapy cannot erase the sense of all homosexual feelings in his patients. But "it can do much to improve a man's way of relating to other men and to strengthen masculine identification."[6] To make up for the damaging consequences of a gender-identity deficit, Nicolosi guides his patients toward discovering the authentic need for attention, affection, and approval, which can be satisfied not through sexual relations but through friendship and brotherly love. Nicolosi concludes *Healing Homosexuality* by noting that both reparative therapy (RT) and "gay affirmative therapy" (GAT), which focuses on allowing the homosexual man to be freed from internalized pressures of society, share an idea of what the homosexual man needs and desires: to give himself permission to love other men.[7] But RT sees sex between men as sabotaging the mutuality needed to grow toward maturity. RT thus frees homosexual men to love other men as equals and as brothers. In Nicolosi's invocation of Christian terminology, it allows them to move from "eros to agape."[8] Although it may be expected that clients will occasionally have homosexual fantasies, they need not act on them. In a secular version of Christian restraint and redemption, Nicolosi's group therapy challenges its members to control their homosexual behavior by seeing the tragedy that underlies it. His techniques consist of male homosocial therapy, which prods and cajoles homosexual male clients into overcoming their "male gender-identity deficit" by bonding in non-sexual ways with other men.

Nicolosi is careful to appear reasonable on the question of reparative therapy for homosexuals, noting that it is not necessary for all homosexuals. He distinguishes those who suffer from homosexuality and argues that they ought to have a chance to receive clinical assistance and that the APA should not stand in their way. This same rhetoric appears in NARTH's position paper in which members portray themselves as an oppressed group which has been silenced by a militant homosexual minority within the APA. In spite of their initial gesture to qualify reparative therapy as suitable for those who elect it, both Nicolosi and NARTH conclude that male homosexuality is fundamentally pathological regardless of whether some homosexuals say they are happy. To fortify his position, Nicolosi invokes scientific neutrality and claims to be much more rational than those who use science to support their political agendas. Thus he claims a putatively objective middle ground by distinguishing himself against both the militant agitators who removed homosexuality from the *DSM-III* and current reactionary forces who seek to ferret out and eliminate the "gay agenda":

> It is not our intention to contribute to reactionary hostility. However, there is a distinction between science and politics, and science should not be made to bow to gay political pressure. The National Association for Research and Therapy of Homosexuality has been recently formed to combat politicization of scientific and treatment issues.[9]

Indeed Nicolosi is presented as an objective scientific authority in a video starring the Christian evangelical telepreacher, D. James Kennedy, in which he repudiates the work of Alfred Kinsey and claims that homosexuals represent a much smaller percentage of the population than Kinsey or his gay advocates assumed.[10] As Edmund Bergler had proclaimed several decades earlier, Nicolosi and Kennedy accuse Kinsey's research of being biased on the grounds that his subjects were disproportionately prisoners, sex offenders, and child molesters. Nicolosi's implicit assumption is that these categories of people are synonymous to homosexuals. As in much of Christian anti-gay discourse, lesbians and women are not mentioned but once or twice in the entire hour-long special but are implicated in every mention of male homosexuality.

Nicolosi, who offered "expert" testimony in support of the anti-gay Oregon Citizens Alliance 1992 ballot initiative to remove protection against discrimination on the basis of sexual orientation, appears later in the video to issue a sweeping, nonspecific repudiation of recent research purporting to find a biological correlation to male homosexuality. This segment ends with D. James Kennedy stating that most homosexuals who want to change have been fed the lie that they cannot be freed through Christ from the bonds of sin. With Christ as simultaneously the ultimate male role model and the ultimate object of Christian desire, no wonder one "repaired" homosexual man appears in the tape rhapsodizing, "If there's any man I love it's Jesus Christ."

Nicolosi's vision of a world of men in need of repair can be linked to the Promise Keepers, an evangelical Christian-based men's movement with alarmingly negative implications for women. Among the Promise Keepers, women are simultaneously exalted as the bastions of moral virtue and yet demonized as smothering or negligent mothers responsible for the pathological imbalances of their sons. While fathers are also blamed in the more recent models of homosexuality-as-psychopathology, mothers continue to be blamed for their overbearing and emasculating desires. The virtuous woman, in both Nicolosi's and the Promise Keepers' vision, is the understanding or forgiving wife and the patient girlfriend, whose main role is to abet the spiritual, moral, and psychological healing of men. But she cannot heal her man alone. As the second of the seven tenets of the Promise Keepers states, "a promise keeper is committed to pursuing vital relationships with a few other men, understanding that he needs brothers to help him keep his promises."

The flipside of Kennedy's discourse is that, since homosexuality is not innate, it can spread, especially through the pernicious vehicle of the Rainbow Curriculum to teach the value of cultural diversity and tolerance whereby, in Kennedy's view, unwitting children are taught to masturbate and to accept homosexuality as normal. It is Kennedy's fear of a queer planet that fuels the urgency of his rhetoric. The same fear echoed in the words of a Columbus, Ohio, radio evangelist, whom I heard one morning in 1995 while driving to work. He warned that we must all watch out for "satanic attacks" that could strike us at any moment when we are vulnerable. The possibility of homosexual urges striking any man makes the "minuscule" one percent statistic of homosexuals in the United States cause for only momentary relief.

In the 1990s, a number of groups have appeared whose aim is to "heal" homosexuals. One of the most prominent is the Transformation Ministries branch of Exodus International, a nondenominational Christian group dedicated to helping homosexuals overcome their homosexuality and to join a growing movement of "ex-gays." The organization follows strict scriptural reading of the Bible and has been aided by the Christian Coalition in advertising campaigns to encourage gays and lesbians to put an end to their unhealthy desires. The Ministries claim a success rate of thirty percent, but they have allowed no long term studies to be done.[11]

During the very week in October 1998 when a gay college student was brutally beaten and murdered by two heterosexual men who entrapped him, a series of full-page advertisements appeared in national newspapers across the United States urging gays and lesbians to turn to God and give up their sinful ways.[12] Indeed, although the ads couched their message in the language of love and forgiveness, their authors at the Christian Coalition and the Family Research Council, during this same week, reiterated their opposition to proposed hate crimes legislation in the wake of the death of Matthew Shepard. Shepard had been pistol whipped and then tied to a fence for two days; he suffered hypothermia and died several hours after he was discovered by a jogger, who took him to a hospital. As he lay in a coma in the Fort Collins, Colorado hospital, a crowd of anti-gay protesters shouted slogans of hate and paraded an effigy of Shepard with the words "Kill Fags" written on it.

President Bill Clinton decried the killing and called for federal legislation to include sexual orientation as a basis for prosecuting hate crimes. The following day, Steven A. Schwalm, policy analyst for the Family Research Council, referred to hate-crimes laws as "having everything to do with silencing political opposition to [homosexuality]." He went on to say that hate-crimes legislation "would criminalize pro-family beliefs."[13] The simultaneity of these events—the killing, the "ex-gays" advertising campaign, and the vocal opposition to hate-crimes legislation—speaks volumes about the level of hostility towards homosexuality, much of which is driven by religious right organizations.

It is against the marriage of anti-homosexual Christian evangelical rhetoric and a longer-term psychoanalytic consensus dating from much earlier in the twentieth century that openly gay scientists Simon LeVay and Dean Hamer argue that homosexuality has a natural and innate cause, somehow rooted in the body and thus beyond the conscious control of the individual. LeVay and Hamer's political and professional motivations are intermeshed and deeply shaped, both epistemologically and practically, by the devastating effects of recent anti-homosexual crusades as well as by the coincidental emergence of the AIDS epidemic.

Fuel was added to the fire of anti-homosexual political crusades when in the early 1980s a mysterious and deadly disease appeared to be afflicting the gay male population in staggering numbers. Immediately, anti-homosexual Christians described AIDS as God's punishment against those who led a sinful and promiscuous lifestyle. Initially named GRID (Gay Related Immune Deficiency), AIDS became synonymous with homosexuality in the minds of many Americans, including sympathetic and concerned people as well as the vast numbers of folks who took part in local vigilante campaigns to keep HIV-infected people out of certain jobs, out of neighborhoods, schools, hospitals, even going so far as to terrorize people with AIDS by burning down their houses, threatening their safety, and justifying these actions as a matter of ensuring public safety. AIDS revivified and intensified already existing homophobia in vast sectors of American culture as it literalized the long-standing conflation of homosexuality with disease. It licensed homophobic campaigns not unlike those of earlier historical moments when moral vigilance crusaders identified homosexuality as a dangerous scourge threatening the health and well-being of a putatively "normal" population. But AIDS made the contemptuous rhetoric all the more urgent and hegemonic since the disease was obviously deadly and was effectively spread through sexual contact. It allowed opponents to speak of homosexuality as a "deadly lifestyle" and thus to propose its elimination as matter of life or death.

During the 1980s, Paul Cameron, as head of the right-wing Family Research Council, wrote a series of articles that emphasized the relationship between homosexuality, child molestation, venereal disease, and self-destruction.[14] Trained as a psychologist, Cameron sought to present his material in scientific terms and published almost exclusively in a journal called *Psychological Reports.* In a 1989 article on the "effect of homosexuality upon public health and social order," Cameron reported the findings of a study that he had designed to refute what he believed was a dangerous and growing assumption that homosexuality was healthy for individuals and for society. Cameron took aim specifically at a study funded by the National Research Council that focused on sexual behavior and intravenous drug use. Its authors had sought to assess the risks associated with the spread of HIV, the virus that leads to AIDS. They had concluded that homosexuals per se "were not dangers to the society at large."[15] Cameron and his co-authors, by contrast, concluded that "from the standpoints of individual health, public health and social order, participating in homosexual activity could be viewed as dangerous to society and incompatible with full health."[16] Through the political activities of the Family Research Council, this and other articles penned by its chairman were used to oppose gay and lesbian rights legislation, sex education campaigns that included any mention of homosexuality, and further funding for research on AIDS that the FRC believed would promote homosexuality.

In 1992, Cameron produced a pamphlet entitled *Medical Consequences of What Homosexuals Do,* which was distributed during the Colorado Amendment 2 campaign. The proposed amendment to the state's constitution would have "prohibit[ed] the State of Colorado and any of its political subdivisions from adopting or enforcing any law or policy which provides that homosexual, lesbian, or bisexual orientation, conduct, or relationships constitutes or entitles a person to claim any minority or protected status, quota preferences, or discrimination." Lurid in its detail, the pamphlet focused on "rectal sex," "fecal sex," and "urine sex," as well as sadomasochistic practices that Cameron linked to the self-destructive lifestyle of homosexuals. In a warning to the public, the pamphlet added that to accept homosexuality in any way was to invite additional burdens on tax-payers who will have to pay for the health care of homosexuals who knowingly endanger their own health. The pamphlet also reiterated that homosexuals are generally inclined toward recruiting innocent youths into their deadly lifestyle. If granted "special rights," they would be able to impose themselves on children and to carry out their plan to destroy the American family.[17]

What relation do these historical and political events have to recent scientific research purporting to have found biological correlations to homosexuality? Let us consider some of the changes over the past few decades by broadening out for a moment to analyze the relation of scientific knowledge to society generally. Then I will try to analyze how this relation positions lesbians, gay men, and queers today with respect to being studied by scientists and to using scientific arguments to counter increasingly virulent attacks on homosexuality.

We are living now in the age of the magical sign of the gene. There is a great deal of hope riding on this "holy grail" of the late twentieth century. Scientists promise that if we can figure out the exact function and location of specific genes within the human body, the human population could be rid of diseases and defects.[18] And even more compelling, knowledge of genetics is marketed as an avenue for self-knowledge—knowledge of our proficiencies, our possibilities, our limits, our histories and our futures.[19] We are told by scientists working on the Human Genome Project that genes can explain to us who we are at the most fundamental level of DNA. Lobbyists for the Human Genome Project (with its present annual budget exceeding $135 million) market this new "Manhattan Project" as, on the one hand, a means to unify humans as a population sharing many genetic traits and, on the other, as a means of making distinctions between types of people. No doubt, this latter option offers great appeal among insurance companies and employers who would like to be able to be deny coverage to those who have "pre-existing" (i.e. genetic dispositions to) disease.[20] Likewise, people like Frederick Goodwin, of the National Institutes of Mental Health, are interested in locating the genetic and neurochemical bases for violence and propose the screening of inner-city children who seem to be "incorrigible."[21] Furthermore, genetic explanations for social inequalities are attractive at a time when the welfare state is under attack and the brutality of poverty diminishes the life choices of an entire generation of children of color living in our cities.[22]

The promises of genetics are grandiose. Not only will the world be rid of disease, but knowledge of genetics will help us to maximize biological resources at a moment of fear over global agricultural scarcity.[23] For Americans, genetic research promises to do even more than fortify our human and natural resources: it promises to save our economy in the face of fierce global competition. Biotechnology is to the 1990s what nuclear weapons development was to the 1960s—the putative guarantor of America's economic and political influence over the destiny of the planet. Never mind that metanational corporations dealing in biotechnology and genetic research will be selling our genes back to us once they isolate and patent key fragments.

I mention the magical sign of the gene and its political economy because over the past several years two scientific teams have reported a "genetic" basis for homosexuality. In 1992, the psychologist Michael

Bailey and the psychiatrist Richard Pillard reported that, among the identical twins they studied, when one identified himself as gay or bisexual, in about half the cases the other did so as well.[24] About twenty-two percent of the fraternal twin brothers they studied were both gay or bisexual, as were about eleven percent of those who were raised as brothers through adoption. Even with these limited findings, the headlines in the popular press cried out: "Scientists Find That Homosexuality is Genetic." Although Bailey and Pillard's research has been criticized on numerous grounds, including that the twins they studied were not reared apart, perhaps the most troubling issue raised by their study was that they gave no explanation as to how they were using or measuring the term *sexual orientation*. The categories of homosexual, heterosexual, and bisexual were taken on face value as the subjects defined themselves, as if we (or they) all agree on the meanings of these terms. Furthermore, the study was not based upon random sampling techniques but recruited its subjects through gay newspapers, thus effectively weeding out men who may engage in homosexuality from time to time but do not read gay magazines or would be loathe to answer such an advertisement. Critics of this method of self-selection suggest that instead of finding a correlation to sexual orientation per se (i.e., the sexual desire of a man for other men), Bailey and Pillard's twin studies could just as well indicate that there is a genetic underpinning to coming out of the closet. In other words, their research may only indicate the presence of a gene for self-assertiveness or bravery.[25] Because the research required the co-operation of the gay subjects' brothers, it also weeded those men who were not out of the closet to their families or who came from homophobic families with brothers who would never agree to be part of such a study. Using the same problematic methods, the later study of female identical twins produced virtually the same statistical findings.[26] But even with these problems of method and conjecture, both studies were touted in the mainstream press as evidence for a genetic basis for homosexuality because the concordance rate for sexual orientation was higher in identical twins than in fraternal, and higher in fraternal twins than in biologically unrelated brothers. Each pair of identical twins was reared together and yet no method was used for determining the influence of social environment and familial relations on sexual orientation. In other words, the researchers did not consider how parents and relatives might treat identical twins differently (i.e., as more alike) than dizygotic or unrelated adopted siblings who were reared together, nor what affect this might have on sexual orientation. Furthermore, since a good half of the identical twins did not show concordance for sexual orientation, the news coverage declaring that scientists had found that homosexuality was genetically determined was misleading.

It is interesting to note that neither of the principal researchers involved in the so-called "gay twins" studies were geneticists or molecular biologists, in spite of the media representations of them. As with other demographic heredity studies (e.g., family pedigree studies from the early twentieth century and early work on the genetic marker for Huntington's chorea), the twin studies researchers took neither tissue nor blood samples of subjects to analyze their DNA or genetic material. Even as psychiatrist Richard Pillard was featured in *Newsweek* holding the magical icon of his study, the molecular model, the actual properties of the participants' DNA did not even enter into the discussion.[27] Self-reported homosexuality was taken as a clear-cut phenotypic trait from which to infer the presence of genetic material that was passed down from previous generations. It was on the basis of subjects' self-identification that the researchers determined that homosexuality was genetic, but in no more than 50 percent of the cases. Nevertheless, the magical sign of the gene was invoked to make sense of this research, and to represent the researchers as engaged scientists.

What else has gone on in science and culture in the last twenty years that has made this new research on sexual orientation emerge? In 1973, when Anne Koedt made her impassioned statement denouncing biology as destiny, no one had ever heard of AIDS. Since then, the AIDS epidemic has profoundly and devastatingly transformed the nature of lesbian and gay life in the United States. Our relations with one another, our understandings of ourselves, our sense of sexual possibilities, and our ideas about political mobilization have undergone massive transformations in the face of the deadly HIV and the social neglect and homophobic contempt that have accompanied it. Our bodies are bound up in medical discourse and practices, once again, but this time under new, urgent, and deadly conditions. And these new conditions produce new ways of imagining the body in relation to subjectivity. It is not surprising that the privileged domain of the body, where our innermost secrets and sexual passions are thought to reside, is being imagined as a source of meanings in the face of this social atrocity. These days, even as they are theoretically and materially disintegrating, we imagine our bodies as a point of origin for exploring contemporary and very pressing questions of the self. Neuroscientist Simon LeVay's own story of what compelled him to undertake research on sexual orientation is a tale of grieving, of trying to make sense of himself as a gay man in the face of deep depression about the loss of his lover to AIDS. By his own account, LeVay's shift in focus from work on the neuroanatomy of vision to the neuroanatomy of sex and sexual orientation was a crucial part of his recovery process.[28]

There is a more palpable, material relationship between the epidemic and much of this new research. Indeed, AIDS provided LeVay with the very brain tissue he used to conduct his research on the hypothalamus.[29] It was men who died of AIDS who constituted the majority of his subject population, and it was their autopsied brain tissue he used to produce his distinction between the categories of homosexual and heterosexual upon which his findings are based. What was the basis LeVay used for determining which tissue belonged to homosexual and which to heterosexual men? In contrast to Bailey and Pillard's study, which relied on the self-reports of subjects as to their sexual orientation, in LeVay's study, a single line in the subject's medical charts stating his mode of HIV transmission became the grounds for classifying a man as either gay or not. Those whose charts indicated the mode of transmission was "male-to-male" sexual contact were defined as gay, and those with other modes of transmission (IV drug use, blood transfusions, etc.) were, by default, presumed to be heterosexual. Of course, these other cases might just as well have been men who occasionally engaged in homosexual sex but who reported a different mode of transmission for whatever reasons. In other words, the journey of the human immunodeficiency virus was relied upon to account for the complexity of these men's sexual subjectivities in a masterful instance of scientific reductivism. Were it not for the early deaths of gay men through HIV infection, together with the ensuing epidemiological protocol of documenting modes of transmission in one's medical chart, LeVay's study could not have been conducted. And although LeVay's "objective" method for determining sexual orientation contrasts with Bailey and Pillard's "subjective" method (i.e., voluntary self-reporting), neither approach takes into account the complexity of how sexual orientation is variously defined and experienced in the course of an individual's lifetime and across historical periods and cultural contexts. But my main point here is that AIDS provided the actual bodies for the hypothalamus study, and it provided a way to classify those bodies. It also provided the impetus for Simon LeVay to recover from his depression through the healing power of neuroscientific research, during what then-president George Bush officially proclaimed the "Decade of the Brain."

AIDS also made possible the now-famous chromosomal study reported in July 1993.[30] Researchers at the National Cancer Institute (NCI) reported the discovery of DNA markers linking male homosexuality with a region on the X chromosome, the chromosome boys get from their mothers (prompting the facetious t-shirt I saw at the gay beach in Provincetown, "Love you, Mom. Thanks for the genes."). Unlike the twins studies, this one did involve blood samples but, again, relied mainly on the self-reporting of gay volunteers who recounted a greater number of lesbians and gay men on their mothers' side of the family than their fathers'. Although it was no doubt colored by the fact that in general in American culture, many of us know more about our mother's family than our father's, this self-reporting led researchers to look for the marker of homosexuality on the X chromosome. This study, like the others before it, was not based on random sampling, so there is no way of knowing how often this marker exists among men who practice homosexuality often or seldom but would never identify as gay. Furthermore, Hamer's team did not check the heterosexual brothers of his gay subjects to see if they too carry the marker for homosexuality. Similarly, few of the subjects' mothers' DNA were checked for the marker either because they were dead, their sons had lost track of them, or they couldn't be tested because they were unaware that their sons were gay. If Hamer were to have found the marker in a significant number of heterosexual brothers or mothers, his findings of a "gene for homosexuality" would have been seriously weakened.

But the relationship of this study to the AIDS epidemic is worthy of note: the money used to fund this research had been earmarked for NCI research on Kaposi's Sarcoma (KS) and lymphoma. To support his research, Hamer applied to the National Cancer Institute proposing a study of whether homosexuals had a genetic susceptibility to KS. According to National Institutes of Health director Harold Varmus, it was only in the course of Hamer's study on KS and homosexuality that the linkage between sexual orientation and DNA markers on the X chromosome was discovered.[31] By funding this study, the NCI entertained the possibility that there was a genetic relationship between KS and male homosexuality. In this move, the NCI researchers reiterated, perhaps inadvertently, the idea that AIDS is a gay disease that affects particular types of people who are genetically predisposed to it. As Evelynn Hammonds has noted, researchers at the NCI and the Human Genome Project have money to study genetic predispositions; now they are looking for problems to solve.[32] KS and homosexuality are just two of those "problems." Hamer, in his statements to the gay and popular media, has stressed that he is merely curious about the possible genetic correlates to homosexuality not because it is pathological but because it is a benign trait like eye-color or handedness. Yet in his proposals for funding, male homosexuality and disease are clearly associated with one another. The innocence of scientific curiosity thus works discursively in an uneasy relationship to the otherwise quite obvious funding politics of scientific research on the controversial topics of homosexuality and AIDS.[33]

There is yet another way that AIDS figures into this new cultural and scientific context, and it has to do with the nature of the current homophobic backlash against gays and lesbians. Right-wing Christian fundamentalists have declared that homosexuality is to the 1990s what abortion was to the 1980s: the enemy in a battle of moral cleansing to determine the future of the world. In 1993 I attended a lecture at the Ohio State University sponsored by the Fellowship of Christian Students entitled "Gay Agony: Can Homosexuals Be Healed?" The guest speaker was Ken Unger, who had just come from an appearance on Pat Robertson's 700 Club. He began his lecture by saying that the compulsive disorder of homosexuality brought AIDS into the world. But, he urged, it is not too late to change, to recover from this compulsion, to turn to others for fellowship and guidance, and to overcome this deeply rooted sexual addiction. Throughout the entire lecture, homosexuality and AIDS were virtually synonymous. Lesbians were never mentioned explicitly in the lecture but are clearly implied in the Christian fundamentalist conflation of homosexuality with disease, moral degeneracy, and death. This illustrates a crucial point: AIDS provides a rationale for both this kind of homophobia and a gay rights opposition to it. Indeed, the speaker proclaimed that, contrary to what the liberal-dominated media says, there is no sound "glandular" or genetic evidence of the immutability of homosexuality. Beseechingly, he repeated, "you can change, you can change." It is in the face of this hostile homophobia, dressed up as Christian compassion, that LeVay's and the NCI research are being proposed as tools of political opposition. But the limitations of the gay rights-through-biology defense are striking: "Biology makes us act this way. We can't be cured. We can't seduce your children." There is little in this approach that particularly affirms the value of resisting heteronormativity.[34]

In addition to well over a decade of governmental neglect and in-difference about AIDS, by the 1990s a growing grassroots backlash against lesbians and gay men became manifestly evident. As I out-lined in the introduction to this book, lesbians and gay men are now the targets of hostility in alarming proportions. In such a climate, any-one who is perceived to be associated with homosexuality may be the victim of harassment and violence. Indeed, a 1998 survey of nearly 500 college students revealed that one-quarter of them admitted to harassing people they thought were gay. Undertaken by a forensic psychologist at the Washington Institute for Mental Illness Research and Training, the study further showed that among men, eighteen percent said they had physically assaulted or threatened someone they thought was gay or lesbian. About thirty-two percent admitted to ver-bal harassment. The figures for women were lower but showed a simi-lar pattern. Almost half of the students claimed they would assault again and either lacked remorse or saw nothing wrong with their be-havior. Many explained their behavior in terms of self-defense based on the assumption that gays are sexual predators. Dr. Karen Franklin, the study's author, stated: "Indeed, assaults on gay men and lesbians were so socially acceptable that respondents often advocated or de-fended such behavior out loud in classrooms, while I was administer-ing my survey."[35] It is in these times of peril and of feeling beleaguered that our bodies, presented to us through the authority of science, ap-pear to be refuges for staking a desperate claim for tolerance. As if the knowledge of a gene for homosexuality would stop the basher's club from crashing down on our heads.

An idiosyncratic reading of civil rights law provides the backdrop to why hope is invested in the biological proof of homosexuality. Gay scientists and some gay leaders argue that homosexuality is an immu-table characteristic, which they liken to race or skin color. Thus the reasoning follows that homosexuals, like African Americans, ought to be protected from discrimination. In the first place this way of think-ing ignores the scientific consensus that clear-cut or mutually exclu-sive racial differences do not exist at the genetic or biological level; race, it is agreed, is primarily a social or demographic concept that at best describes cultural groups with arbitrary and varying bound-aries.[36] But in a larger political sense, the use of race as an analogy to sexual orientation relies on a strange and limited reading of the his-tory of the civil rights movement as well as of the current status of racial minorities. The civil rights movement, after all, focused its anti-racism efforts on grassroots actions, public marches, demonstrations, and the courts. The main goal was equality and respect for all people, regardless of race, religion, or creed; arguments valorizing the biological immutability of race were by no means central. The civil rights movement was most effective through championing social diversity and promoting humane respect for cultural differences, not by African Americans beseeching those in authority to see them as biologically different. In the 1960s, biological arguments about race had long been seen as the handmaidens of racism, just as those about gender were identified to be a central part of the architecture of sexism.

The argument for homosexual immutability betrays a misreading of the scientific research itself. Nothing in any of these studies can fully support the idea that homosexuality is biologically immutable; each study leaves open the possibility that homosexuality is the result of a combination of biological and environmental factors, and several suggest that homosexuality may be tied to a predisposition in temperament that could manifest itself in a number of ways.[37] All agree that biological, social, and psychological factors interact to produce and change the signs of homosexuality. Furthermore, these studies cannot comment effectively on the frequency of homosexuality in the general population. Nor do they offer much in the way of understanding women's complex relationship to questions of sexuality in general, let alone sexual orientation. Most of the recent studies on genetics and homosexuality have not focused specifically on lesbianism. However, LeVay and Hamer, for example, have stated that their findings might offer insights into neuroanatomical and genetic correlations to lesbianism, and they note that lesbianism merits scientific inquiry. It is likely that such discursive gestures are related to Hamer and LeVay's interests in using scientific knowledge as a strategy in gay and lesbian rights organizing. By extrapolating their findings to include lesbians, LeVay and Hamer seek to establish some semblance of unity of position and purpose among gay men and lesbians. Both men gave testimony at the court case challenging the constitutionality of Colorado's Amendment 2, and both testified that there was strong evidence that sexual orientation was rooted in the body rather than being a simple matter of choice.[38] They hoped to convince the court that neither gay men nor lesbians were able to seduce otherwise normal children. But, in the case of lesbians, they had little more than hope that future scientific research would substantiate such a claim.

Based on reading both the mainstream and gay community media coverage of this recent research, I would venture that its most enthusiastic supporters are middle-class white gay men. The new affinity and hope invested in the biology of homosexuality might be seen as the swan song of economically comfortable white men (quietly lip-synched by straight, politically liberal essentialists) who know the lyrics to each verse and who, but for their homosexual desire, have many reasons to regard biological determinism and a hierarchically organized social order with great affection. Maybe biology is a more comforting way to narrate their desires than to make sense of them in terms of cultural and historical contradictions, conflicts, and contingencies. But, to be fair, there are many forces that work to undermine gay and lesbian rights and to further demonize dissenters from normative heterosexuality and the two-sex system upon which it is based. I imagine that, under these circumstances, the chimerical domain of the body, imagined as the ultimate *real* of our existence and yet in whose ineffable logic we imagine ourselves to be controlled, will continue to be a resource for opposing theocratic crusades that will not be satisfied until the entire nation is "born again" and until all its citizens publicly denounce sexual and moral diversity.

I want to close by coming back to the question of the relationship between scientific knowledge and sexual subjectivity. I have tried to suggest that, throughout this century, the nature of this relationship has been as political as it has been personal. That is, different queer people have thought about scientific knowledge in different ways, and some have been more likely to be swept up by its promises and reassurances than others. Their personal stakes have varied. And the kinds of scientific knowledge to which they have been drawn and those which they have questioned varied widely as well. In each of the episodes I described here, including the present, scientific inquiry about homosexuality is politically situated in relation to cultural anxieties. One way to shore up anxieties has been to insist that there be a definitive line drawn between "normal" heterosexuals and diseased (or, at best, merely anomalous) homosexuals. This is the dynamic in relation to which variant subjectivity has been largely—but not thoroughly—fashioned. Thus we can read the recent scientific studies, produced by scientifically credentialed gay activists like LeVay, Pillard, and Hamer, as expressions of a kind of separatism that finds power through claiming biological uniqueness. The idea of biology being destiny is less chilling, and perhaps even liberating, to these gay scientists. Indeed, as Evelyn Fox Keller has noted in reference to molecular biologists, scientists—gay, straight, or otherwise—have an intimate relationship to a newly imagined "nature" at the dawn of a new millennium.[39] Particularly in the genetics laboratory, where genes are engineered and bodies can be elementally reconfigured, scientists may feel that "nature" really is more liberating if only because it is more manipulable than ever before. This sense of animated and manipulated nature no doubt acquires some of its appeal in the context of attacks on the welfare state. Many such attacks underscore a sense that the "nurture" side of arguments about the cause of social problems and about ameliorative strategies is either passé or moot. If it is all in the genes, then there is no use in trying to solve people's problems by ameliorating the conditions in which they live. Turning to nature may be a symptom of a loss of faith in social reform. As we move into a new century, human engineering, once conceptualized as a way of ameliorating social problems by altering institutions and intervening in social relations, may be revised to mean altering unhealthy or unruly individuals at the genetic level.

At the same time that Keller's ideas about a newly created nature in the laboratory may appeal to gay scientists and the public, both Dean Hamer and Simon LeVay, in their respective books and public presentations, argue against the prospect of engineering homosexuality out of the genome. They appear to be more attracted to the foundational narrative of genetics which would cast homosexuality as an eternal, transhistorical, trans-species trait rather than as a novel or even undesirable perversion to be weeded out. But regardless of LeVay and Hamer's attempts to control the implications of their research, there is a growing popular trend toward regarding biological evidence for things like homosexuality as a possible means for targeting "carriers" and removing them from the gene pool.[40]

Among those gay men who are economically and socially powerful in the world, conceding that nature makes them gay is apparently less damaging than it might seem to working-class gay teenagers. A social worker who works with gay suicidal teens recently remarked that the biology-is-destiny line can be deadly. Thinking they are "afflicted" with homosexual desire as a kind of disease or biological defect rather than thinking of it as a desire they somehow choose is, for many gay teenagers, one more reason to commit suicide rather than to live in a world so hostile to their desires.[41]

In *The Epistemology of the Closet*, Eve Sedgwick invites us to "denaturalize the present" and to call into question any idea that "homosexuality as we know it today" is singular, knowable, or unified. Instead, she is interested in the "performative space of contradiction" in what could be our present understandings of homosexuality; she wants to bring out the multiplicity of narratives of "homosexuality as we know it today."[42] What would it mean if "homosexuality as we know it to-day" became reduced in the popular imagination to a strip of DNA, or to a region of the brain, or to a hormonal condition? What would we lose in the defensive move to believe science to be our rational savior and to base our politics in biology? What does science do *for* us? What does it do *to* us? And where can we turn for new questions of the self and new ways of *performing*—as opposed to biologically manifesting—deviance?

What might be the postmodern queer relationship to scientific thinking and argumentation on the subject of homosexuality? What do we learn from looking back at a decidedly "modern" project aimed at figuring out the truth about homosexuality? If we do indeed live in a postmodern moment that can be characterized as a time of deep epistemological skepticism, coinciding with the dissolution of fixed identities and the elaboration of new models of the body's complexi-ties, then what will become of invoking science to make arguments in favor of homosexuality or for changing the terms of sexuality so that the binary oppositions between homosexuality and heterosexuality and between masculinity and femininity are destabilized to the point of being nearly meaningless? Part of the question comes down to thinking about what bodies themselves presently signify. Contempo-rary well-meaning attempts to locate homosexuality in the body share a tendency with contemptuous anti-homosexual detractors to believe that the difference between "us" and "them" is deeply ingrained and politically useful.

In spite of its inability, refusal, or failure to produce distinct signs of homosexuality, the body continues to occupy a central role in scien-tific and popular understandings about lesbianism and homosexuality. Even after a history of baroque and futile attempts, scientists appar-ently refuse to give up the search for signs of homosexuality in the body. Again, the body is seen as simultaneously truthful and determi-native, binding the person with whom it is associated to a set of pro-ficiencies, weaknesses, and desires. As a product of "nature," the body rules the subject who submits to its needs and who, according to a rather peculiar reading of civil rights doctrine, is free of blame and released from the pressure to reform. Thus, while it may no longer be probed for evidence of degeneracy or innate sex inversion, the body continues to be treated as an important source of information for speculating about the sexual practices of certain individuals and for categorizing these individuals accordingly. Evidently, as long as we find a cultural urge to single out the homosexual as a specific type of person—whether that be under the banner of homophobic contempt or its rhetorical opposite, gay rights—the idea of the homosexual body persists. In one view, it must be controlled and repaired. In another, it must be honored and obeyed. It would appear that the a century-old tendency toward binary thinking which separates a friendly "us" from a dangerous "them" makes great use of the body as a site where difference is imagined to materialize.

But to religious groups who oppose homosexuality, the body has little relevance. In the view of fundamentalist Christians, we are all sinners and we can all be redeemed, regardless of what is in our genes. In light of recent right-wing attacks on biological explanations for homosexuality, it is apparent that basing arguments for homosexual rights in genetics or biology is a flawed strategy, especially if not everyone who experiences homosexual desire shows the requisite biological marker that is presumed to cause homosexuality. Lesbians and gay men have good reason to be skeptical about grounding arguments for rights in biology. Many prefer instead to argue for the inherent virtues of human cultural diversity and for protecting individuals' rights to associate with whom they please so long as it is in a consensual fashion. This may, in the end, be a far more productive strategy and one that would accommodate the idea that, for some people, homosexual orientation is deeply rooted and they ought not be targeted for "healing." For others, such as those who fell in the middle of Kinsey's six-point scale or those who in Katharine Bement Davis's study reported "intense emotional attachments" to other women, or in fact anyone interested in consensual sexual experimentation involving homosexuality, this strategy would be inclusive and pliable. Moreover, it would efface the binary thinking that has had much to do with enforcing a rigid ideal of heterosexuality and that has caused undue suffering.

Now, at the turn of a new millennium, refusing the equation of homosexuality with sin and criminality is just as important as it had been a century ago when sexologists began to recast it primarily in medical terms. Enacting refusals to these equations is the work of the present and the future. But we would do well to consider the claims of gay and lesbian liberationists as well as those of a new generation of queer critics who argue that the categories by which we organize sexuality are themselves to blame for much pain, suffering, and violence. Imposing a restrictive and fear-inspiring "normalcy" has had countless minute and monumental effects in the past, especially on

queer people but also on any who have lived under regimes of thinking that have made homosexuality a dreaded specter. If we continue
to look to science and medicine at all, perhaps it should be to investigate how we might all consist of recombinant elements that make the
binary face-off between homosexuality and heterosexuality a thing of
the past. None of the pleasures of undecidability long ascribed to gender and sexual dissenters will be lost in such a move. Moreover, we
may find the emergence of new modes of sexual subjectivity in light
of scientific inquiry, as well as political struggle, that truly value diversity rather than reducing the vast complexity of life to hierarchically
arranged and opposing types.

NOTES

INTRODUCTION

1. *Ward v. Ward* (Florida District Court of Appeals, First District, August 30, 1996; reported in *Florida Law Weekly,* vol. 21 (September 1996): D1 961. The adolescent child had been cared for from birth by her mother, Mary Ward. In September 1995 a circuit court in Escambia County, Florida, transferred custody to John Ward, the child's father, who had been convicted and had served his prison sentence for the second-degree murder of his first wife. The court cited his marriage to a "good woman," Ward's third wife, following Mary, as grounds for granting him custody and also noted that Mary was a lesbian who lived with her female partner, which the court deemed as detrimental to the child. In August 1996 the appellate court in Tallahassee declined to overturn this ruling.

2. Michel Foucault, *History of Sexuality, Volume One: An Introduction,* trans. Robert Hurley (New York: Vintage Books, 1980), 27, 35, 37, 105–7.

3. Foucault, *History of Sexuality,* 47.

4. Michel Foucault, *Discipline and Punish: The Birth of the Prison,* trans. Alan Sheridan (New York: Vintage Books, 1979), 27.

5. For a more developed explanation of Foucault's idea of discourse, see Michel Foucault, "The Order of Discourse," *Untying the Text,* ed. Robert Young, trans. Ian McLeod (London: Routledge, 1981), 48–78. Marie-Christine Leps has outlined Foucault's method of discourse analysis brilliantly in the introduction to her volume on the modern fascination with the criminal, *Apprehending the Criminal: The Production of Deviance in Nineteenth-Century Discourse* (Durham, N.C.: Duke University Press, 1992), 7–14.

6. Notable historical texts on lesbian and gay history are Jonathan Ned Katz, *Gay/Lesbian Almanac: A New Documentary* (New York: Harper, 1983); Jonathan Ned Katz, *Gay American History: Lesbians and Gay Men in the U.S.A.* (New York: Thomas Y. Crowell, 1976); George Chauncey, *Gay New York: Gender, Urban Culture, and the Making of the Gay Male World, 1890–1940* (New York: Basic Books, 1994); Martin Bauml Duberman, *About Time: Exploring the Gay Past* (New York: Gay Presses of New York, 1986); John D'Emilio, *Sexual Politics, Sexual Communities: The Making of a Homosexual Minority in the United States, 1940–1970* (Chicago: University of Chicago Press, 1983); Martin Bauml Duberman, Martha Vicinus, and George Chauncey, Jr., eds., *Hidden from History: Reclaiming the Gay and Lesbian Past* (New York: Meridian, 1989); Allan Berube, *Coming Out Under Fire: The History of Gay Men and Women in World War Two* (New York: Free Press, 1990); Jeffrey Weeks, *Sex, Politics and Society: The Regulation of Sexuality Since 1800* (London: Longman Group, 1981); Jeffrey Weeks, *Sexuality and its Discontents: Meanings, Myths and Modern Sexualities* (London:

Routledge & Kegan Paul, 1985); Lillian Faderman, *Odd Girls and Twilight Lovers: A History of Lesbian Life in Twentieth-Century America* (New York: Columbia University Press, 1991). Outstanding works on the historical construction of lesbian and gay identities are Joan Nestle, *A Restricted Country* (Ithaca: 1987); Audre Lorde, *Zami: A New Spelling of My Name* (Watertown, Mass.: Persephone Press, 1982); Elizabeth Lapovsky Kennedy and Madeline D. Davis, *Boots of Leather, Slippers of Gold: The History of a Lesbian Community* (New York: Routledge, 1993); Donna Penn, "The Meanings of Lesbianism in Post-War America," *Gender & History* 3, no. 2 (Summer 1991): 15–22; George Chauncey, Jr., "Christian Brotherhood or Sexual Perversion? Homosexual Identities and the Construction of Sexual Boundaries in the World War One Era," *Journal of Social History* 19 (1985): 189–211. Significant works that situate the history of homosexuality within a larger history of sexuality are John D'Emilio and Estelle Freedman, *Intimate Matters: A Social History of Sexuality in the United States* (New York: Harper and Row, 1988); Ann Snitow, Christine Stansell, and Sharon Thompson, eds., *Powers of Desire: The Politics of Sexuality* (New York: Monthly Review, 1983); Carole S. Vance, ed., *Pleasure and Danger: Exploring Female Sexuality* (New York: Routledge & Kegan Paul, 1984); Kathy Peiss and Christina Simmons, eds., *Passion and Power: Sexuality in History* (Philadelphia: Temple University Press, 1989). Excellent analyses of the powerful operations of medicine and law in the naming of homosexuality as pathological include Estelle Freedman, "'Uncontrolled Desires': The Response to the Sexual Psychopath, 1920–1960" and George Chauncey, Jr., "From Sexual Inversion to Homosexuality: Medicine and the Changing Conceptualization of Female 'Deviance,'" in Peiss and Simmons, eds. *Passion and Power*. An extraordinarily moving account about the perils of psychotherapy is given in Martin Bauml Duberman, *Cures: A Gay Man's Odyssey* (New York: Dutton, 1991). Notable accounts of the lives of passing and transgendered people include San Francisco Lesbian and Gay History Project, "'She Even Chewed Tobacco': A Pictorial Narrative of Passing Women in America," in *Hidden From History*, 183–94; Louis Sullivan, *From Female to Male: The Life of Jack Bee Garland* (Boston: Alyson, 1990); and Susan Stryker and Jim Van Buskirk, *Gay by the Bay: A History of Queer Culture in the San Francisco Bay Area* (San Francisco: Chronicle Books, 1996); Gay and Lesbian Historical Project of Northern California, "MTF Transgender Activism in the Tenderloin and Beyond, 1966–1975: Commentary and Interview with Elliot Blackstone," *GLQ* 4, no. 2 (1998): 349–72.

7. Though they were originally lumped together in sexological writing on "contrary sexual instinct," homosexuality, transsexuality, and intersexuality have been distinguished more recently from one another in scientific as well as subcultural and academic discourses. As readers will see, I locate the shared origins of these now-discerned "sexual anomalies" and "gender disorders" but, as the book proceeds, I narrow my focus to homosexuality (i.e., sexual relations between members of the same sex). However, as I also note, in spite of their more recent specification, the fact that these anomalies were originally undifferentiated in sexological writings has lasting effects. That is, most medico-scientific discourse and popular perceptions concerning lesbianism and male homosexuality continue to closely associate these with gender anomalies and even sex-inverted anatomical conditions. What is urgently needed at this stage in the field of the history of sexuality are works that analyze the

interlocking discourses as well as the significant divergences between commentary on gender inversion, transsexuality, and intersexuality. For important works moving in this direction, see Joanne Meyerowitz, "Sex Change and the Popular Press: Historical Notes on Transsexuality in the United States, 1930–1955," *GLQ* 4, no. 2 (1998): 159–88; Susan Stryker, "The Transgender Issue: An Introduction," *GLQ* 4, no. 2 (1998): 145–58; Alice Domurat Dreger, *Hermaphrodites and the Medical Invention of Sex* (Cambridge, Mass.: Harvard University Press, 1998); Suzanne Kessler, *Lessons from the Intersexed* (New Brunswick, N.J.: Rutgers University Press, 1998); and Anne Fausto-Sterling, *Body Building: How Biologists Construct Sexuality* (New York: Basic Books, forthcoming).

8. Foucault, *History of Sexuality*, 43.

9. Ibid., 43–44.

10. Ibid., 101.

11. Michel Foucault, "Nietzsche, History, Genealogy," *The Foucault Reader*, ed. Paul Rabinow (New York: Pantheon Books, 1984), 81. In this essay, Foucault examines several of Nietzsche's most important works on genealogy and history, including *On the Genealogy of Morals* (1887) in *Basic Writings of Nietzsche*, ed. and trans. Walter Kaufmann (New York: Modern Library, 1968); *The Gay Science* (1882), trans. Walter Kaufmann (New York: Random House, 1974); *Human, All Too Human* (1878; New York: Gordon Press, 1974).

12. Friedrich Nietzsche, *The Use and Abuse of History* (1874), trans. Adrian Collins (Indianapolis: Bobbs-Merrill, 1957), 11–12, 13.

13. Hayden White, "The Burden of History," *Tropics of Discourse: Essays in Cultural Criticism* (Baltimore: Johns Hopkins University Press, 1978), 49–50.

CHAPTER ONE

1. Richard von Krafft-Ebing, *Psychopathia Sexualis: A Medico-Forensic Study*, 10th ed. (New York: Samuel Login, 1908), 1–2. The original edition is *Psychopathia Sexualis, mit besonderer Berücksichtigung der konträren Sexualempfindung: Eine klinisch-forensische Studie* (Stuttgart: Enke, 1886). Krafft-Ebing revised and expanded the text over twelve editions. All references are to the tenth edition.

2. Michel Foucault offers an outline of the proliferation of studies of life undertaken during this period in the fields of natural history, biology, and the human sciences in *The Order of Things: An Archaeology of the Human Sciences* (New York: Random House, 1970).

3. Edward J. Dudley and Maximillian E. Novak, eds., *The Wild Man Within: An Image in Western Thought Since the Renaissance* (Pittsburgh: University of Pittsburgh Press, 1972); Hayden White, "Forms of Wildness: Archaeology of an Idea" and "The Noble Savage Theme as Fetish," *Tropics of Discourse*, 150–96; Michel Foucault, *Madness and Civilization: A History of Insanity in the Age of Reason*, trans. Richard Howard (New York: Vintage Books, 1965); Arthur O. Lovejoy, *The Great Chain of Being: A Study of the History of an Idea* (Cambridge, Mass.: Harvard University Press, 1936); Richard Bernheimer, *Wild Men in the Middle Ages* (Cambridge, Mass.: Harvard University Press, 1952); R. G. Collingwood, *The Idea of Nature* (Oxford: Oxford University Press, 1945).

4. See, for example, Eilean Hooper-Greenhill, *Museums and the Shaping of Knowl-*

edge (New York: Routledge, 1992), 167–90; Barbara Maria Stafford, *Artful Science: Enlightenment Entertainment and the Eclipse of Visual Education* (Cambridge: MIT Press, 1994).

5. Relevant analyses of this tradition are Patrick Brantlinger, *Rule of Darkness: British Literature and Imperialism, 1830–1914* (Ithaca, N.Y.: Cornell University Press, 1988); Mary B. Campbell, *The Witness and the Other World: Exotic European Travel Writings, 400–1600* (Ithaca, N.Y.: Cornell University Press, 1988); Mary Louise Pratt, *Imperial Eyes: Travel Writing and Transculturation* (New York: Routledge, 1992); Edward Said, *Orientalism* (New York: Vintage, 1978); Raymond Schwab, *Oriental Renaissance: Europe's Rediscovery of India and the East, 1680–1880,* trans. Gene Petterson-Black and Victor Reinking (New York: Columbia University Press, 1984); David Spurr, *The Rhetoric of Empire: Colonial Discourse in Journalism, Travel Writing, and Imperial Administration* (Durham, N.C.: Duke University Press, 1993); Barbara Stafford, *Voyage Into Substance: Art, Science, Nature, and the Illustrated Travel Account, 1760–1840* (Cambridge, Mass.: MIT Press, 1984); Ann Laura Stoler, *Race and the Education of Desire: Foucault's History of Sexuality and the Colonial Order of Things* (Durham, N.C.: Duke University Press, 1995); and Nicholas Thomas, *Colonialism's Culture: Anthropology, Travel, and Government* (Princeton: Princeton University Press, 1994).

6. See, for example, Carl Linne (Linnaeus), *Systema naturae* (1735), ed. M. S. J. Engel-Ledeboer and H. Engel (Nieuwkoop: B. de Graaf, 1964) and *Systema Naturae. Regnum Animale* (1758; London: British Museum, 1956); George Louis Leclerc, comte de Buffon, *Histoire naturelle,* 44 volumes (1744–1804), and *Oeuvres completes de Buffon,* ed. M. A. Richard (Paris: Baudouin, 1828).

7. See Jean-Jacques Rousseau, *The Social Contract* (1743), trans. Maurice Cranston (New York: Penguin Books, 1968) and *A Discourse On Inequality* (1755), trans. Maurice Cranston (New York: Penguin Books, 1986).

8. Hayden White, "The Forms of Wildness: Archaeology of an Idea" and "The Noble Savage Theme as Fetish," in *Tropics of Discourse,* 150–82, 183–96.

9. See George W. Stocking, Jr., *Race, Culture, and Evolution: Essays in the History of Anthropology* (London: Collier-Macmillan, 1976); George W. Stocking, Jr., *Victorian Anthropology* (New York: Free Press, 1987); George W. Stocking, Jr., ed., "Bones, Bodies, Behavior," *Bones, Bodies, Behavior: Essays in Biological Anthropology* (Madison: University of Wisconsin Press, 1988), 3–17; Harold E. Paglario, ed., *Racism in the Eighteenth Century* (Cleveland: Case Western Reserve University, 1973); William Stanton, *The Leopard's Spots: Scientific Attitudes Toward Race in America, 1815–59* (Chicago: University of Chicago Press, 1960); Nancy Leys Stepan, *The Idea of Race in Science: Great Britain, 1800–1960* (Hamden, Conn.: Archon Books, 1982); Stephen J. Gould, *Ontogeny and Phylogeny* (Cambridge, Mass.: Harvard University Press, 1977); Ann Laura Stoler, *Race and the Education of Desire;* Jean Comaroff, "The Diseased Heart of Africa: Medicine, Colonialism and the Black Body," in *Knowledge, Power & Practice: The Anthropology of Medicine and Everyday Life,* ed. Shirley Lindenbaum and Margaret Lock (Berkeley: University of California, 1993), 305–29; Patrick Brantlinger, "Victorians and Africans: The Genealogy of the Myth of the Dark Continent," *Critical Inquiry* 12 (1985): 166–203; Michael Adas, *Machines as Measures of Men: Science, Technology, and Ideologies of Western Dominance* (Ithaca: Cornell University Press, 1989).

10. Prominent primary works in this areas are Buffon, *Oeuvres completes;* Georges Cuvier, *Leçons d'anatomie comparée* (Paris, 1800–1805); James Cowles Prichard, *Researches into the Physical History of Man,* ed. George W. Stocking, Jr. (1813; Chicago: University of Chicago Press, 1973); P. Cabanis, *Rapports du physique et du moral de l'homme,* vols. 3 and 4 of *Oeuvres completes* (Paris, 1823 [1802]); Etienne Geoffroy Saint-Hilaire and Frederic Cuvier, *Histoire naturelle des mammiferes,* vols. 1 and 2 (Paris: A. Belin, 1824); Samuel George Morton, *Crania Americana; or, A Comparative View of the Skulls of Various Aboriginal Nations of North and South America* (Philadelphia: J. Dobson; London: Simpkin, Marshall & Company, 1839); W. Cooke Taylor, *The Natural History of Society in the Barbarous and Civilized State: An Essay Towards Discovering the Origin and Course of Human Improvement,* 2 vols. (London: Longman, Orme, Brown, Green & Longmans, 1840); James Cowles Prichard, *The Natural History of Man: Comprising Inquiries into the Modifying Influence of Physical and Moral Agencies on the Different Tribes of the Human Family,* 2d ed. (London: H. Bailliere, 1845); Robert Knox, *The Races of Men: A Philosophical Enquiry into the Influences of Race Over the Destinies of Nations* (London, 1862 [1850]); R. G. Latham, *The Natural History of the Varieties of Man* (London: J. Van Voorst, 1850); Josiah Clark Nott and G. Gliddon, *Types of Mankind: Or, Ethnological Researches, based upon the Ancient Monuments, Paintings, Sculptures, and Crania of Races,* 6th ed. (Philadelphia: Lippincott, Grambo & Co., 1854); Charles Pickering, *The Races of Man and their Geographical Distribution* (London: H. G. Bohn, 1863 [1851]); Joseph Arthur, comte de Gobineau, *The Moral and Intellectual Diversity of the Races, with Particular Reference to their Respective Influence in the Civil and Political History of Mankind* (Philadelphia: Lippincott, 1856); Louis Agassiz, *Contributions to the Natural History of the United States,* 4 vols. (Boston: Little, Brown, 1862); Paul Broca, *On the Phenomenon of Hybridity in the Genus Homo,* trans. and ed. C. Carter Blake (London: Longman, Green, Longman, & Roberts, 1864); Joseph B. Davis, *Crania Britannica: Delineations and Descriptions of the Skulls of the Aboriginal and Early Inhabitants of the British Islands,* 2 vols. (London: Subscribers, 1865); Sir John Lubbock (Lord Avebury), *Pre-historic Times, as Illustrated by Ancient Remains, and the Manners and Customs of Modern Savages* (London: Williams and Norgate, 1865); Sir John Lubbock (Lord Avebury), *The Origin of Civilization and the Primitive Condition of Man,* ed. Peter Riviere (1870; Chicago: University of Chicago Press, 1978); W. Swainson, *On the Natural History and Classification of Quadrapeds* (London: Longman, Rees, Orme, Brown, Green and Longman, 1835); Edward Burnett Tylor, *Researches into the Early History of Mankind and the Development of Civilization,* 3d ed., ed. Paul Bohannan (1870; Chicago: University of Chicago Press, 1964); Edward Burnett Tylor, *Primitive Culture,* 2 vols., 2d ed. (New York: H. Holt and Company, 1877); Edward Turnipseed, "Some Facts in Regard to the Anatomical Difference between the Negro and White Races," *American Journal of Obstetrics and Diseases of Women and Children* 10 (1877): 32.

11. The literature in this area is most developed on the subject of scientific theories of the criminal. See Marie-Christine Leps, *Apprehending the Criminal: The Production of Deviance in Nineteenth-Century Discourse* (Durham, N.C.: Duke University Press, 1992); Robert Nye, *Crime, Madness, and Politics in Modern France: The Medical Concept of National Decline* (Princeton, N.J.: Princeton University Press, 1984); John Jacob Tobias, *Crime and Industrial Society in the Nineteenth Century* (New York:

Schocken Books, 1967); Allan Sekula, "The Body and the Archive," *October* 39 (Winter 1986): 3–64; Leslie Camhi, "Stealing Femininity: Department Store Kleptomania as Sexual Disorder," *differences* 5, no. 1 (1993): 26–50. Leading primary works on the subject of inborn criminality include Moriz Benedikt, *Anatomical Studies Upon Brains of Criminals* (1881; New York: Da Capo Press, 1981); Cesare Lombroso and Gillaume Ferrero, *The Female Offender* (London: T. Fisher Unwin, 1895); Cesare Lombroso, *Criminal Man, According to the Classification of Cesare Lombroso, Briefly Summarized by His Daughter, Gina Lombroso-Ferrero,* with an introduction by Cesare Lombroso (New York: Putnam's, 1911; reprinted Montclair, N.J.: Patterson Smith, 1972); Richard L. Dugdale, *"The Jukes": A Study in Crime, Pauperism, Disease and Heredity; also Further Studies of Criminals* (New York: G. P. Putnam's Sons, 1877); Havelock Ellis, *The Criminal* (London: Walter Scott, 1890); Hamilton D. Wey, "Criminal Anthropology," *National Prison Association, Proceedings 1890,* 274–90 (Pittsburgh: Shaw Brothers, 1891). On the scientific construction of the "feebleminded," see Mark Haller, *Eugenics: Hereditarian Attitudes in American Thought* (New Brunswick: Rutgers University Press, 1985); Nicole Hahn Rafter, *White Trash: The Eugenics Family Studies, 1877–1919* (Boston: Northeastern University Press, 1988); Daniel J. Kevles, *In the Name of Eugenics: Genetics and the Uses of Human Heredity* (Berkeley: University of California Press, 1985); Stephen J. Gould, *The Mismeasure of Man* (New York: W. W. Norton & Company, 1981); John David Smith, *Minds Made Feeble: The Myth and Legacy of the Kallikaks* (Rockville, Md.: Aspen Systems Corp., 1985). A prominent primary work is Henry H. Goddard, *The Kallikak Family: A Study in the Heredity of Feeblemindedness* (New York: Macmillan, 1912). For analyses of scientific studies of prostitution, see Judith R. Walkowitz, *Prostitution and Victorian Society: Women, Class, and the State* (New York: Cambridge University Press, 1980); Laura Engelstein, *The Keys to Happiness: Sex and the Search for Modernity in Fin-de-Siècle Russia* (Ithaca: Cornell University Press, 1992), 130–44; Sander L. Gilman, "Black Bodies, White Bodies: Toward an Iconography of Female Sexuality in Late Nineteenth-Century Art, Medicine, and Literature," *Critical Inquiry* 12, no. 1 (Autumn 1985): 204–42; Alain Corbin, *Women for Hire: Prostitution and Sexuality in France after 1850,* trans. Alan Sheridan (Cambridge: Harvard University Press, 1990). Prominent primary works on the physical stigmata associated with prostitution are Alexandre Jean-Baptiste Parent-Duchatelet, *On Prostitution in the City of Paris* (London, 1840); Ambroise Tardieu, *Étude médico-légale sur les attentats aux moeurs,* 7th ed. (Paris: 1878 [1857]; Louis Martineu, *Leçons sur les déformations vulvaires et anales produites par la masturbation, le saphisme, la défloration, et la sodomie,* 2d ed., rev. (Paris, 1886); Pauline Tarnowsky, *Étude anthropométrique sur les prostituées et les voleuses* (Paris, 1889); Adrien Charpy, "Des organes genitaux externes chez les prostituées," *Annales des dermatologie* 3 (1970–71): 271–79.

12. Foucault, *The History of Sexuality,* 105–7. See also, Foucault, "Governmentality," *Ideology and Consciousness* 6 (1979): 5–21 and "The Subject and Power," afterword to *Michel Foucault: Beyond Structuralism and Hermeneutics,* ed. Hubert Dreyfus and Paul Rabinow (Chicago: University of Chicago Press, 1982), 208–26.

13. Foucault, *History of Sexuality,* 53.

14. Ibid.

15. I borrow Gayle Rubin's term 'sex/gender system' as an analytical device for understanding the organization of human beings into discrete sexes and genders in

the service of larger psychological, cultural, and economic systems that structure accepted patterns of kinship, exchange, and power in any given cultural context. Gayle
Rubin, "The Traffic in Women: Notes on the Political Economy of Sex," in *Toward
an Anthropology of Women*, ed. Rayna Rapp Reiter (New York: Monthly Review Press,
1975), 157–210.

16. In a fashion slightly different from Foucault's *scientia sexualis*, feminist theorists and historians have attended to the ways that norms of gender and sexuality
were both produced by and generative of a range of scientific practices that focused
specifically on the aberrations presumed to be represented by the female body. For a
critique of Foucault's blindness to the significance of gender in his formulation, see
Teresa de Lauretis, "The Technology of Gender," *Technologies of Gender: Essays on
Theory, Film, and Fiction* (Bloomington, Indiana: Indiana University Press, 1987), 1–30.

17. For a detailed analysis of the historically and culturally specific nature of the
modern two-sex system, see Thomas Laqueur, *Making Sex: Body and Gender From the
Greeks to Freud* (Cambridge: Harvard University Press, 1990).

18. For analyses of sexual science focused on female bodies, see Londa Schiebinger, *Nature's Body: Gender and the Making of Modern Science* (Boston: Beacon Press,
1993) and "Skeletons in the Closet: The First Illustrations of the Female Skeleton in
Eighteenth-Century Anatomy," in *The Making of the Modern Body*, ed. Thomas La-
queur and Catherine Gallagher (Berkeley: University of California Press, 1987),
42–82; Cynthia Eagle Russett, *Sexual Science: The Victorian Construction of Womanhood*
(Cambridge: Harvard University Press, 1989); Ludmilla Jordanova, *Sexual Visions:
Images of Gender in Science and Medicine Between the Eighteenth and Twentieth Centuries*
(Madison: University of Wisconsin Press, 1989); Ornella Moscucci, *The Science of
Woman: Gynaecology and Gender in England, 1800–1929* (New York: Cambridge Uni-
versity Press, 1990); Elizabeth Fee, "The Sexual Politics of Victorian Social Anthro-
pology," in *Clio's Consciousness Raised: New Perspectives on the History of Women*, ed.
Mary Hartman and Lois Banner (New York: Harper and Row, 1974), 86–102; Martha
Vicinus, ed., *Suffer and Be Still: Women in the Victorian Age* (Bloomington: Indiana
University Press, 1972); Carroll Smith-Rosenberg and Charles E. Rosenberg,
"The Female Animal: Medical and Biological Views of Women and Her Role in
Nineteenth-Century America," *American Quarterly* 25 (1973): 131–53; Graham
Barker-Benfield, *The Horrors of a Half-Known Life: Male Attitudes toward Women and
Sexuality in Nineteenth-Century America* (New York: Harper and Row, 1976).

19. The earliest studies undertaken by the fathers of comparative anatomy were
devoted to identifying and measuring physical features, and especially the genitals,
of "Hottentot" women from southern Africa, based on the assumption that these
women were inherently perverse by virtue of their race. French comparative anatomist Georges Cuvier and his colleague, Henri de Blainville, believed that a careful
study of the bodies of African women would confirm that primitives were essentially
immodest, sexually untamed, and lacking in reason. After her death, they literally
dissected the genitals of Saartje Bartmann, a southern African woman who had been
displayed in a cage for the entertainment of European popular audiences and the
observations of scientists. The dissection was done to confirm, among other things,
that "primitive" peoples, and especially females of these groups, lacked the discipline
and decency of civilized Europeans and exhibited perverse sexuality. Thus modern

notions of perversion were written onto and out of the bodies of female primitives who were remarkable for their "excessive" genitalia, which signaled the general immodesty of all primitive peoples. For more on Saartje Bartmann, see Georges Cuvier, "Faites sur le cadavre d'une femme connue à Paris et à Londres sous la nom de Venus Hottentotte," *Memoires du Musee nationale d'histoire naturelle* (3) (1817): 259–74; Henri de Blainville, "Sur une femme de la race hottentote," *Bulletin du Société philomatique de Paris* (1816): 183–90. See also John Marshall, "On the Brain of a Bushwoman; and on the Brains of Two Idiots of European Descent," *Philosophical Transactions of the Royal Society of London* (1864): 501–8; Johannes Müller, "Ueber die ausseren Geslechtstheile der Buschmanninnen," *Archiv für Anatomie, Physiologie und der Wissenschaftliche Medicin* (1834): 319–45. For critical works on Bartmann's place in the history of comparative anatomy, see Anne Fausto-Sterling, "Gender, Race, and Nation: The Comparative Anatomy of 'Hottentot' Women in Europe, 1815–1817," in Jennifer Terry and Jacqueline Urla, eds., *Deviant Bodies: Critical Perspectives on Difference in Science and Popular Culture* (Bloomington: Indiana University Press, 1995), 19–48; Stephen Jay Gould, "The Hottentot Venus," *The Flamingo's Smile: Reflections in Natural History* (New York: W. W. Norton & Company, 1985), 291–305; Bernth Lindfors, "The Hottentot Venus and Other African Attractions in Nineteenth-Century England," *Australasian Drama Studies* 1 (1983): 83–104.

20. Ella Shohat, "Imaging Terra Incognita: The Disciplinary Gaze of the Empire," *Public Culture* 3, no. 2 (1991): 41–70.

21. See, for example, W. H. Flower and James Murie, "Account of the Dissection of a Bushwoman," *Journal of Anatomy and Physiology* 1 (1867): 189–208; *Anthropological Review* 5 (July 1867): 319–324; *Anthropological Review* 8 (January 1870): 89–318; Edward Turnipseed, "Some Facts in Regard to the Anatomical Difference between the Negro and White Races."

22. See, for example, Isaac Baker Brown, *On the Curability of Certain Forms of Insanity, Epilepsy, Catalepsy and Hysteria in Females* (London: Robert Hardwicke, 1866). For analyses of this phenomenon see Sander L. Gilman, "Black Bodies, White Bodies"; Mary Poovey, "'Scenes of an Indelicate Character': The Medical 'Treatment' of Victorian Women," *Representations* 14 (1986): 137–68; Carol Groneman, "Nymphomania: The Historical Construction of Female Sexuality," in Terry and Urla, eds., *Deviant Bodies,* 219–49. For evidence of the persistence of this trend well into the twentieth century, see Jennifer Terry, "Lesbians Under the Medical Gaze: Scientists Search for Remarkable Differences," *Journal of Sex Research* 27, no. 3 (1990): 317–40.

23. See *Herculine Barbin: Being the Recently Discovered Memoirs of a Nineteenth-Century French Hermaphrodite,* introduced by Michel Foucault, trans. Richard McDougall (New York: Pantheon Books, 1980) for a disturbing illustration of the regime enforcing the two-sex system.

24. Karl Friedrich Otto Westphal, "Die kontrare Sexualempfindung: Symptom eines neuropatholgischen (psychopathischen) Zustandes," *Archiv für Psychiatrie und Nervenkrankheiten* 2 (1869): 73–108. For a broad overview of the medicalization of homosexuality in the United States, see Bert Hansen, "American Physicians' 'Discovery' of Homosexuals, 1880–1900: A New Diagnosis in a Changing Society," in Charles E. Rosenberg and Janet Golden, eds., *Framing Disease: Studies in Cultural History* (New Brunswick: Rutgers University Press, 1992), 104–33.

25. Charles Darwin, *On the Origin of Species* (1859; Cambridge, Mass.: Harvard University Press, 1966). See also Charles Darwin, *Journal of Researches into the Natural History and Geology of the Countries Visited During the Voyage of H.M.S. "Beagle"* (London: Henry Colburn, 1839); Charles Darwin, *The Descent of Man, and Selections in Relation to Sex,* 2 vols. (London: Murray, 1871).

26. Among the leading authors applying evolutionary thought to explain human progress and regression were Francis Galton, Darwin's cousin, and Herbert Spencer. See, for example, Herbert Spencer, *Descriptive Sociology: Or, Groups of Sociological Facts, Classified and Arranged by Herbert Spencer* (London: Williams and Norgate, 1874) and *Illustrations of Universal Progress: A Series of Discussions* (New York: D. Appleton and Company, 1880); Sir Francis Galton, *Narration of an Explorer in Tropic South Africa* (London: J. Murray, 1853); *Hereditary Genius: An Inquiry into its Laws and Consequences* (New York: Appleton, 1884); and *Inquiries into Human Faculty and its Development* (London: J. M. Dent and Company, 1908).

27. For analyses of "Social Darwinism," see Robert C. Bannister, *Social Darwinism: Science and Myth in Anglo-American Social Thought* (Philadelphia: Temple University Press, 1979); Ruth S. Cowan, "Nature and Nurture: The Interplay of Biology and Politics in the Work of Francis Galton," *Studies in the History of Biology* 1 (1977): 133–208; Derek Forrest, *Francis Galton: The Life and Works of a Victorian Genius* (London: Elek, 1974); R. Halliday, "Social Darwinism: A Definition," *Victorian Studies* 14 (1971): 389–405; Greta Jones, *Social Darwinism and English Thought: The Interaction Between Biological and Sociological Theory* (Atlantic Highlands, N.J.: Humanities Press, 1980); J. A. Rogers, "Darwinism and Social Darwinism," *Journal of the History of Ideas* 33 (1972): 265–80. For analyses of degeneration theory, see J. Edward Chamberlin and Sander L. Gilman, eds., *Degeneration: The Dark Side of Progress* (New York: Columbia University Press, 1985); Daniel Pick, *Faces of Degeneration: A European Disorder, c. 1848–1918* (New York: Cambridge University Press, 1989); and Richard D. Walter, "What Became of the Degenerate? A Brief History of a Concept," *Journal of the History of Medicine and Allied Sciences* 2 (1956): 422–29.

28. For historical analyses of early sex variant subcultures in the United States and Europe, see George Chauncey, *Gay New York;* Jonathan Ned Katz, *Gay American History;* and *Gay/Lesbian Almanac;* Barry Adam, *The Rise of the Lesbian and Gay Movement* (Boston: G. K. Hall, 1987); Jeffrey Weeks, "Inverts, Perverts, and Mary-Annes: Male Prostitution and the Regulation of Homosexuality in England in the Nineteenth and Early Twentieth Centuries," in Duberman, Vicinus, and Chauncey, eds., *Hidden from History,* 195–211; Randolph Trumbach, "London's Sodomites: Homosexual Behavior and Western Culture in the Eighteenth Century," *Journal of Social History* 11 (1977): 1–33 and "Sodomitical Subcultures, Sodomitical Roles and the Gender Revolution of the Eighteenth Century: The Recent Historiography," in *'Tis Nature's Fault: Unauthorized Sexuality During the Enlightenment,* ed. R. P. Maccubin (New York: Cambridge University Press, 1987).

CHAPTER TWO

1. Richard von Krafft-Ebing, *Psychopathia Sexualis,* 541.

2. Sigmund Freud, "The Sexual Aberrations," in *Three Contributions to the Theory of Sex* (1905) *Standard Edition* 7:123.

3. See Jeffrey Weeks, *Sex, Politics, and Society: The Regulation of Sexuality Since 1800* (New York: Longman, 1981), 99–100.

4. For relevant histories of the rise of scientific medicine, see Paul Starr, *The Social Transformation of American Medicine: The Rise of a Sovereign Profession and the Making of a Vast Industry* (New York: Basic Books, 1982); Charles E. Rosenberg, "Disease and Social Order in America: Perceptions and Expectations" in *AIDS: The Burdens of History,* ed. Elizabeth Fee and Daniel M. Fox (Berkeley: University of California Press, 1988), 12–32. See also William G. Rothstein, *American Medical Schools and the Practice of Medicine* (New York: Oxford University Press, 1987); Nathan Reingold, "Definitions and Speculations: The Professionalization of Science in America in the Nineteenth Century," in *The Pursuit of Knowledge in the Early American Republic,* ed. Alexandra Oleson and Sanborn C. Brown (Baltimore: Johns Hopkins University Press, 1976), 33–69; Barbara Ehrenreich and Deirdre English, *Witches, Midwives, and Nurses: A History of Women Healers* (Old Westbury, N.J.: The Feminist Press, 1973).

5. See, for example, Karl Heinrich Ulrichs, *Forschungen über das Rathsel der mann-mannlichen Liebe,* 4 vols., ed. Hubert Kennedy (Berlin: Verlag rosa Winkel, 1994 [1864–79]); Ulrichs, *The Riddle of "Man-Manly" Love: The Pioneering Work on Male Homosexuality,* 2 vols., trans. Michael A. Lombardi-Nash (Buffalo Prometheus, 1994); Magnus Hirschfeld, *Die Homosexualität des Mannes und des Weibes* (Berlin: Louis Marcus, 1914); Hirschfeld, *Sexual Anomalies and Perversions: Physical and Psychological Development and Treatment* (New York: Random House, 1942 [1936]).

6. See Richard von Krafft-Ebing, *Psychopathia Sexualis;* Jean-Martin Charcot and Valentin Magnan, "Inversions du sens génital et autres perversions génitales," *Archives de Neurologie* 7 (January–February 1882): 55–60 and 12 (November 1882): 292–322.

7. Hubert C. Kennedy, "Karl Heinrich Ulrichs: First Theorist of Homosexuality," in *Science and Homosexualities,* ed. Vernon A. Rosario (New York: Routledge, 1996), 26–45; Hubert C. Kennedy, "The 'Third Sex' Theory of Karl Heinreich Ulrichs," in *Historical Perspectives on Homosexuality,* ed. Salvatore J. Licata and Robert P. Petersen (New York: Haworth Press and Stein and Day, 1981), 103–11; Hubert C. Kennedy, *Ulrichs: The Life and Work of Karl Heinrich Ulrichs, Pioneer of the Modern Gay Movement* (Boston: Alyson Press, 1988); Jonathan Ned Katz, *The Invention of Heterosexuality* (New York: Penguin Books, 1995), 51–52.

8. Theophile Gautier, *Mademoiselle de Maupin,* ed. and trans. Joanna Richardson (1835) (Harmondsworth, Eng.: Penguin Books, 1981).

9. The term "fourth sex" virtually disappeared from scientific and popular discourse about homosexuality, but reappeared in a sensationalistic exposé of lesbianism published in 1964 by male journalist Jess Stearn, who used the term to refer to lesbians. Jess Stearn, *The Grapevine* (Garden City, N.J.: Doubleday & Company, Inc., 1964).

10. For example, British writer Edward Carpenter popularized the idea of a third sex in *The Intermediate Sex* (London: Sonnenschein, 1908); Carpenter, "The Intermediate Sex," *Love's Coming of Age* (London: 1923).

11. *Homosexuality* was a hybrid term combining elements from Greek (homo, or the same) and Latin (sexual). It was coined publicly by Karoly Maria Benkert (pseud. Kertbeny) in 1869, but competed with a number of other terms to describe similar

NOTES TO PAGES 45-49

or closely related phenomena. Synonyms for homosexuality included uranianism, psychical hermaphroditism, sexual intermediacy, and a host of terms originating out of particular sexual acts including tribadism, sapphism, and pederasty. Krafft-Ebing's nomenclature for types of homosexuality was particularly creative and obtuse, including "pure homosexuality," "tardy homosexuality," "viraginity," "psychosexual hermaphrodism," and "gynandrism." This array of vocabulary provides evidence of the discursive complexity, and no small amount of confusion, surrounding the phenomena of homosexuality. But by the turn of the century, most sexologists adopted "homosexuality" as a standard term to encompass both sexual inversion and the desire of an individual for a member of the same sex. For more on Kertbeny's efforts to repeal anti-homosexual laws and his coining of "homosexuality," see Manfred Herzer, "Kertbeny and the Nameless Love," *Journal of Homosexuality* 12 (1985): 1–26; Vern L. Bullough, *Science in the Bedroom: A History of Sex Research* (New York: Basic Books, 1994), 39; Vern Bullough, *Sexual Variance in Society and History* (New York: John Wiley and Sons, 1976), 637.

12. Karl Friedrich Otto Westphal, "Die konträre Sexualempfindung."

13. Richard von Krafft-Ebing, *Psychopathia Sexualis*, 414.

14. For an analysis of the influence of self-identified homosexuals on Krafft-Ebing, see Harry Oosterhuis, "Richard von Krafft-Ebing's 'Step-Children of Nature': Psychiatry and the Making of Homosexual Identity," in *Science and Homosexualities*, ed. Vernon A. Rosario III (New York: Routledge, 1997), 67–88.

15. For a similar line of reasoning, see Jean-Martin Charcot and Valentin Magnan, "Inversions du sens génital et autres perversions génitales."

16. Krafft-Ebing, *Psychopathia Sexualis*, 327.

17. Oosterhuis, "Richard von Krafft-Ebing's 'Step-Children of Nature,'" 71.

18. Krafft-Ebing, *Psychopathia Sexualis*, 542. For more on abulia, see John H. Smith, "Abulia: Sexuality and Diseases of the Will in the Late Nineteenth Century," *Genders* 6 (Fall 1989): 102–24.

19. E. R. Lankester, *Degeneration: A Chapter in Darwinism* (London: Macmillan, 1880); E. S. Talbot, *Degeneracy: Its Causes, Signs and Results* (London: Walter Scott, 1898).

20. Herbert Spencer, "Progress: Its Law and Cause" and "Manners and Fashion."

21. A number of authors compared homosexuality in primitive and civilized societies to make arguments to support the naturalist position, but in most cases they too regarded homosexuality in advanced societies as a feature of distinct individuals, tying it to a specific identity distinct from the common cultural organization of sexuality in the modern West. See, for example, Richard Burton, "Terminal Essay: The Book of the Thousand Nights and a Night" (1886), rpt. in *Homosexuality: A Cross Cultural Approach*, ed. Donald Webster Cory (New York: Julian Press, Inc., 1956), 207–46; Paolo Mantegazza, *The Perversions of Love* (1932), rpt. in Cory, ed., *Homosexuality*, 248–66; Ferdinand Karsch-Haack, *Das gleichgeschlechtliche Leben der Naturvolker* (Munich: Ernst Reinhardt, 1911); Edward Westermarck, "Homosexual Love," *The Origin and Development of Moral Ideas* (London: Macmillan, 1906); Gilbert V. Hamilton, "A Study of Sexual Tendencies in Monkeys and Baboons," *Journal of Animal Behavior* 4 (1914): 295–318; Edward Carpenter, *Intermediate Types Among Primitive*

412   NOTES TO PAGE 50

Folk: A Study in Social Evolution (London: Allen and Unwin, 1914). For an excellent historical analysis of sexologists' appropriation of homosexuality among non-European peoples to construct modern homosexual identity, see Rudi C. Bleys, *The Geography of Perversion: Male-to-Male Sexual Behavior Outside the West and the Ethnographic Imagination, 1750–1918* (New York: New York University Press, 1995).

22. Krafft-Ebing, *Psychopathia Sexualis,* 274.

23. Havelock Ellis, though he had minimal medical training, was a prolific commentator on matters of sex. As a way to achieve legitimacy on the subjects of sex and sexuality, Ellis worked hard to achieve a single medical qualification that was the most basic to acquire (the Licentiate of the Society of Apothecaries). He abandoned the practice of medicine after a few months. When he was made a Fellow of the Royal College of Physicians just before he died, he had to be admitted under a special regulation because he had so few medical credentials. For details on Ellis's career and his complex positioning between Victorian and modern social mores, see Lesley A. Hall, "'Somehow Very Distasteful': Doctors, Men and Sexual Problems Between the Wars," *Journal of Contemporary History* 20, no. 4 (October 1985): 553–74, 556; Andrew P. Lyons and Harriet D. Lyons, "Savage Sexuality and Secular Morality: Malinowski, Ellis, Russell," *Canadian Journal of Anthropology* 5 (1) (Fall 1986): 51–64; Vern L. Bullough, *Science in the Bedroom,* 75–85.

24. Havelock Ellis, *The Criminal.*

25. Havelock Ellis, *Sexual Inversion* (London: Watford University Press, 1897). *Sexual Inversion* was first published in German in 1896, and named J. A. Symonds, who had died in 1893, as a co-author. John Addington Symonds, whose close friends included Walt Whitman and Edward Carpenter, had approached Ellis in 1892 to ask if he "would take a book from me on 'Sexual Inversion' for his Science Series?" In his correspondence with Ellis, who gladly accepted the offer of collaboration, Symonds wrote that "it [sexual inversion] is being fearfully mishandled by pathologists and psychiatrical professors, who know nothing whatsoever about its real nature. . . . The legal and social persecution of abnormal nature requires revision. . . . The theory of morbidity is more humane, but it is not less false, than that of sin or vice." Symonds provided the majority of the research for *Sexual Inversion.* The first English version appeared in 1897 with Symonds as co-author, but his family and his executor, Horatio Brown, bought up and destroyed almost all the existing copies out of fear of scandal. A revised English version omitting Symonds's name first appeared in 1897. All subsequent editions listed Ellis as the sole author. For more on Symonds and his collaboration with Ellis, see Katz, *Gay American History,* 356, 364, and Phyllis Grosskurth, *John Addington Symonds: A Biography* (London: Longmans, Green, 1964). *Sexual Inversion* was revised three times, once in a 1901 edition, again in a 1915 edition, and again in a 1926 edition, to which all subsequent references in this chapter are made.

26. In 1914 Ellis was one of a group of founding members of the British Society for the Study of Sex Psychology, whose first president was Edward Carpenter. The group changed its name in 1920 to the British Sexological Society and had famous supporters and members including George Bernard Shaw, E. M. Forster, Bertrand Russell, Edward Westermarck, Radclyffe Hall, and Una Troubridge. For more on the Society, see Weeks, *Sex, Politics, and Society,* 181–84.

27. Ellis, *Sexual Inversion*, 320.

28. For a more detailed discussion of Ellis's progressive-mindedness, see Paul Robinson, *The Modernization of Sex* (New York: Harper and Row, 1967).

29. Ellis, *Sexual Inversion*, 268–69.

30. Ibid., 13.

31. Hirschfeld's most important works on homosexuality are [T. Ramien, pseud.] *Sappho und Sokrates, oder Wie erklärt sich die Liebe der Männer und der Frauen zu Personen des eigenen Geschlecht?* (Leipzig: Max Spohr, 1896), republished in *Documents of the Homosexual Rights Movement in Germany, 1836–1927* (New York: Arno, 1975); "The Homosexual as an Intersex," in *The Homosexuals as Seen by Themselves and Thirty Authorities*, ed. A. M. Krich (New York: Citadel Press, 1954), 119–34; "Homosexuality," in *Encylopedia Sexualis*, ed. Victor Robinson (New York: Dingwall-Rock, 1936), 321–34; *Die Homosexualität des Mannes und des Weibes* (Berlin: Louis Marcus, 1914). See also his *Sex in Human Relationships*, trans. John Rodker (New York: AMS Press, 1975) and *Sexual Anomalies and Perversions* (New York: Random House, 1942). For a thorough analysis of Hirschfeld's life and work, see James D. Steakley, *The Homosexual Emancipation Movement in Germany* (New York: Arno Press, 1975) and "Per scientiam ad justitiam: Magnus Hirschfeld and the Sexual Politics of Innate Homosexuality," in *Science and Homosexualities*, ed. Vernon A. Rosario (New York: Routledge, 1996), 133–54.

32. Steakley, "Per scientiam ad justitiam," 139, 141.

33. See Cesare Lombroso, *Criminal Man;* Paolo Mantegazza, *Anthropological Studies of the Sexual Relations of Mankind*, trans. James Bruce (New York: Anthropological Press, 1932 [1886]).

34. Hirschfeld, *Sappho und Sokrates*, 14, quoted in Steakley, "Per scientiam ad justitiam," 141.

35. Hirschfeld, *Die Homosexualität des Mannes und des Weibes*, translated and quoted by Stcakley in "Per scientiam ad justitiam," 142.

36. The German psychiatrist Wilhelm Stekel accused Hirschfeld of being "propagandistic" and lacking in objectivity in his research on homosexuality around the time that Hirschfeld and the Scientific-Humanitarian Committee were campaigning against Paragraph 175. Wilhelm Stekel, "Is Homosexuality Curable?" *Psychoanalytic Review* 17 (1930): 433, translated from German version published in 1929.

37. Hirschfeld, "Ursachen und Wesen des Uranismus," *Jahrbuch für sexuelle Zwischenstufen* 5 (1903): 1–193, 68, translated and quoted by Steakley in "Per scientiam ad justitiam," 149.

38. Otto Weininger, *Sex and Character*, translated from sixth German edition (New York: G. P. Putnam's Sons, 1903), 45–46.

39. Freud's early critique of theories of hereditary neuroses was articulated in Sigmund Freud, "Heredity and the Aetiology of Neuroses" (1896), *Standard Edition* 3:141–58; "The Aetiology of Hysteria" (1896), *Standard Edition* 3:189–224; and "Sexuality in the Aetiology of the Neuroses" (1898), *Standard Edition* 3:261–86. In addition to Freud, other prominent psychoanalysts argued the homosexuality arose from psychological factors, rejecting congenital or hereditary etiologies of homosexuality. See, for example, Sandor Ferenczi, "More about Homosexuality" (1909), in *Final Contributions to the Problems and Methods of Psychoanalysis* (New York: Basic Books,

1955); Abraham Brill, "The Conception of Homosexuality," *Journal of the American Medical Association* 61, no. 5 (1913): 335–40; Wilhelm Stekel, *Bisexual Love* (Boston: Badger, 1922). Later psychoanalytic works in this vein include Louis S. London, "Analysis of a Homosexual Neurosis," *The Urologic and Cutaneous Review* 37 (1933): 93; Louis S. London, *Mental Therapy* (New York: Liveright, 1937).

40. Freud, "Mourning and Melancholia" (1917), *Standard Edition* 14:237–58.

41. See, for example, Sigmund Freud, "Psychopathology of Everyday Life" (1901), *Standard Edition* 6; "Jokes and their Relation to the Unconscious" (1905), *Standard Edition* 8:9–236.

42. See, for example, Sigmund Freud, "The Sexual Aberrations." For a trenchant and subversive analysis of the implication of Freud's suggestion here, see Teresa de Lauretis, "Freud, Sexuality, and Perversion," in *The Practice of Love: Lesbian Sexuality and Perverse Desire* (Bloomington: Indiana University Press, 1994), 3–28.

43. See especially Freud, "The Sexual Aberrations."

44. Ibid., 123, n. 1.

45. Freud's reworking of the ideas of constitutional homosexuality were articulated in "The Sexual Aberrations." He further commented on biological factors in some cases of homosexuality in "'Civilized' Sexual Morality and Modern Nervous Illness" (1908), *Standard Edition* 9:179–204 and "The Psychogenesis of a Case of Homosexuality in a Female," *Standard Edition* (1920) 18:146–72.

46. For useful analyses of Freud's complicated thinking on the subject of homosexuality, see Kenneth Lewes, *The Psychoanalytic Theory of Male Homosexuality* (New York: Meridian, 1988), and George Chauncey, Jr., "From Sexual Inversion to Homosexuality."

47. Freud, "The Sexual Aberrations," 135–36.

48. Ibid., 142, 144.

49. Ibid. 144–55.

50. For an explication of Freud's four typical senarios from which male homosexuality arose, see Lewes, *Psychoanalytic Theory of Male Homosexuality,* 36–38. The relevant case histories are Sigmund Freud, "Leonardo da Vinci and a Memory of his Childhood," (1910) *Standard Edition* 11:59–138; "Analysis of a Phobia in a Five-Year-Old Boy ('Little Hans')," (1909) *Standard Edition* 10:3–149; *Three Essays on the Theory of Sexuality* (1905), *Standard Edition* 7:123–246; "Certain Neurotic Mechanisms in Jealousy, Paranoia, and Homosexuality" (1922), *Standard Edition* 18:221–34; "A Case of Paranoia Running Counter to the Psychoanalytic Theory of the Disease" (1915), *Standard Edition* 14:263–72; "From the History of an Infantile Neurosis ('The Wolf Man')" (1918), *Standard Edition* 17:3–22.

51. The complexities faced by girls in overcoming their original homosexual love object are discussed at length in Freud's later essay, "Femininity" (1933), *Standard Edition* 22:112–35.

52. See, for example, Sigmund Freud, *Three Essays on the Theory of Sexuality* (1905); "Leonardo da Vinci and a Memory of his Childhood"; "Letter to An American Mother (1935)," *American Journal of Psychiatry* 107 (1951): 786–87; "'Civilized' Sexuality Morality and Modern Nervous Illness" (1908); *Civilization and Its Discontents* (1930) *Standard Edition* 21: 64–145.

53. Friedrich Engels, for example, posited three main stages of social evolution which he denoted as primitive, barbaric, civilized that parallel Freud's notions. Engels' functionalist theory of cultural evolution traced "advanced" cultures (i.e., European industrialized societies) back to primitive origins. He theorized that in their original natural state primitive peoples were promiscuous and had little or no constraints placed upon their sexual activity. Similar to Freud's stage of childhood polymorphous perversity, in primitive society sexual instincts were not yet channeled and threatened to become uncontrollable if repression was not instituted. Thus, to ensure social stability and co-existence, constraints had to be placed on sexual activity, most notably through the institution of incest taboos. The barbaric stage which followed was marked by the institution of increasingly more discriminating incest taboos. Modest forms of repressing sexual instincts worked, in Engels' depiction of the barbaric stage, to ensure political stability and economic relations of subsistence and simple exchange necessary to early pastoral or agrarian societies. One can identify a parallel between Engels' barbaric stage and Freud's Oedipal stage wherein repressions of the sexual instincts are necessary for ensuring the proper individuation of the child from its mother. The most recent stage of cultural evolution in Engels' framework was that associated with the emergence of capitalism. In this stage, monogamous marriage was instituted and legally enforced, providing a basic framework necessary for the accumulation of capital and the social reproduction of classes. This latter stage was not, in Engels' view, favorable, especially because it resulted in the oppression of women. He looked back fondly at forms of primitive communism, and it is, of course, clear from his collaboration with Marx that Engels spoke of capitalist societies as "advanced" but not as inherently superior to earlier stages of history. His prescription of communism to relieve the ills of capitalism was, without doubt, based upon a progressive telos which urged forward motion and maturity, decried regression, and argued for the development of communism as a more advanced stage of cultural evolution. What he shared with Freud was a teleological perspective, but both authors were deeply ambivalent about the repressive effects that resulted in normative notions of progress and maturity. See Friedrich Engels, *The Origin of the Family, Private Property and the State* (New York: International Publishers, 1972).

In addition, Norbert Elias, in his history of the "civilizing process," echoed Freud's three-stage framework for understanding the relationship between civilization and sexuality by noting the rituals imposed upon children in their acquisition of manners. Norbert Elias, *The History of Manners*, Vol. 1 of *The Civilizing Process*, trans. Edmund Jephcott (New York: Pantheon Books, 1978).

54. Krafft-Ebing, *Psychopathia Sexualis*, 576–78.

55. August Forel, *The Sexual Question*, trans. C. F. Marshall (New York: Rebman Company, 1905), 251.

56. Ibid., 251–53.

57. Ellis, *Sexual Inversion*, 213–15.

58. This line of reasoning is elaborated in Sigmund Freud, "The Psychogenesis of a Case of Female Homosexuality"; "Some Psychological Consequences of the Anatomical Distinction Between the Sexes" (1925), *Standard Edition* 19:243–58; and "Female Sexuality" (1931), *Standard Edition* 21:223–43. For an analysis of the endemic

bisexuality in girls' relationship to the mother, see Nancy Chodorow, "Oedipal Asymmetries and Heterosexual Knots," *Social Problems* 23, no. 4 (1976): 454–68.

59. See also J. H. W. Van Ophuijsen, "Contributions to the Masculinity Complex in Women," *International Journal of Psychoanalysis* 5 (1924): 39–49.

60. Karl Abraham, "Manifestations of the Female Castration Complex," in *Selected Papers on Psychoanalysis*, ed. Leonard and Virginia Woolf (London, 1927).

61. Freud, "The Psychogenesis of a Case of Female Homosexuality," in *Standard Edition* 18: 158.

62. For example, see Helene Deutsch, "On Female Homosexuality," *Psychoanalytic Quarterly* 1 (1932): 484. Rpt. in *The Psychoanalytic Reader*, ed. Robert Fliess (New York: International Universities Press, 1948), 208–30.

63. See, for example, Freud, "A Case of Paranoia Running Counter to the Psychoanalytic Theory of the Disease."

64. Freud, "The Sexual Aberrations," 142, 145.

65. The efforts of homosexual men and women who sought allies among physicians were not in vain; they mark the beginning of a long-term struggle to decriminalize homosexual acts that often involved support from sympathetic medical authorities. Most significant legal reforms to lighten the sentences for sodomy did not occur until 1929 in Germany and much later in Britain and the United States. Paragraph 143 of the Prussian legal code (which later became paragraph 175 after the unification of Germany in 1871) condemned homosexual acts among men. It was reformed in 1929 to decriminalize sodomy among consenting adult men until Hitler came to power and reinstated strict laws making homosexuality punishable by death. In the 1950s, the Wolfenden Committee in England and the American Law Institute in the United States recommended abolition of criminal penalties for homosexual sodomy, except in cases involving violence, children, or public solicitation to commercial vice. Their recommendation was adopted first in Illinois in 1961 and later several other U.S. states and in England in 1967. For background on the repeal of paragraph 175 in Germany, see Oosterhuis, "Richard von Krafft-Ebing's 'Step-Children of Nature,'" 67–88, and for a broad overview of laws used to prosecute homosexuality in England, see Jeffrey Weeks, *Sex, Politics, and Society*, 99–102, and in the United States, see Katz, *Gay/Lesbian Almanac*, 54–58, 68–133.

66. There is considerable evidence that homosexual men and women appropriated the naturalistic model for describing their sexualities. See, for example, the case histories compiled in the fourteen editions of Krafft-Ebing's *Psychopathia Sexualis* and in Ellis's *Sexual Inversion*, which, among other volunteered histories, featured Edward Carpenter's sexual history, presented anonymously as "Case VI," 46–47. See also Edward Carpenter, *Homogenic Love* (Manchester, England: Manchester Labour Press, 1895); *Love's Coming of Age: A Series of Papers on the Relations of the Sexes* (Manchester, England: Labour Press, 1896).

67. The quotation is from a letter dated 1899 that appears in Jean Chalon, *Portrait of a Seductress: The World of Natalie Barney*, trans. Carol Barko (New York: Crown, 1979), 47.

68. See, for example, the standard protocols of sound scientific method as outlined in Committee on the Conduct of Science, National Academy of Sciences,

"Methods and Values in Science," *On Being a Scientist* (Washington, D.C.: National Academy Press, 1989).

CHAPTER THREE

1. G. Frank Lydston, "Sexual Perversion, Satyriasis, and Nymphomania," *Philadelphia Medical and Surgical Reporter* 61, no. 11 (September 14, 1889): 285.

2. Charles H. Hughes, "Homo Sexual Complexion Perverts in St. Louis. Note on a Feature of Sexual Psychopathy," *Alienist and Neurologist* 28, no. 4 (November 1907): 487–88.

3. William Lee Howard, "Effeminate Men and Masculine Women," *New York Medical Journal* 71 (May 5, 1900): 686–87; rpt. in *Root of Bitterness: Documents of the Social History of Women,* 2d ed., ed. Nancy F. Cott, Jeanne Boydston, Ann Braude, Lori Ginzberg, and Molly Ladd-Taylor (Boston: Northeastern University Press, 1996), 339.

4. Margaret Otis, "A Perversion Not Commonly Noted," *Journal of Abnormal Psychology* 8 (1913): 112–14.

5. For an overview of censorship campaigns from this period, see Paul Boyer, *Purity in Print: The Vice-Society Movement and Book Censorship in America* (New York, 1968).

6. See Denslow Lewis, *The Gynecological Consideration of the Sexual Act: And an Appendix with an Account of Denslow Lewis,* ed. Marc H. Hollender (Weston, Mass.: MTSL Press, 1970); Denslow is quoted by Hollender in the introduction.

7. See William Noyes, review of *Sexual Inversion, Psychological Review* 4 (1897): 447. The Comstock Act was used to confiscate texts deemed to be obscene and to prosecute those who circulated them. Ironically, given that European medical texts of the time explicitly advocated sexual restraint, many were banned on the grounds that they contained pornographic descriptions of sex. Nevertheless, nineteenth-century American physicians generally concurred that the public should be protected from exposure to perversion, even in texts written by medical experts.

8. See review of *Sexual Inversion, American Journal of Insanity* 59 (1902): 182.

9. See Arthur Schopenhauer, "Die Metaphysik der Geschlechtsliebe"; esp. appendix to chapter 44 of *Die Welt als Wille und Vorstellung* (Zurich: Diogenes, 1977), 2: 657–64.

10. See, for example, James G. Kiernan, "Perverted Sexual Instinct," *Chicago Medical Journal and Examiner* 48 (March 1884): 263–65. In 1883, New York doctors J. C. Shaw and G. N. Ferris reported eighteen European and seven American cases in J. C. Shaw and G. N. Ferris, "Perverted Sexual Instinct," *Journal of Nervous and Mental Disease* 10, no. 2 (April 1883): 185–204. The American cases were previously published in Allen W. Hagenbach, "Masturbation as a Cause of Insanity," *The Journal of Nervous and Mental Disease* 6 (1879): 603–12; "Dr. H," "'Gynomania': A Curious Case of Masturbation," *The Medical Record* 19, no. 12 (March 19, 1881): 336; G. Adler Blumer, "A Case of Perverted Sexual Instinct," *American Journal of Insanity* (1882): 22–35; William A. Hammond, *Sexual Impotence in the Male* (New York: Bermingham, 1883); and P. M. Wise, "Case of Sexual Perversion," *The Alienist and Neurologist* 4 no. 1 (January 1883): 87–91.

11. See Blumer, "A Case of Perverted Sexual Instinct."

12. See Lydston, "Sexual Perversion, Satyriasis, and Nymphomania," 285. See also Lydston, "Asexualization in the Prevention of Crime," *Medical News* 68 (May 23, 1896): 576.

13. Lydston was not alone in performing such experimental procedures for curbing homosexual desire. Although I have been unable to ascertain actual or even approximate numbers of such cases, I do know that Lydston borrowed techniques developed by the American gynecologist Isaac Baker Brown, who performed hundreds of genital surgeries, most of them on women, including extirpation of the ovaries and clitoridectomies, in order to curb what he considered excessive lust. Among his patients so afflicted were women with a history of homosexual relations. For histories of psychosexual surgery to curb sexual perversions including homosexuality, see Graham Barker-Benfield, *The Horrors of a Half-Known Life;* Jeffrey Moussaieff Masson, *A Dark Science: Women, Sexuality and Psychiatry in the Nineteenth Century* (New York: Farrar, Strauss, and Giroux, 1986); Vern L. Bullough and Martha Voght, "Homosexuality and the 'Secret Sin' in Pre-Freudian America," *Journal of the History of Medicine and Allied Sciences* 28, no. 2 (April 1973): 143–55; Carol Groneman, "Nymphomania."

14. See James G. Kiernan, "Psychical Treatment of Congenital Sexual Inversion," *Review of Insanity and Nervous Disease* 4 no. 4 (June 1894): 295. For similar attitudes, see Kiernan, "Sexual Perversion," *Detroit Lancet* 7, no. 11 (May 1884): 483–84 and "Perverted Sexual Instinct."

15. For a report of Pilcher's castrations, see F. C. Cave, "Report of Sterilization in the Kansas State Home for Feeble-minded," *Journal of Psycho-Asthenics* 15 (1911): 123–25.

16. See F. E. Daniel, "Should Insane Criminals or Sexual Perverts Be Allowed To Procreate?" *Texas Medical Journal* (August 1893): 255–71, rpt. in *Psychological Bulletin, Medico-Legal Journal* (December 1893), and *Texas Medical Journal* 27, no. 10 (April 1912): 371–72, 376–81, quoted in Katz, *Gay American History,* 135–36.

17. See Harry Clay Sharp, "The Sterilization of Degenerates," *Indiana Board of State Charities* (National Christian League for Promotion of Purity, 1908), 1–2, 6. See also Sharp, "Human Sterilization," *Journal of the American Medical Association* 4, no. 12 (1909), quoted in Katz, *Gay American History,* 143–44. For early American reports on experimental surgeries to curb homosexual behavior, see Charles H. Hughes in "The Gentlemen Degenerate. A Homosexual's Self-Description and Self-Applied Title. Pudic Nerve Section Fails Therapeutically," *Alienist and Neurologist* 25, no. 1 (Feb. 1, 1904): 68–70 and Charles H. Hughes, "An Emasculated Homo-sexual. His Antecedent and Post-Operative Life," *Alienist and Neurologist* 35 (1914): 277–80. On the effects of surgical castration on criminal and sexual behavior in general, see Hunter McGuire and G. Frank Lydston, "Sexual Crimes among Southern Negroes"; Lydston, "Asexualization in the Prevention of Crime"; Martin W. Barr, *Mental Defectives: Their History, Treatment, and Training* (Philadelphia: P. Blakiston's Sons & Company, 1904), 195–96; F. C. Cave, "Report of Sterilization in the Kansas State Home for Feebleminded." A classic source on the use of genital surgery to control women's perverse sexual behavior is Isaac Baker Brown, *On the Curability of Certain Forms of Insanity, Epilepsy, Catalepsy and Hysteria in Females.* On the history of coercive genital surgeries to control women, see Carol Groneman, "Nymphomania."

18. For background on the content of states' eugenic sterilization laws and rates of sterilization by category of diagnosis, see Mark Haller, *Eugenics*, 50, 135–41. For more on the eugenics movement in the United States and legislative campaigns to legalize sterilization, see Paul Popenoe and Roswell Hill Johnson, *Applied Eugenics* (New York: Macmillan, 1920); Nicole Hahn Rafter, *White Trash;* John David Smith, *Minds Made Feeble;* Daniel Kevles, *In the Name of Eugenics;* Stefan Kuhl, *The Nazi Connection: Eugenics, American Racism, and German National Socialism* (New York: Oxford University Press, 1994); Stephen J. Gould, "Carrie Buck's Daughter," in *The Flamingo's Smile*, 306–18; Garland E. Allen, "Eugenics and American Social History, 1880–1950," *Genome* 31 (1989): 885–89; Phillip R. Reilly, *The Surgical Solution: A History of Involuntary Sterilization in the United States* (Baltimore, Md.: Johns Hopkins University Press, 1991); and Stephen Trombley, *The Right to Reproduce: A History of Coercive Sterilization* (London: Weidenfeld and Nicolson, 1988). For later reports on castrations of convicted sex criminals, see Marie E. Kopp, "Surgical Treatment as Sex Crime Prevention Measure," *Journal of Criminal Law and Criminology* 28 (January–February 1938): 692–706; Karl M. Bowman, *Final Report on California Sexual Deviation Research* (Sacramento: California State Assembly, 1954).

19. P. M. Wise, "Case of Sexual Perversion." For a follow-up report on the case, see James G. Kiernan, "Original Communications. Insanity. Lecture on Sexual Perversion," *Detroit Lancet* 7, no. 11 (May 1884): 482–83.

20. For Slater's own account of her life, see the *Narrative of Lucy Ann Lobdell, the Female Hunter of Delaware and Sullivan Counties* (New York: published for the author, 1855). The text is available at the Library of Congress. Among tales of adventure, the short narrative makes a feminist appeal for women's equality with men. It is quoted at length in Katz, *Gay American History,* 214–21. For additional cases of women who passed as men around this same time, see Katz, 225–78.

21. Slater died in the Willard Asylum around 1890. According to an undated newspaper clipping attached to the doctor's record of Slater, his "crazy" wife suffered from poor health after his death. See also James G. Kiernan, "Psychological Aspects of the Sexual Appetite," *Alienist and Neurologist* 12 (April 1891): 202–3. For text of the clipping, see Katz, *Gay American History,* 601, n. 27.

22. Allan McLane Hamilton, "The Civil Responsibility of Sexual Perverts," *American Journal of Insanity* 52, no. 4 (April 1896): 503–9. The case is excerpted in Katz, *Gay American History,* 60–64, with the quotation appearing on 61.

23. For reports of the Alice Mitchell case, see T. G. Comstock, "Alice Mitchell of Memphis; A Case of Sexual Perversion or 'Urning' (a Paranoiac)," *Medical Times: The Journal of the American Medical Profession* 20 (1892): 170–73; Krafft-Ebing, *Psychopathia Sexualis,* 550. Subsequent mention of the case occurred in O. D. Cauldwell, "Lesbian Lover Murder," *Sexology* (July 1950) and Frank Caprio, *Female Homosexuality: A Psychodynamic Study of Lesbianism,* foreword by Karl M. Bowman (New York: Evergreen Black Cat, Grove Press, 1962), 175–76. For an analysis of the interlocking narratives about the Mitchell case in legal, medical, and popular texts, see Lisa Duggan, "The Trials of Alice Mitchell: Sexology and the Lesbian Subject in Turn-of-the-Century America," *Signs* 18, no. 4 (Summer 1993): 791–814.

24. See, for example, Cesare Lombroso and Gillaume Ferrero, *The Female Offender;* Pauline Tarnowsky, *Étude anthropométrique sur les prostituées et les voleuses;*

Georges Cuvier, "Faites sur le cadavre d'une femme connue à Paris et à Londres sous le mon de Venus Hottentotte," *Memoires du Musée Nationale d'histoire Naturelle* 3 (1817): 259–74; Henri de Blainville, "Sur une femme de la race Hottentotte," *Bulletin du Societe Philomatique de Paris* (1816): 183–90; W. H. Flower and James Murie, "Account of the Dissection of a Bushwoman." See also John Marshall, "On the Brain of a Bushwoman."

25. William A. Hammond, "The Disease of the Scythians," *American Journal of Neurology and Psychiatry* 1, no. 3 (August 1882): 339–55.

26. Dr. A. B. Holder, "The Bote: Description of a Peculiar Sexual Perversion found among North American Indians," *New York Medical Journal* 50, no. 23 (December 7, 1889): 623–25.

27. Alfred Louis Kroeber, "Handbook of the Indians of California," *U.S. Bureau of American Ethnology Bulletin,* no. 78 (Washington, D.C.: U.S. Govt. Printing Office, 1925), 46, 190, 497, 500–501, 647, 728–29, 748–49, 803.

28. In 1907, a St. Louis neurologist, Charles Hughes, appropriated the term "miscegenation" to describe the intermingling of black and white homosexual men. Charles H. Hughes, "The Homo Sexual Complexion Perverts in St. Louis."

29. See Lawrence Birken, *Consuming Desire: Sexual Science and the Emergence of a Culture of Abundance, 1871–1914* (Ithaca: Cornell University Press, 1988), which traces the discursive shift among sexologists from an early emphasis on (re)production and sexual restraint in the nineteenth century to the twentieth-century valorization of capitalist consumption and hedonism in the United States. For background on the growth of American cities and changes in sexual norms, see Christine Stansell, *City of Women: Sex and Class in New York, 1789–1860* (New York: Alfred Knopf, 1986); Kathy Peiss, *Cheap Amusements: Working Women and Leisure in the Turn of the Century New York* (Philadelphia: Temple University Press, 1986); and Joanne J. Meyerowitz, *Women Adrift: Independent Wage Earners in Chicago, 1880–1930* (Chicago: University of Chicago Press, 1988).

30. Krafft-Ebbing, *Psychopathia Sexualis,* 7.

31. The Comstock Act was officially titled "An Act for the Suppression of Trade in, and Circulation of Obscene Literature and Articles of Immoral Use."

32. For background on anti-vice vigilance movements, see Timothy Gilfoyle, "The Moral Origins of Political Surveillance: The Preventive Society in New York City, 1867–1918," *American Quarterly* 38, no. 4 (1986): 635–52 and *City of Eros: New York, Prostitution, and the Commercialization of Sex* (New York: W. W. Norton and Company, 1992); David Pivar, *Purity Crusade, Sexual Morality, and Social Control, 1868–1900* (Westport, Conn.: Greenwood, 1973); and Paul S. Boyer, *Purity in Print.*

33. For more on the anti-homosexual activities of the New York Society for the Suppression of Vice, see Chauncey, *Gay New York,* 138–49, 230–31.

34. See George M. Beard, *Practical Treatise on Nervous Exhaustion* (New York: W. Wood, 1880); *American Nervousness* (1881; rpt. New York: Arno Press, 1972); and *Sexual Neurasthenia (Nervous Exhaustion): Its Hygiene, Causes, Symptoms, and Treatment, with a Chapter on Diet for the Nervous,* ed. A. D. Rockwell (NY: Treat, 1884). For more on Beard's significance and his reception by European doctors, see Charles E. Rosenberg, "The Place of George M. Beard in Nineteenth-Century Psychiatry," *Bulletin of the History of Medicine* 26 (1962): 245–59 and John H. Smith, "Abulia."

NOTES TO PAGES 91–94

35. See J. L. Caspar and Carl Liman, *Handbuch der Gerlichtichen Medicin* (Berlin: Hirschwald, 1889), 1:173. The text was partially translated by the British homosexual John Addington Symonds, who collaborated with Havelock Ellis on the first edition of *Sexual Inversion*. See John Addington Symonds, *A Problem of Modern Ethics* (London: no publisher, 1896), 116, quoted in Jonathan Katz, *Gay American History*, 574, n. 40.

36. Paul Näcke, "Der homosexuelle Markt in New-York," *Archiv für Kriminal-Anthropologie und Kriminalistik* 22 (1906): 277, quoted in Katz, *Gay American History*, 48.

37. Havelock Ellis, *Sexual Inversion*, 3d ed., 350–51.

38. Allan McLane Hamilton, "Insanity in its Medico-Legal Bearings," in *A System of Legal Medicine*, ed. A. M. Hamilton and Lawrence Godkin, 3 vols. (New York: Treat, 1894–97), 2:49–50; Lydston, "Sexual Perversion, Satyriasis, and Nymphomania," 285. For other sources by physicians commenting on the preponderance of homosexuality in American cities around the turn of the century, see Katz, *Gay American History*, 39–53.

39. The eugenical impetus to mark a sharp distinction between degenerates and normal people led to the deployment of techniques by criminal anthropologists and physicians to determine the visible characteristics that distinguished the "primitive" races as well as a host degenerate types from the general population. Well into the twentieth century, many feared these signs would be harder to detect because of "interbreeding." For examples in the scientific literature that reveal ongoing anxiety about racial passing see Earnest A. Hooton, "Observations and Queries as to the Effect of Race Mixture on Certain Physical Characteristics," Jon Alfred Mjoen, "Harmonic and Disharmonic Racecrossings," Maurice Fishberg, "Intermarriage Between Jews and Christians," W. F. Willcox, "Distribution and Increase of Negroes in the United States," Frederick L. Hoffman, "The Problems of Negro-White Intermixture and Intermarriage," in *Eugenics in Race and State*, Vol. 2: *Scientific Papers of the Second International Congress of Eugenics* (Baltimore: The Williams and Wilkins Company, 1923). See also W. A. Plecker, "Virginia's Effort to Preserve Racial Integrity" and Irene Barnes Taeuber, "Assortative Mating for Color in the American Negro," in *A Decade of Progress in Eugenics: Scientific Papers of the Third International Congress of Eugenics (1932)* (Baltimore: The Williams and Wilkins Company, 1934), 105–12, 124–28. For an ethnographic and anthropometric analysis of racial passing conducted by an African American female graduate student of Earnest Hooton in the 1930s, see Caroline Bond Day, *A Study of Some Negro-White Families in the United States* (Cambridge, Mass.: Peabody Museum/Harvard University Press, 1932). For later discussions of the nature and extent of racial passing in the United States, see John H. Burma, "The Measurement of Negro 'Passing,'" *American Journal of Sociology* 52 (1946–47): 18–22; E. W. Eckard, "How Many Negroes 'Pass'?" *American Journal of Sociology* 52 (1946–47): 498–500.

40. Irving C. Rosse, "Sexual Hypochondriasis and Perversion of the Genesic Instinct," *Journal of Nervous and Mental Disease*, whole ser. vol. 19, new ser. vol. 17, no. 11 (November 1892): 799–807. The article is excerpted in Katz, *Gay American History*, 40–41.

41. Ibid., 806.

42. Ibid., 802.

43. For comparisons of homosexuality in animals and humans from this general period, see Edward J. Kempf, "The Social and Sexual Behavior of Infra-human Primates with Some Comparable Facts in Human Behavior," *The Psychoanalytic Review* 4 (April 1918): 127–54; Gilbert V. Hamilton, "A Study of Sexual Tendencies in Monkeys and Baboons."

44. Rosse, 799.

45. Ibid., 807.

46. Charles H. Hughes, "Postscript to Paper on 'Erotopathia': An Organization of Colored Erotopaths," *Alienist and Neurologist* 14, no. 4 (October 1893): 731–32. Another account of the secret practices of inverts was published by psychologist Colin A. Scott in 1896. Writing on "Sex and Art," with the assistance of his mentor, G. Stanley Hall of Clark University, Scott described "coffee clatches" attended by "peculiar societies of inverts," where men wore women's aprons and gathered to "knit, gossip and crochet." Scott also noted the presence of "fairies" in New York City, who like their European counterparts, had a secret organization that assembled extravagant drag balls. In contrast to Hughes, Scott said nothing about race-mixing within invert societies. See Colin A. Scott, "Sex and Art" in the *American Journal of Psychology* 7, 2 (January 1896): 216.

47. Hughes, "Erotopathia," 732.

48. Charles H. Hughes, "The Homo Sexual Complexion Perverts in St. Louis."

49. Quoted in Hirschfeld, *Die Homosexualität des Mannes und des Weibes*, 550–54, which is also quoted in Katz, *Gay American History*, 51.

50. For more on the backlash against lesbianism in the context of the New Woman, see Esther Newton, "The Mythic Mannish Lesbian: Radclyffe Hall and the New Woman," in *Hidden from History*, ed. Duberman, Vicinus, and Chauncey, 281–93; Carroll Smith-Rosenberg, "Discourses of Sexuality and Subjectivity: The New Woman, 1870–1936," in *Hidden from History*, 264–80; Carroll Smith-Rosenberg, "The New Woman as Androgyne: Social Disorder and Gender Crisis, 1870–1936," in *Disorderly Conduct: Visions of Gender in Victorian America* (New York: Alfred A. Knopf, 1985), 245–96; Nancy Cott, *The Grounding of Modern Feminism* (New Haven: Yale University Press, 1987).

51. William Lee Howard, "Effeminate Men and Masculine Women."

52. L. Pierce Clark, *A Critical Digest of Some of the New Work Upon Homosexuality in Man and Woman,* reprinted from *State Hospital Bulletin* (November 1914), (Utica, N.Y.: State Hospital Press, 1914).

53. Herbert J. Claiborne, "Hypertrichosis in Women: Its Relation to Bisexuality (Hermaphroditism): With Remarks on Bisexuality in Animals, Especially Man," *New York Medical Journal* 99 (1914): 1181.

54. Douglas C. McMurtrie, "Principles of Homosexuality and Sexual Inversion in the Female," *American Journal of Urology* 9 (1913): 147.

55. George Chauncey, Jr., "From Sexual Inversion to Homosexuality," 107.

56. For more on the pro-nativist attitudes of the time, see John Higham, *Strangers in the Land: Patterns of American Nativism, 1860–1925* (New Brunswick: Rutgers University Press, 1955).

57. Edward A. Ross, "The Causes of Race Superiority," *Annals of the American Academy of Political and Social Science* 18 (July 1, 1901): 67–89. For an example of scientific studies of "Old American" stock, see Ales Hrdlicka, *The Old Americans* (Baltimore: The Williams and Wilkins Co., 1925).

58. For the text of Roosevelt's 1905 speech see Myer Solis-Cohen in *Life Knowledge or Women's Responsibilities and Duties at all Periods of Life* (Philadelphia: Uplift Publishing Company, 1909), 147, 149. Other writings on the subject include Theodore Roosevelt, "Race Decadence," *Outlook* 97 (April 8, 1911); Roosevelt, "A Premium on Race Suicide," *Outlook* 105 (September 20, 1911); Roosevelt, "The Greatest American Problem," *Delineator* (June 1907): 966–67; Miriam King and Steven Ruggles, "American Immigration, Fertility, and Race Suicide at the Turn of the Century," *Journal of Interdisciplinary History* 20 (1990): 347–69; Thomas G. Dyer, *Theodore Roosevelt and the Idea of Race* (Baton Rouge: Louisiana University Press, 1980).

59. For background on the appeal of eugenics across a broad political spectrum in the United States, see Diane B. Paul, "Eugenics and the Left," *Journal of the History of Ideas* (October 1984): 567–90 and *Controlling Human Heredity: 1865 to the Present* (Atlantic Highlands, N.J.: Humanities Press, 1995); Michael Freeden, "Eugenics and Progressive Thought: A Study in Ideological Affinity," *Historical Journal* 22 (1979): 645–71; and Kevles, *In the Name of Eugenics*, chapter 2. For an analysis of the complex and precarious alliance between feminists and eugenicists, see Linda Gordon, *Woman's Body, Woman's Right: A Social History of Birth Control in America* (New York: Penguin Books, 1974), 274–90; Ellen Chesler, *Woman of Valor: Margaret Sanger and the Birth Control Movement in America* (New York: Simon and Schuster, 1992); Alice Wexler, *Emma Goldman: An Intimate Life* (New York: Pantheon Books, 1984); Richard Drinnon, *Rebel in Paradise* (Boston: Beacon Press, 1961); Carole R. McCann, *Birth Control Politics in the United States, 1916–1945* (Ithaca Cornell University Press, 1994).

60. Such an attitude was reiterated in 1929, when the Los Angeles psychiatrist Aaron Rosanoff wrote: "The conventional attitude toward homosexual behavior is quite irrational. It is regarded as a sin and a crime, and homosexuals, like heterosexuals, are officially permitted no other outlet for their sexual energies than through marriage. This results not only in untold misery to the patients and their wives, but also in the perpetuation by heredity of homosexual traits—the very thing that conventional society would wish to avoid. It would seem more rational not only to ignore homosexual behavior, as being a matter of concern only to the individual, but also actually to encourage it, on eugenic grounds, to the full extent of the tendencies in that direction existing in the subjects concerned." Aaron Rosanoff, "Human Sexuality, Normal and Abnormal, from a Psychiatric Point of View," *Urologic and Cutaneous Review* 33 (1929): 523–50.

61. See Havelock Ellis, "Sexual Inversion in Women," *Alienist and Neurologist* 16, no. 2 (April 1895): 158. See also, Ellis, "A Note on the Treatment of Sexual Inversion," *Alienist and Neurologist* 17 (July 1896): 258–59.

62. See John Duncan Quackenbos, "Hypnotic Suggestion in the Treatment of Sexual Perversions and Moral Anaesthesia: A Personal Experience," *Transactions of the New Hampshire Medical Society* (1899): 69, 72, 75, 78–80, quoted in Katz, *Gay American History*, 144–45.

63. For more on the agenda of social ameliorationists involving sexuality, see Allan Brandt, *No Magic Bullet: A Social History of Venereal Disease in the United States Since 1800* (New York: Oxford University Press, 1985); John C. Burnham, "The Progressive Era Revolution in American Attitudes Toward Sex," *Journal of American History* 59 (March 1973): 885–908; Timothy Gilfoyle, *City of Eros;* Donna Haraway, *Primate Visions: Gender, Race, and Nature in the World of Modern Science* (New York: Routledge, 1989); Paul Robinson, *Modernization of Sex.*

64. For more on the idiom of adjustment and the widespread application of social engineering during the Progressive period, see Haraway, *Primate Visions,* 66–67. For works dealing with Progressive responses to marriage and divorce patterns see Elaine Tyler May, *Great Expectations: Marriage and Divorce in Post-Victorian America* (Chicago: University of Chicago Press, 1980) and William L. O'Neill, *Divorce in the Progressive Era* (New Haven: Yale University Press, 1967).

65. Besides focusing on sexual maladjustments, the mental hygiene movement also concentrated on preventing and treating mental deficiency, criminality, psychoneuroses, epilepsy, juvenile delinquency, family unhappiness, divorce, alcoholism, and, following World War One, shell-shock. Inspired by *A Mind that Found Itself,* Clifford Beers's 1910 expose on the awful conditions under which asylum patients lived, the National Committee for Mental Hygiene also agitated for reform of state mental hospitals that paralleled the prison reform movement of the time. Both sought to eliminate the barbaric and cruel conditions faced by patients and inmates, and favored methods for rehabilitating them. See Clifford Beers, *A Mind that Found Itself: An Autobiography* (Garden City, N.Y.: Doubleday, Doran and Co., 1937). For more on the mental hygiene movement and the expansion of the psychiatric profession during this period, see Elizabeth Lunbeck, *The Psychiatric Persuasion: Knowledge, Gender, and Power in Modern America* (Princeton, N.J.: Princeton University Press, 1994). For background on the expansion of the mental hygiene movement following World War One, see Walter Bromberg, *Psychiatry Between the Wars, 1918–1945: A Recollection* (Westport, Conn.: Greenwood Press, 1982).

66. For background on Freud's influence on American psychiatry see Nathan G. Hale, Jr., *Freud and the Americans: The Beginning of Psychoanalysis in the United States, 1876–1917* (New York, 1971) and *The Rise and Crisis of Psychoanalysis in the United States: Freud and the Americans, 1917–1985* (New York: Oxford University Press, 1995).

67. For more on Meyer's background, see Adolf Meyer, *The Commonsense Psychiatry of Dr. Adolf Meyer,* ed. Alfred Lief (New York: McGraw-Hill, 1948); Walter Bromberg, *Psychiatry Between the Wars;* Wendell Muncie, *Psychobiology and Psychiatry,* 2d ed. (St. Louis: C. V. Mosby, 1948), 522; J. K. Hall, ed., *One Hundred Years of American Psychiatry* (New York: Columbia University Press, 1944), 168–69, 500.

68. For an analysis of the historical emergence of the term personality, see Warren I. Susman, "'Personality' and the Making of Twentieth Century Culture," in *New Directions in American Intellectual History,* ed. John Higham and Paul K. Conklin (Baltimore: Johns Hopkins University Press, 1979), 212–26. For its history in terms of American psychiatric thought, see Lunbeck, *The Psychiatric Persuasion,* 68–69; and Ruth Leys, "Types of One: Adolf Meyer's Life Chart and the Representation of Individuality," *Representations* 34 (Spring 1991): 1–28, 6. For analyses of the contrasting

definitions of personality in the disciplines of psychology and psychiatry, see Kurt Danziger, *Constructing the Subject: Historical Origins of Psychological Research* (Cambridge: Cambridge University Press, 1990), 159–64.

69. For a brief analysis of Meyer's sexual conservatism, see Hale, *Rise and Crisis of Psychoanalysis*, 170–71.

70. See, for example, Adolf Meyer, "The Role of Mental Factors in Psychiatry," *American Journal of Insanity* 65 (1908–9): 39. For more on Meyer's general contributions to American psychiatry, see Henry Alden Bunker, "Psychiatric Literature," in *One Hundred Years of American Psychiatry*, ed. J. K. Hall, 228–32; John C. Whitehorn, "Psychiatric Research," in *One Hundred Years of American Psychiatry*, 168–69, 172; A. H. Chapman, *Harry Stack Sullivan: His Life and his Work* (New York: G. P. Putnam's Sons, 1976), 39–41. For an analysis of Meyer's functionalist psychiatry and its contentious relationship with both behaviorism and psychoanalysis, see Ruth Leys, "Meyer, Watson, and the Dangers of Behaviorism," *Journal of the History of the Behavioral Sciences* 20, no. 2 (1984): 128–49; Leys, "Meyer, Jung, and the Limits of Association," *Bulletin of the History of Medicine* 59, no. 3 (1985): 345–60; Leys, "Meyer's Dealings with Ernest Jones: A Chapter in the History of the American Response to Psychoanalysis," *Journal of the History of Behavioral Sciences* 17, 4 (1981): 445–65.

71. For an interpretation of Meyer's attempt to reconcile individual freedom and social determinism, see Leys, "Types of One."

72. See Abraham A. Brill, "The Conception of Homosexuality."

73. See Hirschfeld, *Homosexualität des Mannes und des Weibes*. A translated passage on adjustment therapy is quoted in Katz, *Gay American History*, 151–53.

74. See, for example, Aaron J. Rosanoff, "A Theory of Chaotic Sexuality," *American Journal of Psychiatry* 92 (1935): 35–41; Clarence P. Oberndorf, "Diverse Forms of Homosexuality," *Urologic and Cutaneous Review* 33 (1929): 518–23; and Abraham L. Wolbarst, "Sexual Perversions: Their Medical and Social Implications," *Medical Journal and Record* 134 (1931): 5–9, 62–65.

75. Hirschfeld reported his anecdotal findings in *Die Homosexualität des Mannes und des Weibes*, 550–54.

76. Otto Spengler, Letter published in *Monatsberichte des Wissenschaftlich-humanitaren Komitees* 5 (1906): 151, also quoted in Katz, *Gay American History*, 381.

77. Georg Merzbach, *Monatsberichte des Wissenschaftlich-humanitaren Komitees* 6 (1907): 76–77, also quoted in Katz, *Gay American History*, 381–82.

78. Anonymous, Letter from Boston, *Monatsberichte des Wissenschaftlich-humanitaren Komitees* 6 (1907): 98–99; reprinted in Hirschfeld, *Die Homosexualität des Mannes und des Weibes*, 553, also quoted in Katz, *Gay American History*, 382–83.

79. Edward I. Prime Stevenson [Xavier Mayne, pseud.], *The Intersexes: A History of Similisexualism as a Problem in Social Life* (1908; New York: Arno, 1975), quoted in Katz, *Gay American History*, 146–48.

80. Earl Lind, *Autobiography of an Androgyne* (New York: Medico-Legal Press, 1918).

81. The founding charter of the Chicago Society for Human Rights is reprinted, together with founding member Henry Gerber's oral history of its establishment, in Katz, *Gay American History*, 385–93.

82. Katz, *Gay American History*, 389.

83. Margaret Otis, "A Perversion Not Commonly Noted." For an analysis of how racial distinctions between African American and white women inmates functioned as the privileged difference in discourse about incarcerated females, see Estelle Freedman, "The Prison Lesbian: Race, Class, and the Construction of the Aggressive Female Homosexual, 1915–1965," *Feminist Studies* 22, no. 2 (Summer 1996): 397–423. For an analysis of the growing concern about same-sex relationships between school girls during this period, see Nancy Sahli, "'Smashing': Women's Relations Before the Fall," *Chrysalis* 8 (1979): 17–27. Warnings about lesbianism in convents, boarding schools, prisons, and brothels were reiterated often. See, for example, Jacobus X. [pseud.], *Crossways of Sex: A Study in Eroto-Pathology* (New York: American Anthropological Society, n.d.); Maurice Chideckel, *Female Sex Perversion: The Sexually Aberrated Woman as She Is* (New York: Eugenics Publishing Company, 1938); and La Forest Potter, *Strange Loves: A Study of Sexual Abnormalities* (New York: Padell Book Company, 1933).

84. For more on the Albion situation, see Ruth Alexander, *The Girl Problem: Female Sexual Delinquency in New York, 1900–1930* (Ithaca: Cornell University Press, 1995).

85. Charles A. Ford, "Homosexual Practices of Institutionalized Females," *Journal of Abnormal and Social Psychiatry* 23 (1929): 442–48.

86. *The Social Evil in Chicago; A Study of Existing Conditions with Recommendations* (Chicago: Gunthorp-Warren, 1911), 39, 56, 126, 139, 240, 247, 290–91, 295–98, 305, 348.

CHAPTER FOUR

1. Of the major marital hygiene surveys of the 1920s, husbands were consulted in only one, conducted by the psychiatrist Gilbert V. Hamilton and published as *A Research in Marriage* (New York: Albert and Charles Boni, Inc., 1929). In the 1930s, subsequent psychometricians labored to hear from both men and women on the subject. The most prominent marital happiness survey of the 1930s was that of Lewis M. Terman, *Psychological Factors in Marital Happiness* (New York: McGraw-Hill, 1938).

2. Ben Lindsey and Wainwright Evans, *The Companionate Marriage* (New York: Boni and Liveright, 1927).

3. Ibid., v, 394–95.

4. Lisa Duggan, "The Social Reinforcement of Heterosexuality and Lesbian Resistance in the 1920s," in *Class, Race and Sex: The Dynamics of Control,* ed. Amy Swerdlow and Hanah Lessinger (Boston: G. K Hall, 1983), 82. See also Christina Simmons, "Companionate Marriage and the Lesbian Threat," *Frontiers* 4, no. 3 (Fall 1979): 54–59.

5. Lindsey and Evans, *Companionate Marriage,* 10.

6. Th. H. Van de Velde, *Ideal Marriage: Its Physiology and Technique* (New York: Random House, 1926), 11.

7. Th. H. Van de Velde, *Sexual Tensions in Marriage: Their Origins, Prevention and Treatment* (New York: Random House, 1928), 13.

8. Ibid.

9. Ibid., 12.

10. Floyd Dell, *Love in the Machine Age: A Psychological Study of the Transition from Patriarchal Society* (New York: Farrar, 1930).

11. For examples of feminist and leftist critiques, see Charlotte Perkins Gilman, *Herland* (1915; New York: Pantheon Books, 1979) and *Women and Economics*, ed. Carl N. Degler (1898; New York: Harper and Row, 1966); Emma Goldman, *Living My Life* (New York: Dover, 1971); Crystal Eastman, *Crystal Eastman: On Women and Revolution*, ed. Blanche Weisen Cook (New York: Oxford University Press, 1978); Elaine Showalter, ed., *These Modern Women: Autobiographical Essays from the Twenties* (Old Westbury, N.Y.: Feminist Press, 1978). Historical analysis of the "first wave" feminist critique of traditional marriage and family relations is presented in Nancy Cott, *Grounding of Modern Feminism;* Mary Ryan, *Womanhood in America: From Colonial Times to the Present*, 2d ed. (New York: New Viewpoints, 1979); Paula Fass, *The Damned and the Beautiful: American Youth in the 1920s* (New York, 1977); and Candace Falk, *Love, Anarchy, and Emma Goldman*, 2d ed. (New Brunswick: Rutgers University Press, 1990).

12. For historical analyses of the backlash against feminism and lesbianism during the 1920s, see Esther Newton, "The Mythic Mannish Lesbian"; Carroll Smith-Rosenberg, "Discourses of Sexuality and Subjectivity"; Nancy Sahli, "'Smashing'"; Lisa Duggan, "Social Enforcement of Heterosexuality," and Rayna Rapp and Ellen Ross, "The Twenties' Backlash: Compulsory Heterosexuality, the Consumer Family, and the Waning of Feminism," in *Class, Race and Sex: The Dynamics of Control*, ed. Amy Swerdlow and Hanah Lessinger (Boston: G. K. Hall, 1983), 93–107.

13. For example, see John F. W. Meagher, "Homosexuality: Its Psychobiological and Psychopathological Significance," *The Urologic and Cutaneous Review* 33 (1929): 510–18; Noah E. Aronstam, M. D., "The Well of Loneliness: An Impression," *The Urologic and Cutaneous Review* 33 (1929), 543. For subsequent elaborations on these themes, see Maurice Chideckel, *Female Sex Perversion;* Edwood L. Fantis, "Homosexuality in Growing Girls," *Sexology* 2 (February 1935): 349; Edward Podolsky, "'Homosexual Love' in Women," *Popular Medicine* 1 (February 1935): 375.

14. Katharine Bement Davis, *Factors in the Sex Lives of Twenty-two Hundred Women* (New York: Harper and Brothers, 1929). An earlier study had been undertaken by Clelia Mosher, a graduate student at the University of Wisconsin in 1892, which surveyed college-educated married women in order to allow Mosher to give better sexual advice to young women who sought her counsel prior to marrying. Mosher used a questionnaire and interviews to ask her subjects about their sexual knowledge, their sexual relations with their husbands, and their experiences of orgasm. She found that, among the forty-seven women who responded, few knew much about sex before they married, a majority desired sexual intercourse, and most regularly experienced orgasm during sex. Although about half of her subjects stated that pleasure itself was a worthy reason for sexual relations, it appears she did not ask any questions about sexual relations between women. The study was unearthed by Stanford historian Carl Degler in 1974, who discussed it in his famous article "What Ought to Be and What Was: Women's Sexuality in the Nineteenth Century," *American Historical Review* 79 (December 1974): 1467–90, and was subsequently published as Clelia Duel Mosher, *The Mosher Survey: Sexual Attitudes of Forty-Five Victorian*

Women, ed. James Mahood and Kristine Wenburg (New York: Arno Press, 1980). Bullough describes the Mosher research in *Science in the Bedroom,* 107–9.

15. On falling birth rates in the nineteenth-century, see Daniel Scott Smith, "Family Limitation, Sexual Control, and Domestic Feminism in Victorian America," *Feminist Studies* 1 (Winter–Spring 1973): 40–57; Gordon, *Woman's Body,* 47–115.

16. For data on age at first marriage, see John Modell et al., "The Timing of Marriage in the Transition to Adulthood," in John Demos and Saranne Boocock, eds., *Turning Points: Historical and Sociological Essays on the Family* (Chicago: University of Chicago Press, 1978), 12. Other studies show that approximately eighteen percent of women born between 1900 and 1909 married but were childless, and 7.3 percent remained single and childless. See Cott, *Grounding of Modern Feminism,* 138, n. 35, analyzing Paul C. Glick, Table 2, "Updating the Life Cycle of the Family," *Journal of Marriage and the Family* 39 (Feb. 1977): 8.

17. In his study of 5,940 women, Alfred Kinsey found that women who were born from 1900 to 1909 (i.e., those who became sexually active in the 1920s) had more premarital coitus than had their mothers' generation. Fourteen percent of women born before 1900 reported having premarital sexual intercourse before the age of twenty-five, compared to thirty-six percent born from 1900 to 1909. Furthermore, Kinsey found that college-educated women were more likely than others to be sexually active, reversing a trend from those born before 1900. The birth cohort for pre-1900 consisted of 456 women, and the 1900–1909 cohort was 784 women. See Alfred Kinsey et al., *Sexual Behavior in the Human Female* (Philadelphia: W. B. Saunders Co., 1953), 242–45, 298–301, 339, 422–24, 461, 529, 553.

18. For a detailed biography of Katharine Bement Davis, see Ellen Fitzpatrick, ed., *Katharine Bement Davis, Early Twentieth-Century Women, and the Study of Sex Behavior* (New York: Garland, 1987), introduction.

19. Katharine Bement Davis described the work of the Laboratory of Social Hygiene in her introduction to Jean Weidensall, *The Mentality of the Criminal Woman* (Baltimore, Md.: Warwick and York, 1916), ix–xiv. Weidensall, who also received her Ph.D. from University of Chicago, directed the Laboratory until it closed in 1918. For more on Davis's experiences at Bedford Hills, see Estelle Freedman, *Their Sister's Keepers* (Ann Arbor, Mich.: University of Michigan Press, 1981) and Nicole Hahn Rafter, *Partial Justice: Women in State Prisons, 1800–1935* (Boston: Northeastern University Press, 1985).

20. In 1912, the Bureau started what became a six-year research project on prostitution in New York City, under the direction of former director of the Chicago Vice Commission, George Kneeland (Davis wrote a chapter on prostitutes at Bedford Hills). This was followed by a study by Abraham Flexner on prostitution in Europe, another by Howard Woolston on prostitution in the United States, and another by Raymond Fosdick on the treatment of prostitutes by European and American police departments. George Kneeland, *Commercialized Prostitution in New York City* (New York: Century, 1913); Abraham Flexner, *Prostitution in Europe* (New York: Century, 1913); Raymond B. Fosdick, *European Police Systems* (New York: Century, 1915); Fosdick, *American Police Systems* (New York: Century, 1921); and Howard B. Woolston, *Prostitution in the United States* (New York: Century, 1921).

21. The American Social Hygiene Association was formed in 1914 through the

merger of the American Vigilance Association and the American Federation of Sex Hygiene. Somewhat more conservative than Rockefeller's Bureau of Social Hygiene, its founding mission was "to promote social health, to advocate high moral standards, to suppress commercialized vice, and to conduct inquiries concerning prostitution and venereal diseases." The Bureau of Social Hygiene had similar aims but also actively advocated sex education. Members of the ASHA and BSH corresponded frequently and tended to cooperate with one another.

22. Katharine Bement Davis to John D. Rockefeller, Jr., April 27, 1927, Box 7, Folder 44, Office of Messrs. Rockefeller, Rockefeller Boards, Rockefeller Archive Center, Pontico Hills, Tarrytown, N.Y.

23. Davis, *Factors*, ix.

24. Ibid., ix.

25. Ibid.

26. Ibid., 78.

27. Marie Kopp, Katharine Davis, and research assistants Ruth Pointer and Ruth Topping were unmarried during the time of the research. Writing for a popular audience in 1928, Davis discussed the situation of single women and defended their efforts to acquire college educations and make social contributions for the greater good of society. The article reported on data gathered during the *Factors* research as to the many reasons single women gave for not marrying. Davis did not in any way disparage marriage, and in fact offered a reassuring tone by stating that "a large majority have no deeply rooted sex antagonism nor aversion to marriage," and by further dispelling beliefs that women chose careers over marriage and that women had few chances to meet men. She simply reported that such a fate was far from disastrous and suggested that it might be ascertained by asking college-educated men why they preferred to marry women without college educations. See Katharine Bement Davis, "Why They Failed to Marry," *Harper's Magazine* 156 (March 28): 460–69, reprinted in Fitzpatrick, ed., *Katharine Bement Davis*.

Reflecting on her own life in an alumnae magazine of the University of Chicago, Davis, at the age of 73, wrote about her experience as a single woman. She humorously described the marriage proposals that she had declined and spoke of her personal life as basically unglamorous: "I have always been friendly with boys and men, I like them, we have been good chums. . . . But I was never the sort with whom men are always falling love. True, I have had a few proposals of marriage, most women have, I fancy. . . . No man ever loved me enough to blow out his brains for me, and I never ran off with any other woman's husband. So you will find no love stories at all in this tale of my life. It is too bad! I will confess now that I would have liked children and grandchildren. I miss them. More than I do a husband. But when I think about it I console myself with the reflection that at least I have been spared any desire to go to Reno." She offers no anecdotes about other intimate relationships she may have had with women or men, leaving the reader to her imagination. Katharine Bement Davis, "Three Score Years and Ten: An Autobiographical Biography," *University of Chicago Magazine* 26 (December 1933): 58; reprinted in *Katharine Bement Davis*, ed. Fitzpatrick.

28. Davis, *Factors*, 277–78.

29. Davis focused on masturbation in an early report of the research, noting that,

among unmarried women, 603 of 1,000 indulged in masturbation at some time. She did not draw conclusions from this fact, preferring instead to simply reveal the responses of her subjects. But her manner of defining masturbation in the questionnaire was designed to be unthreatening, so that subjects would answer the questions honestly, a decision that went a long way toward removing the stigma from masturbation. For example, she defined auto-erotic activity as "sex reveries or day dreaming" that led to "mild excitement or to orgasm, without manipulating the organs," and masturbation was defined as "self-induced sex pleasure [with or without manipulation] carried to the point of orgasm" (which she, in turn, defined as a "convulsive contraction of the muscles of the interior sex organs, followed by definite relaxation"). She further stated that the harms of masturbation had been greatly exaggerated, and she cited eminent specialists who maintained that "masturbation is a normal stage in the development of the sex nature and must be passed through if sexual development is to be complete." Such sentiments were similar to her perspectives on lesbianism, which she defined in unthreatening terms in order to elicit a range of experiences between women, and which posited a definition of lesbianism that, contrary to the dominant beliefs of the day, was not pathological. Katharine Bement Davis, "A Study of Certain Auto-Erotic Practices," *Mental Hygiene* 8, no. 3 (July 1924): 668–723.

30. Davis, *Factors*, 298.

31. Conversely, among the married women without college degrees, a small percentage engaged in homosexuality with overt practices (15.3 percent), compared to those with college degrees who engaged in overt homosexual relations (30.9 percent of the whole group of married women). Davis, *Factors*, 308–9.

32. Ibid., 306, 312.

33. These findings were cited in Frances M. Strakoch, *Factors in the Sex-Life of 700 Psychopathic Women* (Utica: State Hospitals Press, 1934), as well as in other published studies on sex factors in marital happiness, including those of Gilbert V. Hamilton, Robert Latou Dickinson and Lura Beam, Carney Landis, and Louis M. Terman, all of which concerned themselves with whether sexual satisfaction was key to the success of a marriage. See Gilbert V. Hamilton, *A Research in Marriage;* Robert Latou Dickinson and Lura Beam, *A Thousand Marriages: A Medical Study of Sex Adjustment* (Baltimore: The Williams & Wilkins Company, 1931) and *The Single Woman: A Medical Study in Sex Education* (Baltimore: The Williams & Wilkins Company, 1934); Carney Landis, et al., *Sex in Development: A Study of the Growth and Development of the Emotional and Sexual Aspects of Personality Together With Physiological, Anatomical, and Medical Information on a Group of 153 Normal Women and 142 Female Psychiatric Patients* (New York: Paul B. Hoeber, Inc., 1940); Carney Landis, M. Marjorie Bolles and D. Anthony D'Esopo, "Psychological and Physical Concomitants of Adjustment in Marriage," *Human Biology* 12 (1940): 559–65; Lewis M. Terman, *Psychological Factors in Marital Happiness.*

34. Memorandum by Ruth Topping to Lawrence Dunham, February 15, 1930, Rockefeller Foundation Archives, Record Group 176–89, Series 3, Subseries 2, Box 8, Folder 179, Rockefeller Archives Center, Pontico Hills, Tarrytown, New York.

35. Memorandum of Bureau of Social Hygiene to Katharine Bement Davis, July 12, 1933, Rockefeller Foundation Archives, Record Group 176–89, Series 3, Subseries 2, Box 8, Folder 179.

36. For details about the U.S. obscenity case brought against Radclyffe Hall, see Morris L. Ernst and Alan U. Schwartz, *Censorship: The Search for the Obscene* (New York: Macmillan, 1964), Una Troubridge, *The Life of Radclyffe Hall* (New York: Citadel, 1963); Jonathan Ned Katz, *Gay American History*, 398–404.

37. For a detailed history of the establishment of the Committee on Research in Problems of Sex, see Sophie Aberle and George W. Corner, *Twenty-five Years of Sex Research: History of the National Research Council Committee for Research in Problems of Sex, 1922–1947* (Philadelphia: W. B. Saunders, 1953).

38. Donna Haraway discusses the emergence of the National Research Council as an important player in the era of Progressive reform when the scientific study of social systems and behavior became the organizing principle for scores of philanthropic ventures on the grounds that such knowledge would be useful to industry and thus to the nation as a whole. Haraway, *Primate Visions*, 67–68.

39. Request for an Appropriation of $20,000 to the Bureau of Social Hygiene to Be Used in Promoting the Working Out of a Plan for Research in the Field of Sex, Rockefeller Family Archives, Rockefeller Boards, Record Group 1.

40. The CRPS's original statement of purpose was "To conduct, stimulate, foster, systematize and coordinate research on sex problems to the end that conclusions now held may be evaluated and our scientific knowledge in this field increased as rapidly as possible." See First Annual Report of the Committee for Research on Sex Problems of the Division of Medical Sciences, National Research Council, March 1, 1923, Rockefeller Foundation Archives, Record Group 176–89, Series 3, Subseries 2, Box 8, Folder 189, p. 3.

41. See Memorandum of Lawrence Dunham, March 16, 1928, National Research Council Committee on Sex Research, 1927–1928, Rockefeller Foundation Archives, Record Group 176–89, Series 3, Subseries 2, Box 8, Folder 185. For additional evidence of the focus on biological research, see the First and Second Annual Reports of the CRPS, Rockefeller Foundation Archives, Record Group 176–89, Series 3, Subseries 2, Box 8, Folder 189.

42. Prior to 1940, the CRPS received and rejected four proposals aimed specifically at studying homosexuality. The most significant of these was a study proposed in 1935 by the Committee for the Study of Sex Variants, which I discuss at length in chapters 6 and 7. In its early years, the CRPS funded many of its own members, a practice they justified because the Committee was set up as a research team to operate in the field of legitimate sex research. Although this would appear to be a conflict of interest, the CRPS was never challenged on these grounds and in fact defended the policy as a way to gain scientific legitimacy, believing their own members were the most responsible in the field. Among those CRPS members who received funding were Robert Yerkes and Adolf Meyer. For more on the internal workings of the CRPS, see Aberle and Corner, *Twenty-Five Years of Sex Research,* and Haraway, *Primate Visions*, 71, 94, 417.

43. In a 1928 letter to Lawrence Dunham, director of the Bureau of Social Hygiene, Earl Zinn of the CRPS stated that "because of its implications for the social sciences, the NRC realized that it could not sponsor this [Hamilton's] project." This reasoning was reiterated later in a memorandum written by Dunham, detailing a telephone call with Vernon Kellog of the NRC. See Letter by Zinn to Dunham,

March 2, 1928, National Research Council Committee on Sex Research, Rockefeller Foundation Archives, Record Group 195–200, Series 3, Subseries 2, Box 9, Folder 200; and Memorandum of Dunham, March 16, 1928, National Research Council Committee on Sex Research, 1927–1928, Rockefeller Foundation Archives, Record Group 176–189, Series 3, Subseries 2, Box 8, Folder 185.

44. Of course, women's greater dissatisfaction in marriage may be due to their socially reinforced restriction to it, compared to men who sought sexual satisfaction outside of marriage at a higher rate. Hamilton, *A Research in Marriage*, 83, 171, 192, 542–44.

45. Hamilton's studies of nonhuman primates integrated psychoanalytic concepts developed by Freud and psychological concepts developed by Yerkes. See Gilbert V. Hamilton, "Study of Sexual Tendencies in Monkeys and Baboons." For a similar psychoanalytical interpretation of data acquired from homosexuality in nonhuman primates, see Edward J. Kempf, "Social and Sexual Behavior of Infra-human Primates."

46. See Gilbert V. Hamilton, *An Introduction to Objective Psychopathology* (St. Louis: The C. V. Mosby Company, 1925), 316–20; Hamilton, *A Research in Marriage*, 18.

47. Hamilton remarked: "Practically all of the available evidence of my present research suggests that it is in the little girl's relationship to her father or brothers that we are most likely to find the conditioning factors which make for subsequent inability to achieve the orgasm in heterosexual copulation and, in a limited number of cases, for overt homosexuality." Hamilton, *A Research in Marriage*, 295.

48. Ibid., 496–97.

49. Gilbert V. Hamilton and Kenneth MacGowan, *What's Wrong with Marriage: A Study of Two Hundred Husbands and Wives* (New York: Albert and Charles Boni, 1929).

50. Apparently, Hamilton's zeal to publicize his research led him to conduct his own promotional campaign in the popular press that raised the ire of the BSH and the Rockefeller Foundation. In a letter to L. B. Dunham (BSH), Zinn (CRPS) apologized profusely for Hamilton, promising that there would be no further mention of the BSH in publicity about Hamilton's book, referencing *Ladies Home Journal* and *Harper's Magazine* as places he contacted to make sure they omitted the BSH from mention in reviews of *A Research in Marriage*. This apology was passed on in a letter from Dunham to Colonel Arthur Woods of the Rockefeller Foundation, explaining that Hamilton was "peeved" at the BSH for not letting him use the name. Relations between Hamilton and the BSH were strained even before this, when staff members of the BSH perceived Hamilton to be taking advantage of them by appropriating their office furniture and allowing his staff to take vacations before the year was out, thus adding a month of clerical support that was not allocated to him. See Letter by Zinn to Dunham, July 23, 1928, NRC Committee on Sex, Rockefeller Foundation Archives, Record Group 198–200, Series 3, Subseries 2, Box 9, Folder 200; and Dunham to Woods, July 25, 1928, NRC Committee on Sex, Rockefeller Foundation Archives, Record Group 198–200, Series 3, Subseries 2, Box 9, Folder 200.

51. The CRPS, in 1928, established regulations for the guidance of persons in charge of funded research projects that stipulated, among other things, that "because of the popular interest in sex problems and the news value of such subject matter, it

is suggested that no popular reports of results or publicity statements be issued without the approval of the Committee. This does not apply to scientific reports in accredited journals. Here the investigator has entire freedom. However, the Committee would appreciate being informed in advance as to the publication plans so as to secure reprints (other than those supplied to the Committee by the investigator) if desired. The Committee should not be given publicity other than acknowledgment of support, . . . except through Committee action." Regulations proposed by the CRPS, 1927–28, NRC Committee on Sex Research, Rockefeller Foundation Archives, Record Group 176–89, Series 3, Subseries 2, Box 8, Folder 189.

52. Robert Latou Dickinson and Lura Beam, *A Thousand Marriages* and *The Single Woman.*

53. Dickinson's ties to social hygiene organizations were many, although he was not a formal member of any boards or committees other than the Committee on Maternal Health. The National Committee on Maternal Health chairman, Haven Emerson, M.D. was a professor of public health administration at Columbia University and was affiliated with the National Committee for Mental Hygiene. Board member William F. Snow, M.D. was affiliated with the American Social Hygiene Association. Robert T. Frank, an expert on female sex hormones, received funding for research from the National Research Council's Committee on Research in Problems of Sex. See National Research Council Committee on Sex Research, Rockefeller Foundation Archives, Record Group 201–13, Series 3, Subseries 2, Box 10, Folder 202; and Louise Stevens Bryant Collection, Box 6, Smith College, Northampton, Massachusetts.

54. Louise Stevens Bryant, "Preface," in Robert Latou Dickinson and Lura Beam, *The Single Woman,* v. The news column of the *Journal of the American Medical Association* reported in 1926 that the Committee was conducting clinically based research and was offering an honorarium to women in order to secure complete histories, though the amount was not mentioned. The column indicated that the research project "aims to keep patients under supervision for at least one year, and strictly limits itself to advising patients who present medical indications. It is expected that the study of these histories will help answer, scientifically, such questions as 'What are the effects of contraception on subsequent fertility?' and 'What are the relative values of contraceptives as to reliability, simplicity, and harmlessness?'" News column from *Journal of the American Medical Association* 86 (April–June 1926): 1918.

55. For historical accounts of the rocky relationship between Dickinson and Sanger, see Linda Gordon, *Woman's Body, Woman's Right,* 263–73; James Reed, *From Private Vice to Public Virtue: The Birth Control Movement and American Society Since 1830* (New York: Basic Books, 1978), 176–78; Carole R. McCann, *Birth Control Politics in the United States,* 75, 79–81, 213.

56. Gordon, *Woman's Body, Woman's Right,* 262.

57. Reed, *From Private Vice to Public Virtue,* 167.

58. Dickinson contributed some of the Committee's most significant publications, including Robert Latou Dickinson and Louise Steven Bryant, *Control of Contraception: An Illustrated Medical Manual,* (Baltimore: The Williams and Wilkins Company, 1932); Robert Latou Dickinson, *Human Sex Anatomy* (Baltimore: The Williams and Wilkins Company, 1933); Robert Latou Dickinson, *Human Sex Anatomy: A Topographical Hand Atlas* (Baltimore: The Williams and Wilkins Company, 1949).

59. Dickinson participated in the Second and Third International Congresses of Eugenics held at the American Museum of Natural History in New York City in 1921 and 1932. He also wrote several articles on the merits of sterilization particularly among those in the lower socio-economic strata including blacks, poor whites, immigrants, and "mental defectives." See, for example, Robert Latou Dickinson, "Sterilization Without Unsexing," *Journal of the American Medical Association* 92 (February 2, 1929): 373–79; Dickinson, "Simple Sterilization By Cautery Stricture at the Intrauterine Tubal Openings, Compared with Other Openings," *Surgery, Gynecology, and Obstetrics* 23 (1916): 203–14.

60. Quoted in Reed, *From Private Vice to Public Virtue*, 195.

61. The Committee of Fourteen was an extra-governmental anti-vice organization that was established in 1905. During World War I it sent agents to spy on homosexual men in well-known cruising spots along Riverside Drive, Broadway, Central Park West, and Fifth Avenue. The Committee stepped up its surveillance operations following the war. In 1917, it worked with Comstock's Society for the Suppression of Vice in their attempts to close down bathhouses in Manhattan that were frequented by homosexual men and female prostitutes. It is unclear whether Sarah Truslow Dickinson had anything directly to do with the Committee's anti-homosexual campaigns; her main focus was on stemming prostitution. See Reed, *From Private Vice to Public Virtue*, 155. For more on the Committee of Fourteen's anti-homosexual activities, see Chauncey, *Gay New York*, 147–48, 170–72, 176, 210, 236, 240.

62. Robert Latou Dickinson, "A Gynecologist Looks at Prostitution Abroad: With Reference to Electrocautery Treatment of Gonorrheal Cervicitis and Urethritis," *American Journal of Obstetrics and Gynecology* (1928): 590–602.

63. Prior to starting his private practice, Dickinson worked as a medical examiner for New York City. During this time he conducted routine physical exams for city employees. Out of these exams, Dickinson used information from several thousand routine exams in order to do a study of male sex anatomy which contributed to his famous *Human Sex Anatomy*. Reed, *From Private Vice to Public Virtue*, 152. Later in his life, Dickinson became interested in the subject of male homosexuality, having encountered it in cases of married women who complained about husbands showing a greater interest in men than in them. In 1946, he approached Alfred Kinsey with the idea of doing a study of the genitals of male homosexuals to determine whether they showed distinct signs of masturbation and homosexual behavior, an idea Kinsey politely criticized on the grounds that Dickinson's methods for assembling a subject population were inadequate since they did not take account of the random occurrence of homosexuality across the broader male population. See Dickinson's unpublished paper, "Masturbation: Physical Signs in Males," submitted to Kinsey in December 1946, Miscellaneous Papers; and Letter of Kinsey to Dickinson, January 1, 1947, Dickinson Correspondence, Robert Latou Dickinson Collection, Countway Library, Harvard Medical School, Boston, Massachusetts.

64. Robert Latou Dickinson, "Marital Maladjustment: The Business of Preventive Gynecology," *Long Island Medical Journal* 2 (1908): 1–4. For subsequent writings concerning the role of doctor as marriage counselor, see Dickinson, "Premarital Consultation," *Journal of the American Medical Association* 117 (November 17, 1941):

1687–92; and Dickinson, "Premarital Examination as Routine Preventive Gynecology," *American Journal of Obstetrics and Gynecology* 16 (1928): 631.

65. See Havelock Ellis, Preface to *A Thousand Marriages*, x; and Robert Latou Dickinson and Walter Truslow, "Averages in Attitude and Trunk Development in Women and Their Relation to Pain," *Journal of the American Medical Association* (December 14, 1912): 2128–32.

66. For example, as a way of treating "obstinate" or "rebellious" gonorrhea particularly in prostitutes, Dickinson advised the use of "fine wire cautery," using an electrified nasal cautery tool which had a narrow loop of platinum wire about one centimeter long. This wire was heated and inserted into the patient's vagina and used to carve strips along the cervical canal or to puncture cysts. Dickinson suggested that the tool be wired to a child's train transformer for electrical power, but warned that this could result in an electrical shock. He also warned that some women might be "sensitive" to pain so they might need to be bleached with adrenalin combined with novocaine. The incision process required repeated treatment two to three weeks later. As an alternative, he recommended a technique involving the total destruction of cervical glands through hot-wired cauterization. After witnessing the compulsory detention and treatment of prostitutes in Europe, Dickinson recommended the same procedures here because he believed that prostitutes were to blame for the higher incidence of gonorrhea. Like other social hygienists of his day, Dickinson recommended that doctors fulfill their duty to treating gonorrhea before it further infected middle-class families through prostitutes who were blamed for infecting married gentlemen. He argued that detaining prostitutes was a good place to start since they could be held in jail over the course of their treatment, thus curtailing the spread of the disease and also providing scientists and doctors with information about the effectiveness of treatment. Like many of the medical authorities who advocated the regulation of prostitution, Dickinson did not advocate any such detention for the men who frequented prostitutes. Robert Latou Dickinson, "A Gynecologist Looks at Prostitution Abroad: With Reference to Electrocautery Treatment of Gonorrheal Cervicitis and Urethritis."

67. For a more laudatory assessment of Dickinson's "daring innovations," see Reed, *From Private Vice to Public Virtue*, 157.

68. Robert Latou Dickinson, "Studies of the Levator Ani Muscle," *American Journal of Obstetrics* 22 (1889): 259–261.

69. The results were published in Dickinson, *Human Sex Anatomy*.

70. Dickinson and Truslow, "Averages in Attitude and Trunk Development in Women and Their Relation to Pain," 2131.

71. In *A Thousand Marriages*, Dickinson stated that evidence of arousal during examinations could reveal aspects of a woman's sex life that she declined to mention in conversation with the doctor: "When noted at examination, the degree of apparent erotic excitation may serve to check up on the statements of the patient, being important chiefly where sexual excitability or response is flatly denied." In addition, Dickinson stated that a patient's general behavior could evince tell-tale signs of arousal and thus be important for assessing a woman's problems. Such signs included "habitual rhythmic swing of the hips in walking, restless behavior on the table (other than nervousness); unnecessary exposure (exhibitionism); marked corrugation of the are-

ola or quick erectibility of the follicles and nipples in non-pregnant and non-nursing women; marked vulvar hypertrophies and varicosities; free glairy secretion; discoloration of congestion; protrusion of one or more bulbs of the vestibule; projection and excursion and (infrequently) erection of the clitoris; general vaginal congestion; jumpiness of pelvic floor muscles, either irritable or rhythmic; purplish or deep red congestion of cervix with outpour of clear mucous; varicosities of broad ligaments, and particularly the combinations of these signs—free mucous discharge being the most common symptom." Dickinson and Beam, *A Thousand Marriages*, 54.

72. Although he was a maverick, the American Gynecological Society elected Dickinson president in 1920. His presidential address in that year encouraged gynecologists to work in the fields of contraception, infertility, sterilization, and artificial insemination. Dickinson, "A Program for American Gynecology: Presidential Address," *American Journal of Obstetrics and Gynecology* 1 (1920): 2–10.

73. The case was *United States v. One Package* 13 F. Supp. 334 (E.D.N.Y. 1936), affirmed 82 F. 2d 737 (2d Cir. 1936). For more on the case see, Reed, *From Private Vice to Public Virtue*, 121.

74. Examples of his near-obsession with graphic accuracy are published in Dickinson's *Human Sex Anatomy* and *Human Sex Anatomy: A Topographical Hand Atlas*, both of which contain vivid images of female and male genitalia.

75. Dickinson was a nature enthusiast and produced several sketchbooks of scenery from around the New York area. He placed great value on exercise and contact with the great outdoors, the lack of which, in his view, caused urban dwellers to suffer health problems. His valorization of nature, as well as his respect for natural history, was evident in his medical practice. Indeed, his detailed illustrations harked back to an early tradition of natural history that relied on graphic representations as a basis for making classifications and establishing scientific truth. That he loved to sketch both nature and women's bodies suggests that Dickinson, conscious or not, was faithful to the origins of natural history whereby exotic things were the focus of intense classificatory zeal and thus were depicted in ever-minute detail. Like Linnaeus, in Dickinson, the illustrator and the scientist were one, and the objects of greatest fascination were those associated with the mysteries of nature, including women. Dickinson was author and illustrator of the *Palisades Guide* (New York: American Geographical Society, 1921) and co-author and illustrator of *The New York Walk Book* (New York: American Geographical Society, 1923). For sources that examine the relationship between natural history and studies of female anatomy, see Anne Fausto-Sterling, "Gender, Race, and Nation: The Comparative Anatomy of 'Hottentot' Women in Europe, 1815–1817," in *Deviant Bodies: Critical Perspectives on Difference in Science and Popular Culture*, ed. Jennifer Terry and Jacqueline Urla (Bloomington, Indiana: Indiana University Press, 1995), 19–48; Londa Schiebinger, *Nature's Body*.

76. He was likened to da Vinci and Ellis in "Dickinson Collection Comes to Cleveland Museum of Health," *Museum News of the Cleveland Health Museum* (June-July 1945): 2, in the Robert Latou Dickinson Collection, Countway Library, Harvard Medical School, Boston, Massachusetts.

77. See Reed, *From Private Vice to Public Virtue*, 156–57 and R.L.D.: The Life of Robert Latou Dickinson, 1861–1950, unpublished manuscript, Robert Latou Dickinson Collection, Countway Library, Harvard Medical School.

78. Dickinson regarded German marital counseling centers as models for marriage clinics in the United States. These centers had been developed during the Weimar period in order to make sure that prospective husbands and wives would be checked for tuberculosis, venereal disease, and mental illness. In the late 1930s, the German clinics were modified to become more restrictive under Nazi medicine, and both men and women were checked for any ills that threatened a healthy marriage, including any disabilities which were assumed to be hereditary. In Germany, by 1932, half of the big cities with over 50,000 people had marital counseling centers. But it was not until after the Nuremberg racial purity laws were passed in 1935 that visits to the centers became obligatory and counseling was dramatically expanded. Eventually, almost every local health office had an advisory center to counsel people toward or away from marriage. The standard practice under Nazi racial hygiene was to have physicians conduct an extensive medical examination including the extraction of blood samples, lung x-rays, and neurological tests. If the individual passed this examination, she or he would acquire a certificate to marry which was good for only six months. Very few certificates were denied, and those who did not pass were allowed to appeal to their local genetic health court. However, those who did not comply with the advisory center's decision could be sentenced to prison—that is, if two people married and either or both of them were deemed "unfit," regardless of whether they were sterilized. Under this mandatory routine, the duties of doctors and public health officials expanded dramatically. For more about these practices see, Robert N. Proctor, *Racial Hygiene: Medicine under the Nazis* (Cambridge: Harvard University Press, 1988), 138–42; Atina Grossman, *Reforming Sex: The German Movement for Birth Control and Abortion Reform, 1920–1950* (New York: Oxford University Press, 1995). For an account of the connection between American eugenics organizations and Nazi marriage clinics, see Stefan Kuhl, *The Nazi Connection.*

79. See Dickinson, "Premarital Examination as Routine Preventive Gynecology," 631. In the 1910s, Dickinson consulted for the California-based Human Betterment Foundation on the subject of sterilizing mental patients in state hospitals and on the idea of premarital screening to discourage the unfit from reproducing. Many of his ideas about marriage counseling techniques were developed in dialogue with other eugenicists in Germany and Britain, including Havelock Ellis. And while he appeared to be a moderate when it came to more egregious policies of involuntary sterilization, as late as 1948, and well after most American scientists publicly denounced Nazi eugenics campaigns, Dickinson applauded German policies of premarital screening to prevent hereditary disorders and feeblemindedness. Letter from Robert Dickinson to Karl Bruegger, 20 March 1948, Robert Latou Dickinson Papers, Countway Library, Harvard University Medical School; and Reed, *From Private Vice to Public Virtue,* 195.

80. Dickinson, "Premarital Consultation."

81. Dickinson and Beam, *The Single Woman,* v, 422.

82. Dickinson, "Medical Analysis of *A Thousand Marriages*," *Journal of the American Medical Association* 97, no. 8 (August 22, 1931): 531. This article summarized the larger volume on the subject.

83. On the basis of observing clinical patients who came to him for various gynecological treatments, Dickinson asserted that the clearest correlation between genital

characteristics and experience occurred in cases where he suspected the patient masturbated. In a 1902 article which made him an American authority on female masturbation, he noted that in 427 women whose genitals he carefully sketched, the enlargement and hypertrophy of the labia minora were pathological and "clearcut evidences of traction, pressure or friction." Dickinson, "Hypertrophies of the Labia Minora and Their Significance," *American Gynecology* 1 (1902): 225–54. In 1931, he wrote that "the story of years of active self-excitation both as contemporary practice and as historical development" could be deduced from certain labial contours, enlargements and varicosities, the range of excursions of the clitoris, reactions of the pelvic floor, and thickening of the tissues of the mammary glands. Dickinson, "Medical Analysis of *A Thousand Marriages*," 531.

84. For Dickinson's proposed amendment to the female sexuality research of Katherine Bement Davis and Gilbert V. Hamilton, see Robert Latou Dickinson and Henry H. Pierson, "The Average Life of American Women," *Journal of the American Medical Association* 85, no. 15 (October 15, 1925): 1113–17.

85. In his own words, "It therefore came about that data of the body, the mind and the emotional life were all collected together—always proceeding from body to mind." Dickinson, "Medical Analysis of *A Thousand Marriages*," 530.

86. The studies were not without serious methodological problems. First, the subjects were not selected randomly nor did they represent a cross-section of women. These were women who saw the doctor in private practice for gynecological reasons, and thus they tended to be women of some means with a greater degree of education than average. Secondly, Dickinson's methods of recording cases were not consistent but changed over the course of the forty-eight years during which he documented the cases. Specifically, in the early years of his practice, he did not ask patients about their sex lives, nor did he keep consistent records about the sexual experiences he suspected they had. It was not until later in his career, after he noticed that women often blurted out information about their intimate sexual experiences during routine gynecological exams, that he began to incorporate questions about their sexual behavior into his standard procedure. To finesse this inconsistency, in *A Thousand Marriages* and *The Single Woman* he broke his samples down into two main groups: those for whom he had made records about their sexual experiences and those, from his early practice and from the practices of several colleagues, who functioned as "control groups," having no separate records of their sexual experiences. They were not in any scientific sense "controls," since women in these groups were not asked the full range of questions inquired of the others. When it came to specific data on sexuality, Dickinson in many cases speculated retrospectively on how they were different or similar to the more recent cases. Furthermore, neither he nor Beam made clear who belonged to which group in their specific narrative descriptions or their comprehensive analyses of cases.

87. In *The Single Woman* (205–6), the authors summarized four cases of homosexuality in husbands and included a lengthy letter from one husband to another, intercepted and sent to Dickinson by a wife, which contained hints of the writer's anxiety about his excessive sex drive and habit of masturbation. Though there is no explanation as to why it appears among case records of homosexuality in single women, ap-

parently it is the husband's possible homosexuality that was in question. This is just one of many examples pointing up the idiosyncrasies of the Dickinson/Beam volumes.

88. Dickinson and Beam, *The Single Woman*, 208.

89. Ibid., 204.

90. Ibid., 208.

91. Ibid.

92. Ibid., 212.

93. Lura Beam was involved intimately for almost thirty-five years with Louise Stevens Bryant, who had been executive secretary of the National Committee on Maternal Health. Although they never explicitly called themselves lesbians, the nature of their relationship was known to close associates, including Dickinson. In letters written during the mid-1920s to "Larry," her nickname for Lura, Bryant extolled her affection: "I love and adore you and miss you fearfully all the time," and "Now I am a real Amazon. I love you." Louise Stevens Bryant to Lura Beam, ca. 1922 and January 16, 1925, Louise Stevens Bryant Collection, Box 1, Folder 18, Smith College, Northampton, Massachusetts. Beam's testament of her lasting adoration for Bryant can be found in Lura Beam, *Bequest from a Life: A Biography of Louise Stevens Bryant* (Baltimore: Waverly Press, 1963).

94. Dickinson and Beam, *The Single Woman*, 431.

95. For more on the New York City gay subculture during this period, see Chauncey, *Gay New York*.

CHAPTER FIVE

1. Karl Heinrich Ulrichs, *The Riddle of "Man-Manly" Love: The Pioneering Work on Male Homosexuality*, 2 vols., translated by Michael A. Lombardi-Nash (Buffalo: Prometheus, 1994); Havelock Ellis, *Sexual Inversion;* Sigmund Freud, "The Sexual Aberrations." Hirschfeld's promotion of the idea of sexual intermediacy, adapted from evolutionary theory, including that of Charles Darwin, is discussed in Steakley, "Per scientiam ad justitiam," 143–45.

2. Ernst Laqueur, Elisabeth Dingemanse, P. C. Hart, and S. E. de Jongh, "Female Sex Hormone in Urine of Men," *Klinische Wochenschrift* 6 (1927): 1859. The 1927 discovery was anticipated in a 1921 report by Viennese gynecologist Otfried Fellner suggesting, on the basis of experiments on rabbits that indicated extracts of the male testes produced effects on the growth of the uterus, that rabbit testes contained female sex hormones. See Otfried Fellner, *Pflugers Archiv* (1921): 189. In 1929, American gynecologist Robert Frank reported female sex hormones in male bodies "whose masculine character and ability to impregnate females" were clear. See Robert T. Frank, *The Female Sex Hormone* (Springfield, Ill. and Baltimore: Charles C. Thomas, 1929), 120.

3. H. Siebke, "Presence of Androkinin in Female Organism," *Archiv für Gynaekologie* 146 (1931): 417–62.

4. Bernhard Zondek, "Mass Excretion of Oestrogenic Hormone in the Urine of the Stallion," *Nature* 133 (1934): 209–10; Zondek, "Oestrogenic Hormone in the Urine of the Stallion," *Nature* 133 (1934): 494.

5. Robert T. Frank, *Female Sex Hormone*, 292; A. S. Parkes, "Terminology of Sex Hormones," *Nature* 141 (1938): 12; Parkes, "Androgenic Activity of Ovarian Extracts," *Nature* 139 (1937): 965.

6. For excellent historical analyses of endocrinology see Nelly Oudshoorn, *Beyond the Natural Body: An Archaeology of Sex Hormones* (London: Routledge, 1994), 24–27; and Diana Long Hall, "Biology, Sex Hormones and Sexism in the 1920s," *Philosophical Forum* 5 (Fall-Winter 1973–74): 82.

7. C. A. Wright, "Further Studies of Endocrine Aspects of Homosexuality," *Medical Record* 147 (May 18, 1938): 449–52.

8. M. Reiss, "The Role of Sex Hormones in Psychiatry," *Journal of Mental Science* 86 (1940): 364.

9. Saul Rosenzweig and R. G. Hoskins, "A Note on the Ineffectualness of Sex-Hormone Medication in a Case of Pronounced Homosexuality," *Psychosomatic Medicine* 3, no. 1 (1941): 87–89.

10. S. J. Glass and Roswell H. Johnson, "Limitations and Complications of Organotherapy in Male Homosexuality," *Journal of Endocrinology* 4, no. 11 (1944): 541–43.

11. For a review of hormonal treatments to alter homosexual orientation that continued well into the latter half of the twentieth century, see Heino Meyer-Bahlburg, "Psychoendocrine Research on Sexual Orientation: Current Status and Future Options," *Progress in Brain Research* 61 (1984): 375–99. See also Meyer-Bahlburg, "Sex Hormones and Male Homosexuality in Comparative Perspective," *Archives of Sexual Behavior* (1977): 297–326.

12. Although he often faced vociferous opposition from colleagues in anthropology who adhered to biological and hereditarian schemes for understanding human cultural diversity, Boas gained influence as the century unfolded, and his contributions to larger political debates about race were significant in opposing racist anthropological theories that underpinned anti-immigrant nativism, eugenic sterilization laws, and proposals to restrict marriages among the "unfit." For example, see Franz Boas, "Some Criticisms of Physical Anthropology" (1899), "Influence of Hereditary and Environment Upon Growth" (1913), and "New Evidence in Regard to the Instability of Human Types" (1916), in *Race, Language and Culture* (New York: Macmillan, 1940), 76–85, 165–71; and *The Mind of Primitive Man* (New York: Macmillan, 1911). For historical analyses of Boas's interventions in political debates during the first half of the century, see Lee D. Baker, "The Location of Franz Boas within the African American Struggle," *Critique of Anthropology* 14, no. 2 (1994): 199–217, and Elazar Barkan, "Mobilizing Scientists Against Nazi Racism," in *Bones, Bodies, Behavior,* ed. George W. Stocking, Jr. (Madison: University of Wisconsin Press, 1988), 180–205.

13. For analyses of how anthropology during the twentieth century became a means for analyzing the nature of advanced industrialized societies by comparing them to "primitive" societies, see George E. Marcus and Michael M. K. Fischer, *Anthropology as Cultural Critique: An Experimental Moment in the Human Sciences* (Chicago: University of Chicago Press, 1986) and James Clifford and George E. Marcus, eds., *Writing Culture: The Poetics and Politics of Ethnography* (Berkeley: University of California Press, 1985).

14. Ruth Benedict's research on southwestern American Indian tribes marked the

emergence of the subdiscipline of cultural psychology which developed into the Culture and Personality school. Psychological anthropology sought to determine the nature of the interaction between the individual and his or her culture. It was especially used to analyze divergent behavior patterns of individuals who lived in the same culture. See especially Ruth Benedict, *Patterns of Culture* (Boston: Houghton Mifflin, 1934), 262–65; "Anthropology and the Abnormal," *Journal of General Psychology* 10 (1934): 59–82; "Sex in Primitive Society," *American Journal of Orthopsychiatry* 9 (1939): 570–75.

15. Margaret Mead, *Coming of Age in Samoa: A Psychological Study of Primitive Youth* (1928; rpt. New York: William Morrow, 1961); *Growing Up in New Guinea: A Comparative Study of Primitive Education* (1930; rpt. New York: William Morrow, 1975).

16. Margaret Mead, *Sex and Temperament in Three Primitive Societies* (New York: Dell Publications, 1935). Mead lectured on the cultural specificity of sex differences throughout the 1930s and 1940s, subsequently publishing her main ideas on the subject in *Male and Female: A Study of the Sexes in a Changing World* (New York: William Morrow & Company, 1949).

17. Among the popular writings of Mead were her famous *Redbook* columns, which began in 1961 and continued regularly until shortly before her death on November 15, 1978. See Jane Howard, *Margaret Mead: A Life* (New York: Simon and Schuster, 1984), 389–92.

18. The anthropologist Carole Vance, in "Anthropology Rediscovers Sexuality," discusses Mead's work in the context of what she calls *cultural influence* models of sexuality. According to this paradigm, "sexuality is seen as the basic material on which culture works—a kind of natural Play Doh which is universal, a naturalized category which remains closed to investigation and analysis." Cultural influence models focused on variations of human expression regarding gender and sexuality, thus rejecting blatant forms of universalizing. But, as Vance notes, "the bedrock of sexuality is assumed . . . to be universal and biologically determined," appearing as "sex drive" or "impulse," and cultures are either restrictive or permissive (878). In other words, the meaning of behavior is assumed to be the same in each culture, with "variation" referring only to greater or lesser degrees of repression or expression. The presence of homosexuality in a culture was, for Mead and other cultural influence theorists, a sign of greater tolerance of variation. But Vance argues that drawing this conclusion assumes that all cultures give the same meaning to homosexuality, and, moreover, that its presence is indeed a signifier of tolerance. Vance suggests that both conclusions are flawed due to the imposition of culturally specific Western norms onto other cultural contexts.

19. Jeffrey Weeks critically analyzes Mead's contributions to a more tolerant understanding of variation which at the same time kept heterosexuality fundamentally in place as the "natural" order of sexuality. See Weeks, *Sexuality and its Discontents*, 104–108.

20. Mead, *Male and Female*, 130.

21. Ibid., 135–36.

22. Mead, *Sex and Temperament*, 259.

23. Ibid., 270.

24. Ibid., 271.

25. Her deep affection and sympathy for her mentor, Ruth Benedict, contributed to Mead's passion for championing the cause of social tolerance toward those whose lives deviated from conventions of marriage and childrearing. Benedict, who suffered from one unhappy marriage to a man and had discreet love relationships with other women, earned Mead's unwavering dedication as a student, friend, and colleague. Mead's own sexual orientation has been a matter of considerable speculation. She was married to several men over the course of her life and had one child, and she always had very close female friends. A friend commented that Mead "fell in love with women's souls and men's bodies. She was spiritually homosexual, psychologically bisexual, and physically heterosexual." In response to her cousin's asking what she thought about homosexuality, Mead said: "They make the best companions in the world." But she was remembered by a lesbian artist who saw Mead often in the 1950s as "uncomfortable about overt lesbianism." The artist, when asked, replied that she did not believe Mead was a lesbian: "Not everyone is sexual, you know. For some people, and I think she was one of them, work can take the place of sex." Mead's friend Leo Rosten mentioned that "she spent a great deal of time with groups that included homosexuals . . . but I don't think that was her own special bent. Pleasure, for her, was an interruption of celebration. If she had a choice, I always thought, she'd rather exchange ideas than kisses." All quotations are from Jane Howard, *Margaret Mead*, 367. For other worthy biographical accounts of Mead's life, see Margaret Mead, *Blackberry Winter: My Early Years* (New York: William Morrow, 1972); Mary Catherine Bateson, *A Daughter's Eye: A Memoir of Margaret Mead and Gregory Bateson* (NY: Morrow, 1984).

26. Mead, *Male and Female*, 367–84.

27. Mead's opinions on sexual variations tended to become more conservative over time. Compare, for example, *Sex and Temperament* to "An Anthropologist Looks at the Report," in *Problems of Sexual Behavior*, ed. Charles Walter Clarke (New York: American Social Hygiene Association, 1948, 58–69). In the latter piece, she criticizes Alfred Kinsey's *Sexual Behavior in the Human Male*, charging, among other things, that Kinsey was amoral and reduced sexuality to a mere bodily function. She wasn't particularly pleased that he declined to criticize homosexuality in his presentation of statistics about its frequency in the U.S. middle-class population.

28. Among the proliferation of studies on sex variation in Native American cultures were Leslie Spier, "Klamath Ethnography," *University of California Publications in American Archaeology and Ethnology* 27 (1930): 51–53. Spier observed cases of cross-dressing and role inversion among men, but women who lived as men and adopted some of their habits retained women's dress. See also C. Daryll Forde, "Ethnology of Yuma Indians," *University of California Publications in American Archaeology and Ethnology* 28, no. 4 (1931): 83–278, reporting on transvestites and female inverts among the Yuma tribe of California where "casual secret homosexuality" was practiced among both women and men. Edward Winslow Gifford, "The Cocopa," *University of California Publications in American Archaeology and Ethnology* 31 (1933): 277–94, noted anatomically female transvestites among the Cocopa who behaved like boys when they were young and then like men later, piercing their noses, hunting, doing battle, and marrying women. Gifford claimed that although they lacked breasts, did not men-

struate, and had the muscular build of men, they had female genitalia. For other articles on homosexuality, transvestism, and sex inversion, see Willard Williams Hill, "The Status of the Hermaphrodite and Transvestite in Navaho Culture," *American Anthropologist* 37 (1935): 273–79; Hill, "Note on the Pima Berdache," *American Anthropologist* 40 (1938): 338–40; George Devereux, "Institutionalized Homosexuality of the Mohave Indians," *Human Biology* 9 (1937): 498–527; Ruth Benedict, *Patterns of Culture;* Benedict, "Sex in Primitive Society." For excerpts of these articles, see Katz, *Gay American History,* 312–25.

29. Terman's earlier work on intelligence can be found in Lewis M. Terman, *The Measurement of Intelligence* (Boston: Houghton Mifflin, 1916). His collaboration with Catherine Cox Miles on the subject of genius expanded into a five volume series entitled *Genetic Studies of Genius* (Stanford: Stanford University Press, 1956). Miles's dissertation constituted volume two of the series, entitled *The Early Mental Traits of 300 Geniuses* (Stanford: Stanford University Press, 1926). Biographical works on Terman include Henry L. Minton, *Lewis M. Terman: Pioneer in Psychological Testing* (New York: New York University Press, 1988); May V. Seagoe, *Terman and the Gifted* (Los Altos, Calif.: William Kaufmann, Inc., 1975), the former offering an incisive and critical analysis of Terman's life and work, and the latter a prosaic and laudatory treatment.

30. In the 1926–27 funding cycle, Terman received an initial $2,900 to study "the development of tests of masculinity-femininity in the non-intellectual aspects of mentality." From 1925 through the early 1940s, the Committee on Research of Problems of Sex gave Terman a total of $60,000 to conduct this longitudinal psychological study of what he called "sex correlated" differences among human personalities. For more on the details of funding, see National Research Council Committee on Sex Research, Rockefeller Foundation Archives, Series 3, Subseries 2, Box 8, Folder 188 and Aberle and Corner, *Twenty-five Years of Sex Research.*

31. Lewis M. Terman and Catherine Cox Miles, *Sex and Personality: Studies in Masculinity and Femininity* (New York: McGraw-Hill, 1936). A preliminary report of the study appeared as Terman and Miles, "Sex Differences in the Association of Ideas," *American Journal of Psychology* 41, no. 2 (April 1929): 165–206.

32. The Attitude Interest Analysis Survey was published separately as Lewis M. Terman and Catherine Cox Miles. *Attitude-Interest Analysis Test* (New York: McGraw-Hill, 1936).

33. For other examples of uses of the M-F test, see W. Leslie Barnette, "Study of an Adult Male Homosexual and Terman-Miles M-F Scores," *American Journal of Orthopsychiatry* 12 (1942): 346–51, which detailed the case of a passive male homosexual with a high femininity rating who was "intellectually and socially a valuable individual to society"; and James Page and John Warkentin, "Masculinity and Paranoia," *Journal of Abnormal and Social Psychology* 33 (1938): 527–31, which concluded that paranoia was "in some way related to passive homoeroticism."

34. Terman and Miles, *Sex and Personality,* 495.

35. For critical assessments of the methods and findings of the M-F test, see Henry Minton, "Femininity in Men and Masculinity in Women: American Psychology and Psychiatry Portray Homosexuality in the 1930s," *Journal of Homosexuality* 13, no. 1 (Fall 1986): 8–14; Miriam Lewin, "'Rather Worse Than Folly': Psychology

Measures Femininity and Masculinity, 1: From Terman and Miles to the Guilfords," in *In the Shadows of the Past: Psychology Portrays the Sexes: A Social and Intellectual History*, ed. Miriam Lewis (New York: Columbia University Press, 1984), 155–78; Joseph H. Pleck, "The Theory of Male Sex Role Identity: Its Rise and Fall, 1936 to the Present," in *In the Shadows of the Past*, 205–25; Jill G. Morawski, "Measurement of Masculinity and Femininity: Engendering Categorical Realities," in *Women's Place in Psychology*, ed. Janis S. Bohan (Boulder, Colo.: Westview Press, 1992), 199–226, and "The Troubled Quest for Masculinity, Femininity, and Androgyny," *Review of Personality and Social Psychology* 7 (1987): 44–69; Janice Irvine, *Disorders of Desire: Sex and Gender in Modern American Sexology* (Philadelphia: Temple University Press, 1990), 232–34.

36. For critical assessments of Terman's work in the area of intelligence testing, see Stephen J. Gould, *The Mismeasure of Man;* A. A. Roback, *History of American Psychology* (1952; New York: Collier Books, 1964), 456–62; Michael Sokal, *Psychological Testing and American Society, 1890–1930* (New Brunswick: Rutgers University Press, 1987).

37. Terman and Miles, *Sex and Personality*, 10.

38. Ibid., 240–41.

39. Ibid., 282–83.

40. Ibid., 248, 250.

41. Ibid., 243.

42. For more on the data from lesbian subjects, see Joseph Pleck, "The Theory of Male Sex Role Identity," 210.

43. Terman's bias toward constitutional determinism, notwithstanding his tempered tone in *Sex and Personality*, persisted from his early research on intelligence through his research on homosexuality. He believed that hereditary and biological factors played a big role in personality development, as evidenced in his early writings on intelligence. Indeed, his involvement with eugenics institutions and conferences was extensive, as a prominent participant in the 1921 and 1932 International Eugenics Congresses held at the American Museum of Natural History in New York City, and as a supporter of the California-based Human Betterment Foundation that advocated eugenic sterilization well into the 1940s. Terman opposed behaviorism and the cultural relativism of Margaret Mead, Ruth Benedict, and those associated with the Chicago School of Sociology, including William I. Thomas. For background on debates between Terman and the behaviorists, see Kimball Young, Fred B. Lindstrom and Ronald A. Hardert, ed., "Kimball Young," *Sociological Perspectives* 32, no. 2 (1989): 215–26, no. 3: 383–402; A. A. Roback, *History of American Psychology*, 461–62. For Terman's perspectives on hereditary factors in behavior, see Lewis M. Terman, "Testing for the Crime Germ," *Sunset* 60 (1928): 24–25, 54–56; Terman, "A Study in Precocity and Prematuration," *American Journal of Psychology* 16 (April 1905): 148. For background on Terman's involvement in eugenics campaigns, see Mark H. Haller, *Eugenics*, 99–113, 165–66; Gould, *The Mismeasure of Man;* Daniel J. Kevles, *In the Name of Eugenics*, 79–82, 129.

44. Terman and Miles, *Sex and Personality*, 467.

45. Terman's research on marital happiness was also funded by the National Research Council's Committee on Research in Problems of Sex; it surveyed 800 married

and 105 divorced upper-middle-class white couples contacted through the Los Angeles-based Human Betterment Foundation and the Institute for Family Relations, both headed by eugenics enthusiast Paul Popenoe. See Lewis M. Terman and P. Buttenwieser, "Personality Factors in Marital Compatibility," *Journal of Social Psychology* 6 (1935): 143–71, 267–89; Lewis M. Terman and W. B. Johnson, "Personality Characteristics of Happily Married, Unhappily Married, and Divorced Persons," *Character and Personality* 3 (1935): 290–311; Lewis M. Terman, *Psychological Factors in Marital Happiness;* Lewis M. Terman, "The Effect of Happiness or Unhappiness on Self-Report Regarding Attitudes, Reaction Patterns, and Facts of Personal History," *Psychological Bulletin* 36 (1939): 197–202. For an in-depth analysis of Terman's research on marital compatibility, see Minton, *Lewis M. Terman.*

46. Terman and Miles, *Sex and Personality,* 469.

47. Ibid., 451.

CHAPTER SIX

1. George W. Henry, *Sex Variants: A Study in Homosexual Patterns,* 2 vols. (New York: Paul Hoeber & Sons, 1941), v. The 1941 edition included two volumes, one on case studies of male subjects and the other on female subjects. A second edition appeared in 1948 as one large volume, which kept the case histories intact but omitted some of the appendices from the 1941 edition, most importantly the "Glossary of Homosexuality" and the faceless photographs of some of the subjects. Throughout this chapter, the page citations are to the 1948 edition of *Sex Variants.* For useful overviews of the CSSV's efforts especially in relation to the development of lesbian and gay sexual identities, see Henry L. Minton, "Femininity in Men and Masculinity in Women," and "Community Empowerment and the Medicalization of Homosexuality: Constructing Sexual Identities in the 1930s," *Journal of the History of Sexuality* 6, no. 3 (1996): 435–58.

2. Henry, *Sex Variants,* xii.

3. Ibid., xii.

4. Hirschfeld had suggested such an idea earlier but he tended to emphasize the natural difference of homosexuals, grounded mainly in an evolutionary argument that they belonged to a third sex between males and females. See Steakley, "Per scientiam ad justitiam," 142–43.

5. Hirschfeld used the term *sexual variants* roughly interchangeably with *sexual intermediates,* and it appears that the CSSV adopted the term *sex variants* from him. See, for example, Hirschfeld, "Die Intersexuelle Konstitution," discussed in Steakley, "Per scientiam ad justitiam," 144–46.

6. Minutes of Committee for the Study of Sex Variants, 18 October 1935, Lewis M. Terman Papers, Stanford University. For background on the controversy involving the Committee for Maternal Health over the issue of birth control, see James Reed, *From Private Vice to Public Virtue,* 168.

7. Dickinson to Terman, 28 January 1935, Lewis M. Terman papers, Stanford University Archives, Stanford, California.

8. Jan Gay, *On Going Naked* (New York: Holburn House, 1932). Her children's books include *The Shire Colt* (Garden City, N.Y.: Doubleday, Doran and Company, Inc., 1931); *Pancho and his Burro* (New York: W. Morrow and Company, 1930); *The*

Mutt Book (New York: Harper and Bros., 1932); and *Town Cats* (New York: Alfred Knopf, 1932). For more biographical information on Jan Gay, see her obituary in the *New York Times*, 13 September 1960, and "Proposal of Jan Gay to the Guggenheim Foundation" (for research on Alcoholics Anonymous), 25 October 1950, on file in the Jan Gay correspondence file at the Kinsey Institute, Bloomington, Indiana, and miscellaneous notes from the Thomas Painter file at the Kinsey Institute.

9. Memorandum attached to Dickinson letter to. Terman, 11 February 1935, Lewis Terman Papers, Stanford University. Between 1927 and 1937, Gay traveled to Mexico, Europe, the Near East, and both coasts of South America, which she financed by working as a secretary and a translator for the National Railways of Mexico and then by writing travel books for children. From 1927 through 1929, she stayed in Brazil, Argentina, and Chile, which later led to a ten-year association with the Latin American Institute from 1940–1950. There she did research and public relations work and developed a curriculum to prepare men and women for the diplomatic service and for foreign trade.

10. A similar lay study was undertaken by a lesbian named Barry Barryman in Salt Lake City in the 1920s. The author, who was a professional photographer and later a machinist during World War Two, interviewed twenty-five lesbians, most of whom were her friends and lovers. The study included data on about eighty male homosexuals who were connected to the lesbian subculture in Salt Lake City and were members of a bohemian literary club. Barryman used a standardized questionnaire for interviews and classified individuals according to degrees of masculinity and femininity in both personality and body form, loosely adopting the methods set forth by Hirschfeld. The subjects ranged in age from nineteen to fifty-six, and included teachers, nurses, waitresses, secretaries, a mining engineer, a beauty operator, a barber, a concessions operator, a temporarily unemployed drifter, and a farm laborer. Three were married housewives but identified as lesbians, including one who was married to a gay man. All were white women who were described as coming from "good," "untainted," and "respectable" stock. Most of them were Mormons and two were from large polygamous families. They tended to be secretive about their lesbianism, probably to avoid public opprobrium. They uniformly denied masturbation, which they found repugnant, and many stated that they realized their lesbianism after childhood. Each subject was summarized in a case history format, and Barryman classified ten as having "masculine psychology" and eight as having "feminine psychology," while five "fluctuated" between masculine and feminine. Barryman observed the majority to have broad shoulders, small breasts, and narrow hips, features that underscored the author's premise that lesbians had a hereditary or congenital predisposition to sex inversion and homosexuality. Barryman, like some of her interviewees, tended to downgrade qualities associated with femininity, especially when they were found in men. But the subjects echoed Hirschfeld's naturalist framework, refusing to think of themselves as perverts or as pathologically afflicted. The study, like that initiated by Jan Gay, offers evidence of Hirschfeld's influence on lesbians and gay men in the United States, even as his thinking was, for the most part, marginalized by American physicians and scientists. For more on the Salt Lake City study, see Vern L. Bullough and Bonnie Bullough, "Lesbianism in the 1920s and 1930s: A

New Found Study," *Signs* 2 (1977): 895–904. The questionnaire and responses are on file at the Gay and Lesbian Archives in West Hollywood, California.

11. In addition, Drs. Jean Corwin, Clark Wissler, and W. G. Ogburn were contacted but declined the invitation. Minutes of Sex Variant Committee Meeting, 29 March 1935, Lewis M. Terman papers, Stanford University Archives, Stanford, California. For reasons I have been unable to determine, Earnest Hooton, Clarence Cheney, Marion Kenworthy, and Philip E. Smith appeared on early letterhead but were not included among the Committee members listed in *Sex Variants*.

12. Minutes of CSSV meeting, 10 October 1935, Terman papers. See also letter of Robert Yerkes to Warren Weaver of the National Research Council, April 27, 1936, Rockefeller Foundation Archives, Series 200 (U.S.), Box 39, Folder 440, in which Yerkes reported that "since the Committee for Research in Problems of Sex of the NRC lacks adequate funds for the support of the projects recommend by the Committee for the Study of Sex Variants, Inc., it hereby expresses its sympathy with the aims of said Committee and its willingness to assist in any practical matter."

13. Minutes, 18 October 1935; letter from Eugen Kahn to Terman, 1 February 1940, Terman papers.

14. Minutes, 18 October 1935, Terman papers.

15. The Sex Variant Committee was also turned down in its requests for funds from the Commonwealth Foundation, the Rockefeller Foundation, and the New York Foundation. Minutes, 18 October 1935; letter from Eugen Kahn to Terman, 1 February 1940, Terman papers.

16. Henry, *Sex Variants* (1941), vi. Dickinson's suggestion was mentioned in CSSV Minutes, 18 October 1935, Terman papers.

17. Eugen Kahn to Lewis Terman, 6 June 1938, Terman papers.

18. For a description of one such hospital, see William Logie Russell, *The New York Hospital: A History of the Psychiatric Service, 1771–1936* (New York: Columbia University Press, 1945). Though Russell makes no mention of it, this hospital, which included the Payne-Whitney clinic, is where the CSSV research took place.

19. For background on constitutional psychology and medicine, see Ernst Kretschmer, *Physique and Character: An Investigation of the Nature of Constitution and of the Theory of Temperament* (New York: Harcourt, Brace and Company, 1925); George Draper, *Human Constitution: A Consideration of its Relationship to Disease* (Philadelphia: W. B. Saunders Company, 1924); and George Draper, C. W. Dupertuis, and J. L. Caughey, Jr., *Human Constitution in Clinical Medicine* (New York: Paul B. Hoeber, Inc., 1944). As it was developed by Kretschmer in Germany during the 1920s, constitutional psychology combined photography, extensive physical examinations, and anthropometric measurements to classify individuals according to several different physique types that corresponded to types of personality. Kretschmer observed the *athletic* or muscular type, the *pyknic* or round type, and the *asthenic* or long, slender type, and noted that manic-depressive patients tended to be pyknics while schizophrenics were either athletic or asthenic. Among the "schizoids," which included men with homosexual tendencies, he found "eunuchoid stigmata" consisting of excessive length of extremities, "feminine" trunk proportions, large hip measurements, scantiness of body hair, graceful bones, and either abnormally small or abnormally

large penises and testicles. He noted the syndrome of "masculinism" in certain schizophrenic women whom he reported to have excessively long extremities, narrow hips, broad shoulders, small and underdeveloped breasts, excessive body hair, lack of fat, and small uteri. Similar characteristics were noted in constitutional studies of homosexuals undertaken in the United States during the 1920s and 1930s. See, for example, Arthur Weil, "Körpermasse der Homosexuellen als Ausdrucksform ihrer speziellen Konstitution," *Archiv für Entwicklungsmechanik der Organismen* 49 (1921): 538–44; Frances M. Strakosch, *Factors in the Sex-Life of 700 Psychopathic Women;* George W. Henry and Hugh M. Galbraith, "Constitutional Factors in Homosexuality," *American Journal of Psychiatry* 13 (1934): 1249–1270, and George W. Henry, "Psychogenic and Constitutional Factors in Homosexuality; Their Relation to Personality Disorders," *Psychiatric Quarterly* 8 (1934): 243–64.

20. For examples of Hooton's use of constitutional or physique studies, see Earnest A. Hooton, *The American Criminal: An Anthropological Study,* 3 vols. (Cambridge: Harvard University Press, 1939); *Crime and the Man* (Cambridge: Harvard University Press, 1939); *Up From Ape* (New York: Macmillan, 1931); *Apes, Men and Morons* (New York: G. P. Putnam's Sons, 1937); *Twilight of Man* (New York: G. P. Putnam's Sons, 1939); *Why Men Behave Like Apes, and Vice Versa* (Princeton: Princeton University Press, 1940); Body Build and Life Record of 2631 Harvard Alumni of the Classes 1884–1912, typescript, Tozzer Library, Harvard University; *Handbook of Body Types in the United States Army,* 2 vols. (Washington, D.C.: Department of Army, Office of the Quartermaster General, Military Planning Division, Research and Development Branch, Environmental Protection Service, 1951). Hooton deployed his ideas of physique types to analyses of evolution and race mixture. See, for example, Hooton, "Race Mixture Studies of Dr. Earnest A. Hooton," *Eugenical News* 13 (1927): 81; "Racial Types in America and their Relation to Old World Types," in *The American Aborigines,* ed. Diamond Jenness (New York: Russell and Russell, 1972), 131–63; "Radcliffe Investigates Race Mixture," *Harvard Alumni Bulletin* (April 3, 1930): 768–76; "Some Early Drawings of Hottentot Women," in *Harvard African Studies (Varia Africana II)* 2 (1918): 83–99; "Progress in the Study of Race Mixtures with Special Reference to Work Carried on at Harvard University," in *Proceedings of the American Philosophical Society* 65 (1926): 312–25; "Race Mixture in the United States," *Pacific Review* 2 (1921): 116–27.

21. The social psychologist Dorothy Swaine Thomas concentrated her research on child development as well as on the psychological aspects of traumatic social phenomena. She wrote books on the social aspects of the business cycle, the social behavior of childhood traced longitudinally, internal migration in the United States and Sweden, population distribution and economic growth during and after industrialization in the United States (1870–1950), and the social and psychological aspects of Japanese internment in the United States. See Dorothy Swaine Thomas, *Social Aspects of the Business Cycle* (New York: Knopf, 1927); Dorothy Swaine Thomas, Alice Loomis, Ruth E. Arrington, *Observational Studies of Social Behavior* (New Haven: Institute of Human Relations, Yale University, 1933); Thomas, *Social and Economic Aspects of Swedish Population Movements, 1750–1933* (New York: Macmillan, 1941); Thomas et al., *The Spoilage: Japanese-American Evacuation and Resettlement During World War II* (Berkeley: University of California Press, 1946), and Thomas, Charles

Kikuchi, and James Sakoda, *The Salvage: Japanese-American Evacuations and Resettlement* (Berkeley: University of California Press, 1952).

The sociologist Maurice Davie wrote extensively on race relations and cultural assimilation in the United States. He was also interested in the adaptation of organisms to their environment as it related to mental disorders in humans, and suggested that modern society bred nervousness. For selected works, see Maurice Davie, "On the Examination of Immigrants Abroad" (1921); "A Constructive Immigration Policy," (1923); "Immigration and the Declining Birth Rate," (1924); "Social Aspects of Psychiatry," (1936); "Minorities, a Challenge to American Democracy," (1939); "The Cultural 'Syncretism' of Nationality Groups," (1940); "Our Vanishing Minorities," (1952); "The Negro and the War," (1943) in *The Papers of Maurice R. Davie,* ed. Ruby Jo Reeves Kennedy (New Haven: Yale University Press, 1961). See also Davie, *World Immigration, With Special Reference to the United States* (New York: Macmillan, 1946); *Negroes in American Society* (New York: Whittlesey House, 1949).

22. For more on the social geography and history of New York's gay subculture and crackdowns against it during the late 1920s and 1930s, see Chauncey, *Gay New York.* For an analysis of the transformation of Greenwich Village during the 1920s that discusses, in generally negative terms, the influx of "free lovers" and homosexuals into the Village, see Caroline Ware, *Greenwich Village: 1920-1930: A Comment on American Civilization in the Post-War Years* (1935; Berkeley: University of California Press, 1994). Margaret Anderson, *My Thirty Years War* (New York: Covici, Friede Publishers, 1930), offers a lively view of lesbianism in the context of bohemian life in New York City; Charles Henri Ford and Parker Tyler, *The Young and the Evil* (1933; rpt. London: GMP Publishers, 1989), is a thinly veiled fictional portrayal of the authors' involvement in gay life in the city. For background on the homosexual subculture of Harlem, see Eric Garber, "A Spectacle in Color: The Lesbian and Gay Subculture of Jazz Age Harlem," *Hidden from History,* ed. Duberman, Vicinus, and Chauncey, 318–31, and "'T'Aint Nobody's Bizness': Homosexuality in 1920s Harlem," in *Black Men/White Men,* ed. Michael J. Smith (San Francisco: Gay Sunshine Press, 1983); Langston Hughes, *The Big Sea: An Autobiography* (1940; rpt. New York: Thunder's Mouth Press, 1986).

23. For evidence of this trend in fiction writing, see Jeannette Foster, *Sex Variant Women in Literature* (New York: Vantage Press, Inc., 1956) and James Levin, *The Gay Novel in America* (New York: Garland Publications, 1991). Texts posing as scientific assessments of homosexuality were published during the 1930s, using a sensationalistic style to attract lay readers while also seeking to avoid being classified as pornographic. See, for example, La Forest Potter, *Strange Loves,* and Maurice Chideckel, *Female Sex Perversion.* For background on the censorship trials of *The Well of Loneliness,* see Morris L. Ernst and Alan U. Schwartz, *Censorship,* and for background on the 1926 closing of the Broadway production of Edouard Bourdet's *La Prisonniere,* which featured lesbianism in two of the lead female characters, see Brooks Atkinson, *Broadway,* and Vito Russo, *The Celluloid Closet: Homosexuality in the Movies* (New York: Harper and Row, 1981), 55.

24. For details about the backlash against homosexuals during the Great Depression, see Chauncey, *Gay New York,* 331–58.

25. In its early days, the Sex Variant Committee also considered sponsoring a

study of homosexuality in the merchant marine and Coast Guard, which was to take place at the U.S. Marine Hospital at Ellis Island in New York Harbor. The study proposed very similar techniques to those used in Jan Gay's study, but all expenses were to be paid by the U.S. Public Health Service and U.S. Marine Corps. Another proposed project focused on delinquent boys at the New York State Training School for Boys in Warwick to be supervised by Clarence O. Cheney, who was the School's staff psychiatrist from 1934 to 1935. Following the research protocols of the main study undertaken by Jan Gay and George Henry, Cheney's project involved interviewing and examining 100 boys known to have participated either in "active" or "passive" homosexuality and in comparing them to a control group of twenty-five boys who had no history of homosexuality. Neither the merchant marine nor the Warwick School projects were completed, mostly due to lack of funds. In addition to these proposals, the Sex Variant Committee also contemplated a number of other projects. One involved collaborating with psychiatrist Joseph Wortis, who proposed a study of a group of male homosexuals, under the supervision of Sex Variant Committee member Adolf Meyer and Havelock Ellis. While the approach of the study was psychoanalytic, Wortis also wanted to have the subjects x-rayed and physically examined. The Sex Variant Committee was receptive to cooperating, but it did not pursue the project mainly because it overlapped with the research project undertaken by Jan Gay, Robert Latou Dickinson, and George Henry. Dickinson also proposed a study of "intersexuality" or "hermaphroditism," which he believed had been poorly studied in the past, and which he thought was closely related to homosexuality. For Dickinson, this project was to combine the expertise of endocrinologists, psychiatrists, and gynecologists. Another proposal presented to the Sex Variant Committee which never went forward was made by George Henry who, after finishing five years of research on sex variance, was interested in the particular problems of sex offenders. Neither the intersex nor the sex offender studies were fully pursued. For more on these proposed studies, see Memorandum attached to Dickinson letter to Terman, 18 September 1935, Terman papers; Minutes, 18 October 1935, Terman Papers.

26. Memorandum attached to Dickinson letter to Terman, 11 February 1935, Terman papers.

27. Attachment to letter to Terman from Dickinson, 11 February 1935, Lewis M. Terman papers, Stanford University Archives, Stanford, California.

28. Henry graduated from Wesleyan College in 1912 and from Johns Hopkins University Medical School in 1916, where he was a student of Adolf Meyer and where he subsequently worked before being hired in 1924 to direct the psychiatric clinic at Bloomingdale Hospital in White Plains, New York. He did postgraduate work at the University of Berlin and the University of Amsterdam from 1929 to 1930. Prior to concentrating on homosexuality, he wrote several psychiatric textbooks and articles on practical aspects of hospital-based psychiatry. He also conducted research on metabolic and gastrointestinal processes in relation to psychiatric disorders in animals and humans. See George W. Henry, *Essentials of Psychiatry* (Baltimore: The Williams and Wilkins Company, 1925); *Essentials of Psychopathology* (Baltimore: The Williams and Wilkins Company, 1935); "Basal Metabolism and Emotional States," *Journal of Nervous and Mental Disorders* 70 (1929): 598–605; "Blood Calcium and Phosphorus in Personality Disorders," *Archives of Neurology and Psychiatry* 16 (1926):

48–59; "The Care and Treatment of Mental Disease: Yesterday and To-day," *Modern Hospital* (November 1929); "Catatonia in Birds, Induced by Bulbocapnine," *Psychiatric Quarterly* 8 (1931): 68–81; "A Comparative Study of the Action of Bulbocapnine and some other Drugs in Producing Catatonic States," *Acta Psychiatrica et Neurologica* 5 (1930): 463–71; "Gastrointestinal Motor Functions in Manic-Depressive Psychoses, Roentgenologic Observations," *American Journal of Psychiatry* 11 (1931): 19–28; "Gastrointestinal Motor Functions in Schizophrenia, Roentgenologic Observations," *American Journal of Psychiatry* 7 (1927): 135–52; "The Neuro-Psychiatric Out-Patient Clinic," *General Bulletin*, The Society of the New York Hospital (March 1927); "Practical Applications of Psychiatry in General Hospitals," *Medical Journal and Record* (October 1929); "Some Modern Aspects of Psychiatry in General Hospital Practice," *American Journal of Psychiatry* 9 (1929): 481–500.

Very little is known about George Henry's personal life except that in 1926, the *New York Times* reported that he left his position at Bloomingdale Hospital to go West to get a divorce after his first wife, Blanche, found fervent love letters written in code to him by Elizabeth Mangam, his assistant technician at the hospital. Blanche confronted him with the amorous lines composed in inverted alphabet, and he promptly walked out on her at midnight on January 30th. She tracked him down at his parent's house in Oswego, New York but then lost him again, the *Times* reported. In her divorce suit charging abandonment, Blanche alleged that this affair had gone on for eighteen months and that she had walked in on them kissing as Miss Mangam sat on the doctor's lap. Very shortly after this marriage of eight years ended, George Henry married Miss Eleanor Siebert, with whom he had two daughters and to whom he dedicated *Sex Variants*. *New York Times*, 21 February 1926; *New York Times*, 4 May 1926.

29. Proposal for Study of Homosexuality, G. W. Henry file, Payne–Whitney Clinic Archives, New York Hospital, New York.

30. George Henry to William Russell, 27 May 1935, and Russell to Henry, 20 June 1935, George W. Henry File, Payne–Whitney Archives. This arrangement was extended through 1942, when the Clinic became concerned that Henry and his assistant, Alfred Gross, were not following the procedures that Payne–Whitney had stipulated. This was well after the Sex Variant Study was completed and published and Henry had begun to study homosexual men deferred from Selective Service recruitment stations. Beginning in July 1942, the head of the Payne–Whitney Psychiatric Department notified Henry that the Clinic was short on lab space and needed to take back the labs allocated for use by the Sex Variant Committee. Just about two weeks after this original memo was sent, Clinic administrators voiced concern over the fact that Henry seemed to be absent from the Clinic and Gross seemed to be overseeing the research. This led Payne–Whitney administrators to investigate aspects of the research on draft deferrals, and they subsequently reported a number of indiscretions including the fact that some x-rays were paid for by Payne–Whitney and that subjects' were being taken through parts of the Clinic which were off-limits. In what appears to be a growing desire to sever its affiliation with Henry's externally directed research, the Clinic administrators voiced concern that subjects' confidentiality was not sufficiently protected. By May 1943, the pressure mounted to remove Gross from the research and to discontinue Henry's research altogether because of "practices which

might well bring psychiatry into public disfavor and lead to most unfortunate types of publicity." Apparently, this, in part, stemmed from an allegation that Alfred Gross had written letters to two homosexual subjects asking them for dates at the Stork Club. Shortly thereafter, Henry moved his research on homosexuality out of Payne-Whitney Clinic. See memo to Henry from Diethelm, 10 July 1942; letter to Bourne from Diethelm, 29 July 1942; letter to Bourne from Kopetzky, 19 August 1942; memo to Diethelm from Sargent, 10 September 1942; memo to Miss Lewis from Diethelm, 14 October 1942; letter to Diethelm from John P. Millet, 26 June 1943; letter to Diethelm from Dr. Thomas Rennie, 23 July 1943; letter to Henry from Diethelm, 5 January 1944, George Henry file, Payne-Whitney Clinic Archives, New York Hospital, New York, New York.

31. These included Drs. L. Mary Moench (ob/gyn New York Hospital), Robert Latou Dickinson (Committee on Maternal Health), Joseph C. Roper (ob/gyn New York Hospital), and D. Anthony D'Esopo (ob/gyn Vanderbilt Clinic/Columbia University), who performed gynecological exams on most of the women. Dr. William Cary (ob/gyn New York Hospital) and Dr. Hotchkiss (surgery New York Hospital) examined semen samples to assess rates of fertility and sterility among some of the male subjects. Drs. Arthur Grace (New York Hospital) and Ephraim Shorr (New York Hospital) did general physical and dermatological exams. Radiologists Dr. Robert P. Ball (Presbyterian Hospital/Columbia University) and Dr. John Russell Carty (New York Hospital) x-rayed most of the subjects. And George Henry was assisted by Dr. August E. Witzel (Brooklyn State Hospital) in doing the psychiatric interviews. Henry, *Sex Variants* (1948), xix.

32. Relations between Gay and Painter were at times strained. In his reminiscences on file at the Kinsey Institute, Painter recalled that "Jan was the dominant type. She preferred to dominate male homosexuals, using them as stooges, messenger boys and furniture movers. She also insisted frequently on entertaining her friends in the nude, which was no treat for most of them. When Zhenya left her she proceeded to get drunk more and more habitually till finally she disappeared into Mexico and has not been heard of since. . . . When not on any of these tangents, i.e. clothed and sociable, she was very pleasant, intelligent and agreeable." I found no evidence of Gay's attitudes toward Painter. Apparently he was correct in assessing her alcoholism; she later became involved in Alcoholics Anonymous in San Francisco and attempted to receive funding from the Guggenheim Foundation to study its effectiveness, particularly among lesbians and gay men. For further notes on Painter's impressions of Gay, see Thomas Painter file, Kinsey Institute, Bloomington, Indiana. See also "Proposal of Jan Gay to the Guggenheim Foundation" (for research on Alcoholics Anonymous), 25 October 1950, on file in the Jan Gay correspondence file at the Kinsey Institute.

33. The pedigree chart was developed and used widely by eugenicists in the United States. For examples of pedigree charts and the making of the eugenics family studies, see Henry H. Laughlin, "How to Make a Eugenic Family Study," *Eugenics Record Office Bulletin No. 13* (1915). See also Arthur H. Estabrook and Charles B. Davenport, *The Nam Family: A Study in Cacogenics* (Cold Spring Harbor, N.Y.: Eugenics Record Office, 1912).

34. These were based on ideas developed in Lewis M. Terman and Catherine

Cox Miles, "Sex Differences in the Association of Ideas"; *Attitude-Interest Analysis Test; Sex and Personality*. Terman and Miles were invited to join the Committee on the basis of their development of the M-F test.

35. After completing the Sex Variant study, Dickinson proposed a male counterpart study to the gynecology of homosexuality which was never completed, in part because Dickinson's younger colleague and friend, Alfred Kinsey, gently pointed out its myriad methodological flaws. The proposed study is "Masturbation, Physical Signs in Males," unpublished notes dated December 1946, Robert Latou Dickinson Papers, Countway Library, Harvard Medical School. For Kinsey's gentle critique, see letter from Kinsey to Dickinson, dated 1 January 1947, Miscellaneous Correspondence, Robert Latou Dickinson Papers, Countway Library.

36. See, for example, Lombroso and Ferrero, *The Female Delinquent*; Pauline Tarnowsky, *Étude anthropométrique sur les prostituées et les voleuses;* Earnest Hooton, *The American Criminal.* For analyses of anthropometric and physique studies of deviants, see Laura Engelstein, *The Keys to Happiness,* 128–64; David Horn, "This Norm Which is Note One," in *Deviant Bodies,* ed. Terry and Urla, 109–28; Allan Sekula, "The Body and the Archive."

37. Dickinson produced vivid images of female and male genitalia in *Human Sex Anatomy* and *Human Sex Anatomy: A Topographical Hand Atlas.*

38. Among his own small number of subjects, Ellis observed in 1901 that many had a tendency toward arrested development and physical infantilism. He discerned small external genitalia and small uteri and ovaries among inverted women, but, in contrast to Dickinson's findings, Ellis stated that "women with a large clitoris seem[ed] rarely to be a masculine type" (*Sexual Inversion,* 256). Ellis compared his findings with those of colonial doctors, anthropologists, and European travel writers who claimed to identify the signs of lesbianism around the world. One doctor with the British Indian Medical Service observed swollen vulvas on the bodies of female inmates in the central jail of Bengal and reported that these women, known to have engaged in tribadism, had "indelible stigmata of early masturbation and later sapphism," including very large clitorises which were "readily erectile," and elongated and erectile nipples. Ellis concurred with colonial officials in assuming that these signs were the result rather than the precipitating cause of lesbianism. *Sexual Inversion,* 210.

39. Allan Berube discusses procedures for examining the bodies of homosexual men for signs of sexual practices which were used during recruitment screening of U.S. troops for service in World War Two. According to the 1942 screening regulations, examiners were to check recruits for any signs of "feminine bodily characteristics" or "effeminacy in dress and manner," as well as for a "patulous [or expanded] rectum." Later on, the military adopted other tests to determine whether a man was a "true" homosexual (i.e., was penetrated either in anal sex or fellatio) rather than an incidental pervert. One test was the "gag-reflex" test which involved inserting a tongue depressor into the mouth of a man. If he gagged, he was not a homosexual; if he did not, there was a good chance that he was gay. This test presumed that those men who preferred to penetrate their male partners were not truly homosexual but were only occasionally vulnerable to perversion in certain contexts. This kind of test parallels, to some degree, the stimulus/response examinations to which the sex vari-

ant women were subjected in order to see if they would be sexually aroused by Dr. Moench's examination. Like the gag-reflex test, these exams watched for behavioral responses and assumed that if the subject showed certain signs, a determination of sexual orientation could be made. See Nicolai Gioscia, "The Gag Reflex and Fellatio," *American Journal of Psychiatry* 107 (November 1950): 380. See also A. C. Cornsweet and M. F. Hayes, "Conditioned Response to Fellatio," *American Journal of Psychiatry* 108 (July 1945): 76–78. Both articles are discussed by Allan Berube, *Coming Out Under Fire,* 19, 152–53, 160.

40. This remark appeared in Dickinson and Beam, *A Thousand Marriages,* 54.

41. Robert Latou Dickinson, "Hypertrophies of the Labia Minora." In 1931, he wrote that "the story of years of active self-excitation both as contemporary practice and as historical development" could be deduced from certain labial contours, enlargements, and varicosities, the range of excursions of the clitoris, reactions of the pelvic floor, and thickening of the tissues of the mammary glands. Dickinson, "Medical Analysis of *A Thousand Marriages,*" 531.

42. Miscellaneous Sketch Books (1935), Robert Latou Dickinson Papers, Countway Library, Harvard Medical School.

43. Dickinson, "Premarital Examination as Routine Preventive Gynecology," *American Journal of Obstetrics and Gynecology* 16, no. 5 (November 1928): 646.

44. This list of characteristics resembled those reported earlier by Havelock Ellis, who found that inverted women tended to have firm muscles and deeper voices, swaggered when they walked, and were usually good whistlers, in contrast to inverted men who mostly were incapable of whistling at all. Ellis, *Sexual Inversion,* 256.

45. Henry, *Sex Variants,* 1023.

46. Ibid., 1025.

47. This understanding of sex roles as the product not of nature but of performative acts resonates with Judith Butler's theorization of gender as the sedimentation of repetitious performance, although Henry was wholly unaware of the centrality of parody to his recommendation. See Judith Butler, *Gender Trouble: Feminism and the Subversion of Identity* (New York: Routledge, 1990).

48. Henry, *Sex Variants,* 1026.

49. Ibid.

50. Ibid, 1026.

51. Ibid., 1027.

CHAPTER SEVEN

1. Henry, *Sex Variants,* xiv.

2. Ibid., xii. In an early report to the Committee on the sex variant research, Henry described the types of male and female homosexuals he was studying and outlined the form of the systems and psychiatric exams each "patient" received. According to the minutes from this meeting, Henry "pointed out that these patients are not on the defensive. They consider themselves well adjusted homosexuals. They regret that they are not like others, however, and tend to blame society for its attitude toward them." This is an early indication that for all of Henry's sympathy toward the subjects, he also saw them as pathologically bitter for the stigma they suffer. This notion recurred later in Henry's subsequent work in pastoral psychology which fol-

lowed the Sex Variant research in the 1950s. Minutes of Sex Variant Committee Meeting, 18 October 1935.

3. Jeannette Foster, librarian at the Kinsey Institute for Sex Research from 1948–1952, and excavator and critic of lesbian themes in literature, credited George Henry and the Committee for the Study of Sex Variants in the early pages of her now-famous *Sex Variant Women in Literature* for fashioning the term "sex variant." (The book was originally published in 1956 at Foster's expense because it was so difficult to find a publisher.) George Henry wrote the preface to Foster's book, applauding her efforts at finding sex variance in the more imaginative realms outside of science, which dissected subjects and often obliterated their wholeness. Before embarking on her study of relations between women in literature, Foster explored the implications of such a term: "Since new viewpoints and methods of study are constantly altering our sex vocabulary, some preliminary definitions seem advisable. First, what is meant by sex variant? The term was selected because it is not as yet rigidly defined nor charged with controversial overtones. Intrinsically, variant means no more than differing from a chosen standard, and in the field of sex experience the standard generally accepted is adequate heterosexual adjustment. But even this phrase lacks precision. Lawyer, clergyman, physician, psychoanalyst, biologist, sociologist, each will interpret it from his particular viewpoint." Foster was fond of the term variance because of its flexibility and openness, which allowed her to conduct the hermeneutical practice of finding love (if not explicit sex) between women over centuries of Western fiction and poetry.

4. Hirschfeld's survey was organized into three sections corresponding to stages of the individual's development: hereditary, childhood, and present state. In addition to inquiring about neuroses and sexual inversion in parents, grandparents and relatives, it also asked questions about mental traits and sexual practices in the subject's childhood. The stage of adulthood was broken down into questions about physical characteristics (mannerisms, genitalia, hair, facial features), mental characteristics, sexual orientation, preferred practices, opinions about homosexuality, and aspects of the homosexual subculture. The questionnaire concluded with a special request that subjects present themselves to a competent physician for physical examination to look for unusual characteristics of the larynx and the pelvis, as well as other "possible signs of degeneration." Hirschfeld, while inclined to see homosexuality as a natural variation, also entertained the notion that it might be linked to degeneration in some cases. For a copy of the questionnaire, see Herman Nunberg and Ernst Federn, eds., *Minutes of the Vienna Psychoanalytic Society*, Vol. 1 (1906–1908) (New York: International Universities Press, Inc., 1962), 372–73. For background on its development and use, see Steakley, "Per scientiam ad justitiam," 147–48.

5. Henry, *Sex Variants*, xii.

6. Ibid., xiii.

7. For a more developed theoretical analysis of the problems inherent in understanding variant or deviant subjects through authoritative practices and discursive protocols of medical inquiry, see Jennifer Terry, "Theorizing Deviant Historiography," in *Feminists Revision History*, ed. Ann-Louise Shapiro (New Brunswick: Rutgers University Press, 1994).

8. Foucault, *The History of Sexuality, Volume One*, 101.

9. The glossary, compiled by Gershon Legman, opened with an essay on the history of words referring to homosexuality and was followed by a list of mostly slang terms for homosexual practices and identities. Many were of the terms were euphemistic and humorous codes developed within the subculture. Legman noted words and phrases used by lesbians and gay men amongst themselves, distinguishing these from terms used about homosexuality from outside the subculture. A quick glance at the list reveals that most of the terms attributed to outsiders (by a double asterisk) are terms of derogation, like *pervert, degenerate, neuter, Lesbo, fairy,* and *freak.* Other terms such as *privy-queen* (one who frequents toilets looking for "trade") and *top sergeant* (a masculine Lesbian "who takes or is imagined to take the superior position in tribady") were marked with a single asterisk as insider terms, which carried mixed meanings depending upon their context of use. Besides defining familiar terms like *gay* ("an adjective used almost exclusively by homosexuals to denote homosexuality, sexual attractiveness, promiscuity or lack of restraint") and *queer* (a synonym for homosexual), the glossary also listed slang words which denoted an array of types of homosexuals. A *chicken* was a young boy with little homosexual experience, a *wolf* preferred to be the penetrator and a *punk* or a *lamb* was the recipient in anal sex with another man. A *queen* was simply an effeminate male homosexual. The famous *bull dike* was an aggressive mannish (upper-case) Lesbian. A *bronco*, drawn from the cowboy term for unbroken horse, was a young homosexual man who was "normal [i.e. masculine], rough and sometimes intractable to the wishes of the homosexual." *Hustlers* or *trade* were usually masculine men, either heterosexual or homosexual, who sold themselves to other men, and *rough trade* were the particularly "uncultured" and rough version. Like *goofers*, they seldom, if ever, allowed themselves to be penetrated either in the mouth or anus since these were acts which rendered them effeminate. *Sea-food* was a code name for sailors. A *dowager* was an elegant elderly homosexual man, and a *drag queen* was a professional female impersonator who often engaged in *camping* or noisy, flamboyant, *flaming* ("obviously homosexual") and bizarre behavior "calculated to announce, express, or burlesque one's own homosexuality or that of another." Other names were based on the kinds of places certain individuals frequented and revealed the public nature of male homosexuality. For example, a *tea room queen* frequented toilets to find "persons amenable to his erotic or erotico-financial plans." A *church mouse* was a homosexual man who frequented churches and cathedrals in order to grope or cruise the young men there. Legman, concerned that male homosexuals not be seen as sacrilegious, stated that churches were chosen not because they were places of worship but merely because "crowds of standing and preoccupied people, as in cathedrals, subways, elevators and theaters, are ideal for the homosexual's purpose." Other terms connoting particular types of homosexuals were appropriations of kinship designations which were used to describe people and their relationships in familial terms. For example, a *cousin* was defined as the homosexual lover of another invert. An *auntie* was a middle-aged or elderly homosexual. A *daddy* or a *papa* was "a Lesbian of the masculine type, especially one who lives or consorts with a Lesbian of the feminine type, a *mama*." A *husband* was "the normal or else more aggressive member of a homosexual liaison," while a *wife* was "the less aggressive member of a homosexual alliance." Other terms were used to designate

certain types of people based on their preferred sexual practices. For example, a *pee-pee lover* was a "homosexual, particularly a fellator, who fancie[d] young boys." A *railroad queen* cruised the *jungles* where homosexual tramps lived. A *one-way man* was a male prostitute who, if heterosexual, would allow a client to perform oral sex on him but, if homosexual, would only allow a client to penetrate him. Logically, a *two-way man* allowed himself to be either penetrated or to be the penetrator. A *trapeze artist* was either a *cunnilinctor* (one who performs oral sex on a woman), a *cunnilinctrice* (a woman on whom oral sex is performed), or a woman who performed mutual oral sex or *sixty-nine* with another woman. Both the *jockey* and the *horsewoman*, like the *top sergeant*, were Lesbians who preferred to be on top during tribadism. Other terms denoted an individual's relationship to homosexual identity. For example, a *double-life man* was someone who was actively bisexual. Much of the homosexual argot consisted of euphemistically coded references to particular sexual practices. As a way of disguising their literal meaning, many used metaphors of travel which had the effect of figuring the body as a terrain to journey. For example, taking a *trip around the world* meant to lick a person over every surface of their body before performing oral sex on their genitals. To *make the blind see* meant to perform fellatio on an uncircumcised penis (a *blind piece*), and *to go way down South in Dixie* referred to performing oral sex either on men or women. To *go up the old dirt road* or to *kneel at the altar* referred to the practice of anal penetration of a man by another man. To *yodel in the canyon of love*, or to *sneeze in the cabbage* or to *go under the house* referred to oral sex between lesbians, the latter being an adaptation from African American slang. *Sixty-nine* or *soixante neuf* referred to mutual oral sex and *50/50* referred to alternating fellatio and anal sex. Other terms described characteristics of the genitals, and interestingly, most of these referred to male anatomy and were used mostly by homosexual men. For example, a circumcised penis was obliquely referred to as *low neck and short sleeves*, *lace curtain* was a long foreskin, *eggs in the basket* was the term for testicles, and *leather* referred to the anus. There were no terms listed for women's breasts but *muff* and *pussy* were mentioned. *Cunt* referred to "the internal and external female genitals," but was also appropriated by homosexual men to mean a boy's mouth or rectum when that boy was seen exclusively as a sexual object.

Various kinds of relationships to the gay and lesbian subculture and to homosexual identity also fit into this special vocabulary. In a clever inversion of its dominant meaning, to *discover one's gender* meant "to come out; to become progressively more homosexual with experience" while to *lose one's gender* meant "to leave homosexual practices and become heterosexual." *Ga-ga* referred to the first of seven recognized stages of homosexuality which culminated in the *deeper tones of lavender* when one discovered his or her *gender*, or *let one's hair down*. A homosexual who had *come out* completely was said to be *wise* and to *know the words and music*, or to understand and use typically homosexual locutions. Suggesting there was a tragedy to concealing one's homosexuality, the term to *wear a mourning veil* was typically the practice of a *hidden queen* who tried to mask his homosexuality.

This colorful and amusing list of sexually explicit terms was a sign of the richness of the urban subculture of homosexual men and lesbians. For historians, the glossary, like the lengthy narratives of the subjects, provides evidence of a lively group of people for whom homosexuality was not a curse of abjection, nor a product solely of a pathologizing discourse. On the contrary, camp humor was peppered throughout the glossary.

10. For the remainder of this chapter, all of the cited pages in the text are from *Sex Variants* (1948).

11. Perhaps for this reason, some major university libraries still keep *Sex Variants* locked in cabinets and available only by special request. In the original 1941 edition of *Sex Variants,* Henry stated that its distribution would be limited to doctors in order to assist them in becoming "the mental hygiene leaders of their communities." As if to defend against vigilante opposition, he specifically stated that the volumes were not going to be available to the general public. However, just seven years later, the 1948 edition of *Sex Variants* enjoyed a larger print run and thus a broader readership as it was purchased by many college and university libraries around the United States. Both editions of *Sex Variants* were published by Paul B. Hoeber Press, which published medical textbooks as a division of Harper and Row. Henry's subsequent volume based on the sex variant research was published by a textbook press for both educational and popular consumption and entitled *All the Sexes: A Study of Masculinity and Femininity* (New York: Rinehart & Company, Inc., 1955). It enjoyed even greater public readership, and parts of it were reprinted as popular pulp-style pocketbooks with forewords by clergymen who applauded the books for their instructive value among spiritual counselors. See George W. Henry, *Masculinity and Femininity* (New York: Collier Books, 1964); and *Society and the Sex Variant* (New York: Collier Books, 1965).

12. Sex Variant Committee member Maurice Davie, chair of the Yale sociology department, seriously questioned Painter's study, calling it "impressionistic and full of presumptions, and far from scientific in its approach." Davie, a stickler for careful social science research, recommended that the Sex Variant Committee appoint an advisory committee to oversee Painter's work. See CSSV Minutes, 18 October 1935, Terman papers. Painter's study, entitled "Homosexual Prostitution in Contemporary America," was edited in Alfred Kinsey, Wardell B. Pomeroy, Clyde E. Martin, and Paul H. Gebhard, *Sexual Behavior in the Human Male* (Philadelphia: Warner B. Saunders Co., 1948). Robert Dickinson's extensive handwritten notes on the study are on file in the Robert Latou Dickinson Papers at the Francis A. Countway Library of Medicine, Harvard University Medical School, dated 12 November 1941.

13. In January 1943, Kinsey wrote to Gay, following Dickinson's suggestion that they get together "and discuss our common interest in this problem [of human sexual behavior]." Kinsey briefly outlined his research, which he promised would go "further into the homosexual than any other study made in this country; but it is by no means confined to the homosexual alone" and involves tens of thousands of histories in great detail, without making evaluations as to the ethical or social desirability of any type of behavior. Kinsey stated that his study "attempts to try and understand the viewpoint of all sorts of people who are involved in all sorts of behavior," remarking that "I understand [from reports of both Legman and Dickinson] that your experience with the Henry study was disappointing. . . . Consequently, I should not blame you for not being interested in even looking at any other study which is under

way." But Kinsey wanted to make the effort to contact Gay anyway, on Dickinson's insistence. See letter from Kinsey to Jan Gay, 22 January 1943, Jan Gay correspondence file, Kinsey Institute. Gay responded several years later in August of 1946, voicing interest in Kinsey's research, to which Kinsey responded immediately to tell Gay that he would really appreciate her help in New York City in gathering data during November of 1946, and to state that Tom Painter told her about Kinsey's research. See letter from Kinsey to Gay, 13 August 1946. It appears that Gay, who had been director of admissions and public relations for the Latin American Institute and then Webber College, did not follow through on Kinsey's request. Several years later, in October 1950, Gay wrote Kinsey from her new home in Sausalito, California, requesting a letter of recommendation for a fellowship proposal she was preparing to submit to the Guggenheim Foundation to research the treatment and rehabilitation of alcoholics. "My interest here, as in the earlier studies in homosexuality, is a personal one and embraces almost as wide an acquaintance among participants." Gay included the proposal, which focused on the evaluation of group therapy techniques and dynamics of Alcoholics Anonymous. See letter from Gay to Kinsey, 25 October 1950, Kinsey Institute. Kinsey declined, stating, "I am afraid I am not the person to recommend you. . . . I met you only for a short time and know nothing more about you than general hearsay. I know nothing of your specific scientific training and have had no opportunity to observe you in scientific work. Your one volume on nudism is the only completed work that I know. Consequently, I think someone better qualified than I should make the recommendation. Meanwhile, I wish you the best of things and hope we may become better acquainted in time." Kinsey to Gay, 31 August 1950, Kinsey Institute.

CHAPTER EIGHT

1. For details of Eve Addams's case, see Chauncey, *Gay New York*, 240–43.

2. For further analysis of this sentiment, see Lewis A. Erenberg, "From New York to Middletown: Repeal and the Legitimization of Night Life in the Great Depression," *American Quarterly* 38 (1986): 761–78.

3. For more on the damaging effects of the repeal of Prohibition on gay subcultures in New York City, see Chauncey, *Gay New York*, 327–45.

4. For more on Walker's ill-repute, see J. Brooks Atkinson, *Broadway* (New York: Macmillan, 1970), 248.

5. Chauncey, *Gay New York*, 333.

6. Quoted in *The New York Herald Tribune*, September 26, 1937.

7. The most famous of the original psychopath statutes was the Briggs Law, passed in Massachusetts in 1921, requiring psychiatric evaluation of recidivist felons and those convicted of capital offenses. The innovative law led to many convicts being labeled as psychopaths. In 1918, psychiatrist Bernard Glueck diagnosed nearly a fifth of the inmates in Sing-Sing prison as constitutionally inferior or psychopathic, and from 1919 to 1926 the percentage of inmates at Ossining Prison classified as "psychopathic" jumped from 11.6 to 50.8 percent. See Bernhard Glueck, "A Study of 608 Admissions to Sing-Sing Prison," *Mental Hygiene* 2, no.1 (January 1918): 85–123 and Special Committee of the State Commission of Prisons, "The Psychopathic Delin-

quent," in *31st Annual Report of the State Commissioner of Prisons* (Ossining, N. Y., 1926). Among the most important texts of criminal psychopathy from the 1930s are Franz Alexander and Bruno Straub, *The Criminal, the Judge, and the Public,* trans. Gregory Zilboorg (New York: Macmillan, 1931); Eugen Kahn, *Psychopathic Personalities,* trans. H. Flanders Dunbar (New Haven: Yale University Press, 1931); Benjamin Karpman, *Case Studies in the Psychopathy of Crime,* 2 vols. (Washington, D.C.: Mimeoform Press, 1933; rpt. ed., New York: Mental Science Publishing Co., 1939). See also Karpman, "The Principles and Aims of Criminal Psychopathy," *Journal of Criminal Psychopathology* 1 (January 1940): 172–218.

8. Estelle Freedman, "'Uncontrolled Desires': The Response to the Sexual Psychopath, 1920–1960," in *Passion and Power: Sexuality in History,* ed. Peiss and Simmons (Philadelphia: Temple University Press, 1989), 202.

9. Ibid., 200.

10. For more on the changing perceptions of male sexuality during the 1930s, see Pleck, "The Theory of Male Sex Role Identity," in *In the Shadows of the Past,* ed. Lewin, 205–25.

11. Chauncey, *Gay New York,* 334.

12. For background on proposals to legalize prostitution in the United States during the nineteenth century, see Graham Barker-Benfield, *The Horrors of a Half-Known Life: Male Attitudes toward Women and Sexuality in Nineteenth-Century America* (New York: Harper & Row, 1976). For similar analyses in European history, see Judith R. Walkowitz, *Prostitution and Victorian Society: Women, Class, and the State* (New York: Cambridge University Press, 1980) and *City of Dreadful Delight: Narratives of Sexual Danger in Late-Victorian London* (Chicago: University of Chicago Press, 1992); Alain Corbin, *Women for Hire: Prostitution and Sexuality in France After 1850,* trans. Alan Sheridan (Cambridge: Harvard University Press, 1990).

13. See, for example, Hunter McGuire and G. Frank Lydston, "Sexual Crimes Among Southern Negroes," *Virginia Medical Monthly* 20 (May 1893): 122–23.

14. See, for example, Fritz Wittels, "The Criminal Psychopath in the Psychoanalytic System," *Psychoanalytic Review* 24 (July 1937): 276–91.

15. See, for example, the case of "J.S.," an 18-year-old shipping clerk, admitted to Bellevue Hospital in October 1939. As the psychiatrist reported, "One night he followed an unknown girl home and struck her in the face. He had previously shunned the company of girls and denied any sexual experiences—that is, he denied heterosexual, homosexual episodes or masturbation. He was tense and had but little insight into his behavior but no other evidence of psychopathology was apparent. He said the girl attracted him, that he followed her home and completely lost control of himself and struck her." The psychiatrists gave J. S. a diagnosis of "no psychosis," and the judge suspended his sentence. See Donald Shaskan, "One Hundred Sex Offenders," *American Journal of Orthopsychiatry* 9 (1939): 569. Reporting statistics on sex offenses in 1939, Frosch and Bromberg omitted any discussion of coercive rape of adult women, focusing instead primarily on pedophilia and offenses involving homosexuality. See Jack Frosch and Walter Bromberg, "The Sex Offender: A Psychiatric Study," *American Journal of Orthopsychiatry* 9 (1939): 761–77.

16. For an overview of the plan, see Winfred Overholser, "Legal and Administrative Problems," *Mental Hygiene* 22, no. 1 (January 1938): 20–24.

17. This legislative language is quoted in Joseph Wortis, "Sex Taboos, Sex Offenders and the Law," *American Journal of Orthopsychiatry* 9 (1939): 555.

18. See George W. Henry and Alfred A. Gross, "Social Factors in the Case Histories of One Hundred Underprivileged Homosexuals," *Mental Hygiene* 22, no. 4 (October 1938): 595.

19. See, for example, B. Pollens, *The Sex Criminal* (New York: The Macauly Company, 1938); Karl M. Bowman, "Psychiatric Aspects of the Problem," *Mental Hygiene* 22, no. 1 (January 1938): 10–20; Jack Frosch and Walter Bromberg, "The Sex Offender"; Joseph Wortis, "Sex Taboos, Sex Offenders and the Law"; Donald Shaskan, "One Hundred Sex Offenders"; George W. Henry and Alfred A. Gross, "Social Factors in the Case Histories of One Hundred Underprivileged Homosexuals"; George W. Henry and Alfred A. Gross, "Social Factors in Delinquency," *Mental Hygiene* 24, no. 1 (January 1940): 54–78; George W. Henry and Alfred A. Gross, "The Homosexual Delinquent," *Mental Hygiene* 25, no. 3 (July 1941): 420–42; George W. Henry and Alfred A. Gross, "The Sex Offender: A Consideration of Therapeutic Principles," *National Probation Association Yearbook* (1940): 114–37; Ira S. Wile, "Sex Offenders Against Young Children," *Journal of Social Hygiene* 25, no. 1 (1939): 33.

20. Austin H. MacCormick, "New York's Present Problem," *Mental Hygiene* 22 (January 1938): 4.

21. Henry and Gross, "Social Factors in the Case Histories of One Hundred Underprivileged Homosexuals."

22. Frosch and Bromberg reviewed conviction statistics from 1937 to 1939 in New York City and found that recidivism rates were low among most sex offenders, including homosexuals engaged in consensual acts with adults. The highest rates were among pedophiles, where "54 of the total 120 cases [from 1937 to 1939] had a history of a previous offense of some sort, more than half of them being of sexual type." See Frosch and Bromberg, "The Sex Offender," 765. Another report from 1938 reported that a slightly lower rate of recidivism existed among sex offenders compared to those charged with non-sex related crimes. See *Sex Crimes in New York: A Study by the staff of the Citizens Committee on the Control of Crime in New York (1938)*, cited in Donald Shaskan, "One Hundred Sex Offenders," 567.

23. For background, see Timothy Gilfoyle, *City of Eros*, and Allan Brandt, *No Magic Bullet*.

24. For a history of the expansion of psychiatry away from the confines of asylum-based treatment of the patently insane into the realm of public discourse and the treatment of common psychiatric problems of everyday life, see Elizabeth Lunbeck, *The Psychiatric Persuasion*.

25. The 1937 symposium was published as "The Challenge of Sex Offenders," *Mental Hygiene* 22 (January 1938): 1–24, with contributions by psychiatrists Edward A. Strecker, Karl M. Bowman, Winfred Overholser, and New York City Commissioner of Crime Austin MacCormick.

26. Edward A. Strecker, "Introduction" to "The Challenge of Sex Offenders," *Mental Hygiene* 22, no. 1 (January 1938): 2–3.

27. Ibid., 3.

28. Austin H. MacCormick, "New York's Present Problem," *Mental Hygiene* 22,

no. 1 (January 1938): 4–10. For his progressive perspective on prisoner rehabilitation, see Austin H. MacCormick, *The Education of Adult Prisoners: A Survey and a Program* (New York: National Society of Penal Information, 1931).

29. Karl M. Bowman, "Psychiatric Aspects of the Problem," 11–12.

30. Michel Foucault has analyzed this shift from a focus on the crime to a focus on the criminal's personality that distinguished modern forensic psychiatry in "The Dangerous Individual," in *Michel Foucault: Politics, Philosophy, Culture,* ed. Lawrence D. Kritzman and translated by Alain Baudot and Jane Couchman (New York: Routledge, 1988), 125–51.

31. Bowman, "Psychiatric Aspects of the Problem," 12.

32. Concentrating on indigenous peoples of the Trobriand Islands in Northwest Melanesia, Bronislaw Malinowski observed that Trobriand parents were indifferent to their children's sexual behavior. Thus, he advanced a functionalist argument that the absence of childhood sexual repression among "savages" served specific cultural needs. Consequently, sexual repression in advanced industrial societies functioned to support complex processes of civilization. See Bronislaw Malinowski, *Sex and Repression in Savage Society* (London: Kegan Paul, Trench, Trubner, 1927); Malinowski, *The Sexual Life of Savages in Northwestern Melanesia* (London: Kegan Paul, Trench, Trubner, 1927). For more on Malinowski, see Andrew P. Lyons and Harriet D. Lyons, "Savage Sexuality and Secular Morality."

33. See especially Sigmund Freud, "My Views on the Part Played by Sexuality in the Aetiology of the Neuroses" (1906), *Standard Edition* 7: 271–79; "The Sexual Enlightenment of Children"; "Analysis of a Phobia in a Five-Year-Old Boy ('Little Hans')"; "On the Sexual Theories of Children" (1908), *Standard Edition* 9: 207–26; "Family Romances" (1909), *Standard Edition* 9: 237–41; "The Infantile Genital Organization" (1923), *Standard Edition* 19: 141–45; "Some Psychical Consequences of the Anatomical Distinctions Between the Sexes." See also Albert Moll, *The Sexual Life of the Child* (New York: Macmillan Company, 1929).

34. Bowman, "Psychiatric Aspects of the Problem," 13–15, 19.

35. Bernhard Zondek, "Mass Excretion of Oestrogenic Hormone in the Urine of the Stallion."

36. Bowman explored questions of gender in relation to everyday psychological problems in Karl M. Bowman, *Personal Problems of Men and Women* (New York: Greenberg Press, 1931).

37. Bowman, "Psychiatric Aspects of the Problem," 15.

38. George W. Henry, "Psychogenic and Constitutional Factors in Homosexuality: Their Relation to Personality Disorders," *Psychiatric Quarterly* 8 (January 1934): 243–64. See also George W. Henry and Hugh M. Galbraith, "Constitutional Factors in Homosexuality," *American Journal of Psychiatry* 13 (May 1934): 1249–70, which analyzed the same mental patients and came to the same conclusions.

39. George W. Henry, "Psychogenic and Constitutional Factors in Homosexuality," 259.

40. Ibid., 260.

41. Henry, "Psychogenic Factors in Overt Homosexuality," 889.

42. Ibid., 905.

43. Ibid.

44. E. E. Mayer, Comment on George Henry's "Psychogenic Factors in Homosexuality," *American Journal of Psychiatry* 93 (January 1937): 906.

45. For demographic data on the ethnicity, religious background, intellectual level, and birthplace of the 709 felony sex offenders convicted from 1937 to 1939 in New York City, see Jack Frosch and Walter Bromberg, "The Sex Offender." This study showed that, contrary to popular belief, American-born white men were arrested for the majority of sex offenses. Of the sixty-four men arrested for felonies related to homosexual activity, forty-one were born in the United States, forty-four were white, and twenty were black.

46. George W. Henry and Alfred A. Gross, "Social Factors in the Case Histories of One Hundred Underprivileged Homosexuals," 595.

47. Ibid., 611.

48. Joseph Wortis, "Sex Taboos, Sex Offenders and the Law," *American Journal of Orthopsychiatry* 9 (1939): 554–64 and Ruth Benedict, "Sex in Primitive Society," *American Journal of Orthopsychiatry* 9 (1939): 570–75.

49. Wortis, "Sex Taboos, Sex Offenders, and the Law," 563.

50. Benedict, "Sex in Primitive Society," 570.

51. Ibid., 572.

52. Bowman, "Psychiatric Aspects of the Problem," 16.

53. Wortis, "Sex Taboos, Sex Offenders, and the Law," 564.

54. This is outlined in Lauretta Bender and Samuel Paster, "Homosexual Trends in Children," *American Journal of Orthopsychiatry* 22 (1941): 730–44. For other analyses from this period that tied homosexuality to problems of children's gender identification, see Louis S. London, "Analysis of a Homosexual Neurosis," and Helene Deutsch, "On Female Homosexuality."

55. Wilhelm Stekel, "Is Homosexuality Curable?" 450. The article originally appeared in German in *Der Nervenartz* 2, no. 6 (1929). Stekel was the only member in attendance at the 1908 Vienna Psychoanalytic Society meeting who openly and adamantly opposed any association with Hirschfeld "for personal as well as objective reasons." He expressed his contempt more openly as the years went on. See Nunberg and Federn, *Minutes*, 372.

56. For an account of increasing psychoanalytic hostility toward homosexuals, see Lewes, *The Psychoanalytic Theory of Male Homosexuality*, 95–172.

57. W. Beran Wolfe, *A Woman's Best Years* (Garden City, New York: Garden City Publishing, 1935), 157.

58. Karl A. Menninger, "Comment on paper by George S. Sprague, 'Varieties of Homosexual Manifestations,'" *American Journal of Psychiatry* 92 (1935): 150–51.

59. Freud's 1935 letter was published some sixteen years later in "Letter to An American Mother," *American Journal of Psychiatry* 107 (1951): 786–87.

60. Abraham Brill, "Sexual Manifestations in Neurotic and Psychotic Symptoms," *Psychiatric Quarterly* 14 (1933): 13.

61. See, for example, Joseph Wortis, "A Note on the Body Build of the Male Homosexual," *American Journal of Orthopsychiatry* 8 (1937): 1121–25; Wortis, "Intersexuality and Effeminacy in the Male Homosexual," *American Journal of Orthopsychiatry* 10 (1940): 567–70; and Hyman S. Barahal, "Constitutional Factors in Psychotic Male Homosexuals," *Psychiatric Quarterly* 13 (1939): 391–400. A subsequent refuta-

tion of constitutional and hereditary theories was presented in Roy A. Darke, "Heredity as an Etiological Factor in Homosexuality," *The Journal of Nervous and Mental Disease* 107 (January–June 1948): 251–68.

62. Lieut. Herbert Greenspan and Comdr. John D. Campbell, "The Homosexual as Personality Type," *American Journal of Psychiatry* 101 (1945): 687.

63. Ibid., 688.

64. For more on military psychiatry during World War Two and immediately afterwards, see Allan Berube, *Coming Out Under Fire: The History of Gay Men and Women in World War Two* (New York: Free Press, 1990), chapter one.

65. Louis W. Max, "Breaking Up a Homosexual Fixation by the Conditioned Reaction Technique: A Case Study," *Psychological Bulletin* 32 (1935): 794.

66. Newdigate M. Owensby, "The Correction of Homosexuality," *Urologic and Cutaneous Review* 45, no. 8 (1941): 495. See also Owensby, "Homosexuality and Lesbianism Treated with Metrazol," *Journal of Nervous and Mental Disease* 92, no. 1 (1940): 65–66.

CHAPTER NINE

1. Quoted material drawn from Alfred Kinsey et al., *Sexual Behavior in the Human Male,* 664 and from California State Assembly, *Preliminary Report of the Subcommittee on Sex Crimes of the Assembly Interim Committee on Judicial System and Judicial Process,* 1949 Session, Appendix, 176.

2. Edmund Bergler, "The Myth of a National Disease: Homosexuality and the Kinsey Report," *The Psychiatric Quarterly* 22 (1948): 66–88, excerpted in *The Homosexuals: As Seen By Themselves and 30 Authorities,* ed. A. Krich (New York: Citadel Press, 1954), 247–48.

3. Alfred Kinsey, "Homosexuality: Criteria for a Hormonal Explanation of the Homosexual," *The Journal of Clinical Endocrinology* 1, no. 5 (May 1941): 425.

4. Ibid., 424.

5. Ibid., 425.

6. Alfred Kinsey et al., *Sexual Behavior in the Human Male* and *Sexual Behavior in the Human Female* (Philadelphia: W. B. Saunders Co., 1953).

7. Kinsey et al., *Sexual Behavior in the Human Male,* 393.

8. For more on the background of Kinsey's research, see Janice Irvine, *Disorders of Desire,* 34–66; Regina Markell Morantz, "The Scientist as Sex Crusader: Alfred C. Kinsey and American Culture," *American Quarterly* 29 (Winter 1977): 563–89; Wardell B. Pomeroy, *Dr. Kinsey and the Institute for Sex Research* (New York: Harper and Row, 1972); Cornelia V. Christenson, *Kinsey: A Biography* (Bloomington, Ind.: Institute for Sex Research, 1971); Stephanie H. Kenen, "Who Counts When You're Counting Homosexuals? Hormones and Homosexuality in Mid-Twentieth Century America," in *Science and Homosexualities,* ed. Vernon A. Rosario (New York: Routledge Press, 1997), 197–218.

9. Kinsey et al., *Sexual Behavior in the Human Male,* 623–31.

10. Ibid., 357–62, 382–84, 455–460, 482–84.

11. Kinsey, "Homosexuality," 425. Kinsey stated that "an individual who engages in a sexual relation with another male without, however, coming to climax, or an individual who is erotically aroused by a homosexual stimulus without ever having

overt relations, has certainly had a homosexual experience." But, he continued, "such relations and reactions, however, are not included in the incidence data [reported] . . . because the volume as a whole has been concerned with the number and sources of male orgasms." However, his famous 7–point scale of heterosexual-homosexual ratings did include homosexual contacts "in which the subject fails to reach climax." See Kinsey et al., *Sexual Behavior in the Human Male,* 623.

12. Christenson, *Kinsey: A Biography.*

13. Kinsey et al., *Sexual Behavior in the Human Female,* 452–55, 474–79, 490–501.

14. Ibid., 468.

15. Morantz, "The Scientist as Sex Crusader."

16. Henry, *Sex Variants,* 1075–76, 1081.

17. Kinsey et al., *Sexual Behavior in the Human Female,* 468.

18. See, for example, Clyde V. Kiser, "A Statistician Looks at the Report," in *Problems of Sexual Behavior,* ed. Charles Walter Clarke (New York: American Social Hygiene Association, 1948), 28–36; G. Ramsey, "A Survey Evaluation of the Kinsey Report," *Journal of Clinical Psychology* 6 (1950): 133–43.

19. A. Hobbs and R. Lambert, "An Evaluation of *Sexual Behavior in the Human Male,*" *American Journal of Psychiatry* 104 (1948): 758–65; A. Hobbs and W. Kephart, "Professor Kinsey: His Facts and His Fantasy," *American Journal of Psychiatry* 110 (1954): 614–20.

20. Lewis M. Terman, "Kinsey's 'Sexual Behavior in the Human Male': Some Comments and Criticisms," *Psychological Bulletin* 45 (1948): 443–59.

21. Ashley Montagu, "Understanding Our Sexual Desires," in *About the Kinsey Report: Observations by Eleven Experts on 'Sexual Behavior in the Human Male,'* ed. Donald Porter Geddes and Enid Curie (New York: Signet Books, 1948), 65.

22. Mead reiterated this same criticism when Kinsey released his volume on female sexual behavior, which Mead believed ought to be prohibited from being a best seller because "the sudden removal of a previously guaranteed reticence has left many young people singularly defenseless in just those areas where their desire to conform was protected by a lack of knowledge of the extent of nonconformity." Margaret Mead, "An Anthropologist Looks at the Report," quoted in Wardell Pomeroy, *Dr. Kinsey and the Institute for Sex Research,* 362.

23. Karl Menninger, "One View of the Kinsey Report," *General Practitioner* 8 (1953): 67–72, reprinted in *Pastoral Psychology* also in 1953.

24. O. Spurgeon English, "Sex and Human Love," in *About the Kinsey Report: Observations by Eleven Experts on 'Sexual Behavior in the Human Male,'* ed. Donald Porter Geddes and Enid Curie (New York: New American Library), 96–112.

25. Billy Graham, "The Bible and Dr. Kinsey," and William S. Kroger, "Female Specialist Repudiates Kinsey," in *I Accuse Kinsey! Startling Exposé of Kinsey's Sex Reports,* ed. E. J. Daniels (Orlando, Florida: Christ for the World Publishers, 1954), 103–12, 127–32; the Kroger quotation is on 128.

26. For articulations of this critique from within psychoanalytic circles, see R. Knight, "Psychiatric Issues in the Kinsey Report," in *Sex Habits of American Men: A Symposium on the Kinsey Report,* ed. R. Deutsch (New York: Grosset and Dunlap, 1948); P. Hoch and J. Zubin, eds., *Psychosexual Development in Health and Disease* (New York: Grune and Stratton, 1949); and D. Levy, "Discussion of Clinical and Psycho-

analytic Approach," in *Psychosexual Development in Health and Disease,* ed. Hoch and Zubin.

27. Lawrence Kubie, "Psychiatric Implications of the Kinsey Report," *Psychosomatic Medicine* 10 (1948): 95–106; rpt. in *Sexual Behavior in American Society: An Appraisal of the First Two Kinsey Reports,* ed. Jerome Himelhoch and Sylvia Fleis Fava (New York: W. W. Norton and Company, Inc., 1955), 270–93.

28. See, for example, Jule Eisenbud, "A Psychiatrist Looks at the Report," in *Problems of Sexual Behavior,* ed. Charles Walter Clarke, 20–27; Aron Krich, "Before Kinsey: Continuity in American Sex Research," *Psychoanalytic Review* 63 (1966): 69–90.

29. Krich, "Before Kinsey," 86–87.

30. Kubie, "Psychiatric Implications of the Kinsey Report," 292; see also S. Margolin, "Review of *Sexual Behavior in the Human Male,*" *Psychoanalytic Quarterly* 17 (1948): 265–72.

31. Krich, "Before Kinsey," 86.

32. Ibid., 87; Kubie, "Psychiatric Implications of the Kinsey Report," 275.

33. Wilhelm Stekel, "Is Homosexuality Curable?"

34. Edmund Bergler, "Present Situation in the Genetic Investigation of Homosexuality," *Marriage Hygiene* 4, no. 1 (1937): 16–29.

35. Bergler elaborated the ideas outlined in his 1942 lecture in several books published in the 1950s. See, Edmund Bergler, *The Writer and Psychoanalysis* (Garden City, N.Y.: Doubleday, 1950); *Counterfeit Sex: Homosexuality, Impotence, Frigidity* (New York: Grune and Stratton, 1951); *Fashion and the Unconscious* (New York: R. Brunner, 1953); *Homosexuality: Disease or Way of Life?* (New York: Hill and Wang, 1956); and *One Thousand Homosexuals: Conspiracy of Silence, or Curing and Deglamorizing Homosexuals?* (Paterson, N.J.: Pageant Books, Inc., 1959).

36. Bergler, *Homosexuality,* 8–9, 271.

37. In addition, other authors who exhibited the deep-rooted psychopathology of homosexual masochism included Somerset Maugham and Stendhal. See Bergler, *The Writer and Psychoanalysis* (1950), much of which was repeated in *Homosexuality: Disease or Way of Life?*

38. Among Bergler's books, *Homosexuality: Disease or Way of Life?* was released in numerous editions, including a pocketbook-sized 7th edition in 1971, nine years after his death.

39. See, for example, Irving Bieber, "Clinical Aspects of Male Homosexuality," and Cornelia B. Wilbur, "Clinical Aspects of Female Homosexuality,"in *Sexual Inversion: The Multiple Roots of Homosexuality,* ed. Judd Marmour (New York: Basic Books, 1965), 248–67, 268–81; Frank S. Caprio, *Female Homosexuality;* Louis S. London and Frank S. Caprio, *Sexual Deviations: A Psychodynamic Approach* (Washington, D.C.: The Linacre Press, Inc., 1950); Louis S. London, *Sexual Deviations in the Male and Female* (New York: Bell Publishing Company, 1957); Charles W. Socarides, *The Overt Homosexual* (New York: Grune and Stratton, 1968). For more recent texts arguing that homosexuality can be cured, see Joseph Nicolosi, *Reparative Therapy of Male Homosexuality* (Northvale, N.J.: Jason Aronson, Inc., 1991) and *Healing Homosexuality: Case Stories in Reparative Therapy* (Northvale, N.J.: Jason Aronson, Inc., 1993).

40. Bergler, *Homosexuality,* 146–52.

41. Bergler, *Fashion and the Unconscious.*

42. Bergler, *Homosexuality,* 13–26, 277.

43. Edmund Bergler and William S. Kroger, *Kinsey's Myth of Female Sexuality: The Medical Facts* (New York: Grune and Stratton, 1954).

44. Bergler, *Homosexuality,* 246–47.

45. Ibid., 247.

46. For examples of particularly hostile exchanges between Bergler and his patients, see Bergler, *Homosexuality,* 44–60, 255–56.

47. Ibid., 271.

48. For later examples of this, see Irving Bieber et al., *Homosexuality: A Psychoanalytic Study of Male Homosexuals* (New York: Vintage Books, 1962); Charles Socarides, "Theoretical and Clinical Aspects of Overt Male Homosexuality," *Journal of the American Psychiatric Association* 8 (1960): 552–66; Socarides, "Homosexuality," *International Journal of Psychiatry* 10 (1972): 118–25; Socarides, *Homosexuality* (New York: Aronson, 1978).

49. This argument was articulated again at length after Kinsey's death in 1957 in Bergler, *One Thousand Homosexuals.*

50. Bergler, "The Myth of a National Disease."

CHAPTER TEN

1. D. S. Bailey, *Homosexuality and the Western Christian Tradition* (New York: Longmans, Green and Company, 1955).

2. Philip Wylie, *Generation of Vipers* (New York: Farrar and Rinehart, Inc., 1942).

3. Ibid., 188–89.

4. Select publications include Edward A. Strecker, "Everyday Psychology of the Normal Child," *Mental Hygiene* 17, no. 1 (January 1933): 65–81; "Introduction to 'The Challenge of Sex Offenders'"; *Beyond the Clinical Frontiers: A Psychiatrist Views Crowd Behavior* (New York: W. W. Norton and Company, Inc., 1940); "The Man and the Mob," *Mental Hygiene* 24, no. 4 (October 1940): 529–51; "Mental Hygiene and Mass Man," *Mental Hygiene* 25, no. 1 (January 1941): 3–5; *Fundamentals of Psychiatry* (Philadelphia: Lippincott, 1942); "Military Psychiatry: World War I," in *One Hundred Years of American Psychiatry,* edited by J. K. Hall (New York: Columbia University Press, 1944); "The Contribution of Psychiatry to Democratic Morals," *Rhode Island Journal of Medicine* 27 (1944): 383–84; "Psychiatry Speaks to Democracy," *Mental Hygiene* 29, no. 4 (October 1945): 591–605; Strecker and Kenneth E. Appel, "Morale," *American Journal of Psychiatry* 99 (September 1942): 163; Strecker and Appel, *Psychiatry in Modern Warfare* (New York: Macmillan, 1945); Strecker and Francis T. Chambers, Jr., *Alcohol: One Man's Meat* (New York: Macmillan, 1938).

5. For news coverage of Strecker's lectures against "momism," see, for example, "'Moms' Denounced as Peril to Nation," *New York Times,* April 28, 1945.

6. Edward A. Strecker, *Their Mother's Sons: The Psychiatrist Examines an American Problem* (New York and Philadelphia: J. B. Lippincott Company, 1946) and Edward A. Strecker and Vincent T. Lathbury, *Their Mother's Daughters* (Philadelphia: J. B. Lippincott Company, 1956).

7. Strecker, *Sons,* 131.

8. Ibid., 128–31. Similar ideas about overly attached mothers causing homosexu-

ality in their sons persisted in subsequent psychoanalytic studies of homosexuality. See, for example, Irving Bieber's notion of the "CBI mother"—or *close, binding, and intimate* mother—whose extraordinary and perverse intimacy interfered with her son's normal heterosexual pursuits and emasculated him through debilitating guilt. Bieber discussed the CBI mothers in Society of Medical Psychoanalysts, *Homosexuality: A Psychoanalytic Study of Male Homosexuals* (New York: Vintage Books, 1962).

9. Strecker, *Sons,* 18.

10. Ibid., 128–32.

11. Strecker and Lathbury, *Daughters,* 153.

12. Arguments linking lesbianism to pathological behavior of both mothers and fathers persisted into the 1960s. See, for example, Richard C. Robertiello, "Clinical Notes: Results of Separation from Iposexual Parents During the Oedipal Period, [and] A Female Homosexual Panic," *Psychoanalytic Review* 51, no. 4 (1964–65): 670–72; Robertiello, *Voyage from Lesbos: The Psychoanalysis of a Female Homosexual* (New York: Citadel, 1959.); Cornelia B. Wilbur, "Clinical Aspects of Female Homosexuality."

13. Frederic Wertham, *Seduction of the Innocent* (New York: Rinehart, 1954).

14. Ibid., 10.

15. For a rich analysis of Wertham's contribution to postwar campaigns against indecency in Canada and the United States, see Mary Louise Adams, "Youth, Corruptibility, and English-Canadian Postwar Campaigns against Indecency, 1948–1955," *Journal of the History of Sexuality* 6, no. 11 (1995): 89–117, 103.

16. Wertham, *Seduction,* 177.

17. Ibid., 191.

18. Ibid., 34.

19. See also Marshall C. Greco and James C. Wright, "The Correctional Institution in the Etiology of Chronic Homosexuality," *American Journal of Orthopsychiatry* 14 (1944): 295–307, in which the authors stated that those who suffer from "chronic homosexuality" were the hapless victims of seduction, and who, if they exhibited any feminine characteristics, did so as a matter of conditioning rather than because of heredity or biological factors. The answer, then, was to eliminate "the conditioning experience which we believe to be causal."

20. See, for example, Benjamin Karpman's analysis of lesbianism, in which he asserted that lesbians were more "unscrupulous" and "psychopathic" than homosexual men and that they tended to cultivate a quasi-familial relationship as a way of entrapping hapless prey: "Once they get hold of a victim they do not let her go until she is emotionally bled white." Like male homosexuality, lesbianism was the result of rejection by one parent and a tendency to become fixated on the parent of the same sex; this fixation was then displaced onto adult relationships in which the lesbian either assumed the role of a controlling parent or remained forever a demanding and frustrated child. Benjamin Karpman, *The Sexual Offender and his Offenses* (New York: Julian Press, 1954), 310.

21. For example, see David George Kin, *Women without Men: True Stories of Lesbian Love in Greenwich Village* (New York: Brookwood Publishing Corp., 1958), written in sensationalistic style and described by the author as "fictionalized case histories of female Bohemians who lost contact with social and cultural reality, and deviated from the sexual as well as the moral and spiritual norms" (4). Inverting Hemingway's

famous title, *Men Without Women,* Kin's book is one of many anti-homosexual sensationalist/exploitation texts from the period, describing homosexuality as "merely the symptom of a loveless, competitive society" in which lesbians live in terrible isolation and form "sterile" relationships with other women (5). For other texts purporting to be nonfiction exposés on lesbianism, see Jess Stearn, *The Grapevine; Confessions of a Lesbian Prostitute,* as told to Robert Leslie, with an introduction by Leonard Lowag (New York: Dalhousie Press, Inc., 1965); Lucius B. Steiner, *Sex Behavior of the Lesbian* (Hollywood, Calif.: The Genell Corporation, 1964); W. D. Sprauge, *Sex and the Secretary* (New York: Lancer Books, 1964); Dale Brittenham, *The Female Homosexual* (Los Angeles: Medco Books, 1965).

22. For a history of the rise of homosexual subcultures in the postwar period, see John D'Emilio, *Sexual Politics, Sexual Communities.* For popular sensationalistic accounts, see Jack Lait and Lee Mortimer, *New York: Confidential* (Chicago: Ziff-Davis Publishing Company, 1948); Lee Mortimer, *Washington Confidential Today* (New York: Paperback Library, 1962).

23. For additional analyses, see George Chauncey, "The Postwar Sex Crime Panic," in William Graebner, ed. *True Stories from the American Past* (1993), 160–78, and Estelle Freedman, "'Uncontrolled Desires.'"

24. For statistics and summaries of arrests for crimes against children in California from 1945–1949, see *California Sexual Deviation Research,* report to the California State Assembly prepared by Frank F. Tallman and Karl M. Bowman (January 1953), 31–34, 47–52.

25. The letter is quoted in Estelle Freedman, "Uncontrollable Desires," 207. Freedman notes that a burglar confessed to the killing of the young Chicago girl and that there was no mention of "degeneracy" in the press coverage of his conviction. See Freedman, 221, note 25.

26. Karl M. Bowman and Bernice Engle, "Review of Scientific Literature on Sexual Deviation," in *California Deviation Research,* report presented to the California State Assembly (January 1953), 116.

27. Hoover testified before a subcommittee of the U.S. House Judiciary Committee considering a bill to make it illegal to cross state lines to escape prosecution for degenerate acts with a minor. For a discussion of Hoover's postwar campaign against sex offenders, see Sheldon S. Levy, "Interactions of Institution and Policy Groups: The Origins of Sex Crime Legislation," *Lawyer and Law Notes* 5 (Spring 1951): 32.

28. For background on the purging of lesbians from the armed forces, see Allen Berube and John D'Emilio, "The Military and the Lesbians During the McCarthy Years," *Signs* 9, no. 4 (Summer 1984): 759–75.

29. The states that funded research on sex offenders were California, New York, New Jersey, Nevada, Pennsylvania, and Oregon. For background on state laws against sex crimes during this period, see Karl Bowman, "Review of Sex Legislation and Control of Sex Offenders in the United States of America," *International Review of Criminal Policy* 4 (July 1953): 20–39; Alan H. Swanson, "Sexual Psychopath Statutes: Summary and Analysis," *Journal of Criminal Law, Criminology and Police Science* 51 (July–August 1960): 228–35. As Freedman notes, the new sexual psychopath laws passed during the postwar period "did not necessarily name specific criminal acts, nor did they differentiate between violent and nonviolent, or consensual and noncon-

sensual, behaviors. Rather, they targeted a kind of personality, or an identity, that could be discovered only by trained psychiatrists. . . . The laws rested on the premise that even minor offenders (such as exhibitionists), if psychopaths, posed the threat of potential sexual violence" (Freedman, "Uncontrolled Desires," 209).

30. Karl Bowman, "The Problem of the Sex Offender," *American Journal of Psychiatry* 108 (1951): 253.

31. Electroshock and pharmacologically induced shock treatments were used on homosexual patients in state hospitals and private psychiatric clinics from the 1940s through the 1960s. One common routine was to tamper with the conditioned reflex of individual male patients by showing them slides of sexy men followed by nausea-inducing drugs and then by administering testosterone before showing slides of sexy women. Other experiments included inducing anxiety about homosexuality in a patient while reducing or "desensitizing" anxiety toward heterosexuality. Such treatments, on the whole, were unsuccessful in ending homosexual orientation or desire. Similarly, lobotomies to lessen or eliminate overt homosexual activity were unsuccessful and, in many cases, the patient's sex drive intensified. For examples, see Samuel Liebman, "Homosexuality, Transvestism, and Psychosis: Study of a Case Treated with Electroshock," *Journal of Nervous and Mental Disease* 99, 6 (1944): 945–57; Joseph W. Friedlander and Ralph S. Banay, "Psychosis Following Lobotomy in a Case of Sexual Psychopathology," *Archives of Neurology and Psychiatry* 59 (1948): 303–21; J. Srnec and K. Freund, "Treatment of Male Homosexuality through Conditioning," *International Journal of Sexology* (Bombay) 7, no. 2 (1953): 92–93; Moses Zlotlow and Albert E. Paganini, "Autoerotic and Homoerotic Manifestations in Hospitalized Male Postlobotomy Patients," *Psychiatric Quarterly* 33, 3 (1959): 495–97; Michael M. Miller, "Hypnotic-Aversion Treatment of Homosexuality," *Journal of the National Medical Association* 55, no. 5 (1963): 411–15; Joseph R. Cautela, "Covert Sensitization," *Psychological Reports* 20, no. 2 (1967): 464–65; Ivan Toby Rutner, "A Double-barrel Approach to Modification of Homosexual Behavior," *Psychological Reports* 26, no. 2 (1970): 356–58.

32. Karl Bowman and Bernice Engle, "A Psychiatric Evaluation of Laws of Homosexuality," *American Journal of Psychiatry* 112 (February 1956): 577–83.

33. California State Assembly, *Preliminary Report of the Subcommittee on Sex Crimes,* Appendix, 103–22.

34. George W. Henry and Alfred A. Gross, "Social Factors in the Case Histories of One Hundred Underprivileged Homosexuals"; Henry and Gross, "Social Factors in Delinquency."

35. George W. Henry and Alfred A. Gross, "The Sex Offender"; Henry, "Pastoral Counseling for Homosexuals," *Pastoral Psychology* 2, no. 18 (November 1951): 33–39.

36. In 1945, George Henry was approached by the Quakers to establish the Quaker Emergency Committee, which worked with the magistrate court of New York City by assisting those arrested for nonviolent offenses related to homosexuality to readjust to society. Rather than being incarcerated, these offenders, many of whom were young men, were offered parole so long as they would agree to psychiatric examinations as well as counseling and assistance by social workers to be productive and stable members of society. In 1948, after a disagreement with the Quakers, Henry

and Gross founded the George W. Henry Foundation, which was incorporated in New York state as a tax-exempt nonprofit organization in 1951. The Quakers changed the name of the Quaker Emergency Committee to the Quaker Readjustment Center, adopting a more conservative approach to treating homosexuality, with conservative psychiatrist Frederic Wertham as director. First located in the Lower East Side and then moved to West 20th Street in New York City, the George W. Henry Foundation's express purpose was to "help those who by reason of their sexual maladjustment are in trouble with themselves, the law or society." Its staff, board members, and officers were predominantly psychiatrists, clergy, social workers who represented a variety of religions, though most were connected to the Episcopal church. About half of the Foundation's clients were male parolees referred from the New York municipal courts, and half voluntarily sought counseling and assistance to come to terms with their homosexual desires. Most were indigent and could not afford the services of lawyers or psychiatrists, but some middle-class men who heard about the services offered by the Foundation sought counsel when they were faced with threats of blackmail or public exposure. The Foundation operated with very little money, most of which came from the City of New York and from charitable contributions. Most of the professionals who worked with the organization did so on a voluntary or minimally remunerated basis. Over the course of Foundation's existence, Henry's annual reports took an increasingly explicit religious tone, reflecting his own Episcopalian appreciation of brotherly love, compassion, and forgiveness, which he combined with a Protestant work ethic that saw productivity and discipline as essential to the building of self-esteem. These reports, always composed by Henry during the Lenten season, "when the church admonishes us to take stock of our ways and works," featured a mantra that summarized the basic moral assumption upon which the Foundation's work was based: "All of us need a job and a friend." After George Henry's death in 1964, the Foundation continued under the direction of psychiatrist Ruth Berkeley, who had been a former student of Henry's at Cornell Medical College.

CHAPTER ELEVEN

1. Michael Rogin, "Political Repression in the United States," and "Kiss Me Deadly: Communism, Motherhood, and Cold War Movies," in *Ronald Reagan, the Movie and Other Episodes in Political Demonology* (Berkeley: University of California Press, 1987), 64–77, 237–38.

2. In 1938, the Foreign Agents Registration Act, commonly called the Smith Act, was passed as a measure allowing for the deportation of "aliens" who failed to register with the Justice Department. Like the House Committee on Un-American Activities, founded in the same year, the Smith Act was intended to counter both pro-Nazi and pro-communist influences in the U.S. By 1941, both the Smith Act and HUAC enjoyed broad popular support in the context of America's war against Germany, but from their inception in 1938, they mainly targeted left-wing rather than right-wing groups. See David Caute, *The Great Fear: The Anti-communist Purge under Truman and Eisenhower* (New York: Simon and Schuster, 1978), 25. For background on the ealier "Red Scare," see Robert K. Murray, *Red Scare: A Study in National Hysteria, 1919–1920* (Minneapolis: University of Minnesota Press, 1955); William Preston, Jr., *Aliens*

and Dissenters: Federal Suppression of Radicals, 1903–1933 (Cambridge, Mass.: Harvard University Press, 1966).

3. For histories of American anti-communism during the late 1940s and 1950s, see David Caute, *The Great Fear;* Victor Navasky, *Naming Names* (New York: Viking Press, 1980); David M. Oshinsky, *A Conspiracy So Immense: The World of Joe McCarthy* (New York; D. I. Fine, 1983); Herbert Mitgang, *Dangerous Dossiers: Exposing the Secret War against America's Greatest Authors* (New York: Free Press, 1988); Athan Theoharis, *Seeds of Repression: Harry S. Truman and the Origins of McCarthyism* (Chicago: Quadrangle Books, 1971) and *Spying on Americans: Political Surveillance from Hoover to the Huston Plan* (Philadelphia: Temple University Press, 1978).

4. George F. Kennan, "Moscow Embassy Telegram #511" (February 22, 1946), in *Containment: Documents on American Policy and Strategy,* ed. Thomas H. Etzold and John Lewis Gaddis (New York: Columbia University Press, 1978), 63. See also NSC 68, *United States Objectives and Programs for National Security* (April 14, 1950), a top secret document written by Kennan under the pseudonym "X," reprinted in *Containment Documents on American Policy and Strategy,* 385–442.

5. John D'Emilio, "The Homosexual Menace: The Politics of Sexuality in Cold War America," in *Passion and Power: Sexuality in History,* ed. Kathy Peiss and Christina Simmons (Philadelphia: Temple University Press, 1989), 226–40.

6. For historical analyses of the postwar cult of domesticity, see Elaine Tyler May, *Homeward Bound: American Families in Cold War America* (New York: Basic Books, 1988); Stephanie Coontz, *The Way We Never Were: American Families and the Nostalgia Trap* (New York: Basic Books, 1992); Eugenia Kaledin, *Mothers and More: American Women in the 1950s* (Boston: Twayne Publishers, 1984); Wini Breines, *Young, White, and Miserable: Growing Up Female in the Fifties* (Boston: Beacon Press, 1992). See also Paul S. Boyer, *By the Bomb's Early Light: American Thought and Culture at the Dawn of the Atomic Age* (New York: Pantheon, 1985); Geoffrey S. Smith, "National Security and Personal Isolation: Sex, Gender, and Disease in the Cold-War United States," *The International History Review* 14, no. 2 (May 1992): 307–37.

7. See, for example, Ferdinand Lundberg and Marynia F. Farnham, *Modern Woman and the Lost Sex* (New York: Harper, 1947).

8. For analyses of earlier links between motherhood and civic duty, see Linda Kerber, *Women of the Republic: Intellect and Ideology in Revolutionary America* (Chapel Hill: University of North Carolina Press, 1980); Mary Beth Norton, *Liberty's Daughters: The Revolutionary Experience of American Women, 1750–1800* (Boston: Little, Brown and Company, 1980); Susan Zeiger, "'She Didn't Raise Her Boy to be a Slacker': Motherhood, Conscription, and the Culture of the First World War," *Feminist Studies* 22, no. 1 (Spring 1996): 7–39.

9. The conservative ideological campaign to encourage women to take up wifely and maternal duties was not as powerful as its purveyors would have hoped. Many women, especially in the working class, continued to work outside the home. In addition, a significant number resisted the pressure to be reduced to the role of housewife and mother. For accounts of women who resisted the conservative "family boom," see Joanne J. Meyerowitz, ed., *Not June Cleaver: Women and Gender in Postwar America, 1945–1960* (Philadelphia: Temple University Press, 1994).

NOTES TO PAGES 333–340

10. Cold War films centering around a domineering mom who skews her son's psychosexual development toward treasonous behavior include *My Son John* (1952; director Leo McCarey) and *The Manchurian Candidate* (1962; director John Frankenheimer). For political analyses of these films, see Michael Rogin, "Kiss Me Deadly," · 236–71.

11. See, for example, *Kiss Me Deadly* (1955; director Robert Aldrich), in which a diabolic dame lures Mickey Spillane's hard-boiled detective, Mike Hammer, into a web of deception over the whereabouts of a box containing radioactive material. Hammer nearly falls for the dame but in the end escapes her destructive power in a typical culmination of detective fiction, this time with an atomic twist: the tough male protagonist, having been seduced and nearly destroyed, comes to his senses and casts off the sultry vixen just in time to watch her go up in nuclear flames. See Rogin, "Kiss Me Deadly," 249.

12. Executive Order 9835, published in the *New York Times*, March 26, 1947.

13. For more on the relationship between Truman's promotion of the Marshall Plan and his manipulation of anti-communist sentiments, see Richard M. Freeland, *The Truman Doctrine and the Origins of McCarthyism: Foreign Policy, Domestic Politics, and Internal Security, 1946–1948,* 3d ed. (New York: New York University Press, 1985).

14. *New York Times*, March 1, 1950, p. 1.

15. Smith, "National Security and Personal Isolation," 316.

16. Buckley was quoted in Nicholas von Hoffman, *Citizen Cohn* (New York: 1988), 136.

17. Arthur Schlesinger, *The Vital Center: The Politics of Freedom* (Boston: Houghton Mifflin, 1949).

18. Arthur Schlesinger, *The Politics of Hope* (Boston: Houghton Mifflin Company, 1963), 237–46.

19. Quoted in Smith, "National Security and Personal Isolation," 318.

20. *New York Times*, March 26, 1950, and August 5, 1950.

21. For a description of the Cold Warriors' use of the Raedl case, see Ralph S. Brown, *Loyalty and Security: Employment Tests in the United States* (New Haven: Yale University Press, 1958), 256.

22. *Cong. Rec.,* 81st Cong., 2d sess., March 31, 1950, v. 96, pt. 4: 4527–28.

23. Ibid., 4528.

24. *Cong. Rec.,* 81st Cong., 2d sess., May 15, 1950, v. 96, pt. 15 (Appendix): A3661.

25. Ibid.

26. *New York Times,* April 15, 1950.

27. *Cong. Rec.,* 81st Cong., 2d sess., April 4, 1950, v. 96, pt. 4: 4670.

28. *Cong. Rec.,* 81st Cong., 2d sess., April 19, 1950, v. 96, pt. 4: 5402.

29. The Washington, D.C., vice squad estimated, through a combination of guessing and crude arithmetic, that there were 5,000 to 6,000 "active" homosexuals in the city, of which 75 percent were government employees. To calculate how many homosexuals there were in the city, a list was made from police records which was then multiplied by five and then names of friends of those picked up by the police were added. The initial list was no more than 200. Officials guessed that three out of

every four homosexuals were federal employees, based, ironically, on a stereotype of homosexual men as being intelligent and highly capable of performing well in white collar jobs. These methods were discussed by journalist Max Lerner in the *New York Post,* July 18, 1950, reprinted in Katz, *Gay American History,* 97–98.

30. *New York Post,* July 11, 1950. The article was reprinted in Max Lerner, *The Unfinished Country: A Book of American Symbols* (New York: Simon and Schuster, 1959), 313–16. It is also quoted at length in Katz, *Gay American History,* 94–96.

31. Ibid.

32. *Cong. Rec.,* 81st Cong., 2d sess., December 15, 1950, v. 96, pt. 12: 16587–88.

33. U.S. Senate, 81st Cong., 2d sess., Committee on Expenditures in Executive Departments, "Employment of Homosexuals and Other Sex Perverts in Government" (Washington, D.C., 1950).

34. Executive Order 10241, published in the *New York Times,* April 29, 1951.

35. Executive Order 10450 issued on April 27, 1953.

36. Brown, *Loyalty and Security,* 258.

37. Executive Order 10491 issued on October 14, 1953.

38. Executive Order 10548 issued on August 2, 1954.

39. Jack Lait and Lee Mortimer, *USA: Confidential* (New York: Crown Publishers, 1952) and *Washington: Confidential* (New York: Crown Publishers, 1951).

40. R. G. Waldeck, "The Homosexual International," published in *Cong. Rec.,* 82d Cong., 2d sess., May 1, 1952, v. 98, pt. 10 (Appendix): A2652.

41. For an analysis of the association between Jews and homosexuals inside European diplomatic circles from the seventeenth through the nineteenth century, see Hannah Arendt, *The Origins of Totalitarianism* (New York: Harcourt, Brace, Jovanovich, 1973), especially chapter 2, "The Jews, the Nation-State, and the Birth of Anti-Semitism," 11–53.

42. Waldeck, "The Homosexual International," *Cong. Rec.,* 82d Cong., 2d sess., May 1, 1952, v. 98, pt. 10 (Appendix): A2654.

43. Ibid.

44. Colin J. Williams and Martin S. Weinberg, *Homosexuals and the Military* (New York: Harper and Row, 1971); Berube, *Coming Out Under Fire,* 255–65.

45. U.S. Department of Navy, *Report of the Board Appointed to Prepare and Submit Recommendations to the Secretary of the Navy for the Revision of Policies, Procedures, and Directives Dealing with Homosexuals, 21 December 1956–15 March 1957* (also known as the *Crittendon Report*), Captain S. H. Crittendon, chairman, vol. A, app. 22.

46. For an account of the Boise scandal, see John Gerassi, *The Boys of Boise: Furor, Vice, and Folly in an American City* (New York: Macmillan, 1966).

47. For details of the congressional and legal censorship Kinsey confronted, see Vern Bullough, *Science in the Bedroom,* 183–85.

48. Smith, "National Security and Personal Isolation," 322. For more on Roy Cohn's life, see also Nicholas von Hoffman, *Citizen Cohn.*

49. For more on Hoover's private files and the allegations of his homosexuality, see Katz, *Gay/Lesbian Almanac,* 530–31; John M. Crewdson, "Files from Hoover Backers Reported," *New York Times,* February 2, 1974; Crewdson, "Censored Version of Secret Hoover Files on Official's Misconduct," *New York Times,* November

24, 1976; and John M. Goshko, "Inside Hoover's Sex Files," *New York Post*, November 24, 1976.

CHAPTER TWELVE

1. J. D. Mercer, *They Walk in Shadow* (New York: Comet Books, 1959), 11–12.

2. For a thorough history of homophile politics and organizations, see D'Emilio, *Sexual Politics, Sexual Communities.*

3. D'Emilio, *Sexual Politics*, 73.

4. For more background on the DOB, see Del Martin and Phyllis, *Lesbian/ Woman* (New York: Bantam Books, 1983), 210–46.

5. Kinsey et al., *Sexual Behavior in the Human Female*, 476–87.

6. "The Case of the Well-Meaning Lyncher," *One Magazine* (November 1953): 10–11.

7. This critique was also articulated by psychiatrist Robert Lindner, who in 1956 argued against the "myth of conformity" which gripped the nation and contributed to a dangerous trend toward the loss of individuality and the rise of totalitarianism. In a contradictory fashion, Lindner valorized homosexuals for their refusal to conform to repressive sexual mores, while at the same time he identified homosexuality as a symptom of pathology in many of his case histories of disturbed individuals. See Robert Lindner, "Homosexuality and the Contemporary Scene," in *Must You Conform?* (New York: Holt, Rinehart and Winston, 1956).

8. Alfred A. Gross, Henry's assistant, was guilty of similar attitudes. See Alfred A. Gross, *Strangers in our Midst: Problems of the Homosexual in American Society* (Washington, D.C.: Public Affairs Press, 1962).

9. George Henry, from the Fifth Annual Report of the George W. Henry Foundation, April 1, 1953, quoted in *One* (November 1953): 10–11.

10. Evelyn Hooker, "The Adjustment of the Male Overt Homosexual," *Journal of Projective Techniques* 21 (1957): 18–31; also published in *Mattachine Review* (December 1957): 32–39 and (January 1958): 4–11; and reprinted in Hendrik M. Rutenbeek, ed., *The Problem of Homosexuality in Modern Society* (NY, 1963); see also, Hooker, "A Preliminary Analysis of Group Behavior in Homosexuals," *Journal of Psychology* 42 (1956): 217–25.

11. Donald Webster Cory [pseud.], *The Homosexual in America: A Subjective Approach* (New York: Greenberg, 1951), xiii.

12. Ibid., 14. In 1964, Cory extended his argument to apply to lesbianism, heartily endorsing the work of DOB and urging full civil rights for lesbians, who, like gay men, were victims of unjust discrimination. See Donald Webster Cory, *The Lesbian in America* (New York: Tower Publications, 1964).

13. In 1957, the Wolfenden Report was released in England, recommending the elimination of criminal penalties for private consensual acts between adults. See J. D. Mercer, *They Walk in Shadow*, 401–14. For an ambitious text similar to Mercer's, see Daniel West, *The Other Man: A Study of the Social, Legal, and Clinical Aspects of Homosexuality* (New York: Whiteside and William Morrow & Co., 1955).

14. Mercer, *They Walk in Shadow*, 7.

15. Compare, for example, the writings of Karl Ulrichs and Edward Carpenter

to J. D. Mercer and, more recently, to gay neuroanatomist Simon LeVay. Ulrichs, *The Riddle of "Man-Manly" Love;* Carpenter, *The Intermediate Sex;* Simon LeVay, "Evidence for Anatomical Differences in the Brains of Homosexual Men," *Science* 253 (1991): 1034–37 and *The Sexual Brain* (Cambridge, Mass.: MIT Press, 1993).

16. Frank E. Kameny, "Does Research into Homosexuality Matter?," *The Ladder* (May 1965): 14–20. See also Frank E. Kameny, "Emphasis on Research has had its Day," *The Ladder* (Oct. 1965): 10–13, 23.

17. Florence Conrad, "Research is Here to Stay," *The Ladder* (July/August 1965): 15–21.

18. Letter signed L.H.N. [Lorraine Hansberry Nemiroff], *The Ladder* 1, no. 8 (May 1957): 26, 28, quoted in Katz, *Gay American History*, 425. Barbara Grier identified Hansberry as the author of the letter in her "Lesbiana" column, *The Ladder* 14, nos. 5–6 (February-March 1970).

19. Letter signed "L.N." [Lorraine (Hansberry) Nemiroff], *The Ladder* 1, no. 11 (August 1957): 30.

20. Jess Stearn, *The Sixth Man* (London: W. H. Allen, 1962), 23, 25.

21. Jess Stearn, *The Grapevine*.

22. R. E. L. Masters, *The Homosexual Revolution* (New York: Belmont Books, 1962).

23. Ibid., 187.

24. Bieber's claims are published in Society of Medical Psychoanalysts, *Homosexuality: A Psychoanalytic Study of Male Homosexuals*. See also Bieber, "Clinical Aspects of Male Homosexuality."

25. See Cornelia B. Wilbur, "Clinical Aspects of Female Homosexuality."

26. Charles W. Socarides, *The Overt Homosexual*, 7–8. See also Socarides, "Homosexuality," and "Theoretical and Clinical Aspects of Overt Male Homosexuality."

27. Socarides, *Homosexuality*, xvi.

28. Ibid., 4.

29. For a detailed history of this struggle, see Ronald Bayer, *Homosexuality and American Psychiatry: The Politics of Diagnosis* (New York: Basic Books, 1981).

30. Del Martin and Phyllis Lyon, *Lesbian/Woman* (San Francisco: Glide Publications, 1972). This book was published in an expanded edition in 1983 by Bantam Books. All further citations to the book are to this 1983 edition.

31. Del Martin and Phyllis Lyon, *Lesbian/Woman*, 268–69.

32. Willer is quoted in Martin and Lyon, *Lesbian/Woman*, 247.

33. "A Letter from Mary" is quoted in Martin and Lyon, *Lesbian/Woman*, 260.

34. Ibid., 266–67.

35. Radclyffe Hall, *The Well of Loneliness* (New York: Avon Books, 1981), 437.

36. Martin and Lyon, *Lesbian/Woman*, 274.

37. See, for example, Gunter Dörner, "Hormonal Induction and Prevention of Female Homosexuality," *Journal of Endocrinology* 42 (1968): 163–64 and *Hormones and Brain Differentiation* (Amsterdam: Elsevier, 1976).

38. These ideas are presented in Gunter Dörner et al., "A Neuroendocrine Predisposition for Homosexuality in Men," *Archives of Sexual Behavior* 4 (1975): 1–8 and "Stressful Events in Prenatal Life of Bi- and Homosexual Men," *Experiments in Clinical Endocrinology* 81 (1983): 83–87.

39. See, for example, Richard C. Friedman, "Hormones and Sexual Orientation in Men," *American Journal of Psychiatry* 134 (1977): 571–72; Friedman and Leonore O. Stern, "Juvenile Aggressivity and Sissiness in Homosexual and Heterosexual Males," *Journal of the American Academy of Psychoanalysis* 8 (1980): 427–40; Richard Green, *The 'Sissy Boy Syndrome' and the Development of Homosexuality* (New Haven: Yale University Press, 1987); and Robert C. Stoller, "Boyhood Gender Aberrations: Treatment Issues," *Journal of the American Psychoanalytic Association* 26 (1978): 541–58.

40. Published in the *Washington Post*, September 27, 1965, reprinted in *The Challenge and Progress of Homosexual Law Reform* (San Francisco, 1968).

41. J. L. Simmons, "Public Stereotypes of Deviants," *Social Problems* 13 (1965): 223–32.

42. Elizabeth A. Rooney and Don C. Gibbons, "Social Reactions to 'Crimes Without Victims,'" *Social Problems* 13 (1966): 400–10.

43. The study was conducted by the National Opinion Research Center and published in *Drum* 25 (August 1967). For background and full results of the study see Albert D. Klassen, Colin J. Williams, and Eugene E. Levitt, *Sex and Morality in the U.S.: An Empirical Enquiry under the Auspices of the Kinsey Institute*, introduction by Hubert J. O'Gorman (Middletown, Conn.: Weslyan University Press, 1989), especially chapters 7–10 (165–245).

44. Darrell J. Steffensmeier, "Factors Affecting Reactions toward Homosexuals" (Ph.D. diss., University of Iowa, 1970).

45. The poll is discussed in Klassen et al., *Sex and Morality in the U.S.*, 168–245.

46. Ibid., 183.

47. Martin Duberman, *Cures: A Gay Man's Odyssey.*

EPILOGUE

1. Anne Koedt, "Lesbianism and Feminism," in *Radical Feminism*, ed. Anne Koedt, Ellen Levine, Anita Rapone (New York: Quadrangle Books, 1973), 248.

2. Chandler Burr, "Homosexuality and Biology," *The Atlantic Monthly* 271, no. 3 (March 1993): 47–65, 48. Burr elaborated on this in *A Separate Creation: The Search for the Biological Origins of Sexual Orientation* (New York: Hyperion, 1997).

3. See Joseph Nicolosi, *Reparative Therapy of Male Homosexuality* and *Healing Homosexuality: Case Stories in Reparative Therapy.*

4. Nicolosi, *Reparative Therapy*, xvi.

5. Ibid., xvii.

6. Ibid., xviii.

7. Nicolosi, *Healing Homosexuality*, 214–15.

8. Ibid., 220.

9. Ibid., ix. See also the Position Paper of the National Association for Research and Therapy of Homosexuality (founded May 1992) available from NARTH, 16542 Ventura Blvd., Suite 416, Encino, California 91436; tel. (818) 789–4440.

10. The fifty-minute *Gay Rights Special* was produced in 1994 by Coral Ridge Ministries, 5555 North Federal Highway, Fort Lauderdale, Florida 33308. It aired on the CRM's weekly television program and is available on video.

11. For more on Exodus International, see John Leland and Mark Miller, "Can Gays Convert?" *Newsweek*, August 17, 1998, 46–50. For information about cam-

paigns aimed at "deprogramming" gay and lesbian teens against their will, see Ingrid Ricks, "Mind Games," *The Advocate* (National Lesbian and Gay Newsmagazine), December 28, 1993, 38–40; see also Newsletter (Spring 1995) of the National Center for Lesbian Rights, 870 Market Street, Suite 570, San Francisco, California 94102.

12. Matthew Shepard's death was reported in *The New York Times*, October 12, 1998.

13. Steven Schwalm is quoted in "Gay Man Dies from Attack," *New York Times*, October 13, 1998.

14. See Paul Cameron, "Homosexual Molestation of Children/Sexual Interaction of Teacher and Pupil," *Psychological Reports* 57 (1985): 1227–36; Paul Cameron, Kay Proctor, William Coburn, and Nels Forde, "Sexual Orientation and Sexually Transmitted Disease," *Nebraska Medical Journal* 70 (1985): 292–99; Paul Cameron, K. Proctor, William Coburn, Nels Forde, H. Larson, and Kirk Cameron, "Child Molestation and Homosexuality," *Psychological Reports* 58 (1985): 327–37.

15. C. F. Turner, H. G. Miller, and L. E. Moses, eds., *Sexual Behavior and Intravenous Drug Use* (Washington, D.C.: National Academy Press, 1989), 396.

16. Paul Cameron, Kirk Cameron, and Kay Proctor, "The Effect of Homosexuality Upon Public Health and Social Order," *Psychological Reports* 64 (1989): 1167. Four percent of Cameron's sample of 4,340 adult respondents, gathered from metropolitan areas in the United States, were reported to be homosexual and bisexual. According to the authors, this four percent "more frequently exposed themselves to biological hazards (e.g. sadomasochism, fisting, bestiality, ingestion of feces)," had larger numbers of sexual partners, engaged more frequently in "socially disruptive sex" (e.g. cheating in marriage, making obscene phone calls, and deliberately infecting others with disease), and more frequently reported engaging in "socially disruptive activities" (e.g., shoplifting, tax cheating, "criminality").

17. *The Medical Consequences of What Homosexuals Do* was produced by the Family Research Institute, Inc., P. O. Box 2091, Washington, D.C. 20013.

18. See, for example, Thomas C. Caskey, "DNA-based Medicine: Prevention and Therapy," in *The Code of Codes: Scientific and Social Issues in the Human Genome Project*, ed. Daniel J. Kevles and Leroy Hood (Cambridge: Harvard University Press, 1992), 112–35; Walter Gilbert, "A Vision of the Grail," in *The Code of Codes*, 83–97; Leroy Hood, "Biology and Medicine in the Twenty-first Century," in *The Code of Codes*, 281–99.

19. This is elaborated in Donna Haraway, "The Promise of Monsters: A Regenerative Politics for Inappropriate/d Others," in *Cultural Studies*, ed. Lawrence Grossberg, Cary Nelson, Paula Treichler (New York: Routledge, 1992), 295–337.

20. For relevant critiques of the Human Genome Project, see Richard Lewontin, "The Dream of the Human Genome," in *Cultures on the Brink: Ideologies of Technology*, ed. Gretchen Bender and Timothy Druckrey (Seattle: Bay Press, 1994), 107–27 and Ruth Hubbard and Elijah Wald, *Exploding the Gene Myth: How Genetic Information is Produced and Manipulated by Scientists, Physicians, Employers, Insurance Companies, Educators, and Law Enforcers* (Boston: Beacon Press, 1993).

21. Frederick Goodwin, "Conduct Disorder as a Precursor to Adult Violence and Substance Abuse: Can the Progression be Halted?" (address presented to the American Psychiatric Association Annual Convention, Washington, D.C., May 1992).

22. See Charles Murray and Richard Herrnstein, *The Bell Curve: Intelligence and Class Structure in American Life* (New York: The Free Press, 1994) and their critics in Steven Fraser, ed., *The Bell Curve Wars: Race, Intelligence, and the Future of America* (New York: Basic Books, 1995); Russell Jacoby and Naomi Glauberman, eds., *The Bell Curve Debate: History, Documents, Opinions* (New York: Times Books, 1995).

23. Jack Kloppenburg, Jr. *Seeds and Sovereignty: The Use and Control of Genetic Resources* (Durham, N.C.: Duke University Press, 1988); Alistair Smith, "Biodiversity and Food Security," *Science as Culture* 2: 591–601.

24. J. Michael Bailey and Richard C. Pillard, "A Genetic Study of Male Sexual Orientation," *Archives of General Psychiatry* 48 (1991): 1089–96.

25. For a critique of Bailey and Pillard, see William Byne and Bruce Parsons, "Human Sexual Orientation: The Biological Theories Reappraised," *Archives of General Psychiatry* 50 (1993): 228–39.

26. J. Michael Bailey, Richard C. Pillard, Michael C. Neale, and Yvonne Agyei, "Heritable Factors Influence Sexual Orientation in Women," *Archives of General Psychiatry* 50 (1993): 217–23.

27. Christine Gorman, "Are Gay Men Born that Way?" *Newsweek* 138, no. 10 (1991): 48.

28. Joe Dolce, "And How Big is Yours?" (Interview with Simon LeVay), *The Advocate* 630 (June 1, 1993): 38–44.

29. Simon LeVay, "Evidence for Anatomical Differences in the Brains of Homosexual Men."

30. Dean H. Hamer, Stella Hu, Victoria Magnuson, Nan Hu, and Angela Pattatucci, "A Linkage Between DNA Markers on the X Chromosome and Male Sexual Orientation," *Science* 261 (1993): 321–27. See also Hamer et al., "Evidence for Homosexuality Gene." *Science* 261 (1993): 291–92.

31. Varmus is quoted in John Crewdson, "Author [Dean Hamer] Defends Findings against Allegations," *Chicago Tribune*, June 25, 1995.

32. Evelynn M. Hammonds, Remarks at Out/Write Conference on Lesbian and Gay Writing and Publishing (Boston, Massachusetts, 1993).

33. The NIH and NCI have been under some attack for funding studies like Hamer's, whose findings appear to bear no relationship to cancer research. When questioned by Senator Bob Smith (R-N.H.) as to why the NIH and NCI seemed to be funding research that had little or nothing to do with cancer, Varmus stated that Hamer's research was indeed intended to uncover any possible links between male homosexuality and KS. A companion study on lesbians proposed by Hamer and his collaborator, Angela Pattatucci, similarly sought funding to investigate a genetic link between lesbianism and breast cancer. As a condition for funding in both of these cases, researchers had to hypothesize a link between homosexuality and disease. Furthermore, proponents of the studies defend them from attacks by the tax-paying public on the grounds that they contribute to medical knowledge. Thus, the discursive web that historically tied homosexuality together with disease is tightened once again, this time in the context of high-tech genetics research and taxpayer revolt. See Crewdson, "Author [Dean Hamer] Defends Findings against Allegations," *Chicago Tribune*, June 25, 1995.

34. For critiques of new gay science, see Donna Minkowitz, "Trial by Science: In

the Fight Over Amendment 2, Biology is Back and Gay Allies are Claiming It," *Village Voice*, November 30, 1993, 27–30; and Janet E. Halley, "Sexual Orientation and the Politics of Biology: A Critique of the Argument from Immutability," *Stanford Law Review* 46, no. 3 (1994): 503–68.

35. Karen Franklin is quoted in "A Pattern of Abuse," *New York Times*, August 25, 1998, a little more than a month before Matthew Shepard was beaten and killed.

36. See Gloria Marshall, "Racial Classifications: Popular and Scientific," in *The "Racial" Economy of Science*, ed. Sandra Harding (Bloomington: Indiana University Press, 1993), 116–27, and Elazar Barkan, *The Retreat of Scientific Racism: Changing Concepts of Race in Britain and the United States Between the World Wars* (Cambridge: Cambridge University Press, 1992).

37. Simon LeVay, *The Sexual Brain;* LeVay and Dean H. Hamer, "Evidence for a Biological Influence in Male Homosexuality," *Scientific American* 270, no. 5 (May 1994): 44–49.

38. The issue of whether or not sexual orientation is a biologically determined characteristic has played a significant role in a number of recent political and legal battles over anti-gay discrimination. In the state court challenge to Colorado's Amendment 2, the Colorado judge who overturned the amendment as unconstitutional concluded that "the preponderance of credible evidence suggests that there is a biologic or genetic 'component' of sexual orientation." Similar arguments to those made by Hamer and LeVay in Colorado have been made in the debates over whether to allow gays and lesbians to serve openly in the military. See Crewdson, "Author Defends Findings," and Daniel J. Kevles, "The X Factor: The Battle Over the Ramification of a Gay Gene," *New Yorker* (April 3, 1995): 85–90.

39. Evelyn Fox Keller, "Nature, Nurture, and the Human Genome Project," in *The Code of Codes*, ed. Kevles and Hood, 281–99.

40. Hubbard and Wald, *Exploding the Gene Myth.*

41. Frank Acqueno, Remarks at Out/Write Conference on Lesbian and Gay Writing and Publishing, Boston, Massachusetts (1993).

42. Eve Kosofsky Sedgwick, *Epistemology of the Closet* (Berkeley: University of California Press, 1990).

BIBLIOGRAPHY

Aberle, Sophie, and George W. Corner. *Twenty-five Years of Sex Research: History of the National Research Council Committee for Research in Problems of Sex, 1922–1947.* Philadelphia: W. B. Saunders, 1953.

Abraham, Karl. "Manifestations of the Female Castration Complex." In *Selected Papers on Psychoanalysis,* edited by Leonard and Virginia Woolf. London, 1927.

Adam, Barry. *The Rise of the Lesbian and Gay Movement.* Boston: G. K. Hall, 1987.

Adams, Mary Louise. "Youth, Corruptibility, and English-Canadian Postwar Campaigns against Indecency, 1948–1955." *Journal of the History of Sexuality* 6, no. 11 (1995): 89–117.

Adas, Michael. *Machines as Measures of Men: Science, Technology, and Ideologies of Western Dominance.* Ithaca: Cornell University Press, 1989.

Adler, Herman Morris. "Unemployment and Personality: A Study of Psychopathic Cases." *Mental Hygiene* 1 (January 1917): 16–24.

Agassiz, Louis. *Contributions to the Natural History of the United States.* 4 vols. Boston: Little, Brown, 1862.

Alexander, Franz, and Bruno Straub. *The Criminal, the Judge, and the Public.* Translated by Gregory Zilboorg. New York: Macmillan, 1931.

Alexander, Ruth. *The Girl Problem: Female Sexual Delinquency in New York, 1900–1930.* Ithaca: Cornell University Press, 1995.

Allen, Garland E. "Eugenics and American Social History, 1880–1950." *Genome* 31 (1989): 885–89.

Anderson, Margaret. *My Thirty Years War.* New York: Covici, Friede Publishers, 1930.

Anon. Letter from Boston. *Monatsberichte des Wissenschaftlich-humanitaren Komitees* 6 (1907): 98–99.

Arendt, Hannah. *The Origins of Totalitarianism.* New York: Harcourt, Brace, Jovanovich, 1973.

Aronstam, Noah E., M. D. "The Well of Loneliness: An Impression." *The Urologic and Cutaneous Review* 33 (1929): 543.

Atkinson, J. Brooks. *Broadway.* New York: Macmillan, 1970.

Bailey, D. S. *Homosexuality and the Western Christian Tradition.* New York: Longmans, Green and Company, 1955.

Bailey, J. Michael, and Richard C. Pillard. "A Genetic Study of Male Sexual Orientation." *Archives of General Psychiatry* 48 (1991): 1089–96.

Bailey, J. Michael, Richard C. Pillard, Michael C. Neale, and Yvonne Agyei. "Heritable Factors Influence Sexual Orientation in Women." *Archives of General Psychiatry* 50 (1993): 217–23.

Baker, Lee D. "The Location of Franz Boas Within the African American Struggle." *Critique of Anthropology* 14, no. 2 (1994): 199–217.

Bannister, Robert C. *Social Darwinism: Science and Myth in Anglo-American Social Thought.* Philadelphia: Temple University Press, 1979.

Barahal, Hyman S. "Constitutional Factors in Psychotic Male Homosexuals." *Psychiatric Quarterly* 13 (1939): 391–400.

———. "Testosterone in Psychotic Male Homosexuals." *Psychiatric Quarterly* 14, no. 2 (1940): 319–30.

Barkan, Elazar. "Mobilizing Scientists Against Nazi Racism." In *Bones, Bodies, Behavior,* edited by George W. Stocking, Jr., 180–205. Madison: University of Wisconsin Press, 1988.

———. *The Retreat of Scientific Racism: Changing Concepts of Race in Britain and the United States Between the World Wars.* Cambridge: Cambridge University Press, 1992.

Barker-Benfield, Graham. *The Horrors of a Half-Known Life: Male Attitudes toward Women and Sexuality in Nineteenth-Century America.* New York: Harper and Row, 1976.

Barnette, W. Leslie. "Study of an Adult Male Homosexual and Terman-Miles M-F Scores." *American Journal of Orthopsychiatry* 12 (1942): 346–51.

Barr, Martin W. *Mental Defectives: Their History, Treatment, and Training.* Philadelphia: P. Blakiston's Sons & Company, 1904.

Bateson, Mary Catherine. *A Daughter's Eye: A Memoir of Margaret Mead and Gregory Bateson.* New York: Morrow, 1984.

Bayer, Ronald. *Homosexuality and American Psychiatry: The Politics of Diagnosis.* New York: Basic Books, 1981.

Beam, Lura. *Bequest from a Life: A Biography of Louise Stevens Bryant.* Baltimore: Waverly Press, 1963.

Beard, George M. *American Nervousness: Its Causes and Consequences.* 1881. Reprint, New York: Arno Press, 1972.

———. *Practical Treatise on Nervous Exhaustion.* New York: W. Wood, 1880.

———. *Sexual Neurasthenia (Nervous Exhaustion): Its Hygiene, Causes, Symptoms, and Treatment.* 1884. Reprint, New York: Arno Press, 1972.

Beers, Clifford. *A Mind that Found Itself: An Autobiography.* Garden City, N.Y.: Doubleday, Doran and Co., 1937.

Bender, Lauretta, and Samuel Paster. "Homosexual Trends in Children." *American Journal of Orthopsychiatry* 22 (1941): 730–44.

Benedict, Ruth. "Anthropology and the Abnormal." *Journal of General Psychology* 10 (1934): 59–82.

———. *Patterns of Culture.* Boston: Houghton Mifflin, 1934.

———. "Sex in Primitive Society." *American Journal of Orthopsychiatry* 9 (1939): 570–75.

Benedikt, Moriz. *Anatomical Studies Upon Brains of Criminals.* 1881. New York: Da Capo Press, 1981.

Bergler, Edmund. *Counterfeit Sex: Homosexuality, Impotence, Frigidity.* New York: Grune and Stratton, 1951.

———. *Fashion and the Unconscious.* New York: R. Brunner, 1953.

————. *Homosexuality: Disease or Way of Life?.* New York: Hill and Wang, 1956.

————. "The Myth of a National Disease: Homosexuality and the Kinsey Report" *The Psychiatric Quarterly* 22 (1948): 66–88. Excerpt reprinted in *The Homosexuals: As Seen By Themselves and 30 Authorities,* edited by A. Krich, 247–48. New York: Citadel Press, 1954.

————. *One Thousand Homosexuals: Conspiracy of Silence, or Curing and Deglamorizing Homosexuals?* Paterson, N.J.: Pageant Books, Inc., 1959.

————. "Present Situation in the Genetic Investigation of Homosexuality." *Marriage Hygiene* 4, no. 1 (1937): 16–29.

————. *The Writer and Psychoanalysis.* Garden City, N.Y.: Doubleday, 1950.

Bergler, Edmund, and Eduard Hitschmann. *Frigidity in Women.* Washington, D.C.: Nervous and Mental Disease Publishing Company, 1936.

Bergler, Edmund, and William S. Kroger. *Kinsey's Myth of Female Sexuality: The Medical Facts.* New York: Grune and Stratton, 1954.

Bernheimer, Richard. *Wild Men in the Middle Ages.* Cambridge, Mass.: Harvard University Press, 1952.

Berube, Allan. *Coming Out Under Fire: The History of Gay Men and Women in World War Two.* New York: Free Press, 1990.

Berube, Allan, and John D'Emilio. "The Military and the Lesbians During the McCarthy Years." *Signs* 9, no. 4 (Summer 1984): 759–75.

Bieber, Irving. "Clinical Aspects of Male Homosexuality." In *Sexual Inversion: The Multiple Roots of Homosexuality,* edited by Judd Marmour, 248–67. New York: Basic Books, 1965.

Bieber, Irving, et al., *Homosexuality: A Psychoanalytic Study of Male Homosexuals.* New York: Vintage Books, 1962.

Birke, Lynda I. A. *Women, Feminism and Biology: The Feminist Challenge.* Sussex: Wheatsheaf Books, 1986.

Birken, Lawrence. *Consuming Desire: Sexual Science and the Emergence of a Culture of Abundance, 1871–1914.* Ithaca: Cornell University Press, 1988.

Blainville, Henri de. "Sur une femme de la race hottentote." *Bulletin du Societe philomatique de Paris* (1816): 183–90.

Bleys, Rudi C. *The Geography of Perversion: Male-to-Male Sexual Behavior Outside the West and the Ethnographic Imagination, 1750–1918.* New York: New York University Press, 1995.

Blumer, G. Adler. "Case of Perverted Sexual Instinct." *American Journal of Insanity* 39 (1882): 22–35.

Boas, Franz. *The Mind of Primitive Man.* New York: Macmillan, 1911.

————. "Some Criticisms of Physical Anthropology" (1899), "Influence of Hereditary and Environment Upon Growth" (1913), and "New Evidence in Regard to the Instability of Human Types" (1916). In *Race, Language and Culture,* 76–85, 165–71. New York: Macmillan, 1940.

Bourdet, Edouard. *The Captive (La Prisonniere).* Translated by Arthur Hornblow, Jr. with an introduction by J. Brooks Atkinson. New York: Brentano's, 1926.

Bowman, Karl M. *Final Report on California Sexual Deviation Research.* Sacramento: California State Assembly, 1954.

————. *Personal Problems of Men and Women.* New York: Greenberg Press, 1931.

————. "The Problem of the Sex Offender." *American Journal of Psychiatry* 108 (1951): 250–57.

————. "Psychiatric Aspects of the Problem." *Mental Hygiene* 22, no. 1 (January 1938): 10–20.

————. "Review of Sex Legislation and Control of Sex Offenders in the United States of America." *International Review of Criminal Policy* 4 (July 1953): 20–39.

Bowman, Karl, and Bernice Engle. "A Psychiatric Evaluation of Laws of Homosexuality." *American Journal of Psychiatry* 112 (February 1956): 577–83.

————. "Review of Scientific Literature on Sexual Deviation," in *California Deviation Research,* report presented to the California State Assembly (January 1953).

Boyer, Paul S. *By the Bomb's Early Light: American Thought and Culture at the Dawn of the Atomic Age.* New York: Pantheon, 1985.

————. *Purity in Print: The Vice-Society Movement and Book Censorship in America.* New York: Scribner's, 1968.

Brandt, Allan. *No Magic Bullet: A Social History of Venereal Disease in the United States Since 1800.* New York: Oxford University Press, 1985.

Brantlinger, Patrick. *Rule of Darkness: British Literature and Imperialism, 1830–1914.* Ithaca, N.Y.: Cornell University Press, 1988.

————. "Victorians and Africans: The Genealogy of the Myth of the Dark Continent." *Critical Inquiry* 12 (1985): 166–203.

Breines, Wini. *Young, White, and Miserable: Growing Up Female in the Fifties.* Boston: Beacon Press, 1992.

Brill, Abraham. "The Conception of Homosexuality." *Journal of the American Medical Association* 61, no. 5 (1913): 335–40.

————. "Sexual Manifestations in Neurotic and Psychotic Symptoms." *Psychiatric Quarterly* 14 (1933): 9–16.

Brittenham, Dale. *The Female Homosexual.* Los Angeles: Medco Books, 1965.

Broca, Paul. *On the Phenomenon of Hybridity in the Genus Homo.* Translated and edited by C. Carter Blake. London: Longman, Green, Longman, & Roberts, 1864.

Bromberg, Walter. *Psychiatry Between the Wars, 1918–1945: A Recollection.* Westport, Conn.: Greenwood Press, 1982.

Brown, Isaac Baker. *On the Curability of Certain Forms of Insanity, Epilepsy, Catalepsy and Hysteria in Females.* London: Robert Hardwicke, 1866.

Brown, Ralph S. *Loyalty and Security: Employment Tests in the United States.* New Haven: Yale University Press, 1958.

Buffon, George Louis Leclerc, comte de. *Natural History, General and Particular.* 1741. 9 volumes. Translated by William Smellie. London: A Strahan, 1791.

————. *Oeuvres completes de Buffon.* Edited by M. A. Richard. Paris: Baudouin, 1828.

Bullough, Vern L. *Science in the Bedroom: A History of Sex Research.* New York: Basic Books, 1994.

————. *Sexual Variance in Society and History.* New York: John Wiley and Sons, 1976.

Bullough, Vern L., and Bonnie Bullough. "Lesbianism in the 1920s and 1930s: A New Found Study." *Signs* 2 (1977): 895–904.

Bullough, Vern L., and Martha Voght. "Homosexuality and the 'Secret Sin' in Pre-Freudian America." *Journal of the History of Medicine and Allied Sciences* 28, no. 2 (April 1973): 143–55.

Bunker, Henry Alden. "Psychiatric Literature." In *One Hundred Years of American Psychiatry*, edited by J. K. Hall, 228–32.

Burma, John H. "The Measurement of Negro 'Passing.'" *American Journal of Sociology* 52 (1946–47): 18–22.

Burnham, John C. "The Progressive Era Revolution in American Attitudes Toward Sex." *Journal of American History* 59 (March 1973): 885–908.

Burr, Chandler. "Homosexuality and Biology." *The Atlantic Monthly* 271, no. 3 (March 1993): 47–65.

———. *A Separate Creation: The Search for the Biological Origins of Sexual Orientation.* New York: Hyperion, 1997.

Burton, Richard. "Terminal Essay: The Book of the Thousand Nights and a Night." 1886. Reprinted in *Homosexuality: A Cross Cultural Approach*, edited by Donald Webster Cory, 207–46. New York: Julian Press, Inc., 1956.

Butler, Judith. *Gender Trouble: Feminism and the Subversion of Identity.* New York: Routledge, 1990.

Byne, William, and Bruce Parsons. "Human Sexual Orientation: The Biological Theories Reappraised." *Archives of General Psychiatry* 50 (1993): 228–39.

Cabanis, P. *Rapports du physique et du moral de l'homme* (1802), vols. 3 and 4 of *Oeuvres completes.* Paris, 1823.

California State Assembly, *Preliminary Report of the Subcommittee on Sex Crimes of the Assembly Interim Committee on Judicial System and Judicial Process*, 1949 Session.

Cameron, Paul. "Homosexual Molestation of Children/Sexual Interaction of Teacher and Pupil." *Psychological Reports* 57 (1985): 1227–36.

Cameron, Paul, Kirk Cameron, and Kay Proctor. "The Effect of Homosexuality Upon Public Health and Social Order." *Psychological Reports* 64 (1989): 1167–79.

Cameron, Paul, Kay Proctor, William Coburn, and Nels Forde. "Sexual Orientation and Sexually Transmitted Disease." *Nebraska Medical Journal* 70 (1985): 292–99.

Cameron, Paul, Kay Proctor, William Coburn, Nels Forde, H. Larson, and Kirk Cameron. "Child Molestation and Homosexuality," *Psychological Reports* 58 (1985): 327–37.

Camhi, Leslie. "Stealing Femininity: Department Store Kleptomania as Sexual Disorder." *differences* 5, no. 1 (1993): 26–50.

Campbell, Mary B. *The Witness and the Other World: Exotic European Travel Writings, 400–1600.* Ithaca, N.Y.: Cornell University Press, 1988.

Caprio, Frank S. *Female Homosexuality: a Psychodynamic Study of Lesbianism.* 2nd. ed. Foreword by Karl M. Bowman. New York: Evergreen Black Cat, Grove Press, 1962.

Carpenter, Edward. *Homogenic Love.* Manchester, England: Manchester Labour Press, 1895.

———. *Love's Coming of Age: A Series of Papers on the Relations of the Sexes.* Manchester, England: Manchester Labour Press, 1896.

———. *The Intermediate Sex.* London: Sonnenschein, 1908.

———. "The Intermediate Sex." *Love's Coming of Age.* London: 1923.

———. *Intermediate Types Among Primitive Folk: A Study in Social Evolution.* London: Allen and Unwin, 1914.

"The Case of the Well-Meaning Lyncher." *One Magazine* (November 1953): 10–11.

Caskey, Thomas C. "DNA-based Medicine: Prevention and Therapy," in *The Code of Codes: Scientific and Social Issues in the Human Genome Project,* edited by Daniel J. Kevles and Leroy Hood, 112–35. Cambridge, Mass.: Harvard University Press, 1992.

Caspar, J. L., and Carl Liman. *Handbuch der Gerlichtichen Medicin.* Vol. 1. Berlin: Hirschwald, 1889.

Cauldwell, O. D. "Lesbian Lover Murder." *Sexology* (July 1950).

Caute, David. *The Great Fear: The Anti-communist Purge under Truman and Eisenhower.* New York: Simon and Schuster, 1978.

Cautela, Joseph R. "Covert Sensitization." *Psychological Reports* 20, no. 2 (1967): 464–65.

Cave, F. C. "Report of Sterilization in the Kansas State Home for Feeble-minded." *Journal of Psycho-Asthenics* 15 (1911): 123–25.

The Challenge and Progress of Homosexual Law Reform. Prepared by the Council on Religion and the Homosexual, Daughters of Bilitis Society for Individual Rights, Tavern Guild of San Francisco. San Francisco: Council on Religion and the Homosexual, 1968.

Chalon, Jean. *Portrait of a Seductress: The World of Natalie Barney.* Translated by Carol Barko. New York: Crown, 1979.

Chamberlin, J. Edward, and Sander L. Gilman, eds. *Degeneration: The Dark Side of Progress.* New York: Columbia University Press, 1985.

Chapman, A. H. *Harry Stack Sullivan: His Life and his Work.* New York: G. P. Putnam's Sons, 1976.

Charcot, Jean-Martin, and Valentin Magnan. "Inversions du sens génital et autres perversions génitales." *Archives de Neurologie* 7 (January-February 1882): 55–60 and 12 (November 1882): 292–322.

Chauncey, George, Jr. "Christian Brotherhood or Sexual Perversion? Homosexual Identities and the Construction of Sexual Boundaries in the World War One Era." *Journal of Social History* 19 (1985): 189–211.

———. "From Sexual Inversion to Homosexuality: Medicine and the Changing Conceptualization of Female Deviance." In *Passion and Power,* edited by Kathy Peiss and Christina Simmons, 87–117.

———. *Gay New York: Gender, Urban Culture, and the Making of the Gay Male World, 1890–1940.* New York: Basic Books, 1994.

———. "The Postwar Sex Crime Panic." In William Graebner, ed. *True Stories from the American Past,* edited by William Graebner, 160–78. New York: McGraw-Hill, 1993.

Charpy, Adrien. "Des organes genitaux externes chez les prostituées." *Annales des dermatologie* 3 (1970–71): 271–79.

Chesler, Ellen. *Woman of Valor: Margaret Sanger and the Birth Control Movement in America.* New York: Simon and Schuster, 1992.

Chideckel, Maurice. *Female Sex Perversion: The Sexually Aberrated Woman as She Is.* New York: Eugenics Publishing Company, 1938.

Chodorow, Nancy. "Oedipal Asymmetries and Heterosexual Knots," *Social Problems* 23, no. 4 (1976): 454–68.

Christenson, Cornelia V. *Kinsey: A Biography.* Bloomington, Ind.: Institute for Sex Research, 1971.

Claiborne, Herbert J. "Hypertrichosis in Women: Its Relation to Bisexuality (Hermaphroditism): With Remarks on Bisexuality in Animals, Especially Man." *New York Medical Journal* 99 (1914): 1178–83.

Clark, L. Pierce. *A Critical Digest of Some of the Newer Work Upon Homosexuality in Man and Woman.* Utica, N.Y.: State Hospital Press, 1914.

Clifford, James, and George E. Marcus, eds. *Writing Culture: The Poetics and Politics of Ethnography.* Berkeley: University of California Press, 1985.

Collingwood, R. G. *The Idea of Nature.* Oxford: Oxford University Press, 1945.

Comaroff, Jean. "The Diseased Heart of Africa: Medicine, Colonialism and the Black Body." In *Knowledge, Power & Practice: The Anthropology of Medicine and Everyday Life,* edited by Shirley Lindenbaum and Margaret Lock, 305–29. Berkeley: University of California Press, 1993.

Comstock, T. G. "Alice Mitchell of Memphis; A Case of Sexual Perversion or 'Urning' (a Paranoiac)." *Medical Times: The Journal of the American Medical Profession* 20 (1892): 170–73.

Confessions of a Lesbian Prostitute as told to Robert Leslie, with an introduction by Leonard Lowag. New York: Dalhousie Press, Inc., 1965.

Conrad, Florence. "Research is Here to Stay." *The Ladder* (July/August 1965): 15–21.

Coontz, Stephanie. *The Way We Never Were: American Families and the Nostalgia Trap.* New York: Basic Books, 1992.

Corbin, Alain. *Women for Hire: Prostitution and Sexuality in France after 1850.* Translated by Alan Sheridan. Cambridge: Harvard University Press, 1990.

Cornsweet, A. C., and M. F. Hayes. "Conditioned Response to Fellatio." *American Journal of Psychiatry* 108 (July 1945): 76–78.

Cory, Donald Webster [pseud.]. *The Homosexual in America: A Subjective Approach.* New York: Greenberg, 1951.

———. *The Lesbian in America.* Introduction by Albert Ellis. New York: Tower Publications, 1964.

Cott, Nancy. *The Grounding of Modern Feminism.* New Haven: Yale University Press, 1987.

Cowan, Ruth S. "Nature and Nurture: The Interplay of Biology and Politics in the Work of Francis Galton." *Studies in the History of Biology* 1 (1977): 133–208.

Crewdson, John. "Author [Dean Hamer] Defends Findings against Allegations." *Chicago Tribune,* June 25, 1995.

———. "Files from Hoover Backers Reported." *New York Times,* February 2, 1974.

———. "Censored Version of Secret Hoover Files on Official's Misconduct." *New York Times,* November 24, 1976.

Cuvier, Georges. "Faites sur le cadavre d'une femme connue a Paris et a Londres sous la nom de Venus Hottentotte." *Memoires du Musée nationale d'histoire naturelle* 3 (1817): 259–74.

———. *Lecons d'anatomie comparée.* Paris, 1800–1805.

Daniel, F. E. "Should Insane Criminals or Sexual Perverts Be Allowed To Procreate?" *Texas Medical Journal* (August 1893): 255–71.

Daniels, E. J., ed. *I Accuse Kinsey! Startling Exposé of Kinsey's Sex Reports.* Orlando, Florida: Christ for the World Publications, 1954.

Danziger, Kurt. *Constructing the Subject: Historical Origins of Psychological Research.* Cambridge: Cambridge University Press, 1990.

Darke, Roy A. "Heredity as an Etiological Factor in Homosexuality." *The Journal of Nervous and Mental Disease* 107 (January–June 1948): 251–68.

Darwin, Charles. *The Descent of Man, and Selections in Relation to Sex.* 2 vols. London: Murray, 1871.

———. *Journal of Researches into the Natural History and Geology of the Countries Visited During the Voyage of H.M.S. "Beagle."* London: Henry Colburn, 1839.

———. *On the Origin of Species.* 1859. Cambridge, Mass.: Harvard University Press, 1966.

Davie, Maurice. *Negroes in American Society.* New York: Whittlesey House, 1949.

———. "On the Examination of Immigrants Abroad" (1921); "A Constructive Immigration Policy" (1923), 34–72; "Immigration and the Declining Birth Rate" (1924); "Social Aspects of Psychiatry" (1936); "Minorities, a Challenge to American Democracy" (1939); "The Cultural 'Syncretism' of Nationality Groups" (1940); "Our Vanishing Minorities" (1952); "The Negro and the War" (1943). In *The Papers of Maurice R. Davie,* edited by Ruby Jo Reeves Kennedy. New Haven: Yale University Press, 1961.

———. *World Immigration, With Special Reference to the United States.* New York: Macmillan, 1946.

Davis, Joseph B. *Crania Britannica: Delineations and Descriptions of the Skulls of the Aboriginal and Early Inhabitants of the British Islands.* 2 vols. London: Subscribers, 1865.

Davis, Katharine Bement. *Factors in the Sex Lives of Twenty-two Hundred Women.* New York: Harper and Brothers, 1929.

———. "A Study of Certain Auto-Erotic Practices." *Mental Hygiene* 8, no. 3 (July 1924): 668–723.

———. "Three Score Years and Ten: An Autobiographical Biography." *University of Chicago Magazine* 26 (December 1933): 58. Reprinted in *Katharine Bement Davis,* ed. Fitzpatrick.

———. "Why They Failed to Marry." *Harper's Magazine* 156 (March 1928): 460–69. Reprinted in *Katharine Bement Davis,* ed. Fitzpatrick.

Day, Caroline Bond. *A Study of Some Negro-White Families in the United States.* Cambridge, Mass.: Peabody Museum/Harvard University Press, 1932.

Degler, Carl. "What Ought to Be and What Was: Women's Sexuality in the Nineteenth Century." *American Historical Review* 79 (December 1974): 1467–90.

de Lauretis, Teresa. *The Practice of Love: Lesbian Sexuality and Perverse Desire.* Bloomington: Indiana University Press, 1994.

———. "The Technology of Gender." In *Technologies of Gender: Essays on Theory, Film, and Fiction,* 1–30. Bloomington, Indiana: Indiana University Press, 1987.

Dell, Floyd. *Love in the Machine Age: A Psychological Study of the Transition from Patriarchal Society.* New York: Farrar, 1930.

D'Emilio, John. "The Homosexual Menace: The Politics of Sexuality in Cold War

America." In *Passion and Power*, edited by Kathy Peiss and Christina Simmons, 226–40.

———. *Sexual Politics, Sexual Communities: The Making of a Homosexual Minority in the United States, 1940–1970.* Chicago: University of Chicago Press, 1983.

D'Emilio, John, and Estelle Freedman. *Intimate Matters: A Social History of Sexuality in the United States.* New York: Harper and Row, 1988.

Deutsch, Helene. "On Female Homosexuality," (1932). In *The Psychoanalytic Reader*, edited by Robert Fliess, 208–30. New York: International Universities Press, 1948.

Devereux, George. "Institutionalized Homosexuality of the Mohave Indians." *Human Biology* 9 (1937): 498–527.

"Dickinson Collection Comes to Cleveland Museum of Health." *Museum News of the Cleveland Health Museum* (June–July 1945): 2.

Dickinson, Robert Latou. "A Gynecologist Looks at Prostitution Abroad: With Reference to Electrocautery Treatment of Gonorrheal Cervicitis and Urethritis." *American Journal of Obstetrics and Gynecology* 16 (1928): 590–602.

———. "Hypertrophies of the Labia Minora and Their Significance." *American Gynecology* 1 (1902): 225–54.

———. *Human Sex Anatomy.* Baltimore: The Williams and Wilkins Company, 1933.

———. *Human Sex Anatomy: A Topographical Hand Atlas.* Baltimore: The Williams and Wilkins Company, 1949.

———. "Marital Maladjustment: The Business of Preventive Gynecology." *Long Island Medical Journal* 2 (1908): 1–4.

———. "Medical Analysis of *A Thousand Marriages.*" *Journal of the American Medical Association* 97, no. 8 (August 22, 1931): 531.

———. *The New York Walk Book.* New York: American Geographical Society, 1923.

———. *Palisades Guide.* New York: American Geographical Society, 1921.

———. "Premarital Consultation." *Journal of the American Medical Association* 117 (November 17, 1941): 1687–92.

———. "Premarital Examination as Routine Preventive Gynecology." *American Journal of Obstetrics and Gynecology* 16 (1928): 631–49.

———. "A Program for American Gynecology: Presidential Address." *American Journal of Obstetrics and Gynecology* 1 (1920): 2–10.

———. "Simple Sterilization By Cautery Stricture at the Intra-uterine Tubal Openings, Compared with Other Openings." *Surgery, Gynecology, and Obstetrics* 23 (1916): 203–14.

———. "Sterilization Without Unsexing." *Journal of the American Medical Association* 92 (February 2, 1929): 373–79.

———. "Studies of the Levator Ani Muscle." *American Journal of Obstetrics* 22 (1889): 259–61.

Dickinson, Robert Latou, and Lura Beam. *The Single Woman: A Medical Study in Sex Education.* Baltimore: The Williams & Wilkins Company, 1934.

———. *A Thousand Marriages: A Medical Study of Sex Adjustment.* Baltimore: The Williams & Wilkins Company, 1931.

Dickinson, Robert Latou, and Louise Stevens Bryant. *Control of Contraception:*

An Illustrated Medical Manual. Baltimore: The Williams and Wilkins Company, 1932.

Dickinson, Robert Latou, and Henry H. Pierson. "The Average Life of American Women." *Journal of the American Medical Association* 85, no. 15 (October 15, 1925): 1113–17.

Dickinson, Robert Latou, and Walter Truslow. "Averages in Attitude and Trunk Development in Women and Their Relation to Pain." *Journal of the American Medical Association* 59, no. 24 (December 14, 1912): 2128–32.

Dolce, Joe. "And How Big is Yours?" Interview with Simon LeVay. *The Advocate* 630 (June 1, 1993): 38–44.

Dörner, Gunter. "Hormonal Induction and Prevention of Female Homosexuality." *Journal of Endocrinology* 42 (1968): 163–64.

———. *Hormones and Brain Differentiation.* Amsterdam: Elsevier, 1976.

Dörner, Gunter et al. "A Neuroendocrine Predisposition for Homosexuality in Men." *Archives of Sexual Behavior* 4 (1975): 1–8.

———. "Stressful Events in Prenatal Life of Bi- and Homosexual Men." *Experiments in Clinical Endocrinology* 81 (1983): 83–87.

Draper, George. *Human Constitution: A Consideration of its Relationship to Disease.* Philadelphia: W. B. Saunders Company, 1924.

Draper, George, C. W. Dupertuis, and J. L. Caughey, Jr. *Human Constitution in Clinical Medicine.* New York: Paul B. Hoeber, Inc., 1944.

Dreger, Alice Domurat. *Hermaphrodites and the Medical Invention of Sex.* Cambridge, Mass.: Harvard University Press, 1998.

Drinnon, Richard. *Rebel in Paradise.* Boston: Beacon Press, 1961.

Duberman, Martin Bauml. *About Time: Exploring the Gay Past.* New York: Gay Presses of New York, 1986.

———. *Cures: A Gay Man's Odyssey.* New York: Dutton Press, 1991.

Duberman, Martin Bauml, Martha Vicinus, and George Chauncey, Jr., eds. *Hidden from History: Reclaiming the Gay and Lesbian Past.* New York: Meridian, 1989.

Dudley, Edward J., and Maximillian E. Novak, eds. *The Wild Man Within: An Image in Western Thought Since the Renaissance.* Pittsburgh: University of Pittsburgh Press, 1972.

Dugdale, Richard L. *"The Jukes": A Study in Crime, Pauperism, Disease and Heredity; also Further Studies of Criminals.* New York: G. P. Putnam's Sons, 1877.

Duggan, Lisa. "The Social Enforcement of Heterosexuality and Lesbian Resistance in the 1920s." In *Class, Race and Sex: The Dynamics of Control,* edited by Amy Swerdlow and Hanah Lessinger, 75–92. Boston: G. K. Hall, 1983.

———. "The Trials of Alice Mitchell: Sexology and the Lesbian Subject in Turn-of-the-Century America." *Signs* 18, no. 4 (Summer 1993): 791–814.

Dyer, Thomas G. *Theodore Roosevelt and the Idea of Race.* Baton Rouge: Louisiana University Press, 1980.

Eastman, Crystal. *Crystal Eastman: On Women and Revolution.* Edited by Blanche Weisen Cook. New York: Oxford University Press, 1978.

Eckard, E. W. "How Many Negroes 'Pass'?" *American Journal of Sociology* 52 (1946–47): 498–500.

Ehrenreich, Barbara, and Deirdre English. *Witches, Midwives, and Nurses: A History of Women Healers*. Old Westbury, N.J.: The Feminist Press, 1973.

Eisenbud, Jule. "A Psychiatrist Looks at the Report." In *Problems of Sexual Behavior*, edited by Charles Walter Clarke, 20–27. New York: American Social Hygiene Association, 1948.

Elias, Norbert. *The History of Manners*. Volume 1 of *The Civilizing Process*. Translated by Edmund Jephcott. 1939. New York: Pantheon Books, 1978.

Ellis, Havelock. *The Criminal*. London: Walter Scott, 1890.

———. "A Note on the Treatment of Sexual Inversion." *Alienist and Neurologist* 17 (July 1896): 258–59.

———. *Sexual Inversion*. London: Watford University Press, 1897.

———. *Sexual Inversion*. Vol. 2 of *Studies in the Psychology of Sex*. 4 vols. 2d ed. Philadelphia: F. A. Davis Company, 1901.

———. *Sexual Inversion*. Vol. 2 of *Studies in the Psychology of Sex*. 4 vols. 3d ed. Philadelphia: F. A. Davis Company, 1915.

———. "Sexual Inversion in Women." *Alienist and Neurologist* 16, no. 2 (April 1895): 141–58.

Ellis, Havelock, and John Addington Symonds. *Sexual Inversion*. Vol. 1. *Studies in the Psychology of Sex*. London: Wilson and Macmillan, 1897. Reprinted New York: Arno Press, 1975.

Engels, Friedrich. *The Origin of the Family, Private Property and the State*. New York: International Publishers, 1972.

Engelstein, Laura. *The Keys to Happiness: Sex and the Search for Modernity in Fin-de-Siècle Russia*. Ithaca: Cornell University Press, 1992.

English, O. Spurgeon. "Sex and Human Love." In *About the Kinsey Report: Observations by Eleven Experts on 'Sexual Behavior in the Human Male'*, edited by Donald Porter Geddes and Enid Curie, 96–112. New York: New American Library.

Erenberg, Lewis A. "From New York to Middletown: Repeal and the Legitimization of Night Life in the Great Depression." *American Quarterly* 38 (1986): 761–78.

Ernst, Morris L., and Alan U. Schwartz. *Censorship: The Search for the Obscene*. New York: Macmillan, 1964.

Estabrook, Arthur H., and Charles B. Davenport. *The Nam Family: A Study in Cacogenics*. Cold Spring Harbor, N.Y.: Eugenics Record Office, 1912.

Faderman, Lillian. *Odd Girls and Twilight Lovers: A History of Lesbian Life in Twentieth-Century America*. New York: Columbia University Press, 1991.

Falk, Candace. *Love, Anarchy, and Emma Goldman*. 2d ed. New Brunswick: Rutgers University Press, 1990.

Fantis, Edwood L. "Homosexuality in Growing Girls." *Sexology* 2 (February 1935): 349.

Fass, Paula. *The Damned and the Beautiful: American Youth in the 1920s*. New York: Oxford University Press, 1977.

Fausto-Sterling, Anne. *Body Building: How Biologists Construct Sexuality*. New York: Basic Books, forthcoming.

———. "Gender, Race, and Nation: The Comparative Anatomy of 'Hottentot' Women in Europe, 1815–1817." In *Deviant Bodies: Critical Perspectives on Difference in Science and Popular Culture*, edited by Jennifer Terry and Jacqueline Urla, 19–48. Bloomington, Indiana: Indiana University Press, 1995.

Fee, Elizabeth. "The Sexual Politics of Victorian Social Anthropology." In *Clio's Consciousness Raised: New Perspectives on the History of Women*, edited by Mary Hartman and Lois Banner, 86–102. New York: Harper and Row, 1974.

Fellner, Otfried. *Pflugers Archiv* (1921): 189.

Ferenczi, Sandor. "More about Homosexuality." 1909. In *Final Contributions to the Problems and Methods of Psychoanalysis*. New York: Basic Books, 1955.

Fishberg, Maurice. "Intermarriage Between Jews and Christians." In *Eugenics in Race and State*, Vol. 2: *Scientific Papers of the Second International Congress of Eugenics (1921)*, 125–33. Baltimore: The Williams and Wilkins Company, 1923.

Fitzpatrick, Ellen, ed. *Katharine Bement Davis, Early Twentieth-Century Women, and the Study of Sex Behavior*. New York: Garland, 1987.

Flexner, Abraham. *Prostitution in Europe*. New York: Century, 1913.

Flower, W. H., and James Murie. "Account of the Dissection of a Bushwoman." *Journal of Anatomy and Physiology* 1 (1867): 189–208; *Anthropological Review* 5 (July 1867): 319–24; *Anthropological Review* 8 (January 1870): 89–318.

Ford, Charles A. "Homosexual Practices of Institutionalized Females." *Journal of Abnormal and Social Psychiatry* 23 (1929): 442–48.

Ford, Charles Henri, and Parker Tyler. *The Young and the Evil*. 1933. Reprinted London: GMP Publishers, 1989.

Forde, C. Daryll. "Ethnology of Yuma Indians." *University of California Publications in American Archaeology and Ethnology* 28, no. 4 (1931): 83–278.

Forel, August. *The Sexual Question*. Translated by C. F. Marshall. New York: Rebman Company, 1905.

Forrest, Derek. *Francis Galton: The Life and Works of a Victorian Genius*. London: Elek, 1974.

Fosdick, Raymond B. *American Police Systems*. New York: Century, 1921.

———. *European Police Systems*. New York: Century, 1915.

Foster, Jeannette. *Sex Variant Women in Literature*. New York: Vantage Press, Inc., 1956.

Foucault, Michel. "The Dangerous Individual." In *Michel Foucault: Politics, Philosophy, Culture*, edited by Lawrence D. Kritzman and translated by Alain Baudot and Jane Couchman, 125–51. New York: Routledge, 1988.

———. *Discipline and Punish: The Birth of the Prison*. Translated by Alan Sheridan. New York: Vintage Books, 1979.

———. "Governmentality." *Ideology and Consciousness* 6 (1979): 5–21.

———. *The History of Sexuality, Volume One: An Introduction*. Translated by Robert Hurley. New York: Vintage Books, 1978.

———. *Madness and Civilization: A History of Insanity in the Age of Reason*. Translated by Richard Howard. New York: Vintage Books, 1965.

———. "Nietzsche, History, Genealogy." In *The Foucault Reader*, edited by Paul Rabinow, 76–100. New York: Pantheon Books, 1984.

———. *The Order of Things: An Archaeology of the Human Sciences*. New York: Random House, 1970.

————. "The Order of Discourse." In *Untying the Text,* edited by Robert Young and translated by Ian McLeod, 48–78. London: Routledge Press, 1981.

————. "The Subject and Power." Afterword to *Michel Foucault: Beyond Structuralism and Hermeneutics,* edited by Hubert Dreyfus and Paul Rabinow, 208–26. Chicago: University of Chicago Press, 1982.

Frank, Robert T. *The Female Sex Hormone.* Springfield, Ill. and Baltimore: Charles C. Thomas, 1929.

Fraser, Steven, ed., *The Bell Curve Wars: Race, Intelligence, and the Future of America.* New York: Basic Books, 1995.

Freeden, Michael. "Eugenics and Progressive Thought: A Study in Ideological Affinity." *Historical Journal* 22 (1979): 645–71.

Freedman, Estelle. "The Prison Lesbian: Race, Class, and the Construction of the Aggressive Female Homosexual, 1915–1965." *Feminist Studies* 22, no. 2 (Summer 1996): 397–423.

————. *Their Sister's Keepers.* Ann Arbor, Mich.: University of Michigan Press, 1981.

————. "'Uncontrolled Desires': The Response to the Sexual Psychopath, 1920–1960." In *Passion and Power,* edited by Kathy Peiss and Christina Simmons, 199–225.

Freeland, Richard M. *The Truman Doctrine and the Origins of McCarthyism: Foreign Policy, Domestic Politics, and Internal Security, 1946–1948.* 3d ed. New York: New York University Press, 1985.

Freud, Sigmund. *The Standard Edition of the Complete Psychological Works of Sigmund Freud,* 24 vols. Edited by James Strachey. London: Hogarth Press, 1953.

————. "The Aetiology of Hysteria." 1896. *Standard Edition* 3: 189–224.

————. "Analysis of a Phobia in a Five-Year-Old Boy ('Little Hans')." 1909. *Standard Edition* 10: 3–149.

————. "A Case of Paranoia Running Counter to the Psychoanalytic Theory of Disease." 1915. *Standard Edition* 14: 263–72.

————. "Certain Neurotic Mechanisms in Jealousy, Paranoia, and Homosexuality." 1922. *Standard Edition* 18: 221–34.

————. *Civilization and its Discontents.* 1930. *Standard Edition* 21: 64–145.

————. "'Civilized' Sexual Morality and Modern Nervous Illness." 1908. *Standard Edition* 9: 177–204.

————. "Family Romances." 1909. *Standard Edition* 9: 237–41.

————. "Female Sexuality." 1931. *Standard Edition* 21: 223–43.

————. "Femininity." 1933. *Standard Edition* 22: 112–35.

————. "From the History of an Infantile Neurosis ('Wolf Man')." 1915. *Standard Edition* 17: 3–22.

————. "Heredity and the Aetiology of Neuroses." 1896. *Standard Edition* 3: 141–58.

————. "The Infantile Genital Organization." 1923. *Standard Edition* 19: 141–45.

————. *Jokes and the Relation to the Unconscious.* 1905. *Standard Edition* 8: 9–236.

————. "Leonardo da Vinci and a Memory of his Childhood." 1910. *Standard Edition* 11: 59–138.

————. "Letter to An American Mother." 1935. *American Journal of Psychiatry* 107 (1951): 786–87.

————. "Mourning and Melancholia." 1917. *Standard Edition* 14: 237–58.

————. "My Views on the Part Played by Sexuality in the Aetiology of the Neuroses." 1906. *Standard Edition* 7: 271–79.

————. "On the Sexual Theories of Children." 1908. *Standard Edition* 9: 207–26.

————. "The Psychogenesis of a Case of Female Homosexuality." 1920. *Standard Edition* 18: 146–72.

————. *Psychopathology of Everyday Life*. 1901. *Standard Edition* 6.

————. "The Sexual Aberrations." 1905. *Standard Edition* 7: 135–72.

————. "The Sexual Enlightenment of Children." 1907. *Standard Edition* 9: 131–39.

————. "Sexuality in the Aetiology of the Neuroses." 1898. *Standard Edition* 3: 261–86.

————. "Some Psychical Consequences of the Anatomical Distinctions Between the Sexes." 1925. *Standard Edition* 19: 243–58.

————. *Three Contributions to the Theory of Sex*. 1905. *Standard Edition* 7: 123–246.

Friedlander, Joseph W., and Ralph S. Banay. "Psychosis Following Lobotomy in a Case of Sexual Psychopathology." *Archives of Neurology and Psychiatry* 59 (1948): 303–21.

Friedman, Richard C. "Hormones and Sexual Orientation in Men." *American Journal of Psychiatry* 134 (1977): 571–72.

Friedman, Richard C., and Leonore O. Stern, "Juvenile Aggressivity and Sissiness in Homosexual and Heterosexual Males." *Journal of the American Academy of Psychoanalysis* 8 (1980): 427–40.

Frosch, Jack, and Walter Bromberg. "The Sex Offender: A Psychiatric Study." *American Journal of Orthopsychiatry* 9 (1939): 761–77.

Galton, Sir Francis. *Hereditary Genius: An Inquiry into its Laws and Consequences*. New York: Appleton, 1884.

————. *Inquiries into Human Faculty and its Development*. London: J. M. Dent and Company, 1908.

————. *Narration of an Explorer in Tropic South Africa*. London: J. Murray, 1853.

Garber, Eric. "A Spectacle in Color: The Lesbian and Gay Subculture of Jazz Age Harlem." In *Hidden from History: Reclaiming the Gay and Lesbian Past*, edited by Martin Bauml Duberman, Martha Vicinus, George Chauncey, 318–31. New York: Meridian, 1989.

————. "'T'Aint Nobody's Bizness': Homosexuality in 1920s Harlem." In *Black Men/White Men*, edited by Michael J. Smith. San Francisco: Gay Sunshine Press, 1983.

Gautier, Theophile. *Mademoiselle de Maupin*. 1835. Edited and translated by Joanna Richardson. Harmondsworth, Eng.: Penguin Books, 1981.

Gay and Lesbian Historical Project of Northern California. "MTF Transgender Activism in the Tenderloin and Beyond, 1966–1975: Commentary and Interview with Elliot Blackstone." *GLQ* vol. 4, no. 2 (1998): 349–72.

Gay, Jan. *The Mutt Book*. New York: Harper and Bros., 1932.

————. *On Going Naked*. New York: Holburn House, 1932.

————. *Pancho and his Burro*. New York: W. Morrow and Company, 1930.

————. *The Shire Colt*. Garden City, N.Y.: Doubleday, Doran and Company, Inc., 1931.

————. *Town Cats.* New York: Alfred Knopf, 1932.

Gerassi, John. *The Boys of Boise: Furor, Vice, and Folly in an American City.* New York: Macmillan, 1966.

Gifford, Edward Winslow. "The Cocopa." *University of California Publications in American Archaeology and Ethnology* 31 (1933): 277–94.

Gilbert, Walter. "A Vision of the Grail," in *The Code of Codes: Scientific and Social Issues in the Human Genome Project,* edited by Daniel J. Kevles and Leroy Hood, 83–97. Cambridge, Mass.: Harvard University Press, 1992.

Gilfoyle, Timothy. *City of Eros: New York, Prostitution, and the Commercialization of Sex.* New York: W. W. Norton and Company, 1992.

————. "The Moral Origins of Political Surveillance: The Preventive Society in New York City, 1867–1918." *American Quarterly* 38, no. 4 (1986): 635–52.

Gilman, Charlotte Perkins. *Herland.* 1915. Reprinted by New York: Pantheon Books, 1979.

————. *Women and Economics.* 1898. Edited by Carl N. Degler. New York: Harper and Row, 1966.

Gilman, Sander L. "Black Bodies, White Bodies: Toward an Iconography of Female Sexuality in Late Nineteenth-Century Art, Medicine, and Literature." *Critical Inquiry* 12, no. 1 (Autumn 1985): 204–42.

Gioscia, Nicolai. "The Gag Reflex and Fellatio." *American Journal of Psychiatry* 107 (November 1950): 380.

Glass, S. J., and Roswell H. Johnson. "Limitations and Complications of Organotherapy in Male Homosexuality." *Journal of Endocrinology* 4, no. 11 (1944): 541–43.

Glueck, Bernhard. "A Study of 608 Admissions to Sing-Sing Prison." *Mental Hygiene* 2, no. 1 (January 1918): 85–123.

Gobineau, Joseph Arthur, comte de. *The Moral and Intellectual Diversity of the Races, with Particular Reference to their Respective Influence in the Civil and Political History of Mankind.* Philadelphia: Lippincott, 1856.

Goddard, Henry H. *The Kallikak Family: A Study in the Heredity of Feeblemindedness.* New York: Macmillan, 1912.

Goldman, Emma. *Living My Life.* 2 vols. New York: Dover, 1971.

Goodwin, Frederick. "Conduct Disorder as a Precursor to Adult Violence and Substance Abuse: Can the Progression be Halted?" Address presented to the American Psychiatric Association Annual Convention, Washington, D.C., May 1992.

Gordon, Linda. *Woman's Body, Woman's Right: A Social History of Birth Control in America.* New York: Penguin Books, 1974.

Gorman, Christine. "Are Gay Men Born that Way?" *Newsweek* 138, no. 10 (1991): 48.

Goshko, John M. "Inside Hoover's Sex Files." *New York Post,* November 24, 1976.

Gould, Stephen Jay. "The Hottentot Venus." In *The Flamingo's Smile: Reflections in Natural History,* 291–305. New York: W. W. Norton & Company, 1985.

————. "Carrie Buck's Daughter." In *The Flamingo's Smile,* 306–18.

————. *The Mismeasure of Man.* New York: W. W. Norton & Company, 1981.

————. *Ontogeny and Phylogeny.* Cambridge, Mass.: Harvard University Press, 1977.

Graham, Billy. "The Bible and Dr. Kinsey." In *I Accuse Kinsey! Startling Exposé of Kinsey's Sex Reports,* edited by E. J. Daniels, 103–12.

Greco, Marshall C., and James C. Wright. "The Correctional Institution in the Etiology of Chronic Homosexuality." *American Journal of Orthopsychiatry* 14 (1944): 295–307.

Green, Richard. *The 'Sissy Boy Syndrome' and the Development of Homosexuality.* New Haven: Yale University Press, 1987.

Greenspan, Lieut. Herbert, and Comdr. John D. Campbell. "The Homosexual as Personality Type." *American Journal of Psychiatry* 101 (1945): 682–89.

Groneman, Carol. "Nymphomania: The Historical Construction of Female Sexuality." In *Deviant Bodies,* edited by Jennifer Terry and Jacqueline Urla, 219–49.

Gross, Alfred A. *Strangers in our Midst: Problems of the Homosexual in American Society.* Washington, D.C.: Public Affairs Press, 1962.

Grosskurth, Phyllis. *John Addington Symonds: A Biography.* London: Longmans, Green, 1964.

Grossmann, Atina. *Reforming Sex: The German Movement for Birth Control and Abortion Reform, 1920–1950.* New York: Oxford University Press, 1995.

Hackfield, A. W. "Ameliorative Effects of Therapeutic Castration on Habitual Sex Offenders." *Journal of Nervous and Mental Disease* 82, no. 1 (July 1935): 15–29 and 82, no. 2 (August 1935): 169–81.

Hagenbach, Allen W. "Masturbation as a Cause of Insanity." *The Journal of Nervous and Mental Disease* 6 (1879): 603–12.

Hale, Nathan G., Jr. *Freud and the Americans: The Beginning of Psychoanalysis in the United States, 1876–1917.* New York: Oxford University Press, 1971.

———. *The Rise and Crisis of Psychoanalysis in the United States: Freud and the Americans, 1917–1985.* New York: Oxford University Press, 1995.

Hall, Diana Long. "Biology, Sex Hormones and Sexism in the 1920s." *Philosophical Forum* 5 (Fall-Winter 1973–74): 81–96.

Hall, J. K., ed. *One Hundred Years of American Psychiatry.* New York: Columbia University Press, 1944.

Hall, Lesley A. "'Somehow Very Distasteful': Doctors, Men and Sexual Problems Between the Wars." *Journal of Contemporary History* 20, no. 4 (October 1985): 553–74.

Hall, Radclyffe. *The Well of Loneliness.* 1928. Reprinted by New York: Avon Books, 1981.

Haller, Mark. *Eugenics: Hereditarian Attitudes in American Thought.* New Brunswick: Rutgers University Press, 1985.

Halley, Janet E. "Sexual Orientation and the Politics of Biology: a Critique of the Argument from Immutability." *Stanford Law Review* 46, no. 3 (1994): 503–68.

Halliday, R. "Social Darwinism: A Definition." *Victorian Studies* 14 (1971): 389–405.

Hamer, Dean H., Stella Hu, Nan Hu, Angela Pattatucci, and Victoria Magnuson. "Evidence for Homosexuality Gene." *Science* 261 (1993): 291–92.

———. "A Linkage Between DNA Markers on the X Chromosome and Male Sexual Orientation." *Science* 261 (1993): 321–27.

Hamilton, Allan McLane. "The Civil Responsibility of Sexual Perverts." *American Journal of Insanity* 52 (1896): 503–11.

———. "Insanity in its Medico-Legal Bearings." In *A System of Legal Medicine,* edited by A. M. Hamilton and Lawrence Godkin. 3 vols. New York: Treat, 1894–97.

Hamilton, Gilbert V. *An Introduction to Objective Psychopathology.* St. Louis: The C. V. Mosby Company, 1925.

———. *A Research in Marriage.* New York: Albert and Charles Boni, Inc., 1929.

———. "A Study of Sexual Tendencies in Monkeys and Baboons." *Journal of Animal Behavior* 4 (1914): 295–318.

Hamilton, Gilbert V., and Kenneth MacGowan. "Physical Disabilities in Wives." In *Sex in Civilization,* edited by V. F. Calverton and S. D. Schmalhausen, introduction by Havelock Ellis, 562–79. New York: The Macaulay Company, 1929.

———. *What's Wrong with Marriage: A Study of Two Hundred Husbands and Wives.* New York: Albert and Charles Boni, 1929.

Hammond, William A. "The Disease of the Scythians." *American Journal of Neurology and Psychiatry* 1, no. 3 (August 1882): 339–55.

———. *Sexual Impotence in the Male.* New York: Bermingham, 1883.

Hansen, Bert. "American Physicians' 'Discovery' of Homosexuals, 1880–1900: A New Diagnosis in a Changing Society." In *Framing Disease: Studies in Cultural History,* edited by Charles E. Rosenberg and Janet Golden, 104–33. New Brunswick: Rutgers University Press, 1992.

Haraway, Donna J. *Primate Visions: Gender, Race, and Nature in the World of Modern Science.* New York: Routledge, 1989.

———. "The Promise of Monsters: A Regenerative Politics for Inappropriate/d Others." In *Cultural Studies,* edited by Lawrence Grossberg, Cary Nelson, Paula Treichler, 295–337. New York: Routledge, 1992.

Henry, George W. *All the Sexes: A Study of Masculinity and Femininity.* New York: Rinehart & Company, Inc., 1955.

———. "Basal Metabolism and Emotional States." *Journal of Nervous and Mental Disorders* 70 (1929): 598–605.

———. "Blood Calcium and Phosphorus in Personality Disorders." *Archives of Neurology and Psychiatry* 16 (1926): 48–59.

———. "The Care and Treatment of Mental Disease: Yesterday and To-day." *Modern Hospital* (November 1929).

———. "Catatonia in Birds, Induced by Bulbocapnine." *Psychiatric Quarterly* 8 (1931): 68–81.

———. "A Comparative Study of the Action of Bulbocapnine and some other Drugs in Producing Catatonic States." *Acta Psychiatrica et Neurologica* 5 (1930): 463–71.

———. *Essentials of Psychiatry.* Baltimore: The Williams and Wilkins Company, 1925.

———. *Essentials of Psychopathology.* Baltimore: The Williams and Wilkins Company, 1935.

———. "Gastrointestinal Motor Functions in Manic-Depressive Psychoses, Roentgenologic Observations." *American Journal of Psychiatry* 11 (1931): 19–28.

———. "Gastrointestinal Motor Functions in Schizophrenia, Roentgenologic Observations." *American Journal of Psychiatry* 7 (1927): 135–52.

———. *Masculinity and Femininity.* New York: Collier Books, 1964.

———. "The Neuro-Psychiatric Out-Patient Clinic." *General Bulletin,* The Society of the New York Hospital (March 1927).

———. "Pastoral Counseling for Homosexuals." *Pastoral Psychology* 2, no. 18 (November 1951): 33–39.

―――. "Practical Applications of Psychiatry in General Hospitals." *Medical Journal and Record* 130 (October 1929): 383–85.

―――. "Psychogenic and Constitutional Factors in Homosexuality: Their Relation to Personality Disorders." *Psychiatric Quarterly* 8 (1934): 243–64.

―――. *Sex Variants: A Study in Homosexual Patterns.* 2 vols. New York: Paul B. Hoeber, the Medical Book Department of Harper & Brothers, 1941.

―――. *Sex Variants: A Study in Homosexual Patterns.* 2d ed. in one volume. New York: Paul B. Hoeber, 1948.

―――. *Society and the Sex Variant.* New York: Collier Books, 1965.

―――. "Some Modern Aspects of Psychiatry in General Hospital Practice." *American Journal of Psychiatry* 9 (1929): 481–500.

Henry, George W., and Alfred A. Gross. "The Homosexual Delinquent." *Mental Hygiene* 25, no. 3 (July 1941): 420–42.

―――. "The Sex Offender: A Consideration of Therapeutic Principles." *National Probation Association Yearbook* (1940): 114–37.

―――. "Social Factors in the Case Histories of One Hundred Underprivileged Homosexuals." *Mental Hygiene* 22, no. 4 (October 1938): 591–611.

―――. "Social Factors in Delinquency." *Mental Hygiene* 24, no. 1 (January 1940): 54–78.

Henry, George W., and Hugh M. Galbraith. "Constitutional Factors in Homosexuality." *American Journal of Psychiatry* 13 (1934): 1249–70.

Herculine Barbin: Being the Recently Discovered Memoirs of a Nineteenth-Century French Hermaphrodite. Introduced by Michel Foucault and translated by Richard McDougall. New York: Pantheon Books, 1980.

Herzer, Manfred. "Kertbeny and the Nameless Love." *Journal of Homosexuality* 12 (1985): 1–26.

Higham, John. *Strangers in the Land: Patterns of American Nativism, 1860–1925.* New Brunswick: Rutgers University Press, 1955.

Hill, Willard Williams. "Note on the Pima Berdache." *American Anthropologist* 40 (1938): 338–40.

―――. "The Status of the Hermaphrodite and Transvestite in Navaho Culture." *American Anthropologist* 37 (1935): 273–79.

Hirschfeld, Magnus. "The Homosexual as an Intersex." In *The Homosexuals As Seen By Themselves and Thirty Authorities,* edited by A. M. Krich, 119–34. New York: Citadel Press, 1954.

―――. *Die Homosexualität des Mannes und des Weibes.* Berlin: Louis Marcus, 1914. 2d ed., 1920.

―――. "Homosexuality." In *Encylopedia Sexualis,* edited by Victor Robinson, 321–34. New York: Dingwall-Rock, 1936.

―――. "Die Intersexuelle Konstitution." *Jahrbuch für sexuelle Zwischenstufen* 23 (1923): 3–27.

―――. [T. Ramien, pseud.]. *Sappho und Sokrates, oder Wie erklärt sich die Liebe der Männer und der Frauen zu Personen des eigenen Geschlecht?* Leipzig: Max Spohr, 1896. Reprinted in *Documents of the Homosexual Rights Movement in Germany, 1836–1927.* New York: Arno, 1975.

————. *Sex in Human Relationships*. Translated by John Rodker. New York: AMS Press, 1975.

————. *Sexual Anomalies and Perversions: Physical and Psychological Development and Treatment*. 1936. New York: Random House, 1942.

————. "Ursachen und Wesen des Uranismus." *Jahrbuch für sexuelle Zwischenstufen* 5 (1903): 1–193.

Hobbs, A., and R. Lambert. "An Evaluation of *Sexual Behavior in the Human Male*." *American Journal of Psychiatry* 104 (1948): 758–65.

Hobbs, A., and W. Kephart. "Professor Kinsey: His Facts and His Fantasy." *American Journal of Psychiatry* 110 (1954): 614–20.

Hoch, P., and J. Zubin, eds. *Psychosexual Development in Health and Disease*. New York: Grune and Stratton, 1949.

Hoffman, Frederick L. "The Problems of Negro-White Intermixture and Intermarriage." In *Eugenics in Race and State*, Vol. 2: *Scientific Papers of the Second International Congress of Eugenics (1921)*, 175–88. Baltimore: The Williams and Wilkins Company, 1923.

Holder, A. B. "The Bote: Description of A Peculiar Sexual Perversion Found Among North American Indians." *New York Medical Journal* 50, no. 23 (December 7, 1889): 623–25.

Hood, Leroy. "Biology and Medicine in the Twenty-first Century." In *The Code of Codes*, edited by Daniel J. Kevles and Leroy Hood, 281–99.

Hooker, Evelyn. "The Adjustment of the Male Overt Homosexual." *Journal of Projective Techniques* 21 (1957): 18–31. Reprinted in *Mattachine Review* (December 1957): 32–39 and (January 1958): 4–11 and reprinted in *The Problem of Homosexuality in Modern Society*, edited by Hendrik M. Ruitenbeek. New York: Dutton, 1963.

————. "A Preliminary Analysis of Group Behavior in Homosexuals." *Journal of Psychology* 42 (1956): 217–25.

Hooper-Greenhill, Eilean. *Museums and the Shaping of Knowledge*. New York: Routledge, 1992.

Hooton, Earnest A. *The American Criminal: An Anthropological Study*. 3 vols. Cambridge: Harvard University Press, 1939.

————. *Apes, Men and Morons*. New York: G. P. Putnam's Sons, 1937.

————. "Body Build and Life Record of 2631 Harvard Alumni of the Classes 1884–1912." Typescript. Tozzer Library, Harvard University.

————. *Crime and the Man*. Cambridge: Harvard University Press, 1939.

————. *Handbook of Body Types in the United States Army*. 2 vols. Washington, D.C.: Department of Army, Office of the Quartermaster General, Military Planning Division, Research and Development Branch, Environmental Protection Service, 1951.

————. "Observations and Queries as to the Effect of Race Mixture on Certain Physical Characteristics." In *Eugenics in Race and State*, Vol 2: *Scientific Papers of the Second International Congress of Eugenics (1921)*, 64–74. Baltimore: The Williams and Wilkins Company, 1923.

————. "Progress in the Study of Race Mixtures with Special Reference to Work

Carried on at Harvard University." *Proceedings of the American Philosophical Society* 65 (1926): 312–25.

———. "Race Mixture Studies of Dr. Earnest A. Hooton." *Eugenical News* 13 (1927): 81.

———. "Race Mixture in the United States." *Pacific Review* 2 (1921): 116–27.

———. "Racial Types in America and their Relation to Old World Types." In *The American Aborigines*, edited by Diamond Jenness, 131–63. New York: Russell and Russell, 1972.

———. "Radcliffe Investigates Race Mixture." *Harvard Alumni Bulletin* (April 3, 1930): 768–76.

———. "Some Early Drawings of Hottentot Women." In *Harvard African Studies (Varia Africana II)* 2 (1918): 83–99.

———. *Twilight of Man.* New York: G. P. Putnam's Sons, 1939.

———. *Up From Ape.* New York: The Macmillan Company, 1931.

———. *Why Men Behave Like Apes, and Vice Versa.* Princeton: Princeton University Press, 1940.

Horn, David G. "This Norm Which is Note One." In *Deviant Bodies*, edited by Jennifer Terry and Jacqueline Urla, 109–28.

Howard, Jane. *Margaret Mead: A Life.* New York: Simon and Schuster, 1984.

Howard, William Lee. "Effeminate Men and Masculine Women." *New York Medical Journal* 71 (May 5, 1900): 686–87. Reprinted in *Root of Bitterness: Documents of the Social History of Women.* 2d ed. Edited by Nancy F. Cott, Jeanne Boydston, Ann Braude, Lori Ginzberg, and Molly Ladd-Taylor, 338–40. Boston: Northeastern University Press, 1996.

Hrdlicka, Ales. *The Old Americans.* Baltimore: The Williams and Wilkins Company, 1925.

Hubbard, Ruth, and Elijah Wald. *Exploding the Gene Myth: How Genetic Information is Produced and Manipulated by Scientists, Physicians, Employers, Insurance Companies, Educators, and Law Enforcers.* Boston: Beacon Press, 1993.

Hughes, Charles H. "An Emasculated Homo-sexual. His Antecedent and Post-Operative Life." *Alienist and Neurologist* 35 (1914): 277–80.

———. [Dr. H.]. "'Gynomania': A Curious Case of Masturbation." *The Medical Record* 19, no. 12 (March 19, 1881): 336.

———. "Homo Sexual Complexion Perverts in St. Louis: Note on a Feature of Sexual Psychopathy." *Alienist and Neurologist* 28, no. 4 (November 1907): 487–88.

———. "Postscript to Paper on 'Erotopathia': An Organization of Colored Erotopaths." *Alienist and Neurologist* 14, no. 4 (October 1893): 731–32.

Hughes, Langston. *The Big Sea: An Autobiography.* 1940. New York: Thunder's Mouth Press, 1986.

Irvine, Janice. *Disorders of Desire: Sex and Gender in Modern American Sexology.* Philadelphia: Temple University Press, 1990.

Jacoby, Russell, and Naomi Glauberman, eds. *The Bell Curve Debate: History, Documents, Opinions.* New York: Times Books, 1995.

Jacobus X [pseud.]. *Crossways of Sex: A Study in Eroto-Pathology.* New York: American Anthropological Society, n.d.

Jones, Greta. *Social Darwinism and English Thought: The Interaction Between Biological and Sociological Theory*. Atlantic Highlands, N.J.: Humanities Press, 1980.

Jones, James. *Alfred C. Kinsey: A Public/Private Life*. New York: W. W. Norton and Company, 1997.

Jordanova, Ludmilla. *Sexual Visions: Images of Gender in Science and Medicine Between the Eighteenth and Twentieth Centuries*. Madison: University of Wisconsin Press, 1989.

Kahn, Eugen. *Psychopathic Personalities*. Translated by H. Flanders Dunbar. New Haven: Yale University Press, 1931.

Kaledin, Eugenia. *Mothers and More: American Women in the 1950s*. Boston: Twayne Publishers, 1984.

Kameny, Frank E. "Does Research into Homosexuality Matter?" *The Ladder* (May 1965): 14–20.

Karpman, Benjamin. *Case Studies in the Psychopathology of Crime*. 2 vols. Washington, D.C.: Mimeoform Press, 1933; rpt. New York: Mental Science Publishing Co., 1939.

———. "The Principles and Aims of Criminal Psychopathology." *Journal of Criminal Psychopathology* 1, no. 3 (January 1940): 172–218.

———. *The Sexual Offender and his Offenses*. New York: Julian Press, 1954.

Karsch-Haack, Ferdinand. *Das gleichgeschlechtliche Leben der Naturvölker*. Munich: Ernst Reinhardt, 1911.

Katz, Jonathan Ned. *Gay American History: Lesbians and Gay Men in the U.S.A.* New York: Thomas Y. Crowell, 1976; reprinted New York: New American Library, 1992.

———. *Gay/Lesbian Almanac: A New Documentary*. New York: Harper and Row, 1983; reprinted New York: Richard Gallen, 1994.

———. *The Invention of Heterosexuality*. New York: Penguin Books, 1995.

Keller, Evelyn Fox. "Nature, Nurture, and the Human Genome Project." In *The Code of Codes*, edited by Daniel J. Kevles and Leroy Hood, 281–99.

Kempf, Edward J. "The Social and Sexual Behavior of Infra-human Primates with Some Comparable Facts in Human Behavior." *The Psychoanalytic Review* 4 (April 1918): 127–54.

Kenen, Stephanie H. "Who Counts When You're Counting Homosexuals? Hormones and Homosexuality in Mid-Twentieth Century America." In *Science and Homosexualities*, edited by Vernon A. Rosario, 197–218.

Kennedy, Elizabeth Lapovsky, and Madeline D. Davis. *Boots of Leather, Slippers of Gold: The History of a Lesbian Community*. New York: Routledge, 1993.

Kennedy, Hubert C. "Karl Heinrich Ulrichs: First Theorist of Homosexuality." In *Science and Homosexualities*, edited by Vernon A. Rosario, 26–34.

———. "The 'Third Sex' Theory of Karl Heinreich Ulrichs." In *Historical Perspectives on Homosexuality*, edited by Salvatore J. Licata and Robert P. Petersen, 103–11. New York: Haworth Press and Stein and Day, 1981.

———. *Ulrichs: The Life and Work of Karl Heinrich Ulrichs, Pioneer of the Modern Gay Movement*. Boston: Alyson Press, 1988.

Kennan, George F. "Moscow Embassy Telegram #511." February 22, 1946.

Reprinted in *Containment: Documents on American Policy and Strategy,* edited by Thomas H. Etzold and John Lewis Gaddis, 50–63. New York: Columbia University Press, 1978.

———. *United States Objectives and Programs for National Security.* April 14, 1950. Reprinted in *Containment: Documents on American Policy and Strategy,* edited by Thomas H. Etzold and John Lewis Gaddis, 385–442.

Kerber, Linda. *Women of the Republic: Intellect and Ideology in Revolutionary America.* Chapel Hill: University of North Carolina Press, 1980.

Kessler, Suzanne. *Lessons from the Intersexed.* New Brunswick, N.J.: Rutgers University Press, 1998.

Kevles, Daniel J. *In the Name of Eugenics: Genetics and the Uses of Human Heredity.* Berkeley: University of California Press, 1985.

———. "The X Factor: The Battle Over the Ramification of a Gay Gene." *New Yorker* (April 3, 1995): 85–90.

Kiernan, James G. "Original Communications. Insanity. Lecture on Sexual Perversion." *Detroit Lancet* 7, no. 11 (May 1884): 482–83.

———. "Perverted Sexual Instinct." *Chicago Medical Journal and Examiner* 48 (March 1884): 263–65.

———. "Psychical Treatment of Congenital Sexual Inversion." *Review of Insanity and Nervous Disease* 4, no. 4 (June 1894): 295.

———. "Psychological Aspects of the Sexual Appetite." *Alienist and Neurologist* 12 (April 1891): 202–3.

———. "Sexual Perversion." *Detroit Lancet* 7, no. 11 (May 1884): 483–84.

Kin, David George. *Women without Men: True Stories of Lesbian Love in Greenwich Village.* New York: Brookwood Publishing Corp., 1958.

King, Miriam, and Steven Ruggles. "American Immigration, Fertility, and Race Suicide at the Turn of the Century." *Journal of Interdisciplinary History* 20 (1990): 347–69.

Kinsey, Alfred. "Homosexuality: Criteria for a Hormonal Explanation of the Homosexual." *The Journal of Clinical Endocrinology* 1, no. 5 (May 1941): 424–28.

Kinsey, Alfred, Wardell B. Pomeroy, Clyde E. Martin, Paul H. Gebhard. *Sexual Behavior in the Human Female.* Philadelphia: W. B. Saunders Co., 1953.

———. *Sexual Behavior in the Human Male.* Philadelphia: W. B. Saunders Co., 1948.

Kiser, Clyde V. "A Statistician Looks at the Report." In *Problems of Sexual Behavior,* edited by Charles Walter Clarke, 28–36. New York: American Social Hygiene Association, 1948.

Klassen, Albert D., Colin J. Williams, and Eugene E. Levitt. *Sex and Morality in the U.S.: An Empirical Enquiry under the Auspices of the Kinsey Institute.* Introduction by Hubert J. O'Gorman. Middletown, Conn.: Weslyan University Press, 1989.

Kloppenburg, Jack, Jr. *Seeds and Sovereignty: The Use and Control of Genetic Resources.* Durham, N.C.: Duke University Press, 1988.

Knight, R. "Psychiatric Issues in the Kinsey Report." In *Sex Habits of American Men: A Symposium on the Kinsey Report,* edited by R. Deutsch. New York: Grosset and Dunlap, 1948.

Kneeland, George. *Commercialized Prostitution in New York City.* New York: Century, 1913.

Knox, Robert. *The Races of Men: A Philosophical Enquiry into the Influences of Race Over the Destinies of Nations.* 1850. London, 1862.

Koedt, Anne. "Lesbianism and Feminism." In *Radical Feminism,* edited by Anne Koedt, Ellen Levine, Anita Rapone, 246–58. New York: Quadrangle Books, 1973.

Kopp, Marie E. "Surgical Treatment as Sex Crime Prevention Measure." *Journal of Criminal Law and Criminology* 28 (January–February 1938): 692–706.

Krafft-Ebing, Richard von. *Psychopathia Sexualis, mit besonderer Berücksichtigung der konträren Sexualempfindung: Eine klinisch-forensische Studie.* Stuttgart: Enke 1886.

———. *Psychopathia Sexualis: A Medico-Forensic Study.* 10th ed. New York: Samuel Login, 1908.

Kretschmer, Ernst. *Physique and Character: An Investigation of the Nature of Constitution and of the Theory of Temperament.* New York: Harcourt, Brace and Company, 1925.

Krich, Aron. "Before Kinsey: Continuity in American Sex Research." *Psychoanalytic Review* 63 (1966): 69–90.

Kroger, William S. "Female Specialist Repudiates Kinsey." In *I Accuse Kinsey!* edited by E. J. Daniels, 127–32.

Kroeber, Alfred Louis. *Handbook of the Indians of California.* U.S. Bureau of American Ethnology Bulletin, no. 78. Washington, D.C.: U.S. Govt. Printing Office, 1925.

Kubie, Lawrence. "Psychiatric Implications of the Kinsey Report." *Psychosomatic Medicine* 10 (1948): 95–106. Reprinted in *Sexual Behavior in American Society: An Appraisal of the First Two Kinsey Reports,* edited by Jerome Himelhoch and Sylvia Fleis Fava, 270–93. New York: W. W. Norton and Company, Inc., 1955.

Kuhl, Stefan. *The Nazi Connection: Eugenics, American Racism, and German National Socialism.* New York: Oxford University Press, 1994.

Lait, Jack, and Lee Mortimer. *New York: Confidential.* Chicago: Ziff-Davis Publishing Company, 1948.

———. *USA: Confidential.* New York: Crown Publishers, 1952.

———. *Washington: Confidential.* New York: Crown Publishers, 1951.

Landis, Carney, M. Marjorie Bolles and D. Anthony D'Esopo. "Psychological and Physical Concomitants of Adjustment in Marriage." *Human Biology* 12 (1940): 559–65.

Landis, Carney, Agnes T. Landis, M. Marjorie Bolles, Harriet F. Metzger, Marjorie Wallace Pitts, D. Anthony D'Esopo, Howard C. Moloy, Sophia J. Kleegman, Robert Latou Dickinson. *Sex in Development: A Study of the Growth and Development of the Emotional and Sexual Aspects of Personality together with Physiological, Anatomical, and Medical Information on a Group of 153 Normal Women and 142 Female Psychiatric Patients.* New York: Paul B. Hoeber, Inc., 1940.

Lankester, E. R. *Degeneration: A Chapter in Darwinism.* London: Macmillan, 1880.

Laqueur, Ernst, Elisabeth Dingemanse, P. C. Hart, and S. E. de Jongh. "Female Sex Hormone in Urine of Men." *Klinische Wochenschrift* 6 (1927): 1859.

Laqueur, Thomas. *Making Sex: Body and Gender From the Greeks to Freud.* Cambridge: Harvard University Press, 1990.

Latham, R. G. *The Natural History of the Varieties of Man.* London: J. Van Voorst, 1850.

Laughlin, Henry H. "How to Make a Eugenic Family Study." *Eugenics Record Office Bulletin No. 13* (1915).

Leland, John, and Mark Miller. "Can Gays Convert?" *Newsweek*, August 17, 1998: 46–50.

Leps, Marie-Christine. *Apprehending the Criminal: The Production of Deviance in Nineteenth-Century Discourse.* Durham, N.C.: Duke University Press, 1992.

Lerner, Max. *The Unfinished Country: A Book of American Symbols.* New York: Simon and Schuster, 1959.

LeVay, Simon. "Evidence for Anatomical Differences in the Brains of Homosexual Men." *Science* 253 (1991): 1034–37.

———. *The Sexual Brain.* Cambridge, Mass.: MIT Press, 1993.

LeVay, Simon, and Dean H. Hamer. "Evidence for a Biological Influence in Male Homosexuality." *Scientific American* 270, no. 5 (May 1994): 44–49.

Levin, James. *The Gay Novel in America.* New York: Garland Publications, 1991.

Levy, D. "Discussion of Clinical and Psychoanalytic Approach." In *Psychosexual Development in Health and Disease,* edited by P. Hoch and J. Zubin. New York: Grune and Stratton, 1949.

Levy, Sheldon S. "Interactions of Institution and Policy Groups: The Origins of Sex Crime Legislation." *Lawyer and Law Notes* 5 (Spring 1951): 32.

Lewes, Kenneth. *The Psychoanalytic Theory of Male Homosexuality.* New York: Meridian, 1988.

Lewin, Miriam. "'Rather Worse Than Folly': Psychology Measures Femininity and Masculinity, 1: From Terman and Miles to the Guilfords." In *In the Shadows of the Past: Psychology Portrays the Sexes: A Social and Intellectual History,* edited by Miriam Lewin, 155–78. New York: Columbia University Press, 1984.

Lewis, Denslow. *The Gynecological Consideration of the Sexual Act: And an Appendix with an Account of Denslow Lewis.* Edited by Marc H. Hollender. Weston, Mass.: MTSL Press, 1970.

Lewontin, Richard. "The Dream of the Human Genome." In *Cultures on the Brink: Ideologies of Technology,* edited by Gretchen Bender and Timothy Druckrey, 107–27. Seattle: Bay Press, 1994.

Leys, Ruth. "Meyer's Dealings with Ernest Jones: A Chapter in the History of the American Response to Psychoanalysis." *Journal of the History of Behavioral Sciences* 17, no. 4 (1981): 445–65.

———. "Meyer, Jung, and the Limits of Association." *Bulletin of the History of Medicine* 59, no. 3 (1985): 345–60.

———. "Meyer, Watson, and the Dangers of Behaviorism." *Journal of the History of the Behavioral Sciences* 20, no. 2 (1984): 128–49.

———. "Types of One: Adolf Meyer's Life Chart and the Representation of Individuality." *Representations* 34 (Spring 1991): 1–28.

Liebman, Samuel. "Homosexuality, Transvestism, and Psychosis: Study of a Case Treated with Electroshock." *Journal of Nervous and Mental Disease* 99, no. 6 (1944): 945–57.

Lind, Earl. *Autobiography of an Androgyne.* New York: Medico-Legal Press, 1918.

Lindfors, Bernth. "The Hottentot Venus and Other African Attractions in Nineteenth-Century England." *Australasian Drama Studies* 1 (1983): 83–104.

Lindner, Robert. "Homosexuality and the Contemporary Scene." In *Must You Conform?,* 29–76. New York: Holt, Rinehart and Winston, 1956.

Lindsey, Ben, and Wainwright Evans. *The Companionate Marriage.* New York: Boni and Liveright, 1927.

Linne, Carl (Linnaeus). *Systema naturae.* 1735. Edited by M. S. J. Engel-Ledeboer and H. Engel. Nieuwkoop: B. de Graaf, 1964.

———. *Systema Naturae. Regnum Animale.* 1758. London: British Museum (Natural History), 1956.

Lombroso, Cesare. *Criminal Man.* 1889. New York: Putnam, 1911.

———. *Criminal Man, According to the Classification of Cesare Lombroso, Briefly Summarized by His Daughter, Gina Lombroso-Ferrero.* Introduction by Cesare Lombroso. New York: Putnam's, 1911; reprinted by Montclair, N.J.: Patterson Smith, 1972.

Lombroso, Cesare, and Gillaume Ferrero. *The Female Offender.* London: T. Fisher Unwin, 1895.

London, Louis S. "Analysis of a Homosexual Neurosis." *The Urologic and Cutaneous Review* 37 (1933): 93.

———. *Mental Therapy.* New York: Liveright, 1937.

———. *Sexual Deviations in the Male and Female.* New York: Bell Publishing Company, 1957.

London, Louis S., and Frank S. Caprio. *Sexual Deviations: A Psychodynamic Approach.* Washington, D.C.: The Linacre Press, Inc., 1950.

Lorde, Audre. *Zami: A New Spelling of My Name.* Watertown, Mass.: Persephone Press, 1982.

Lovejoy, Arthur O. *The Great Chain of Being: A Study of the History of an Idea.* Cambridge, Mass.: Harvard University Press, 1936.

Lubbock, Sir John (Lord Avebury). *The Origin of Civilization and the Primitive Condition of Man.* 1870. Edited by Peter Riviere. Chicago: University of Chicago Press, 1978.

———. *Pre-historic Times, as Illustrated by Ancient Remains, and the Manners and Customs of Modern Savages.* London: Williams and Norgate, 1865.

Lunbeck, Elizabeth. *The Psychiatric Persuasion: Knowledge, Gender, and Power in Modern America.* Princeton, N.J.: Princeton University Press, 1994.

Lundberg, Ferdinand, and Marynia F. Farnham. *Modern Woman and the Lost Sex.* New York: Harper, 1947.

Lydston, G. Frank. "Asexualization in the Prevention of Crime." *Medical News* 68 (May 23, 1896): 576.

———. "Sexual Perversion, Satyriasis, and Nymphomania." *Philadelphia Medical and Surgical Reporter* 61. no. 11 (September 14, 1889): 281–85.

Lyons, Andrew P., and Harriet D. Lyons. "Savage Sexuality and Secular Morality: Malinowski, Ellis, Russell." *Canadian Journal of Anthropology* 5, no. 1 (Fall 1986): 51–64.

MacCormick, Austin H. *The Education of Adult Prisoners: A Survey and a Program.* New York: National Society of Penal Information, 1931.

———. "New York's Present Problem." *Mental Hygiene* 22, no. 1 (January 1938): 4–10.

Malinowski, Bronislaw. *Sex and Repression in Savage Society.* London: Kegan Paul, Trench, Trubner, 1927.

———. *The Sexual Life of Savages in Northwestern Melanesia.* London: Kegan Paul, Trench, Trubner, 1927.

Mantegazza, Paolo. *Anthropological Studies of the Sexual Relations of Mankind.* 1886. Translated by James Bruce. New York: Anthropological Press, 1932.

———. *The Perversions of Love.* 1932. Reprinted in *Homosexuality: A Cross Cultural Approach,* edited by Donald Webster Cory, 248–66. New York: Julian Press, 1956.

Marcus, George E., and Michael M. K. Fischer. *Anthropology as Cultural Critique: An Experimental Moment in the Human Sciences.* Chicago: University of Chicago Press, 1986.

Margolin, S. "Review of *Sexual Behavior in the Human Male.*" *Psychoanalytic Quarterly* 17 (1948): 265–72.

Marshall, John. "On the Brain of a Bushwoman; and on the Brains of Two Idiots of European Descent." *Philosophical Transactions of the Royal Society of London* (1864): 501–8.

Marshall, Gloria. "Racial Classifications: Popular and Scientific." In *The "Racial" Economy of Science,* edited by Sandra Harding, 116–27. Bloomington: Indiana University Press, 1993.

Martin, Del, and Phyllis Lyon. *Lesbian/Woman.* San Francisco: Glide Publications, 1972. Rev. and enl. ed., N.Y.: Bantam Books, 1983.

Martineau, Louis. *Leçons sur les déformations vulvaires et anales produites par la masturbation, le saphisme, la défloration, et la sodomie.* 2d ed., rev. Paris, 1886.

Masson, Jeffrey Moussaieff. *A Dark Science: Women, Sexuality and Psychiatry in the Nineteenth Century.* New York: Farrar, Strauss, and Giroux, 1986.

Masters, R. E. L. *The Homosexual Revolution.* New York: Belmont Books, 1962.

Max, Louis W. "Breaking Up a Homosexual Fixation by the Conditioned Reaction Technique: A Case Study." *Psychological Bulletin* 32 (1935): 734.

May, Elaine Tyler. *Great Expectations: Marriage and Divorce in Post-Victorian America.* Chicago: University of Chicago Press, 1980.

———. *Homeward Bound: American Families in Cold War America.* New York: Basic Books, 1988.

McCann, Carole R. *Birth Control Politics in the United States, 1916–1945.* Ithaca: Cornell University Press, 1994.

McGuire, Hunter, and G. Frank Lydston. "Sexual Crimes Among Southern Negroes." *Virginia Medical Monthly* 20 (May 1893): 122–23.

McMurtrie, Douglas C. "Principles of Homosexuality and Sexual Inversion in the Female." *American Journal of Urology* 9 (1913): 147.

Mead, Margaret. "An Anthropologist Looks at the Report." In *Problems of Sexual Behavior,* edited by Charles Walter Clarke, 58–69. New York: American Social Hygiene Association, 1948.

———. *Blackberry Winter: My Early Years.* New York: William Morrow, 1972.

———. *Coming of Age in Samoa: A Psychological Study of Primitive Youth.* 1928. New York: William Morrow, 1961.

———. *Growing Up in New Guinea: A Comparative Study of Primitive Education.* 1930. New York: William Morrow, 1975.

———. *Male and Female: A Study of the Sexes in a Changing World.* New York: William Morrow & Company, 1949.

————. *Sex and Temperament in Three Primitive Societies.* New York: Dell Publications, 1935.

Meagher, John F. W. "Homosexuality: Its Psychobiological and Psychopathological Significance." *The Urologic and Cutaneous Review* 33 (1929): 505–18.

Menninger, Karl A. "Comment on paper by George S. Sprague, 'Varieties of Homosexual Manifestations.'" *American Journal of Psychiatry* 92 (1935): 150–51.

————. "One View of the Kinsey Report." *General Practitioner* 8 (1953): 67–72.

Mercer, J. D. *They Walk in Shadow: A Study of Sexual Variations with Emphasis on the Ambisexual and Homosexual Components and our Contemporary Sex Laws.* New York: Comet Books, 1959.

Merzbach, Georg. Letter. *Monatsberichte des Wissenschaftlich-humanitaren Komitees* 6 (1907): 76–77.

Meyer, Adolf. *The Commonsense Psychiatry of Adolf Meyer.* Edited by Alfred Lief. New York: McGraw-Hill, 1948.

————. *Psychobiology: A Science of Man.* Compiled and edited by Eunice E. Winters and Anna Mae Bowers. Springfield, Ill.: Charles C. Thomas, 1957.

————. "The Role of Mental Factors in Psychiatry." *American Journal of Insanity* 65 (1908–9): 39.

Meyer-Bahlburg, Heino. "Psychoendocrine Research on Sexual Orientation: Current Status and Future Options." *Progress in Brain Research* 61 (1984): 375–99.

————. "Sex Hormones and Male Homosexuality in Comparative Perspective." *Archives of Sexual Behavior* (1977): 297–326.

Meyerowitz, Joanne J. "Sex Change and the Popular Press: Historical Notes on Transsexuality in the United States, 1930–1955." *GLQ* vol. 4, no. 2 (1998): 159–88.

————. *Women Adrift: Independent Wage Earners in Chicago, 1880–1930.* Chicago: University of Chicago Press, 1988.

Meyerowitz, Joanne J., ed. *Not June Cleaver: Women and Gender in Postwar America, 1945–1960.* Philadelphia: Temple University Press, 1994.

Mjoen, Jon Alfred. "Harmonic and Disharmonic Racecrossings." In *Eugenics in Race and State,* Vol. 2: *Scientific Papers of the Second International Congress of Eugenics (1921),* 41–61. Baltimore: The Williams and Wilkins Company, 1923.

Miles, Catherine Cox. *The Early Mental Traits of 300 Geniuses.* Stanford: Stanford University Press, 1926.

Miller, Michael M. "Hypnotic-Aversion Treatment of Homosexuality." *Journal of the National Medical Association* 55, no. 5 (1963): 411–15.

Minkowitz, Donna. "Trial by Science: In the Fight over Amendment 2, Biology is Back and Gay Allies are Claiming It." *Village Voice,* November 30, 1993, 27–30.

Minton, Henry. "Community Empowerment and the Medicalization of Homosexuality: Constructing Sexual Identities in the 1930s." *Journal of the History of Sexuality* 6, no. 3 (1996): 435–58.

————. "Femininity in Men and Masculinity in Women: American Psychology and Psychiatry Portray Homosexuality in the 1930s." *Journal of Homosexuality* 13, no. 1 (Fall 1986): 8–14.

————. *Lewis M. Terman: Pioneer in Psychological Testing.* New York: New York University Press, 1988.

Mitgang, Herbert. *Dangerous Dossiers: Exposing the Secret War against America's Greatest Authors.* New York: Free Press, 1988.

Modell, John, et al. "The Timing of Marriage in the Transition to Adulthood." In John Demos and Saranne Boocock, eds., *Turning Points: Historical and Sociological Essays on the Family.* Chicago: University of Chicago Press, 1978.

Moll, Albert. *The Sexual Life of the Child.* New York: Macmillan Company, 1929.

Montagu, Ashley. "Understanding Our Sexual Desires." In *About the Kinsey Report: Observations by Eleven Experts on 'Sexual Behavior in the Human Male',* edited by Donald Porter Geddes and Enid Curie, 59–69. New York: Signet Books, 1948.

Morantz, Regina Markell. "The Scientist as Sex Crusader: Alfred C. Kinsey and American Culture." *American Quarterly* 29 (Winter 1977): 563–89.

Morawski, Jill G. "Measurement of Masculinity and Femininity: Engendering Categorical Realities." In *Women's Place in Psychology,* edited by Janis S. Bohan, 199–226. Boulder, Colo.: Westview Press, 1992.

———. "The Troubled Quest for Masculinity, Femininity, and Androgyny." *Review of Personality and Social Psychology* 7 (1987): 44–69.

Mortimer, Lee. *Washington Confidential Today.* New York: Paperback Library, 1962.

Morton, Samuel George. *Crania Americana; or, A Comparative View of the Skulls of Various Aboriginal Nations of North and South America.* Philadelphia: J. Dobson; London: Simpkin, Marshall & Company, 1839.

Moscucci, Ornella. *The Science of Woman: Gynaecology and Gender in England, 1800–1929.* New York: Cambridge University Press, 1990.

Mosher, Clelia Duel. *The Mosher Survey: Sexual Attitudes of Forty-Five Victorian Women.* Edited by James Mahood and Kristine Wenburg. New York: Arno Press, 1980.

Muller, Johannes. "Über die ausseren Geslechtstheile der Buschmanninnen." *Archiv für Anatomie, Physiologie under Wissenschaftliche Medicin* (1834): 319–45.

Muncie, Wendell. *Psychobiology and Psychiatry.* 2d ed. St. Louis: C. V. Mosby, 1948.

Murray, Charles, and Richard Herrnstein. *The Bell Curve: Intelligence and Class Structure in American Life.* New York: The Free Press, 1994.

Murray, Robert K. *Red Scare: A Study in National Hysteria, 1919–1920.* Minneapolis: University of Minnesota Press, 1955.

Näcke, Paul. "Der homosexuelle Markt in New-York." *Archiv für Kriminal-Anthropologie und Kriminalistik* 22 (1906): 277.

National Academy of Sciences. "Methods and Values in Science." In *On Being a Scientist.* Washington, D.C.: National Academy Press, 1989.

National Association for Research and Therapy of Homosexuality. Position Paper. Encino, Calif.: NARTH, 1992.

Navasky, Victor. *Naming Names.* New York: Viking Press, 1980.

Nestle, Joan. *A Restricted Country.* Ithaca: Firebrand Books, 1987.

Newton, Esther. "The Mythic Mannish Lesbian: Radclyffe Hall and the New Woman." In *Hidden from History,* edited by Duberman, Vicinus, and Chauncey, 281–93.

Nicolosi, Joseph. *Healing Homosexuality: Case Stories in Reparative Therapy.* Northvale, N.J.: Jason Aronson, Inc., 1993.

————. *Reparative Therapy of Male Homosexuality.* Northvale, N.J.: Jason Aronson, Inc., 1991.

Nietzsche, Friedrich. *The Gay Science.* 1882. Translated by Walter Kaufmann. New York: Random House, 1974.

————. *Human, All Too Human.* 1878. New York: Gordon Press, 1974.

————. *On the Genealogy of Morals.* 1887. In *Basic Writings of Nietzsche,* edited and translated by Walter Kaufmann. New York: Modern Library, 1968.

————. *The Use and Abuse of History.* 1874. Translated by Adrian Collins. Indianapolis, Indiana: Bobbs-Merrill Company, Inc., 1957.

Norton, Mary Beth. *Liberty's Daughters: The Revolutionary Experience of American Women, 1750–1800.* Boston: Little, Brown and Company, 1980.

Nott, Josiah Clark, and G. Gliddon. *Types of Mankind: Or, Ethnological Researches, based upon the Ancient Monuments, Paintings, Sculptures, and Crania of Races.* 6th ed. Philadelphia: Lippincott, Grambo & Co., 1854.

Noyes, William. Review of Havelock Ellis' *Sexual Inversion. Psychological Review* 4 (1897): 447.

Nunberg, Herman, and Ernst Federn, eds. *Minutes of the Vienna Psychoanalytic Society.* Vol. 1, 1906–1908. Translated by M. Nunberg. New York: International Universities Press, Inc., 1962.

Nye, Robert. *Crime, Madness, and Politics in Modern France: The Medical Concept of National Decline.* Princeton, N.J.: Princeton University Press, 1984.

Oberndorf, Clarence P. "Diverse Forms of Homosexuality." *The Urologic and Cutaneous Review* 33 (1929): 518–23.

Oosterhuis, Harry. "Richard von Krafft-Ebing's 'Step-Children of Nature': Psychiatry and the Making of Homosexual Identity." In *Science and Homosexualities,* edited by Vernon A. Rosario, 67–88.

O'Neill, William L. *Divorce in the Progressive Era.* (New Haven: Yale University Press, 1967.

Oshinsky, David M. *A Conspiracy So Immense: The World of Joe McCarthy.* New York: D. I. Fine, 1983.

Otis, Margaret Otis. "A Perversion Not Commonly Noted." *Journal of Abnormal Psychology* 8 (1913): 112–14.

Oudshoorn, Nelly. *Beyond the Natural Body: An Archaeology of Sex Hormones.* London: Routledge, 1994.

Overholser, Winfred. "Legal and Administrative Problems." *Mental Hygiene* 22, no. 1 (January 1938): 20–24.

Owensby, Newdigate M. "The Correction of Homosexuality." *The Urologic and Cutaneous Review* 45, no. 8 (1941): 494–96.

————. "Homosexuality and Lesbianism Treated with Metrazol." *Journal of Nervous and Mental Disease* 92, no. 1 (1940): 65–66.

Page, James, and John Warkentin. "Masculinity and Paranoia." *Journal of Abnormal and Social Psychology* 33 (1938): 527–31.

Paglario, Harold E., ed. *Racism in the Eighteenth Century.* Cleveland: Case Western Reserve University, 1973.

Parent-Duchatelet, Alexandre Jean-Baptiste. *On Prostitution in the City of Paris.* London, 1840.

Parkes, A. S. "Androgenic Activity of Ovarian Extracts." *Nature* 139 (1937): 965.

———. "Terminology of Sex Hormones." *Nature* 141 (1938): 12.

Paul, Diane B. *Controlling Human Heredity, 1865 to the Present.* Atlantic Highlands, N.J.: Humanities Press, 1995.

———. "Eugenics and the Left." *Journal of the History of Ideas* (October 1984): 567–90.

Peiss, Kathy. *Cheap Amusements: Working Women and Leisure in the Turn of the Century New York.* Philadelphia: Temple University Press, 1986.

Peiss, Kathy, and Christina Simmons, eds. *Passion and Power: Sexuality in History.* Philadelphia: Temple University Press, 1989.

Penn, Donna. "The Meanings of Lesbianism in Post-War America." *Gender & History* 3, no. 2 (Summer 1991): 15–22.

Pick, Daniel. *Faces of Degeneration: A European Disorder, c. 1848–1918.* New York: Cambridge University Press, 1989.

Pickering, Charles. *The Races of Man and their Geographical Distribution.* 1851. London: H. G. Bohn, 1863.

Pivar, David. *Purity Crusade, Sexual Morality, and Social Control, 1868–1900.* Westport, Conn.: Greenwood, 1973.

Pleck, Joseph H. "The Theory of Male Sex Role Identity: Its Rise and Fall, 1936 to the Present." In *In the Shadows of the Past,* edited by Lewin, 205–25.

Plecker, W. A. "Virginia's Effort to Preserve Racial Integrity." In *A Decade of Progress in Eugenics: Scientific Papers of the Third International Congress of Eugenics (1932),* 105–12. Baltimore: The Williams and Wilkins Company, 1934.

Podolsky, Edward. "'Homosexual Love' in Women." *Popular Medicine* 1 (February 1935): 375.

Pollens, B. *The Sex Criminal.* New York: The Macauly Company, 1938.

Pomeroy, Wardell B. *Dr. Kinsey and the Institute for Sex Research.* New York: Harper and Row, 1972.

Potter, La Forest. *Strange Loves: A Study of Sexual Abnormalities.* New York: Padell Book Company, 1933.

Poovey, Mary. "'Scenes of an Indelicate Character': The Medical 'Treatment' of Victorian Women." *Representations* 14 (1986): 137–68.

Popenoe, Paul, and Roswell Hill Johnson. *Applied Eugenics.* New York: Macmillan, 1920.

Pratt, Mary Louise. *Imperial Eyes: Travel Writing and Transculturation.* New York: Routledge, 1992.

Preston, William, Jr. *Aliens and Dissenters: Federal Suppression of Radicals, 1903–1933.* Cambridge, Mass.: Harvard University Press, 1966.

Prichard, James Cowles. *The Natural History of Man: Comprising Inquiries into the Modifying Influence of Physical and Moral Agencies on the Different Tribes of the Human Family.* 2d ed. London: H. Bailliere, 1845.

———. *Researches into the Physical History of Man.* 1813. Edited by George W. Stocking, Jr. Chicago: University of Chicago Press, 1973.

Proctor, Robert N. *Racial Hygiene: Medicine under the Nazis.* Cambridge: Harvard University Press, 1988.

Quackenbos, John Duncan. "Hypnotic Suggestion in the Treatment of Sexual Perversions and Moral Anaesthesia: A Personal Experience." *Transactions of the New Hampshire Medical Society* (1899): 69–91.

Rafter, Nicole Hahn. *Partial Justice: Women in State Prisons, 1800–1935*. Boston: Northeastern University Press, 1985.

———. *White Trash: The Eugenics Family Studies (1877–1919)*. Boston: Northeastern University Press, 1988.

Ramsey, G. "A Survey Evaluation of the Kinsey Report." *Journal of Clinical Psychology* 6 (1950): 133–43.

Rapp, Rayna, and Ellen Ross. "The Twenties' Backlash: Compulsory Heterosexuality, the Consumer Family, and the Waning of Feminism." In *Class, Race and Sex: The Dynamics of Control*, edited by Amy Swerdlow and Hanah Lessinger, 93–107. Boston: G. K. Hall, 1983.

Reed, James. *From Private Vice to Public Virtue: The Birth Control Movement and American Society Since 1830*. New York: Basic Books, 1978.

Reilly, Phillip R. *The Surgical Solution: A History of Involuntary Sterilization in the United States*. Baltimore: Johns Hopkins University Press, 1991.

Reingold, Nathan. "Definitions and Speculations: The Professionalization of Science in America in the Nineteenth Century." In *The Pursuit of Knowledge in the Early American Republic*, edited by Alexandra Oleson and Sanborn C. Brown, 33–69. Baltimore: Johns Hopkins University Press, 1976.

Reiss, M. "The Role of Sex Hormones in Psychiatry." *Journal of Mental Science* 86 (1940): 364.

Review of *Sexual Inversion*. *American Journal of Insanity* 59 (1902): 182.

Ricks, Ingrid. "Mind Games." *The Advocate* (National Lesbian and Gay Newsmagazine), December 28, 1993, 38–40.

"R.L.D.: The Life of Robert Latou Dickinson, 1861–1950." Unpublished manuscript, Robert Latou Dickinson Collection, Countway Library, Harvard Medical School.

Roback, A. A. *History of American Psychology*. 1952. New York: Collier Books, 1964.

Robertiello, Richard C. "Clinical Notes: Results of Separation from Iposexual Parents During the Oedipal Period, [and] A Female Homosexual Panic." *Psychoanalytic Review* 51, no. 4 (1964–65): 670–72.

———. *Voyage from Lesbos: The Psychoanalysis of a Female Homosexual*. New York: Citadel, 1959.

Robinson, Paul. *The Modernization of Sex*. New York: Harper and Row, 1976.

Rogers, J. A. "Darwinism and Social Darwinism." *Journal of the History of Ideas* 33 (1972): 265–80.

Rogin, Michael. "Kiss Me Deadly: Communism, Motherhood, and Cold War Movies." In *Ronald Reagan, the Movie and Other Episodes in Political Demonology*, 236–71. Berkeley: University of California Press, 1987.

———. "Political Repression in the United States." In *Ronald Reagan, the Movie and Other Episodes in Political Demonology*, 64–77.

Rooney, Elizabeth A., and Don C. Gibbons. "Social Reactions to 'Crimes Without Victims.'" *Social Problems* 13 (1966): 400–10.

Roosevelt, Theodore. "The Greatest American Problem." *Delineator* (June 1907): 966–67.

————. "A Premium on Race Suicide." *Outlook* 105 (September 20, 1911).

————. "Race Decadence." *Outlook* 97 (April 8, 1911).

Rosanoff, Aaron. "Human Sexuality, Normal and Abnormal, From a Psychiatric Point of View." *Urologic and Cutaneous Review* 33 (1929): 523–50.

————. "A Theory of Chaotic Sexuality." *American Journal of Psychiatry* 92 (1935): 35–41.

Rosario, Vernon, ed. *Science and Homosexualities.* New York: Routledge, 1997.

Rosenberg, Charles E. "Disease and Social Order in America: Perceptions and Expectations." In *AIDS: The Burdens of History,* edited by Elizabeth Fee and Daniel M. Fox, 12–32. Berkeley: University of California Press, 1988.

————. "The Place of George M. Beard in Nineteenth-Century Psychiatry." *Bulletin of the History of Medicine* 26 (1962): 245–59.

Rosenzweig, Saul, and R. G. Hoskins. "A Note on the Ineffectualness of Sex-Hormone Medication in a Case of Pronounced Homosexuality." *Psychosomatic Medicine* 3, no. 1 (1941): 87–89.

Ross, Edward A. "The Causes of Race Superiority." *Annals of the American Academy of Political and Social Science* 18 (July 1, 1901): 67–89.

Rosse, Irving C. "Sexual Hypochondriasis and Perversion of the Genesic Instinct." *Journal of Nervous and Mental Disease,* whole ser. vol. 19, new ser. vol. 17, no. 11 (November 1892): 799–807.

Rothstein, William G. *American Medical Schools and the Practice of Medicine.* New York: Oxford University Press, 1987.

Rousseau, Jean-Jacques. *A Discourse On Inequality.* 1755. Translated by Maurice Cranston. New York: Penguin Books, 1986.

————. *The Social Contract.* 1743. Translated by Maurice Cranston. New York: Penguin Books, 1968.

Rubin, Gayle. "The Traffic in Women: Notes on the Political Economy of Sex." In *Toward an Anthropology of Women,* edited by Rayna Rapp Reiter, 157–210. New York: Monthly Review Press, 1975.

Russell, William Logie. *The New York Hospital: A History of the Psychiatric Service, 1771–1936.* New York: Columbia University Press, 1945.

Russett, Cynthia Eagle. *Sexual Science: The Victorian Construction of Womanhood.* Cambridge: Harvard University Press, 1989.

Russo, Vito. *The Celluloid Closet: Homosexuality in the Movies.* New York: Harper and Row, 1981.

Rutner, Ivan Toby. "A Double-barrel Approach to Modification of Homosexual Behavior." *Psychological Reports* 26, no. 2 (1970): 356–58.

Ryan, Mary. *Womanhood in America: From Colonial Times to the Present.* 2d ed. New York: New Viewpoints, 1979.

Sahli, Nancy. "'Smashing': Women's Relations Before the Fall." *Chrysalis* 8 (1979): 17–27.

Said, Edward. *Orientalism.* New York: Vintage, 1978.

Saint-Hilaire, Etienne Geoffroy, and Frederic Cuvier. *Histoire naturelle des mammiferes.* Vols. 1 and 2. Paris: A. Belin, 1824.

San Francisco Lesbian and Gay History Project. "'She Even Chewed Tobacco': A

Pictorial Narrative of Passing Women in America." In *Hidden From History,* edited by Duberman, Vicinus, and Chauncey, 183–94.

Schiebinger, Londa. *Nature's Body: Gender and the Making of Modern Science.* Boston: Beacon Press, 1993.

———. "Skeletons in the Closet: The First Illustrations of the Female Skeleton in Eighteenth-Century Anatomy." In *The Making of the Modern Body,* edited by Thomas Laqueur and Catherine Gallagher, 42–82. Berkeley: University of California Press, 1987.

Schlesinger, Arthur. *The Politics of Hope.* Boston: Houghton Mifflin Company, 1963.

———. *The Vital Center: The Politics of Freedom.* Boston: Houghton Mifflin, 1949.

Schmidt, G. "Allies and Persecutors: Science and Medicine in the Homosexuality Issues." *Journal of Homosexuality* 10, nos. 3 and 4 (1984): 127–40.

Schopenhauer, Arthur. "Die Metaphysik der Geschlechtsliebe." In *Die Welt als Wille und Vorstellung,* 8, vols. 1 and 2. Zurich: Diogenes, 1977.

Schwab, Raymond. *Oriental Renaissance: Europe's Rediscovery of India and the East, 1680–1880.* Translated by Gene Petterson–Black and Victor Reinking. New York: Columbia University Press, 1984.

Scott, Colin A. "Sex and Art." *American Journal of Psychology* 7, no. 2 (January 1896): 216.

Seagoe, May V. *Terman and the Gifted.* Los Altos, Calif.: William Kaufmann, Inc., 1975.

Sedgwick, Eve Kosofsky. *Epistemology of the Closet.* Berkeley: University of California Press, 1990.

Sekula, Allan. "The Body and the Archive." *October* 39 (Winter 1986): 3–64.

Sharp, Harry Clay. "Human Sterilization." *Journal of the American Medical Association* 4, no. 12 (1909).

———. "The Sterilization of Degenerates." *Indiana Board of State Charities* (National Christian League for Promotion of Purity) (1908), 1–2, 6.

Shaskan, Donald. "One Hundred Sex Offenders." *American Journal of Orthopsychiatry* 9 (1939): 565–69.

Shaw, J. C., and G. N. Ferris. "Perverted Sexual Instinct." *Journal of Nervous and Mental Disease* 10, no. 2 (April 1883): 185–204.

Shohat, Ella. "Imaging Terra Incognita: The Disciplinary Gaze of the Empire." *Public Culture* 3, no. 2 (1991): 41–70.

Showalter, Elaine, ed. *These Modern Women: Autobiographical Essays from the Twenties.* Old Westbury, N.Y.: Feminist Press, 1978.

Siebke, H. "Presence of Androkinin in Female Organism." *Archiv für Gynaekologie* 146 (1931): 417–62.

Simmons, Christina. "Companionate Marriage and the Lesbian Threat." *Frontiers* 4, no. 3 (Fall 1979): 54–59.

Simmons, J. L. "Public Stereotypes of Deviants." *Social Problems* 13 (1965): 223–32.

Slater, Lucy Ann [Lucy Ann Lobdell and Joe Lobdell, pseuds.]. *Narrative of Lucy Ann Lobdell, the Female Hunter of Delaware and Sullivan Counties.* New York: published for the author, 1855.

Smith, Alistair. "Biodiversity and Food Security." *Science as Culture* 2: 591–601.

Smith, Daniel Scott. "Family Limitation, Sexual Control, and Domestic Feminism in Victorian America." *Feminist Studies* 1 (Winter–Spring 1973): 40–57.

Smith, Geoffrey S. "National Security and Personal Isolation: Sex, Gender, and Disease in the Cold-War United States." *The International History Review* 14, no. 2 (May 1992): 307–37.

Smith, John David. *Minds Made Feeble: The Myth and Legacy of the Kallikaks.* Rockville, Md.: Aspen Systems Corp., 1985.

Smith, John H. "Abulia: Sexuality and Diseases of the Will in the Late Nineteenth Century." *Genders* 6 (Fall 1989): 102–24.

Smith-Rosenberg, Carroll. "Discourses of Sexuality and Subjectivity: The New Woman, 1870–1936." In *Hidden from History,* edited by Duberman, Vicinus, and Chauncey, 264–80.

———. "The New Woman as Androgyne: Social Disorder and Gender Crisis, 1870–1936." In *Disorderly Conduct: Visions of Gender in Victorian America,* 245–96. New York: Alfred A. Knopf, 1985.

Smith-Rosenberg, Carroll, and Charles E. Rosenberg. "The Female Animal: Medical and Biological Views of Women and Her Role in Nineteenth-Century America." *American Quarterly* 25 (1973): 131–53.

Snitow, Ann, Christine Stansell, and Sharon Thompson, eds. *Powers of Desire: The Politics of Sexuality.* New York: Monthly Review, 1983.

Socarides, Charles. *Homosexuality.* New York: Aronson, 1978.

———. "Homosexuality." *International Journal of Psychiatry* 10 (1972): 118–25.

———. *The Overt Homosexual.* New York: Grune and Stratton, 1968.

———. "Theoretical and Clinical Aspects of Overt Male Homosexuality." *Journal of the American Psychiatric Association* 8 (1960): 552–66.

The Social Evil in Chicago; A Study of Existing Conditions with Recommendations. Chicago: Gunthorp-Warren, 1911.

Society of Medical Psychoanalysts. *Homosexuality: A Psychoanalytic Study of Male Homosexuals.* New York: Vintage Books, 1962.

Sokal, Michael. *Psychological Testing and American Society, 1890–1930.* New Brunswick: Rutgers University Press, 1987.

Solis-Cohen, Myer. *Life Knowledge or Women's Responsibilities and Duties at all Periods of Life.* Philadelphia: Uplift Publishing Company, 1909.

Special Committee of the State Commission of Prisons. "The Psychopathic Delinquent." In *31st Annual Report of the State Commissioner of Prisons.* Ossining, N. Y., 1926.

Spencer, Herbert. *Descriptive Sociology: Or, Groups of Sociological Facts, Classified and Arranged by Herbert Spencer.* London: Williams and Norgate, 1874.

———. *Illustrations of Universal Progress: A Series of Discussions.* New York: D. Appleton and Company, 1880.

———. "Progress: Its Law and Cause" (1857) and "Manners and Fashion" (1854). In *Illustrations of Universal Progress: A Series of Discussions.* New York: D. Appleton and Company, 1880.

Spengler, Otto. Letter. *Monatsberichte des Wissenschaftlich-humanitaren Komitees* 5 (1906): 151.

Spier, Leslie. "Klamath Ethnography." *University of California Publications in American Archaeology and Ethnology* 27 (1930): 51–53.

Sprauge, W. D. *Sex and the Secretary.* New York: Lancer Books, 1964.

Spurr, David. *The Rhetoric of Empire: Colonial Discourse in Journalism, Travel Writing, and Imperial Administration.* Durham, N.C.: Duke University Press, 1993.

Srnec, J., and K. Freund. "Treatment of Male Homosexuality through Conditioning." *International Journal of Sexology* (Bombay) 7, no. 2 (1953): 92–93.

Stafford, Barbara Maria. *Artful Science: Enlightenment Entertainment and the Eclipse of Visual Education.* Cambridge: MIT Press, 1994.

———. *Voyage into Substance: Art, Science, Nature, and the Illustrated Travel Account, 1760–1840.* Cambridge, Mass.: MIT Press, 1984.

Stansell, Christine. *City of Women: Sex and Class in New York, 1789–1860.* New York: Alfred Knopf, 1986.

Stanton, William. *The Leopard's Spots: Scientific Attitudes Toward Race in America, 1815–59.* Chicago: University of Chicago Press, 1960.

Starr, Paul. *The Social Transformation of American Medicine: The Rise of a Sovereign Profession and the Making of a Vast Industry.* New York: Basic Books, 1982.

Steakley, James D. *The Homosexual Emancipation Movement in Germany.* New York: Arno Press, 1975.

———. "Per scientiam ad justitiam: Magnus Hirschfeld and the Sexual Politics of Innate Homosexuality." In *Science and Homosexualities,* edited by Vernon A. Rosario, 133–54.

Stearn, Jess. *The Grapevine.* Garden City, N.J.: Doubleday & Company, Inc., 1964.

———. *The Sixth Man.* London: W. H. Allen, 1962.

Steffensmeier, Darrell J. "Factors Affecting Reactions Toward Homosexuals." Ph.D. diss. Iowa University, 1970.

Steinach, Eugen. "Pubertats druesen und Zwitterbildung." *Archiv für Entwicklungsdynamik* 42 (1916): 307–32.

———. *Sex and Forty Years of Biological and Medical Experiments.* New York: Viking, 1930.

Steiner, Lucius B. *Sex Behavior of the Lesbian.* Hollywood, Calif.: The Genell Corporation, 1964.

Stekel, Wilhelm. *Bisexual Love.* Boston: Badger, 1922.

———. "Is Homosexuality Curable?" *Psychoanalytic Review* 17 (1930): 443–51.

Stepan, Nancy Leys. *The Idea of Race in Science: Great Britain, 1800–1960.* Hamden, Conn.: Archon Books, 1982.

Stevenson, Edward I. Prime [Xavier Mayne, pseud.]. *The Intersexes: A History of Similisexualism as a Problem in Social Life.* 1908. New York: Arno, 1975.

Stocking, George W., Jr., ed. "Bones, Bodies, Behavior." In *Bones, Bodies, Behavior: Essays in Biological Anthropology,* 3–17. Madison: University of Wisconsin Press, 1988.

———. *Race, Culture, and Evolution: Essays in the History of Anthropology.* London: Collier-Macmillan, 1976.

———. *Victorian Anthropology.* New York: Free Press, 1987.

Stoler, Ann Laura. *Race and the Education of Desire: Foucault's History of Sexuality and the Colonial Order of Things.* Durham, N.C.: Duke University Press, 1995.

Stoller, Robert C. "Boyhood Gender Aberrations: Treatment Issues." *Journal of the American Psychoanalytic Association* 26 (1978): 541–58.

Strakosch, Frances M. *Factors in the Sex-Life of 700 Psychopathic Women.* Utica: State Hospitals Press, 1934.

Strecker, Edward A. *Beyond the Clinical Frontiers: A Psychiatrist Views Crowd Behavior.* New York: W. W. Norton and Company, Inc., 1940.

———. "The Contribution of Psychiatry to Democratic Morals." *Rhode Island Journal of Medicine* 27 (1944): 383–84.

———. "Everyday Psychology of the Normal Child." *Mental Hygiene* 17, no. 1 (January 1933): 65–81.

———. *Fundamentals of Psychiatry.* Philadelphia: Lippincott, 1942.

———. "Introduction to 'The Challenge of Sex Offenders.'" *Mental Hygiene* 22, no. 1 (January 1938): 1–3.

———. "The Man and the Mob." *Mental Hygiene* 24, no. 4 (October 1940): 529–51.

———. "Mental Hygiene and Mass Man." *Mental Hygiene* 25, no. 1 (January 1941): 3–5.

———. "Military Psychiatry: World War I." In *One Hundred Years of American Psychiatry,* edited by J. K. Hall. New York: Columbia University Press, 1944.

———. "Psychiatry Speaks to Democracy." *Mental Hygiene* 29, no. 4 (October 1945): 591–605.

———. *Their Mother's Sons: The Psychiatrist Examines an American Problem.* New York and Philadelphia: J. B. Lippincott Company, 1946.

Strecker, Edward A., and Kenneth E. Appel. "Morale." *American Journal of Psychiatry* 99 (September 1942): 163.

———. *Psychiatry in Modern Warfare.* New York: Macmillan, 1945.

Strecker, Edward A., and Francis T. Chambers, Jr.. *Alcohol: One Man's Meat.* New York: Macmillan, 1938.

Strecker, Edward A., and Vincent T. Lathbury. *Their Mother's Daughters.* Philadelphia: J. B. Lippincott Company, 1956.

Stryker, Susan. "The Transgender Issue: An Introduction." *GLQ* vol. 4, no. 2 (1998): 145–58.

Styker, Susan, and Jim Van Buskirk. *Gay By the Bay: A History of Queer Culture in the San Francisco Bay Area.* San Francisco: Chronicle Books, 1996.

Sullivan, Louis. *From Female to Male: The Life of Jack Bee Garland.* Boston: Alyson, 1990.

Susman, Warren I. "'Personality' and the Making of Twentieth Century Culture." In *New Directions in American Intellectual History,* edited by John Higham and Paul K. Conklin, 212–26. Baltimore: Johns Hopkins University Press, 1979.

Swainson, W. *On the Natural History and Classification of Quadrapeds.* London: Longman, Rees, Orme, Brown, Green and Longman, 1835.

Swanson, Alan H. "Sexual Psychopath Statutes: Summary and Analysis." *Journal of Criminal Law, Criminology and Police Science* 51 (July–August 1960): 228–35.

Symonds, John Addington. *A Problem of Modern Ethics.* Unpublished manuscript, 1896.

Taeuber, Irene Barnes. "Assortative Mating for Color in the American Negro." In

A Decade of Progress in Eugenics: Scientific Papers of the Third International Congress of Eugenics (1932), 124–28. Baltimore: The Williams and Wilkins Company, 1934.

Talbot, E. S. *Degeneracy: Its Causes, Signs and Results.* London: Walter Scott, 1898.

Tallman, Frank F., and Karl M. Bowman. *California Sexual Deviation Research.* Report to the California State Assembly. Sacramento, Calif.: January 1953.

Tardieu, Ambroise. *Étude médico-légale sur les attentats aux moeurs.* 1857. 7th ed. Paris: 1878.

Tarnowsky, Pauline. *Étude anthropométrique sur les prostituées et les voleuses.* Paris, 1889.

Taylor, W. Cooke. *The Natural History of Society in the Barbarous and Civilized State: An Essay Towards Discovering the Origin and Course of Human Improvement.* 2 vols. London: Longman, Orme, Brown, Green & Longmans, 1840.

Terman, Lewis M. "The Effect of Happiness or Unhappiness on Self-Report Regarding Attitudes, Reaction Patterns, and Facts of Personal History." *Psychological Bulletin* 36 (1939): 197–202.

———. *Genetic Studies of Genius.* 5 vols. Stanford: Stanford University Press, 1956.

———. "Kinsey's *Sexual Behavior in the Human Male:* Some Comments and Criticisms." *Psychological Bulletin* 45 (1948): 443–59.

———. *The Measurement of Intelligence.* Boston: Houghton Mifflin, 1916.

———. *Psychological Factors in Marital Happiness.* New York: McGraw-Hill, 1938.

———. "A Study in Precocity and Prematuration." *American Journal of Psychology* 16 (April 1905): 145–83.

———. "Testing for the Crime Germ." *Sunset* 60 (1928): 24–25, 54–56.

Terman, Lewis M., and P. Buttenweiser. "Personality Factors in Marital Compatibility." *Journal of Social Psychology* 6 (1935): 143–71, 267–89.

Terman, Lewis M., and W. B. Johnson. "Personality Characteristics of Happily Married, Unhappily Married, and Divorced Persons." *Character and Personality* 3 (1935): 290–311.

Terman, Lewis M., and Catherine Cox Miles. *Attitude-Interest Analysis Test.* New York: McGraw-Hill, 1936.

———. *Sex and Personality: A Study of Masculinity and Femininity.* New York: McGraw-Hill, 1936.

———. "Sex Differences in the Association of Ideas." *American Journal of Psychology* 41, no. 2 (April 1929): 165–206.

Terry, Jennifer. "Lesbians Under the Medical Gaze: Scientists Search for Remarkable Differences." *Journal of Sex Research* 27, no. 3 (1990): 317–40.

———. "Theorizing Deviant Historiography." In *Feminists Revision History,* edited by Ann-Louise Shapiro, 276–303. New Brunswick: Rutgers University Press, 1994.

Terry, Jennifer, and Jacqueline Urla, eds. *Deviant Bodies: Critical Perspectives on Difference in Science and Popular Culture.* Bloomington: Indiana University Press, 1995.

Theoharis, Athan. *Seeds of Repression: Harry S. Truman and the Origins of McCarthyism.* Chicago: Quadrangle Books, 1971.

———. *Spying on Americans: Political Surveillance from Hoover to the Huston Plan.* Philadelphia: Temple University Press, 1978.

Thomas, Dorothy Swaine. *Social Aspects of the Business Cycle.* New York: Knopf, 1927.

————. *Social and Economic Aspects of Swedish Population Movements, 1750–1933.* New York: Macmillan, 1941.

Thomas, Dorothy Swaine, Charles Kikuchi and James Sakoda. *The Salvage: Japanese-American Evacuations and Resettlement.* Berkeley: University of California Press, 1952.

Thomas, Dorothy Swaine, Richard S. Nishimoto, Rosalie A. Hankey, James M. Sakoda, Morton Grodzins, Frank Miyamoto. *The Spoilage: Japanese-American Evacuation and Resettlement During World War II.* Berkeley: University of California Press, 1946.

Thomas, Dorothy Swaine, Alice Loomis, Ruth E. Arrington. *Observational Studies of Social Behavior.* New Haven: Institute of Human Relations, Yale University, 1933.

Thomas, Nicholas. *Colonialism's Culture: Anthropology, Travel, and Government.* Princeton: Princeton University Press, 1994.

Tobias, John Jacob. *Crime and Industrial Society in the Nineteenth Century.* New York: Schocken Books, 1967.

Trombley, Stephen. *The Right to Reproduce: A History of Coercive Sterilization.* London: Weidenfeld and Nicolson, 1988.

Troubridge, Una. *The Life of Radclyffe Hall.* New York: Citadel, 1963.

Trumbach, Randolph. "London's Sodomites: Homosexual Behavior and Western Culture in the Eighteenth Century." *Journal of Social History* 11 (1977): 1–33.

————. "Sodomitical Subcultures, Sodomitical Roles and the Gender Revolution of the Eighteenth Century: The Recent Historiography." In *'Tis Nature's Fault: Unauthorized Sexuality During the Enlightenment,* edited by Robert Purks Maccubin. New York: Cambridge University Press, 1987.

Turner, C. F., H. G. Miller, and L. E. Moses, eds. *Sexual Behavior and Intraveneous Drug Use.* Washington, D.C.: National Academy Press, 1989.

Turnipseed, Edward. "Some Facts in Regard to the Anatomical Difference between the Negro and White Races." *American Journal of Obstetrics and Diseases of Women and Children* 10 (1877): 32.

Tylor, Edward Burnett. *Primitive Culture.* 2 vols. 2d ed. New York: H. Holt and Company, 1877.

————. *Researches into the Early History of Mankind and the Development of Civilization.* 1870. 3d ed. Edited by Paul Bohannan. Chicago: University of Chicago Press, 1964.

Ulrichs, Karl Heinrich. *Forschungen über das Rathsel der mann-mannlichen Liebe.* 1864–79. 4 vols. Edited by Hubert Kennedy. Berlin: Verlag Rosa Winkel, 1994.

————. *The Riddle of "Man-Manly" Love: The Pioneering Work on Male Homosexuality.* 2 vols. Translated by Michael A. Lombardi-Nash. Buffalo: Prometheus, 1994.

U.S. Department of Navy. *Report of the Board Appointed to Prepare and Submit Recommendations to the Secretary of the Navy for the Revision of Policies, Procedures, and Directives Dealing with Homosexuals, 21 December 1956–15 March 1957.* Also known as the *Crittendon Report.* Captain S. H. Crittendon, chairman.

U.S. Senate, 81st Cong., 2d sess., Committee on Expenditures in Executive Departments. "Employment of Homosexuals and Other Sex Perverts in Government." Washington, D.C.: Government Publishing Office, 1950.

Vance, Carole S. "Anthropology Rediscovers Sexuality: A Theoretical Comment." *Social Science and Medicine* 33, no. 8 (1991): 875–84.

Vance, Carole S., ed. *Pleasure and Danger: Exploring Female Sexuality.* New York: Routledge & Kegan Paul, 1984.

Van de Velde, Th. H. *Ideal Marriage: Its Physiology and Technique.* New York: Random House, 1926.

———. *Sexual Tensions in Marriage: Their Origins, Prevention and Treatment.* New York: Random House, 1928.

Van Ophuijsen, J. H. W. "Contributions to the Masculinity Complex in Women." *International Journal of Psychoanalysis* 5 (1924): 39–49.

Vicinus, Martha, ed. *Suffer and Be Still: Women in the Victorian Age.* Bloomington: Indiana University Press, 1972.

Visher, John W. "A Study in Constitutional Psychopathic Inferiority." *Mental Hygiene* 6, no. 4 (October 1922): 729–45.

von Hoffman, Nicholas. *Citizen Cohn.* New York: Doubleday, 1988.

Waldeck, R. G. "The Homosexual International." Published in *Congressional Record,* 83 Cong., 2d sess., 1952, 98: A2652.

Walkowitz, Judith R. *City of Dreadful Delight: Narratives of Sexual Danger in Late-Victorian London.* Chicago: University of Chicago Press, 1992.

———. *Prostitution and Victorian Society: Women, Class, and the State.* New York: Cambridge University Press, 1980.

Walter, Richard D. "What Became of the Degenerate? A Brief History of a Concept." *Journal of the History of Medicine and Allied Sciences* 2 (1956): 422–29.

Ware, Caroline. *Greenwich Village: 1920–1930: A Comment on American Civilization in the Post-War Years.* 1935. Berkeley: University of California Press, 1994.

Weeks, Jeffrey. "Inverts, Perverts, and Mary-Annes: Male Prostitution and the Regulation of Homosexuality in England in the Nineteenth and Early Twentieth Centuries." In *Hidden from History,* edited by Duberman, Vicinus, and Chauncey, 195–211.

———. *Sex, Politics and Society: The Regulation of Sexuality Since 1800.* London: Longman Group, 1981.

———. *Sexuality and its Discontents: Meanings, Myths and Modern Sexualities.* London: Routledge & Kegan Paul, 1985.

Weidensall, Jean. *The Mentality of the Criminal Woman.* Baltimore, Md.: Warwick and York, 1916.

Weil, Arthur. "Körpermasse der Homosexuellen als Ausdrucksform ihrer speziellen Konstitution." *Archiv für Entwicklungsmechanik der Organismen* 49 (1921): 538–44.

Weininger, Otto. *Sex and Character.* Translated from the 6th German edition. New York: G. P. Putnam's Sons, 1903.

Wertham, Frederic. *Seduction of the Innocent.* New York: Rinehart, 1954.

West, Daniel. *The Other Man: A Study of the Social, Legal, and Clinical Aspects of Homosexuality.* New York: Whiteside and William Morrow & Co., 1955.

Westermarck, Edward. "Homosexual Love." *The Origin and Development of Moral Ideas.* London: Macmillan, 1906.

Westphal, Karl Friedrich Otto. "Die konträre Sexualempfindung: Symptom eines neuropatholgischen (psychopathischen) Zustandes." *Archiv für Psychiatrie und Nervenkrankheiten* 2 (1869): 73–108.

Wexler, Alice. *Emma Goldman: An Intimate Life.* New York: Pantheon Books, 1984.

Wey, Hamilton D. "Criminal Anthropology." In *National Prison Association, Proceedings 1890,* 274–90. Pittsburgh: Shaw Brothers, 1891.

White, Hayden. "The Burden of History." In *Tropics of Discourse: Essays in Cultural Criticism,* 27–50. Baltimore: Johns Hopkins University Press, 1978.

———. "The Forms of Wildness: Archaeology of an Idea." In *Tropics of Discourse,* 150–82.

———. "The Noble Savage Theme as Fetish." In *Tropics of Discourse,* 183–96.

Whitehorn, John C. "Psychiatric Research." In *One Hundred Years of American Psychiatry,* edited by J. K. Hall, 168–72.

Wilbur, Cornelia B. "Clinical Aspects of Female Homosexuality." In *Sexual Inversion: the Multiple Roots of Homosexuality,* edited by Judd Marmour, 268–81. New York: Basic Books, 1965.

Wile, Ira S. "Sex Offenders against Young Children." *Journal of Social Hygiene* 25, no. 1 (1939): 33.

Willcox, W. F. "Distribution and Increase of Negroes in the United States." In *Eugenics in Race and State,* Vol. 2: *Scientific Papers of the Second International Congress of Eugenics (1921),* 166–73. Baltimore: The Williams and Wilkins Company, 1923.

Williams, Colin J., and Martin S. Weinberg. *Homosexuals and the Military.* New York: Harper and Row, 1971.

Wise, P. M. "Case of Sexual Perversion." *The Alienist and Neurologist* 4, no. 1 (January 1883): 87–91.

Wittels, Fritz. "The Criminal Psychopath in the Psychoanalytic System." *Psychoanalytic Review* 24 (July 1937): 276–91.

Wolbarst, Abraham L. "Sexual Perversions: Their Medical and Social Implications." *Medical Journal and Record* 134 (1931): 5–9, 62–5.

Wolfe, W. Beran. *A Woman's Best Years.* Garden City, New York: Garden City Publishing, 1935.

Woolston, Howard B. *Prostitution in the United States.* New York: Century, 1921.

Wortis, Joseph. "Intersexuality and Effeminacy in the Male Homosexual." *American Journal of Orthopsychiatry* 10 (1940): 567–70.

———. "A Note on the Body Build of the Male Homosexual." *American Journal of Orthopsychiatry* 8 (1937): 1121–25.

———. "Sex Taboos, Sex Offenders and the Law." *American Journal of Orthopsychiatry* 9 (1939): 554–64.

Wright, C. A. "Further Studies of Endocrine Aspects of Homosexuality." *Medical Record* 147 (May 18, 1938): 449–52.

Wylie, Philip. *Generation of Vipers.* New York: Farrar and Rinehart, Inc., 1942.

Young, Kimball, Fred B. Lindstrom, and Ronald A. Hardert, ed. "Kimball Young." *Sociological Perspectives* 32, no. 2 (1989): 215–26, no. 3: 383–402.

Zeiger, Susan. "'She Didn't Raise Her Boy to be a Slacker': Motherhood, Conscription, and the Culture of the First World War." *Feminist Studies* 22, no. 1 (Spring 1996): 7–39.

Zlotlow, Moses, and Albert E. Paganini. "Autoerotic and Homoerotic Manifestations in Hospitalized Male Postlobotomy Patients." *Psychiatric Quarterly* 33, no. 3 (1959): 495–97.

Zondek, Bernhard. "Mass Excretion of Oestrogenic Hormone in the Urine of the Stallion." *Nature* 133 (1934): 209–10.

———. "Oestrogenic Hormone in the Urine of the Stallion." *Nature* 133 (1934): 494.

ARCHIVES CONSULTED

Karl M. Bowman Papers, Dorothy Swaine Thomas Papers, Bancroft Library, University of California at Berkeley.

Louise Stevens Bryant Papers, Sophia Smith Collection, Smith College.

Columbia University Medical School Archive, New York City.

Robert Latou Dickinson Papers, Countway Library, Harvard Medical School, Boston, Massachusetts.

Kinsey Institute for Research in Sex, Gender, and Reproduction, Indiana University, Bloomington, Indiana.

Adolf Meyer Papers, The Johns Hopkins University, Baltimore, Maryland.

New York Academy of Medicine, New York City.

New York Psychiatric Institute, New York City.

Payne-Whitney Clinic, New York Hospital, New York City.

Papers of the Bureau of Social Hygiene and the National Research Council's Committee on Research in Problems of Sex, Rockefeller Archives Center, Pontico Hills, New York.

Lewis Terman Papers, Stanford University, Stanford, California.

UCLA Special Collections.

INDEX

HQ 76.3 .U5 T45 1999

Terry, Jennifer,

An American obsession

 State Library of Ohio

SEO Library Center
40780 SR 821 * Caldwell, OH 43724

DEMCO